Sociological Theory:

A BOOK OF READINGS

THE MACMILLAN COMPANY
NEW YORK • CHICAGO
DALLAS • ATLANTA • SAN FRANCISCO
LONDON • MANILA

BRETT-MACMILLAN LTD.
TORONTO

Sociological Theory:

A BOOK OF READINGS

EDITED BY

Lewis A. Coser
BRANDEIS UNIVERSITY

Bernard Rosenberg
COLLEGE OF THE CITY OF NEW YORK

THE MACMILLAN COMPANY
NEW YORK

Second Printing 1959

LIBRARY OF CONGRESS CATALOG CARD NUMBER: 57–9021

CONTENTS

INTRODUCTION

ALFRED NORTH WHITEHEAD may have put the case a little too sharply when he observed that it is a sign of maturity for a science to forget its ancestors. However, it is certainly true that recollection of their work should be selective. One of the weaknesses of traditional histories of sociological thought is that they have attempted to present a synoptic overview of past sociological theory without a conscious effort at selection. Such lack of intellectual discrimination has no place in an ordered perspective. It tends to level figures of very uneven stature and thus to confuse the student who may be feeling his way toward a standard of significance. Attention should be directed here and deflected there. It is our conviction that the student of sociology, as distinct from the historian of ideas, must above all be introduced to those aspects of the works of the past that have proved viable. We know of no better criterion in art or in science, or in a discipline struggling to move from one category to the other.

All writing, however novel, inevitably contains much that is relevant only to the period, place, and society of its composition. Hence, there should be no reluctance to deal with sociological thought by deliberately choosing from the welter of divergent and antagonistic ideas those which seem most relevant for contemporary research and expanding theory.

We are convinced that sociology as a science can develop only if it is able to point to a genuine accumulation of empirically validated results. Unrelated research findings—the quest for "facts" which, once found, do not speak for themselves—are more likely to produce a miscellany of curiosa than the lineaments of a science. Therefore, we shall attempt, in a necessarily limited and elliptical way, to indicate how large such an accumulation of results interlaced with theory has actually grown up in sociology.

We shall show how certain concepts and theories first suggested by an earlier generation have been developed further at a later date; we shall also be obliged to point out that, in some cases, earlier formulations have been neglected by later theorists who painfully rediscovered what would have been known to them if they had undertaken a careful inventory of their theoretical inheritance. To a small extent this book should serve as such an inventory.

The presentation of texts and the discussion of concepts will differ rather drastically from those found in most books on sociological theory. We shall not be concerned with the assessment of the whole work of any theorists but only with those parts of it which seem most pertinent within the context of present-day inquiry. What once loomed large may by now, in this framework have shriveled to a different dimension. If Ratzenhofer and Gumplowicz can be forgotten completely, Comte and Spencer cannot. Yet neither positivism nor evolutionism is any longer the specter that haunts sociology. Thus, when discussing Herbert Spencer, we shall not have occasion to deal extensively with his evolutionary theories, but deserved weight will be given to his pioneering analysis of structure and function. Similarly, when presenting the work of William Graham Sumner, our emphasis will be on his treatment of different types of controlling norms rather than on the brand of Social Darwinism with which he was historically associated.

The disadvantages of such a method are fairly obvious. The uninitiated reader will not be able to form a fully rounded view of any of the authors we present, although he may be stimulated to do so at his leisure. It seems to us that the advantages of our approach outweigh its disadvantages: instead of being confronted with a jumble of information which he is only too likely to forget in short order, the student will be presented with theoretical conceptions the relevance of which (to current research) will be made apparent to him. Even though he will not receive a complete picture of every writer (which in any case no single book of readings could supply), he will, we hope, attain an integrated view of the development of the science of sociology. This book, then, is not conceived as an exhaustive inventory of sociological ideas, but as a selective and suggestive introduction to those theoretical ideas which inform the work of contemporary sociology. The lines of filiation and mutual influence of the key concepts which sociology utilizes today will, we trust, be made reasonably clear to the student.

The relations between theory and research have been the subject of sustained interest in the last several decades of American sociology. "Rediscovering" certain European theorists such as Max Weber, Emile Durkheim, and Georg Simmel, and influenced by repeated onslaughts on the part of a younger generation of theoretically oriented sociologists against the busywork of fact gatherers, American sociology has produced what might be called a renaissance of sociological theory. We fear, however, that in the initial exuberance of theoretical discovery there has occasionally been a tendency to revert to some of the most gross errors of an earlier period of theorizing, a tendency to engage in large-scale system-building, the construction of imposing theories which contain few if any testable propositions. Such development of generalizations on so high a level of abstraction that their immediate relevance and utility are almost completely obscured is not likely to advance creative research. We feel that such system-building often has led to the unfortunate tendency of epigones to substitute pigeonholing in impressively labeled categories for creative investigation. No insight is gained by translating known facts into new terminology.

It is our intention in the following selections to make clear that leading theorists of the past were concerned with the development of theories *about* relevant aspects of the social reality which they faced, rather than with the building of airtight but empty scholastic systems. Because their theories were constructed in such a way, they were able to survive the tests of time and of usefulness. Thus, William Graham Sumner's distinction between folkways, mores, and institutions still can serve useful purposes, while the impressive generalizations developed by his contemporary Lester Frank Ward are of interest only to specialists in the history of ideas.

Theorists "in the grand manner" fell into disrepute after World War I. With the growth of radical empiricism, social scientists retrenched and pursued a will-o'-the-wisp—theory-free investigations of phenomena of less and less consequence. Some old-timers continued to theorize, and for a time they were regarded with a kind of tolerant odium. Today, on the surface at least, this situation has greatly changed. It is generally conceded that theory is an indispensable part of the scientific enterprise. A *sub rosa* cleavage persists, but this has more to do with the absence of sophistication on both sides than with the presence of a philosophical issue. What we can say, with the wisdom of hindsight, is that the revulsion against theory as such was misconceived. If such men as Durkheim and Weber still provide us with our best clues, it is because a generation or two of nose counting has supplied us with none that are better. Between their time and ours, *techniques* have been devised, if not perfected, which permit us to pursue lines of investigation programmatically stated by the founders of our science. It is at this point that fruitful lines of continuity can be re-established. We regard it as our principal task to highlight and trace what seem to us such heartening lines as are now in the process of formation.

In the selections that follow the reader will thus not find discussions of integrated systems but only of special propositions, specific concepts, or examples of substantive theorizing. Inevitably an element of personal bias has crept into the process of selection, but we hope we have kept such bias under control.

The editors are aware that much present-day theorizing feeds, though sometimes unconsciously, on theoretical propositions developed long before the rise of formal sociology, or developed independently of it. How can one treat, say, the sociology of power and authority without discussing Machiavelli and Hobbes? How is it possible to touch the sociology of order without reference to de Bonald, de Maistre, and Burke? Yet we have decided to include in our selections only the work of theorists who may be specifically labeled as belonging to sociology, social psychology, and social anthropology. This decision was made on purely pragmatic grounds; it was felt that inclusion of other thinkers would transcend the boundaries which we have set for ourselves and thus burst the limitations of a single volume.

Similar reasons have prompted the decision to include only those European authors whose writings are available in American translation. We deplore the fact that theoretical contributions of great importance, such as the sociological writings of Max Scheler and of Maurice Halbwachs, are as yet not available to American students. We regret that the majority of young sociologists—despite the ritualistic requirements of language examinations—are unable to acquaint themselves with theoretical writings in other languages. But we must accept the fact that by and large only those European works which have been translated have had a decisive influence on American sociological thinking. For this reason, and also because of the space limitations alluded to earlier, we have reluctantly decided to omit—except in one case—all hitherto untranslated works.

A word as to the organization of this book. The reader will note that we have planned in terms of concepts rather than in terms of substantive areas of investigation. Thus he will find chapters dealing with the concept of reference group or the concept of anomie rather than with, say, minority relations or the sociology of the family. We followed this plan because we feel that undue concern with substantive areas of research detracts from the central fact that concepts which are useful in the search for regularities of behavior in one field may also be of import in another seemingly unrelated area. Thus recent investigations have shown that reference-group theory developed in research on military structure may also provide important clues in such seemingly unrelated fields as the sociology of class relations, prejudice, and political behavior, as well as in the sociological interpretation of personality. The customary departmental organization has tended to obscure important interrelations and to hamper the cross-field application of theoretical clues originally developed in one particular area. A student familiar with the central concepts of sociology will be less likely to draw upon *ad hoc* hypotheses to explain a puzzling problem in his own research; he will, we hope, be able to draw upon his conceptual knowledge to explain problems in his particular area—even though these concepts have never as yet been applied to it.

To be sure, a simple array of concepts does not constitute a theory. Concepts, as Robert K. Merton has argued, "constitute the definitions (or prescriptions) of what is to be observed; they are the variables between which empirical relationships are to be sought"; yet it is clear that no theory can be developed without concepts. Only logical interrelations between various concepts may lead to the development of a theory. But for our purposes it seems that the most convenient mode of exposition is to focus on a series of concepts and to observe how various authors have been able, through the utilization of such concepts, to institute theories accounting for uniformities of behavior which these concepts have led them to discover.

A final cautionary word to the student using this volume may be in order. Some of our selections are rather short, while other authors are represented by lengthy excerpts from their work. Such differences are not meant to suggest relative merit. We have often decided to use short excerpts from writings that are easily available in other form, while giving more space to relatively inaccessible material. On the other hand, we often found that, while certain authors have the gift of succinctly stating their main contention, others require more space to develop their train of thought in successive steps.

This book is not meant to help the student pass his examination requirements; it is intended to familiarize him with a heritage of vast knowledge so that he can put it to future use in his own work. The work of the future can be fruitful only if it is informed by the contributions of the past. As T. S. Eliot once wrote: "Someone said 'The dead writers are remote from us because we *know* so much more than they do.' Precisely, and they are that which we know."

ACKNOWLEDGMENTS

We wish to express our special gratitude to two colleagues. Professor Robert K. Merton of Columbia University read our first draft and made a number of important suggestions which helped shape our orientation and the nature of our final selections. Professor Robert Bierstedt of the College of the City of New York read several drafts of our manuscript and gave us most constructive advice. But for them, what seemed to be an almost unmanageable body of concepts could not have been brought into its present form.

We also wish to thank our wives, Rose Laub Coser and Sarah Helen Rosenberg, who have so graciously contributed to the clarification of our thinking.

Nor are we unmindful of the help given us by students in more than one classroom. The eagerness with which many of them received and entertained general ideas has gladdened us, and suggested more strongly than anything else that American sociological theory may have a bright future.

L. A. C.

B. R.

Sociological Theory:

A BOOK OF READINGS

1.
DEFINITION OF THE FIELD

THE PRECURSORS of sociological theory are as old as civilization. At least since man attained mastery of the arts of reading and writing, he has speculated about himself, his world, and their relationship to each other. In both Oriental and Occidental antiquity, with the development of high civilization as well as literacy, philosophers often anticipated ideas that required millennia to develop on a "modern" basis. To some extent, there has never been anything new under the sun, and all philosophy *is* but a footnote to Plato. Even physical science may be shorn of its novelty if we remember, for example, that an atomic theory of matter was advanced well before the Christian era by Democritus and Lucretius.

And yet all is flux. Change, transitoriness, impermanence, process are to be seen all around and within us. Applied exclusively to man, the simultaneous presence of fixity and its opposite is summed up by a contemporary philosopher, Kurt Riezler, in the title of his book, *Human Nature: Mutable and Immutable*. Moreover, everything in the present may be traced to something or, more often, to many things in the past which, in their turn, do not spring upon the world *ex nihilo*. As the ancients knew, nothing comes from nothing.

The task we have set ourselves in this chapter is to deal, far from definitively, with what sociological theory is, how the enterprise was conceived and, especially, what motivated a number of men in different parts of the western world to originate it. We have explained in the introduction why, despite our qualms about overlooking early genius, it was not deemed advisable to trace our concepts back through all of history. It would take more than one book, probably more than one small library, to do the job, and even then it would be one for scholars whose competence lies principally in the history of ideas. Also, such a procedure would involve us in an infinite regress. For "X" was influenced by "Y" and "Y" by "Z"—and so on almost into infinity.

So we begin at a point in time when sociology is programmatically freed from social philosophy. That point comes in the nineteenth century; its avatar is a volatile Frenchman named Isidore Auguste François Marie Xavier

1

Comte (1798–1857). To say that sociology as a specific field of inquiry originates with Comte is not to deny that his system was the meeting place of many minds. Harry Elmer Barnes states the case correctly when he points out that Comte's "chief contribution lay in his remarkable capacity for synthesis and organization rather than in the development of new and original social doctrines." [1] Among those from whom Comte derived much, Barnes mentions Aristotle, Bossuet, Kant, Hume, Turgot, Vico, de Maistre, Saint-Pierre, Condorcet, Montesquieu, and Saint-Simon. The list could easily be enlarged. It would demonstrate that Comte was an erudite man with powers of encyclopedic absorption, who greatly benefited from the intellectual labor of others.

However, after all the major sources have been uncovered, there remains a social situation which must be considered if we are to understand Comte's unique synthesis. The founder of sociology lived in a period of tremendous upheaval, of disorganization and reorganization, when many men confidently believed that the world which was collapsing before them could be remade after their hearts' desire. Science had performed wonders in subduing nature. Never before did man know so much about organic and inorganic matter. Only the species itself was proving intractable. What could be more logical than the extension of methods already established as successful in natural science to the one unit of study left untouched by them?

Comte surveyed the history of science. In so doing, he noted its progression: first, astronomy and celestial mechanics, the subject farthest removed from man; then, physics, chemistry, and biology—in that order— gradually approaching man as matter and as an organism. The time now seemed ripe for a science of sciences, something that would embrace man and all his works. Comte saw it as the culmination of trends that had been set in motion a few centuries before. At last disinterested observation and experimentation might be used in a deliberate effort to understand human beings as social animals of a very distinctive sort. Problems of enormous complexity and the possible means of ameliorating or solving them were both at hand.

Comte thought that human intelligence had evolved to the point where social physics or sociology, as a source of knowledge about man, was feasible. With that knowledge, the good society could be created. Clearly, Comte's underlying motivation for the study of sociology was humanitarian. He stated his credo in those words: "*Savoir pour prévoir et prévoir pour pouvoir*" (To know in order to predict and to predict in order to control). Comte felt that only if man was equipped with the necessary knowledge which neither metaphysics nor theology would yield could he hope to deal with his increasingly vexatious problems.

It was one of Comte's firmest beliefs that each branch of knowledge passes through three stages: the theological or fictitious, the metaphysical or abstract, and the scientific or positive. This is the famous Law of the Three Stages. The human mind in its theological state seeks the essential nature of things, first and final causes, absolute truth. It "supposes all phenomena to be produced by the immediate action of supernatural beings." The metaphysical state is merely a modification of the theological. In it, the mind supposes that abstract forces rather than supernatural beings are inherent in and produce all phenomena.

In the final, the positive state, the mind has given over the vain search for Absolute notions, the origin and destination of the universe, and the causes of phenomena, and applies itself to the study of their laws—that is, their invariable relations of succession and resemblance. Reasoning and observation, duly combined, are the means of this knowledge . . . There is no science which, having attained the positive stage, does not bear the marks of having passed through the others. Some time since it was (whatever it might be) composed, as we can now perceive, of metaphysical abstractions; and further back in the course of time, it took its form from theological conceptions. We shall have only too much occasion to see, as we proceed, that our most advanced sciences still bear very evident marks of the two earlier periods through which they have passed.

The progress of the individual mind is not only an illustration, but an indirect evidence of that of the general mind. The point of departure of the individual and of the race being the same, the phases of the mind of a man correspond to the epochs of the mind of the race. Now, each of us is aware, if he looks back upon his own history, that he was a theologian in his childhood, a metaphysician in his youth, and a natural philosopher in his manhood. All men who are up to their age can verify this for themselves.[2]

That the individual in his own life cycle relives all of human history is a familiar idea. We find the outstanding Swiss psychologist Jean Piaget expressing it in our own day when he explains socialization, perhaps too optimistically, as a process of moving from theocracy through gerontocracy to democracy.[3] The crux of this idea, stated in surprisingly similar terms by Comte and Piaget, was summed up by nineteenth-century biologists who said that "ontogeny recapitulates phylogeny." The pathfinders of sociological thought were always tempted to use biology as a model for their work. They flourished in an age when every cultivated person had to reckon with the doctrine of evolution and to ponder the theories of men like Lamarck, Cuvier, Wallace, and Darwin.

It is not surprising, therefore, that Comte, Herbert Spencer (1820–1903), his opposite number in Great Britain, and all their American followers, starting with Lester Frank Ward (1841–1913), came to be known as social evolutionists. Like the others, Comte has frequently and justifiably been taxed for his "organicism" (the tendency to see society as an organism, which is less pronounced in Comte than in some other organicists who located a "central sensorium," a medulla oblongata, a cerebrum, and a cerebellum as societal divisions). If sociology is merely biology on a different level of abstraction, then indeed there is little justification for the new and unpedigreed science. But this aspect of Comte, along with other residues of mysticism, has been abandoned by all sociologists who "are up to their age."

We are the residuary legatees of another vision which Comte saw and inspired others of his time to see. This is the vision of society and the state, not as an organismic but as an *organic* whole. Man had already been viewed from many angles and was to be subjected to more minute analysis. Without questioning the legitimacy of such procedure, Comte proposed that man be viewed sociologically, that is to say, holistically. To see human beings in their total social setting was the peculiar task of sociology as Comte understood it. Although he believed in progress, Comte was convinced that the overview provided by sociology would enable man to plan his future scientifically and thus facilitate what might not otherwise take place so surely or so pointedly. Nothing bespeaks his intention more eloquently than his first book, appropriately entitled *A Program of Scientific Work Required for the Reorganization of Society.*

Herbert Spencer was certainly no radical social reformer; neither was he quite the intransigent enemy of change that his detractors have pictured him to be. Spencer favored intelligent social change and believed that the instrument for such innovation would be sociology. This he emphasizes in "Our Need for It," which is Chapter One of his famous treatise, *The Study of Sociology.* In opposition to mere common sense, a social science is called for to supply evidence on the basis of which rational decisions can be made. Spencer's books are rich with examples that still give them the ring of contemporaneity. For instance:

How obvious it appears that when minds go deranged, there is no remedy but replacing the weak internal control by a strong external control. Yet the "non-restraint system" has had far more success than the system of straight-waistcoats. Dr. Batty Tuke, a physician of much experience in treating the insane, has lately testified that the desire to escape is great when locks and keys are used, but almost disappears when they are disused: the policy of unlocked doors has had 95% of success and 5% of failure. And in further evidence of the mischief often done by measures supposed to be curative, here is Dr. Maudsley, also an authority on such questions, speaking of "asylum-made lunatics." Again, is it not clear that the repression of crime will be effectual in proportion as the punishment is severe? Yet the great amelioration in our penal code, initiated by Romilly, has not been followed by increased criminality but by decreased criminality; and the testimonies of those who have had most experience—Machonochie in Norfolk Island, Dickson in Western Australia, Obermeir in Germany, Montesinos in Spain—unite to show that in proportion as the criminal is left to suffer no other penalty than that of maintaining himself under such restraints only as are needful for public safety, the reformation is great: exceeding indeed, all anticipation.[4]

It has taken the dominant school of twentieth-century American sociology some time to learn what Spencer kept hammering at a hundred years ago: that common sense is but a poor guide to reality. Men think they know how to go about curing their social ills, although they would never depend on untutored laymen to treat the simpler physical ailments that afflict them. Spencer puts it classically in his *Study*:

You see that this wrought-iron plate is not quite flat; it sticks up a little here toward the left—"cockles," as we say. How shall we flatten it? Obviously, you reply, by hitting down on the part that is prominent. Well, here is a hammer, and I give the plate a blow as you advise. Harder, you say. Still no effect. Another stroke: well, there is one, and another, and another. The prominence remains, you see: the evil is as great as ever—greater, indeed. But this is not all. Look at the warp which the plate has got near the opposite edge. Where it was flat before it is now curved. A pretty bungle we have made of it. Instead of curing the original defect, we have produced a second. Had we asked an artisan practised in "planishing," as it is called, he would have told us that no good was to be done, but only mischief, by hitting down on the projecting part. He would have taught us how to give variously–directed and specially–adjusted blows with a hammer elsewhere: so attacking the evil not by direct but by indirect actions. The required process is less simple than you thought. Even a sheet of metal is not to be successfully dealt with after those common-sense methods in which you have so much confidence. What, then, shall we say about a society? "Do you think I am easier to be played upon than a pipe?" asks Hamlet. Is humanity more readily straightened than an iron plate? [5]

The relevance of this statement is made very clear if we place it side by side with some recent observations of Robert K. Merton, who ranks among the two or three greatest contemporary American theorists. When Merton defends his interpretation or "codification" of structural-functionalism (see Chapter 14), he does so in terms similar to those of Spencer. Merton distinguishes between "manifest" and "latent" functions, stressing the latter. "It is precisely the latent functions of a practice or belief which are *not* common knowledge, for these are unintended and generally unrecognized social and psychological consequences. As a result, findings concerning latent functions represent a greater increment in knowledge than findings concerning manifest functions. They represent also greater departures from 'common sense' knowledge about social life," [6] . . . and therein lies their value.

Spencer must also be credited with having been able to meet the principal objections to sociology as such, objections raised in his time and continuously reiterated thereafter.[7] The complaint is that each man is unique, that the course of his life is unpredictable, and that therefore no generalizations about men can be made. Spencer replies, characteristically, with an analogy:

What Biography is to Anthropology, History is to Sociology . . . The kind of relation which the sayings and doings that make up the ordinary account of a man's life, bear to an account of his bodily and mental evolution, structural and functional, is like the kind of relation borne by that narrative of a nation's actions and fortunes its historian gives us, to a description of its institutions, regulative and operative, and the ways in which their structures and functions have gradually established themselves. And if it is an error to say that there is no Science of Man, because the events of a man's life cannot be foreseen, it is equally an error to say that there is no Science of Society, because there can be no prevision of the occurrences which make up ordinary history.

There is much more here than mere counterassertion: a cogent argument is carefully unfolded and repays study even today.

In all probability, Spencer was thinking of Thomas Carlyle when he declared that a certain class of people was unprepared to interpret sociological phenomena scientifically. Carlyle believed that certain extraordinary individuals were responsible for the determination of human history. To Spencer such a philosophy of history corresponded to the mentality of savages and children. It was precisely to combat Supernaturalism and the Great-Man Theory of history, that Spencer, like Comte before him, felt the urgent need for a usable social science. Said Spencer, "If you want roughly to estimate anyone's mental calibre, you cannot do it better than by observing the ratio of generalities to personalities in his talk—how far simple truths about individuals are replaced by truths abstracted from numerous experiences of men and things. And when you have thus measured many, you find but a scattered few likely to take anything more than a biographical view of human affairs." [9] And it is to the scattered few that he calls for help in establishing a hitherto neglected, more mature, point of view.

The founders of sociology were actuated by a common dissatisfaction. They all sensed that something was missing from the armamentarium of Western scholarship, and each was willing, without deprecating it, to relinquish his original area of interest—history, philology, economics, theology, chemistry, political science, or psychology—in an effort to transcend the limitations of all such disciplines. Such men were scattered and few; other thinkers clung tenaciously to their several specialties. Most scholars were, and not a few still are, openly disdainful of the sociological upstart. As John Stuart Mill pointed out to his friend, Auguste Comte, it was, after all, a bastard science which combined the Latin root *socius* with the Greek *logos*. Like all illegitimate children, sociology has constantly had to justify its existence. In providing a *raison d'être*, no one excels the early masters. Only when sight is lost of their reasoning does the field itself become hazy and undefinable.

Surely the most persistent criticism sociological theory has had to meet is that concepts such as "society" are unreal abstractions. Nowadays the impeachment is somewhat subtilized. Yet it is basically what it was when Georg Simmel (1858–1918) and Emile Durkheim (1858–1917) thought they had laid the ghost. Their argument must be pondered in detail. No more than an inkling can be given here, but for the case in brief or *in extenso,* we are well advised to follow Georg Simmel:

Let us grant for the moment that only individuals "really" exist. Even then, only a false conception of science could infer from this "fact" that any knowledge which somehow aims at synthesizing these individuals deals with merely speculative abstractions and unrealities. Quite on the contrary, human thought always and everywhere synthesizes the given into units that serve as subject matters of the sciences. They have no counterpart whatever in immediate reality. Nobody, for instance, hesitates to talk of the development of the Gothic style. Yet nowhere is there such a thing as "Gothic style," whose existence could be shown. Instead, there are particular works of art which along with individual elements, also contain stylistic elements; and the two cannot be clearly separated. The Gothic style as a topic of historical knowledge is an *intellectual* phenomenon. It is abstracted from reality; it is not itself a given reality. Innumerable times, we do not even want to know how individual things behave in detail; we form new units out of them. When we inquire into the Gothic style, its laws, its development, we do not describe any particular cathedral or palace. Yet the *material* that makes up the unit we are investigating—"Gothic style"—we gain only from a study of the details of cathedrals and palaces. Or we ask how the "Greeks" and the "Persians" behaved in the battle of Marathon. If it were true that only individuals are "real," historical cognition would reach its goal only if it included the behavior of each individual Greek and each individual Persian. If we knew his whole life history, we could psychologically understand his behavior during the battle. Yet even if we could manage to satisfy such a fantastic claim, we would not have solved our problem at all. For this problem does not concern this or that individual Greek or Persian; it concerns all of them. The notion, the "Greeks" or the "Persians," evidently constitutes a totally different phenomenon, which results from a certain intellectual synthesis, not from the observation of isolated individuals. To be sure, each of these individuals was led to behave as he did by a development which is somehow different from that of every other individual. In reality, none of them behaved precisely like any other. And, in no individual, is what he shares with others clearly separable from what distinguishes him from others. Both aspects, rather, form the inseparable unity of his personal life. Yet in spite of all this, out of all these individuals we form the more comprehensive units, "the Greeks" and "the Persians."

Even a moment's reflection shows that similar concepts constantly supersede individual existences. If we were to rob our cognition of all such intellectual syntheses because only individuals are "real," we would deprive human knowledge of its least dubious and most legitimate contents. The stubborn assertion that after all there exist nothing but individuals which alone, therefore, are the concrete objects of science, cannot prevent us from speaking of the histories of Catholicism and Social Democracy, of cities, and political territories, of the feminist movement, of the conditions of craftsmen, and of thousands of other synthetic events and collective phenomena—and therefore, of society in general. It certainly is an abstract concept. But each of the innumerable articulations and arrangements covered by it is an object that can be investigated and is worth investigation. And none of them consists of individual existences that are observed in all their details.[10]

If Simmel sought to dissociate sociology from psychology, so has every methodologist of the new science since that time. Evidently the battle must be refought in every generation; as we write, it is far from having subsided. That social problems should be dealt with on the social level is still a doubtful proposition in many quarters. Let us see how the French genius, Emile Durkheim, who moved from Kantian philosophy to neo-Comtean sociology, handled this question in a typical passage from his invaluable book, *The Rules of Sociological Method*:

But, it will be said that, since the only elements making up society are individuals, the first origins of sociological phenomena cannot but be psychological. In reasoning thus, it can be established just as easily that organic phenomena may be explained by inorganic phenomena. It is very certain that there are in the living cell only molecules of crude matter. But these molecules are in contact with one another, and this association is the cause of the new phenomena which characterize life, the very germ of which cannot possibly be found in any of the separate elements. A whole is not identical with the sum of its parts . . .

By reason of this principle, society is not a mere sum of individuals. Rather, the system formed by their association represents a specific reality which has its own characteristics. Of course, nothing collective can be produced if individual consciousnesses are not assumed; but this necessary condition is by itself insufficient. These consciousnesses must be combined in a certain way; social life results from this combination and is, consequently, explained by it. . . . The group thinks, feels and acts quite differently from the way in which its members would were they isolated. If, then, we begin with the individual, we shall be able to understand nothing of what takes place in the group. In a word, there is between psychology and sociology the same break in continuity as between biology and the physicochemical sciences. (*Elsewhere in the same treatise, Durkheim admits there is such a thing as biochemistry and there may be such a thing as social psychology. Editors.*) Consequently, every time that a social phenomenon is directly explained by a psychological phenomenon, we may be sure that the explanation is false.[11]

Durkheim knew that biology, economics, and psychology took up various phases of human activity and shed light upon them. But they only told part of the story. It seemed to him that the older social sciences overlooked those ways of acting, thinking, and feeling which are not mere products of the individual's consciousness. These ways may eventually, and in most cases do, conform to what a person feels subjectively. However, they are not his creations. He inherits them—they are, we would now say, culturally transmitted to him—through formal and informal education. Society provides a large number of predefined conventions which must be obeyed on pain of ridicule, isolation, incarceration, or death. Norms govern our lives, they are exterior to us, and we are constrained to accept them. What follows from these premises is something sociologists have come to know as the normative determination of human behavior.

Thus, the category of facts which interested Durkheim and prompted him to become a sociologist par excellence were those pertaining to an external force whose coercive power largely controls mankind. That force Durkheim identified collectively as society and more particularly as a multitude of habits of thought, modes of dress, languages, and traditions considered appropriate to one's class and country which most men were obliged to accept most of the time. There is always a body of established beliefs and practices that constitutes a social order into which the individual is born. These are not merely legal and moral regulations, religious faiths, and financial systems. They also include "social currents such as any great movement of indignation, pity or enthusiasm in a crowd." [12] These currents do not originate in any one mind; they carry each person along in spite of himself. In the same class are opinions on religious, political, literary, or general esthetic matters formed either by society as a whole or by certain limited, but influential, circles. There is a continuous effort to impose responses on man that he could not have produced spontaneously. This is most obvious when, during the period of greatest plasticity, the child's views are shaped by education; they are more subtly conditioned when he grows to adulthood. Durkheim saw education, broadly defined, as the means by which social beings are constituted. Their social milieu fashions them in its own image.

It was Durkheim's opinion that collective habits inhere in the successive acts which they determine. These habits receive permanent expression in a formula which is repeated from mouth to mouth and fixed in writing. "Such is the origin and nature of legal and moral rules, popular aphorisms and proverbs, articles of faith wherein religious or political groups condense their beliefs, standards of taste, etc." [13] According to Durkheim, this is also the proper subject matter of sociology.

Durkheim's paramount theoretical problem then became: how can "the proper subject matter of sociology" be isolated from individual, non-social causes? And his answer is altogether relevant, for it was to relate statistical data such as birth rates, marriage rates, or suicide rates to underlying attitudes, to the state of "collective consciousness." This was Durkheim's prescription for neutralizing individual circumstances and disentangling social phenomena from all foreign matter. Durkheim conceded that individual differences are, in a marginal sense, of interest to social psychology. He refused as a sociologist to be preoccupied with them to the exclusion of an anterior collectivity.

If men are constrained by exterior norms that exist prior to, but are ultimately incorporated in, consciousness, then their acts are largely predetermined, and Durkheim believed this to be the case. He by no means considered the individual to lack self-control. His point of view was closer to that of Hegel, who held that freedom consists in the recognition of its nonexistence. To Durkheim this meant the necessity of going "back along the chain of causes and effects until we find a point where the action of man may be effectively brought to bear." In effect, he admonished us to study the regularities in society, and thereby to protect ourselves through our ability to predict, and thus to advance toward a higher state of human development. Durkheim thought that social phenomena down to the most minute ceremonial detail present an astonishing uniformity; if we learn their nature, it will be possible to control them and free ourselves.

By 1917, when the celebrated sociological innovators, William I. Thomas (1863–1947) and Florian Znaniecki published their monumental study, *The Polish Peasant in Europe and America* (2nd ed., 1927) much more was known about the nature of science than could have been apparent in any earlier generation. The widely read "Methodological Note" to Thomas and Znaniecki's famous work reflects a new degree of sophistication. Nevertheless, it faithfully echoes many sound formulations originally set forth by Comte. Thomas and Znaniecki found that the twentieth century even more than the nineteenth urgently needed "a conscious and rational technique" to deal with social processes that tended to get out of hand:

> The marvelous results attained by a rational technique in the sphere of material reality invite us to apply some analogous procedure to social reality. Our success in controlling nature gives us confidence that we shall eventually be able to control the social world in the same measure.
>
> While our realization that nature can be controlled only by treating it as independent of any immediate act of our will or reason is four centuries old, our confidence in "legislation" and "moral suasion" shows that this idea is not generally realized with regard to the social world. But the tendency to rational control is growing in this field also and constitutes at present an insistent demand on the social sciences.[14]

Thomas and Znaniecki held forty years ago that the moment had arrived for substituting conscious technique for half-conscious routine, although they saw only a halting development of this technique. It was still beset with the weaknesses that Comte had noted, for . . . "even now we find in it many implicit or explicit ideas and methods corresponding to stages of human thought passed hundreds and even thousands of years ago." They observed the continued presence of magic as an anachronism that takes the form of "meeting a crisis by an arbitrary act of will decreeing the disappearance of the undesirable or the appearance of the desirable phenomena, and using arbitrary physical action to enforce the decree."[15] This situation differed but little from the one symbolized by Spencer's wrought-iron plate.

Thomas and Znaniecki take note of a later phase which, while better than the first, is still faulty. This is a phase based upon "common sense" and represented by "practical sociology." The cardinal fallacy of this transitional technique is that it supposes a full knowledge of that social reality with which all human beings have an empirical acquaintance. Such an attitude reminds Thomas and Znaniecki of the ancient assumption "that we know the physical world because we live and act in it, and that therefore we have the right of generalizing without a special and thorough investigation, on the mere basis of 'common sense.'" The illusion of omniscience stems from total reliance upon sense perception and results in such scientific errors as the geocentric system in astronomy and the medieval concept of motion. But in the world surveyed by Thomas and Znaniecki men were more willing to deny their senses in defining the inorganic than in understanding the superorganic. They still are.

These pioneer authors who wished to promote sociological theory to a mature state viewed their main problem as that of causal explanation. To them, the determination and systematization of data constituted only a first step in scientific investigation. They boldly faced the task of attempting to understand and control the process of *becoming,* which, they pointed out must be analyzed into a plurality of facts representing a succession of cause and effect. Therefore, "The idea of social theory is the analysis of the totality of social becoming into such causal processes and a systematization permitting us to understand the connections between these processes." [16] In casting about for the best possible method of causal explanation, Thomas and Znaniecki rejected a fallacy prevalent in their time, according to which science simply takes the facts as they are without any methodological prepossessions "entirely a posteriori from pure experience." However, they declared, "A fact by itself is already an abstraction; we isolate a certain limited aspect of the concrete process of becoming, rejecting, at least provisionally, all its indefinite complexity. The question is only whether we perform this abstraction methodically or not, whether we know what and why we accept and reject or simply take uncritically the old abstractions of 'common sense.'" [17] It is a measure of how knowledgeable *they* had become that in 1917 Thomas and Znaniecki could take so advanced a position. Not all of their confreres have yet caught up with it.

Sociology enjoys more general acceptance and academic respectability in the United States at present than in any other part of the world. One reason it has flourished in this country is that from the time of such men as Lester Frank Ward, practicality has made a powerful appeal to American sociologists. The technological side of science—in this case applied sociology or "human engineering"—always had more opportunity to develop in this environment than theory, which was often dismissed contemptuously as abstract, fine-spun and arid. We have suggested that the early European protagonists of sociology usually envisaged practical application of their theories, but they considered such consequences only as ultimate objectives after the development of the science to which they dedicated themselves. In the United States, on the other hand, there was considerable interest in a social science that would provide immediate solutions to complicated problems of the moment. American sociologists could, of course, draw upon a large European reservoir for the analysis of social phenomena. Yet they were more likely to be guided in their investigations by specific problems such as crime, immigration, vice, or feminist unrest. To Thomas and Znaniecki this seemed like putting the cart before the horse. Their insight is all the more remarkable since with their joint study of the *Polish Peasant* they themselves were plunging into the vortex of American social problems. But they were guided in their inquiry by the concepts sociology had already put at their disposal and which they further developed. Their analysis transcends the specific phenomenon under study and through its theoretical elaboration gives us generalizations applicable to a wide range of social situations. Indeed, the "Methodological Note" with which they introduce their major work contains severe strictures against immediate reference to practical aims. It points out the fallacies that result from trying to understand difficult situations without any guiding theoretical framework.

Granting that we should be able to foresee future developments and prepare for them, accumulate a stock of secure and objective information to be applied if the need arises, the authors favored the growth of an exact and empirical science "ready for eventual application. And such a science can be constituted only if we treat it as an end in itself, not as a means to anything else, and if we give it time and opportunity to develop along all the lines of investigation possible, even if we do not see what may be the eventual applications of one or another of its results." [18]

To be sure, there are many urgent social problems which cry out for solution, but, as historians of science (not to mention Thomas and Znaniecki) have often pointed out, practical problems are most often solved in the long run by those who concentrate on most unpractical theoretical work, while those who steep themselves in practicality and common sense remain powerless to make a dent even in those problems which they set out to overcome.

On the other hand, there has been a noticeable tendency to claim with exaggerated and unwarranted enthusiasm that *the* sociological theory is to emerge within a very short time from the development of a master scheme now in the process of elaboration. A certain degree of skepticism seems to be warranted. The speculative mind concerned only with theory in the large is likely to leave behind a system of Byzantine style, a large architectonic scheme admirable perhaps for its logical consistency but otherwise of no relevance to the workaday development of a growing science.

There is a real need today for a science of society, and the features of such a science can by now be perceived rather clearly. But much more difficult theoretical work—in constant interplay with research—is still required to transform into solid achievement what is as yet largely a promise. It seems to us that the pioneers of sociological theory have succeeded in establishing that there *is* a social reality subject to its own partly validated laws of development, a reality which requires analysis on its own terms, and that these terms cannot be reduced to psychology, economics, or any of the other sciences of man. It now remains for us so to codify the results of our research that in the course of time ever more encompassing theories can be initiated to account for uniformities in the social sphere. We heartily concur with Robert K. Merton when he says:

Sociological theory must advance on these interconnected planes: through special theories adequate to limited ranges of social data, and the evolution of a more general conceptual scheme adequate to consolidate groups of special theories.

To concentrate entirely on the master conceptual scheme for deriving all subsidiary theories is to run the risk of producing twentieth-century equivalents of large philosophical systems of the past, with all their varied suggestiveness, all their architectonic splendor and all their scientific sterility.[19]

NOTES

1. Harry Elmer Barnes, *An Introduction to the History of Sociology*, Chicago, 1948, p. 83.
2. Auguste Comte, *The Positive Philosophy*, London, 1893 (3rd ed.) Vol. 1, p. 2.
3. Jean Piaget, *The Moral Judgment of the Child*, Glencoe, Illinois, 1948.
4. Herbert Spencer, *The Study of Sociology*, New York, 1875, pp. 13–14.
5. *Ibid.*, pp. 270–271.
6. Robert K. Merton, *Social Theory and Social Structure*, Glencoe, Illinois, 1949, p. 68.
7. For a recent example see *The American Scholar Forum*, Spring 1952, and a rejoinder, "Social Science and the Humanists" by Bernard Rosenberg in *The American Scholar*, Spring 1953, pp. 203–214.
8. Spencer, *op. cit.*, p. 58.
9. *Ibid.*, p. 32.
10. Georg Simmel, *The Sociology of Georg Simmel*, translated and edited by Kurt H. Wolff, Glencoe, Illinois, 1950, pp. 4–6.
11. Emile Durkheim, *The Rules of Sociological Method*, Chicago, 1938, pp. 102–104.
12. *Ibid.*, p. 4.
13. *Ibid.*, p. 7.
14. William Isaac Thomas and Florian Znaniecki, *The Polish Peasant in Europe and America*, New York, 1927, p. 1.
15. *Ibid.*, p. 3.
16. *Ibid.*, p. 36.
17. *Ibid.*, p. 37.
18. *Ibid.*, p. 15.
19. Merton, *op. cit.*, p. 10.

PART I

General Concepts

2.
CULTURE

WHAT DISTINGUISHES man from non-man? That, as La Rochefoucauld suggested, he drinks whether thirsty or not and makes love in every season? That he has a soul? That he is a rational animal or a gregarious creature? There are both thoughtful and whimsical answers to this question, but in the cool light of science most of them are seen to be misleading, superficial, or simply erroneous.

All ethnological and sociological reflection begins by asking what differentiates man from other species. Anything that follows from that reflection stands or falls on the validity of a single answer: that man alone is in possession of culture. In *Primitive Culture* Sir Edward Tylor (1832–1917), who, with Herbert Spencer, probably did most to give British social science its special flavor, first advanced the classic definition of culture. It was a simple but inclusive definition which stated or implied that the proper domain of anthropology lay in everything man made and taught to future generations who could also accumulate and transmit their knowledge. This is what Tylor meant by "culture." By reason of his peculiar endowment, man, unlike any other species, is able to recreate the natural environment. Man makes tools and rules and patterns his life according. He becomes at one and the same time a slave to and the master of his own past creations.

The eminent American anthropologist, A. L. Kroeber, in his famous essay on "The Superorganic" in 1917 fully embraced the Tylorian point of view and strongly criticized "biologism" (the reduction of human behavior to biological mechanisms), a major tendency of his day and ours. Tylor's opposite number in the United States, Lewis Henry Morgan (1818–1881), had advanced similar views (which reappear even more forcefully in the contemporary work of a gifted disciple, Leslie White). These premises, in turn, are conceptually identical with those of the great French sociologist, Emile Durkheim (1858–1917), who used "society" to mean what the anthropologists understood by "culture."

In the twentieth century cultural anthropologists such as Bronislaw Malinowski (1884–1942) and Leslie White have stressed the linguistic basis of man's capacity to develop culture. This is most evident in the readings

17

we have selected. Men are organisms in symbolic communication with each other. Therefore, they have culture. We are distinctively a symbol-making and symbol-using species. All else follows from this primary datum, as White has so trenchantly shown us. Neither material culture—which Malinowski brought more to the fore than did Tylor—nor non-material culture—habits, ideas, and beliefs—could exist without the symbol.

Clyde Kluckhohn's valuable summary suggests how far social science has gone in achieving a general acceptance of this key concept.

Culture Defined * (*Tylor*)

Culture or Civilization, taken in its wide ethnographic sense, is that complex whole which includes knowledge, belief, art, morals, law, custom, and any other capabilities and habits acquired by man as a member of society. The condition of culture among the various societies of mankind, in so far as it is capable of being investigated on general principles, is a subject apt for the study of laws of human thought and action. On the one hand, the uniformity which so largely pervades civilization may be ascribed, in great measure, to the uniform action of uniform causes; while on the other hand its various grades may be regarded as stages of development or evolution, each the outcome of previous history, and about to do its proper part in shaping the history of the future. To the investigation of these two great principles in several departments of ethnography, with especial consideration of the civilization of the lower tribes as related to the civilization of the higher nations, the present volumes are devoted.

Our modern investigators in the sciences of inorganic nature are foremost to recognize, both within and without their special fields of work, the unity of nature, the fixity of its laws, the definite sequence of cause and effect through which every fact depends on what has gone before it, and acts upon what is to come after it. They grasp firmly the Pythagorean doctrine of pervading order in the universal Kosmos. They affirm, with Aristotle, that nature is not full of incoherent episodes, like a bad tragedy. They agree with Leibnitz in what he calls 'my axiom, that nature never acts by leaps (la nature n'agit jamais par saut),' as well as in his 'great principle, commonly little employed, that nothing happens without its sufficient reason.' Nor, again, in studying the structure and habits of plants and animals, or in investigating the lower functions even of man, are these leading ideas un-

* Reprinted from *Primitive Culture* by Edward B. Tylor, Vol. I, pp. 1–6, John Murray, London, 1891.

acknowledged. But when we come to talk of the higher processes of human feeling and action, of thought and language, knowledge and art, a change appears in the prevalent tone of opinion. The world at large is scarcely prepared to accept the general study of human life as a branch of natural science, and to carry out, in a large sense, the poet's injunction to 'Account for moral as for natural things.' To many educated minds there seems something presumptuous and repulsive in the view that the history of mankind is part and parcel of the history of nature, that our thoughts, wills, and actions accord with laws as definite as those which govern the motion of waves, the combination of acids and bases, and the growth of plants and animals.

The main reasons of this state of the popular judgment are not far to seek. There are many who would willingly accept a science of history if placed before them with substantial definiteness of principle and evidence, but who not unreasonably reject the systems offered to them, as falling too far short of a scientific standard. Through resistance such as this, real knowledge always sooner or later makes its way, while the habit of opposition to novelty does such excellent service against the invasions of speculative dogmatism, that we may sometimes even wish it were stronger than it is. But other obstacles to the investigation of laws of human nature arise from considerations of metaphysics and theology. The popular notion of free human will involves not only freedom to act in accordance with motive, but also a power of breaking loose from continuity and acting without cause,— a combination which may be roughly illustrated by the simile of a balance sometimes acting in the usual way, but also possessed of the faculty of turning by itself without or against its weights. This view of an anomalous action of the will which it need hardly be said is incompatible with scientific argument, subsists as an opinion patent or latent in men's minds, and strongly affecting their theoretic views of history, though it is not, as a rule, brought prominently forward in systematic reasoning. Indeed the definition of human will, as strictly according with motive, is the only possible scientific basis in such enquiries. Happily, it is not needful to add here yet another to the list of dissertations on supernatural intervention and natural causation, on liberty, predestination, and accountability. We may hasten to escape from the regions of transcendental philosophy and theology, to start on a more hopeful journey over more practicable ground. None will deny that, as each man knows by the evidence of his own consciousness, definite and natural cause does, to a great extent, determine human action. Then, keeping aside from considerations of extra-natural interference and causeless spontaneity, let us take this admitted existence of natural cause and effect as our standing-ground, and travel on it so far as it will bear us. It is on this same basis that physical science pursues, with ever-increasing success, its quest of laws of nature. Nor need this restriction hamper the scientific study of human life, in which the real difficulties are the practical ones of enormous complexity of evidence, and imperfection of methods of observation.

Now it appears that this view of human will and conduct, as subject to definite law, is indeed recognized and acted upon by the very people who oppose it when stated in the abstract as a general principle, and who then complain that it annihilates man's free will, destroys his sense of personal responsibility, and degrades him to a soulless machine. He who will say these things will nevertheless pass much of his own life in studying the motives which lead to human action, seeking to attain his wishes through them, framing in his mind theories of personal character, reckoning what are likely to be the effects of new combinations, and giving to his reasoning the crowning character of true scientific enquiry, by taking it for granted that in so far as his calculation turns out wrong, either his evidence must have been false or incomplete, or his judgment upon it unsound. Such a one will sum up the experience of years spent in complex relations with society, by declaring his persuasion that there is a reason for everything in life, and that where events look unaccountable, the rule is to wait and watch in hope that the key to the problem may some day be found. This man's observation may have been as narrow as his inferences are crude and prejudiced, but nevertheless he has been an inductive philosopher 'more than forty years without knowing it.' He has practically acknowledged definite laws of human thought and action, and has simply thrown out of account in his own studies of life the whole fabric of motiveless will and uncaused spontaneity. It is assumed here that they should be just so thrown out of account in wider studies, and that the true philosophy of history lies in extending and improving the methods of the plain people who form their judgments upon facts, and check them upon new facts. Whether the doctrine be wholly or but partly true, it accepts the very condition under which we search for new knowledge in the lessons of experience, and in a word the whole course of our rational life is based upon it.

'One event is always the son of another, and we must never forget the parentage,' was a remark made by a Bechuana chief to Casalis the African missionary. Thus at all times historians, so far as they have aimed at being more than mere chroniclers, have done their best to show not merely succession, but connexion, among the events upon their record. Moreover, they have striven to elicit general principles of human action, and by these to explain particular events, stating expressly or taking tacitly for granted the existence of a philosophy of history. Should any one deny the possibility of thus establishing historical laws, the answer is ready with which Boswell in such a case turned on Johnson: 'Then, sir, you would reduce all history to no better than an almanack.' That nevertheless the labours of so many eminent thinkers should have as yet brought history only to the threshold of science, need cause no wonder to those who consider the bewildering complexity of the problems which come before the general historian. The evidence from which he is to draw his conclusions is at once so multifarious and so doubtful, that a full and distinct view of its bearing on a particular question is hardly to be attained, and thus the temptation becomes all but irresistible to garble it in support of some rough and ready theory of the course of events. The philosophy of history at large, explaining the past and predicting the future phenomena of man's life in the world by reference to general laws, is in fact a subject with which, in the present state of knowledge, even genius aided by wide research seems but hardly able to cope. Yet there are departments of it which, though difficult enough, seem comparatively accessible. If the field of enquiry be narrowed from History as a whole to that branch of it which is here called Culture, the history, not of tribes or nations, but of the condition of knowledge, religion, art, custom, and the like among them, the task of investigation proves to lie within far more moderate compass. We suffer still from the same kind of difficulties which beset the wider argument, but they are much diminished. The evidence is no longer so wildly heterogeneous, but may be more simply classified and compared, while the power of getting rid of extraneous matter, and treating each issue on its own proper set of facts, makes close reasoning on the whole more available than in general history. This may appear from a brief preliminary examination of the problem, how the phenomena of Culture may be classified and arranged, stage by stage, in a probable order of evolution.

The Superorganic * (*Kroeber*)

A way of thought characteristic of our western civilization has been the formulation of complementary antitheses, a balancing of exclusive opposites. One of these pairs of ideas with which our world has been laboring for some two thousand years is expressed in the words *body* and *soul*. Another couplet

* Reprinted from *The Nature of Culture* by Alfred Louis Kroeber, pp. 23–30, by permission of The University of Chicago Press. Copyright, 1952, by The University of Chicago.

that has served its useful purpose, but which science is now often endeavoring to rid itself of, at least in certain aspects, is the distinction of the *physical* from the *mental*. A third discrimination is that of the *vital* from the *social,* or in other phraseology, of the *organic* from the *cultural*. The implicit recognition of the difference between organic qualities and processes and social qualities and processes is of long standing. The formal distinction is however recent. In fact the full import of the significance of the antithesis may be said to be only dawning upon the world. For every occasion on which some human mind sharply separates organic and social forces, there are dozens of other times when the distinction between them is not thought of, or an actual confusion of the two ideas takes place.

One reason for this current confusion of the organic and social is the predominance, in the present phase of the history of thought, of the idea of evolution. This idea, one of the earliest, simplest, and also vaguest ever attained by the human mind, has received its strongest ground and fortification in the domain of the organic; in other words, through biological science. At the same time, there is an evolution, or growth, or gradual development, apparent also in other realms than that of plant and animal life. We have theories of stellar or cosmic evolution; and there is obvious, even to the least learned, a growth or evolution of civilization. In the nature of things there is little danger of the carrying over of the Darwinian or post-Darwinian principles of the evolution of life into the realm of burning suns and lifeless nebulae. Human civilization or progress, on the other hand, which exists only in and through living members of the species, is outwardly so similar to the evolution of plants and animals, that it has been inevitable that there should have been sweeping applications of the principles of organic development to the facts of cultural growth. This of course is reasoning by analogy, or arguing that because two things resemble each other in one point they will also be similar in others. In the absence of knowledge, such assumptions are justifiable as assumptions. Too often, however, their effect is to predetermine mental attitude, with the result that when the evidence begins to accumulate which could prove or disprove the assumption based on analogy, this evidence is no longer viewed impartially and judiciously, but is merely distributed and disposed of in such a way as not to interfere with the established conviction into which the original tentative guess has long since turned.

This is what has happened in the field of organic and social evolution. This distinction between them, which is so obvious that to former ages it seemed too commonplace to remark upon, except incidentally and indirectly, has been largely obscured in the last fifty years through the hold which thoughts connected with the idea of organic evolution have had on minds of the time. It even seems fair to say that this confusion has been greater and more general among those to whom study and scholarship are a daily pursuit than to the remainder of the world.

And yet many aspects of the difference between the organic and that in human life which is not organic, are so plain that a child can grasp them, and that all human beings, including the veriest savages, constantly employ the distinction. Everyone is aware that we are born with certain powers and that we acquire others. There is no need of argument to prove that we derive some things in our lives and make-up from nature through heredity, and that other things come to us through agencies with which heredity has nothing to do. No one has yet been found to assert that any human being is born with an inherent knowledge of the multiplication table; nor, on the other hand, to doubt that the children of a negro are born negroes through the operation of hereditary forces. Some qualities in every individual are however clearly debatable ground; and when the development of civilization as a whole and the evolution of life as a whole are compared, the distinction of the processes involved has too often been allowed to lapse.

Some millions of years ago, it is currently taught, natural selection, or some other evolutionary agency, first caused birds to appear in the world. They sprang from reptiles. Conditions were such that the struggle for existence on the earth was hard; while in the air there were safety and room. Gradually, either by a series of almost imperceptible gradations through a long line of successive generations, or by more marked and sudden leaps in a shorter period, the group of birds was evolved from its reptilian ancestors. In this development, feathers were acquired and scales lost; the grasping faculty of the front legs was converted into an ability to sustain the body in the air. The advantages of resistance enjoyed by a cold-blooded organization were given up for the equivalent or greater compensation of the superior activity that goes with warm-bloodedness. The net result of this chapter of evolutionary history was that a new power, that of aerial locomotion, was added to the sum total of faculties possessed by the highest group of animals, the vertebrates. The vertebrate animals as a whole, however, were not affected. The majority of them are without the power of flight as their ancestors were millions of years ago. The birds, in turn, had lost certain faculties which they once possessed, and presumably would still possess were it not for the acquisition of their wings.

In the last few years human beings have also attained the power of aerial locomotion. But the process by which this power was attained, and its effects on the species, are as different from those which characterized the acquisition of flight by the first birds as it is possible for them to be. Our means of flying are outside of our bodies. A bird is born with a pair of wings, but we have invented the aeroplane. The bird renounced a potential pair of hands to get his wings; we, because our new faculty is not part of our congenital make-up, keep all the organs and capacities of our fore-fathers but add to them the new ability. The process of the development of civilization is clearly one of accumulation: the old is retained, in spite of the incoming of the new. In organic evolution, the introduction of new features is generally possible only through the loss or modification of existing organs or faculties.

In short, the growth of new species of animals takes place through, and in fact consists of, changes in their organic constitution. As regards the growth of civilization, on the other hand, the one example cited is sufficient to show that change and progress can take place through an invention without any such constitutional alteration of the human species.

There is another way of looking at this difference. It is clear that as a new species originates, it is derived wholly from the individual or individuals that first showed the particular traits distinguishing the new species. When we say that it is derived from these individuals we mean, literally, that it is descended. In other words, the species is composed only of such individuals as contain the "blood"—the germ-plasm—of particular ancestors. Heredity is thus the indispensable means of transmission. When however an invention is made, the entire human race is capable of profiting thereby. People who have not the slightest blood kinship to the first designers of aeroplanes can fly and are flying today. Many a father has used, enjoyed, and profited by the invention of his son. In the evolution of animals, the descendant can build upon the inheritance transmitted to him from his ancestors, and may rise to higher powers and more perfect development; but the ancestor is, in the very nature of things, precluded from thus profiting from his descendant. In short, organic evolution is essentially and inevitably connected with hereditary processes; the social evolution which characterizes the progress of civilization, on the other hand, is not, or not necessarily, tied up with hereditary agencies.

The whale is not only a warm-blooded mammal, but is recognized as the remote descendant of carnivorous land animals. In some few million years, as such genealogies are usually reckoned, this animal lost his legs for running, his claws for holding and tearing, his original hair and external ears that would be useless or worse in water, and acquired fins and fluke, a cylindrical body, a layer of fat, and the power of holding his breath. There was much that the species gave up; more, on the whole, perhaps than it gained. Certainly some of its parts have degenerated. But there was one new power that it did achieve: that of roaming the ocean indefinitely.

The parallel and also contrast is in the human acquisition of the identical faculty. We do not, in gradual alteration from father to son, change our arms into flippers and grow a tail. We do not enter the water at all to navigate it. We build a boat. And what this means is that we preserve our bodies and our natal faculties intact, unaltered from those of our fathers and remotest ancestors. Our means of marine travel is outside of our natural endowment. We make it and use it: the original whale had to turn himself into a boat. It took him countless generations to attain to his present condition. All individuals that failed to conform to type left no offspring; or none that went into the blood of the whales of today.

Again, we may compare human and animal beings when groups of them reach a new and arctic environment, or when the climate of the tract where the race is established slowly becomes colder and colder. The non-human mammal species comes to have heavy hair. The polar bear is shaggy; his Sumatran relative sleek. The arctic hare is enveloped in soft fur; the jack-rabbit in comparison is shabbily thin and moth-eaten. Good furs come from the far north, and they lose in richness, in quality, and in value, in proportion as they are stripped from animals of the same species that inhabit milder regions. And this difference is racial, not individual. The jack-rabbit would quickly perish with the end of summer in Greenland; the caged polar bear suffers from temperature warmth within the massive coat which nature has fastened on him.

Now there are people who look for the same sort of inborn peculiarities in the Arctic Eskimo and Samoyed; and find them, because they look for them. That the Eskimo is furry, no one can assert: in fact, we are hairier than he. But it is asserted that he is fat-protected—like the blubber-covered seal that he lives on; and that he devours quantities of meat and oil because he needs them. The true amount of his fat, compared with that of other human beings, remains to be ascertained. He probably has more than the European; but probably no more than the normal full-blooded Samoan and Hawaiian from under the tropics. And as to his diet, if this is seal and seal and seal all winter long, it is not from any congenital craving of his stomach, but because he does not know how to get himself anything else. The Alaskan miner, and the arctic and antarctic explorer, do not guzzle blubber. Wheat-flour, eggs, coffee, sugar, potatoes, canned vegetables—whatever the exigencies of their vocation and the cost of transportation permit—make up their fare. The Eskimo is only too anxious to join them; and both he and they can thrive on the one diet as on the other.

In fact, what the human inhabitant of intemperate latitudes does, is not to develop a peculiar digestive system, any more than he grows hair. He changes his environment, and thereby is able to retain his original body unaltered. He builds a closed house, which keeps out the wind and retains the heat of his body. He makes a fire or lights a lamp. He skins a seal or a caribou of the furry hide with which natural selection or other processes of organic evolution have endowed these beasts; he has his wife make him a shirt and trousers, boots and gloves, or two sets of them; he puts them on; and in a few years, or days, he is provided with the protection which it took the polar bear and the arctic hare, the sable and the ptarmigan, untold periods to acquire. What is more, his baby, and his baby's baby, and his hundredth descendant are born as naked, and unarmed physically, as he and his hundredth ancestor were born.

That this difference in method of resisting a difficult environment, as followed respectively by the polar bear species and the human Eskimo race, is absolute, need not be asserted. That the difference is deep, is unquestionable. That it is as important as it is often neglected, it is the object of this essay to establish.

It has long been the custom to say that the difference is that between body and mind; that animals have their physiques adapted to their circumstances, but that man's superior intelligence enables him to rise superior to such lowly needs. But this is not the most significant point of difference. It is true that without the much greater mental faculties of man, he could not achieve the attainments the lack of which keeps the brute chained to the limitations of his anatomy. But the greater human intelligence in itself does not cause the differences that exist. This psychic superiority is only the indispensable condition of what is peculiarly human; civilization. Directly, it is the civilization in which every Eskimo, every Alaskan miner or arctic discoverer is reared, and not any greater inborn faculty, that leads him to build houses, ignite fire, and wear clothing. The distinction between animal and man which counts is not that of the physical and mental, which is one of relative degree, but that of the organic and social which is one of kind. The beast has mentality, and we have bodies; but in civilization man has something that no animal has.

That this distinction is actually something more than that of the physical and mental, appears from an example that may be chosen from the non-bodily: speech.

On the surface, human and animal speech, in spite of the enormously greater richness and complexity of the former, are much alike. Both express emotions, possibly ideas, in sounds formed by bodily organs and understood by the hearing individual. But the difference between the so-called language of brutes and that of men is infinitely great; as a homely illustration will set forth.

A newly-born pup is brought up in a litter of kittens by a fostering cat. Familiar anecdotes and newspaper paragraphs to the contrary, the youngster will bark and growl, not purr or miaow. He will not even try to do the latter. The first time his toe is stepped on, he will whine, not squeal, just as surely as when thoroughly angered he will bite as his never-beheld mother did, and not even attempt to claw as he has seen his foster-mother do. For half his life seclusion may keep him from sight or sound or scent of another dog. But then let a bark or a snarl reach him through the restraining wall, and he will be all attention—more than at any voice ever uttered by his cat associates. Let the bark be repeated, and interest will give way to excitement, and he will answer in kind, as certainly as, put with a bitch, the sexual impulses of his species will manifest themselves. It cannot be doubted that dog speech is ineradicably part of dog nature, as fully contained in it without training or culture, as wholly part of the dog organism, as are teeth or feet or stomach or motions or instincts. No degree of contact with cats, or deprivation of association with his own kind, can make a dog acquire cat speech, or lose his own, any more than it can cause him to switch his tail instead of wagging it, to rub his sides against his master instead of leaping against him, or to grow whiskers and carry his drooping ears erect.

Let us take a French baby, born in France of French parents, themselves descended for numerous generations from French-speaking ancestors. Let us, at once after birth, entrust the infant to a mute nurse, with instructions to let no one handle or see her charge, while she travels by the directest route to the interior heart of China. There she delivers the child to a Chinese couple, who legally adopt it, and rear it as their son. Now suppose three or ten or thirty years passed. Is it needful to discuss what the growing or grown Frenchman will speak? Not a word of French; pure Chinese, without a trace of accent and with Chinese fluency; and nothing else.

It is true that there is a common delusion, frequent even among educated people, that some hidden influence of his French-talking ancestors will survive in the adopted Chinaman: that it is only necessary to send him to

France with a batch of real Chinamen, and he will acquire his mother's tongue with appreciably greater facility, fluency, correctness, and naturalness than his Mongolian companions. That a belief is common, however, is as likely to stamp it a common superstition as a common truth. And a reasonable biologist, in other words, an expert qualified to speak of heredity, will pronounce this answer to this problem in heredity, superstition. He might merely choose a politer phrase.

Now there is something deep-going here. No amount of association with Chinese would turn our young Frenchman's eyes from blue to black, or slant them, or flatten his nose, or coarsen or stiffen his wavy, oval-sectioned hair; and yet his speech is totally that of his associates, in no measure that of his blood kin. His eyes and his nose and his hair are his from heredity; his language is non-hereditary—as much so as the length to which he allows his hair to grow, or the hole which, in conformity to fashion, he may or may not bore in his ears. It is not so much that speech is mental and facial proportions are physical; the distinction that has meaning and use is that human language is non-hereditary and social, eye-color and nose-shape hereditary and organic. By the same criterion, dog speech, and all that is vaguely called the language of animals, is in a class with men's noses, the proportions of their bones, the color of their skin, and the slope of their eyes, and not in a class with any human idiom. It is inherited, and therefore organic. By a human standard, it is not really language at all, except by the sort of metaphor that speaks of the language of the flowers.

It is true that now and then a French child would be found that under the conditions of the experiment assumed, would learn Chinese more slowly, less idiomatically, and with less power of expression, than the average Chinaman. But there would also be French babies, and as many, that would acquire the Chinese language more quickly, more fluently, with richer power of revealing their emotions and defining their ideas, than the normal Chinese. These are individual differences, which it would be absurd to deny, but which do not affect the average, and are not to the point. One Englishman speaks better English, and more of it, than another, and he may also through precocity, learn it much sooner; but one talks English no more and no less truly than the other.

There is one form of animal expression in which the influence of association has sometimes been alleged to be greater than that of heredity. This is the song of birds. There is a good deal of conflicting opinion, and apparently of evidence, on this point. Many birds have a strong inherent impulse to imitate sounds. It is also a fact that the singing of one individual stimulates the other—as with dogs, wolves, cats, frogs, and most noisy animals. That in certain species of birds capable of a complex song the full development will not often be reached in individuals raised out of hearing of their kind, may probably be admitted. But it seems to be clear that every species has a song or call distinctively its own; that this minimum is attainable without association by every normal member of the singing sex, as soon as conditions of age, food, and warmth are proper, and the requisite stimulus of noise, or silence, or sex development, is present. That there has been serious conflict of opinion as to the nature of bird song, will ultimately be found to be chiefly due to the pronouncement of opinions on the matter by those who read their own mental states and activities into animals—a common fallacy that every biological student is now carefully trained against at the outset of his career. In any event, whether one bird does or does not in some degree "learn" from another, there is no fragment of evidence that bird song is a tradition, that like human speech or human music it accumulates and develops from age to age, that it is inevitably altered from generation to generation by fashion or custom, and that it is impossible for it ever to remain the same: in other words, that it is a social thing or due to a process even remotely akin to those affecting the constituents of human civilization.

It is also true that there is in human life a series of utterances that are of the type of animal cries. A man in pain moans without purpose of communication. The sound is literally pressed from him. A person in supreme fright may shriek. We know that his cry is unintended, what the physiologist calls a reflex action. The true shriek is as liable to escape the victim pinned before the approaching engineerless train, as him who is pursued by thinking and planning enemies. The woodsman crushed by a rock forty miles from the nearest human being, will moan like the run-over city dweller surrounded by a crowd waiting for the speeding ambulance. Such cries are of a class with those of animals. In fact, really to understand the "speech" of brutes, we must think ourselves into a condition in which our utterances would be totally restricted to such instinctive cries—"inarticulate" is their general though often inaccurate designation. In an exact sense, they are not language at all.

This is precisely the point. We undoubtedly have certain activities of utterance, certain faculties and habits of sound production, that are truly parallel with those of animals; and we also have something more that is quite different and without parallel among the animals. To deny that something purely animal underlies human speech, is fatuous; but it would be equally narrow to believe that because our speech springs from an animal foundation, and originated in this foundation, it therefore is nothing but animal mentality and utterances greatly magnified. A house may be built on rock; without this base it might be impossible for it to have been erected; but no one will maintain that therefore the house is nothing but improved and glorified stone.

As a matter of fact, the purely animal element in human speech is small. Apart from laughter and crying, it finds rare utterance. Our interjections are denied by philologists as true speech, or at best but half admitted. It is a fact that they differ from full words in not being voiced, generally, to convey a meaning—nor to conceal one. But even these particles are shaped and dictated by fashion, by custom, by the type of civilization to which we belong, in short by social and not by organic elements. When I drive the hammer on my thumb instead of on the head of the nail, an involuntary "damn" may escape me as readily if I am alone in the house, as if companions stand on each side. Perhaps more readily. So far, the exclamation does not serve the purpose of speech and is not speech. But the Spaniard will say "carramba" and not "damn"; and the Frenchman, the German, the Chinaman, will avail himself of still different expression. The American says "outch" when hurt. Other nationalities do not understand this syllable. Each people has its own sound; some even two—one used by men and the other by women. A Chinaman will understand a laugh, a moan, a crying child, as well as we understand it, and as well as a dog understands the snarl of another dog. But he must learn "outch," or it is meaningless. No dog, on the other hand, ever has given utterance to a new snarl, unintelligible to other dogs, as a result of having been brought up in different associations. Even this lowest element of human speech, then, this involuntary half-speech of exclamations, is therefore shaped by social influences.

Herodotus tells of an Egyptian king, who, wishing to ascertain the parent tongue of humanity, had some infants brought up in isolation from their own kind, with only goats as companions and for sustenance. When the children, grown older, were revisited, they cried the word "bekos," or, subtracting the ending which the normalizing and sensitive Greek could not endure omitting from anything that passed his lips, more probably "bek." The king then sent to all countries to learn in what land this vocable meant something. He ascertained that in the Phrygian idiom it signified bread, and, assuming that the children were crying for food, concluded that they spoke Phrygian in voicing their "natural" human speech, and that this tongue must therefore be the original one of mankind. The king's belief in an inherent and congenital language of man, which only the blind accidents of time had distorted into a multitude of idioms, may seem simple; but naive as it is, inquiry would reveal crowds of civilized people still adhering to it.

This however is not our moral to the tale. That lies in the fact that the one and only word attributed to the children, "bek," was, if the story has any authenticity whatsoever, only a reflection or imitation—as the commentators of Herodotus long since conjectured—of the bleating of the goats that were the children's only associates and instructors. In short, if it is allowable to deduce any inference from so apocryphal an anecdote, what it proves is that there is no natural and therefore no organic human language.

Thousands of years later another sovereign, the Mogul emperor Akbar, repeated the experiment with the intent of ascertaining the "natural" religion of mankind. His band of children were shut up in a house. When, the necessary time having elapsed, the doors were opened in the presence of the expectant and enlightened ruler, his disappointment was great: the children trooped out as dumb as deaf-mutes. Faith dies hard, however; and we may suspect that it would take a third trial, under modern chosen and controlled conditions, to satisfy some natural scientists that speech, for the human individual and for the human race, is wholly an acquired and not a hereditary thing, entirely outward and not at all inward—a social product and not an organic growth.

Human and animal speech, then, though one roots in the other, are in the nature of a different order. They resemble each other only as the flight of a bird and of an aeronaut are alike. That the analogy between them has frequently deceived, proves only the guilelessness of the human mind. The operative processes are wholly unlike; and this, to him who is desirous of understanding, is far more important than the similarity of effect. The savage and the peasant who cure by cleaning the knife and leaving the wound unattended, have observed certain indisputable facts. They know that cleanness aids, dirt on the whole impedes recovery. They know the knife as the cause, the wound as the effect; and they grasp, too, the correct principle that treatment of the cause is in general more likely to be effective than treatment of the symptom. They fail only in not inquiring into the process that may be involved. Knowing nothing of the nature of sepsis, of bacteria, of the agencies of putrefaction and retardation of healing, they fall back on agencies more familiar to themselves, and use, as best they may, the process of magic intertwined with that of medicine. They carefully scrape the knife; they oil it; they keep it bright. The facts from which they work are correct; their logic is sound enough; they merely do not distinguish between two irreconcilable processes—that of magic and that of physiological chemistry—and apply one in place of another. The student of today who reads the civilizationally moulded mind of men into the mentality of a dog or ape, or who tries to explain civilization—that is, history—by organic factors, commits an error which is less antiquated and more in fashion, but of the same kind and nature.

The Symbol * (*White*)

THE ORIGIN AND BASIS OF HUMAN BEHAVIOR

"In the Word was the Beginning . . . the beginning of Man and of Culture."

I

In July, 1939, a celebration was held at Leland Stanford University to commemorate the hundredth anniversary of the discovery that the cell is the basic unit of all living tissue. Today we are beginning to realize and to appreciate the fact that the symbol is the basic unit of all human behavior and civilization.

All human behavior originates in the use of symbols. It was the symbol which transformed our anthropoid ancestors into men and made them human. All civilizations have been generated, and are perpetuated, only by the use of symbols. It is the symbol which transforms an infant of Homo sapiens into a human being; deaf mutes who grow up without the use of symbols are not human beings. All human behavior consists of, or is dependent upon, the use of symbols. Human behavior is symbolic behavior; symbolic behavior is human behavior. The symbol is the universe of humanity.

II

The great Darwin declared in *The Descent of Man* that "there is no fundamental difference between man and the higher mammals in their mental faculties," that the difference between them consists "*solely* in his [man's] almost infinitely larger power of associating together the most diversified sounds and ideas . . . the mental powers of higher animals do not differ *in kind*, though greatly *in degree*, from the corresponding powers of man" (Chs. 3, 18; emphasis ours).

* From *The Science of Culture*, pp. 22–33. Copyright, 1949, by Leslie A. White. Published by Farrar, Straus & Cudahy, Inc.

This view of comparative mentality is held by many scholars today. Thus, F. H. Hankins, a prominent sociologist, states that "in spite of his large brain, it cannot be said that man has any mental traits that are peculiar to him . . . All of these human superiorities are merely relative or differences of degree." Professor Ralph Linton, an anthropologist, writes in *The Study of Man*: "The differences between men and animals in all these [behavior] respects are enormous, but they seem to be differences in quantity rather than in quality." "Human and animal behavior can be shown to have so much in common," Linton observes, "that the gap [between them] ceases to be of great importance." Dr. Alexander Goldenweiser, likewise an anthropologist, believes that "In point of sheer psychology, mind as such, man is after all no more than a talented animal" and that "the difference between the mentality here displayed [by a horse and a chimpanzee] and that of man is merely one of degree." [1]

That there are numerous and impressive similarities between the behavior of man and that of ape is fairly obvious; it is quite possible that chimpanzees and gorillas in zoos have noted and appreciated them. Fairly apparent, too, are man's behavioral similarities to many other kinds of animals. Almost as obvious, but not easy to define, is a difference in behavior which distinguishes man from all other living creatures. I say 'obvious' because it is quite apparent to the common man that the non-human animals with which he is familiar do not and cannot enter, and participate in, the world in which he, as a human being, lives. It is impossible for a dog, horse, bird, or even an ape, to have *any* understanding of the meaning of the sign of the cross to a Christian, or of the fact that black (white among the Chinese) is the color of mourning. No chimpanzee or laboratory rat can appreciate the difference between Holy water and distilled water, or grasp the meaning of *Tuesday, 3,* or *sin*. No animal save man can distinguish a cousin from an uncle, or a cross cousin from a parallel cousin. Only man can commit the crime of incest or adultery; only he can remember the Sabbath and keep it Holy. It is not, as we well know, that the lower animals can do these things but to a lesser degree than ourselves; they cannot perform these acts of appreciation and distinction *at all*. It is, as Descartes said long ago, "not only that the brutes have less Reason than man, but that they have none at all." [2]

But when the scholar attempts to *define* the mental difference between man and other animals he sometimes encounters difficulties which he cannot surmount and, therefore, ends up by saying that the difference is merely one of degree: man has a bigger mind, "larger power of association," wider range of activities, etc. We have a good example of this in the distinguished physiologist, Anton J. Carlson. After taking note of "man's present achievements in science, in the arts (including oratory), in political and social institutions," and noting "at the same time the apparent paucity of such behavior in other animals," he, as a common man "is tempted to conclude that in these capacities, at least, man has a qualitative superiority over other mammals." But, since, as a scientist, Professor Carlson cannot *define* this qualitative difference between man and other animals, since as a physiologist he cannot explain it, he refuses to admit it—" . . . the physiologist does not accept the great development of articulate speech in man as something qualitatively new; . . ."—and suggests helplessly that some day we may find some new "building stone," an "additional lipoid, phosphatid, or potassium ion," in the human brain which will explain it, and concludes by saying that the difference between the mind of man and that of non-man is "probably only one of degree." [3]

The thesis that we shall advance and defend here is that there is a *fundamental* difference between the mind of man and the mind of non-man. This difference is one of kind, not one of degree. And the gap between the two types is of the greatest importance—at least to the science of comparative behavior. Man uses symbols; no other creature does. An organism has the ability to symbol or it does not; there are no intermediate stages.

III

A symbol may be defined as a thing the value or meaning of which is bestowed upon it by those who use it. I say 'thing' because a symbol may have any kind of physical form; it may have the form of a material object, a color, a sound, an odor, a motion of an object, a taste.

The meaning, or value, of a symbol is in no instance derived from or determined by properties intrinsic in its physical form: the color appropriate to mourning may be yellow, green, or any other color; purple need not be the color of royalty; among the Manchu rulers of China it was yellow. The meaning of the word "see" is not intrinsic in its phonetic (or pictorial) properties. "Biting one's thumb at" [4] someone might mean anything. The meanings of symbols are derived from and determined by the organisms who use them; meaning is bestowed by human organisms upon physical things or events which thereupon become symbols. Symbols "have their signification," to use John Locke's phrase, "from the arbitrary imposition of men." [5]

All symbols must have a physical form otherwise they could not enter our experience. This statement is valid regardless of our theory of experiencing. Even the exponents of "Extra-Sensory Perception" who have challenged Locke's dictum that "the knowledge of the existence of any other thing [besides ourselves and God] we can have only by sensation" [6] have been obliged to work with physical rather than ethereal forms. But the meaning of a symbol cannot be discovered by mere sensory examination of its physical form. One cannot tell by looking at an *x* in an algebraic equation what it stands for; one cannot ascertain with the ears alone the symbolic value of the phonetic compound *si*; one cannot tell merely by weighing a pig how much gold he will exchange for; one cannot tell from the wave length of a color whether it stands for courage or cowardice, "stop" or "go"; nor can one discover the spirit in a fetish by any amount of physical or chemical examination. The meaning of a symbol can be grasped only by non-sensory, symbolic means.

The nature of symbolic experience may be easily illustrated. When the Spaniards first encountered the Aztecs, neither could speak the language of the other. How could the Indians discover the meaning of santo, or the significance of the crucifix? How could the Spaniards learn the meaning of *calli,* or appreciate Tlaloc? These meanings and values could not be communicated by sensory experience of physical properties alone. The finest ears will not tell you whether *santo* means "holy" or "hungry." The keenest senses cannot capture the value of holy water. Yet, as we all know, the Spaniards and the Aztecs did discover each other's meanings and appreciate each other's values. But not with sensory means. Each was able to enter the world of the other only by virtue of a faculty for which we have no better name than *symbol.*

But a thing which in one context is a symbol is, in another context, not a symbol but a sign. Thus, a word is a symbol only when one is concerned with the distinction between its meaning and its physical form. This distinction *must* be made when one bestows value upon a sound-combination or when a previously bestowed value is discovered for the first time; it *may* be made at other times for certain purposes. But after value has been bestowed upon, or discovered in, a word, its meaning becomes identified, in use, with its physical form. The word then functions as a sign, rather than as a symbol. Its meaning is then grasped with the senses.

We define a *sign* as a physical thing or event whose function is to indicate some other thing or event. The meaning of a sign may be inherent in its physical form and its context, as in the case of the height of a column of mercury in a thermometer as an indication of temperature, or the return of robins in the spring. Or, the meaning of a sign may be merely identified with its physical form as in the case of a hurricane signal or a quarantine flag. But in either case, the meaning of the sign may be ascertained by sensory means. The fact that a thing may be both a symbol (in one context) and a sign (in another context) has led to confusion and misunderstanding.

Thus Darwin says: "That which distinguishes man from the lower animals is not the understanding of articulate sounds, for as everyone knows, dogs understand many words and sentences." (Ch. III, *The Descent of Man*)

It is perfectly true, of course, that dogs, apes, horses, birds, and perhaps creatures even lower in the evolutionary scale, can be taught to respond in a specific way to a vocal command. Little Gua, the infant chimpanzee in the Kelloggs' experiment, was, for a time, "considerably superior to the child in responding to human words." [7] But it does not follow that no difference exists between the meaning of "words and sentences" to a man and to an ape or dog. Words are both signs and symbols to man; they are merely signs to a dog. Let us analyze the situation of vocal stimulus and response.

A dog may be taught to roll over at the command "Roll over!" A man may be taught to stop at the command "Halt!" The fact that a dog can be taught to roll over in Chinese, or that he can be taught to "go fetch" at the command "roll over" (and, of course, the same is true for a man) shows that there is no necessary and invariable relationship between a particular sound combination and a specific reaction to it. The dog or the man can be taught to respond in a certain manner to any arbitrarily selected combination of sounds, for example, a group of nonsense syllables, coined for the occasion. On the other hand, any one of a great number and variety of responses may become evocable by a given stimulus. Thus, so far as the *origin* of the relationship between vocal stimulus and response is concerned, the nature of the relationship, i.e., the meaning of the stimulus, is not determined by properties intrinsic in the stimulus.

But, once the relationship has been established between vocal stimulus and response, the meaning of the stimulus becomes *identified with the sounds*; it is then *as if* the meaning were intrinsic in the sounds themselves. Thus, 'halt' does not have the same meaning as 'hilt' or 'malt,' and these stimuli are distinguished from one another with the auditory mechanism. A dog may be conditioned to respond in a certain way to a sound of a given wave length. Sufficiently alter the pitch of the sound and the response will cease to be forthcoming. The meaning of the stimulus has become identified with its physical form; its value is appreciated with the senses.

Thus in *sign* behavior we see that in *establishing* a relationship between a stimulus and a response the properties intrinsic in the stimulus do not determine the nature of the response. But, *after the relationship has been established* the meaning of the stimulus is *as if* it were *inherent* in its physical form. It does not make any difference what phonetic combination we select to evoke the response of terminating self-locomotion. We may teach a dog, horse, or man to stop at any vocal command we care to choose or devise. But once the relationship has been established between sound and response, the meaning of the stimulus become identified with its physical form and is, therefore, perceivable with the senses.

So far we have discovered no difference between the dog and the man; they appear to be exactly alike. And so they are as far as we have gone. But we have not told the whole story yet. No difference between dog and man is discoverable so far as learning to respond appropriately to a vocal stimulus is concerned. But we must not let an impressive similarity conceal an important difference. A porpoise is not yet a fish.

The man differs from the dog—and all other creatures—in that *he can and does play an active role in determining what value the vocal stimulus is to have, and the dog cannot.* The dog does not and cannot play an active part in determining the value of the vocal stimulus. Whether he is to roll over or go fetch at a given stimulus, or whether the stimulus for roll over be one combination of sounds or another is a matter in which the dog has nothing whatever to "say." He plays a purely passive role and can do nothing else. He learns the meaning of a vocal command just as his salivary glands may learn to respond to the sound of a bell. But man plays an active role and thus becomes a creator: let x equal three pounds of coal and it does equal three pounds of coal; let removal of the hat in a house of worship indicate respect and it becomes so. This creative faculty, that of freely, actively, and arbitrarily bestowing value upon things, is one of the most commonplace as well as *the* most important characteristic of man. Children employ it freely in their play: "Let's pretend that this rock is a wolf."

The difference between the behavior of man and other animals then, is that the lower animals may receive new values, may acquire new meanings, but they cannot create and bestow them. Only man can do this. To use a crude analogy, lower animals are like a person who has only the receiving apparatus for wireless messages: he can receive messages but cannot send them. Man can do both. And this difference is one of kind, not of degree: a creature can either "arbitrarily impose signification," can either create and bestow values, or he cannot. There are no intermediate stages. This difference may appear slight, but, as a carpenter once told William James in discussing differences between men, "It's very important." All *human* existence depends upon it and it alone.

The confusion regarding the nature of words and their significance to men and the lower animals is not hard to understand. It arises, first of all, from a failure to distinguish between the two quite different contexts in which words function. The statements, "The meaning of a word cannot be grasped with the senses," and "The meaning of a word can be grasped with the senses," though contradictory, are nevertheless equally true. In the *symbol* context the meaning cannot be perceived with the senses; in the sign context it can. This is confusing enough. But the situation has been made worse by using the words 'symbol' and 'sign' to label, not the *different contexts*, but *one and the same thing*: the word. Thus a word is a symbol *and* a sign, two different things—because it may function in two contexts, esthetic and commercial.

IV

That man is unique among animal species with respect to mental abilities, that a fundamental difference of kind—not of degree—separates man from all other animals is a fact that has long been appreciated, despite Darwin's pronouncement to the contrary. Long ago, in his *Discourse on Method*, Descartes pointed out that "there are no men so dull and stupid . . . as to be incapable of joining together different words . . . on the other hand, there is no other animal, however perfect . . . which can do the like." John Locke, too, saw clearly that "the power of abstracting is not at all in them [i.e., beasts], and that the having of general ideas is that which puts a perfect distinction between man and brutes, and is an excellency which the faculties of brutes do by no means attain to . . . they have no use of words or any other general signs." [8] The great British anthropologist, E. B. Tylor, remarked upon "the mental gulf that divides the lowest savage from the highest ape . . . A young child can understand what is not proved to have entered the mind of the cleverest dog, elephant, or ape." [9] And, of course, there are many today who recognize the "mental gulf" between man and other species.

Thus, for over a century we have had, side by side, two traditions in comparative psychology. One has declared that man does not differ from other animals in mental abilities except in degree. The other has seen clearly that man is unique in at least one respect, that he possesses an ability that no other animal has. The difficulty of *defining* this difference adequately has kept this question open until the present day. The distinction between *sign* behavior and *symbol* behavior as drawn here may, we hope, contribute to a solution of this problem once and for all.

V

Very little indeed is known of the organic basis of the symbolic faculty: we know next to nothing of the neurology of "symbolling." And very few scientists—anatomists, neurologists or physical anthropologists—appear to be interested in the subject. Some, in fact, seem to be unaware of the existence of such a problem. The duty and task of giving an account of the neural basis of symbolling does not, however, fall within the province of the sociologist or the cultural anthropologist. On the contrary, he should scrupulously exclude it as irrelevant to his problems and interests; to introduce it would bring only confusion. It is enough for the sociologist or cultural anthropologist to take the ability to use symbols, possessed by man alone, as given. The use to which he puts this fact is in no way affected by his, or even the anatomist's, inability to describe the symbolic process in neurological terms. However, it is well for the social scientist to be acquainted with the little that neurologists and anatomists do know about the structural basis of symbolling. We, therefore, review briefly the chief relevant facts here.

The anatomist has not been able to discover why men can use symbols and apes cannot. So far as is known the only difference between the brain of man and the brain of an ape is a quantitative one: ". . . man has no new kinds of brain cells or brain cell connections," as A. J. Carlson has remarked. Nor does man, as distinguished from other animals, possess a specialized "symbol-mechanism." The so-called speech areas of the brain should not be identified with symbolling. The notion that symbolling is identified with, or dependent upon, the ability to utter articulate sounds is not uncommon. Thus, L. L. Bernard lists as "the fourth great organic asset of man . . . his vocal apparatus . . . characteristic of him alone." But this is an erroneous conception. The great apes have the mechanism necessary for the production of articulate sounds. "It seemingly is well established," write R. M. and A. W. Yerkes in *The Great Apes,* "that the motor mechanism of voice in this ape [chimpanzee] is adequate not only to the production of a considerable variety of sounds, but also to definite articulations similar to those of man." And the physical anthropologist, E. A. Hooton, asserts that "all of the anthropoid apes are vocally and muscularly equipped so that they could have an articulate language if they possessed the requisite intelligence." Furthermore, as Descartes and Locke pointed out long ago, there are birds who do actually utter articulate sounds, who duplicate the sounds of human speech, but who of course are quite incapable of symbolling. The "speech areas" of the brain are merely areas associated with the muscles of the tongue, with the larynx, etc. But, as we know, symbolling is not at all confined to the use of these organs. One may symbol with any part of the body that he can move at will.[10]

To be sure, the symbolic faculty was brought into existence by the natural processes of organic evolution. And we may reasonably believe that the focal point, if not the locus, of this faculty is in the brain, especially the forebrain. Man's brain is much larger than that of an ape, both absolutely and relatively. The brain of the average adult human male is about 1500 c.c. in size; brains of gorillas seldom exceed 500 c.c. Relatively, the human brain weighs about $\frac{1}{50}$th of the entire body weight, while that of a gorilla varies from $\frac{1}{150}$th to $\frac{1}{200}$th part of that weight.[11] And the forebrain especially is large in man as compared with the ape. Now in many situations we know that quantitative changes give rise to qualitative differences. Water is transformed into steam by additional quantities of heat. Additional power and speed lift the taxiing airplane from the ground and transform terrestrial locomotion into flight. The difference between wood alcohol and grain alcohol is a qualitative expression of a quantitative difference in the proportions of carbon and hydrogen. Thus a marked growth in size of the brain in many may have brought forth a *new* kind of function.

REFERENCES
1. Hankins, pp. 56, 327; Linton, 1936, pp. 79, 68, 60; Goldenweiser, 1937, p. 39.
2. Descartes, p. 189.
3. Carlson, pp. 477–79.
4. "Do you bite your thumb at us, sir?"—*Romeo and Juliet,* Act I, Sc. 1.
5. Locke, Book III, Ch. 9.
6. *Ibid.,* Book IV, Ch. 11.
7. Kellogg, p. 289.
8. Locke, Book II, Chs. 11, 10.
9. Tylor, 1881, pp. 54, 123.
10. Carlson, p. 477; Bernard, L. L., 1927a, p. 399; Yerkes, p. 301; Hooton, 1931, p. 167.
11. Hooton, 1931, p. 153.

Culture * (*Malinowski*)

MAN VARIES in two respects: in physical form and in social heritage, or culture. The science of physical anthropology, employing a complex apparatus of definitions, descriptions and terminologies and somewhat more precise

* By Bronislaw Malinowski, reprinted from *Encyclopaedia of the Social Sciences,* Vol. IV, pp. 621–626, with permission of the publisher, The Macmillan Company. Copyright, 1930, by The Macmillan Company.

methods than common sense and untutored observation, has succeeded in cataloguing the various branches of mankind according to their bodily structure and physiological characteristics. But man varies also in an entirely different aspect. A pure blooded Negro infant, transported to France and brought up there, would differ profoundly from what he would have been if reared in the jungle of his native land. He would have been given a different social heritage: a different language, different habits, ideas and beliefs; he would have been incorporated into a different social organization and cultural setting. This social heritage is the key concept of cultural anthropology, the other branch of the comparative study of man. It is usually called culture in modern anthropology and social science. The word culture is at times used synonymously with civilization, but it is better to use the two terms distinctively, reserving civilization for a special aspect of more advanced cultures. Culture comprises inherited artifacts, goods, technical processes, ideas, habits and values. Social organization cannot be really understood except as a part of culture; and all special lines of inquiry referring to human activities, human groupings and human ideas and beliefs can meet and become cross fertilized in the comparative study of cultures.

Man in order to live continually alters his surroundings. On all points of contact with the outer world he creates an artificial, secondary environment. He makes houses or constructs shelters; he prepares his food more or less elaborately, procuring it by means of weapons and implements; he makes roads and uses means of transport. Were man to rely on his anatomical equipment exclusively, he would soon be destroyed or perish from hunger and exposure. Defense, feeding, movement in space, all physiological and spiritual needs, are satisfied indirectly by means of artifacts even in the most primitive modes of human life. The man of nature, the *Naturmensch,* does not exist.

This material outfit of man—his artifacts, his buildings, his sailing craft, his implements and weapons, the liturgical paraphernalia of his magic and religion—are one and all the most obvious and tangible aspects of culture. They define its level and they constitute its effectiveness. The material equipment of culture is not, however, a force in itself. Knowledge is necessary in the production, management and use of artifacts, implements, weapons and other constructions and is essentially connected with mental and moral discipline, of which religion, laws and ethical rules are the ultimate source. The handling and possession of goods imply also the appreciation of their value. The manipulation of implements and the consumption of goods also require cooperation. Common work and common enjoyment of its results are always based on a definite type of social organization. Thus material culture requires a complement less simple, less easily catalogued or analyzed, consisting of the body of intellectual knowledge, of the system of moral, spiritual and economic values, of social organization and of language. On the other hand, material culture is an indispensable apparatus for the molding or conditioning of each generation of human beings. The secondary environment, the outfit of material culture, is a laboratory in which the reflexes, the impulses, the emotional tendencies of the organism are formed. The hands, arms, legs and eyes are adjusted by the use of implements to the proper technical skill necessary in a culture. The nervous processes are modified so as to yield the whole range of intellectual concepts, emotional types and sentiments which form the body of science, religion and morals prevalent in a community. As an important counterpart to these mental processes there are the modifications in the larynx and tongue which fix some of the crucial concepts and values by associating them with definite sounds. Artifact and custom are equally indispensable and they mutually produce and determine one another.

Language is often regarded as something distinct from both man's material possessions and his system of customs. This view is frequently coupled with a theory by which meaning is regarded as a mystical content of the word, which can be transmitted in utterance from one mind to another. But the meaning of a word is not mysteriously contained in it but is rather an active effect of the sound uttered within a context of situation. The utterance of sound is a significant act indispensable in all forms of human concerted action. It is a type of behavior strictly comparable to the handling of a tool, the wielding of a weapon, the performance of a ritual or the concluding of a contract. The use of words is in all these forms of human activity an indispensable correlate of manual and bodily behavior. The meaning of words consists in what they achieve by concerted action, the indirect handling of the environment through the direct action upon other organisms. Speech therefore is a bodily habit and is comparable to any other type of custom. The learning of language consists in the development of a system of conditioned reflexes which at the same time become conditioned stimuli. Speech is the production of articulate sounds, developed in childhood out of the inarticulate infantile utterances which constitute the child's main endowment in dealing with his environment. As the individual grows his increase of linguistic knowledge runs parallel with his general development. A growing knowledge of technical processes is bound up with the learning of technical terms; the development of his tribal citizenship and social responsibility is accompanied by the acquisition of a sociological vocabulary and of polite speech, commands and legal phraseology; the growing experience of religious and moral values is associated with the development of ritual and ethical formulae. The full knowledge of language is the inevitable correlate of the full attainment of a tribal and cultural status. Language thus is an integral part of culture; it is not, however, a system of tools but rather a body of vocal customs.

Social organization is often regarded by sociologists as remaining outside culture, but the organization of social groups is a complex combination of material equipment and bodily customs which cannot be divorced from either its material or psychological substratum. Social organization is the standardized manner in which groups behave. But a social group consists always of individuals. The child, attached to its parents through the satisfaction of all its needs, grows up within the shelter of the parental house, hut or tent. The domestic hearth is the center around which the various necessities of warmth, comfort, food and companionship are satisfied. Later in every human society communal life is associated with the local settlement, the town, village or compound; it is localized within definite boundaries and associated with private and public activities of an economic, political and religious nature. In every organized activity therefore human beings are bound together by their connection with a definite portion of environment, by their association with a common shelter and by the fact that they carry out certain tasks in common. The concerted character of their behavior is the result of social rules, that is, customs, either sanctioned by explicit measures or working in an apparently automatic way. The sanctioned rules—laws, customs and manners—belong to the category of acquired bodily habits. The essence of moral values by which man is driven to definite behavior by inner compulsion has in religious and metaphysical thought been ascribed to conscience, the will of God or an inborn categorical imperative; while some sociologists have explained it as due to a supreme moral being—society, or the collective soul. Moral motivation when viewed empirically consists in a disposition of the nervous system and of the whole organism to follow within given circumstances a line of behavior dictated by inner constraint which is due neither to innate impulses nor yet to obvious gains or utilities. The inner constraint is the result of the gradual training of the organism within a definite set of cultural conditions. The impulses, desires and ideas are within each society welded into specific systems, in psychology called sentiments. Such sentiments define the attitudes of a man toward the members of his group, above all his nearest kindred; toward the material objects of his surroundings; toward the country which he inhabits; toward the community with which he works; toward the realities of his magical, religious or metaphysical *Weltanschauung.* Fixed values or sentiments often condition human behavior so that man prefers death to surrender or compromise, pain to pleasure, abstention to satisfaction of desire. The formation of sentiments and thus of values is always based on the cultural apparatus in a society. Sentiments are formed over a long space of time and through a very gradual training or conditioning of the organism. They are based on forms of organization, very often world wide, such as the Christian church, the community of Islam, the empire, the flag—all symbols or catchwords, behind which, however, there exist vast and living cultural realities.

The understanding of culture is to be found in the process of its production by succeeding generations and in the way in which it produces in each new generation the appropriately molded organism. The metaphysical concepts of a group mind, collective sensorium or consciousness are due to an apparent antinomy of sociological reality: the psychological nature of human culture on the one hand and on the other the fact that culture transcends the individual. The fallacious solution of this antinomy is the theory that human minds combine or integrate and form a superindividual and yet essentially spiritual being. Durkheim's theory of moral constraint by the direct influence of the social being, the theories based on a collective unconscious and archetype of culture, such concepts as consciousness of kind or the inevitability of collective imitation, account for the psychological yet superindividual nature of social reality by introducing some theoretical metaphysical short cut.

The psychological nature of social reality is, however, due to the fact that its ultimate medium is always the individual mind or nervous system. The collective elements are due to the sameness of reaction within the small groups which act as units of social organization by the process of conditioning and to the medium of material culture within which the conditioning takes place. The small groups which act as units because of their mental sameness are then integrated into the larger schemes of social organization by the principles of territorial distribution, cooperation and division into strata of material culture. Thus the reality of the superindividual consists in the body of material culture, which remains outside any individual and yet influences him in the ordinary physiological manner. There is nothing mystical therefore in the fact that culture is at the same time psychological and collective.

Culture is a reality *sui generis* and must be studied as such. The various sociologies which treat the subject matter of culture by way of the organic simile or in the likeness of a collective mind are irrelevant. Culture is a well organized unity divided into two fundamental aspects—a body of artifacts and a system of customs—but also obviously into further subdivisions or units. The analysis of culture into its component elements, the relation of these elements to one another and their relation to the needs of the human organism, to the environment and to the universally acknowledged human ends which they subserve are important problems of anthropology.

Anthropology has dealt with its material by two different methods, controlled by two incompatible conceptions of the growth and history of culture. The evolutionary school has regarded the growth of culture as a series of spontaneous metamorphoses proceeding according to definite laws and producing a fixed sequence of successive stages. This school took for granted the divisibility of culture into simple elements and it treated these elements as if they were units of the same order; it presented theories of the evolution of fire making side by side with accounts of how religion developed, versions of the origin and development of marriage and doctrines as to the development of pottery. Stages of economic development and steps in the evolution of domestic animals, of cutting implements and of ornamental design were formulated. Yet there is no doubt that, although certain implements have changed, passed through a sequence of stages and obeyed more or less definite laws of evolution, the family, marriage or religious beliefs are not subject to any simple, dramatic metamorphoses. The fundamental institutions of human culture have changed not by way of sensational transformations but rather through an increasing differentiation of form in accordance with an increasingly definite function. Until the nature of the various cultural phenomena, their function and their form are understood and described more fully, it seems premature to speculate on possible origins and stages. The concepts of origins, stages, laws of development and growth of culture have remained nebulous and essentially non-empirical. The method of evolutionary anthropology was based primarily on the concept of survival, since this allowed the student to reconstruct past stages from present day conditions. The concept of survival, however, implies that a cultural arrangement can outlive its function. The better a certain type of culture is known, the fewer survivals there appear to be in it. Evolutionary inquiry should therefore be preceded by a functional analysis of culture.

The same criticism applies to the historical or diffusionist school, which attempts to reconstruct the history of human cultures mainly by tracing their diffusion. This school denies the importance of spontaneous evolution and maintains that cultures have been produced mainly by the imitation or taking over of artifacts and customs. The method of the school consists in a careful mapping out of cultural similarities over large portions of the globe and in speculative reconstructions as to how the similar units of culture have wandered from one place to another. The disputes of historical anthropologists (for there is little consensus between Elliot Smith and F. Boas; W. J. Perry and Pater Schmidt; Clark Wissler and Graebner; or Frobenius and Rivers) refer mostly to the questions as to where a type of culture originated, whither it moved and how it was transported. The difference is primarily due to the way in which each school conceives, on the one hand, the divisions of culture into its component parts and, on the other, the process of diffusion. This method of division of culture into its component units, which are then supposed to diffuse, is even less satisfactory. The concepts of cultural traits, trait complexes and *Kulturkomplexe* are indiscriminately applied to single utensils or implements, such as the boomerang, the bow or the dire drill, or to vague characteristics of material culture, such as megalithity, sexual suggestiveness of the cowrie shell or certain details of objective form. Agriculture, the worship of fertility and enormous yet vague principles of social grouping, such as dual organization, the clan system or a type of religious cult, are regarded as single traits, that is, units of diffusion. But culture cannot be regarded as a fortuitous agglomerate of such traits. Only elements of the same order can be treated as identical units of argument; only compatible elements compound into a homogeneous whole. Insignificant details of material culture, on the one hand, social institutions and cultural values, on the other, must be treated differently. They are not invented in the same way, cannot be carried, diffused or implanted in the same manner.

The weakest point in the method of the historical school is the way in which its members establish the identity of cultural elements. For the whole problem of historical diffusion is raised by the occurrence of really or apparently identical traits or complexes in different areas. In order to establish the identity of two elements of culture the diffusionist uses the criteria of what might be called irrelevant form and fortuitous concatenation of elements respectively. The irrelevancy of form is a fundamental concept because form, which is dictated by inner necessity, could have developed independently. Complexes, naturally concatenated, could also be the product of independent evolution—hence the need to consider only fortuitously connected traits. Accidental concatenation, however, and irrelevant detail of form can, according to Graebner and his followers, be only the result of direct diffusion. But irrelevance of form and fortuitousness of concatenation are both negative assertions, which in the last instance mean that the form of an artifact or an institution cannot be accounted for or the concatenation between several elements of culture found. The historical method uses absence of knowledge as its basis of argument. To be valid its results must be preceded by a functional study of the given culture, which should exhaust all the possibilities of explaining form by function and of establishing relationships between the various elements of culture.

If culture in its material aspects is primarily a body of instrumental artifacts, it seems at first sight improbable that any culture should harbor a great many irrelevant traits, survivals or fortuitous complexes either dumped down by some itinerant alien culture or handed over as survivals, useless fragments of a vanished stage. Still less is it likely that customs, institutions or moral values should present this necrotic or irrelevant character in which the evolutionary and diffusionist schools are primarily interested.

Culture consists of the body of commodities and instruments as well as of customs and bodily or mental habits which work directly or indirectly for the satisfaction of human needs. All the elements of culture, if this conception be true, must be at work, functioning, active, efficient. The essentially dynamic character of cultural elements and of their relations suggests that it is in the study of cultural function that the most important task of anthropology consists. The primary concern of functional anthropology is with the function of institutions, customs, implements and ideas. It holds that the cultural process is subject to laws and that the laws are to be found in the function of the real elements of culture. The atomizing or isolating treatment of cultural traits is regarded as sterile, because the significance of culture consists in the relation between its elements, and the existence of accidental or fortuitous culture complexes is not admitted.

To formulate a number of fundamental principles an example may be taken from material culture. The simplest artifact, extensively used in the simplest cultures, a plain stick, roughly trimmed, some five to six feet long, such as can be used for digging up roots or in the cultivation of the soil, for punting or in walking, is an ideal element or trait of culture for it has a fixed, simple form, is apparently a self-contained unit and is very important in every culture. To define the cultural identity of a stick by its form, by describing its material, its length, its weight, its color or any other physical characteristics—by describing it in fact according to the final criterion of form as it is used by the diffusionist—would be a methodically erroneous procedure. The digging stick is handled in its own way; it is used in a garden or in the bush for a special purpose; it is procured and discarded in a somewhat careless manner—for a single specimen has usually very small economic value. But the digging stick looms large in the economic scheme of every community in which it is used as well as in folklore, mythology and customs. A stick of identical form can be used in the same culture as a punting pole, a walking staff or a rudimentary weapon. But in each of these specific uses the stick is embedded in a different cultural context; that is, put to different uses, surrounded with different ideas, given a different cultural value and as a rule designated by a different name. In each case it forms an integral part of a different system of standardized human activities. In brief, it fulfils a different function. It is the diversity of function not the identity of form that is relevant to the student of culture. The stick exists as a part of culture only in so far as it is used in human activities, in so far as it serves human needs; and therefore the digging stick, the walking staff, the punting pole, although they may be identical in physical nature, are each a distinct element of culture. For the simplest as well as the most elaborate artifact is defined by its function, the part which it plays within a system of human activities; it is defined by the ideas which are connected with it and by the values which surround it.

This conclusion receives its importance from the fact that the systems of activities to which material objects are referred are not fortuitous but are organized, well determined, comparable systems found throughout the world of cultural diversity. The cultural context of the digging stick, the system of agricultural activities, always presents the following component parts: a portion of territory is legally set aside for the use of a human group by the rules of land tenure. A body of traditional usages exists regulating the way in which this territory is to be cultivated. Technical rules, ceremonial and ritual usages determine in every culture what plants are to be grown; how the ground is to be cleared, the soil prepared and fertilized; how the work is to proceed; how, when and by whom the magical acts or religious ceremonies are to be performed; how, finally, the crops are to be harvested, distributed, stored and consumed. Likewise the group of people who own the territory, the plant and the produce, who work together, enjoy and consume the results of their labors, are always well defined.

These are the characteristics of the institution of gardening as it is universally found wherever the environment is favorable to the cultivation of the soil and the level of culture sufficiently high to allow it. The fundamental identity of this organized system of activities is due primarily to the fact that it is built up around the satisfaction of a deep human need—the regular provision of staple food of a vegetable nature. The satisfaction of this need by agriculture, which insures possibility of control, regularity of production and relative abundance, is so superior to any other food providing activity that it was bound to diffuse or to develop wherever conditions were favorable and the level of culture sufficiently high.

The fundamental uniformity in institutionalized gardening is due to yet another cause, the principle of limited possibilities, first laid down by Goldenweiser. Given a definite cultural need, the means of its satisfaction are small in number, and therefore the cultural arrangement which comes into being in response to the need is determined within narrow limits. Given the human need for a support, a rudimentary weapon and an implement for exploring in the dark, the material most suitable is wood, the only adequate shape thin and long, and a plentiful supply is accessible. Yet a sociology or cultural theory of the walking staff is possible, for the staff displays a diversity of uses, ideas and mystical associations and in its ornamental, ritual and symbolic, developments becomes a part of important institutions such as magic, chieftainship and kingship.

The Study of Culture * (*Kluckhohn*)

Culture, as used by American anthropologists, is of course a technical term which must not be confused with the more limited concept of ordinary language and of history and literature. The anthropological term designates those aspects of the total human environment, tangible and intangible, which have been created by men. "A culture" refers to the distinctive way of life of a group of people, their complete "design for living." The Japanese constitute a nation or a society. This entity may be directly observed. "Japanese culture," however, is an abstraction from observed regularities or trends toward regularity in the modes of response of this people.

Recent anthropological research in the United States has by no means been limited to the study of cultures. The community studies of W. Lloyd Warner and other American anthropologists are well known. There have been published some pioneer investigations in quantitative comparative

* Reprinted from "The Study of Culture" by Clyde Kluckhohn, Chapter V of *The Policy Sciences* edited by Daniel Lerner and Harold D. Lasswell with permission of the publishers, Stanford University Press. Copyright 1951 by the Board of Trustees of Leland Stanford Junior University. Publication assisted by a grant from Carnegie Corporation of New York.

sociology in which the theory is drawn from sociology, psychoanalysis, and behavioristic psychology as well as from anthropology.[1] An increasing number of American anthropologists have been concerned with interrelations between the cultural and the psychological.[2] Others have been developing the interstitial area between biology and anthropology.[3] Still others have concentrated upon the physical environment as a conditioning and limiting factor in cultural development and function.[4]

Nevertheless, culture remains the master concept of American anthropology, with the partial exception of physical anthropology. For ethnologists, folklorists, anthropological linguists, archaeologists, and social anthropologists, culture is always a point of departure or a point of reference if not invariably the point of central emphasis. During the past fifteen years there have been significant refinements both in the theory of culture and in methods and techniques for the study of cultures.

THEORY

Many different definitions of culture are current. A review of these and their development will shortly be published.[5] They vary in degree of looseness or precision, in the stressing of one conceptual element as opposed to another. There have also been some recent controversies on epistemological and ontological questions.[6] Neglecting, however, the finer details of terminology and some philosophical nuances, most American anthropologists would agree substantially with the following propositions of Herskovits[7] on the theory of culture:

1. Culture is learned;[8]
2. Culture derives from the biological,[9] environmental, psychological, and historical components of human existence;
3. Cuture is structured;
4. Culture is divided into aspects;
5. Culture is dynamic;
6. Culture is variable;
7. Culture exhibits regularities that permit its analysis by the methods of science;
8. Culture is the instrument whereby the individual adjusts to his total setting, and gains the means for creative expression.[10]

A perhaps not unrepresentative brief definition is that of Kluckhohn and Kelly: "A culture is an historically created system of explicit and implicit designs for living, which tends to be shared by all or specially designated members of a group at a specified point in time." [11] Some comments may clarify this definition. Each culture is a precipitate of history from the materials supplied by human biology and the natural environment to which human organisms must make certain minimal adjustments for survival. The selectivity out of the potentialities afforded by human nature and physical surroundings and within the limits set by biological and physical nature is channeled by the historical process. The conventional or arbitrary element (that is, the purely cultural) arises in part out of the accidents of history, including both chance internal events and contacts with other peoples. The word "system" has important implications. The fact that cultures have organization as well as content is now generally recognized. Nor can culture be used as a conceptual instrument for prediction unless due account is taken of this systemic property. The word "tends" warns against reifying an abstraction. One cannot drop a perpendicular from even the most accurate description of a culture or any specific carrier of that culture. No individual thinks, feels, or acts precisely as the "blueprints" which constitute a culture indicate that he will or should. Nor are all the "blueprints" meant by the society to apply to each individual. There are sex differentials, age differentials, occupational differentials, and the like. The best conceptual model of the culture can only state correctly the central tendencies of ranges of variation.

The anthropologist's description of a culture may be compared to a map. A map is obviously not a concrete bit of land but rather an abstract representation of a particular area. If a map is accurate and one can read it, one doesn't get lost. If a culture is correctly portrayed, one will realize the existence of the distinctive features of a way of life and their interrelationships.

Culture is omnipresent; it interposes a double screen between, for example, the psychologist and the native or innate or constitutional personality he is trying to discover and describe. One is tempted to paraphrase Zola's remark that science is nature seen through a temperament and say that personality is a temperament which is both seen through and screened by a culture. Because of the mass of tradition and the complexities of human relationships, even the few simple things that people as animals want have been disguised in cultural patterns. An animal eats when he is hungry—if he can, but the human animal waits for lunch time. Three daily meals are as much an artifact as an automobile. Sneezing at first looks like pure biology. But little customs grow up about it, such as saying "excuse me" or

"Gesundheit." People do not sneeze in exactly the same way in different cultures or in various strata of the same society. Sneezing is a biological act caught in a cultural web. It is difficult to point to any activity that is not culturally tailored.

Why do most people, most of the time, adhere to cultural patterns? We cannot give this question the examination it deserves, but two reasons are obvious. First, by following custom one affirms one's solidarity with one's group and escapes a sense of loneliness. Second, patterns are necessary if we are to have a social life, with its attendant division of labor. Imagine people living in the same home and invariably preparing and eating food in different rooms at different times.

The analysis of a culture must encompass both the explicit and the implicit. The explicit culture consists in those regularities in word and deed which may be generalized straight from the evidence of the ear or eye. One has only to observe and to discover the consistencies in one's observations. No arbitrary acts of interpretation on the part of the anthropologist are involved. The implicit culture, however, is an abstraction of the second order. Here the anthropologist infers least common denominators which seem, as it were, to underlie a multiplicity of cultural contents. Only in the most sophisticated and self-conscious of cultures will his attention be called directly to these by carriers of the culture. The implicit culture consists of pure forms. Explicit culture includes both content and structure.

Culture content. Description of culture content consists in stating what is done, said, and made—by whom, when, and under what circumstances. A useful system for categorizing culture content has been supplied by Ralph Linton.[12] The most easily isolable elements in designs for living are called culture *traits.* A random list of a few traits in American culture might include listening to news broadcasts at breakfast, the assembly line, and political bosses in large cities. However, each one of these elements can, if the intensity of analysis requires it, be broken down into smaller separable units called *items.* For instance, the interlarding of "commercials" with news in the morning, the fact that news broadcasts are either five minutes or fifteen minutes in length, the fact that each individual or family ordinarily turns to some preferred announcer or commentator—these are some of the items that might be listed when the American trait of "listening to news broadcasts at breakfast" is broken down. Or the culture trait of the crossbow may be analyzed into items: size, materials, details of workmanship, and the like.

On the other hand, lists of traits may be grouped together according to function. The assembly line, collective bargaining, various social services rendered by management to workers, and numerous other traits make up the *trait complex* of the American industrial system. This trait complex, in turn, is linked with various other trait complexes, such as mining, agriculture, and fishing, to make up a total *activity*—economic production.

Linton has also given us a scheme for the description of culture content from the point of view of relative participation of individuals in the various complexes and activities. Those culture elements which apply to all normal adult members of the society are called *universals*. Those which apply only to distinct categories of individuals are *specialties*. Those which are well-known to all adults (or at least to those adults in certain culturally differentiated groups) but with respect to which there is free choice are *alternatives*. *Variants* are elements or complexes "which are shared by certain individuals but which are not common to all members of the society, or even to all the members of any one group of the socially recognized categories."

Structure. As Ernst Cassirer and Kurt Lewin, among others, have pointed out, scientific progress frequently depends upon changes in what is regarded as real and amenable to objective study. The development of the social sciences has been impeded by a confusion between the "real" and the concrete. Psychologists, typically, are reluctant to concede reality in the social world to anything but individuals. The greatest advance in contemporary anthropological theory is probably the increasing recognition that there is something more to culture than artifacts, linguistic texts, and lists of atomized traits.

Structural relations are characterized by relatively fixed relations between parts rather than by the parts or elements themselves. That relations are as "real" as things is conceded by most philosophers. It is also clear from ordinary experience that an exhaustive analysis of reality cannot be made within the limitations of an atomistic or narrowly positivistic scheme. Take a brick wall. Its "reality" would be granted by all save those who follow an idealism of Berkeley's sort. Then let us take each brick out of the wall. A radical empiricist would be in all consistency obliged to say that we have destroyed nothing. Yet it is clear that while nothing concrete has been annihilated, a form has been eliminated. Similarly, the student of culture change is forced to admit that forms may persist while content changes or that content remains relatively unaltered but is organized into new structures.

An analogy used by Freud for personality is equally applicable to cultural disintegration. If we throw a crystal to the ground, it breaks; however, its dissolution is not haphazard. The fragmentation accords with lines of cleavage predetermined by the particular structure of the crystal, invisible though it was to the naked eye. So, in culture, the mode in which the parts stand to one another cannot be indifferent from the standpoint of understanding and prediction. If a form ceases to exist, the resultant change is different from that of a purely subtractive operation. Each culture is, among other things, a complex of relations, a multiverse of ordered and interrelated parts. Parts do not cause a whole but they comprise a whole, not necessarily in the sense of being perfectly integrated but in the sense of being separable only by abstraction.

All nature consists of materials. But the manner in which matter is organized into entities is as significant as the substance or the function serviced within a given system. Recent organic chemistry has documented this fact. The selfsame atoms present in exactly the same number may constitute either a medicine or a poison, depending solely upon the fashion in which they are arranged. Contemporary genetics and biology have come to the same conclusion. A famous geneticist has written: "All that matters in heredity is its pattern." An extremely positivistic biologist has observed: "These results appear to demonstrate that statistical features of *organization* can be heritable. . . ." [13] A behavioristic psychologist, Clark Hull, finds that behavior sequences are "strictly patterned" and that it is the pattern which is often determinative of adaptive or nonadaptive behavior.

That organization and equilibrium generally prevail in nature, as they seem to do, is doubtless a matter of balance, economy, or least action of energy. If it is assumed that those aspects of behavior which we call cultural are part of a natural and not of a supernatural order, it is to be expected that exactness of relationship, irrespective of dimensions, must be discovered and described in the cultural realm. One of the most original of anthropological linguists, B. L. Whorf, has put well the approach most suited to cultural studies:

In place of apparatus, linguistics uses and develops *techniques*. Experimental does not mean quantitative. Measuring, weighing, and pointer-reading devices are seldom needed in linguistics, for quantity and number play little part in the realm of pattern, where there are no variables but, instead, abrupt alternations from one configuration to another. The mathematical sciences require exact measurement, but what linguistics requires is, rather, exact "patternment" —an exactness of relation irrespective of dimensions. Quantity, dimension, magnitude are metaphors since they do not properly belong in this spaceless, relational world. I might use this simile: Exact measurement of lines and angles will be needed to draw exact squares of other regular polygons, but measurement, however precise, will not help us to draw an exact circle. Yet it is necessary only to discover the principle of the compass to reach by a leap the ability to draw perfect circles. Similarly, linguistics has developed techniques which, like compasses, enable it without any true measurement at all to specify *exactly* the patterns with which it is concerned. Or I might perhaps liken the case to the state of affairs within the atom, where also entities appear to alternate from configuration to configuration rather than to move in terms of measurable positions. As alternants, quantum phenomena must be treated by a method of analysis that substitutes a point in a pattern under a set of conditions for a point in a pattern under another set of conditions—a method similar to that used in analysis of linguistic phenomena.[14]

There is nothing mystical about saying that cultures have organization as well as content. This point may be driven home by an analogy used by the Gestalt psychologists. Take a musical succession made up of three notes. If one is told that the notes are A, C, and G, one receives information that is fundamental but does not enable one to predict the type of sensation which will be experienced in hearing the notes. One needs further information on relationships. Are the notes to be played in that order? What duration will each receive? How will the emphasis, if any, be distributed? Will the instrument be a piano or a violin?

The analysis of a culture has also only begun when all its items, traits, trait complexes, and activities have been noted. Both the Navaho and the Hopi Indians make dry paintings. In a distribution chart, both of these cultures would be marked "present" as to this trait. Yet the place of this event in the sequence of rites which constitute their great ceremonials is very different. Moreover, the relationship of this trait to the purposes of the whole ceremonial is not envisioned in the same way by the two tribes. In short, the full significance of any single element in a cultural design will be seen only when that element is viewed in the total matrix of its relationship to other elements and indeed to other designs. Naturally, this includes accent or emphasis as well as position. Accent is manifested sometimes through frequency, sometimes through intensity. Both the Navaho and the Diegueno Indians use a certain narcotic plant. Any Navaho, however, can live a full and normal life without ever happening to see this plant used. In contrast, a Diegueno, in former times, could hardly fail to witness the usage many times a year. Both the Navaho and the Hopi have an initiation rite for boys wherein the boys are whipped on the naked back by older men with staves of yucca. But the importance of intensity of this occasion is exceedingly different in the two cases. Many adult Navahos never go through this rite. Among the Hopi, however, this is an absolute prerequisite to full participation in the society. If a Navaho man has been initiated, his references in conversation to this event are likely to be quite casual. The ordinary Hopi will evidence considerable emotion in any discussion of the subject.

If cultural forms are so significant, why has attention to their systematic analysis lagged so far behind the description of culture content? In the first place, some students have overemphasized a consideration in which there is some truth. They have said that what we understand in patterns is the applicability of forms, not the basic meanings. Up to a point, however, motivations need not be sought beyond the border of the pattern itself. An American wants or feels obliged to give at Christmas time. He thinks, "Ah, everyone can use handkerchiefs." The recipient may say to himself, "What will I do with all these handkerchiefs? Oh, well, what did I send him? And anyway it's the spirit that counts. I am glad he thought of me." Giving handkerchiefs at Christmas is often patently absurd from the immediate functional point of view, but it nobly fulfills the pattern. The latent function, of course, is to show that you take your culture seriously.

In the second place, there is probably among Western peoples some resentment of patterns as such. This may be connected with our traditional notions of individualism and of freedom of the will. Americans, at least, dislike grammar because it imposes a pattern (rigidity, determinism) on the medium of expression which most individuals know best. Explicitness with regard to grammar is more than wearying—there is the hint of a personal insult because of interference with the "spontaneity" of personal expression.

In the third place, informants are much less helpful in explaining the patterns of their culture than they are in describing its content. The manner of response has become "second nature." The *structure* of behavior tends to be automatic—one doesn't think about it and one doesn't want to. As Edward Sapir has noted, "There are large sections of culture that act as a bar to the free exercise of rationality. One may observe that adults have compromised rationality with their culture—and they resent a re-examination of these questions by their children." Or, as W. I. Thomas says, "Social habit systems tend to acquire a relatively fixed and unreflective character resembling instinctive reflex responses."

However, during the last twenty years, American anthropologists have been forced—in part by their attempts to make predictions, especially in the field of applied anthropology—to realize that a list of traits never gets beyond the signatory stage. One can say correctly that Plains Indian culture included buffalo food, nomadism, the tipi, the travois, geometric decoration in painting, quill work, the sun dance, and military societies. Such a series of signs is useful, indeed indispensable, in making historical reconstructions from plotted distributions or in determining the influence of geography upon culture content. The travois, for example, is an invaluable clue to such problems. From the internal standpoint, the culture could get along very nicely without the travois. The list does not define adequately the distinctive features of the life of the Plains Indians. Of all the traits catalogued, only the sun dance and the medicine bundle complex are crucial to the emotionally felt structure of the culture. A trait list indicates but does not define. It is like saying, "John Smith is the attorney who lives at 84 Washington Street." One can have a whole encyclopedia of signatory knowledge and still be unable to answer most of the questions posed by serious students of human life. A trait list, even when sorted as to universals, alternatives, specialties, and variants, is only a relatively objective beginning: it helps one merely to a comparatively superficial and external comprehension.

Various approaches. American social scientists have therefore developed ways of conceptualizing cultural structure. They vary in frames of references and in serving different but equally legitimate intellectual interests. When one's attention is directed primarily to the degree of sanction and emotional feeling attached to the following-out of certain sequences in prescribed ways or with prescribed emphasis, one may utilize the well-known categories of Sumner and Keller: folkways and mores. This distinction was one of the earliest systematic discriminations of cultural structure and has proved of considerable utility. But the focal issue is that of *degree* of sanction, and this must often be decided upon extremely arbitrary grounds. Moreover, it is not always clear whether a *mos* or a folkway is established on the basis of behavioral or normative modalities. Finally, mores and folkways tend to imply a static culture.

One can also segregate a complex of patterns in accordance with the varying roles which different patterns play in the total economy of the overall designs for living. Here one may distinguish situational, instrumental, and integrative patterns.[15] Situational patterns are those which crystallize around the foci supplied by certain invariant "givens" of biological and physical nature. For example, each culture must have patterns that take account of age and sex differences in the members of the society, of the fact of biological kinship, and the like. Instrumental patterns are those that are manifestly functional: those for food production, for the building of shelter, etc. Integrative patterns supply definitions of the situation that rationalize the deeper uncertainties of human existence, such as death. They also provide for symbolic and other types of social solidarity. These patterns operate to lessen the potential conflict and obstruction between the various statuses and roles of different individuals. Ideally, these patterns bring it about that all the statuses of the society intermesh like a series of interlocking gears. Without integrative patterns, individuals would, because of mutual obstruction and conflict, be unable to fulfill their roles as defined by the first two groups of patterns.

A. L. Kroeber,[16] with his eye alike upon history, function, and psychology, has distinguished systemic, total-culture, and style patterns. *Systemic patterns* are "nexuses of culture traits which have assumed a definite and coherent structure, which function successfully, and which acquire historic weight and persistence." [17] Kroeber cites plow agriculture, monotheism, and the alphabet as examples:

> The pattern of plow agriculture comprises the plow itself; animals to draw it; domestication of these beasts; grains of the barley or wheat types sown by broadcast scattering, without attention to the individual seed, seedling, or plant; fields larger than gardens and of some length; and fertilization with dung primarily from draft animals.[18]

Such a pattern "is modifiable superficially, but modifiable only with difficulty as to its underlying plan." Kroeber compares the concept of mammalian dentition in biology. It is clear that systemic patterns are cross-cultural rather than limited to a single culture.

A *style pattern* is "a way of achieving definiteness and effectiveness in human relations by choosing or evolving one line of procedure out of several possible ones and sticking to it." The style pattern of Greek mathematics was geometric. The style pattern of the modern industrial world includes machine versus manual manufacture but also credit and mass production. "Every style is necessarily prelimited; it is an essential commitment to one manner, to the exclusion of others."

The *total-culture pattern* is similar to the notions of ethos and *Zeitgeist*. It is such a concept which Ruth Benedict used in *Patterns of Culture* and in her description of the Japanese culture-whole, *The Chrysanthemum and the Sword*. Earlier and later nonanthropological attempts to describe total-culture patterns might be cited. Perhaps Burckhardt's *Renaissance* is the most familiar. Kroeber says:

> The pattern or physiognomy of trend of a great civilization is certainly an important thing to know, but it is difficult to formulate accurately and reliably. Such a pattern has in it breath and complexity, depth and subtlety, universal features but also uniqueness. In proportion as the expression of such a large pattern tends to the abstract, it becomes arid and lifeless; in proportion as it remains attached to concrete facts, it lacks generalization. Perhaps the most vivid and impressive characterizations have been made by frank intuition deployed on a rich body of knowledge and put into skillful words. Yet this does not constitute proof and is at best at the fringe of the approved methods

of science and scholarship. These difficulties will explain why the formulation of whole-culture patterns has not progressed farther, though it is surely one of the most important problems that anthropology and related researches face.[19]

Herskovits has recently presented the interesting concept of *cultural focus*, which

. . . designates the tendency of every culture to exhibit greater complexity, greater variation in the institutions of some of its aspects than in others. So striking is this tendency to develop certain phases of life, while others remain in the background, so to speak, that in the shorthand of the disciplines that study human societies these focal aspects are often used to characterize whole cultures.[20]

He points to the changing emphases in Western civilizations: Egypt—economic and politico-religious concerns; Athens—the quest for truth; Rome—the principle of organization; Middle Ages—the other world, with a hierarchical concept of the universe; Renaissance—secular matters, learning, and the arts; etc. He shows the utility of the concept in explaining why a given people accept one new idea or thing and reject another.

In a series of important papers, Morris Opler [21] has developed and applied a concept of *theme*: "a postulate or position, declared or implied, and usually controlling behavior or stimulating activity, which is tacitly approved or openly promoted in a society." These cultural postulates are conceived as arising from and being related to basic human needs and social structure, but as essential to the description and explanation of the patterning and change which go on within this framework. One of Opler's examples is that of the rivalry between the sexes in Jicarilla Apache culture. He shows how the influence of this thematic principle appears in such diverse aspects of culture content as mythology, sexual life, economy, warfare, ceremonials, kinship behavior, and others.

Most of the concepts thus far discussed blur the distinction between explicit and implicit culture in describing structure.[22] It seems necessary for rigor to separate these categories as sharply as possible. There are, first, epistemological and logical reasons. Any statement about implicit culture is a second-order abstraction, and it is only fair that the terminology should warn the reader of this fact. Second, the implicit culture has a different meaning for the culture carriers. Since the implicit culture is largely unverbalized it tends to be taken for granted as a part of the natural order of things and is extraordinarily resistant to change.

Patterns of the explicit culture.[23] The explicit culture includes all those features of the designs for living of a group which can be described to an outsider by participants in the culture—though actually the field worker gets his basic data as much or more from observation, from participation, and from listening to informal conversation as he does from questioning informants. Explicit culture includes, of course, manifestations of thought and feeling. In other words, the distinction between explicit ánd implicit is not that between objective and subjective. Explicit culture comprises culture content and cultural forms. The latter may conveniently be differentiated into *behavioral patterns, normative patterns, orientations, cultural categories,* and *cultural postulates.*

The problem of pattern is the problem of symmetry, of constancies of form irrespective of wide variations in concrete details of actualization. So far as biological and physical possibilities are concerned, a given act can be carried out, an idea stated, or a specific artifact made in a number of different ways. However, in all societies the same mode of disposing of many situations is repeated over and over. There is, as it were, an inhibition alike of the randomness of trial-and-error behavior, of the undifferentiated character of instinctive behavior, and of responses that are merely functional. A determinate organization prevails.

The contrast between behavioral and normative patterns is basically the familiar one between practices and rules, but the word *pattern* is a reminder that one is dealing not merely with regularities but with structural regularities—with a predictable conjunction of words and acts in a fixed order and with definable intensity and emphasis. Behavioral patterns are modes of conduct; normative patterns, modes of standards. Both are inductive generalizations—what a logician would call "class constructs." The anthropologist arrives at behavioral patterns by discovering what people do in fact do—the central tendencies in ranges of behavioral dispersion. The cultural conceptions of how persons of specified status *ought* to behave in given situations (normative patterns) are obtained from regularities in statements and from evidences of approval or disapproval of certain acts. It is clear that a normative pattern may be either positive or negative. The goodness of fit, or lack thereof, between behavioral and normative patterns is a sensitive index of the coherence of a culture and of the intensity of culture change at the moment.

For a fine analysis some subsidiary concepts are useful. Normative patterns may be subdivided into *compulsory, preferred, typical, alternative,* and *restricted.* If one were to attempt to obtain a mean average from the facts and state *the* normative pattern, one would often have either to accept a form of statement which was cumbersome and imprecise or to neglect the minor mode or modes entirely and consider the major mode as *the* normative pattern. While the major mode is likely to be the most representative single value in such material, most cultures (since their historical and biological origins have been highly heterogeneous) will strongly tend to give bimodal or multimodal distributions. And a single mode is a notoriously unsatisfactory description of any asymmetrical curve. If the trend of the distributions were markedly regular in the direction of flatness (in which case the mean would doubtless be the most representative value), this fact would in itself signify a lack of patterning of norms (or of behaviors).

It is necessary to distinguish the subtypes of behavioral patterns by different terms. "Compulsory," for instance, plainly refers to a standard of value, and only in the case of an extraordinarily well-integrated culture or a culture where the external sanctions were most efficiently enforced could behavioral patterns be characterized as compulsory. Conversely, one hardly expects the system of normative patterns to encompass patterns which are disapproved or prohibited. There can be cognizance of such patterns in the *idea* patterns of the culture, but not in the normative patterns. *Disapproved* and *prohibited* patterns are inevitably behavioral patterns. For example, adultery is not recognized in the normative patterns of the culture of the Navaho Indians. Behaviorally, however, adultery is common and the carrying out of extramarital relations is most distinctly patterned in ways of which the Navaho are explicitly aware. Prostitution has likewise (at least at some times and places) been a disapproved behavioral pattern of Navaho culture.

Where the anthropologist is interested only in the behavioral patterns or where he has an insufficient knowledge of the normative patterns, the behavioral patterns may be described simply as modalities without in any way begging the question of conformance to the corresponding normative patterns. *Major behavioral pattern* will serve as a label for the behavioral pattern which is unequivocally the major mode of a set of correlative patterns. *Minor behavioral pattern* is suggested for those modes which are definitely minor. Where the interest is in conformance and the necessary information is available, *conformant* and *deviant* behavioral patterns may be distinguished. These latter must not be regarded as synonymous with major and minor, for in a rapidly changing culture the deviant patterns are frequently the major behavioral patterns.

More diffuse structures of the explicit culture. Let us now turn to certain aspects of cultural form which, while recognized by the members of the group, are distinct from patterns in that they are more diffuse, more generalized, more all-pervasive. Patterns, whether behavioral or normative, are abstractions having to do with specific series of acts. If we observe and/or hear repeatedly about a series of marriage ceremonies, scalp dances, and a certain type of feast within the same group, we can abstract designs for specific types of behavior. Each pattern is abstracted not only from the knowledge and habits exhibited in a physical act, but also from the attitudes, values, and ideas associated with the knowledge and habits. All of these data are consciously recognized by the participants and can (to at least some extent) be verbally described by them. There is more to be said of explicit attitudes and values, however, than is strictly attachable to specific pattern forms. The group, as it were, holds a store of "points of view," of generalized ways of feeling, thinking, and believing, that are in some sense independent of physical objects, acts, and speech. This body of "mental" attitudes gives special meaning to new traits, brings about shifts in their function, and places them in their proper position in the hierarchy of cultural values.

REFERENCES

1. The most impressive example is G. P. Murdock's *Social Structure* (1949).
2. See, for example, Cora Du Bois, *People of Alor* (1944); and Clyde Kluckhohn and Henry A. Murray (eds.), *Personality in Nature, Society, and Culture* (1948).
3. Cf. John Gillin, *The Ways of Men* (1948), pp. 23–175; and Kluckhohn and Murray, *op. cit.*, pp. 107–61 and 377–471.
4. E.g., J. H. Steward, *Basin-Plateau Aboriginal Sociopolitical Groups* (Smithsonian Institution, Bureau of American Ethnology, Bulletin 120 [1938]); A. L. Kroeber, *Cultural and Natural Areas of Native North America* (1939).
5. A. L. Kroeber and C. Kluckhohn, "The Concept of Culture: A Critical Review of Definitions," *Papers of the Peabody Museum* (Harvard University) Vol. XLI (1950). The approximate consensus of these definitions is as follows: "Culture consists in patterned ways of thinking, feeling, and reacting, acquired and transmitted mainly by symbols, constituting the distinctive achievements of human groups, including their embodiments in artifacts; the essential core of culture consists of traditional (i.e., historically derived and selected) ideas and especially their attached values."
6. See D. Bidney, "Human Nature and the Cultural Process," *American Anthropologist,* XLIX, No. 3 (1947), 375–96.
7. Melville J. Herskovits, *Man and His Works* (1940), p. 625.
8. Perhaps it is too obvious to add that while all culture is learned, not all learning is culture. The individual learns a good deal during his own private life-experience which he does not share with others or transmit to others. It might also be commented that some aspects of culture are learned only through the use of symbols, particularly linguistic symbols. Indeed, an argument can be made for R. Bain's definition of culture as "all social behavior which is mediated by symbols."
9. See Claude Lévi-Strauss, *Les Structures Élémentaires de la Parenté* (1949), especially pp. 1–13.
10. Herskovits leaves implicit the fact that participation in a culture or in any part of it is never emotionally neutral. The attitude of the participant may range from hearty acceptance to belligerent revolt, but even what seems to be passive conformance is emotionally tinged.
11. C. Kluckhohn and W. H. Kelly, "The Concept of Culture," in Ralph Linton (ed.), *The Science of Man in the World Crisis* (1945), pp. 78–107.
12. *The Study of Man* (1936).

13. W. J. Crozier and E. Wolf, "Specific Constants for Visual Excitation," *Proceedings of the National Academy of Sciences*, XXV, No. 4 (1939), 176–79. Italics mine.

14. B. L. Whorf, "Linguistics as an Exact Science," in United States Department of State, Foreign Service Institute, *Four Articles on Metalinguistics* (1949), p. 11.

15. See T. Parsons, *Essays in Sociological Theory* (1949), pp. 44–51.

16. *Anthropology* (1948), pp. 312–18, 329–31.

17. This definition is taken from Kroeber's "Structure, Function, and Pattern in Biology and Anthropology," *Scientific Monthly*, LVI (1943), p. 112.

18. *Anthropology* (1948), p. 313.

19. *Ibid.*, p. 317.

20. *Man and His Works*, p. 542.

21. See especially Opler's "Themes as Dynamic Forces in Culture," in *American Journal of Sociology*, LI (1945), 198–206, and "An Application of the Theory of Themes in Culture," in *Journal of the Washington Academy of Sciences*, XXXVI (1946), 137–66.

22. John Gillin in *The Ways of Men* (1948) makes a distinction between overt and internalized (covert) habits and customs. He then distinguishes "behavioral customs" from "mental customs" ("mental" seems a most unfortunate terminology). While Gillin seems to recognize most of the bases for what are here called explicit and implicit culture, he does not follow these considerations through in his analyses of cultural structure. His book, however, makes original and significant contributions to cultural theory. His distinction between actional and representational customs and his Part IV ("Patterning and Coordination of Culture") break some new ground.

23. The system of analysis about to be presented has been partially developed in two papers by C. Kluckhohn: "Patterning as Exemplified in Navaho Culture," in Leslie Spier *et al.* (eds.), *Language, Culture and Personality* (1941), pp. 109–30; and "Covert Culture and Administrative Problems," *American Anthropologist*, XLV (1943), 213–27. For a critical discussion and a comparison with other American and European explorations into cultural structure see Hans Dietschy, "De Deux Aspects de la Civilisation," *Archives Suisses d'Anthropologie Générale*, XII (1947), 116–31.

3.

INTERACTION

THE CONCEPT of interaction may be said to define the process which constitutes the very core of social life and human behavior. It is one of the tenets of sociology that the behavior of human beings can never be fully understood if one does not realize that the social actions of individuals are always oriented toward other human beings, and that it is the interplay between the action of Self (Ego) and the expected or actual reaction of one or many Others (Alters) which occupies the center of the human stage. Thus, the simplest unit of sociological, as distinct from psychological, analysis consists not of solitary individuals but of at least a pair of individuals mutually influencing each other's behavior.

But were one simply to insist upon the fact that human behavior is behavior in interaction, one would have missed an important part of the story. In a sense interaction seems indeed a universal phenomenon: atoms in a molecule or planets in the solar system react on one another, and within the body cells mutually influence one another and structure the organs by their reciprocal influence. What distinguishes human interaction from other types is above all the fact that this process involves norms, status positions, and reciprocal obligations which always come into play when two or more actors enter into relations with each other. Therefore, sociology is concerned not so much with interaction as such as it is with that form of interaction which is patterned by the social structure within which it takes place.

Georg Simmel (1858–1918), the founder of what has since been called the "formal school" of sociology, was the first to focus the attention of sociologists upon the importance of interactive processes. Simmel contended that it was possible to discover a number of relatively stable forms of interaction underlying the great diversity of concrete social phenomena. Thus it was possible to discover patterned elements of conflict, of cooperation, and of competition in social relationships, though the concrete manifestations of these elements would vary according to the particularities of each concrete social situation. To Simmel it seemed possible to arrive at systematic classification and description of these enduring patterns of reciprocal interaction. This enabled him to counter the claim of those who maintained that no social science was possible since each concrete situation in which individuals were involved was unique and not susceptible of generalization.

Simmel's work has had a deep influence on American social science, especially on the so-called Chicago School. A reading of one of the earliest textbooks in American sociology, the programmatic outline of the field by the Chicago sociologists Robert E. Park (1864–1944) and Ernest W. Burgess, would show this early influence of Simmelian ideas in America.

While Simmel's work thus had an enduring impact in this country, it also proved seminal in his native land. Leopold von Wiese works closely in the Simmelian tradition, especially in his efforts to classify and systematically analyze forms of social interaction. But the influence of Simmel on other German sociologists was also enduring, even though they did not follow Simmel's lead in all respects. The thought of Max Weber (1864–1920), the dean of German sociology, though in crucial ways oriented in quite different directions, was nevertheless based in large part on Simmel's pioneering insistence on the importance of interactive processes. Our selections from Max Weber are meant to indicate this dependence of Weber's thought on Simmelian schemes of analysis.

The great British anthropologist Bronislaw Malinowski (1884–1942) was less directly influenced by Simmel and his successors than the sociologists just mentioned. Yet his conviction that the normative systems of a society as well as its basic obligations and rights must be understood in terms of reciprocal obligations that the members of society have toward each other can be seen as an extension of Simmel's insights. The selections from the French anthropologist Claude Lévi-Strauss and the American sociologist Talcott Parsons are meant to indicate the extent to which recent anthropological and sociological research re-emphasizes or rediscovers the Simmelian emphasis on interaction.

The Dyad and the Triad * (Simmel)

We see that such phenomena as isolation and freedom actually exist as forms of sociological relations, although they often do so only by means of complex and indirect connections. In view of this fact, the simplest sociological formation, methodologically speaking, remains that which operates between two elements. It contains the scheme, germ, and material of innumerable more complex forms. Its sociological significance, however, by no means rests on its extensions and multiplications only. It itself is a sociation. Not only are

* Reprinted from *The Sociology of Georg Simmel*, translated, edited, and with an introduction by Kurt H. Wolff, pp. 122–125, 145–153, by permission of the publisher, The Free Press, Glencoe, Ill. Copyright, 1950, by The Free Press, A Corporation.

many general forms of sociation realized in it in a very pure and characteristic fashion; what is more, the limitation to two members is a condition
under which alone several forms of relationship exist. Their typically sociological nature is suggested by two facts. One is that the greatest variation of
individualities and unifying motives does not alter the identity of these
forms. The other is that occasionally these forms exist as much between two
groups—families, states, and organizations of various kinds—as between two
individuals.

Everyday experiences show the specific character that a relationship
attains by the fact that only two elements participate in it. A common fate
or enterprise, an agreement or secret between two persons, ties each of them
in a very different manner than if even only three have a part in it. This is
perhaps most characteristic of the secret. General experience seems to indicate that this minimum of two, with which the secret ceases to be the
property of the one individual, is at the same time the maximum at which
its preservation is relatively secure. A secret religious-political society which
was formed in the beginning of the nineteenth century in France and Italy,
had different degrees among its members.

The real secrets of the society were known only to the higher degrees;
but a discussion of these secrets could take place only between any two
members of the high degrees. The limit of two was felt to be so decisive that,
where it could not be preserved in regard to knowledge, it was kept at least
in regard to the verbalization of this knowledge. More generally speaking,
the difference between the dyad and larger groups consists in the fact that
the dyad has a different relation to each of its two elements than have larger
groups to their members. Although, for the outsider, the group consisting of
two may function as an autonomous, super-individual unit, it usually does
not do so for its participants. Rather, each of the two feels himself confronted
only by the other, not by a collectivity above him. The social structure here
rests immediately on the one and on the other of the two, and the secession
of either would destroy the whole. The dyad, therefore, does not attain that
super-personal life which the individual feels to be independent of himself.
As soon, however, as there is a sociation of three, a group continues to exist
even in case one of the members drops out.

This dependence of the dyad upon its two individual members causes
the thought of its existence to be accompanied by the thought of its termination much more closely and impressively than in any other group, where
every member knows that even after his retirement or death, the group can
continue to exist. Both the lives of the individual and that of the sociation

are somehow colored by the imagination of their respective deaths. And "imagination" does not refer here only to theoretical, conscious thought, but to a part or a modification of existence itself. Death stands before us, not like a fate that will strike at a certain moment but, prior to that moment, exists only as an idea or prophecy, as fear or hope, and without interfering with the reality of this life. Rather, the fact that we shall die is a quality inherent in life from the beginning. In all our living reality, there is something which merely finds its last phase or revelation in our death: we are, from birth on, beings that will die. We are this, of course, in different ways. The manner in which we conceive this nature of ours and its final effect, and in which we react to this conception, varies greatly. So does the way in which this element of our existence is interwoven with its other elements. But the same observations can be made in regard to groups. Ideally, any large group can be immortal. This fact gives each of its members, no matter what may be his personal reaction to death, a very specific sociological feeling. A dyad, however, depends on each of its two elements alone—in its death, though not in its life: for its life, it needs both, but for its death, only one. This fact is bound to influence the inner attitude of the individual toward the dyad, even though not always consciously nor in the same way. It makes the dyad into a group that feels itself both endangered and irreplaceable, and thus into the real locus not only of authentic sociological tragedy, but also of sentimentalism and elegiac problems.

This feeling tone appears wherever the end of the union has become an organic part of its structure. Not long ago, there came news from a city in northern France regarding a strange "Association of the Broken Dish." Years ago, some industrialists met for dinner. During the meal, a dish fell on the floor and broke. One of the diners noted that the number of pieces was identical with that of those present. One of them considered this an omen, and in consequence of it, they founded a society of friends who owed one another service and help. Each of them took part of the dish home with him. If one of them dies, his piece is sent to the president, who glues the fragments he receives together. The last survivor will fit the last piece, whereupon the reconstituted dish is to be interred. The "Society of the Broken Dish" will thus dissolve and disappear. The feeling within that society, as well as in regard to it, would no doubt be different if new members were admitted and the life of the group thereby perpetuated indefinitely. The fact that from the beginning it is defined as one that will die gives it a peculiar stamp—which the dyad, because of the numerical condition of its structure, has always.

.   .   .

1. THE SOCIOLOGICAL SIGNIFICANCE OF THE THIRD ELEMENT

What has been said indicates to a great extent the role of the third element, as well as the configurations that operate among three social elements. The dyad represents both the first social synthesis and unification, and the first separation and antithesis. The appearance of the third party indicates transition, conciliation, and abandonment of absolute contrast (although, on occasion, it introduces contrast). The triad as such seems to me to result in three kinds of typical group formations. All of them are impossible if there are only two elements; and, on the other hand, if there are more than three, they are either equally impossible or only expand in quantity but do not change their formal type.

2. THE NON-PARTISAN AND THE MEDIATOR

It is sociologically very significant that isolated elements are unified by their common relation to a phenomenon which lies outside of them. This applies as much to the alliance between states for the purpose of defense against a common enemy as to the "invisible church" which unifies all the faithful in their equal relation to the one God. The group-forming, mediation function of a third element will be discussed in a later context. In the cases under examination now, the third element is at such a distance from the other two that there exist no properly sociological interactions which concern all three elements alike. Rather, there are configurations of two. In the center of sociological attention, there is either the relation between the two joining elements, the relation between them as a unit and the center of interest that confronts them. At the moment, however, we are concerned with three elements which are so closely related or so closely approach one another that they form a group, permanent or momentary.

In the most significant of all dyads, monogamous marriage, the child or children, as the third element, often has the function of holding the whole together. Among many "nature peoples," only childbirth makes a marriage perfect or insoluble. And certainly one of the reasons why developing culture makes marriages deeper and closer is that children become independent relatively late and therefore need longer care. Perfection of marriage through childbirth rests, of course, on the value which the child has for the husband, and on his inclination, sanctioned by law and custom, to expel a childless wife. But the actual result of the third element, the child, is that it alone really closes the circle by tying the parents to one another. This can occur in two forms. The existence of the third element may directly start or strengthen the union of the two, as for instance, when the birth of a child increases the spouses' mutual love, or at least the husband's for his wife. Or the relation of each of the spouses to the child may produce a new and indirect bond between them. In general, the common preoccupations of a married couple with the child reveal that their union passes through the child, as it were; the union often consists of sympathies which could not exist without such a point of mediation. This emergence of the inner socialization of three elements, which the two elements by themselves do not desire, is the reason for a phenomenon mentioned earlier, namely, the tendency of unhappily married couples not to wish children. They instinctively feel that the child would close a circle within which they would be nearer one another, not only externally but also in their deeper psychological layers, than they are inclined to be.

When the third element functions as a non-partisan, we have a different variety of mediation. The non-partisan either produces the concord of two colliding parties, whereby he withdraws after making the effort of creating direct contact between the unconnected or quarreling elements; or he functions as an arbiter who balances, as it were, their contradictory claims against one another and eliminates what is incompatible in them. Differences between labor and management, especially in England, have developed both forms of unification. There are boards of conciliation where the parties negotiate their conflicts under the presidency of a non-partisan. The mediator, of course, can achieve reconciliation in this form only if each party believes that the proportion between the reasons for the hostility, in short, the objective situation justifies the reconciliation and makes peace advantageous. The very great opportunity that non-partisan mediation has to produce this belief lies not only in the obvious elimination of misunderstandings or in appeals to good will, etc. It may also be analyzed as follows. The non-partisan shows each party the claims and arguments of the other; they thus lose the tone of subjective passion which usually provokes the same tone on the part of the adversary. What is so often regrettable here appears as something wholesome, namely, that the feeling which accompanies a psychological content when one individual has it, usually weakens greatly when it is transferred to a second. This fact explains why recommendations and testimonies that have to pass several mediating persons before reaching the deciding individual, are so often ineffective, even if their objective content arrives at its destination without any change. In the course of these transfers, affective imponderables get lost; and these not only supplement insufficient objective qualifications, but, in practice, they alone cause sufficient ones to be acted upon.

Here we have a phenomenon which is very significant for the development of purely psychological influences. A third mediating social element deprives conflicting claims of their affective qualities because it neutrally formulates and presents these claims to the two parties involved. Thus this circle that is fatal to all reconciliation is avoided: the vehemence of the one no longer provokes that of the other, which in turn intensifies that of the first, and so forth, until the whole relationship breaks down. Furthermore, because of the non-partisan, each party to the conflict not only listens to more objective terms than it would if it confronted the other without mediation. For now it is important for each to win over even the mediator. This, however, can be hoped for only on purely objective grounds, because the mediator is not the arbitrator, but only guides the process of coming to terms; because, in other words, he must always keep out of any decision—whereas the arbitrator ends up by taking sides. Within the realm of sociological techniques, there is nothing that serves the reconciliation of conflicting parties so effectively as does objectivity, that is, the attempt at limiting all complaints and requests to their objective contents. Philosophically speaking, the conflict is reduced to the objective spirit of each partial standpoint, so that the personalities involved appear as the mere vehicles of objective conditions. In case of conflict, the personal form in which objective contents become subjectively alive must pay for its warmth, color, and depth of feeling with the sharpness of the antagonism that it engenders. The diminution of this personal tone is the condition under which the understanding and reconciliation of the adversaries can be attained, particularly because it is only under this condition that each of the two parties actually realizes what the other must insist upon. To put it psychologically, antagonism of the will is reduced to intellectual antagonism. Reason is everywhere the principle of understanding; on its basis can come together what on that of feeling and ultimate decision of the will is irreconcilably in conflict. It is the function of the mediator to bring this reduction about, to represent it, as it were, in himself; or to form a transformation point where, no matter in what form the conflict enters from one side, it is transmitted to the other only in an objective form; a point where all is retained which would merely intensify the conflict in the absence of mediation.

It is important for the analysis of social life to realize clearly that the constellation thus characterized constantly emerges in all groups of more than two elements. To be sure, the mediator may not be specifically chosen, nor be known or designated as such. But the triad here serves merely as a type or scheme; ultimately all cases of mediation can be reduced to this form. From the conversation among three persons that lasts only an hour, to the permanent family of three, there is no triad in which a dissent between any two elements does not occur from time to time—a dissent of a more harmless or more pointed, more momentary or more lasting, more theoretical or more practical nature—and in which the third member does not play a mediating role. This happens innumerable times in a very rudimentary and inarticulate manner, mixed with other actions and interactions, from which the purely mediating function cannot be isolated. Such mediations do not even have to be performed by means of words. A gesture, a way of listening, the mood that radiates from a particular person, are enough to change the difference between two individuals so that they can seek understanding, are enough to make them feel their essential commonness which is concealed under their acutely differing opinions, and to bring this divergence into the shape in which it can be ironed out the most easily. The situation does not have to involve a real conflict or fight. It is rather the thousand insignificant differences of opinion, the allusions to an antagonism of personalities, the emergence of quite momentary contrasts of interest or feeling, which continuously color the fluctuating forms of all living together; and this social life is constantly determined in its course by the presence of the third person, who almost inevitably exercises the function of mediation. This function makes the round among the three elements, since the ebb and flow of social life realizes the form of conflict in every possible combination of two members.

The non-partisanship that is required for mediation has one of two presuppositions. The third element is non-partisan either if he stands above the contrasting interests and opinions and is actually not concerned with them, or if he is equally concerned with both. The first case is the simpler of the two and involves fewest complications. In conflicts between English laborers and entrepreneurs, for instance, the non-partisan called in could be neither a laborer nor an entrepreneur. It is notable how decisively the separation of objective from personal elements in the conflict (mentioned earlier) is realized here. The idea is that the non-partisan is not attached by personal interest to the objective aspects of either party position. Rather, both come to be weighed by him as by a pure, impersonal intellect, without touching the subjective sphere. But the mediator must be subjectively interested in the persons or groups themselves who exemplify the contents of the quarrel which to him are merely theoretical, since otherwise he would not take over his function. It is, therefore, as if subjective interest set in motion a purely objective mechanism. It is the fusion of personal distance from the objective significance of the quarrel with personal interest in its subjective significance which characterizes the non-partisan position. This position is the more perfect, the more distinctly each of these two elements is developed and the more harmoniously, in its very differentiation, each cooperates with the other.

The situation becomes more complicated when the non-partisan owes his position, not to his neutrality, but to his equal participation in the interests in conflict. This case is frequent when a given individual belongs to two different interest groups, one local, and the other objective, especially occupational. In earlier times, bishops could sometimes intervene between the secular ruler of their diocese and the pope. The administrator who is thoroughly familiar with the special interests of his district will be the most suitable mediator in the case of a collision between these special interests and the general interests of the state which employs him. The measure of the combination between impartiality and interest which is favorable to the mediation between two locally separate groups, is often found in persons who come from one of these groups but live with the other. The difficulty of positions of this kind in which the mediator may find himself, usually derives from the fact that his equal interests in both parties, that is, his inner equilibrium, cannot be definitely ascertained and is, in fact, doubted often enough by both parties.

Yet an even more difficult and, indeed, often tragic situation occurs when the third is tied to the two parties, not by specific interests, but by his total personality; and this situation is extreme when the whole matter of the conflict cannot be clearly objectified, and its objective aspect is really only a pretext or opportunity for deeper personal irreconcilabilities to manifest themselves. In such a case, the third, whom love or duty, fate or habit have made equally intimate with both, can be crushed by the conflict—much more so than if he himself took sides. The danger is increased because the balance of his interests, which does not lean in either direction, usually does not lead to successful mediation, since reduction to a merely objective contrast fails. This is the type instanced by a great many family conflicts. The mediator, whose equal distance to both conflicting parties assures his impartiality, can accommodate both with relative ease. But the person who is impartial because he is equally close to the two, will find this much more difficult and will personally get into the most painful dualism of feelings. Where the mediator is chosen, therefore, the equally uninterested will be

preferred (other things being equal) to the equally interested. Medieval
Italian cities, for instance, often obtained their judges from the outside in
order to be sure that they were not prejudiced by inner party frictions.

This suggests the second form of accommodation by means of an impartial third element, namely, arbitration. As long as the third properly
operates as a mediator, the final termination of the conflict lies exclusively
in the hands of the parties themselves. But when they choose an arbitrator,
they relinquish this final decision. They project, as it were, their will to
conciliation, and this will becomes personified in the arbitrator. He thus
gains a special impressiveness and power over the antagonistic forces. The
voluntary appeal to an arbitrator, to whom they submit from the beginning,
presupposes a greater subjective confidence in the objectivity of judgment
than does any other form of decision. For, even in the state tribunal, it is
only the action of the complaint that results from confidence in just decision,
since the complainant considers the decision that is favorable to him the just
decision. The defendant, on the other hand, must enter the suit whether
or not he believes in the impartiality of the judge. But arbitration results
only when both parties to the conflict have this belief. This is the principle
which sharply differentiates mediation from arbitration; and the more
official the act of conciliation, the more punctiliously is this differentiation
observed.

This statement applies to a whole range of conflicts; from those between capitalist and worker, which I mentioned earlier, to those of great
politics, where the "good services" of a government in adjusting a conflict
between two others are quite different from the arbitration occasionally
requested of it. The trivialities of daily life, where the typical triad constantly
places one into a clear or latent, full or partial difference from two others,
offer many intermediary grades between these two forms. In the inex-
haustibly varying relations, the parties' appeal to the third person, to his
voluntarily or even forcibly seized initiative to conciliate, often gives him a
position whose mediating and arbitrating elements it is impossible to
separate. If one wants to understand the real web of human society with its
indescribable dynamics and fullness, the most important thing is to sharpen
one's eyes for such beginnings and transitions, for forms of relationship which
are merely hinted at and are again submerged, for their embryonic and fragmentary articulations. Illustrations which exemplify in its purity any one of
the concepts denoting these forms, certainly are indispensable sociological
tools. But their relation to actual social life is like that of the approximately
exact space forms, that are used to illustrate geometrical propositions, to the
immeasurable complexity of the actual formations of matter.

After all that has been said, it is clear that from an over-all viewpoint, the existence of the impartial third element serves the perpetuation of the group. As the representative of the intellect, he confronts the two conflicting parties, which for the moment are guided more by will and feeling. He thus, so to speak, complements them in the production of that psychological unity which resides in group life. On the one hand, the non-partisan tempers the passion of the others. On the other hand, he can carry and direct the very movement of the whole group if the antagonism of the other two tends to paralyze their forces. Nevertheless, this success can change into its opposite. We thus understand why the most intellectually disposed elements of a group lean particularly toward impartiality: the cool intellect usually finds lights and shadows in either quarter; its objective justice does not easily side unconditionally with either. This is the reason why sometimes the most intelligent individuals do not have much influence on the decisions in conflicts, although it would be very desirable that such decisions come from them. Once the group has to choose between "yes" and "no" they, above all others, ought to throw their weight into the balance, for then the scale will be the more likely to sink in favor of the right side. If, therefore, impartiality does not serve practical mediation directly, in its combination with intellectuality it makes sure that the decision is not left to the more stupid, or at least more prejudiced, group forces. And in fact, ever since Solon, we often find disapproval of impartial behavior. In the social sense, this disapproval is something very healthy: it is based on a much deeper instinct for the welfare of the whole than on mere suspicion of cowardice—an attack which is frequently launched against impartiality, though often quite unjustifiably.

Whether impartiality consists in the equal distance or in the equal closeness that connects the non-partisan and the two conflicting parties, it is obvious that it may be mixed with a great many other relations between him and each of the two others and their group as a whole. For instance, if he constitutes a group with the other two but is remote from their conflicts, he may be drawn into them in the very name of independence from the parties which already exist. This may greatly serve the unity and equilibrium of the group, although the equilibrium may be highly unstable. It was this sociological form in which the third estate's participation in state matters occurred in England. Ever since Henry III, state matters were inextricably dependent on the cooperation of the great barons who, along with the prelates, had to grant the monies; and their combination had power, often superior power, over the king. Nevertheless, instead of the fruitful collaboration between estates and crown, there were incessant splits, abuses, power shifts, and clashes. Both parties came to feel that these could be ended only by resort to a third element which, until then, had been kept out of state matters; lower vassals, freemen, counties, and cities. Their representatives were invited to councils; and this was the beginning of the House of Commons. The third element thus exerted a double function. First, it helped to make an actuality of government as the image of the state in its comprehensiveness. Secondly, it did so as an agency which confronted hitherto existing government parties objectively, as it were, and thus contributed to the more harmonious employment of their reciprocally exhausted forces for the over-all purpose of the state.

Social Action and Social Interaction * (*Weber*)

1. Social action, which includes both failure to act and passive acquiescence, may be oriented to the past, present, or expected future behaviour of others. Thus it may be motivated by revenge for a past attack, defence against present, or measures of defence against future aggression. The 'others' may be individual persons, and may be known to the actor as such, or may constitute an indefinite plurality and may be entirely unknown as individuals. Thus 'money' is a means of exchange which the actor accepts in payment because he orients his action to the expectation that a large but unknown number of individuals he is personally unacquainted with will be ready to accept it in exchange on some future occasion.

2. Not every kind of action, even of overt action, is 'social' in the sense of the present discussion. Overt action is non-social if it is oriented solely to the behaviour of inanimate objects. Subjective attitudes constitute social action only so far as they are oriented to the behaviour of others. For example, religious behaviour is not social if it is simply a matter of contemplation or of solitary prayer. The economic activity of an individual is only social if, and then only in so far as, it takes account of the behaviour of someone else. Thus very generally in formal terms it becomes social in so far as the actor's actual control over economic goods is respected by others. Concretely it is social, for instance, if in relation to the actor's own consumption the future wants of others are taken into account and this becomes one consideration affecting the actor's own saving. Or, in another connexion, production may be oriented to the future wants of other people.

3. Not every type of contact of human beings has a social character;

* Reprinted from *Max Weber: The Theory of Social and Economic Organization*, translated by A. M. Henderson and Talcott Parsons, edited with an introduction by Talcott Parsons, pp. 111–115, 118–120, by permission of the publisher, The Free Press, Glencoe, Ill. Copyright, 1947, by The Free Press, A Corporation.

this is rather confined to cases where the actor's behaviour is meaningfully oriented to that of others. For example, a mere collision of two cyclists may be compared to a natural event. On the other hand, their attempt to avoid hitting each other, or whatever insults, blows, or friendly discussion might follow the collision, would constitute 'social action.'

4. Social action is not identical either with the similar actions of many persons or with action influenced by other persons. Thus, if at the beginning of a shower a number of people on the street put up their umbrellas at the same time, this would not ordinarily be a case of action mutually oriented to that of each other, but rather of all reacting in the same way to the like need of protection from the rain. It is well known that the actions of the individual are strongly influenced by the mere fact that he is a member of a crowd confined within a limited space. Thus, the subject matter of studies of 'crowd psychology,' such as those of Le Bon, will be called 'action conditioned by crowds.' It is also possible for large numbers, though dispersed, to be influenced simultaneously or successively by a source of influence operating similarly on all the individuals, as by means of the press. Here also the behaviour of an individual is influenced by his membership in the crowd and by the fact that he is aware of being a member. Some types of reaction are only made possible by the mere fact that the individual acts as part of a crowd. Others become more difficult under these conditions. Hence it is possible that a particular event or mode of human behaviour can give rise to the most diverse kinds of feeling—gaiety, anger, enthusiasm, despair, and passions of all sorts—in a crowd situation which would not occur at all or not nearly so readily if the individual were alone. But for this to happen there need not, at least in many cases, be any meaningful relation between the behaviour of the individual and the fact that he is a member of a crowd. It is not proposed in the present sense to call action 'social' when it is merely a result of the effect on the individual of the existence of a crowd as such and the action is not oriented to that fact on the level of meaning. At the same time the borderline is naturally highly indefinite. In such cases as that of the influence of the demagogue, there may be a wide variation in the extent to which his mass clientele is affected by a meaningful reaction to the fact of its large numbers; and whatever this relation may be, it is open to varying interpretations.

But furthermore, mere 'imitation' of the action of others, such as that on which Tarde has rightly laid emphasis, will not be considered a case of specifically social action if it is purely reactive so that there is no meaningful orientation to the actor imitated. The borderline is, however, so indefinite that it is often hardly possible to discriminate. The mere fact that a person is found to employ some apparently useful procedure which he learned from someone else does not, however, constitute, in the present sense, social action. Action such as this is not oriented to the action of the other person, but the actor has, through observing the other, become acquainted with certain objective facts; and it is these to which his action is oriented. His action is then *causally* determined by the action of others, but not meaningfully. On the other hand, if the action of others is imitated because it is 'fashionable' or traditional or exemplary, or lends social distinction, or on similar grounds, it is meaningfully oriented either to the behaviour of the source of imitation or of third persons or of both. There are of course all manner of transitional cases between the two types of imitation. Both the phenomena discussed above, the behaviour of crowds and imitation, stand on the indefinite border-line of social action. The same is true, as will often appear, of traditionalism and charisma. The reason for the indefiniteness of the line in these and other cases lies in the fact that both the orientation to the behaviour of others and the meaning which can be imputed to the actor himself, are by no means always capable of clear determination and are often altogether unconscious and seldom fully self-conscious. Mere 'influence' and meaningful orientation cannot therefore always be clearly differentiated on the empirical level. But conceptually it is essential to distinguish them, even though merely 'reactive' imitation may well have a degree of sociological importance at least equal to that of the type which can be called social action in the strict sense. Sociology, it goes without saying, is by no means confined to the study of 'social action'; this is only, at least for the kind of sociology being developed here, its central subject matter, that which may be said to be decisive for its status as a science. But this does not imply any judgment on the comparative importance of this and other factors.

.   .   .

The term 'social relationship' will be used to denote the behaviour of a plurality of actors in so far as, in its meaningful content, the action of each takes account of that of the others and is oriented in these terms. The social relationship thus *consists* entirely and exclusively in the existence of a *probability* that there will be, in some meaningfully understandable sense, a course of social action. For purposes of definition there is no attempt to specify the basis of this probability.

1. Thus, as a defining criterion, it is essential that there should be at least a minimum of mutual orientation of the action of each to that of the others. Its content may be of the most varied nature; conflict, hostility, sexual attraction, friendship, loyalty, or economic exchange. It may involve the fulfilment, the evasion, or the denunciation of the terms of an agreement;

economic, erotic, or some other form of 'competition'; common membership in national or class groups or those sharing a common tradition of status. In the latter cases mere group membership may or may not extend to include social action; this will be discussed later. The definition, furthermore, does not specify whether the relation of the actors is 'solidary' or the opposite.

2. The 'meaning' relevant in this context is always a case of the meaning imputed to the parties in a given concrete case, on the average or in a theoretically formulated pure type—it is never a normatively 'correct' or a metaphysically 'true' meaning. Even in cases of such forms of social organization as a state, church, association, or marriage, the social relationship consists exclusively in the fact that there has existed, exists, or will exist a probability of action in some definite way appropriate to this meaning. It is vital to be continually clear about this in order to avoid the 'reification' [1] of these concepts. A 'state,' for example, ceases to exist in a sociologically relevant sense whenever there is no longer a probability that certain kinds of meaningfully oriented social action will take place. This probability may be very high or it may be negligibly low. But in any case it is only in the sense and degree in which it does exist or can be estimated that the corresponding social relationship exists. It is impossible to find any other clear meaning for the statement that, for instance, a given 'state' exists or has ceased to exist.

3. The subjective meaning need not necessarily be the same for all the parties who are mutually oriented in a given social relationship; there need not in this sense be 'reciprocity.' 'Friendship,' 'love,' 'loyalty,' 'fidelity to contracts,' 'patriotism,' on one side, may well be faced with an entirely different attitude on the other. In such cases the parties associate different meanings with their actions and the social relationship is in so far objectively 'asymmetrical' from the points of view of the two parties. It may nevertheless be a case of mutual orientation in so far as, even though partly or wholly erroneously, one party presumes a particular attitude toward him on the part of the other and orients his action to this expectation. This can, and usually will, have consequences for the course of action and the form of the relationship. A relationship is objectively symmetrical only as, according to the typical expectations of the parties, the meaning for one party is the same as that for the other. Thus the actual attitude of a child to its father may be at least approximately that which the father, in the individual case, on the average or typically, has come to expect. A social relationship in which the attitudes are completely and fully corresponding is in reality a limiting case. But the absence of reciprocity will, for terminological purposes, be held to exclude the existence of a social relationship only if it actually results in the

absence of a mutual orientation of the action of the parties. Here as elsewhere all sorts of transitional cases are the rule rather than the exception.

4. A social relationship can be of a temporary character or of varying degrees of permanence. That is, it can be of such a kind that there is a probability of the repeated recurrence of the behaviour which corresponds to its subjective meaning, behaviour which is an understandable consequence of the meaning and hence is expected. In order to avoid fallacious impressions, let it be repeated and continually kept in mind, that it is *only* the existence of the probability that, corresponding to a given subjective meaning complex, a certain type of action will take place, which constitutes the 'existence' of the social relationship. Thus that a 'friendship' or a 'state' exists or has existed means this and only this: that we, the observers, judge that there is or has been a probability that on the basis of certain kinds of known subjective attitude of certain individuals there will result in the average sense a certain specific type of action.[2] For the purposes of legal reasoning it is essential to be able to decide whether a rule of law does or does not carry legal authority, hence whether a legal relationship does or does not 'exist.' This type of question is not, however, relevant to sociological problems.

5. The subjective meaning of a social relationship may change, thus a political relationship, once based on solidarity, may develop into a conflict of interests. In that case it is only a matter of terminological convenience and of the degree of continuity of the change whether we say that a new relationship has come into existence or that the old one continues but has acquired a new meaning. It is also possible for the meaning to be partly constant, partly changing.

6. The meaningful content which remains relatively constant in a social relationship is capable of formulation in terms of maxims which the parties concerned expect to be adhered to by their partners, on the average and approximately. The more rational in relation to values or to given ends the action is, the more is this likely to be the case. There is far less possibility of a rational formulation of subjective meaning in the case of a relation of erotic attraction or of personal loyalty or any other affectual type than, for example, in the case of a business contract.

7. The meaning of a social relationship may be agreed upon by mutual consent. This implies that the parties make promises covering their future behaviour, whether toward each other or toward third persons. In such cases each party then normally counts, so far as he acts rationally, in some degree on the fact that the other will orient his action to the meaning of the agreement as he (the first actor) understands it. In part, they orient their action

rationally to these expectations as given facts with, to be sure, varying degrees of subjectively 'loyal' intention of doing their part. But in part also they are motivated each by the value to him of his 'duty' to adhere to the agreement in the sense in which he understands it. This much may be anticipated.[3]

REFERENCES

1. See above, pp. 101-3.
2. Compare above, paras. 6 and 7 under 1.
3. For a further elaboration of this subject, see secs. 9 and 13 below.

The Principle of Give and Take * (*Malinowski*)

In the foregoing we have seen a series of pictures from native life, illustrating the legal aspect of the marriage relationship, of co-operation in a fishing team, of food barter between inland and coastal villages, of certain cere-monial duties of mourning. These examples were adduced with some detail, in order to bring out clearly the concrete working of what appears to me to be the real mechanism of law, social and psychological constraint, the actual forces, motives, and reasons which make men keep to their obligations. If space permitted it would be easy to bring these isolated instances into a coherent picture and to show that in all social relations and in all the various domains of tribal life, exactly the same legal mechanism can be traced, that it places the *binding obligations* in a special category and sets them apart from other types of customary rules. A rapid though comprehensive survey will have to suffice.

To take the economic transactions first: barter of goods and services is carried on mostly within a standing partnership, or is associated with definite social ties or coupled with a mutuality in non-economic matters. Most if not all economic acts are found to belong to some chain of reciprocal gifts and counter-gifts, which in the long run balance, benefiting both sides equally.

I have already given an account of the economic conditions in N. W. Melanesia, in "The Primitive Economics of the Trobriand Islanders" (*Economic Journal,* 1921) and in *Argonauts of the Western Pacific,* 1923. Chapter vi of that volume deals with matters here discussed, i.e., the forms of economic exchange. My ideas about primitive law were not mature at that time, and the facts are presented there without any reference to the present argument—their testimony only the more telling because of that. When, however, I describe a category of offerings as 'Pure Gifts' and place under

* Reprinted from *Crime and Custom in Savage Society* by Bronislaw Malinowski, pp. 39–45, by permission of the publisher, Routledge & Kegan Paul Ltd.

this heading the gifts of husband to wife and of father to children, I am obviously committing a mistake. I have fallen then, in fact, into the error exposed above, of tearing the act out of its context, of not taking a sufficiently long view of the chain of transactions. In the same paragraph I have supplied, however, an implicit rectification of my mistake in stating that "a gift given by the father to his son is said [by the natives] to be a repayment for the man's relationship to the mother" (p. 179). I have also pointed out there that the 'free gifts' to the wife are also based on the same idea. But the really correct account of the conditions—correct both from the legal and from the economic point of view—would have been to embrace the whole system of gifts, duties, and mutual benefits exchanged between the husband on one hand, wife, children, and wife's brother on the other. It would be found then in native ideas that the system is based on a very complex give and take, and that in the long run the mutual services balance.[1]

The real reason why all these economic obligations are normally kept, and kept very scrupulously, is that failure to comply places a man in an intolerable position, while slackness in fulfilment covers him with opprobrium. The man who would persistently disobey the rulings of law in his economic dealings would soon find himself outside the social and economic order—and he is perfectly well aware of it. Test cases are supplied nowadays, when a number of natives through laziness, eccentricity, or a non-conforming spirit of enterprise, have chosen to ignore the obligations of their status and have become automatically outcasts and hangers-on to some white man or other.

The honourable citizen is bound to carry out his duties, though his submission is not due to any instinct or intuitive impulse or mysterious 'group-sentiment,' but to the detailed and elaborate working of a system, in which every act has its own place and must be performed without fail. Though no native, however intelligent, can formulate this state of affairs in a general abstract manner, or present it as a sociological theory, yet every one is well aware of its existence and in each concrete case he can foresee the consequences.

In magical and religious ceremonies almost every act, besides its primary purposes and effects, is also regarded as an obligation between groups and individuals, and here also there comes sooner or later an equivalent repayment or counter-service, stipulated by custom. Magic in its most important forms is a public institution in which the communal magician, who as a rule holds his office by inheritance, has to officiate on behalf of the whole group. Such is the case in the magic of gardens, fishing, war, weather, and canoe-building. As necessity arises, at the proper season, or in certain circumstances he is under an obligation to perform his magic, to keep the taboos, and at times also to control the whole enterprise. For this he is repaid by small offerings, immediately given, and often incorporated into the ritual proceedings. But the real reward lies in the prestige, power, and privileges which his position confers upon him.[2] In cases of minor or occasional magic, such as love charms, curative rites, sorcery, magic of toothache and of pig-welfare, when it is performed on behalf of another, it has to be paid for substantially and the relation between client and professional is based on a contract defined by custom. From the point of view of our present argument, we have to register the fact that all the acts of communal magic are obligatory upon the performer, and that the obligation to carry them out goes with the status of communal magician, which is hereditary in most cases and always is a position of power and privilege. A man may relinquish his position and hand it over to the next in succession, but once he accepts it, he has to carry on the work incumbent, and the community has to give him in return all his dues.

As to the acts which usually would be regarded as religious rather than magical—ceremonies at birth or marriage, rites of death and mourning, the worship of ghosts, spirits, or mythical personages—they also have a legal side clearly exemplified in the case of mortuary performances, described above. Every important act of a religious nature is conceived as a moral obligation towards the object, the ghost, spirit, or power worshipped; it also satisfies some emotional craving of the performer; but besides all this it has also as a matter of fact its place in some social scheme, it is regarded by some third person or persons as due to them, watched and then repaid or returned in kind. When, for example, at the annual return of the departed ghosts to their village you give an offering to the spirit of a dead relative, you satisfy his feelings, and no doubt also his spiritual appetite, which feeds on the spiritual substance of the meal; you probably also express your own sentiment towards the beloved dead. But there is also a social obligation involved: after the dishes have been exposed for some time and the spirit has finished with his spiritual share, the rest, none the worse, it appears, for ordinary consumption after its spiritual abstraction, is given to a friend or relation-in-law still alive, who then returns a similar gift later on.[3] I can recall to my mind not one single act of a religious nature without some such sociological by-play more or less directly associated with the main religious function of the act. Its importance lies in the fact that it makes the act a social obligation, besides its being a religious duty.

I could still continue with the survey of some other phases of tribal life and discuss more fully the legal aspect of domestic relations, already exemplified above, or enter into the reciprocities of the big enterprises, and so on. But it must have become clear now that the detailed illustrations previously given are not exceptional isolated cases, but representative instances of what obtains in every walk of native life.

REFERENCES

1. Compare also the apposite criticism of my expression "pure gift" and of all it implies by M. Marcel Mauss, in *L'Année Sociologique,* Nouvelle Série, vol. i, pp. 171 sqq. I had written the above paragraph before I saw M. Mauss's strictures, which substantially agreed with my own. It is gratifying to a field-worker when his observations are sufficiently well presented to allow others to refute his conclusions out of his own material. It is even more pleasant for me to find that my maturer judgment has led me independently to the same results as those of my distinguished friend M. Mauss.
2. For further data referring to the social and legal status of the hereditary magician, see Chap. xvii on "Magic," in *Argonauts of the Western Pacific,* as well as the descriptions of and sundry references to canoe magic, sailing magic, and *baloma* magic. Compare also the short account of garden magic in "Primitive Economics" (*Economic Journ.,* 1921); of war magic, in *Man,* 1920 (No. 5 of article); and of fishing magic, in *Man,* 1918 (No. 53 of article).
3. Comp. the writer's account of the *Milamala,* the feast of the annual return of the spirits, in "Baloma; the spirits of the dead in the Trobriand Islands" (*Journ. of the R. Anthrop. Institute,* 1916). The food offerings in question are described on p. 378.

The Principle of Reciprocity * (*Lévi-Strauss*)

The conclusions of the famous *Essay on the Gift* are well known. In this study which is considered a classic today, Mauss intended to show first of all, that in primitive societies exchange consists less frequently of economic transactions than of reciprocal gifts; secondly, that these reciprocal gifts have a much more important function in these societies than in ours; finally, that this primitive form of exchange is not wholly nor essentially of an economic character but is what he calls "a total social fact," i.e., an event which has at the same time social and religious, magic and economic, utilitarian and sentimental, legal and moral significance. It is known that in numerous primitive societies, and particularly in those of the Pacific Islands and those of the Northwest Pacific coast of Canada and of Alaska, all the ceremonies observed on important occasions are accompanied by a distribution of valued objects. Thus in New Zealand the ceremonial offering of clothes, jewels, arms, food and various furnishings was a common characteristic of the social life of the Maori. These gifts were presented in the event of births, marriages, deaths, exhumations, peace treaties and misdemeanors, and incidents too numerous to be recorded. Similarly, Firth lists the occasions of ceremonial exchange in Polynesia: "birth, initiation, marriage, sickness,

* Claude Lévi-Strauss, *Les Structures Élémentaires de la Parenté,* chapter v.: "Le Principe de Reciprocité," Presses Universitaires de France, 1949. Abridged and translated by Rose L. Coser and Grace Frazer.

death and other social events . . ." [1] Another observer cites the following occasions for ceremonial exchange in a section of the same region: betrothal, marriage, pregnancy, birth and death; and he describes the presents offered by the father of the young man at the celebration of the betrothal: ten baskets of dry fish, ten thousand ripe and six thousand green coco-nuts, the boy himself receiving in exchange two large cakes.[2]

Such gifts are either exchanged immediately for equivalent gifts, or received by the beneficiaries on the condition that on a subsequent occasion they will return the gesture with other gifts whose value often exceeds that of the first, but which bring about in their turn a right to receive later new gifts which themselves surpass the magnificence of those previously given. The most characteristic of these institutions is the potlatch of the Indians in Alaska and in the region of Vancouver. These ceremonies have a triple function: to give back with proper "interest" gifts formerly received; to establish publicly the claim of a family or social group to a title or privilege, or to announce a change of status; finally, to surpass a rival in generosity, to crush him if possible under future obligations which it is hoped he cannot meet, thus taking from him privileges, titles, rank, authority and prestige.

Doubtless the system of reciprocal gifts only reaches such vast proportions with the Indians of the Northwest Pacific, a people who show a genius and exceptional temperament in their treatment of the fundamental themes of a primitive culture. But Mauss has been able to establish the existence of similar institutions in Melanesia and Polynesia. The main function of the food celebrations of many tribes in New Guinea is to obtain recognition of the new "pangua" through a gathering of witnesses, that is to say, the function which in Alaska, according to Barnett, is served by potlatch. . . . Gift exchange and potlatch is a universal mode of culture, although not equally developed everywhere.

But we must insist that this primitive conception of the exchange of goods is not only expressed in well-defined and localized institutions. It permeates all transactions, ritual or secular, in the course of which objects or produce are given or received. Everywhere we find again and again this double assumption, implicit or explicit, that reciprocal gifts constitute a means of transmission of goods; and that these goods are not offered principally or essentially, in order to gain a profit or advantage of an economic nature: "After celebrations of birth," writes Turner of the Samoan culture, "after having received and given the *oloa* and the *tonga* (that is the masculine gifts and the feminine gifts) the husband and the wife are not any richer than they were before."

Exchange does not bring a tangible result as is the case in the commercial transactions in our society. Profit is neither direct, nor is it inherent in the objects exchanged as in the case of monetary profit or consumption values. Or rather, profit does not have the meaning which we assign to it because in primitive culture, there is something else in what we call a "commodity" than that which renders it commodious to its owner or to its merchant. Goods are not only economic commodities but vehicles and instruments for realities of another order: influence, power, sympathy, status, emotion; and the skillful game of exchange consists of a complex totality of maneuvers, conscious or unconscious, in order to gain security and to fortify one's self against risks incurred through alliances and rivalry.

.   .   .

Writing about the Andaman Islanders, Radcliffe-Brown states: "The purpose of the exchange is primarily a moral one; to bring about a friendly feeling between the two persons who participate." The best proof of the supra-economic character of these exchanges is that, in the potlatch, one does not hesitate sometime to destroy considerable wealth by breaking a "copper," or throwing it in the sea and that greater prestige results from the destruction of riches than from its distribution; for distribution, although it may be generous, demands a similar act in return. The economic character exists, however, although it is always limited and qualified by the other aspects of the institution of exchange. "It is not simply the possession of riches which brings prestige, it is rather their distribution. One does not gather riches except in order to rise in the social hierarchy. . . . However, even when pigs are exchanged for pigs, and food for food, the transactions do not lose all economic significance for they encourage work and stimulate a need for cooperation." [3]

The idea that a mysterious advantage is attached to the obtainment of commodities, or at least certain commodities by means of reciprocal gifts, rather than by production or by individual acquisition is not limited to primitive societies.

In modern society, there are certain kinds of objects which are especially well suited for presents, precisely because of their non-utilitarian qualities. In some Iberian countries these objects can only be found, in all their luxury and diversity, in stores especially set up for this purpose and which are similar to the Anglo-Saxon "gift shops." It is hardly necessary to note that these gifts, like invitations (which, though not exclusively, are also free distributions of food and drink) are "returned"; this is an instance in our society of the principle of reciprocity. It is commonly understood in our society that certain goods of a non-essential consumption value, but to which we attach a great psychological aesthetic or sensual value, such as flowers, candies and luxury articles, are obtainable in the form of reciprocal gifts rather than in the form of purchases or individual consumption.

Certain ceremonies and festivals in our society also regulate the periodic return and traditional style of vast operations of exchange. The exchange of presents at Christmas, during one month each year, to which all the social classes apply themselves with a sort of sacred ardor, is nothing else than a gigantic potlatch, which implicates millions of individuals, and at the end of which many family budgets are confronted by lasting disequilibrium. Christmas cards, richly decorated, certainly do not attain the value of the "coppers"; but the refinement of selection, their outstanding designs, their price, the quantity sent or received, give evidence (ritually exhibited on the mantelpiece during the week of celebration), of the recipient's social bonds and the degree of his prestige. We may also mention the subtle techniques which govern the wrapping of the presents and which express in their own way the personal bond between the giver and the receiver: special stickers, paper, ribbon, etc. Through the vanity of gifts, their frequent duplication resulting from the limited range of selection, these exchanges also take the form of a vast and collective destruction of wealth. There are many little facts in this example to remind one that even in our society the destruction of wealth is a way to gain prestige. Isn't it true that the capable merchant knows that a way to attract customers is by advertising that certain high-priced goods must be "sacrificed"? The move is economic but the terminology retains a sense of the sacred tradition.

.　　　.　　　.

In the significant sphere of the offering of food, for which banquets, teas, and evening parties are the modern customs, the language itself, e.g., "to give a reception," shows that for us as in Alaska or Oceania, "to receive is to give." One offers dinner to a person whom one wishes to honor, or in order to return a "kindness." The more the social aspect takes precedence over the strictly alimentary, the more emphasis is given to style both of food and of the way in which it is presented: the fine porcelain, the silverware, the embroidered table cloths which ordinarily are carefully put away in the family cabinets and buffets, are a striking counterpart of the ceremonial bowls and spoons of Alaska brought out on similar occasions from painted and decorated chests. Above all, the attitudes towards food are revealing: what the natives of the Northwest coast call "rich food" connotes also among ourselves something else than the mere satisfaction of physiological needs. One does not serve the daily menu when one gives a dinner party. Moreover, if the occasion calls for certain types of food defined by tradition, their apparition alone, through a significant recurrence, calls for shared consumption. A bottle of old wine, a rare liqueur, bothers the conscience of the owner; these are delicacies which one would not buy and consume alone without a vague feeling of guilt. Indeed, the group judges with singular harshness the person who does this. This is reminiscent of the Polynesian ceremonial exchanges, in which goods must as much as possible not be exchanged within the group of paternal relations, but must go to other groups and into other villages. To fail at this duty is called "sori tana" —"to eat from one's own basket." And at the village dances, convention demands that neither of the two local groups consume the food which they have brought but that they exchange their provisions and that each eat the food of the other. The action of the person who, as the woman in the Maori proverb *Kai Kino ana Te Arahe,* would secretly eat the ceremonial food, without offering a part of it, would provoke from his or her relations sentiments which would range, according to circumstances, from irony, mocking and disgust to sentiments of dislike and even rage. It seems that the group confusedly sees in the individual accomplishment of an act which normally requires collective participation a sort of social incest.

But the ritual of exchange does not only take place in the ceremonial meal. Politeness requires that one offer the salt, the butter, the bread, and that one present one's neighbor with a plate before serving oneself. We have often noticed the ceremonial aspect of the meal in the lower-priced restaurants in the south of France; above all in those regions where wine is the main industry, it is surrounded by a sort of mystical respect which makes it "rich food." In those little restaurants where wine is included in the price of the meal each guest finds in front of his plate, a modest bottle of a wine more than often very bad. This bottle is similar to that of the person's neighbor, as are the portions of meat and vegetables, which a waiter passes around. However, a peculiar difference of attitude immediately manifests itself in regard to the liquid nourishment and the solid nourishment: the latter serves the needs of the body and the former its luxury, the one serves first of all to feed, the other to honor. Each guest eats, so to speak, for himself. But when it comes to the wine, a new situation arises; if a bottle should be insufficiently filled, its owner would call good-naturedly for the neighbor to testify. And the proprietor would face, not the anger of an individual victim, but a community complaint. Indeed, the wine is a social commodity whereas the *plat du jour* is a personal commodity. The small bottle can hold just one glass, its contents will be poured not in the glass of the owner, but in that of his neighbor. And the latter will make a corresponding gesture of reciprocity.

What has happened? The two bottles are identical in size, their contents similar in quality. Each participant in this revealing scene, when the final count is made, has not received more than if he had consumed his own wine. From an economic point of view, no one has gained and no one had lost. But there is much more in the exchange itself than in the things exchanged.

The situation of two strangers who face each other, less than a yard apart, from two sides of a table in an inexpensive restaurant (to obtain an individual table is a privilege which one must pay for, and which cannot be awarded below a certain price) is commonplace and episodical. However, it is very revealing, because it offers an example, rare in our society (but prevalent in primitive societies) of the formation of a group for which, doubtless because of its temporary character, no ready formula of integration exists. The custom in French society is to ignore persons whose name, occupation and social rank are unknown. But in the little restaurant, such people find themselves placed for two or three half-hours in a fairly intimate relationship, and momentarily united by a similarity of preoccupations. There is conflict, doubtless not very sharp, but real, which is sufficient to create a state of tension between the norm of "privacy" and the fact of community. They feel at the same time alone and together, compelled to the habitual reserve between strangers, while their respective positions in physical space and their relationships to the objects and utensils of the meal, suggest and to a certain degree call for intimacy. These two strangers are exposed for a short period of time to living together. Without doubt not for as long a time nor as intimately as when one shares a sleeping car, or a cabin on a transatlantic crossing, but for this reason also no clear cultural procedure has been established. An almost imperceptible anxiety is likely to arise in the minds of the two guests with the prospect of small disagreements that the meeting could bring forth. When social distance is maintained, even if it is not accompanied by any manifestation of disdain, insolence or aggression, it is in itself a cause of suffering; for such social distance is at variance with the fact that all social contact carries with it an appeal and that this appeal is at the same time a hope for response. Opportunity for escape from this trying yet ephemeral situation is provided by an exchange of wine. It is an affirmation of good grace which dispels the reciprocal uncertainty; it substitutes a social bond for mere physical juxtaposition. But it is also more than that; the partner who had the right to maintain reserve is called upon to give it up; wine offered calls for wine returned, cordiality demands cordiality. The relationship of indifference which has lasted until one of the guests has decided to give it up can never be brought back. From now on it must become a relationship either of cordiality or hostility. There is no possibility of refusing the neighbor's offer of his glass of wine without appearing insulting. Moreover, the acceptance of the offer authorizes another offer, that of conversation. Thus a number of minute social bonds are established by a series of alternating oscillations, in which a right is established in the offering and an obligation in the receiving.

And there is still more. The person who begins the cycle has taken the initiative, and the greater social ease which he has proved becomes an advantage for him. However, the opening always carries with it a risk, namely that the partner will answer the offered libation with a less generous drink, or, on the contrary, that he will prove to be a higher bidder thus forcing the person who offered the wine first to sacrifice a second bottle for the sake of his prestige. We are, therefore, on a microscopic scale, it is true, in the presence of a "total social fact" whose implications are at the same time social, psychological and economic.

This drama, which on the surface seems futile and to which, perhaps, the reader will find that we have awarded a disproportionate importance, seems to us on the contrary to offer material for inexhaustible sociological reflection. We have already pointed out the interest with which we view the non-crystallized forms of social life: the spontaneous aggregations arising from crises, or (as in the example just discussed) simple sub-products of collective life, provide us with vestiges which are still fresh, of very primitive social psychological experiences. In this sense the attitudes of the strangers in the restaurant appear to be an infinitely distant projection, scarcely perceptible but nonetheless recognizable, of a fundamental situation; that in which individuals of primitive tribes find themselves for the first time entering into contact with each other or with strangers. The primitives know only two ways of classifying strangers; strangers are either "good" or "bad." But one must not be misled by a naive translation of the native terms. A "good" group is that to which, without hesitating, one grants hospitality, the one for which one deprives oneself of most precious goods; while the "bad" group is that from which one expects and to which one inflicts, at the first opportunity, suffering or death. With the latter one fights, with the former one exchanges goods.

The general phenomenon of exchange is first of all a total exchange, including food, manufactured objects, as well as those most precious items: women. Doubtlessly we are a long way from the strangers in the restaurant and perhaps it seems startling to suggest that the reluctance of the French peasant to drink his own bottle of wine gives a clue for the explanation of the incest taboo. Indeed, we believe that both phenomena have the same sociological and cultural meaning.

.   .   .

The prohibition of incest is a rule of reciprocity. It means: I will only give up my daughter or my sister if my neighbor will give up his also. The violent reaction of the community towards incest is the reaction of a community wronged. The fact that I can obtain a wife is, in the last analysis, the consequence of the fact that a brother or a father has given up a woman.

In Polynesia Firth distinguishes three spheres of exchange according to the relative mobility of the articles concerned. The first sphere concerns food in its diverse forms; the second, rope and fabrics made of bark; the third, hooks, cables, turmeric cakes and canoes. He adds: "Apart from the three spheres of exchange mentioned a fourth may be recognized in cases where goods of unique quality are handed over. Such for instance was the transfer of women by the man who could not otherwise pay for his canoe. Transfers of land might be put into the same category. Women and land are given in satisfaction of unique obligations. . . ." [4]

It is necessary to anticipate the objection that we are relating two phenomena which are not of the same type; it might be argued that indeed gifts may be regarded even in our own culture as a primitive form of exchange but that this kind of reciprocal interaction has been replaced in our society by exchange for profit except for a few remaining instances such as invitations, celebrations and gifts: that in our society the number of goods that are being transferred according to these archaic patterns represents only a small proportion of the objects of commerce and merchandising, and that reciprocal gifts are merely amusing vestiges which can retain the curiosity of the antiquary; and that it is not possible to say that the prohibition of incest, which is as important in our own society as in any other, has been derived from a type of phenomenon which is abnormal today and of purely anecdotical interest. In other words, we will be accused, as we ourselves have accused McLennan, Spencer, Averbury and Durkheim, of deriving the function from the survival and the general case from the existence of an exceptional one.

.   .   .

This objection can be answered by distinguishing between two interpretations of the term "archaic." The survival of a custom or of a belief can be accounted for in different ways: the custom or belief may be a vestige, without any other significance than that of an historical residue which has been spared by chance; but it may also continue throughout the centuries to have a specific function which does not differ essentially from the original one. An institution can be archaic because it has lost its reason for existing or on the contrary because this reason for existing is so fundamental that its transformation has been neither possible nor necessary.

Such is the case of exchange. Its function in primitive society is essential because it encompasses at the same time material objects, social values and women, while in our culture the original function of exchange of goods has gradually been reduced in importance as other means of acquisition have developed; reciprocity as the basis of getting a spouse, however, has maintained its fundamental function; for one thing because women are the most precious property, and above all because women are not in the first place a sign of social value, but a natural stimulant; and the stimulant of the only instinct whose satisfaction can be postponed, the only one consequently, for which, in the act of exchange, and through the awareness of reciprocity, the transformation can occur from the stimulant to the sign and, thereby, give way to an institution; this is the fundamental process of transformation from the conditions of nature to cultural life.

The inclusion of women in the number of reciprocal transactions from group to group and from tribe to tribe is such a general custom that a volume would not suffice to enumerate the instances in which it occurs. Let us note first of all that marriage is everywhere considered as a particularly favorable occasion for opening a cycle of exchanges. The "wedding presents" in our society evidently enter again into the group of phenomena which we have studied above.

In Alaska and in British Columbia, the marriage of a girl is necessarily accompanied by a potlatch; to such a point that the Comox aristocrats organize mock-marriage ceremonies, where there is no bride, for the sole purpose of acquiring privileges in the course of the exchange ritual. But the relation which exists between marriage and gifts is not arbitrary; marriage is itself an inherent part of as well as a central motive for the accompanying reciprocal gifts. Not so long ago it was the custom in our society to "ask for" a young girl in marriage; the father of the betrothed woman "gave" his daughter in marriage; in English the phrase is still used, "to give up the bride." And in regard to the woman who takes a lover, it is also said that she "gives herself." The Arabic word, *sadaqa*, signifies the alm, the bride's price, law and tax. In this last case, the meaning of the word can be explained by the custom of wife buying. But marriage through purchase is an institution which is special in form only; in reality it is only a modality of the fundamental system as analyzed by Mauss, according to which, in primitive society and still somewhat in ours, rights, goods and persons circulate within a group according to a continual mechanism of services and counter-services. Malinowski has shown that in the Trobriand Islands, even after marriage, the payment of mapula represents, on the part of the man, a counter-service destined to compensate for the services furnished by the wife in the form of sexual gratifications.

.   .   .

Even marriage through capture does not contradict the law of reciprocity; it is rather one of the possible institutionalized ways of putting it into practice. In Tikopia the abduction of the betrothed woman expresses in a dramatic fashion the obligation of the detaining group to give up the girls. The fact that they are "available" is thus made evident.

It would then be false to say that one exchanges or gives gifts at the same time that one exchanges or gives women. Because the woman herself is nothing else than one of these gifts, the supreme gift amongst those that can only be obtained in the form of reciprocal gifts. The first stage of our analysis has been directed towards bringing to light this fundamental characteristic of the gift, represented by the woman in primitive society, and to explain the reasons for it. It should not be surprising then to see that women are included among a number of other reciprocal prestations.

.   .   .

The small nomadic bands of the Nambikwara Indians of western Brazil are in constant fear of each other and avoid each other; but at the same time they desire contact because it is the only way in which they are able to exchange, and thereby obtain articles which they are lacking. There is a bond, a continuity between the hostile relations and the provision of reciprocal prestations: exchanges are peacefully resolved wars, wars are the outcome of unsuccessful transactions. This characteristic is evidenced by the fact that the passing of war into peace or at least of hostility into cordiality operates through the intermediary of ritual gestures: the adversaries feel each other out, and with gestures which still retain something of the attitudes of combat, inspect the necklaces, earrings, bracelets, and feathered ornaments of one another with admiring comments.

And from battle they pass immediately to the gifts; gifts are received, gifts are given, but silently, without bargaining, without complaint, and apparently without linking that which is given to that which is obtained. These are, indeed, reciprocal gifts, not commercial operations. But the relationship may be given yet an additional meaning: two tribes who have thus come to establish lasting cordial relations, can decide in a deliberate manner, to join by setting up an artificial kinship relation between the male members of the two tribes: the relationship of brothers-in-law. According to the matrimonial system of the Nambikwara, the immediate consequence of this innovation is that all the children of one group become the potential spouses of the children of the other group and vice-versa; thus a continuous transition exists from war to exchange and from exchange to intermarriage; and the exchange of betrothed women is merely the termination of an uninterrupted process of reciprocal gifts, which brings about the transition from hostility to alliance, from anxiety to confidence and from fear to friendship.

REFERENCES

1. Raymond Firth, *Primitive Polynesian Economy,* London, 1939, p. 321.
2. H. Ian Hogbin, "Sexual life of the natives of Ongton Java." *Journal of the Polynesian Society,* Vol. 40, p. 28.
3. A. B. Deacon, *Malekula . . . A Vanishing People in the New Hebrides,* London, 1934, p. 637.
4. Firth, *op. cit.,* p. 344.

The Basic Structure of the Interactive Relationship * (*Parsons*)

The interaction of ego and alter is the most elementary form of a social system. The features of this interaction are present in more complex form in all social systems.

In interaction ego and alter are each objects of orientation for the other. The basic differences from orientations to nonsocial objects are two. First, since the outcome of ego's action (e.g., success in the attainment of a goal) is contingent on alter's reaction to what ego does, ego becomes oriented not only to alter's probable *overt* behavior but also to what ego interprets to be alter's expectations relative to ego's behavior, since ego expects that alter's expectations will influence alter's behavior. Second, in an integrated system, this orientation to the expectations of the other is reciprocal or complementary.

Communication through a common system of symbols is the precondition of this reciprocity or complementarity of expectations. The alternatives which are open to alter must have some measure of stability in two respects: first, as realistic possibilities for alter, and second, in their meaning to ego.

* Reprinted by permission of the publishers from Talcott Parsons and Edward A. Shils, editors, *Toward a General Theory of Action,* pp. 105–107. Cambridge, Mass: Harvard University Press, Copyright, 1952, by The President and Fellows of Harvard College.

This stability presupposes generalization from the particularity of the given situations of ego and alter, both of which are continually changing and are never concretely identical over any two moments in time. When such generalization occurs, and actions, gestures, or symbols have more or less the *same* meaning for both ego and alter, we may speak of a common culture existing between them, through which their interaction is mediated.

Furthermore, this common culture, or symbol system, inevitably possesses in certain aspects a normative significance for the actors. Once it is in existence, observance of its conventions is a necessary condition for ego to be "understood" by alter, in the sense of allowing ego to elicit the type of reaction from alter which ego expects. This common set of cultural symbols becomes the medium in which is formed a constellation of the contingent actions of both parties, in such a way that there will simultaneously emerge a definition of a range of *appropriate* reactions on alter's part to each of a range of possible actions ego has taken and vice versa. It will then be a condition of the stabilization of such a system of complementary expectations, not only that ego and alter should *communicate,* but that they should *react appropriately* to each other's action.

A tendency toward consistent appropriateness of reaction is also a tendency toward conformity with a normative pattern. The culture is not only a set of symbols of communication but a *set of norms* for action.

The motivation of ego and alter become integrated with the normative patterns through interaction. The polarity of gratification and deprivation is crucial here. An appropriate reaction on alter's part is a gratifying one to ego. If ego conforms with the norm, this gratification is in one aspect a reward for his conformity with it; the converse holds for the case of deprivation and deviance. The reactions of alter toward ego's conformity with or deviance from the normative pattern thus become sanctions to ego. Ego's expectations vis-à-vis alter are expectations concerning the roles of ego and of alter; and sanctions reinforce ego's motivation to conform with these role-expectations. Thus the complementarity of expectations brings with it the reciprocal reinforcement of ego's and alter's motivation to conformity with the normative pattern which defines their expectations.

The interactive system also involves the process of generalization, not only in the common culture by which ego and alter communicate but in the interpretation of alter's discrete actions vis-à-vis ego as expressions of alter's *intentions* (that is, as indices of the cathectic-evaluative aspects of alter's motivational orientations toward ego). This "generalization" implies that ego and alter agree that certain actions of alter are indices of the *attitudes* which alter has acquired toward ego (and reciprocally, ego toward alter).

Since culture and the latter is internalized in ego's need-dispositions, ego is sensitive not only to alter's overt acts, but to his *attitudes*. He acquires a need not only to obtain specific *rewards* and avoid specific *punishments* but to enjoy the favorable attitudes and avoid the unfavorable ones of alter. Indeed, since he is integrated with the same norms, these are the same as his attitudes toward himself as an object. Thus violation of the norm causes him to feel shame toward alter, guilt toward himself.

It should be clear that as an ideal type this interaction paradigm implies *mutuality* of gratification in a certain sense, though not necessarily equal distribution of gratification. As we shall see in the next chapter, this is also the paradigm of the process of the learning of generalized orientations. Even where special mechanisms of adjustment such as dominance and submission or alienation from normative expectations enter in, the process still must be described and analyzed in relation to the categories of this paradigm. It is thus useful both for the analysis of systems of normative expectations and for that of the actual conformity or deviation regarding these expectations in concrete action.

In summary we may say that this is the basic paradigm for the structure of a solidary interactive relationship. It contains all the fundamental elements of the role structure of the social system and the attachment and security system of the personality. It involves culture in both its communicative and its value-orientation functions. It is the modal point of the organization of all systems of action.

4.

SOCIAL CONTROL

SOCIAL CONTROL refers to those mechanisms by which society exercises its dominion over component individuals and enforces conformity to its norms, i.e., its values. The term was first used by one of the fathers of American sociology, Edward A. Ross (1866–1951), in a series of papers written just before the turn of the century which were later incorporated in the book *Social Control*. It has since become a standard mode of conceptualization in American sociology.

Ross employed the term "social control" in a rather imprecise sense, yet one gathers that he was mainly concerned with those regulative institutions which insure that individual behavior is in conformity with group demands. He showed the important role which belief in the supernatural, ceremonies, public opinion, morals, art, education, law, and related phenomena play in maintaining the normative structure of society.

Ross' contemporary, William G. Sumner (1840–1910), another of the founding fathers of American sociology, attempted in his famous *Folkways* (1906) a somewhat similar task. As the subtitle of the book, "A Study of the Sociological Importance of Usages, Manners, Customs and Morals," indicates, Sumner was primarily concerned with the way in which standardized norms serve to insure individual conformity. "Folkways," in Sumner's terminology, are "habits and customs . . . which become regulative and imperative for succeeding generations . . . they very largely control individual and social undertaking."

These early sociological investigators significantly enlarged our understanding of social control by pointing out that there is a wide range of control mechanisms and that law, which had earlier been seen as the only important mechanism, was one of many, and possibly not even the most important. Yet these analysts never satisfactorily explained the manner in which external control comes to be incorporated into the personality of the individual. When faced with this problem, they tended to use a series of *ad hoc* concepts such as suggestion and imitation. Such concepts not only failed to explain the mechanisms involved; they also proved to be convenient labels for as yet unexplained phenomena.

Further advance came from a number of theorists who, though working independently arrived at substantially similar results. Emile Durkheim, after first having attempted to explain social control solely in terms of exterior constraints, was led in his later work to emphasize that social norms, far from being imposed on the individual from the outside, became in fact *internalized*, that they are "society living in us." Durkheim now maintained that the essence of control lay in the individual's sense of moral obligation to obey a rule—the voluntary acceptance of duty rather than a simple exterior conformity to outside pressure. The moral demands of society, as Durkheim sees them in his mature work, are constitutive elements of the individual personality itself.

While Durkheim was led to stress internalization of societal demands as the most important element in social control, the American social philosopher, George Herbert Mead (1863–1931), and the Austrian psychiatrist, Sigmund Freud (1856–1939), made further significant contributions to our understanding of the internalization of social norms. Mead argued that a person's self-image the "me," develops through his social experience as he becomes aware of the expectations and appraisals of others. The attitude of "significant others" becomes internalized and forms the "generalized other," the "conscience" of the individual. In this manner the expectations of others in the society form the character and "conscience" of the individual. Conscience is a societal creation. Sigmund Freud's construct, the superego, which is too well known to require discussion here, though arrived at from a different point of departure and consistent with a different terminology, may nevertheless be said in this respect to dovetail rather closely with Mead's conceptions. It would seem that to Freud, as to Mead, the internalization of societal norms involves a disciplining of impulse through the incorporation of the expectations of others into the psychic structure.

Finally, our reading from the brilliant Swiss psychologist, Jean Piaget, is meant to point toward yet another road, in many respects similar to Mead's, through which the process of internalization of social norms can be approached. It is Piaget's thesis in his work *The Moral Judgment of the Child* that autonomous moral judgments are internalized only on the basis of cooperative social relationships, whereas "authoritarian" social relationships lead only to conformity with heteronomous commands. Types of individual morality are thus seen as deriving genetically from the types of social structure in which individuals are involved.

Of course, many problems of the relation of the individual to his society remain unsolved; it may still be said that by having brought into focus the internalization of social requirements within the individual, sociology and social psychology have in the last two generations achieved one of the major breakthroughs in social theory and in the understanding of human behavior.

Social Control * (*Ross*)

Even in a mining camp, the issues are not always between man and man. In the keeping of arms or whiskey from the Indians, or in the limiting of gambling, there comes to light a collective interest which only collective action can protect. There are offences that exasperate the group as well as offences that arouse the ire of the individual. In this common wrath and common vengeance lies the germ of a social control of the person.[1]

So far as the fruits of a common enterprise can be reaped in full by the participants, coöperation may be left entirely free; but when the benefits of a coöperation will redound to the group as a whole and be enjoyed by all alike, it is necessary that all be required to assume their due share of the burden. Among the earliest signs of collective pressure is the endeavor to make kickers, cowards, and shirkers take part in joint undertakings which benefit all. Among the Iowa settlers the first symptom of contractile power in the social tissue appeared in the community defence of cases to test squatter land titles.[2] Along the river building of the levee is the first occasion for compulsory coöperation. In Egypt and China, the early river monarchies, the care of the waters had much to do with forming the state.[3] In new lands, defence against the aborigines is the chief community interest and overrides masterfully the timidity or apathy of individual settlers.

In complex coöperation even the willing need an authority over them, for success implies such a delicate poise of numerous individual performances that the Word must go forth and with power. This is why warfare, the great primary coöperation, is usually the mother of discipline.

.   .   .

It is, in fact, impossible to reap the advantages of high organization of any kind—military, political, industrial, commercial, education—save by restraints of one kind or another. If the units of a society are not reliable, the waste and leakage on the one hand, or the friction due to the checks and safeguards required to prevent such loss on the other hand, prove so burdensome as to nullify the advantages of high organization and make complicated social machinery of any kind unprofitable.

Men are therefore in chronic need of better order than the natural moral motives will provide. At this point and at that point they gradually become sensible of a drag on their prosperity. They find themselves in the

* Reprinted from *Social Control* by Edward Alsworth Ross, pp. 49–50, 59–60, and 411–412 with permission of the publisher, The Macmillan Company. Copyright, 1910, by The Macmillan Company.

presence of a degree of discord, collision, and general unreliability which shuts them out of real material advantages. Better order becomes "a long-felt want," and it would be most surprising if this "demand" called forth no "supply." If in their collective capacity men did not find a means of guiding the will or conscience of the individual member of society, they would here betray a lack of enterprise they show nowhere else. The elementary personal struggle threatens the general prosperity just as the swollen river or the wildfire. And if men raise levees and firebrakes against the natural forces, why not against the human passions? Provided it be possible, a group control of conduct is, therefore, just what we should look for. The wonder would be if it were lacking.

Most of us, it is true, are born with a certain fitness for order. Ages of social weathering have allowed a mantle of soft green to creep over the flint of animal ferocity and selfishness. But the layer of soil is too thin. The abundant fruits of righteousness we need to-day must grow on *made* soil. The primitive Teuton is to the modern what the frowning ledges along his Rhine are to the smiling vine-clad terraces into which human labor has transformed them.

An unremitting control is needed, for the moral habit of one generation does not become the instinct of the next.

.   .   .

In respect to their fundamental character, it is possible to divide most of the supports of order into two groups. Such instruments of control as public opinion, suggestion, personal ideal, social religion, art, and social valuation draw much of their strength from the primal moral feelings. They take their shape from sentiment rather than utility. They control men in many things which have little to do with the welfare of society regarded as a corporation. They are aimed to realize not merely a social order but what one might term a *moral* order. These we may call *ethical*.

On the other hand, law, belief, ceremony, education, and illusion need not spring from ethical feelings at all. They are frequently the means deliberately chosen in order to reach certain ends. They are likely to come under the control of the organized few, and be used, whether for the corporate benefit or for class benefit, as the tools of policy. They may be termed *political*, using the word "political" in its original sense of "pertaining to policy."

Now, the prominence of the one group or the other in the regulative scheme depends upon the constitution of the society. The *political* instruments operating through prejudice or fear will be preferred: —

1. In proportion as the population elements to be held together are antipathetic and jarring.
2. In proportion to the subordination of the individual will and welfare by the scheme of control.
3. In proportion as the social constitution stereotypes differences of status.
4. In proportion as the differences in economic condition and opportunity it consecrates are great and cumulative.
5. In proportion as the parasitic relation is maintained between races, classes, or sexes.

In confirmation of these statements, we have but to recall that the chief influences which history recognizes as stiffening State, Church, Hierarchy, Tradition, are conquest, caste, slavery, serfdom, gross inequalities of wealth, military discipline, paternal regimentation, and race antipathies within the bosom of the group. The disappearance of any one of these conditions permits a mellowing and liberalizing of social control.

On the other hand the *ethical* instruments, being more mild, enlightening, and suasive, will be preferred:—

1. In proportion as the population is homogeneous in race.
2. In proportion as its culture is uniform and diffused.
3. In proportion as the social contacts between the elements in the population are many and amicable.
4. In proportion as the total burden of requirement laid upon the individual is light.
5. In proportion as the social constitution does not consecrate distinctions of status or the parasitic relation, but conforms to common elementary notions of justice.

REFERENCES

1. Sir Henry Maine shows that in early law only injuries of the community are crimes. The injuries of the individual are torts and can be settled for. Moreover, "When the Roman community conceived itself to be injured the analogy of a personal wrong received was carried out to its consequences with absolute literalness, and the state avenged itself by a single act on the individual wrongdoer. The result was that in the infancy of the commonwealth every offence vitally touching its security or its interests was punished by a separate enactment of the legislature."—"Ancient Law," p. 360.
2. Jesse Macy, "Institutional Beginnings in a Western State." Johns Hopkins University *Studies in Historical and Political Science,* Vol. II.
3. E. J. Simcox, "Primitive Civilizations," Vol. I, pp. 75–76; Vol. II, pp. 9, 63.

The Mores * (*Sumner*)

66. *More exact definition of the mores*. We may now formulate a more complete definition of the mores. They are the ways of doing things which are current in a society to satisfy human needs and desires, together with the faiths, notions, codes, and standards of well living which inhere in those ways, having a genetic connection with them. By virtue of the latter element the more are traits in the specific character (ethos) of a society or a period. They pervade and control the ways of thinking in all the exigencies of life, returning from the world of abstractions to the world of action, to give guidance and to win revivification. "The mores [*Sitten*] are, before any beginning of reflection, the regulators of the political, social, and religious behavior of the individual. Conscious reflection is the worst enemy of the mores, because mores begin unconsciously and pursue unconscious purposes, which are recognized by reflection often only after long and circuitous processes, and because their expediency often depends on the assumption that they will have general acceptance and currency, uninterfered with by reflection." [1] "The mores are usage in any group, in so far as it, on the one hand, is not the expression or fulfillment of an absolute natural necessity [e.g. eating or sleeping], and, on the other hand, is independent of the arbitrary will of the individual, and is generally accepted as good and proper, appropriate and worthy." [2]

68. *The ritual of the mores*. The mores are social ritual in which we all participate unconsciously. The current habits as to hours of labor, meal hours, family life, the social intercourse of the sexes, propriety, amusements, travel, holidays, education, the use of periodicals and libraries, and innumerable other details of life fall under this ritual. Each does as everybody does. For the great mass of mankind as to all things, and for all of us for a great many things, the rule to do as all do suffices. We are led by suggestion and association to believe that there must be wisdom and utility in what all do. The great mass of the folkways give us discipline and the support of routine and habit. If we had to form judgments as to all these cases before we could act in them, and were forced always to act rationally, the burden would be unendurable. Beneficent use and wont save us this trouble.

80. *The mores have the authority of facts*. The mores come down to us from the past. Each individual is born into them as he is born into the atmosphere, and he does not reflect on them, or criticise them any more than

---

* Reprinted from *Folkways* by William Graham Sumner, Ginn and Company, 1904, paragraphs 66, 68, 80 and 83.

a baby analyzes the atmosphere before he begins to breathe it. Each one is subjected to the influence of the mores, and formed by them, before he is capable of reasoning about them. It may be objected that nowadays, at least, we criticise all traditions, and accept none just because they are handed down to us. If we take up cases of things which are still entirely or almost entirely in the mores, we shall see that this is not so. There are sects of free-lovers amongst us who want to discuss pair marriage (sec. 374). They are not simply people of evil life. They invite us to discuss rationally our inherited customs and ideas as to marriage, which, they say, are by no means so excellent and elevated as we believe. They have never won any serious attention. Some others want to argue in favor of polygamy on grounds of expediency. They fail to obtain a hearing. Others want to discuss property. In spite of some literary activity on their part, no discussion of property, bequest, and inheritance has ever been opened. Property and marriage are in the mores. Nothing can ever change them but the unconscious and imperceptible movement of the mores. Religion was originally a matter of the mores. It became a societal institution and a function of the state. It has now to a great extent been put back into the mores. Since laws with penalties to enforce religious creeds or practices have gone out of use any one may think and act as he pleases about religion. Therefore it is not now "good form" to attack religion. Infidel publications are now tabooed by the mores, and are more effectually repressed than ever before. They produce no controversy. Democracy is in our American mores. It is a product of our physical and economic conditions. It is impossible to discuss or criticise it. It is glorified for popularity, and is a subject of dithyrambic rhetoric. No one treats it with complete candor and sincerity. No one dares to analyze it as he would aristocracy or autocracy. He would get no hearing and would only incur abuse. The thing to be noticed in all these cases is that the masses oppose a deaf ear to every argument against the mores. It is only in so far as things have been transferred from the mores into laws and positive institutions that there is discussion about them or rationalizing upon them. The mores contain the norm by which, if we should discuss the mores, we should have to judge the mores. We learn the mores as unconsciously as we learn to walk and eat and breathe. The masses never learn how we walk, and eat, and breathe, and they never know any reason why the mores are what they are. The justification of them is that when we wake to consciousness of life we find them facts which already hold us in the bonds of tradition, custom, and habit. The mores contain embodied in them notions, doctrines, and maxims, but they are facts. They are in the present tense. They have nothing to do with what ought to be, will be, may be, or once was, if it is not now.

83. *Inertia and rigidity of the mores.* We see that we must conceive of the mores as a vast system of usages, covering the whole of life, and serving all its interests; also containing in themselves their own justification by tradition and use and wont, and approved by mystic sanctions until, by rational reflection, they develop their own philosophical and ethical generalizations, which are elevated into "principles" of truth and right. They coerce and restrict the newborn generation. They do not stimulate to thought, but the contrary. The thinking is already done and is embodied in the mores. They never contain any provision for their own amendment. They are not questions, but answers, to the problem of life. They present themselves as final and unchangeable, because they present answers which are offered as "the truth." No world philosophy, until the modern scientific world philosophy, and that only within a generation or two, has ever presented itself as perhaps transitory, certainly incomplete, and liable to be set aside to-morrow by more knowledge. No popular world philosophy or life policy ever can present itself in that light. It would cost too great a mental strain. All the groups whose mores we consider far inferior to our own are quite as well satisfied with theirs as we are with ours. The goodness or badness of mores consists entirely in their adjustment to the life conditions and the interests of the time and place (sec. 65). Therefore it is a sign of ease and welfare when no thought is given to the mores, but all coöperate in them instinctively. The nations of southeastern Asia show us the persistency of the mores, when the element of stability and rigidity in them becomes predominant. Ghost fear and ancestor worship tend to establish the persistency of the mores by dogmatic authority, strict taboo, and weighty sanctions. The mores then lose their naturalness and vitality. They are stereotyped. They lose all relation to expediency. They become an end in themselves. They are imposed by imperative authority without regard to interests or conditions (caste, child marriage, widows). When any society falls under the dominion of this disease in the mores it must disintegrate before it can live again. In that diseased state of the mores all learning consists in committing to memory the words of the sages of the past who established the formulae of the mores. Such words are "sacred writings," a sentence of which is a rule of conduct to be obeyed quite independently of present interests, or of any rational considerations.

REFERENCES

1. v. Hartman, *Phänom. des Sittl. Bewusseins,* 73.
2. Lazarus in *Ztsft. für Völkerpsy.,* I., 439.

The Internalization of Social Control I * (*Durkheim*)

What are the distinctive characteristics of a moral fact?

All morality appears to us as a system of rules of conduct. But all techniques are equally ruled by maxims that prescribe the behaviour of the agent in particular circumstances. What then is the difference between moral rules and other rules of technique?

(i) We shall show that moral rules are invested with a special authority by virtue of which they are obeyed simply because they command. We shall reaffirm, as a result of a purely empirical analysis, the notion of duty and nevertheless give a definition of it closely resembling that already given by Kant. Obligation is, then, one of the primary characteristics of the moral rule.

(ii) In opposition to Kant, however, we shall show that the notion of duty does not exhaust the concept of morality. It is impossible for us to carry out an act simply because we are ordered to do so and without consideration of its content. For us to become the agents of an act it must interest our sensibility to a certain extent and appear to us as, in some way, *desirable*. Obligation or duty only expresses one aspect abstracted from morality. A certain degree of desirability is another characteristic no less important than the first.

Something of the nature of duty is found in the desirability of morality. If it is true that the content of the act appeals to us, nevertheless its nature is such that it cannot be accomplished without effort and self-constraint. The *élan,* even the enthusiasm, with which we perform a moral act takes us outside ourselves and above our nature, and this is not achieved without difficulty and inner conflict. It is this *sui generis* desirability which is commonly called *good*.

Desirability and obligation are the two characteristics which it is useful to stress, without necessarily denying the existence of others. It will be our main intention to show that all moral acts have these two characteristics, even though they may be combined in different proportions.

. . .

Moral reality appears to us under two different aspects that must be clearly distinguished: the objective and the subjective.

Each people at a given moment of its history has a morality, and it is

* Reprinted from *Sociology and Philosophy* by Emile Durkheim, translated by D. F. Pocock, pp. 35–36 and 40–46, by permission of the publisher, The Free Press, Glencoe, Ill. Copyright, 1953, by The Free Press, A Corporation.

in the name of this ruling morality that tribunals condemn and opinion judges. For a given group there is a clearly defined morality. I postulate, then, supported by the facts, that there is a general morality common to all individuals belonging to a collectivity.

Now, apart from this morality there is an indefinite multitude of others. Each individual moral conscience expresses the collective morality in its own way. Each one sees it and understands it from a different angle. No individual can be completely in tune with the morality of his time, and one could say that there is no conscience that is not in some ways immoral. Each mind, under the influence of its milieu, education or heredity sees moral rules by a different light. One individual will feel the rules of civic morality keenly, but not so strongly the rules of domestic morality, or inversely. Another who feels only very slightly the duties of charity may have a profound respect for contract and justice. The most essential aspects of morality are seen differently by different people.

I do not intend to treat here of both these two sorts of moral reality, but only of the first. I shall deal with objective moral reality, that common and impersonal standard by which we evaluate action. The diversity of individual moral consciences shows how impossible it is to make use of them in order to arrive at an understanding of morality itself. Research into the conditions that determine these individual variations of morality would, no doubt, be an interesting psychological study, but would not help us to reach our particular goal.

Just as I am not concerned with the manner in which this or that particular individual sees morality, I also leave on one side the opinions of philosophers and moralists. I have nothing whatever to do with their systematic attempts to explain or construct moral reality except in so far as one can find in them a more or less adequate expression of the morality of their time. A moralist has a far greater sensibility than the average man to the dominant moral trends of his time, and consequently his consciousness is more representative of the moral reality. But I refuse to accept his doctrines as explanations, as scientific expressions of past or present moral reality.

The subject of my research and the kind of moral reality which I shall study have now been defined. But this reality can be studied in two different ways: (i) We can try to discover and to understand it, or (ii) we can set out to evaluate it at particular times.

Here I do not intend to discuss the second problem. We must begin with the first. Faced with the confusion of present moral ideas, a methodical approach is indispensable. We must begin at the beginning and progress from facts on which common agreement can be reached to see where the divergences occur. In order to judge or appreciate morality, as to evaluate life or nature (for value judgments can apply to the whole realm of reality), one must begin by acquainting oneself with moral reality.

Thus the first condition for the theoretical study of moral reality is to be able to recognize it and to distinguish it from other realities; in brief, to define it. This is not a question of giving it a philosophical definition; that can come when our research has made some headway. All that is possible or profitable is an initial, provisional definition that permits us to agree upon the reality we are dealing with; such a definition is obviously indispensable if we are to know what we are talking about.

The first question that confronts us, as in all rational and scientific research, is: By what characteristics can we recognize and distinguish moral facts?

Morality appears to us to be a collection of maxims, of rules of conduct. But there are also other rules that prescribe our behaviour. All utilitarian techniques are governed by analogous systems of rules, and we must find the distinguishing characteristics of moral rules. If we consider all the rules that govern conduct we shall be able to see whether there are not some that have peculiar and specific characteristics. If we agree that the rules that show these characteristics conform to the popular conception[1] of moral rules we shall be able to apply to them the usual title and to say that here we have the characteristics of moral reality.

To achieve any result at all in this research there is only one method of proceeding. We must discover the intrinsic differences between these moral rules and other rules through their apparent and exterior differences, for at the beginning this is all that is accessible to us. We must find a reagent that will force moral rules to demonstrate their specific character. The reagent we shall employ is this: We shall put these various rules to the test of violation and see whether from this point of view there is not some difference between moral rules and rules of technique.

The violation of a rule generally brings unpleasant consequences to the agent. But we may distinguish two different types of consequence: (i) The first results mechanically from the act of violation. If I violate a rule of hygiene that orders me to stay away from infection, the result of this act will automatically be disease. The act, once it has been performed, sets in motion the consequences, and by analysis of the act we can know in advance what the result will be. (ii) When, however, I violate the rule that forbids me to kill, an analysis of my act will tell me nothing. I shall not find inherent in it the subsequent blame or punishment. There is complete heterogeneity between the act and its consequence. It is impossible to discover *analytically* in the act of murder the slightest notion of blame. The link between act and consequence is here a *synthetic* one.

Such consequences attached to acts by synthetic links I shall call *sanctions*. I do not as yet know the origin or explanation of this link. I merely note its existence and nature, without at the moment going any further.

We can, however, enlarge upon this notion. Since sanctions are not revealed by analysis of the act that they govern, it is apparent that I am not punished *simply because* I did this or that. It is not the intrinsic nature of my action that produces the sanction which follows, but the fact that the act violates the rule that forbids it. In fact, one and the same act, identically performed with the same material consequences, is blamed or not blamed according to whether or not there is a rule forbidding it. The existence of the rule and the relation to it of the act determine the sanction. Thus homicide, condemned in time of peace, is freed from blame in time of war. An act, intrinsically the same, which is blamed today among Europeans, was not blamed in ancient Greece since there it violated no pre-established rule.

We have now reached a deeper conception of sanctions. A sanction is the consequence of an act that does not result from the content of that act, but from the violation by that act of a pre-established rule. It is because there is a pre-established rule, and the breach is a rebellion against this rule, that a sanction is entailed.

Thus there are rules that present this particular characteristic: We refrain from performing the acts they forbid simply because they are forbidden. This is what is meant by the obligatory character of the moral rule. We rediscover by a rigorously empirical analysis the idea of *duty* and obligation almost as Kant understood it.

We have so far only considered negative sanctions (blame, punishment), since in these the characteristic of obligation is most apparent. There are sanctions of another kind. Acts that conform to the moral rule are praised and those who accomplish them are honoured. In this case the public moral consciousness reacts in a different way and the consequence of the act is favourable to the agent, but the mechanism of this social phenomenon is the same. As in the preceding instance the sanction comes, not from the act itself, but from its conformity to a rule that prescribes it. No doubt this type of obligation differs slightly from the former in degree, but we have here two varieties of the same group. There are not two kinds of moral rules, negative and positive commands; both are but two classes within the same category.

We have, then, defined moral obligation, and it is a definition not without interest. It shows how far the latest perfected utilitarian moralities have misconceived the problem of morality. Spencer's morality, for example, betrays a complete ignorance of the nature of obligation. For him punishment is no more than the mechanical consequence of an act (this is most apparent in his *Education* on the subject of school punishment).[2] This erroneous idea that punishment arises automatically from the act itself is widespread. In a recent inquiry into godless morality may be found the letter of a scientist who is interested in philosophy and maintains that the only punishment that a secular moralist can consider is the evil consequence of immoral acts (intemperance ruins the health, etc.).

In this way one evades the moral problem, which is precisely to explain duty, to explain its foundations and in what way it is not a hallucination but a reality.

So far we have followed Kant fairly closely. But if his analysis of moral acts is in part correct, it is nevertheless incomplete and insufficient, since it shows us only one aspect of moral reality.

We cannot perform an act which is not in some way meaningful to us simply because we have been commanded to do so. It is psychologically impossible to pursue an end to which we are indifferent—i.e., that does not appear to us as *good* and does not affect our sensibility. Morality must, then, be not only obligatory but also desirable and desired. This *desirability* is the second characteristic of all moral acts.

This desirability peculiar to moral life participates of the preceding characteristic of obligation, and is not the same as the desirability of the objects that attract our ordinary desires. The nature of our desire for the commanded act is a special one. Our *élan* and aspiration are accompanied by discipline and effort. Even when we carry out a moral act with enthusiasm we feel that we dominate and transcend ourselves, and this cannot occur without a feeling of tension and self-restraint. We feel that we do violence to a part of our being. Thus we must admit a certain element of eudemonism and one could show that desirability and pleasure permeate the obligation. We find charm in the accomplishment of a moral act prescribed by a rule that has no other justification than that it is a rule. We feel a *sui generis* pleasure in performing our duty simply because it is our duty. The notion of good enters into those of duty and obligation just as they in turn enter into the notion of good. Eudemonism and its contrary pervade moral life.

Duty, the Kantian Imperative, is only one abstract aspect of moral reality. In fact, moral reality always presents simultaneously these two aspects which cannot, in fact, be isolated. No act has ever been performed as a result of duty alone; it has always been necessary for it to appear in some respect as good. Inversely there is no act that is purely desirable, since all call for some effort.

Just as the idea of obligation, the first characteristic of moral life, gave us the opportunity to criticize utilitarianism, the second characteristic, that of goodness, shows us the insufficiency of Kant's explanation of moral obligation. Kant's hypothesis, according to which the sentiment of obligation was due to the heterogeneity of reason and sensibility, is not easy to reconcile with the fact that moral ends are in one aspect objects of desire. If to a certain extent sensibility has the same end as reason, it cannot be humbled by submitting to the latter.

Are these, then, the only two characteristics of moral reality? They are not, and I could demonstrate others. The two that I have just noted appear to me to be the most important, constant and universal. I know of no moral rule or morality where they are not found. However, in different instances they combine in varied proportions. There are acts which are accomplished almost exclusively by enthusiasm, acts of moral heroism where the element of obligation is at a minimum and where the idea of goodness predominates. There are others also where the idea of duty finds a minimum of support in the sensibility. The relation between these two elements also varies with time; thus in antiquity it would appear that the notion of duty was on the wane; in the systems of morality, and perhaps in the everyday life of the people, the idea of the Sovereign Good predominated. Generally speaking, I believe it is the same wherever morality is essentially religious. In the same epoch the relation of the two elements may vary in the extreme in different individuals. Different persons feel in different degrees the attraction of one or other of these elements, and it is very rarely indeed that both exert an equal attraction. Each one of us has his moral blind spots. There are those for whom moral acts are above all good and desirable; there are those with a greater feeling for the rule itself who enjoy discipline, loathe anything indeterminate, and wish their lives to follow a rigid program and their conduct to be constantly controlled by inflexible rules.

REFERENCES

1. The scientific notion is not the same as the popular notion, which may be erroneous. Popular opinion may deny the qualification *moral* to rules which show all the signs of being moral precepts. All that is necessary is that the difference be not so great as to render the retention of the more usual term inconvenient. Thus the zoologist may speak of 'fish' even though his conception is not identical with the popular one.
2. *Education, Intellectual, Physical and Moral,* Ch. III, London, 1861, D. F. P.

The Internalization of Social Control II * (*Mead*)

We have discussed at length the social foundations of the self, and hinted that the self does not consist simply in the bare organization of social attitudes. We may now explicitly raise the question as to the nature of the "I" which is aware of the social "me." I do not mean to raise the metaphysical question of how a person can be both "I" and "me," but to ask for the significance of this distinction from the point of view of conduct itself. Where in conduct does the "I" come in as over against the "me"? If one determines what his position is in society and feels himself as having a certain function and privilege, these are all defined with reference to an "I," but the "I" is not a "me" and cannot become a "me." We may have a better self and a worse self, but that again is not the "I" as over against the "me," because they are both selves. We approve of one and disapprove of the other, but when we bring up one or the other they are there for such approval as "me's." The "I" does not get into the limelight; we talk to ourselves, but do not see ourselves. The "I" reacts to the self which arises through the taking of the attitudes of others. Through taking those attitudes we have introduced the "me" and we react to it as an "I."

The simplest way of handling the problem would be in terms of memory. I talk to myself, and I remember what I said and perhaps the emotional content that went with it. The "I" of this moment is present in the "me" of the next moment. There again I cannot turn around quick enough to catch myself. I become a "me" in so far as I remember what I said. The "I" can be given, however, this functional relationship. It is because of the "I" that we say that we are never fully aware of what we are, that we surprise ourselves by our own action. It is as we act that we are aware of ourselves. It is in memory that the "I" is constantly present in experience. We can go back directly a few moments in our experience, and then we are dependent upon memory images for the rest. So that the "I" in memory is there as the spokesman of the self of the second, or minute, or day ago. As given, it is a "me" but it is a "me" which was the "I" at the earlier time. If you ask, then, where directly in your own experience the "I" comes in, the answer is that it comes in as a historical figure. It is what you were a second ago that is the "I" of the "me." It is another "me" that has to take that role. You cannot get the immediate response of the "I" in the process.[1] The "I" is in a certain

* Reprinted from *Mind, Self and Society* by George H. Mead (edited by Charles W. Morris), pp. 173–178, by permission of The University of Chicago Press. Copyright, 1934, by The University of Chicago.

sense that with which we do identify ourselves. The getting of it into experience constitutes one of the problems of most of our conscious experience;
it is not directly given in experience.

The "I" is the response of the organism to the attitudes of the others;[2]
the "me" is the organized set of attitudes of others which one himself assumes. The attitudes of the others constitute the organized "me," and then
one reacts toward that as an "I." I now wish to examine these concepts in
greater detail.

There is neither "I" nor "me" in the conversation of gestures; the whole
act is not yet carried out, but the preparation takes place in this field of
gesture. Now, in so far as the individual arouses in himself the attitudes of
the others, there arises an organized group of responses. And it is due to the
individual's ability to take the attitudes of these others in so far as they can
be organized that he gets self-consciousness. The taking of all of those
organized sets of attitudes gives him his "me"; that is the self he is aware of.
He can throw the ball to some other member because of the demand made
upon him from other members of the team. That is the self that immediately
exists for him in his consciousness. He has their attitudes, knows what they
want and what the consequence of any act of his will be, and he has assumed
responsibility for the situation. Now, it is the presence of those organized
sets of attitudes that constitutes that "me" to which he as an "I" is responding. But what that response will be he does not know and nobody else knows.
Perhaps he will make a brilliant play or an error. The response to that
situation as it appears in his immediate experience is uncertain, and it is that
which constitutes the "I."

The "I" is his action over against that social situation within his own
conduct, and it gets into his experience only after he has carried out the act.
Then he is aware of it. He had to do such a thing and he did it. He fulfills
his duty and he may look with pride at the throw which he made. The "me"
arises to do that duty—that is the way in which it arises in his experience.
He had in him all the attitudes of others, calling for a certain response; that
was the "me" of that situation, and his response is the "I."

I want to call attention particularly to the fact that this response of
the "I" is something that is more or less uncertain. The attitudes of others
which one assumes as affecting his own conduct constitute the "me," and
that is something that is there, but the response to it is as yet not given.
When one sits down to think anything out, he has certain data that are
there. Suppose that it is a social situation which he has to straighten out.
He sees himself from the point of view of one individual or another in the
group. These individuals, related all together, give him a certain self. Well,

what is he going to do? He does now know and nobody else knows. He can get the situation into his experience because he can assume the attitudes of the various individuals involved in it. He knows how they feel about it by the assumption of their attitudes. He says, in effect, "I have done certain things that seem to commit me to a certain course of conduct." Perhaps if he does so act it will place him in a false position with another group. The "I" as a response to this situation, in contrast to the "me" which is involved in the attitudes which he takes, is uncertain. And when the response takes place, then it appears in the field of experience largely as a memory image.

Our specious present as such is very short. We do, however, experience passing events; part of the process of the passage of events is directly there in our experience, including some of the past and some of the future. We see a ball falling as it passes, and as it does pass part of the ball is covered and part is being uncovered. We remember where the ball was a moment ago and we anticipate where it will be beyond what is given in our experience. So of ourselves; we are doing something, but to look back and see what we are doing involves getting memory images. So the "I" really appears experientially as a part of a "me." But on the basis of this experience we distinguish that individual who is doing something from the "me" who puts the problem up to him. The response enters into his experience only when it takes place. If he says he knows what he is going to do, even there he may be mistaken. He starts out to do something and something happens to interfere. The resulting action is always a little different from anything which he could anticipate. This is true even if he is simply carrying out the process of walking. The very taking of his expected steps puts him in a certain situation which has a slightly different aspect from what is expected, which is in a certain sense novel. That movement into the future is the step, so to speak, of the ego, of the "I." It is something that is not given in the "me."

Take the situation of a scientist solving a problem, where he has certain data which call for certain responses. Some of this set of data call for his applying such and such a law, while others call for another law. Data are there with their implications. He knows what such and such coloration means, and when he has these data before him they stand for certain responses on his part; but now they are in conflict with each other. If he makes one response he cannot make another. What he is going to do he does not know, nor does anybody else. The action of the self is in response to these conflicting sets of data in the form of a problem, with conflicting demands upon him as a scientist. He has to look at it in different ways. That action of the "I" is something the nature of which we cannot tell in advance.

The "I," then, in this relation of the "I" and the "me," is something that is, so to speak, responding to a social situation which is within the experience of the individual. It is the answer which the individual makes to the attitude which others take toward him when he assumes an attitude toward them. Now, the attitudes he is taking toward them are present in his own experience, but his response to them will contain a novel element. The "I" gives the sense of freedom, of initiative. The situation is there for us to act in a self-conscious fashion. We are aware of ourselves, and of what the situation is, but exactly how we will act never gets into experience until after the action takes place.

Such is the basis for the fact that the "I" does not appear in the same sense in experience as does the "me." The "me" represents a definite organization of the community there in our own attitudes, and calling for a response, but the response that takes place is something that just happens. There is no certainty in regard to it. There is a moral necessity but no mechanical necessity for the act. When it does take place then we find what has been done. The above account gives us, I think, the relative position of the "I" and "me" in the situation, and the grounds for the separation of the two in behavior. The two are separated in the process but they belong together in the sense of being parts of a whole. They are separated and yet they belong together. The separation of the "I" and the "me" is not fictitious. They are not identical, for, as I have said, the "I" is something that is never entirely calculable. The "me" does call for a certain sort of an "I" in so far as we meet the obligations that are given in conduct itself, but the "I" is always something different from what the situation itself calls for. So there is always that distinction, if you like, between the "I" and the "me." The "I" both calls out the "me" and responds to it. Taken together they constitute a personality as it appears in social experience. The self is essentially a social process going on with these two distinguishable phases. If it did not have these two phases there could not be conscious responsibility, and there would be nothing novel in experience.

REFERENCES

1. The sensitivity of the organism brings parts of itself into the environment. It does not, however, bring the life-process itself into the environment, and the complete imaginative presentation of the organism is unable to present the living of the organism. It can conceivably present the conditions under which living takes place but not the unitary life-process. The physical organism in the environment always remains a thing (MS).
2. [For the "I" viewed as the biologic individual, see Supplementary Essays II, III.]

The Internalization of Social Control III * (*Piaget*)

The analysis of the child's moral judgments has led us perforce to the discussion of the great problem of the relations of social life to the rational consciousness. The conclusion we came to was that the morality prescribed for the individual by society is not homogeneous because society itself is not just one thing. Society is the sum of social relations, and among these relations we can distinguish two extreme types: relations of constraint, whose characteristic is to impose upon the individual from outside a system of rules with obligatory content, and relations of cooperation whose characteristic is to create within people's minds the consciousness of ideal norms at the back of all rules. Arising from the ties of authority and unilateral respect, the relations of constraint therefore characterize most of the features of society as it exists, and in particular the relations of the child to its adult surrounding. Defined by equality and mutual respect, the relations of cooperation, on the contrary, constitute an equilibrial limit rather than a static system. Constraint, the source of duty and heteronomy, cannot, therefore, be reduced to the good and to autonomous rationality, which are the fruits of reciprocity, although the actual evolution of the relations of constraint tends to bring these nearer to cooperation.

In spite of our wish to confine the discussion to the problems connected with child psychology, the reader will not have failed to recognize the affinity of these results with those of the historical or logico-sociological analyses carried out by M. Brunschvicg and M. Lalande. *Le Progrès de la Conscience dans la Philosophie occidentale* is the widest and the most subtle demonstration of the fact that there exists in European thought a law in the evolution of moral judgments which is analogous to the law of which psychology watches the effects throughout the development of the individual. Now to indulge in philosophic enquiry is simply to take increasing cognizance of the currents of thought which enter into and sustain the states of society itself. What the philosopher does is not so much to create something new as to reflect the elaborations of the human mind. It is therefore of the utmost significance that the critical analysis of history which M. Brunschvicg has put to fresh use should have succeeded in bringing to light in the evolution of Western philosophic thought the gradual victory of the norms of reciprocity over those of social conformism.

* Reprinted from *The Moral Judgment of the Child* by Jean Piaget, pp. 401–411, by permission of the publishers, The Free Press, Glencoe, Ill., and Routledge & Kegan Paul Ltd., London. Copyright, 1951, by The Free Press, A Corporation.

As to M. Lalande, what he says on "la dissolution" as also on the social character of logical norms, has shown more than any other work on the subject the duality that lies hidden in the word "social." There are, M. Lalande tells us, two societies: existing or organized society, whose constant feature is the constraint which it exercises upon individual minds, and there is the ideal or assimilative society, which is defined by the progressive identification of people's minds with one another. The reader will recognize here the same distinction as we have been led to observe between the relations of authority and the relations of equality.

Some of M. Lalande's minor contentions would, indeed, stand in the way of our complete agreement with his ideas taken as a whole. It does not seem to us at all certain, for example, that "evolution" in the sense of progressive organization is necessarily bound up with a society based on constraint. The passage from the homogeneous to the heterogeneous which M. Lalande agrees with Spencer in taking as the mark of evolution leads no doubt to social differentiation. But this differentiation is precisely, as the sociologists have pointed out, the condition of a break with the conformity due to constraint, and consequently the condition of personal liberation. Moral equality is not the result of an advance towards homogeneity, assuming that agreement can be reached on the meaning of this word, but of a mobility which is a function of differentiation. The more differentiated the society, the better can its members alter their situation in accordance with their aptitudes, the greater will be the opportunity for intellectual and moral cooperation. We cannot, therefore, take the identification of minds, which, for M. Lalande, is the supreme norm, to be the same thing as cooperation. Without attempting to evaluate this "vector," and limiting ourselves to the mere description of psychological facts, what the morality of the good seems to us to achieve is reciprocity rather than identification. The morality of the autonomous conscience does not tend to subject each personality to rules that have a common content: it simply obliges individuals to "place themselves" in reciprocal relationship with each other without letting the laws of perspective resultant upon this reciprocity destroy their individual points of view.

But what do these minor discrepancies matter since it is thanks to M. Lalande's teaching that we are able to dissociate what the sociologists have so often tended to confuse? And above all, what do the concepts that are used in the interpretation of the facts matter, so long as the method employed is the same? For in the work of M. Lalande we have an example of that rare thing—research on the evolution of norms conducted well within the limits of the psycho-sociological method. Without in any way neglecting the demands of rationality, this great logician has been able to discern in intellectual and moral assimilation processes admitting of analysis in terms of social psychology while implying by their very "direction" the existence of ideal norms immanent in the human spirit.

This concordance of our results with those of historico-critical or logico-sociological analysis brings us to a second point: the parallelism existing between moral and intellectual development. Everyone is aware of the kinship between logical and ethical norms. Logic is the morality of thought just as morality is the logic of action. Nearly all contemporary theories agree in recognizing the existence of this parallelism—from the *a priori* view which regards pure reason as the arbiter both of theoretical reflection and daily practice, to the sociological theories of knowledge and of ethical values. It is therefore in no way surprising that the analysis of child thought should bring to the fore certain particular aspects of this general phenomenon.[1]

One may say, to begin with, that in a certain sense neither logical nor moral norms are innate in the individual mind. We can find, no doubt, even before language, all the elements of rationality and morality. Thus sensori-motor intelligence gives rise to operations of assimilation and construction, in which it is not hard to see the functional equivalent of the logic of classes and of relations. Similarly the child's behaviour towards persons shows signs from the first of those sympathetic tendencies and affective reactions in which one can easily see the raw material of all subsequent moral behaviour. But an intelligent act can only be called logical and a goodhearted impulse moral from the moment that certain norms impress a given structure and rules of equilibrium upon this material. Logic is not co-extensive with intelligence, but consists of the sum-total of rules of control which intelligence makes use of for its own direction. Morality plays a similar part with regard to the affective life. Now there is nothing that allows us to affirm the existence of such norms in the pre-social behaviour occurring before the appearance of language. The control characteristic of sensori-motor intelligence is of external origin: it is things themselves that constrain the organism to select which steps it will take; the initial intellectual activity does actively seek for truth. Similarly, it is persons external to him who canalize the child's elementary feelings, those feelings do not tend to regulate themselves from within.

This does not mean that everything in the *a priori* view is to be rejected. Of course the *a priori* never manifests itself in the form of ready-made innate mechanisms. The *a priori* is the obligatory element, and the necessary connections only impose themselves little by little, as evolution proceeds. It is at the end of knowledge and not in its beginnings that the mind becomes conscious of the laws immanent to it. Yet to speak of directed evolution and asymptotic advance towards a necessary ideal is to recognize the existence of a something which acts from the first in the direction of this evolution. But under what form does this "something" present itself? Under the form of a structure that straightway organizes the contents of consciousness, or under the form of a functional law of equilibrium, unconscious as yet because the mind has not yet achieved this equilibrium, and to be manifested only in and through the multitudinous structures that are to appear later? There seems to us to be no doubt about the answer. There is in the very functioning of sensori-motor operations a search for coherence and organization. Alongside, therefore, of the incoherence that characterizes the successive steps taken by elementary intelligence we must admit the existence of an ideal equilibrium, indefinable as structure but implied in the functioning that is at work. Such is the *a priori*: it is neither a principle from which concrete actions can be deduced nor a structure of which the mind can become conscious as such, but it is a sum-total of functional relations implying the distinction between the existing states of disequilibrium and an ideal equilibrium yet to be realized.

How then will the mind extract norms in the true sense from this functional equilibrium? It will form structures by means of an adequate conscious realization (*prise de conscience*). To ensure that the functional search for organization exhibited by the initial sensori-motor and affective activity give rise to rules of organization properly so called, it is sufficient that the mind should become conscious of this search and of the laws governing it, thus translating into structure what till then had been function and nothing more.

But this coming into consciousness or conscious realization is not a simple operation and is bound up with a whole set of psychological conditions. It is here that psycho-sociological research becomes indispensable to the theory of norms and that the genetic parallelism existing between the formation of the logical and of the moral consciousness can be observed.

In the first place it should be noticed that the individual is not capable of achieving this conscious realization by himself, and consequently does not straight away succeed in establishing norms properly so called. It is in this sense that reason in its double aspect, both logical and moral, is a collective product. This does not mean that society has conjured up rationality out of the void, nor that there does not exist a spirit of humanity that is superior to society because dwelling both within the individual and the social group. It means that social life is necessary if the individual is to become conscious of the functioning of his own mind and thus to transform into norms properly so called the simple functional equilibria immanent in all mental and even all vital activity.

For the individual, left to himself, remains egocentric. By which we mean simply this—just as at first the mind, before it can dissociate what belongs to objective laws from what is bound up with the sum of subjective conditions, confuses itself with the universe, so does the individual begin by understanding and feeling everything through the medium of himself before distinguishing what belongs to things and other people from what is the result of his own particular intellectual and affective perspective. At this stage, therefore, the individual cannot be conscious of his own thought, since consciousness of self implies a perpetual comparison of the self with other people. Thus from the logical point of view egocentrism would seem to involve a sort of alogicality, such that sometimes affectivity gains the ascendant over objectivity, and sometimes the relations arising from personal activity prove stronger than the relations that are independent of the self. And from the moral point of view, egocentrism involves a sort of anomie such that tenderness and disinterestedness can go hand in hand with a naive selfishness, and yet the child not feel spontaneously himself to be better in one case than the other. Just as the ideas which enter his mind appear from the first in the form of beliefs and not of hypotheses requiring verification, so do the feelings that arise in the child's consciousness appear to him from the first as having value and not as having to be submitted to some ulterior evaluation. It is only through contact with the judgments and evaluations of others that this intellectual and affective anomie will gradually yield to the pressure of collective logical and moral laws.

In the second place, the relations of constraint and unilateral respect which are spontaneously established between child and adult contribute to the formation of a first type of logical and moral control. But this control is insufficient of itself to eliminate childish egocentrism. From the intellectual point of view this respect of the child for the adult gives rise to an "annunciatory" conception of truth: the mind stops affirming what it likes to affirm and falls in with the opinion of those around it. This gives birth to a distinction which is equivalent to that of truth and falsehood: some affirmations are recognized as valid while others are not. But it goes without saying that although this distinction marks an important advance as compared to the anomie of egocentric thought, it is none the less irrational in principle. For if we are to speak of truth as rational, it is not sufficient that the contents of one's statements should conform with reality: reason must have taken active steps to obtain these contents and reason must be in a position to control the agreement or disagreement of these statements with reality. Now, in the case under discussion, reason is still very far removed from this autonomy: truth means whatever conforms with the spoken word of the adult. Whether the child has himself discovered the propositions which he asks the adult to sanction with his authority, or whether he merely repeats what the adult has said, in both cases there is intellectual constraint put upon an inferior by a superior, and therefore heteronomy. Thus, far from checking childish egocentrism at its source, such a submission tends on the contrary partly to consolidate the mental habits characteristic of egocentrism. Just as, if left to himself, the child believes every idea that enters his head instead of regarding it as a hypothesis to be verified, so the child who is submissive to the word of his parents believes without question everything he is told, instead of perceiving the element of uncertainty and search in adult thought. The self's good pleasure is simply replaced by the good pleasure of a supreme authority. There is progress here, no doubt, since such a transference accustoms the mind to look for a common truth, but this progress is big with danger if the supreme authority be not in its turn criticized in the name of reason. Now, criticism is born of discussion, and discussion is only possible among equals: cooperation alone will therefore accomplish what intellectual constraint failed to bring about. And indeed we constantly have occasion throughout our schools to notice the combined effects of this constraint and of intellectual egocentrism. What is "verbalism," for example, if not the joint result of oral authority and the syncretism peculiar to the egocentric language of the child? In short, in order to really socialize the child, cooperation is necessary, for it alone will succeed in delivering him from the mystical power of the word of the adult.

An exact counterpart of these findings about intellectual constraint is supplied by the observations on the effect of moral constraint contained in the present book. Just as the child believes in the adult's omniscience so also does he unquestioningly believe in the absolute value of the imperatives he receives. This result of unilateral respect is of great practical value, for it is in this way that there is formed an elementary sense of duty and the first normative control of which the child is capable. But it seemed to us clear that this acquisition was not sufficient to form true morality. For conduct to be characterized as moral there must be something more than an outward agreement between its content and that of the commonly accepted rules: it is also requisite that the mind should tend towards morality as to an autonomous good and should itself be capable of appreciating the value of the rules that are proposed to it. Now in the case under discussion, the good is simply what is in conformity with heteronomous commands. And as in the case of intellectual development, moral constraint has the effect of partly consolidating the habits characteristic of egocentrism. Even when the child's behaviour is not just a calculated attempt to reconcile his individual interest with the letter of the law, one can observe (as we had occasion to do in the game of marbles) a curious mixture of respect for the law and of caprice in its application. The law is still external to the mind, which cannot therefore be transformed by it. Besides, since he regards the adult as the source of the law, the child is only raising up the will of the adult to the rank of the supreme good after having previously accorded this rank to the various dictates of his own desires. An advance, no doubt, but again an advance charged with doubtful consequences if cooperation does not come and establish norms sufficiently independent to subject even the respect due to the adult to this inner ideal. And indeed so long as unilateral respect is alone at work, we see a "moral realism." Resting in part on the externality of rules, such a realism is also kept going by all the other forms of realism peculiar to the egocentric mentality of the child. Only cooperation will correct this attitude, thus showing that in the moral sphere, as in matters of intelligence, it plays a liberating and a constructive role.

Hence a third analogy between moral and intellectual evolution: cooperation alone leads to autonomy. With regard to logic, cooperation is at first a source of criticism; thanks to the mutual control which it introduces, it suppresses both the spontaneous conviction that characterizes egocentrism and the blind faith in adult authority. Thus, discussion gives rise to reflection and objective verification. But through this very fact cooperation becomes the source of constructive values. It leads to the recognition of the principles of formal logic in so far as these normative laws are necessary to common search for truth. It leads, above all, to a conscious realization of the logic of relations, since reciprocity on the intellectual plane necessarily involves elaboration of those laws of perspective which we find in the operations distinctive of systems of relations.

In the same way, with regard to moral realities, cooperation is at first the source of criticism and individualism. For by comparing his own private motives with the rules adopted by each and sundry, the individual is led to judge objectively the acts and commands of other people, including adults. Whence the decline of unilateral respect and the primacy of personal judgment. But in consequence of this, cooperation suppresses both egocentrism and moral realism, and thus achieves an interiorization of rules. A new morality follows upon that of pure duty. Heteronomy steps aside to make way for a consciousness of good, of which the autonomy results from the acceptance of the norms of reciprocity. Obedience withdraws in favour of the idea of justice and of mutual service, now the source of all the obligations which till then had been imposed as incomprehensible commands. In a word, cooperation on the moral plane brings about transformations exactly parallel to those of which we have just been recalling the existence in the intellectual domain.

REFERENCE

1. We have further developed this point at the Ninth International Congress of Psychology which met at New Haven (U.S.A.). See *Ninth International Congress of Psychology, Proceedings and Papers,* p. 339 .

5.

POWER AND AUTHORITY

POWER, that is, broadly speaking, the ability to determine the behavior of others in accord with one's own wishes, is clearly an ubiquitous social phenomenon. There are few social relationships from which the power element is wholly absent. It is therefore all the more remarkable that sociological approaches to the problem of power are of relatively recent origin. Though philosophers and political theorists from the days of Plato and Aristotle have been interested in the social as well as the human consequences of subordination and superordination, sociological contributions marking major departures from earlier perspectives date only from about the turn of the century, more specifically from the writings of Max Weber and Georg Simmel. However, we also owe important insights to Italian sociological theory, especially to the works of Vilfredo Pareto (1848–1923), Roberto Michels (1876–1936) and Gaetano Mosca (1858–1941).

Hence the following pages first present the basic work of Weber and Simmel and then introduce the reader to a sampling of the ways in which their ideas have been utilized and extended by more recent American theorizing.

Many aspects of power relations had already been analyzed by such thinkers as Machiavelli and Hobbes. It has remained for sociologists to point out systematically that the exercise of power, except in marginal cases, involves an element of obedience and that therefore reciprocity is inherent in power relationships. The exercise of social power, though it may rely ultimately upon the ability to apply coercive sanctions in case of noncompliance, involves more than unilateral imposition of will; it also involves acceptance. The excerpts from Georg Simmel's work on subordination and superordination are meant to exemplify this approach and to illustrate Simmel's contention that power relations involve an active reciprocity of orientation.

But if power involves acceptance, such acceptance may be based on a variety of grounds. For example, acceptance of the power of a police official to serve us with a summons and acceptance of the power of a father to discipline children may involve different elements. Hence we must distinguish between different types of voluntary obedience. It is in this respect that the contributions of Max Weber may be considered of crucial relevance. By proposing a classification of types of authority, that is, of ways in which the exercise of power is socially legitimized, he provided us with a method by which different grounds for exacting obedience may be conceptually distinguished and in which they may be related to the normative structure and the role distributions of given societies. His threefold classification of types of authority—"legal" authority, "traditional" authority, and "charismatic" authority—has been criticized in many respects, yet it remains a fundamental point of entry for later theorizing in this area.

H. Goldhamer and E. Shils, contemporary American sociologists working in a broadly Weberian tradition, attempt here to systematize and refine some of the central insights of Max Weber's sociology of power and authority. Chester Barnard, a leading modern analyst of authority and bureaucracy, in his influential analysis of the ways in which authority is exercised, has laid special stress on Simmel's contention that authority must always be looked at in terms of its acceptance by social actors.

The selection from Robert Bierstedt, a perceptive modern analyst of power phenomena, is meant to illustrate the extent to which recent American sociological reflection, while deeply indebted to its European precursors, has succeeded in further clarifying the notion of power. We are now able to distinguish this notion from other concepts, such as leadership and influence, which, though intimately related to it, must yet be considered separately if confusion is to be avoided. In this connection Bierstedt's observation that authority, as distinct from power, is always attached to statuses, not to persons, and is always institutionalized, may be considered especially valuable.

The final selection, from a recent work of H. Gerth and C. W. Mills, is meant to summarize in a few pithy paragraphs much present theory in the area under consideration.

Forms of Domination * (*Simmel*)

DOMINATION, A FORM OF INTERACTION

Nobody, in general, wishes that his influence completely determine the other individual. He rather wants this influence, this determination of the other, to act back upon *him*. Even the abstract will-to-dominate, therefore, is a case of interaction. This will draws its satisfaction from the fact that the acting or suffering of the other, his positive or negative condition, offers itself to the dominator as the product of *his* will. The significance of this solipsistic exercise of domination (so to speak) consists, for the superordinate

* Reprinted from *The Sociology of Georg Simmel,* translated, edited, and with an introduction by Kurt H. Wolff, 1950, pp. 181–186, by permission of the publisher, The Free Press, Glencoe, Ill. Copyright, 1950, by The Free Press, A Corporation.

himself, exclusively in the consciousness of his efficacy. Sociologically speaking, it is only a rudimentary form. By virtue of it alone, sociation occurs as little as it does between a sculptor and his statue, although the statue, too, acts back on the artist through his consciousness of his own creative power. The practical function of this desire for domination, even in this sublimated form, is not so much the exploitation of the other as the mere consciousness of this possibility. For the rest, it does not represent the extreme case of egoistic inconsiderateness. Certainly, the desire for domination is designed to break the *internal* resistance of the subjugated (whereas egoism usually aims only at the victory over his *external* resistance). But still, even the desire for domination has some interest in the other person, who constitutes a value for it. Only when egoism does not even amount to a desire for domination; only when the other is absolutely indifferent and a mere means for purposes which lie beyond him, is the last shadow of any sociating process removed.

The definition of later Roman jurists shows, in a relative way, that the elimination of *all* independent significance of one of the two interacting parties annuls the very notion of society. This definition was to the effect that the *societas leonina* [1] must not be conceived of as a social contract. A comparable statement has been made regarding the lowest-paid workers in modern giant enterprises which preclude all effective competition among rivaling entrepreneurs for the services of these laborers. It has been said that the difference in the strategic positions of workers and employers is so overwhelming that the work contract ceases to be a "contract" in the ordinary sense of the word, because the former are unconditionally at the mercy of the latter. It thus appears that the moral maxim never to use a man as a mere means is actually the formula of every sociation. Where the significance of the one party sinks so low that its effect no longer enters the relationship with the other, there is as little ground for speaking of sociation as there is in the case of the carpenter and his bench.

Within a relationship of subordination, the exclusion of all spontaneity whatever is actually rarer than is suggested by such widely used popular expressions as "coercion," "having no choice," "absolute necessity," etc. Even in the most oppressive and cruel cases of subordination, there is still a considerable measure of personal freedom. We merely do not become aware of it, because its manifestation would entail sacrifices which we usually never think of taking upon ourselves. Actually, the "absolute" coercion which even the most cruel tyrant imposes upon us is always distinctly relative. Its condition is our desire to escape from the threatened punishment or from other consequences of our disobedience. More precise analysis shows that the super-subordination relationship destroys the subordinate's freedom only in the case of direct physical violation. In every other case, this relationship only demands a price for the realization of freedom—a price, to be sure, which we are not willing to pay. It can narrow down more and more the sphere of external conditions under which freedom is clearly realized, but, except for physical force, never to the point of the complete disappearance of freedom. The moral side of this analysis does not concern us here, but only its sociological aspect. This aspect consists in the fact that interaction, that is, action which is mutually determined, action which stems exclusively from personal origins, prevails even where it often is not noted. It exists even in those cases of superordination and subordination—and therefore makes even those cases *societal* forms—where according to popular notions the "coercion" by one party deprives the other of every spontaneity, and thus of every real "effect," or contribution to the process of interaction.

AUTHORITY AND PRESTIGE

Relationships of superordination and subordination play an immense role in social life. It is therefore of the utmost importance for its analysis to clarify the spontaneity and co-efficiency of the subordinate subject and thus to correct their widespread minimization by superficial notions about them. For instance, what is called "authority" presupposes, in a much higher degree than is usually recognized, a freedom on the part of the person subjected to authority. Even where authority seems to "crush" him, it is based not *only* on coercion or compulsion to yield to it.

The peculiar structure of "authority" is significant for social life in the most varied ways; it shows itself in beginnings as well as in exaggerations, in acute as well as in lasting forms. It seems to come about in two different ways. A person of superior significance or strength may acquire, in his more immediate or remote milieu, an overwhelming weight of his opinions, a faith, or a confidence which have the character of objectivity. He thus enjoys a prerogative and an axiomatic trustworthiness in his decisions which excel, at least by a fraction, the value of mere subjective personality, which is always variable, relative, and subject to criticism. By acting "authoritatively," the quantity of his significance is transformed into a new quality; it assumes for his environment the physical state—metaphorically speaking—of objectivity.

But the same result, authority, may be attained in the opposite direction. A super-individual power—state, church, school, family or military organizations—clothes a person with a reputation, a dignity, a power of ultimate decision, which would never flow from his individuality. It is the nature of an authoritative person to make decisions with a certainty and automatic recognition which logically pertain only to impersonal, objective axioms and deductions. In the case under discussion, authority descends upon a person from above, as it were, whereas in the case treated before, it arises from the qualities of the person himself, through a *generatio aequivoca*.[2] But evidently, at this point of transition and change-over [from the personal to the authoritative situation], the more or less voluntary faith of the party subjected to authority comes into play. This transformation of the value of personality into a super-personal value gives the personality something which is beyond its demonstrable and rational share, however slight this addition may be. The believer in authority himself achieves the transformation. He (the subordinate element) participates in a sociological event which requires his spontaneous cooperation. As a matter of fact, the very feeling of the "oppressiveness" of authority suggests that the autonomy of the subordinate party is actually presupposed and never wholly eliminated.

Another nuance of superiority, which is designated as "prestige," must be distinguished from "authority." Prestige lacks the element of super-subjective significance; it lacks the identity of the personality with an objective power or norm. Leadership by means of prestige is determined entirely by the strength of the individual. This individual force always remains conscious of itself. Moreover, whereas the average type of leadership always shows a certain mixture of personal and superadded-objective factors, prestige leadership stems from pure personality, even as authority stems from the objectivity of norms and forces. Superiority through prestige consists in the ability to "push" individuals and masses and to make unconditional followers of them. Authority does not have this ability to the same extent. The higher, cooler, and normative character of authority is more apt to leave room for criticism, even on the part of its followers. In spite of this, however, prestige strikes us as the more voluntary homage to the superior person. Actually, perhaps, the recognition of authority implies a more profound freedom of the subject than does the enchantment that emanates from the prestige of a prince, a priest, a military or spiritual leader. But the matter is different in regard to the *feeling* on the part of those led. In the face of authority, we are often defenseless, whereas the *élan* with which we follow a given prestige always contains a consciousness of spontaneity. Here, precisely because devotion is only to the wholly personal, this devotion seems to flow only from the ground of personality with its inalienable freedom. Certainly, man is mistaken innumerable times regarding the measure of freedom which he must invest in a certain action. One reason for this is the vagueness and uncertainty of the explicit conception by means of which we account for this inner process. But in whatever way we interpret freedom, we can say that some measure of it, even though it may not be the measure we suppose, is present wherever there is the feeling and the conviction of freedom.[3]

LEADER AND LED

The seemingly wholly passive element is in reality even more active in relationships such as obtain between a speaker and his audience or between a teacher and his class. Speaker and teacher appear to be nothing but leaders; nothing but, momentarily, superordinate. Yet whoever finds himself in such or a similar situation feels the determining and controlling re-action on the part of what seems to be a purely receptive and guided mass. This applies not only to situations where the two parties confront one another physically. All leaders are also led; in innumerable cases, the master is the slave of his slaves. Said one of the greatest German party leaders referring to his followers: "I am their leader, therefore I must follow them."

In the grossest fashion, this is shown by the journalist. The journalist gives content and direction to the opinions of a mute multitude. But he is nevertheless forced to listen, combine, and guess what the tendencies of this multitude are, what it desires to hear and to have confirmed, and whither it wants to be led. While apparently it is only the public which is exposed to *his* suggestions, actually he is as much under the sway of the *public's* suggestion. Thus, a highly complex interaction (whose two, mutually spontaneous forces, to be sure, appear under very different forms) is hidden here beneath the semblance of the pure superiority of the one element and a purely passive being-led of the other.

The content and significance of certain personal relations consist in the fact that the exclusive function of one of the two elements is service for the other. But the perfect measure of this devotion of the first element often depends on the condition that the other element surrenders to the first, even though on a different level of the relationship. Thus, Bismarck remarked concerning his relation to William I: "A certain measure of devotion is determined by law; a greater measure, by political conviction; beyond this, a personal feeling of *reciprocity* is required.—My devotion had its principal ground in my loyalty to royalist convictions. But in the special form in which this royalism existed, it is after all possible only under the impact of a certain reciprocity—the reciprocity between master and servant." The most characteristic case of this type is shown, perhaps, by hypnotic suggestion. An outstanding hypnotist pointed out that in every hypnosis the hypnotized has an effect upon the hypnotist; and that, although this effect cannot be easily determined, the result of the hypnosis could not be reached without it. Thus here, too, appearance shows an absolute influence, on the one side, and an absolute being-influenced, on the other; but it conceals an interaction, an exchange of influences, which transforms the pure one-sidedness of superordination and subordination into a *sociological* form.

REFERENCES

1. "Sociation with a lion," that is, a partnership in which all the advantage is on one side.—Tr.
2. "Equivocal birth" or "spontaneous generation."—Tr.
3. Here—and analogously in many other cases—the point is not to define the concept of prestige but only to ascertain the existence of a certain variety of human interactions, quite irrespective of their designation. The presentation, however, often begins appropriately with the concept which linguistic usage makes relatively most suitable for the discovery of the relationship, because it suggests it. This sounds like a merely definitory procedure. Actually, however, the attempt is never to find the content of a concept, but to describe, rather, an actual content, which only occasionally has the chance of being covered, more or less, by an an already existing concept.

Types of Authority * (*Weber*)

All ruling powers, profane and religious, political and apolitical, may be considered as variations of, or approximations to, certain pure types. These types are constructed by searching for the basis of *legitimacy,* which the ruling power claims. Our modern 'associations,' above all the political ones, are of the type of 'legal' authority. That is, the legitimacy of the powerholder to give commands rests upon rules that are rationally established by enactment, by agreement, or by imposition. The legitimation for establishing these rules rests, in turn, upon a rationally enacted or interpreted 'constitution.' Orders are given in the name of the impersonal norm, rather than in the name of a personal authority; and even the giving of a command constitutes obedience toward a norm rather than an arbitrary freedom, favor, or privilege.

The 'official' is the holder of the power to command; he never exercises this power in his own right; he holds it as a trustee of the impersonal and 'compulsory institution.' [1] This institution is made up of the specific patterns of life of a plurality of men, definite or indefinite, yet specified according to rules. Their joint pattern of life is normatively governed by statutory regulations.

The 'area of jurisdiction' is a functionally delimited realm of possible objects for command and thus delimits the sphere of the official's legitimate

* From *From Max Weber: Essays in Sociology,* pp. 294–229, edited by H. H. Gerth and C. W. Mills. Copyright 1946 by Oxford University Press, Inc. Reprinted by permission.

power. A hierarchy of superiors, to which officials may appeal and complain in an order of rank, stands opposite the citizen or member of the association. Today this situation also holds for the hierocratic association that is the church. The pastor or priest has his definitely limited 'jurisdiction,' which is fixed by rules. This also holds for the supreme head of the church. The present concept of [papal] 'infallibility' is a jurisdictional concept. Its inner meaning differs from that which preceded it, even up to the time of Innocent III.

The separation of the 'private sphere' from the 'official sphere' (in the case of infallibility: the *ex cathedra* definition) is carried through in the church in the same way as in political, or other, officialdoms. The legal separation of the official from the means of administration (either in natural or in pecuniary form) is carried through in the sphere of political and hierocratic associations in the same way as is the separation of the worker from the means of production in capitalist economy: it runs fully parallel to them.

No matter how many beginnings may be found in the remote past, in its full development all this is specifically modern. The past has known other bases for authority, bases which, incidentally, extend as survivals into the present. Here we wish merely to outline these bases of authority in a terminological way.

1. In the following discussions the term 'charisma' shall be understood to refer to an *extraordinary* quality of a person, regardless of whether this quality is actual, alleged, or presumed. 'Charismatic authority,' hence, shall refer to a rule over men, whether predominantly external or predominantly internal, to which the governed submit because of their belief in the extraordinary quality of the specific *person*. The magical sorcerer, the prophet, the leader of hunting and booty expeditions, the warrior chieftain, the so-called 'Caesarist' ruler, and, under certain conditions, the personal head of a party are such types of rulers for their disciples, followings, enlisted troops, parties, et cetera. The legitimacy of their rule rests on the belief in and the devotion to the extraordinary, which is valued because it goes beyond the normal human qualities, and which was originally valued as supernatural. The legitimacy of charismatic rule thus rests upon the belief in magical powers, revelations and hero worship. The source of these beliefs is the 'proving' of the charismatic quality through miracles, through victories and other successes, that is, through the welfare of the governed. Such beliefs and the claimed authority resting on them therefore disappear, or threaten to disappear, as soon as proof is lacking and as soon as the charismatically quali-

fied person appears to be devoid of his magical power or forsaken by his god. Charismatic rule is not managed according to general norms, either traditional or rational, but, in principle, according to concrete revelations and inspirations, and in this sense, charismatic authority is 'irrational.' It is 'revolutionary' in the sense of not being bound to the existing order: 'It is written—but I say unto you . . . !'

2. 'Traditionalism' in the following discussions shall refer to the psychic attitude-set for the habitual workaday and to the belief in the everyday routine as an inviolable norm of conduct. Domination that rests upon this basis, that is, upon piety for what actually, allegedly, or presumably has always existed, will be called 'traditionalist authority.'

Patriarchalism is by far the most important type of domination the legitimacy of which rests upon tradition. Patriarchalism means the authority of the father, the husband, the senior of the house, the sib elder over the members of the household and sib; the rule of the master and patron over bondsmen, serfs, freed men; of the lord over the domestic servants and household officials; of the prince over house- and court-officials, nobles of office, clients, vassals; of the patrimonial lord and sovereign prince (*Landesvater*) over the 'subjects.'

It is characteristic of patriarchical and of patrimonial authority, which represents a variety of the former, that the system of inviolable norms is considered sacred; an infraction of them would result in magical or religious evils. Side by side with this system there is a realm of free arbitrariness and favor of the lord, who in principle judges only in terms of 'personal,' not 'functional,' relations. In this sense, traditionalist authority is irrational.

3. Throughout early history, charismatic authority, which rests upon a belief in the sanctity or the value of the extraordinary, and traditionalist (patriarchical) domination, which rests upon a belief in the sanctity of everyday routines, divided the most important authoritative relations between them. The bearers of charisma, the oracles of prophets, or the edicts of charismatic war lords alone could integrate 'new' laws into the circle of what was upheld by tradition. Just as revelation and the sword were the two extraordinary powers, so were they the two typical innovators. In typical fashion, however, both succumbed to routinization as soon as their work was done.

With the death of the prophet or the war lord the question of successorship arises. This question can be solved by *Kürung,* which was originally not an 'election' but a selection in terms of charismatic qualification; or the question can be solved by the sacramental substantiation of charisma, the successor being designated by consecration, as is the case in hierocratic or apostolic succession; or the belief in the charismatic qualification of the charismatic leader's sib can lead to a belief in hereditary charisma, as represented by hereditary kingship and hereditary hierocracy. With these routinizations, *rules* in some form always come to govern. The prince or the hierocrat no longer rules by virtue of purely personal qualities, but by virtue of acquired or inherited qualities, or because he has been legitimized by an act of charismatic election. The process of routinization, and thus traditionalization, has set in.

Perhaps it is even more important that when the organization of authority becomes permanent, the staff supporting the charismatic ruler becomes routinized. The ruler's disciples, apostles, and followers became priests, feudal vassals and, above all, officials. The original charismatic community lived communistically off donations, alms, and the booty of war: they were thus specifically alienated from the economic order. The community was transformed into a stratum of aids to the ruler and depended upon him for maintenance through the usufruct of land, office fees, income in kind, salaries, and hence, through prebends. The staff derived its legitimate power in greatly varying stages of appropriation, infeudation, conferment, and appointment. As a rule, this meant that princely prerogatives became *patrimonial* in nature. Patrimonialism can also develop from pure patriarchalism through the disintegration of the patriarchical master's strict authority. By virtue of conferment, the prebendary or the vassal has as a rule had a personal *right* to the office bestowed upon him. Like the artisan who possessed the economic means of production, the prebendary possessed the means of administration. He had to bear the costs of administration out of his office fees or other income, or he passed on to the lord only part of the taxes gathered from the subjects, retaining the rest. In the extreme case he could bequeath and alienate his office like other possessions. We wish to speak of *status* patrimonialism when the development by appropriation of prerogatory power has reached this stage, without regard to whether it developed from charismatic or patriarchical beginnings.

The development, however, has seldom stopped at this stage. We always meet with a *struggle* between the political or hierocratic lord and the owners or usurpers of prerogatives, which they have appropriated as status groups. The ruler attempts to expropriate the estates, and the estates attempt to expropriate the ruler. The more the ruler succeeds in attaching to himself a staff of officials who depend solely on him and whose interests are linked to his, the more this struggle is decided in favor of the ruler and the more the privilege-holding estates are gradually expropriated. In this connection, the prince acquires administrative means of his own and he keeps them firmly in his own hands. Thus we find political rulers in the Occident, and progressively from Innocent III to Johann XXII, also hierocratic rulers who have finances of their own, as well as secular rulers who have magazines and arsenals of their own for the provisioning of the army and the officials.

The *character* of the stratum of officials upon whose support the ruler has relied in the struggle for the expropriation of status prerogatives has varied greatly in history. In Asia and in the Occident during the early Middle Ages they were typically clerics; during the Oriental Middle Ages they were typically slaves and clients; for the Roman Principate, freed slaves to a limited extent were typical; humanist literati were typical for China; and finally, jurists have been typical for the modern Occident, in ecclesiastical as well as in political associations.

The triumph of princely power and the expropriation of particular prerogatives has everywhere signified at least the possibility, and often the actual introduction, of a rational administration. As we shall see, however, this rationalization has varied greatly in extent and meaning. One must, above all, distinguish between the *substantive* rationalization of administration and of judiciary by a patrimonial prince, and the *formal* rationalization carried out by trained jurists. The former bestows utilitarian and social ethical blessings upon his subjects, in the manner of the master of a large house upon the members of his household. The trained jurists have carried out the rule of general laws applying to all 'citizens of the state.' However fluid the difference has been—for instance, in Babylon or Byzantium, in the Sicily of the Hohenstaufen, or the England of the Stuarts, or the France of the Bourbons—in the final analysis, the difference between substantive and formal rationality has persisted. And, in the main, it has been the work of *jurists* to give birth to the modern Occidental 'state' as well as to the Occidental 'churches.' We shall not discuss at this point the source of their strength, the substantive ideas, and the technical means for this work.

With the triumph of *formalist* juristic rationalism, the legal type of domination appeared in the Occident at the side of the transmitted types of domination. Bureaucratic rule was not and is not the only variety of legal authority, but it is the purest. The modern state and municipal official, the modern Catholic priest and chaplain, the officials and employees of modern banks and of large capitalist enterprises represent, as we have already mentioned, the most important types of this structure of domination.

The following characteristic must be considered decisive for our terminology: in legal authority, submission does not rest upon the belief and devotion to charismatically gifted persons, like prophets and heroes, or upon sacred tradition, or upon piety toward a personal lord and master who is defined by an ordered tradition, or upon piety toward the possible incumbents of office fiefs and office prebends who are legitimized in their own right through privilege and conferment. Rather, submission under legal authority is based upon an *impersonal* bond to the generally defined and functional 'duty of office.' The official duty—like the corresponding right to exercise authority: the 'jurisdictional competency'—is fixed by *rationally established* norms, by enactments, decrees, and regulations, in such a manner that the legitimacy of the authority becomes the legality of the general rule, which is purposely thought out, enacted, and announced with formal correctness.

REFERENCE
1. *Anstalt.*

Power and Status * (*Goldhamer and Shils*)

A person may be said to have *power* to the extent that he influences the behavior [1] of others in accordance with his own intentions. Three major forms of power may be distinguished in terms of the type of influence brought to bear upon the subordinated individual. The power-holder exercises *force* when he influences behavior by a physical manipulation of the subordinated individual (assault, confinement, etc.); *domination* when he influences behavior by making explicit to others what he wants them to do (command, request, etc.); [2] and *manipulation* when he influences the behavior of others without making explicit the behavior which he thereby wants them to perform.[3] Manipulation may be exercised by utilizing symbols or performing acts. Propaganda is a major form of manipulation by symbols. The undermining of confidence in an enterprise by sabotaging its activities may be taken as an example of manipulation by acts.

Most power-holders claim legitimacy for their acts, i.e., they claim the "right to rule" as they do. If the legitimacy of the exercise of power is acknowledged by the subordinated individuals we speak of *legitimate power*; if it is not recognized we call it *coercion* (provided, of course, that the intention of the power-holder is realized). There are three major forms of legitimate power. Legitimate power is regarded as *legal* when the recognition of legitimacy rests on a belief by the subordinated individuals in the legality of the laws, decrees, and directives promulgated by the power-holder; *tradi-*

* Reprinted from "Types of Power and Status" by Herbert Goldhamer and Edward A. Shils, *The American Journal of Sociology,* Vol. XLV, No. 2, September, 1939, pp. 171–182, by permission of The University of Chicago Press.

tional when the recognition of legitimacy rests on a belief in the sanctity of traditions by virtue of which the power-holder exercises his power and in the traditional sanctity of the orders which he issues; and *charismatic* when the recognition of legitimacy rests on a devotion to personal qualities of the power-holder. Usually, of course, these personal qualities are, or appear to the followers to be, extraordinary qualities such as sanctity and heroism.[4]

A person whose general position as a power-holder is recognized as legitimate may exercise force, domination, or manipulation. But, as far as the recognition of the legitimacy of individual acts of power is concerned, it is clear that manipulation cannot be legitimate power, since in the case of manipulation there is no recognition by the subordinated individual that an act of power has been effected. Persons who are subject to force (especially as an initial form of influencing behavior and not as a sanction) frequently do not recognize the legitimacy of such acts of power. Generally, therefore, the recognition of a power-holder as a legitimate exerciser of power rests on the recognition of the legitimacy of his acts of domination. However, this need not mean that he may not also exercise force or manipulation.

Attempted domination may meet with obedience or disobedience. The motivation for obedience and disobedience is *instrumental* to the extent that it is based on an anticipation of losses and gains, and *noninstrumental* to the extent that it is based on ethical or affective imperatives of conduct dictating obedience or disobedience to the command. In the case of obedience these imperatives may derive either (*a*) from a belief that the recognition of power as legitimate, i.e., as legal, traditional, or charismatic, imposes obedience as a norm of conduct or (*b*) from norms of conduct (e.g., the mores) which dictate, not obedience to the power-holder but the performance of the particular acts commanded. In the case of disobedience the imperatives will likewise derive either (*a*) from a belief that the recognition of power as nonlegitimate, i.e., coercive, imposes disobedience as a norm of conduct or (*b*) from norms of conduct which dictate not disobedience to the power-holder but the nonperformance of the particular acts commanded.[5] Although one may recognize the legitimacy of power, yet one may also obey or disobey out of instrumental considerations. This signifies in the case of disobedience that the instrumental considerations outweigh the motivation toward conformity arising from the recognition of legitimacy.

If the attempt of a person to exercise power fails, the power act may be followed either by a substitute power act or by a sanction. A *substitute power act* is intended primarily to attain the original aim of the first act. Substitution may take place both within or between types of power. Thus a command may be substituted for a polite request (both forms of attempted domination), or unsuccessful propaganda may be succeeded by an outright command (manipulation and domination). A *sanction* is a power act initiated primarily as a reprisal for nonconformity with a prior act of power; its intent is punitive and not primarily directed toward achieving the goal of the prior unsuccessful power act. Since persons who are subjected to attempted exercise of force or manipulation do not—unlike persons subjected to commands—either obey or disobey, sanctions may most properly be spoken of as a reprisal for disobedience to a command (domination) rather than as nonconformity to other types of power. However, it may be true that an unsuccessful propagandist or unsuccessful exerciser of force may (irrationally) take actions with punitive intent against persons who fail to succumb to his propaganda or to his attempt to exercise force.

A sanction may be either a deprivation of values already possessed or an obstruction to the attainment of values which would have been realized were it not for the punitive intervention of the power-holder. A sanction may be either a physical loss (beating, confinement, etc.) or a nonphysical loss (fining, confiscation, removal from office, ridicule, etc.).

Disobedience to the command of a power-holder may result not only in consciously intended sanctions but also in unintended penalizations (such as guilt feelings, loss of prestige, etc.), the anticipation of which may motivate the individual to conform. Market operations afford an important case of unintended penalizations. The demands of buyers and sellers upon each other produce a collective compromise expressed in the price level. Intransigent buyers and sellers are not necessarily subject to intended losses, but their intransigence is, in fact, likely to squeeze them out of the market. The conformity of the buyers or sellers to the imperatives of market conditions involves, in this case, conformity not only to the immediate demands of those with whom they have direct relations but through them, indirectly, with all other persons in the market. Unintended consequences may also be derivative penalizations, i.e., they may be unintended results from the infliction of an intended sanction. Thus imprisonment may (even after release) result in the loss of job, prestige, and associations.

Sanctions may be exercised either directly by the power-holder himself or indirectly through others in official or nonofficial positions. Most power-holders of any consequence possess a staff of officials to whom the exercise of sanctions is delegated. Although power-holders may instigate persons without official position (mobs, the public, "the consumer," etc.) to take reprisals against nonconformists, the exercise of sanctions by nonofficials is perhaps most important in the case of unintended and derivative penalizations and in the case of intended sanctions without instigation from official power-holders.

A power relation is *unilateral* if only one party to the relationship exercises power over the other and *bilateral* if both parties exercise power over each other. The power relationships between officers and privates in an army are typically unilateral. A major form of bilateral power relation is the case of bargaining power, to the extent that each party influences the behavior of the other in the intended direction. In bargaining each party attempts to influence the behavior of the other either by depriving him of values already possessed or by obstructing the attainment of values not yet possessed but desired. Bilateral power relations exist not only in the case of domination (as when each party is able to make demands on the other) but also in the case of manipulation. That is, each party may influence the behavior of the other party without making explicit what behavior is desired. Thus parties may mutually influence each other's behavior in a desired direction by propaganda or by acts. The outcome of attempted bilateral domination or manipulation may be complete fulfilment of the intentions of both parties (provided they are not incompatible) or a compromise, i.e., a partial success by both parties or the fulfilment (partially or fully) of the intention of only one party or, finally, modes of behavior completely different from the intention of either party.[6]

The exercise of power is *direct* when the power-holder alters the behavior of others without utilizing an intermediary and *indirect* when a chain of direct power acts is initiated by a power-holder who utilizes one or more subordinate power-holders. The control of an army by a general or of factory workers by a large-scale entrepreneur is largely by means of indirect power. The chain of direct power acts constituting the exercise of indirect power may be composed of different types of direct power acts. Thus the initial act may be a command (domination) to a subordinate power-holder who may alter the behavior of others by propaganda (manipulation) in order to instigate mob violence (force) against certain groups, thus attaining the intention of the initiating power-holder. The personnel utilized in the sequence of direct power acts composing indirect power may be both official and nonofficial.

The amount of power exercised by an individual may be measured either by the ratio of his successful power acts to all of his attempted power acts or by certain criteria specified below. These measures may be used as a basis of comparison between different power-holders. The two "amounts" represent not alternative techniques of measurement but differences in what is measured. Amount in these cases does not mean the same thing. Most investigations of power, in so far as they deal with the amount of power, utilize "amount" in the second sense.

Two principal criteria may be used to measure the amount of power exercised by a power-holder: the number of actions of any given person, in each of any number of selected types of behavior, over which control is realized (or potential)[7]; and the number[8] of persons so controlled. The definition of dictatorship as "a form of government where everything that is not forbidden is obligatory" indicates complete power in terms of the spheres of behavior over which control is exercised.

Concentration of power is not diminished if the power-holder acts through many subordinates, provided he is able to exercise control over them. In fact, however, the utilization of a large subordinate staff is very likely to diffuse power, since the chief power-holder is rarely able to control fully the actions of his subordinates who may therefore exercise a certain amount of independent or initiatory, rather than dependent, power. Further the impossibility of maintaining complete control over the subordinate staff and the reliance which the power-holder must place on them tends to set up a bilateral power relation between the chief power-holder and his subordinates, giving the latter power over the chief power-holder in addition to any independent power they may exercise over the mass. Subordinate power-holders, to the extent that they exercise independent power in the sphere claimed by the chief power-holder, will limit the power of the latter, and to that extent lose their character of subordinates. On the other hand, a plurality of independent power-holders (whether partially or completely independent) may not only limit but also reinforce or not at all affect one another's exercise of power. This will be true only to the extent that the power-holders influence the behavior of others in a manner which does not obstruct the intentions of their co-power-holders. With the growing interdependence of all aspects of social life, however, and consequently the increased probabilities that any act will have more extensive repercussions throughout the society than formerly, it becomes more essential for a power-holder both to control many aspects of behavior that formerly might have seemed quite unnecessary for carrying out his intentions and to prevent others from exercising powers that formerly might not have interfered with his intention. Although one finds in contemporary society, both in public and in private spheres, an increasing concentration of power, the necessity, as enterprises increase in size, of exercising power through the utilization of many subordinate power-holders tends to limit the actual if not the formal concentration of power.

The amount and stability of power exercised will be limited by the means which the power-holder has available for influencing the behavior of others by making them want to do what he wants them to do or by the sanctions which they anticipate that he can bring to bear upon them. Large amounts of power cannot be exercised in a purely coercive fashion, for even though the mass of subordinated individuals do not recognize the power-holder as exercising legitimate power, the necessity of utilizing a large staff would introduce other than purely coercive power into the total power system; for the subordinate power-holders, who exercise dependent power and carry out sanctions for cases of nonconformity among the mass, cannot themselves be controlled by coercion alone. The greater the amount of coercive power exercised, the greater is the dependence of the chief power-holder on his staff. For this reason and because the possible supervision over, and sanctions against, the mass often fall short of the requirements for the exercise of coercive power, the latter frequently has to be augmented and supported by manipulation. This may serve the purpose not only of getting people to act in a desired manner without exercising coercion but also of developing a belief in the legitimacy of the power exercised and thereby also limiting the need for coercive action.

It is sometimes assumed that a person who uses force or is in a position to impose very drastic sanctions in the event of nonconformity with his commands is somehow more powerful than one who exercises power without the use of these means. But, the amount of power exercised by a legitimate power-holder may be as great as, or greater than, the amount exercised by a coercive power-holder. If, however, we restrict comparison only to coercive power-holders, then it is true, all other things being equal, that power varies directly with the severity of the sanctions, that the power-holder can impose.

Men evaluate the objects, acts, and human attributes with which they come into contact. These evaluations may become systematized into a hierarchy of values. The individual makes judgments of others and ranks them on the basis of his hierarchy of values and his knowledge concerning what characteristics these other persons possess. Such a judgment of rank made about either the total person or relatively stable segments of the person constitutes the *social status* of that person (for the individual making the judgment). Societies and individuals use different gestures to express degrees of deference which they accord to varying ranks of social status. These gestures expressing the status of an individual may be called *deference gestures* or more simply, *deference*.

The deference gestures which a person directs toward or about another person are *genuine* when the deferrer holds them appropriate for expressing the status he ascribes to that other individual, and *spurious* when they are not those which he holds as appropriate for expressing the status he ascribes to the other individual.[9] Spurious deference may be the giving of a deference either higher or lower than that which the deferrer considers appropriate for the status in question (or higher or lower than the deferrer customarily gives to a person with the status in question). The first of these two types of spurious deference constitutes a frequent form of manipulation, the spurious deference being intended to induce a desired form of behavior.

Status judgments are *total* when the evaluation is made of the person as a whole and not of any particular role which he performs or any particular attribute which he possesses and *segmental* when the evaluation is made of the person in terms of a particular role which he performs or of a particular attribute which he possesses.

Deference gestures are *specialized* when they are utilized only toward persons performing certain roles (such as saluting in the case of the army); and *nonspecialized* when they are used equally toward persons of the same status irrespective of their roles (as general terms of respect such as "sir"). People often accord generalized deference gestures to persons to whom they accord segmental status because specialized gestures exist only for a very limited number of roles (such as military or ecclesiastical roles). The use of a nonspecialized deference gesture, such as "sir," does not signify, therefore, that the individual using it necessarily does so because he accords high total status. Persons may, however, intentionally use certain nonspecialized deference gestures in order to create a definite impression that a high total status is being accorded when in fact the status actually accorded is only high segmental status. To the extent that this is successfully used to influence behavior it constitutes manipulation.

Deference gestures frequently become highly conventionalized and hence uniform throughout a society or segments of a society. There may, however, be considerable individuation of deference gestures, i.e., a considerable deviation from the conventional forms. Clearly the more individuated such gestures become, the less they will serve to convey to others the deference being accorded by the person making the gestures. Deference gestures vary not only in their degree of individuation but also in the degree to which they discriminate differences in status. Thus in eighteenth-century Germany Fräulein as a mode of address was a highly discriminatory deference gesture, as it was used only in addressing young women of the upper classes.

In some periods societies or special groups within societies have attempted to level status and deference distinctions, even though they have found it impossible to erase differences in those objective characteristics of persons which usually give rise to status and deference distinctions. Such attempts are often found in the early stages of religious sectarian movements (for the members are equal before God and should therefore be equal before one another) and in the early periods of egalitarian revolutions. It would seem that the attempt to level deference distinctions is usually more successful than the attempt to level status distinctions. Thus leveling terms such as *citoyen* are universally applied to all members of the society, and various honorific terms if retained are universally applied and thus lose their discriminatory value. Because of this one finds that in time new deference gestures are evolved to permit expressions of the different degrees of status developed on the basis of the new revolutionary value system.

The status accorded to a person depends on the value hierarchy held by the individual making the status judgment and the individual's knowledge of the characteristics of the person judged. A status judgment that a person makes of another is *true* if based on an accurate knowledge of the characteristics of the person judged, and *false* if based on an incorrect knowledge of the characteristics of the person judged. Thus if a person ranks wealth very high in his hierarchy of values and if he believes another person to be very wealthy, he will rank the latter high in the status scale. If, in fact, the person judged is wealthy, the status accorded him by the person making the judgment is a true status; but if, in fact, the person judged is poor, then the judgment is a false status. To say that a status judgment concerning an individual is "true" does not imply an objectively true status judgment in the sense that any status judgment deviating from it is false. If persons have different value hierarchies and all have approximately the same correct knowledge of the characteristics of the individual being judged, the various different status judgments will all be true status judgments. As long as the value hierarchies of the persons making the judgments differ, the status judgments must differ if they are true.[10]

The status judgments referred to in this article are privately or subjectively made status judgments. A person may make true status judgments but publicly may state that the individual in question has in his opinion a higher or lower status than he privately judges him to have. Such falsifications may be termed spurious status to distinguish them from status judgments based on incorrect knowledge, i.e., false status judgments. Status judgments are often given expression through deference gestures, and falsification of these constitutes, of course, spurious deference.

The present discussion of status might seem to impute to individuals a high degree of awareness of their own value systems and considerable conscious analysis in the process of assigning status to an individual and according him the appropriate deference gestures. Status judgments and deference gestures are, of course, not usually arrived at in such a fashion, although such a process is likely to occur in the case of some types of persons, such as religious and political sectarian leaders who make all evaluations in terms of a few clearly and fervently held principles. Again, it is possible that an individual may apply different value hierarchies in making status judgments of different types of individuals. The possession of a plurality of value hierarchies is perhaps most likely to exhibit itself in making status judgments of the self and of others with the same objective characteristics. To what extent, however, individuals may have more than one independent value hierarchy is difficult to say. Furthermore, for the entire discussion of social values and social status it is of the highest importance to realize that for some individuals and in some periods for a considerable proportion of the population the value hierarchies may be in a condition of great flux resulting in both ambiguity and ambivalence of status judgments. No investigation of status and deference could afford to ignore the complications mentioned above, but the present discussion does not attempt either to analyze the psychological processes by which status judgments and deference gestures are made or to deal with the manifold consequences resulting from ambiguous and ambivalent value systems.

REFERENCES

1. Behavior is here to be understood as both covert and overt behavior. Influence is to be understood as both an alteration of behavior and a maintenance of behavior as it was, but other than what it would have been without the intervention of the power-holder.
2. "Shoulder arms!" and "Please close the door" are both cases of domination, provided, of course, that these utterances succeed in realizing the intention of the speaker. It may be that everyday associations render "Please close the door" as an example of domination somewhat surprising. A polite request, however, is as much a way of getting people to do what one wants them to do as is the most brutally uttered command. Polite requests often enable a person to exercise power over another where a command containing no elements of deference may fail. The relation between the exercise of power over, and the granting of deference to, subordinated individuals is not treated here.
3. Since the distinction between domination and manipulation rests on the degree to which the power-holder makes his intention explicit to the person whose behavior he wants to influence, the two frequently shade off into each other. It often happens, of course, that the context in which the power-holder's behavior takes place is such as to enable him to assume that his intention is quite clear to the person whom he is attempting to influence. It is desirable to include such cases under domination.

   It is clear that manipulation excludes modifications of behavior following the communication of factual representations in discussion. In the case of discussion the intentions of the discussants are evident to each other. This, of course, does not preclude the possibility of manipulatory elements entering into a discussion. As in the cases discussed in the first paragraph, the line between discussion and manipulation may (in certain concrete cases) be difficult to draw.

4. The classification of types of legitimate power is that of Max Weber (cf. *Wirtschaft und Gesellschaft* [Tübingen, 1925], I, 124).

5. Motivation for conformity with, or rejection of, the expressed wish or demand of the power-holder is here considered only in terms of perceptions by the subordinated person of certain selected characteristics of the power-holder and the commanded act. Clearly a number of other factors would be relevant in a complete analysis of why one individual obeys or disobeys another, e.g., the personality of the obeying person. Such factors are not considered here since the above classification is not being used as a basis for a complete causal explanation of obedience or disobedience.

6. The last case is only an *attempted* bilateral power relation since neither party accomplished his intention. The case in which only one party accomplishes his intention is marginal to the definition of bilateral power and may be characterized as being a case of attempted bilateral power with culmination in unilateral power.

7. It would be extremely difficult to determine how much control is possible in a given situation unless the power-holder actually attempts to exercise power. Although for some purposes it would be highly desirable to attempt estimates of the potential amount of power that could be wielded, the amount of power actually exercised would in most cases be the primary interest, and of course would involve the sounder empirical procedure. However, the predictions of the power-holder and those subordinate to him as to how much power the power-holder might wield if so inclined may be an important determinant of the behavior of the power-holder and those subordinated to him.

8. "Number" here may be absolute number or the proportion of controlled persons in the total population. It may also be desirable to represent this as the ratio between those who are controlled to the total number over whom control is attempted.

9. Deference gestures toward a particular person may also be said to be genuine or spurious according to whether they conform (genuine deference) or do not conform (spurious deference) with the deference gestures that the deferrer has used toward others of similar status. This assumes, of course, that the majority of his deference gestures have given true expression to his status judgments.

10. Genuine and spurious deference may of course occur either in the case of a correct or an incorrect knowledge of the objective characteristics of the person to whom the deference is being accorded, i.e., they may occur either in the case of true or of false status judgments. The deference accorded a bogus aristocrat may be genuine but would be based on a false status judgment and hence may, for convenience of reference, be called "mistaken deference." If deference is spurious and based on a false status judgment it may be called "deception deference." Since deception deference involves an error concerning the objective characteristics of the individual to whom the deference is accorded and a falsification of the deference gesture by the deferrer, it is conceivable that the two "errors" may cancel each other and that the person giving deception deference may accord the same deference as a person who has correct knowledge and gives genuine deference. The terms "genuine" and "spurious" deference may be taken as implying true status judgments unless otherwise indicated or qualified by the terms "mistaken" and "deception" deference.

The Acceptance of Authority * (*Barnard*)

We may leave the secondary stages of this analysis for later consideration. What we derive from it is an approximate definition of authority for our purpose: Authority is the character of a communication (order) in a formal

* Reprinted by permission of the publishers from Chester I. Barnard, *The Functions of the Executive*, pp. 163–175, Cambridge, Mass.: Harvard University Press, Copyright, 1938, by The President and Fellows of Harvard College.

organization by virtue of which it is accepted by a contributor to or "member" of the organization as governing the action he contributes; that is, as governing or determining what he does or is not to do so far as the organization is concerned. According to this definition, authority involves two aspects: first, the subjective, the personal, the *accepting* of a communication as authoritative, the aspects which I shall present in this section; and, second, the objective aspect—the character in the communication by virtue of which it is accepted—which I present in the second section, "The System of Coördination."

If a directive communication is accepted by one to whom it is addressed, its authority for him is confirmed or established. It is admitted as the basis of action. Disobedience of such a communication is a denial of its authority for him. Therefore, under this definition the decision as to whether an ordei has authority or not lies with the persons to whom it is addressed, and does not reside in "persons of authority" or those who issue these orders.

This is so contrary to the view widely held by informed persons of many ranks and professions, and so contradictory to legalistic conceptions, and will seem to many so opposed to common experience, that it will be well at the outset to quote two opinions of persons in a position to merit respectful attention. It is not the intention to "argue from authorities"; but before attacking the subject it is desirable at least to recognize that prevalent notions are not universally held. Says Roberto Michels in the monograph "Authority" in the *Encyclopaedia of the Social Sciences,*[1] "Whether authority is of personal or institutional origin it is created and maintained by public opinion, which in its turn is conditioned by sentiment, affection, reverence or fatalism. Even when authority rests on mere physical coercion it is *accepted* [2] by those ruled, although the acceptance may be due to a fear of force."

Again, Major-General James G. Harbord, of long and distinguished military experience, and since his retirement from the Army a notable business executive, says on page 259 of his *The American Army in France*:[3]

A democratic President had forgotten that the greatest of all democracies is an Army. Discipline and morale influence the inarticulate vote that is instantly taken by masses of men when the order comes to move forward—a variant of the crowd psychology that inclines it to follow a leader, but the Army does not move forward until the motion has "carried." "Unanimous consent" only follows cooperation between the *individual* men in the ranks.

These opinion are to the effect that even though physical force is involved, and even under the extreme condition of battle, when the regime is nearly absolute, authority nevertheless rests upon the acceptance or consent of individuals. Evidently such conceptions, if justified, deeply affect an appropriate understanding of organization and especially of the character of the executive functions.

Our definition of authority, like General Harbord's democracy in an army, no doubt will appear to many whose eyes are fixed only on enduring organizations to be a platform of chaos. And so it is—exactly so in the preponderance of attempted organizations. They fail because they can maintain no authority, that is, they cannot secure sufficient contributions of personal efforts to be effective or cannot induce them on terms that are efficient. In the last analysis the authority fails because the individuals in sufficient numbers regard the burden involved in accepting necessary orders as changing the balance of advantage against their interest, and they withdraw or withhold the indispensable contributions.

III

We must not rest our definition, however, on general opinion. The necessity of the assent of the individual to establish authority *for him* is inescapable. A person can and will accept a communication as authoritative only when four conditions simultaneously obtain: (*a*) he can and does understand the communication; (*b*) *at the time of his decision* he believes that it is not inconsistent with the purpose of the organization; (*c*) *at the time of his decision,* he believes it to be compatible with his personal interest as a whole; and (*d*) he is able mentally and physically to comply with it.

(*a*) A communication that cannot be understood *can* have no authority. An order issued, for example, in a language not intelligible to the recipient is no order at all—no one would so regard it. Now, many orders are exceedingly difficult to understand. They are often necessarily stated in general terms, and the persons who issued them could not themselves apply them under many conditions. Until interpreted they have no meaning. The recipient either must disregard them or merely do anything in the hope that that is compliance.

Hence, a considerable part of administrative work consists in the interpretation and reinterpretation of orders in their application to concrete circumstances that were not or could not be taken into account initially.

(*b*) A communication believed by the recipient to be incompatible with the purpose of the organization, as he understands it, could not be accepted. Action would be frustrated by cross purposes. The most common practical example is that involved in conflicts of orders. They are not rare. An intelligent person will deny the authority of that one which contradicts the purpose of the effort as *he* understands it. In extreme cases many individuals would be virtually paralyzed by conflicting orders They would be literally unable to comply—for example, an employee of a water system ordered to blow up an essential pump, or soldiers ordered to shoot their own comrades. I suppose all experienced executives know that when it is necessary to issue orders that will appear to the recipients to be contrary to the main purpose, especially as exemplified in prior habitual practice, it is usually necessary and always advisable, if practicable, to explain or demonstrate why the appearance of conflict is an illusion. Otherwise the orders are likely not to be executed, or to be executed inadequately.

(c) If a communication is believed to involve a burden that destroys the net advantage of connection with the organization, there no longer would remain a net inducement to the individual to contribute to it. The existence of a net inducement is the only reason for accepting *any* order as having authority. Hence, if such an order is received it must be disobeyed (evaded in the more usual cases) as utterly inconsistent with personal motives that are the basis of accepting any orders at all. Cases of voluntary resignation from all sorts of organizations are common for this sole reason. Malingering and intentional lack of dependability are the more usual methods.

(d) If a person is unable to comply with an order, obviously it must be disobeyed, or, better, disregarded. To order a man who cannot swim to swim a river is a sufficient case. Such extreme cases are not frequent; but they occur. The more usual case is to order a man to do things only a little beyond his capacity; but a little impossible is still impossible.

IV

Naturally the reader will ask: How is it possible to secure such important and enduring coöperation as we observe if in principle and in fact the determination of authority lies with the subordinate individual? It is possible because the decisions of individuals occur under the following conditions: (a) orders that are deliberately issued in enduring organizations usually comply with the four conditions mentioned above; (b) there exists a "zone of indifference" in each individual within which orders are acceptable without conscious questioning of their authority; (c) the interests of the persons who contribute to an organization as a group result in the exercise of an influence on the subject, or on the attitude of the individual, that maintains a certain stability of this zone of indifference.

(a) There is no principle of executive conduct better established in good organizations than that orders will not be issued that cannot or will not be obeyed. Executives and most persons of experience who have thought about it know that to do so destroys authority, discipline, and morale.[4] For reasons to be stated shortly, this principle cannot ordinarily be formally admitted, or at least cannot be professed. When it appears necessary to issue orders which are initially or apparently unacceptable, either careful preliminary education, or persuasive efforts, or the prior offering of effective inducements will be made, so that the issue will not be raised, the denial of authority will not occur, and orders will be obeyed. It is generally recognized that those who least understand this fact—newly appointed minor or "first line" executives—are often guilty of "disorganizing" their groups for this reason, as do experienced executives who lose self-control or become unbalanced by a delusion of power or for some other reason. Inexperienced persons take literally the current notions of authority and are then said "not to know how to use authority" or "to abuse authority." Their superiors often profess the same beliefs about authority in the abstract, but their successful practice is easily observed to be inconsistent with their professions.

(*b*) The phrase "zone of indifference" may be explained as follows: If all the orders for actions reasonably practicable be arranged in the order of their acceptability to the person affected, it may be conceived that there are a number which are clearly unacceptable, that is, which certainly will not be obeyed; there is another group somewhat more or less on the neutral line, that is, either barely acceptable or barely unacceptable; and a third group unquestionably acceptable. This last group lies within the "zone of indifference." The person affected will accept orders lying within this zone and is relatively indifferent as to what the order is so far as the question of authority is concerned. Such an order lies within the range that in a general way was anticipated at the time of undertaking the connection with the organization. For example, if a soldier enlists, whether voluntarily or not, in an army in which the men are ordinarily moved about within a certain broad region, it is a matter of indifference whether the order be to go to A or B, C or D, and so on; and goings to A, B, C, D, etc., are in the zone of indifference.

The zone of indifference will be wider or narrower depending upon the degree to which the inducements exceed the burdens and sacrifices which determine the individual's adhesion to the organization. It follows that the range of orders that will be accepted will be very limited among those who are barely induced to contribute to the system.

(*c*) Since the efficiency of organization is affected by the degree to which individuals assent to orders, denying the authority of an organization communication is a threat to the interests of all individuals who derive a net advantage from their connection with the organization, unless the orders are unacceptable to them also. Accordingly, at any given time there is among most of the contributors an active personal interest in the maintenance of the authority of all orders which to them are within the zone of indifference. The maintenance of this interest is largely a function of informal organization. Its expression goes under the names of "public opinion," "organization opinion," "feeling in the ranks," "group attitude," etc. Thus the common sense of the community informally arrived at affects the attitude of individuals, and makes them, as individuals, loath to question authority that is within or near the zone of indifference. The formal statement of this common sense is the fiction that authority comes down from above, from the general to the particular. This fiction merely establishes a presumption among individuals in favor of the acceptability of orders from superiors, enabling them to avoid making issues of such orders without incurring a sense of personal subserviency or a loss of personal or individual status with their fellows.

Thus the contributors are willing to maintain the authority of communications because, where care is taken to see that only acceptable communications in general are issued, most of them fall within the zone of personal indifference; and because communal sense influences the motives of most contributors most of the time. The practical instrument of this sense is the fiction of superior authority, which makes it possible normally to treat a personal question impersonally.

The fiction [5] of superior authority is necessary for two main reasons:

(1) It is the process by which the individual delegates upward, or to the organization, responsibility for what is an organization decision—an action which is depersonalized by the fact of its coördinate character. This means that if an instruction is disregarded, an executive's risk of being wrong must be accepted, a risk that the individual cannot and usually will not take unless in fact his position is at least as good as that of another with respect to correct appraisal of the relevant situation. Most persons are disposed to grant authority because they dislike the personal responsibility which they otherwise accept, especially when they are not in a good position to accept it. The practical difficulties in the operation of organization seldom lie in the excessive desire of individuals to assume responsibility for the organization action of themselves or others, but rather lie in the reluctance to take responsibility for their own actions in organization.

(2) The fiction gives impersonal notice that what is at stake is the good of the organization. If objective authority is flouted for arbitrary or merely temperamental reasons, if, in other words, there is deliberate attempt to twist an organization requirement to personal advantage, rather than properly to safeguard a substantial personal interest, then there is a deliberate attack on the organization itself. To remain outside an organization is

not necessarily to be more than not friendly or not interested. To fail in an obligation intentionally is an act of hostility. This no organization can permit; and it must respond with punitive action if it can, even to the point of incarcerating or executing the culprit. This is rather generally the case where a person has agreed in advance in general what he will do. Leaving an organization in the lurch is not often tolerable.

The correctness of what has been said above will perhaps appear most probable from a consideration of the difference between executive action in emergency and that under "normal" conditions. In times of war the disciplinary atmosphere of an army is intensified—it is rather obvious to all that its success and the safety of its members are dependent upon it. In other organizations, abruptness of command is not only tolerated in times of emergency, but expected, and the lack of it often would actually be demoralizing. It is the sense of the justification which lies in the obvious situation which regulates the exercise of the veto by the final authority which lies at the bottom. This is a commonplace of executive experience, though it is not a commonplace of conversation about it.[6]

II. THE SYSTEM OF COÖRDINATION

Up to this point we have devoted our attention to the subjective aspect of authority. The executive, however, is predominantly occupied not with this subjective aspect, which is fundamental, but with the objective character of a communication which induces acceptance.

I

Authority has been defined in part as a "character of a communication in a formal organization." A "superior" is not in our view an authority nor does he have authority strictly speaking; nor is a communication authoritative except when it is an effort or action of organization. This is what we mean when we say that individuals are able to exercise authority only when they are acting "officially," a principle well established in law, and generally in secular and religious practice. Hence the importance ascribed to time, place, dress, ceremony, and authentication of a communication to establish its official character. These practices confirm the statement that authority relates to a communication "in a formal organization." There often occur occasions of compulsive power of individuals and of hostile groups; but authority is always concerned with something *within* a definitely organized system. Current usage conforms to the definition in this respect. The word "authority" is seldom employed except where formal organization connection is stated or implied (unless, of course, the reference is obviously figurative).

These circumstances arise from the fact that the character of authority in organization communications lies in the *potentiality of assent* of those to whom they are sent. Hence, they are only sent to contributors or "members" of the organization. Since all authoritative communications are official and relate only to organization action, they have no meaning to those whose actions are not included within the coöperative system. This is clearly in accord with the common understanding. The laws of one country have no authority for citizens of another, except under special circumstances. Employers do not issue directions to employees of other organizations. Officials would appear incompetent who issued orders to those outside their jurisdiction.

A communication has the presumption of authority when it originates at sources of organization information—a communications center—better than individual sources. It loses this presumption, however, if not within the scope or field of this center. The presumption is also lost if the communication shows an absence of adjustment to the actual situation which confronts the recipient of it.

Thus men impute authority to communications from superior positions, provided they are reasonably consistent with advantages of scope and perspective that are credited to those positions. This authority is to a considerable extent independent of the personal ability of the incumbent of the position. It is often recognized that though the incumbent may be of limited personal ability his advice may be superior solely by reason of the advantage of position. This is the *authority of position*.

But it is obvious that some men have superior ability. Their knowledge and understanding regardless of position command respect. Men impute authority to what they say in an organization for this reason only. This is the *authority of leadership*. When the authority of leadership is combined with the authority of position, men who have an established connection with an organization generally will grant authority, accepting orders far outside the zone of indifference. The confidence engendered may even make compliance an inducement in itself.

Nevertheless, the determination of authority remains with the individual. Let these "positions" of authority in fact show ineptness, ignorance of conditions, failure to communicate what ought to be said, or let leadership fail (chiefly by its concrete action) to recognize implicitly its dependence upon the essential character of the relationship of the individual to the organization, and the authority if tested disappears.

This objective authority is only maintained if the positions or leaders continue to be adequately informed. In very rare cases persons possessing great knowledge, insight, or skill have this adequate information without occupying executive position. What they say ought to be done or ought not to be done will be accepted. But this is usually personal advice at the risk of the taker. Such persons have influence rather than authority. In most cases genuine leaders who give advice concerning organized efforts are required to accept positions of responsibility; for knowledge of the applicability of their special knowledge or judgment to concrete *organization* action, not to abstract problems, is essential to the worth of what they say as a basis of organization authority. In other words, they have an organization personality, as distinguished from their individual personality,[7] commensurate with the influence of their leadership. The common way to state this is that there cannot be authority without corresponding responsibility. A more exact expression would be that objective authority cannot be imputed to persons in organization positions unless subjectively they are dominated by the organization as respects their decisions.

It may be said, then, that the maintenance of objective authority adequate to support the fiction of superior authority and able to make the zone of indifference an actuality depends upon the operation of the system of communication in the organization. The function of this system is to supply adequate information to the positions of authority and adequate facilities for the issuance of orders. To do so it requires commensurate capacities in those able to be leaders. High positions that are not so supported have weak authority, as do strong men in minor positions.

Thus authority depends upon a coöperative personal attitude of individuals on the one hand; and the system of communication in the organization on the other. Without the latter, the former cannot be maintained. The most devoted adherents of an organization will quit it, if its system results in inadequate, contradictory, inept orders, so that they cannot know who is who, what is what, or have the sense of effective coördination.

This system of communication, or its maintenance, is a primary or essential continuing problem of a formal organization. Every other practical question of effectiveness or efficiency—that is, of the factors of survival—depends upon it. In technical language the system of communication of which we are now speaking is often known as the "lines of authority."

REFERENCES

1. New York: Macmillan.
2. Italics mine.
3. Boston: Little, Brown and Co., 1936.

4. Barring relatively few individual cases, when the attitude of the individual indicates in advance likelihood of disobedience (either before or after connection with the organization), the connection is terminated or refused before the formal question arises.

   It seems advisable to add a caution here against interpreting the exposition in terms of "democracy," whether in governmental, religious, or industrial organizations. The dogmatic assertion that "democracy" or "democratic methods" are (or are not) in accordance with the principles here discussed is not tenable. As will be more evident after the consideration of objective authority, the issues involved are much too complex and subtle to be taken into account in *any* formal scheme. Under many conditions in the political, religious, and industrial fields democratic processes create questions of more or less logical character, in place of the real questions, which are matters of feeling and appropriateness and of informal organization. By oversimplification of issues this may destroy objective authority. No doubt in many situations formal democratic processes may be an important element in the maintenance of authority, i.e., of organization cohesion, but may in other situations be disruptive, and probably never could be, in themselves, sufficient. On the other hand the solidarity of some coöperative systems (General Harbord's army, for example) under many conditions may be unexcelled, though requiring formally autocratic processes.

   Moreover, it should never be forgotten that authority in the aggregate arises from *all* the contributors to a coöperative system, and that the weighting to be attributed to the attitude of individuals varies. It is often forgotten that in industrial (or political) organizations measures which are acceptable at the bottom may be quite unacceptable to the substantial proportion of contributors who are executives, and who will no more perform their essential functions than will others, if the conditions are, to them, impossible. The point to be emphasized is that the maintenance of the contributions necessary to the endurance of an organization requires the authority of *all* essential contributors.

5. The word "fiction" is used because from the standpoint of logical construction it merely explains overt acts. Either as a superior officer or as a subordinate, however, I know nothing that I actually regard as more "real" than "authority."

6. It will be of interest to quote a statement which has appeared since these lines were written, in a pamphlet entitled "Business—Well on the Firing Line" (No. 9 in the series "What Helps Business Helps You," in *Nation's Business*). It reads in part: "Laws don't create Teamplay. It is not called into play by law. For every written rule there are a thousand unwritten rules by which the course of business is guided, which govern the millions of daily transactions of which business consists. These rules are not applied from the top down, by arbitrary authority. They grow out of actual practice—from the bottom up. They are based upon mutual understanding and compromise, the desire to achieve common ends and further the common good. They are observed *voluntarily*, because they have the backing of experience and common sense."

7. See Chapter VII, p. 88.

An Analysis of Social Power * (*Bierstedt*)

Few problems in sociology are more perplexing than the problem of social power. In the entire lexicon of sociological concepts none is more troublesome than the concept of power. We may say about it in general only what St. Augustine said about time, that we all know perfectly well what it is—until someone asks us. Indeed, Robert M. MacIver has recently been induced

* Reprinted from *The American Sociological Review*, XV, 6, pp. 730–738, by permission of the publisher, The American Sociological Society, and the author.

to remark that "There is no reasonably adequate study of the nature of social power."[1] The present paper cannot, of course, pretend to be a "reasonably adequate study." It aims at reasonableness rather than adequacy and attempts to articulate the problem as one of central sociological concern, to clarify the meaning of the concept, and to discover the locus and seek the sources of social power itself.

The power structure of society is not an insignificant problem. In any realistic sense it is both a sociological (*i.e.*, a scientific) and a social (*i.e.*, a moral) problem. It has traditionally been a problem in political philosophy. But, like so many other problems of a political character, it has roots which lie deeper than the *polis* and reach into the community itself. It has ramifications which can be discerned only in a more generalized kind of inquiry than is offered by political theory and which can ultimately be approached only by sociology. Its primitive basis and ultimate locus, as MacIver has emphasized in several of his distinguished books,[2] are to be sought in community and in society, not in government or in the state. It is apparent, furthermore, that not all power is political power and that political power—like economic, financial, industrial, and military power—is only one of several and various kinds of social power. Society itself is shot through with power relations—the power a father exercises over his minor child, a master over his slave, a teacher over his pupils, the victor over the vanquished, the blackmailer over his victim, the warden over his prisoners, the attorney over his own and opposing witnesses, an employer over his employee, a general over his lieutenants, a captain over his crew, a creditor over a debtor, and so on through most of the status relationships of society.[3] Power, in short, is a universal phenomenon in human societies and in all social relationships. It is never wholly absent from social interaction, except perhaps in the primary group where "personal identification" (Hiller) is complete and in those relations of "polite acquaintance" (Simmel) which are "social" in the narrowest sense. All other social relations contain components of power. What, then, is this phenomenon?

Social power has variously been identified with prestige, with influence, with eminence, with competence or ability, with knowledge (Bacon), with dominance, with rights, with force, and with authority. Since the intension of a term varies, if at all, inversely with its extension—*i.e.*, since the more things a term can be applied to the less precise its meaning—it would seem to be desirable to distinguish power from some at least of these other concepts. Let us first distinguish power from prestige.

The closest association between power and prestige has perhaps been made by E. A. Ross in his classic work on social control. "The immediate cause of the location of power," say Ross, "is prestige." And further, "The class that has the most prestige will have the most power." [4] Now prestige may certainly be construed as one of the sources of social power and as one of the most significant of all the factors which separate man from man and group from group. It is a factor which has as one of its consequences the complex stratification of modern societies, to say nothing of the partial stratification of non-literate societies where the chief and the priest and the medicine-man occupy prestigious positions. But prestige should not be identified with power. They are independent variables. Prestige is frequently unaccompanied by power and when the two occur together power is usually the basis and ground of prestige rather than the reverse. Prestige would seem to be a consequence of power rather than a determinant of it or a necessary component of it. In any event, it is not difficult to illustrate the fact that power and prestige are independent variables, that power can occur without prestige, and prestige without power. Albert Einstein, for example, has prestige but no power in any significant sociological sense of the word. A policeman has power, but little prestige. Similarly, on the group level, the Phi Beta Kappa Society has considerable prestige—more outside academic circles than inside, to be sure—but no power. The Communist Party in the United States has a modicum of power, if not the amount so extravagantly attributed to it by certain Senators, but no prestige. The Society of Friends again has prestige but little power.

Similar observations may be made about the relations of knowledge, skill, competence, ability, and eminence to power. They are all components of, sources of, or synonyms of prestige, but they may be quite unaccompanied by power. When power does accompany them the association is incidental rather than necessary. For these reasons it seems desirable to maintain a distinction between prestige and power.

When we turn to the relationship between influence and power we find a still more intimate connection but, for reasons which possess considerable cogency, it seems desirable also to maintain a distinction between influence and power. The most important reason, perhaps, is that influence is persuasive while power is coercive. We submit voluntarily to influence while power requires submission. The mistress of a king may influence the destiny of a nation, but only because her paramour permits himself to be swayed by her designs. In any ultimate reckoning her influence may be more important than his power, but it is inefficacious unless it is transformed into power. The power a teacher exercises over his pupils stems not from his superior knowledge (this is competence rather than power) and not from his opinions (this is influence rather than power), but from his ability to apply the sanction of failure, *i.e.,* to withhold academic credit, to the student who does not fulfill his requirements and meet his standards. The competence may be unappreciated and the influence may be ineffective, but the power may not be gainsaid.

Furthermore, influence and power can occur in relative isolation from each other and so also are relatively independent variables. We should say, for example, that Karl Marx has exerted an incalculable influence upon the twentieth century, but this poverty-stricken exile who spent so many of his hours immured in the British Museum was hardly a man of power. Even the assertion that he was a man of influence is an ellipsis. It is the ideas which are influential, not the man. Stalin, on the other hand, is a man of influence only because he is first a man of power. Influence does not require power, and power may dispense with influence. Influence may convert a friend, but power coerces friend and foe alike. Influence attaches to an idea, a doctrine, or a creed, and has its locus in the ideological sphere. Power attaches to a person, a group, or an association, and has its locus in the sociological sphere. Plato, Aristotle, St. Thomas, Shakespeare, Galileo, Newton, and Kant were men of influence, although all of them were quite devoid of power. Napoleon Bonaparte and Abraham Lincoln were men of both power and influence. Genghis Khan and Adolf Hitler were men of power. Archimedes was a man of influence, but the soldier who slew him at the storming of Syracuse had more power. It is this distinction which gives point to Spengler's otherwise absurd contention that this nameless soldier had a greater impact upon the course of history than the great classical physicist.

When we speak, therefore, of the power of an idea or when we are tempted to say that ideas are weapons or when we assert, with the above-mentioned Bonaparte, that the pen is mightier than the sword, we are using figurative language, speaking truly as it were, but metaphorically and with synecdoche. Ideas are influential, they may alter the process of history, but for the sake of logical and sociological clarity it is preferable to deny to them the attribute of power. Influence in this sense, of course, presents quite as serious and as complex a problem as power, but it is not the problem whose analysis we are here pursuing.

It is relatively easy to distinguish power from dominance. Power is a sociological, dominance a psychological concept. The locus of power is in groups and it expresses itself in inter-group relations; the locus of dominance is in the individual and it expresses itself in inter-personal relations. Power appears in the statuses which people occupy in formal organization; dominance in the roles they play in informal organization. Power is a function of the organization of associations, of the arrangement and juxtaposition of groups, and of the structure of society itself. Dominance, on the other hand, is a function of personality or of temperament; it is a personal trait. Dominant individuals play roles in powerless groups; submissive individuals in powerful ones. Some groups acquire an inordinate power, especially in the political sense, because there are so many submissive individuals who are easily persuaded to join them and who meekly conform to the norms which membership imposes. As an example, one need mention only the growth of the National Socialist Party in Germany. Dominance, therefore, is a problem in social psychology; power a problem in sociology.[5]

It is a little more difficult to distinguish power from "rights" only because the latter term is itself so ambiguous. It appears indeed in two senses which are exactly contradictory—as those privileges and only those which are secured by the state and as those which the state may not invade even to secure. We do not need to pursue the distinctions between various kinds of rights, including "natural rights," which are elaborated in the history of jurisprudence and the sociology of law to recognize that a right always requires some support in the social structure, although not always in the laws, and that rights in general, like privileges, duties, obligations, responsibilities, perquisites, and prerogatives, are attached to statuses both in society itself and in the separate associations of society. One may have a right without the power to exercise it,[6] but in most cases power of some kind supports whatever rights are claimed. Rights are more closely associated with privileges and with authority than they are with power. A "right," like a privilege, is one of the perquisites of power and not power itself.[7]

We have now distinguished power from prestige, from influence, from dominance, and from rights, and have left the two concepts of force and authority. And here we may have a solution to our problem. Power is not force and power is not authority, but it is intimately related to both and may be defined in terms of them. We want therefore to propose three definitions and then to examine their implications: (1) power is latent force; (2) force is manifest power; and (3) authority is institutionalized power. The first two of these propositions may be considered together. They look, of course, like circular definitions and, as a matter of fact, they are. If an independent meaning can be found for one of these concepts, however, the other may be defined in terms of it and the circularity will disappear.[8] We may therefore suggest an independent definition of the concept of force. Force, in any significant sociological sense of the word, means the application of sanctions. Force, again in the sociological sense, means the reduction or limitation or closure or even total elimination of alternatives to the social action of one person or group by another person or group. "Your money or your life" symbolizes a situation of naked force, the reduction of alternatives to two. The execution of a sentence to hang represents the total elimination of alternatives. One army progressively limits the social action of another until only two alternatives remain for the unsuccessful contender—to surrender or die. Dismissal or demotion of personnel in an association similarly, if much less drastically, represents a closure of alternatives. Now all these are situations of force, or manifest power. Power itself is the predisposition or prior capacity which makes the application of force possible. Only groups which have power can threaten to use force and the threat itself is power. Power is the ability to employ force, not its actual employment, the ability to apply sanctions, not their actual application.[9] Power is the ability to introduce force into a social situation; it is the presentation of force. Unlike force, incidentally, power is always successful; when it is not successful it is not, or ceases to be, power. Power symbolizes the force which *may* be applied in any social situation and supports the authority which *is* applied. Power is thus neither force nor authority but, in a sense, their synthesis.

The implications of these propositions will become clearer if we now discuss the locus of power in society. We may discover it in three areas, (1) in formal organization, (2) in informal organization, and (3) in the unorganized community. The first of these presents a fairly simple problem for analysis. It is in the formal organization of associations that social power is transformed into authority. When social action and interaction proceed wholly in conformity to the norms of the formal organization, power is dissolved without residue into authority. The right to use force is then attached to certain statuses within the association, and this right is what we ordinarily mean by authority.[10] It is thus authority in virtue of which persons in an association exercise command or control over other persons in the same association. It is authority which enables a bishop to transfer a priest from his parish, a priest with his "power of the keys" to absolve a sinner, a commanding officer to assign a post of duty to a subordinate officer, a vice-president to dictate a letter to his secretary, the manager of a baseball team to change his pitcher in the middle of an inning, a factory superintendent to demand that a certain job be completed at a specified time, a policeman to arrest a citizen who has violated a law, and so on through endless examples. Power in these cases is attached to statuses, not to persons, and is wholly institutionalized as authority.[11]

In rigidly organized groups this authority is clearly specified and formally articulated by the norms (rules, statutes, laws) of the association. In less rigidly organized groups penumbral areas appear in which authority is less clearly specified and articulated. Sometimes authority clearly vested in an associational status may not be exercised because it conflicts with a moral norm to which both members and non-members of the association adhere in the surrounding community. Sometimes an official may remove a subordinate from office without formal cause and without formal authority because such action, now involving power, finds support in public opinion. Sometimes, on the contrary, he may have the authority to discharge a subordinate, but not the power, because the position of the latter is supported informally and "extra-associationally" by the opinion of the community. An extreme case of this situation is exemplified by the inability of the general manager, Ed Barrow, or even the owner, Colonel Jacob Ruppert, to "fire" Babe Ruth from the New York Yankees or even, when the Babe was at the height of his fame, to trade him.

Sometimes these power relations become quite complicated. In a university organization, for example, it may not be clear whether a dean has the authority to apply the sanction of dismissal to a professor, or, more subtly, whether he has the authority to abstain from offering an increase in salary to a professor in order indirectly to encourage him to leave, or, still more subtly, whether, when he clearly has this authority of abstention, he will be accused of maladministration if he exercises it.[12] It is similarly unclear whether a Bishop of the Episcopal Church has the authority to remove a rector from his parish when the latter apparently has the support of his parishioners.[13] In other words, it sometimes comes to be a matter of unwise policy for an official to exercise the authority which is specifically vested in his position, and it is in these cases that we can clearly see power leaking into the joints of associational structure and invading the formal organization.[14]

It may be observed that the power implied in the exercise of authority does not necessarily convey a connotation of personal superiority. Leo Durocher is not a better pitcher than the player he removes nor, in turn, is he inferior to the umpire who banishes him from the game. A professor may be a "better" scholar and teacher than the dean who dismisses him, a lawyer more learned in the law than the judge who cites him for contempt, a worker a more competent electrician than the foreman who assigns his duties, and so on through thousands of examples. As MacIver has written, "The man who commands may be no wiser, no abler, may be in no sense better than the average of his fellows; sometimes, by any intrinsic standard he is inferior to them. Here is the magic of government." [15] Here indeed is the magic of all social organization.

Social action, as is well known, does not proceed in precise or in absolute conformity to the norms of formal organization. Power spills over the vessels of status which only imperfectly contain it as authority. We arrive, therefore, at a short consideration of informal organization, in which the prestige of statuses gives way to the esteem for persons and in which the social interaction of the members proceeds not only in terms of the explicit norms of the association but also in terms of implicit extra-associational norms whose locus is in the community and which may or may not conflict, at strategic points, with the associational norms. Our previous examples have helped us to anticipate what we have to say about the incidence and practice of power in informal organization. No association is wholly formal, not even the most rigidly organized. Social organization makes possible the orderly social intercourse of people who do not know each other—the crew of a ship and their new captain, the faculty of a university department and a new chairman, the manager of a baseball team and his new recruit, the citizen and the tax collector, the housewife and the plumber, the customer and the clerk. But in any association the members do become acquainted with each other and begin to interact not only "extrinsically" and "categorically," in terms of the statuses they occupy, but also "intrinsically" and "personally," in terms of the roles they play and the personalities they exhibit.[16] Sub-groups arise and begin to exert subtle pressures upon the organization itself, upon the norms which may be breached in the observance thereof, and upon the authority which, however firmly institutionalized, is yet subject to change. These sub-groups may, as cliques and factions, remain within the association or, as sects and splinter groups, break away from it. In any event, no formal organization can remain wholly formal under the exigencies of time and circumstance. Power is seldom completely institutionalized as authority, and then no more than momentarily. If power sustains the structure, opposing power threatens it, and every association is always at the mercy of a majority of its own members. In all associations the power of people acting in concert is so great that the prohibition against "combinations" appears in the statutes of all military organizations and the right of collective petition is denied to all military personnel.

Power appears, then, in associations in two forms, institutionalized authority in the formal organization and uninstitutionalized as power itself in the informal organization. But this does not exhaust the incidence of power with respect to the associations of society. It must be evident that power is required to inaugurate an association in the first place, to guarantee its continuance, and to enforce its norms. Power supports the fundamental order of society and the social organization within it, wherever there is order. Power stands behind every association and sustains its structure. Without power there is no organization and without power there is no order. The intrusion of the time dimension and the exigencies of circumstance require continual re-adjustments of the structure of every association, not excepting the most inelastically organized, and it is power which sustains it through these transitions.[17] If power provides the initial impetus behind the organization of every association, it also supplies the stability which it maintains throughout its history. Authority itself cannot exist without the immediate support of power and the ultimate sanction of force.

As important as power is, however, as a factor in both the formal and informal organization of associations, it is even more important where it reigns, uninstitutionalized, in the interstices between associations and has its locus in the community itself. Here we find the principal social issues of contemporary society—labor vs. capital, Protestant vs. Catholic, CIO vs. AFL, AMA vs. FSA, Hiss vs. Chambers (for this was not a conflict between individuals), Republican vs. Democrat, the regents of the University of California vs. the faculty, Russia vs. the United States, and countless others throughout the entire fabric of society. It is not the task of our present analysis to examine these conflicts in detail but rather to investigate the role of power wherever it appears. And here we have two logical possibilities— power in the relations of like groups and power in the relations of unlike groups. Examples of the former are commercial companies competing for the same market, fraternal organizations of the same kind competing for members, religious associations competing for adherents, newspapers competing for readers, construction companies bidding for the same contracts, political parties competing for votes, and so on through all the competitive situations of society. Examples of the latter are conflicts between organized labor and organized management, between the legislative and executive branches of government, between different sub-divisions of the same bureaucracy (*e.g.*, Army vs. Navy), between university boards of trustees and an association of university professors, and so on through an equally large number of instances. Power thus appears both in competition and in conflict and has no incidence in groups which neither compete nor conflict, *i.e.*, between groups which do not share a similar social matrix and have no social relations, as for example the American Council of Learned Societies and the American Federation of Labor. Power thus arises only in social opposition of some kind.

It is no accident that the noun "power" has been hypostatized from the adjective "potential." It may seem redundant to say so, but power is always potential; that is, when it is used it becomes something else, either force or authority. This is the respect which gives meaning, for example, to the concept of a "fleet in being" in naval strategy. A fleet in being represents power, even though it is never used. When it goes into action, of course, it is no longer power, but force. It is for this reason that the Allies were willing to destroy the battleship *Richelieu,* berthed at Dakar, after the fall of France, at the price of courting the disfavor of the French. Indeed, the young officer attending his introductory lectures on naval strategy, is sometimes surprised to hear what he may consider an excessive and possibly even a perverse emphasis upon the phrase, "Protect the battleships." Why should the battleship, the mightiest engine of destruction afloat, require such care in assuring its protection with sufficient cruiser, destroyer, and air support? The answer is that a battleship is even more effective as a symbol of power than it is as an instrument of force.

If power is one of the imperatives of society it may also be partly a pretense and succeed only because it is inaccurately estimated, or unchallenged. This, of course, is a familiar stratagem in war. But it occurs in the majority of power relationships in society. The threat of a strike may succeed when the strike will not. Blackmail may have consequences more dire than the exposure of the secret. The threat of a minority to withdraw from an association may affect it more than an actual withdrawal. The threat of a boycott may achieve the result desired when the boycott itself would fail. As an example of this last, movie exhibitors sometimes discover that if they ignore a ban imposed upon a picture by a religious censor, the ban not only does not diminish the attendance figures but increases them. In poker parlance—and indeed it is precisely the same phenomenon—a "bluff" is powerful, but the power vanishes when the bluff is called.

We may, in a comparatively brief conclusion, attempt to locate the sources of power. Power would seem to stem from three sources: (1) numbers of people, (2) social organization, and (3) resources. In a previous paper we have discussed in some detail the role of majorities in both unorganized and organized social groups, and in both the formal and informal aspects of the latter, and arrived at the conclusion, among others, that majorities constitute a residual locus of social power. It is neither necessary nor desirable to review this proposition here, beyond reiterating an emphasis upon the power which resides in numbers. Given the same social organization and the same resources, the larger number can always control the smaller and secure its compliance. If majorities, particularly economic and political majorities, have frequently and for long historical periods suffered oppression, it is because they have not been organized or have lacked resources. The power which resides in numbers is clearly seen in elections of all kinds, where the majority is conceded the right to institutionalize its power as authority—a right which is conceded because it can be taken. This power appears in all associations, even the most autocratic. It is the power of a majority, even in the most formally and inflexibly organized associations, which either threaten or sustains the stability of the associational structure.[18]

As important as numbers are as the primary source of social power, they do not in themselves suffice. As suggested above, majorities may suffer oppression for long historical periods, they may, in short, be powerless or possess only the residual power of inertia. We arrive therefore at the second source of social power—social organization. A well organized and disciplined body of marines or of police can control a much larger number of unorganized individuals. An organized minority can control an unorganized majority. But even here majorities possess so much residual power that there are limits beyond which this kind of control cannot be exercised. These limits appear with the recognition that the majority may organize and thus reverse the control. And an organized majority, as suggested in the paper previously referred to, is the most potent social force on earth.

Of two groups, however, equal or nearly equal in numbers and comparable in organization, the one with access to the greater resources will have the superior power. And so resources constitute the third source of social power. Resources may be of many kinds—money, property, prestige, knowledge, competence, deceit, fraud, secrecy, and, of course, all of the things usually included under the term "natural resources." There are also supernatural resources in the case of religious associations which, as agencies of a celestial government, apply supernatural sanctions as instruments of control. In other words, most of the things we have previously differentiated from power itself may now be re-introduced as among the sources of power. It is easily apparent that, in any power conflict, they can tip the balance when the other sources of power are relatively equal and comparable. But they are not themselves power. Unless utilized by people who are in organized association with one another they are quite devoid of sociological significance.

As a matter of fact, no one of these sources in itself constitutes power, nor does any one of them in combination with either of the others. Power appears only in the combination of all three—numbers, organization, and resources.

It may finally be of more than incidental interest to note that there is one, and only one, kind of social situation in which the power of opposing groups is completely balanced. The numbers on each "side" are equal, their social organization is identical, and their resources are as nearly the same as possible. This situation reveals itself in games and contests in which power components are cancelled out and the victory goes to the superior skill.

Whether the game be baseball or bridge there is insistence, inherent in the structure of the game itself, upon an equalization of power and this is the universal characteristic of all sports and the basis of the conception "fair play." [19] It would be foolish, of course, to assert that resources are always equal. The New York Yankees, for example, have financial resources which are not available to the St. Louis Browns and one bridge partnership may have better cards than its opponent. But such inequalities excite disapproval because they deny the nature of sport. The franchise of the Browns may be transferred from St. Louis for this reason, and tournament bridge is duplicate bridge so that all teams will play the same hands. When resources cannot be equalized, the situation ceases to be a game and sentiment supports the "underdog." We thus have here a most familiar but nevertheless peculiar power situation, one in which power is so balanced as to be irrelevant. Sport may be a moral equivalent for war, as William James wanted to believe, but it can never be a sociological equivalent. The two situations are only superficially similar. The difference between a conflict and a contest is that the former is a power phenomenon and the latter is not.

In this paper we have taken a somewhat vague and ambiguous concept, the concept of social power, and have attempted to sharpen the edges of its meaning. Among the proposals offered, the following may serve as a summary: (1) power is a social phenomenon *par excellence,* and not merely a political or economic phenomenon; (2) it is useful to distinguish power from prestige, from influence, from dominance, from rights, from force, and from authority; (3) power is latent force, force is manifest power, and authority is institutionalized power; (4) power, which has its incidence only in social opposition of some kind, appears in different ways in formal organization, in informal organization, and in the unorganized community; and (5) the sources and necessary components of power reside in a combination of numbers (especially majorities), social organization, and resources. All of these are preliminary and even primitive propositions. All of them require additional analysis.

REFERENCES

1. *The Web of Government,* New York: Macmillan, 1947, p. 458. MacIver goes on to say, "The majority of the works on the theme are devoted either to proclaiming the importance of the role of power, like those of Hobbes, Gumplowicz, Ratzenhofer, Steinmetz, Treitschke, and so forth, or to deploring that role, like Bertrand Russell in his *Power." Ibid.* One might make the additional comment that most of the discussions of power place it specifically in a political rather than a sociological context and that in the latter sense the problem has attracted almost no attention.
2. See especially *The Modern State,* London: Oxford University Press, 1926, pp. 221–231, and *The Web of Government, op. cit.,* pp. 82–113, *et passim.*

3. It will be noted that not all of these examples of power exhibit the support of the state. To some of them the state is indifferent, to one it is opposed.
4. *Social Control,* New York: Macmillan, 1916, p. 78.
5. This distinction, among others, illustrates the impropriety of associating too closely the separate disciplines of psychology and sociology. Many psychologists and, unfortunately, some sociologists profess an inability to see that individual and group phenomena are fundamentally different in character and that, for example, "the tensions that cause wars" have little to do with the frustrations of individuals. Just as the personal frustrations of soldiers interfere with the fighting efficiency of a military unit, so the personal frustrations of individuals reduce and sometimes destroy the efficiency of any organized action. Heller has an interesting comment in this connection: "The objective social function of political power may be at marked variance with the subjective intentions of the individual agents who give concrete expression to its organization and activities. The subjective motivations which induce the inhabitant to perform military service or to pay taxes are of minor importance. For political power, no less than every other type of social power, is a cause and effect complex, revolving about the objective social effect and not, at least not exclusively, about the subjective intent and attitude." See his article "Power, Political," *Encyclopaedia of the Social Sciences,* Vol. VI, p. 301. In other words, the subjective factors which motivate an individual to indulge in social action, the ends he seeks and the means he employs, have nothing to do, or at best very little to do, with the objective social consequences of the action. A man may join the army for any number of reasons—to achieve financial security and early retirement, to conform with the law, to escape a delicate domestic situation, to withdraw from an emotional commitment, to see the world, to escape the pressure of mortgage payments, to fight for a cause in which he believes, to wear a uniform, or to do as his friends are doing. None of these factors will affect very much the army which he joins. Similarly, people do not have children because they wish to increase the birth rate, to raise the classification of the municipal post office, or to contribute to the military strength of the state, although the births may objectively have all of these consequences.
6. An example will subsequently be supplied.
7. There is, of course, a further distinction between rights and privileges. Military leave, for example, is a privilege and not a right; it may be requested but it may not be demanded. It may be granted but, on the other hand, it may not.
8. As a matter of purely technical interest, it may be observed that all definitions are ultimately circular. Every system of inference must contain undefined or "primitive" terms in its initial propositions because, if it were necessary to define every term before using it, it would be impossible ever to begin talking or writing or reasoning. An undefined term in one system is not necessarily an indefinable term, however, particularly in another system, and furthermore this kind of circularity is no logical deficiency if the circle, so to speak, *nicht zu klein ist.* This engaging phrase comes from Herbert Feigl, a logician who has examined this problem in a paper on Moritz Schlick, *Erkenntnis* Band 7, 1937–1938, p. 406. Ralph Eaton also discusses this problem in his *General Logic,* p. 298, as do Whitehead and Russell in the Introduction to *Principia Mathematica.*
9. Sanctions, of course, may be positive or negative, require or prohibit the commission of a social act.
10. Authority appears frequently in another sense as when, for example, we say that Charles Goren is an authority on bridge or Emily Post on etiquette. Here it carries the implication of superior knowledge or skill or competence and such persons are appealed to as sources of information or as arbiters. In this sense authority is related to influence but not to power.
11. This is what Max Weber called *legitime Herrschaft,* which Parsons translates as "authority." See *The Theory of Social and Economic Organization,* Parsons editor, New York: Oxford University Press, 1947, p. 152, n. 83.
12. As in a case at the University of Illinois.
13. As in the Melish case in Brooklyn, which is currently a subject for litigation in the courts.

14. That even the most highly and rigidly organized groups are not immune from these invasions of power has been illustrated, in a previous paper, with respect to the Roman Catholic Church, the United States Navy, and the Communist Party. See Robert Bierstedt, "The Sociology of Majorities," *American Sociological Review*, 13 (December, 1948), 700–710.
15. *The Web of Government, op. cit.,* p. 13.
16. The terms in quotation marks are E. T. Hiller's. See his *Social Relations and Structures*, New York: Harper, 1947, Chapters 13, 14, 38.
17. If the power of the members, informally exercised, supports an association through changes in structure, it is the structure itself which supports it through changes in personnel.
18. For an elaboration of this theme see "The Sociology of Majorities," *op. cit.*
19. The game of poker is an exception. Here, unless there are betting limits, resources are not initially equalized among the contestants. In this situation, as in war, deceit is encouraged and becomes a part of the structure of the game. It is for this reason, probably, that poker sometimes carries a connotation of immorality.

Power and Authority: A Summary * (*Gerth and Mills*)

The political order, we have said, consists of those institutions within which men acquire, wield, or influence distributions of power. We ascribe "power" to those who can influence the conduct of others even against their will.

Where everyone is equal there is no politics, for politics involves subordinates and superiors. All institutional conduct, of course, involves distributions of power, but such distributions are the essence of politics. In so far as it has to do with "the state," the political order is the "final authority"; in it is instituted the use of final sanctions, involving physical force, over a given territorial domain. This trait marks off political institutions, such as the state, from other institutional orders.

Since power implies that an actor can carry out his will, power involves obedience. The general problem of politics accordingly is the explanation of varying distributions of power and obedience, and one basic problem of political psychology is why men by their obedience accept others as the powerful. Why do they obey?

A straightforward, although inadequate, answer is given by those who see men in the large as herd animals who must be led by a strong man who stays out in front. The explanation of power and obedience in terms of the strong man may hold in some primitive contexts in which only the strong fighter has a chance to become a military and political chieftain;[1] it may also hold in the "gang," where awe of the strongest holds the others to obedience, and contests over power are decided by fist fights. Beyond such situations,

* From *Character and Social Structure* by Hans Gerth and C. Wright Mills, pp. 193–195, copyright, 1953, by Harcourt, Brace and Company, Inc. Reprinted by permission of the publishers.

however, the problem of power cannot be reduced to a problem of simple physical might.

In Bernard Shaw's *Saint Joan,* the dauphin dryly remarks that he lacked a great deal in almost everything because his ancestors had used it all up. Yet, despite such personal weaknesses, other men looked up to the dauphin and obeyed him. Physical and mental weaklings are often found ruling proud and strong men. We cannot therefore always explain authority and obedience in terms of the characteristics of the power holder. Although Bismarck once said that you can do all sorts of things with bayonets except sit on them, obviously power and obedience involve more than differences in the biological means and the physical implements of violence.[2]

The incongruity of strong men willingly obeying physical weaklings leads us to ask: Why are there stable power relations which are *not* based on the direct and physical force of the stronger? The question has been answered by political scientists and philosophers in terms of a consensus between the subordinates and the powerful. This consensus has been rationally formulated in theories of "contract," "natural law," or "public sentiment."[3] For the social psychologist, such approaches are valuable in that they emphasize the question of voluntary obedience, for from a psychological point of view the crux of the problem of power rests in understanding the origin, constitution, and maintenance of voluntary obedience.

There is an element of truth in Laud's assertation: "There can be no firmness without law; and no laws can be binding if there is no conscience to obey them; penalty alone could never, can never do it."[4] In any given political order, we may expect to find both "conscience" and "coercion," and it is the element of conscience, of voluntary obedience, that engages our attention, even though we keep in mind the fact that regardless of the type and extent of conscience, all states practice coercion.

An adequate understanding of power relations thus involves a knowledge of the grounds on which a power holder claims obedience, and the terms in which the obedient feels an obligation to obey. The problem of the grounds of obedience is not a suprahistorical question; we are concerned rather with reconstructing those central ideas which in given institutional structures in fact operate as grounds for obedience. Often such ideas are directly stated and theoretically elaborated; often they are merely implied, left inarticulate and taken for granted. But, in either case, different reasons for obedience prevail in different political institutions.

In terms of the publicly recognized reasons for obedience—"legitimations" or symbols of justification[5]—the core of the problem of politics consists in understanding "authority." For it is authority that characterizes enduring political orders. The power of one animal over another may occur in terms of brute coercion, accompanied by grunts and growls, but man, as Suzanne Langer has written, can "control [his] inferiors by setting up symbols of [his] power, and the mere idea that words or images convey stands there to hold our fellows in subjection even when we cannot lay our hands on them. . . . Men . . . oppress each other by symbols of might." [6]

Power is simply the probability that men will act as another man wishes. This action may rest upon fear, rational calculation of advantage, lack of energy to do otherwise, loyal devotion, indifference, or a dozen other individual motives. *Authority*, or legitimated power, involves voluntary obedience based on some idea which the obedient holds of the powerful or of his position. "The strongest," wrote Rousseau, "is never strong enough to be always master, unless he transforms his strength into right, and obedience into duty." [7]

Most political analysts have thus come to distinguish between those acts of power which, for various reasons, are considered to be "legitimate," and those which are not. We speak of "naked power" as, for instance, during warfare, after which the successful tries to gain "authority" over the defeated; and we speak of "authority" in cases of legitimate acts of power, and thus, of "public authorities," or "ecclesiastic" or "court authority" and so on. In order to become "duly authorized," power needs to clothe itself with attributes of "justice," "morality," "religion," and other cultural values which define acceptable "ends" as well as the "responsibilities" of those who wield power. Since power is seen as a means, men ask: "Whose power and for what ends?" And most supreme power holders seek to give some sort of answer, to clothe their power in terms of other ends than power for power's sake.

REFERENCES

1. "And when Saul stood among the people, he was higher than any of the people from his shoulders and upward" (I Sam., 10:23).
2. The extent of violence in political orders varies. Thus thirteen out of fourteen nineteenth-century presidents of Bolivia died by violence, but only four out of thirty-three presidents of the United States. Cf. P. A. Sorokin, "Monarchs and Rulers," *Social Forces*, March 1926.
3. See Chapter X: Symbol Spheres, especially Section 1: Symbol Spheres in Six Contexts.
4. Cited by John N. Figgis, *The Divine Right of Kings* (rev. ed.; Cambridge: University Press, 1934), p. 265.
5. See Chapter X: Symbol Spheres.
6. *Fortune*, January 1944, p. 150. See also her *Philosophy in a New Key* (Cambridge: Harvard Univ. Press, 1942), pp. 286–87.
7. J. J. Rousseau, *Social Contract*, rev. tr. by Charles Frankel (New York: Hafner, 1947).

6.

COHESION AND CONFLICT

WHAT MAKES for social order? What accounts for a condition of social cohesion among members of societies or groups? This was one of the earliest questions that sociology attempted to answer. The problem was clearly in the center of Auguste Comte's preoccupations when he formulated the principles of the science which he was the first to call sociology. Comte lived in a society which had been intensely disorganized by the series of social convulsions which began with the French Revolution; hence his quest for a science of order which could help recreate the lost cohesion of French society.

Comte's work now has but little impact on ongoing research (though more careful perusal of the texts might prove rewarding even to present-day researchers), but its impact on the other great pioneer of French sociology, Emile Durkheim, whose work is still of great import today, was considerable. Durkheim began to write after another great disintegrating crisis in French society: defeat in the war with Germany in 1870–71, the Commune, and the birth pangs of the Third Republic. Once again the problem of social cohesion in the face of threatening breakdown was very much the order of the day, and Durkheim's sociology was centrally concerned with this problem. But rather than speculate widely, and often vaguely, as Comte had been wont to do, Durkheim chose to investigate more carefully a series of variables which could be controlled with relative ease. His classic study of suicide is not simply a study of a "social problem" but is an attempt to show how differential suicide rates may be explained in terms of variations in the social cohesion—or solidarity—of different groups. Social solidarity is shown by Durkheim to constitute a key variable in different types of social action. If solidarity is weak, a number of "pathological" consequences—suicide being only one of them—are likely to occur. Inversely, high rates of such "pathological" behavior can be taken as an index of insufficient cohesion in total societies or their sub-groups. It was thus Durkheim's contention that a strong "collective conscience"—or moral integration—among members of a society indicates a degree of societal health, while a weak "collective conscience," a lack of cohesion and integration, indicates that the society suffered from

169

some serious ailment. Social cohesion, Durkheim reasoned, provides psychic support to group members in the various crises of life; it relieves stresses and anxieties and thus cushions the impact of crisis on the individual. Those groups, then, which have little social cohesion cannot adequately protect their members from the impact of such anxieties and tend to have higher suicide rates.

The work of Durkheim has been under attack in various quarters for over half a century. It is easy, for example, to demonstrate the conservative bias in his writings. But his pinpointing of the importance of social cohesion as a sociological variable has been generally recognized as an important center of growth in sociological theorizing.

Our next two selections from the British anthropologists A. R. Radcliffe-Brown (1881–1956) and Bronislaw Malinowski have been placed in this section, though they do in part return to topics which have already been treated in the section on social control. Though these authors dealt with somewhat different phenomena—social sanctions and reciprocal obligations of group members respectively—both were concerned with essentially the same problem that intrigued Durkheim. They attempted to make us see how, and under what conditions, society succeeds in imposing some sort of order upon and cohesion between its members—how, in other words, these members "stick together."

The selections from Karl Marx (1818–1883), George Sorel (1847–1922), and Georg Simmel, as well as the final selections, might seem at first glance to deal with subjects far removed from those treated in the beginning of this section. They discuss social conflict, a phenomenon which might appear to be the very opposite of cohesion. Yet such a common-sense view, certain conservative thinkers to the contrary notwithstanding, is quite mistaken. Indeed, as the excerpts from the work of Karl Marx indicate, social conflict with some brings in its wake social cohesion with others. Social conflict, while seemingly a negative phenomenon which simply "tears down," is seen upon inspection to increase the cohesion of conflicting groups within a society. The modern bourgeoisie, as well as the modern working class, Marx contends, owe their historical existence to the struggle which they conducted against other classes and strata.

To this basic insight George Sorel, the brilliant French social theorist, adds the amplification that a decrease in conflict between classes leads to a decrease of cohesion within those classes, so that a lessening of the violence of class struggle may lead to a weakening of the boundaries between classes and, in the extreme case, to the complete loss of class cohesion and class identity.

Our final three selections from the classic work *Conflict* by Georg Simmel and from recent work by the British anthropologist, Max Gluckman, as well as by one of the authors of this volume, further extend the ideas already partly adumbrated in the Marxian approach, by pointing out that conflict may be a precondition for the orderly functioning of society. These authors see stability as a temporary balance of conflicting forces; they contend that conflict, far from being a sign of disease of the body social, has indeed many positive functions in society, not the least of which may be to bring about increased social solidarity of group members.

Suicide and Social Cohesion * (*Durkheim*)

The aptitude of Jews for suicide is always less than that of Protestants; in a very general way it is also, though to a lesser degree, lower than that of Catholics. Occasionally however, the latter relation is reversed; such cases occur especially in recent times. Up to the middle of the century, Jews killed themselves less frequently than Catholics in all countries but Bavaria; only towards 1870 do they begin to lose their ancient immunity. They still very rarely greatly exceed the rate for Catholics. Besides, it must be remembered that Jews live more exclusively than other confessional groups in cities and are in intellectual occupations. On this account they are more inclined to suicide than the members of other confessions, for reasons other than their religion. If therefore the rate for Judaism is so low, in spite of this aggravating circumstance, it may be assumed that other things being equal, their religion has the fewest suicides of all.

These facts established, what is their explanation?

II

If we consider that the Jews are everywhere in a very small minority and that in most societies where the foregoing observations were made, Catholics are in the minority, we are tempted to find in these facts the cause explaining the relative rarity of voluntary deaths in these two confessions. Obviously, the less numerous confessions, facing the hostility of the surrounding populations, in order to maintain themselves are obliged to exercise severe control over themselves and subject themselves to an especially rigorous discipline. To justify the always precarious tolerance granted them, they have to practice greater morality. Besides these considerations, certain facts seem really to imply that this special factor has some influence. In Prussia, the minority status of Catholics is very pronounced, since they are only a third of the whole population. They kill themselves only one third

* Reprinted from *Suicide: A Study in Sociology* by Emile Durkheim, translated by George Simpson, pp. 156–161, 169–170, and 208–212, by permission of the publishers, The Free Press, Glencoe, Ill., and Routledge & Kegan Paul Ltd., London. Copyright, 1951, by The Free Press, A Corporation.

as often as the Protestants. The difference decreases in Bavaria where two thirds of the inhabitants are Catholics; the voluntary deaths of the latter are here only in the proportion of 100 to 275 of those of Protestants or else of 100 to 238, according to the period. Finally, in the almost entirely Catholic Empire of Austria, only 155 Protestant to 100 Catholic suicides are found. It would seem then that where Protestantism becomes a minority its tendency to suicide decreases.

But first, suicide is too little an object of public condemnation for the slight measure of blame attaching to it to have such influence, even on minorities obliged by their situation to pay special heed to public opinion. As it is an act without offense to others, it involves no great reproach to the groups more inclined to it than others, and is not apt to increase greatly their relative ostracism as would certainly be the case with a greater frequency of crime and misdemeanor. Besides, when religious intolerance is very pronounced, it often produces an opposite effect. Instead of exciting the dissenters to respect opinion more, it accustoms them to disregard it. When one feels himself an object of inescapable hostility, one abandons the idea of conciliating it and is the more resolute in his most unpopular observances. This has frequently happened to the Jews and thus their exceptional immunity probably has another cause.

Anyway, this explanation would not account for the respective situation of Protestants and Catholics. For though the protective influence of Catholicism is less in Austria and Bavaria, where it is in the majority, it is still considerable. Catholicism does not therefore owe this solely to its minority status. More generally, whatever the proportional share of these two confessions in the total population, wherever their comparison has been possible from the point of view of suicide, Protestants are found to kill themselves much more often than Catholics. There are even countries like the Upper Palatinate and Upper Bavaria, where the population is almost wholly Catholic (92 and 96 per cent) and where there are nevertheless 300 and 423 Protestant suicides to 100 Catholic suicides. The proportion even rises to 528 per cent in Lower Bavaria where the reformed religion has not quite one follower to 100 inhabitants. Therefore, even if the prudence incumbent on minorities were a partial cause of the great difference between the two religions, the greatest share is certainly due to other causes.

We shall find these other causes in the nature of these two religious systems. Yet they both prohibit suicide with equal emphasis; not only do they penalize it morally with great severity, but both teach that a new life begins beyond the tomb where men are punished for their evil actions, and

Protestantism just as well as Catholicism numbers suicide among them. Finally, in both cults these prohibitions are of divine origin; they are represented not as the logical conclusion of correct reason, but God Himself is their authority. Therefore, if Protestantism is less unfavorable to the development of suicide, it is not because of a different attitude from that of Catholicism. Thus, if both religions have the same precepts with respect to this particular matter, their dissimilar influence on suicide must proceed from one of the more general characteristics differentiating them.

The only essential difference between Catholicism and Protestantism is that the second permits free inquiry to a far greater degree than the first. Of course, Catholicism by the very fact that it is an idealistic religion concedes a far greater place to thought and reflection than Greco-Latin polytheism or Hebrew monotheism. It is not restricted to mechanical ceremonies but seeks the control of the conscience. So it appeals to conscience, and even when demanding blind submission of reason, does so by employing the language of reason. None the less, the Catholic accepts his faith ready made, without scrutiny. He may not even submit it to historical examination since the original texts that serve as its basis are proscribed. A whole hierarchical system of authority is devised, with marvelous ingenuity, to render tradition invariable. All *variation* is abhorrent to Catholic thought. The Protestant is far more the author of his faith. The Bible is put in his hands and no interpretation is imposed upon him. The very structure of the reformed cult stresses this state of religious individualism. Nowhere but in England is the Protestant clergy a hierarchy; like the worshippers, the priest has no other source but himself and his conscience. He is a more instructed guide than the run of worshippers but with no special authority for fixing dogma. But what best proves that this freedom of inquiry proclaimed by the founders of the Reformation has not remained a Platonic affirmation is the increasing multiplicity of all sorts of sects so strikingly in contrast with the indivisible unity of the Catholic Church.

We thus reach our first conclusion, that the proclivity of Protestantism for suicide must relate to the spirit of free inquiry that animates this religion. Let us understand this relationship correctly. Free inquiry itself is only the effect of another cause. When it appears, when men, after having long received their ready made faith from tradition, claim the right to shape it for themselves, this is not because of the intrinsic desirability of free inquiry, for the latter involves as much sorrow as happiness. But it is because men henceforth need this liberty. This very need can have only one cause: the overthrow of traditional beliefs. If they still asserted themselves with equal energy, it would never occur to men to criticize them. If they still had the same authority, men would not demand the right to verify the source of this authority. Reflection develops only if its development becomes imperative, that is, if certain ideas and instinctive sentiments which have hitherto adequately guided conduct are found to have lost their efficacy. Then reflection intervenes to fill the gap that has appeared, but which it has not created. Just as reflection disappears to the extent that thought and action take the form of automatic habits, it awakes only when accepted habits become disorganized. It asserts its rights against public opinion only when the latter loses strength, that is, when it is no longer prevalent to the same extent. If these assertions occur not merely occasionally and as passing crises, but become chronic; if individual consciences keep reaffirming their autonomy, it is because they are constantly subject to conflicting impulses, because a new opinion has not been formed to replace the one no longer existing. If a new system of beliefs were constituted which seemed as indisputable to everyone as the old, no one would think of discussing it any longer. Its discussion would no longer even be permitted; for ideas shared by an entire society draw from this consensus an authority that makes them sacrosanct and raises them above dispute. For them to have become more tolerant, they must first already have become the object of less general and complete assent and been weakened by preliminary controversy.

Thus, if it is correct to say that free inquiry once proclaimed, multiplies schisms, it must be added that it presupposes them and derives from them, for it is claimed and instituted as a principle only in order to permit latent or half-declared schisms to develop more freely. So if Protestantism concedes a greater freedom to individual thought than Catholicism, it is because it has fewer common beliefs and practices. Now, a religious society cannot exist without a collective *credo* and the more extensive the *credo* the more unified and strong is the society. For it does not unite men by an exchange and reciprocity of services, a temporal bond of union which permits and even presupposes differences, but which a religious society cannot form. It socializes men only by attaching them completely to an identical body of doctrine and socializes them in proportion as this body of doctrine is extensive and firm. The more numerous the manners of action and thought of a religious character are, which are accordingly removed from free inquiry, the more the idea of God presents itself in all details of existence, and makes individual wills converge to one identical goal. Inversely, the greater concessions a confessional group makes to individual judgment, the less it dominates lives, the less its cohesion and vitality. We thus reach the

conclusion that the superiority of Protestantism with respect to suicide results from its being a less strongly integrated church than the Catholic
Church.

This also explains the situation of Judaism. Indeed, the reproach to
which the Jews have for so long been exposed by Christianity has created
feelings of unusual solidarity among them. Their need of resisting a general
hostility, the very impossibility of free communication with the rest of the
population, has forced them to strict union among themselves. Consequently, each community became a small, compact and coherent society
with a strong feeling of self-consciousness and unity. Everyone thought and
lived alike; individual divergences were made almost impossible by the
community of existence and the close and constant surveillance of all over
each. The Jewish church has thus been more strongly united than any other,
from its dependence on itself because of being the object of intolerance.
By analogy with what has just been observed apropos of Protestantism, the
same cause must therefore be assumed for the slight tendency of the Jews
to suicide in spite of all sorts of circumstances which might on the contrary
incline them to it. Doubtless they owe this immunity in a sense to the hostility surrounding them. But if this is its influence, it is not because it imposes a higher morality but because it obliges them to live in greater union.
They are immune to this degree because their religious society is of such
solidarity. Besides, the ostracism to which they are subject is only one of
the causes producing this result; the very nature of Jewish beliefs must
contribute largely to it. Judaism, in fact, like all early religions, consists
basically of a body of practices minutely governing all the details of life
and leaving little free room to individual judgment.

III

Several facts confirm this explanation.

First, of all great Protestant countries, England is the one where suicide
is least developed. In fact, only about 80 suicides per million inhabitants are
found there, whereas the reformed societies of Germany have from 140 to
400; and yet the general activity of ideas and business seems no less great
there than elsewhere. Now, it happens at the same time that the Anglican
church is far more powerfully integrated than other Protestant churches.
To be sure, England has been customarily regarded as the classic land of
individual freedom; but actually many facts indicate that the number of
common, obligatory beliefs and practices, which are thus withdrawn from
free inquiry by individuals, is greater than in Germany. First, the law still

sanctions many religious requirements: such as the law of the observance of Sunday, that forbidding stage representations of any character from Holy Scripture; the one until recently requiring some profession of faith from every member of political representative bodies, etc. Next, respect for tradition is known to be general and powerful in England: it must extend to matters of religion as well as others. But a highly developed traditionalism always more or less restricts activity of the individual. Finally, the Anglican clergy is the only Protestant clergy organized in a hierarchy. This external organization clearly shows an inner unity incompatible with a pronounced religious individualism.

Besides, England has the largest number of clergymen of any Protestant country. In 1876 there averaged 908 church-goers for every minister, compared with 932 in Hungary, 1,100 in Holland, 1,300 in Denmark, 1,440 in Switzerland and 1,600 in Germany. The number of priests is not an insignificant detail nor a superficial characteristic but one related to the intrinsic nature of religion. The proof of this is that the Catholic clergy is everywhere much more numerous than the Protestant. In Italy there is a priest for every 267 Catholics, in Spain for 419, in Portugal for 536, in Switzerland for 540, in France for 823, in Belgium for 1,050. This is because the priest is the natural organ of faith and tradition and because here as elsewhere the organ inevitably develops in exact proportion to its function. The more intense religious life, the more men are needed to direct it. The greater the number of dogmas and precepts the interpretation of which is not left to individual consciences, the more authorities are required to tell their meaning; moreover, the more numerous these authorities, the more closely they surround and the better they restrain the individual. Thus, far from weakening our theory, the case of England verifies it. If Protestantism there does not produce the same results as on the continent, it is because religious society there is much more strongly constituted and to this extent resembles the Catholic Church.

.   .   .

Secondly, we see why, generally speaking, religion has a prophylactic effect upon suicide. It is not, as has sometimes been said, because it condemns it more unhesitatingly than secular morality, nor because the idea of God gives its precepts exceptional authority which subdues the will, nor because the prospect of a future life and the terrible punishments there awaiting the guilty give its proscriptions a greater sanction than that of human laws. The Protestant believes in God and the immortality of the soul no less than the Catholic. More than this, the religion with least inclination to suicide, Judaism, is the very one not formally proscribing it and also the one in which the idea of immortality plays the least role. Indeed, the Bible contains no law forbidding man to kill himself and, on the other hand, its beliefs in a future life are most vague. Doubtless, in both matters, rabbinical teaching has gradually supplied the omissions of the sacred book; but they have not its authority. The beneficent influence of religion is therefore not due to the special nature of religious conceptions. If religion protects man against the desire for self-destruction, it is not that it preaches the respect for his own person to him with arguments *sui generis;* but because it is a society. What constitutes this society is the existence of a certain number of beliefs and practices common to all the faithful, traditional and thus obligatory. The more numerous and strong these collective states of mind are, the stronger the integration of the religious community, and also the greater its preservative value. The details of dogmas and rites are secondary. The essential thing is that they be capable of supporting a sufficiently intense collective life. And because the Protestant church has less consistency than the others it has less moderating effect upon suicide.

. . .

We have thus successively set up the three following propositions:

Suicide varies inversely with the degree of integration of religious society.
Suicide varies inversely with the degree of integration of domestic society.
Suicide varies inversely with the degree of integration of political society.

This grouping shows that whereas these different societies have a moderating influence upon suicide, this is due not to special characteristics of each but to a characteristic common to all. Religion does not owe its efficacy to the special nature of religious sentiments, since domestic and political societies both produce the same effects when strongly integrated. This, moreover, we have already proved when studying directly the manner of action of different religions upon suicide. Inversely, it is not the specific nature of the domestic or political tie which can explain the immunity they confer, since religious society has the same advantage. The cause can only be found in a single quality possessed by all these social groups, though perhaps to varying degrees. The only quality satisfying this condition is that they are all strongly integrated social groups. So we reach the general conclusion: suicide varies inversely with the degree of integration of the social groups of which the individual forms a part.

But society cannot disintegrate without the individual simultaneously detaching himself from social life, without his own goals becoming preponderant over those of the community, in a word without his personality tending to surmount the collective personality. The more weakened the groups to which he belongs, the less he depends on them, the more he consequently depends only on himself and recognizes no other rules of conduct than what are founded on his private interests. If we agree to call this state egoism, in which the individual ego asserts itself to excess in the face of the social ego and at its expense, we may call egoistic the special type of suicide springing from excessive individualism.

But how can suicide have such an origin?

First of all, it can be said that, as collective force is one of the obstacles best calculated to restrain suicide, its weakening involves a development of suicide. When society is strongly integrated, it holds individuals under its control, considers them at its service and thus forbids them to dispose wilfully of themselves. Accordingly it opposes their evading their duties to it through death. But how could society impose its supremacy upon them when they refuse to accept this subordination as legitimate? It no longer then possesses the requisite authority to retain them in their duty if they wish to desert; and conscious of its own weakness, it even recognizes their right to do freely what it can no longer prevent. So far as they are the admitted masters of their destinies, it is their privilege to end their lives. They, on their part, have no reason to endure life's sufferings patiently. For they cling to life more resolutely when belonging to a group they love, so as not to betray interests they put before their own. The bond that unites them with the common cause attaches them to life and the lofty goal they envisage prevents their feeling personal troubles so deeply. There is, in short, in a cohesive and animated society a constant interchange of ideas and feelings from all to each and each to all, something like a mutual moral support, which instead of throwing the individual on his own resources, leads him to share in the collective energy and supports his own when exhausted.

But these reasons are purely secondary. Excessive individualism not only results in favoring the action of suicidogenic causes, but it is itself such a cause. It not only frees man's inclination to do away with himself from a protective obstacle, but creates this inclination out of whole cloth and thus gives birth to a special suicide which bears its mark. This must be clearly understood for this is what constitutes the special character of the type of suicide just distinguished and justifies the name we have given it. What is there then in individualism that explains this result?

It has been sometimes said that because of his psychological constitution, man cannot live without attachment to some object which transcends and survives him, and that the reason for this necessity is a need we must have not to perish entirely. Life is said to be intolerable unless some reason for existing is involved, some purpose justifying life's trials. The individual alone is not a sufficient end for his activity. He is too little. He is not only hemmed in spatially; he is also strictly limited temporally. When, therefore, we have no other object than ourselves we cannot avoid the thought that our efforts will finally end in nothingness, since we ourselves disappear. But annihilation terrifies us. Under these conditions one would lose courage to live, that is, to act and struggle, since nothing will remain of our exertions. The state of egoism, in other words, is supposed to be contradictory to human nature and, consequently, too uncertain to have chances of permanence.

In this absolute formulation the proposition is vulnerable. If the thought of the end of our personality were really so hateful, we could consent to live only by blinding ourselves voluntarily as to life's value. For if we may in a measure avoid the prospect of annihilation we cannot extirpate it; it is inevitable, whatever we do. We may push back the frontier for some generations, force our name to endure for some years or centuries longer than our body; a moment, too soon for most men, always comes when it will be nothing. For the groups we join in order to prolong our existence by their means are themselves mortal; they too must dissolve, carrying with them all our deposit of ourselves. Those are few whose memories are closely enough bound to the very history of humanity to be assured of living until its death. So, if we really thus thirsted after immortality, no such brief perspectives could ever appease us. Besides, what of us is it that lives? A word, a sound, an imperceptible trace, most often anonymous, therefore nothing comparable to the violence of our efforts or able to justify them to us. In actuality, though a child is naturally an egoist who feels not the slightest craving to survive himself, and the old man is very often a child in this and so many other respects, neither ceases to cling to life as much or more than the adult; indeed we have seen that suicide is very rare for the first fifteen years and tends to decrease at the other extreme of life. Such too is the case with animals, whose psychological constitution differs from that of men only in degree. It is therefore untrue that life is only possible by its possessing its rationale outside of itself.

Indeed, a whole range of functions concern only the individual; these are the ones indispensable for physical life. Since they are made for this purpose only, they are perfected by its attainment. In everything concerning them, therefore, man can act reasonably without thought of transcendental purposes. These functions serve by merely serving him. In so far as he has no other needs, he is therefore self-sufficient and can live happily with no other objective than living. This is not the case, however, with the civilized adult. He has many ideas, feelings and practices unrelated to organic needs. The roles of art, morality, religion, political faith, science itself are not to repair organic exhaustion nor to provide sound functioning of the organs. All this supra-physical life is built and expanded not because of the demands of the cosmic environment but because of the demands of the social environment. The influence of society is what has aroused in us the sentiments of sympathy and solidarity drawing us toward others; it is society which, fashioning us in its image, fills us with religious, political and moral beliefs that control our actions. To play our social role we have striven to extend our intelligence and it is still society that has supplied us with tools for this development by transmitting to us its trust fund of knowledge.

Through the very fact that these superior forms of human activity have a collective origin, they have a collective purpose. As they derive from society they have reference to it; rather they are society itself incarnated and individualized in each one of us. But for them to have a raison d'être in our eyes, the purpose they envisage must be one not indifferent to us. We can cling to these forms of human activity only to the degree that we cling to society itself.

Social Sanction * (*Radcliffe-Brown*)

In any community there are certain modes of behavior which are usual and which characterize that particular community. Such modes of behavior may be called usages. All social usages have behind them the authority of the society, but among them some are sanctioned and others are not. A sanction is a reaction on the part of a society or of a considerable number of its members to a mode of behavior which is thereby approved (positive sanctions) or disapproved (negative sanctions). Sanctions may further be distinguished according to whether they are diffuse or organized; the former are spontaneous expressions of approval or disapproval by members of the community acting as individuals, while the latter are social actions carried out according to some traditional and recognized procedure. It is a significant fact that in all human societies the negative sanctions are more definite

* By A. R. Radcliffe-Brown, reprinted from *Encyclopaedia of the Social Sciences*, Vol. XIII, pp. 531–534, with permission of the publisher, The Macmillan Company. Copyright, 1934, by The Macmillan Company.

than the positive. Social obligations may be defined as rules of behavior the failure to observe which entails a negative sanction of some sort. These are thus distinguished from non-obligatory social usages, as, for example, customary technical procedures.

The sanctions existing in a community constitute motives in the individual for the regulation of his conduct in conformity with usage. They are effective, first, through the desire of the individual to obtain the approbation and to avoid the disapprobation of his fellows, to win such rewards or to avoid such punishments as the community offers or threatens; and, second, through the fact that the individual learns to react to particular modes of behavior with judgments of approval and disapproval in the same way as do his fellows, and therefore measures his own behavior both in anticipation and in retrospect by standards which conform more or less closely to those prevalent in the community to which he belongs. What is called conscience is thus in the widest sense the reflex in the individual of the sanctions of the society.

It is convenient to begin a discussion of sanctions by a consideration of the diffuse negative sanctions, comprising reactions toward the particular or general behavior of a member of the community which constitute judgments of disapproval. In such reactions there are not only differences of degree—for disapproval is felt and expressed with different degrees of intensity—but also differences of kind. Such differences are difficult to define and classify. In the English language, for example, there are a large number of words which express disapproval of individual behavior; these vary from discourteous, unmannerly, unseemly and unworthy, through improper, discreditable, dishonorable and disreputable, to outrageous and infamous. Every society or culture has its own ways of judging behavior and these might conveniently be studied in the first instance through the vocabulary. But until comparative study of societies of different types has proceeded further no systematic classification of the kinds of diffuse negative sanction is possible. Provisionally the negative moral or ethical sanction may be defined as a reaction of reprobation by the community toward a person whose conduct is disapproved; moral obligations may thus be considered as rules of conduct which, if not observed, bring about a reaction of this kind. Another distinguishable sanction is that whereby the behavior of an individual is met with ridicule on the part of his fellows; this has been called the satirical sanction. The varieties of diffuse positive sanctions, being less definite than negative sanctions, are therefore still more difficult to classify.

From the diffuse sanctions already described there should be distinguished what may be called (by a wide extension of the term) religious sanctions; these have also been named supernatural sanctions and mystic sanctions, but both these terms have unsatisfactory connotations. The religious sanctions are constituted in any community by the existence of certain beliefs which are themselves obligatory; it is therefore only within a religious community that these sanctions exist. They take the form that certain deeds by an individual produce a modification in his religious condition, in either a desirable (good) or an undesirable (evil) direction. Certain acts are regarded as pleasing to gods or spirits or as establishing desirable relations with them, while others displease them or destroy in some way the desirable harmonious relations. The religious condition of the individual is in these instances conceived to be determined by his relation to personal spiritual beings. The change in the religious condition may elsewhere be regarded as the immediate effect of the act itself, not mediated by its effects on some personal god or spirit, a view common not only in many of the simpler societies, but also found in a special form in Buddhism and in other advanced Indian religions. Sin may be defined as any mode of behavior which falls under a negative religious sanction; there is no convenient term for the opposite of sin, that is, an action which produces religious merit or a desirable ritual condition.

The religious sanctions involve the belief that most unsatisfactory ritual or religious conditions (pollution, uncleanness, sinfulness) can be removed or neutralized by socially prescribed or recognized procedures, such as lustration, sacrifice, penance, confession and repentance. These expiatory rites are also considered to act either immediately, or mediately through their effects on gods or spirits, depending upon whether the sin is regarded as acting in the one way or the other.

While in modern western civilization a sin is usually regarded as necessarily a voluntary action or thought, in many simple societies an involuntary action may fall within the given definition of sin. Sickness—for example, leprosy among the Hebrews—is often regarded as similar to ritual or religious pollution and as therefore requiring expiation or ritual purification. A condition of ritual or religious impurity is normally considered as of immediate or ultimate danger to the individual; it may be believed that he will fall sick and perhaps die unless he can be purified. In some religions the religious sanction takes the form of a belief that an individual who sins in this life will suffer some form of retribution in an after life. In many instances an individual who is ritually unclean is looked upon as a source of danger not only to himself but also those with whom he comes in contact or to the whole community. He may therefore be more or less excluded for a time or even permanently from participation in the social life of the community. Frequently if not always therefore an obligation rests upon the sinner, or unclean person, to undertake the necessary process of purification.

Thus the religious sanctions differ from the other diffuse sanctions by reason of the beliefs and conceptions indicated above, which cannot be defined or described in any simple way. Somewhat similar beliefs underlie magical practises and procedures in relation to luck, but whereas religious observances and the beliefs associated with them are obligatory within a given religious community, the former are comparable with technical procedures, customary but not obligatory.

Organized sanctions are to be regarded as special developments of the diffuse sanctions, frequently under the influence of the beliefs belonging to religion. Organized positive sanctions, or premial sanctions, are rarely developed to any great extent. Honors, decorations, titles, and other rewards for merit, including monetary rewards such as special pensions, given to individuals by a community as a whole, are characteristic of modern societies. In preliterate societies a man who has slain an enemy may be given the right to distinguish himself by wearing some special decoration or in other ways.

Organized negative sanctions, important among which are the penal sanctions of criminal law, are definite recognized procedures directed against persons whose behavior is subject to social disapproval. There are many varieties of such procedures, the most important and widespread being the following: subjection to open expression of reprobation or derision, as, for example, through forcible public exposure by confinement in stocks; partial exclusion, permanent or temporary, from full participation in social life and its privileges, including permanent or temporary loss of civil or religious rights; specific loss of social rank, or degradation, the exact contrary of the positive sanction of promotion; infliction of loss of property by imposition of a fine or by forcible seizure or destruction; infliction of bodily pain; mutilation or branding in which pain is incidental to permanent exposure to reprobation; permanent exclusion from the community, as by exile; imprisonment; and punishment by death. These sanctions are legal sanctions when they are imposed by a constituted authority, political, military or ecclesiastic.

In any given society the various primary sanctions form a more or less systematic whole which constitutes the mechanism of social control. There is an intimate relation between the religious sanctions and the moral sanctions, which varies, however, in different societies, and cannot be stated in any brief formula. The primary legal sanctions of criminal law, in all societies except the highly secularized modern states, show a close connection with religious beliefs.

Besides these primary social sanctions and resting upon them there are certain sanctions which may be termed secondary; these are concerned with the actions of persons or groups in their effects upon other persons or groups. In modern civil law, for example, when an individual is ordered by a court to pay damages, the primary sanction behind the order is the power of the court to make forcible seizure of his property or to imprison or otherwise punish him for contempt of court if he fails to obey. Thus secondary sanctions consist of procedures carried out by a community, generally through its representatives, or by individuals with the approval of the community, when recognized rights have been infringed. They are based upon the general principle that any person who has suffered injury is entitled to satisfaction and that such satisfaction should be in some way proportioned to the extent of the injury.

One class of such procedures consists of acts of retaliation, by which is meant socially approved, controlled and limited acts of revenge. Thus in an Australian tribe when one man has committed an offense against another, the latter is permitted by public opinion, often definitely expressed by the older men, to throw a certain number of spears or boomerangs at the former or in some instances to spear him in the thigh. After he has been given such satisfaction he may no longer harbor ill feelings against the offender. In many preliterate societies the killing of an individual entitles the group to which he belongs to obtain satisfaction by killing the offender or some member of his group. In regulated vengeance the offending group must submit to this as an act of justice and must not attempt further retaliation. Those who have received such satisfaction are felt to have no further grounds for ill feeling.

Satisfaction for injury may be obtained also through the duel, a recognized and controlled combat between individuals, or through similar combats between two groups. Among Australian tribes dueling with spears, boomerangs, clubs and shields or stone knives, with the bystanders ready to interfere if they think things are going too far, is a frequently adopted alternative to one-sided retaliation. In these same tribes there are similar regulated combats between two groups, sometimes in the presence of other groups who see that there is fair play. It is often difficult to draw a dividing line between such group combats and warfare; in fact they may possibly be regarded as a special form of warfare characteristic of primitive rather than of civilized societies. Frequently therefore war may be regarded as a secondary social sanction similar to the duel. A political group maintains recognition of its rights by the threat of war if those rights should be infringed. Even in the simplest societies it is recognized that certain acts are right in war and others are wrong and that a declaration of war may be just in certain circumstances and in others unjust, so that the conduct of warfare is to some extent controlled by diffuse sanctions.

Indemnification is often found as an alternative to retaliation as a means of giving and receiving satisfaction. An indemnity is something of value given by a person or group to another person or group in order to remove or neutralize the effects of an infringement of rights. It may be distinguished from a propitiatory gift by the fact that it is obligatory (i.e. subject to a negative sanction, diffuse or organized) in the particular circumstances. A payment made in anticipation of an invasion of rights with the consent of the person or persons receiving it may be regarded as an indemnity. Thus in many societies taking a woman in marriage is regarded as an invasion of the rights of her family and kin, so that before they consent to part with her they must receive an indemnity or the promise of such. In these cases the process of indemnification bears some similarity to that of purchase, which is a transfer of rights of property for a consideration.

In many preliterate societies procedures of indemnification are carried out under the diffuse sanction of public opinion, which compels an individual to indemnify one whose rights he has infringed. In some societies there is a recognized right of an injured person to indemnify himself by forcible seizure of the property of the offender. When society becomes politically organized, procedures of retaliation and indemnification backed by diffuse sanctions give place to legal sanctions backed by the power of judicial authorities to inflict punishment. Thus arises civil law, by which a person who has suffered an infringement of rights may obtain reparation or restitution from the person responsible.

In a consideration of the functions of social sanctions it is not the effects of the sanction upon the person to whom they are applied that are most important but rather the general effects within the community applying the sanctions. For the application of any sanction is a direct affirmation of social sentiments by the community and thereby constitutes an important, possibly essential, mechanism for maintaining these sentiments. Organized negative sanctions in particular, and to a great extent the secondary sanctions, are expressions of a condition of social dysphoria brought about by some deed. The function of the sanction is to restore the social euphoria by giving definite collective expression to the sentiments which have been affected by the deed, as in the primary sanctions and to some extent in the secondary sanctions, or by removing a conflict within the community itself. The sanctions are thus of primary significance to sociology in that they are reactions on the part of a community to events affecting its integration.

Reciprocity as the Basis of Social Cohesion * (*Malinowski*)

Again, recasting our whole perspective and looking at matters from the sociological point of view, i.e. taking one feature of the constitution of the tribe after another, instead of surveying the various types of their tribal activities, it would be possible to show that the whole structure of Trobriand society is founded on the principle of *legal status*. By this I mean that the claims of chief over commoners, husband over wife, parent over child, and vice versa, are not exercised arbitrarily and one-sidedly, but according to definite rules, and arranged into well-balanced chains of reciprocal services.

Even the chief, whose position is hereditary, based on highly venerable mythological traditions, surrounded with semi-religious awe, enhanced by a princely ceremonial of distance, abasement, and stringent taboos, who has a great deal of power, wealth, and executive means, has to conform to strict norms and is bound by legal fetters. When he wants to declare war, organize an expedition, or celebrate a festivity, he must issue formal summons, publicly announce his will, deliberate with the notables, receive the tribute, services and assistance of his subjects in a ceremonial manner, and finally repay them according to a definite scale.[1] It is enough to mention here what has been previously said about the sociological status of marriage, of the relations between husband and wife, and of the status between relatives-in-law.[2] The whole division into totemic clans, into sub-clans of a local nature and into village communities, is characterized by a system of reciprocal services and duties, in which the groups play a game of give and take.

What perhaps is most remarkable in the legal nature of social relations is that reciprocity, the give-and-take principle, reigns supreme also within the clan, nay within the nearest group of kinsmen. As we have seen already, the relation between the maternal uncle and his nephews, the relations be-

* Reprinted from *Crime and Custom in Savage Society* by Bronislaw Malinowski, pp. 46–49, with permission of the publisher, Routledge & Kegan Paul, Ltd., London.

tween brothers, nay the most unselfish relation, that between a man and his sister, are all and one founded on mutuality and the repayment of services. It is just this group which has always been accused of 'primitive communism.' The clan is often described as the only legal person, the one body and entity, in primitive jurisprudence. "The unit is not the individual, but the kin. The individual is but part of the kin," are the words of Mr. Sidney Hartland. This is certainly true if we take into consideration that part of social life in which the kinship group—totemic clan, phratry, moiety, or class— plays the reciprocity game against co-ordinate groups. But what about the perfect unity within the clan? Here we are offered the universal solution of the "pervading group-sentiment, if not group-instinct," which is said to be specially rampant in the part of the world with which we are concerned, inhabited by "a people dominated by such a group-sentiment as actuates the Melanesian" (Rivers). This, we know, is quite a mistaken view. Within the nearest kinship group rivalries, dissensions, the keenest egotism flourish and dominate indeed the whole trend of kinship relations. To this point I shall have to return presently, for more facts and more definitely telling ones are necessary finally to explode this myth of kinship-communism, of the perfect solidarity within the group related by direct descent, a myth recently revived by Dr. Rivers, and in some danger therefore of gaining general currency.

REFERENCES

1. Comp. for more detail, the various aspects of chieftainship I have brought out in art. cit. "Primitive Economics," op. cit. (*Argonauts*), and the articles on "War" and on "Spirits," also referred to previously.
2. Here again I must refer to some of my other publications, where these matters have been treated in detail, though not from the present point of view. See the three articles published in *Psyche* of October, 1923 ("The Psychology of Sex in Primitive Societies"); April, 1924 ("Psycho-Analysis and Anthropology"); and January, 1925 ("Complex and Myth in Mother-Right"), in which many aspects of sexual psychology, of the fundamental ideas and customs of kinship and relationship, have been described. The two latter articles appear uniform with this work in my *Sex and Repression in Savage Society* (1926).

Class Cohesion through Conflict * (*Marx*)

The organisation of strikes, combinations, trade unions, marches simultaneously with the political struggles of the workers, who now constitute a great political party under the name of Chartists.

* Reprinted from *Poverty of Philosophy* by Karl Marx, translated by H. Quelch, Charles H. Kerr & Company, Chicago, Ill., 1910.

It is under the form of these combinations that the first attempts at association among themselves have always been made by the workers.

The great industry masses together in a single place a crowd of people unknown to each other. Competition divides their interests. But the maintenance of their wages, this common interest which they have against their employer, unites them in the same idea of resistance—combination. Thus combination has always a double end, that of eliminating competition among themselves while enabling them to make a general competition against the capitalist. If the first object of resistance has been merely to maintain wages, in proportion as the capitalists in their turn have combined with the idea of repression, the combinations, at first isolated, have formed in groups, and, in face of constantly united capital, the maintenance of the associations became more important and necessary for them than the maintenance of wages. This is so true that the English economists are all astonished at seeing the workers sacrifice a good part of their wages on behalf of the associations which, in the eyes of these economists, were only established in support of wages. In this struggle—a veritable civil war—are united and developed all the elements necessary for a future battle. Once arrived at that point, association takes a political character.

The economic conditions have in the first place transformed the mass of the people of a country into wageworkers. The domination of capital has created for this mass of people a common situation with common interests. Thus this mass is already a class, as opposed to capital, but not yet for itself. In the struggle, of which we have only noted some phases, this mass unites, it is constituted as a class for itself. The interests which it defends are the interests of its class. But the struggle between class and class is a political struggle.

In the bourgeoisie we have two phases to distinguish, that during which it is constituted as a class under the régime of feudalism and absolute monarchy, and that wherein, already constituted as a class, it overthrew feudalism and monarchy in order to make of society a bourgeois society. The first of these phases was the longest and necessitated the greatest efforts. That also commenced with partial combination against the feudal lords.

Many researches have been made to trace the different historical phases through which the bourgeoisie has passed from the early commune to its constitution as a class.

But when it becomes a question of rendering an account of the strikes, combinations, and other forms in which before our eyes the proletarians effect their organisation as a class, some are seized with fear while others express a transcendental disdain.

Class Identity and Conflict * (*Sorel*)

According to Marx, capitalism, by reason of the innate laws of its own nature, is hurrying along a path which will lead the world of to-day, with the inevitability of the evolution of organic life, to the doors of the world of to-morrow. This movement comprises a long period of capitalistic construction, and it ends by a rapid destruction, which is the work of the proletariat. Capitalism creates the heritage which Socialism will receive, the men who will suppress the present régime, and the means of bringing about this destruction, at the same time that it preserves the results obtained in production.[1] Capitalism begets new ways of working; it throws the working class into revolutionary organisations by the pressure it exercises on wages; it restricts its own political basis by competition, which is constantly eliminating industrial leaders. Thus, after having solved the great problem of the organisation of labour, to effect which Utopians have brought forward so many naive or stupid hypotheses, capitalism provokes the birth of the cause which will overthrow it, and thus renders useless everything that Utopians have written to induce enlightened people to make reforms; and it gradually ruins the traditional order, against which the critics of the idealists had proved themselves to be so deplorably incompetent. It might therefore be said that capitalism plays a part analogous to that attributed by Hartmann to The Unconscious in nature, since it prepares the coming of social reforms which it did not intend to produce. Without any coordinated plan, without any directive ideas, without any ideal of a future world, it is the cause of an inevitable evolution; it draws from the present all that the present can give towards historical development; it performs in an almost mechanical manner all that is necessary, in order that a new era may appear, and that this new era may break every link with the idealism of the present times, while preserving the acquisitions of the capitalistic economic system.[2]

Socialists should therefore abandon the attempt (initiated by the Utopians) to find a means of inducing the enlightened middle class to prepare the *transition to a more perfect system of legislation*; their sole function is that of explaining to the proletariat the greatness of the revolutionary part they are called upon to play. By ceaseless criticism the proletariat must be brought to perfect their organisations; they must be shown how the embryonic forms which appear in their unions[3] may be developed,

* Reprinted from *Reflections on Violence* by Georges Sorel, authorized translation by T. E. Hulme and J. Roth, 1915, pp. 84–91, by permission of the publishers, The Free Press, Glencoe, Ill., and George Allen & Unwin Ltd., London.

so that, finally, they may build up institutions without any parallel in the history of the middle class; that they may form ideas which depend solely on their position as producers in large industries, and which owe nothing to middle-class thought; and that they may acquire *habits of liberty* with which the middle class nowadays are no longer acquainted.

This doctrine will evidently be inapplicable if the middle class and the proletariat do not oppose each other implacably, with all the forces at their disposal; the more ardently capitalist the middle class is, the more the proletariat is full of a warlike spirit and confident of its revolutionary strength, the more certain will be the success of the proletarian movement.

The middle class with which Marx was familiar in England was still, as regards the immense majority, animated by their conquering, insatiable, and pitiless spirit, which had characterised at the beginning of modern times the creators of new industries and the adventurers launched on the discovery of unknown lands. When we are studying the modern industrial system we should always bear in mind this similarity between the capitalist type and the warrior type; it was for very good reasons that the men who directed gigantic enterprises were named *captains of industry*. This type is still found to-day in all its purity in the United States: there are found the indomitable energy, the audacity based on a just appreciation of its strength, the cold calculation of interests, which are the qualities of great generals and great capitalists.[4] According to Paul de Rousiers, every American feels himself capable of "trying his luck" on the battlefield of business,[5] so that the general spirit of the country is in complete harmony with that of the multi-millionaires; our men of letters are exceedingly surprised to see these latter condemning themselves to lead to the end of their days a galley-slave existence, without ever thinking of leading a nobleman's life for themselves, as the Rothschilds do.

In a society so enfevered by the passion for the success which can be obtained in competition, all the actors walk straight before them like veritable automata, without taking any notice of the great ideas of the sociologists; they are subject to very simple forces, and not one of them dreams of escaping from the circumstances of his condition. Then only is the development of capitalism carried on with that inevitableness which struck Marx so much, and which seemed to him comparable to that of a natural law. If, on the contrary, the middle class, led astray by the *chatter* of the preachers of ethics and sociology, return to an *ideal of conservative mediocrity,* seek to correct the *abuses* of economics, and wish to break with the barbarism of their predecessors, then one part of the forces which were to further the development of capitalism is employed in hindering it, an arbitrary and irrational element is introduced, and the future of the world becomes completely indeterminate.

This indetermination grows still greater if the proletariat are converted to the ideas of social peace at the same time as their masters, or even if they simply consider everything from the corporative point of view; while Socialism gives to every economic contest a general and revolutionary colour.

Conservatives are not deceived when they see in the compromises which lead to collective contracts, and in corporative particularism,[6] the means of avoiding the Marxian revolution;[7] but they escape one danger only to fall into another, and they run the risk of being devoured by Parliamentary Socialism.[8] Jaurès is as enthusiastic as the clericals about measures which turn away the working classes from the idea of the Marxian revolution; I believe he understands better than they do what the result of social peace will be; he founds his own hopes on the simultaneous ruin of the capitalistic and the revolutionary spirit.

It is often urged, in objection to the people who defend the Marxian conception, that it is impossible for them to stop the movement of degeneration which is dragging both the middle class and the proletariat far from the paths assigned to them by Marx's theory. They can doubtless influence the working classes, and it is hardly to be denied that strike violences do keep the revolutionary spirit alive; but how can they hope to give back to the middle class an ardour which is spent?

It is here that the role of violence in history appears to us as singularly great, for it can, in an indirect manner, so operate on the middle class as to awaken them to a sense of their own class sentiment. Attention has often been drawn to the danger of certain acts of violence which compromised *admirable social works,* disgusted employers who were disposed to arrange the happiness of their workmen, and developed egoism where the most noble sentiments formerly reigned.

To repay with *black ingratitude* the *benevolence* of those who would protect the workers,[9] to meet with insults the homilies of the defenders of human fraternity, and to reply by blows to the advances of the propagators of social peace—all that is assuredly not in conformity with the rules of the fashionable Socialism of M. and Mme. Georges Renard,[10] but it is a very practical way of indicating to the middle class that they must mind their own business and only that.

I believe also that it may be useful to thrash the orators of democracy and the representatives of the Government, for in this way you insure that none shall retain any illusions about the character of acts of violence. But these acts can have historical value only if they are the *clear and brutal expression of the class war*: the middle classes must not be allowed to imagine that, aided by cleverness, social science, or high-flown sentiments, they might find a better welcome at the hands of the proletariat.

The day on which employers perceive that they have nothing to gain by works which promote social peace, or by democracy, they will understand that they have been ill-advised by the people who persuaded them to abandon their trade of creators of productive forces for the noble profession of educators of the proletariat. Then there is some chance that they may get back a part of their energy, and that moderate or conservative economics may appear as absurd to them as they appeared to Marx. In any case, the separation of classes being more clearly accentuated, the proletarian movement will have some chance of developing with greater regularity than to-day.

The two antagonistic classes therefore influence each other in a partly indirect but decisive manner. Capitalism drives the proletariat into revolt, because in daily life the employers use their force in a direction opposed to the desire of their workers; but the future of the proletariat is not entirely dependent on this revolt; the working classes are organised under the influence of other causes, and Socialism, inculcating in them the revolutionary idea, prepares them to suppress the hostile class. Capitalist force is at the base of all this process, and its action is automatic and inevitable.[11] Marx supposed that the middle class had no need to be incited to employ force, but we are to-day faced with a new and very unforeseen fact—a middle class which seeks to weaken its own strength. Must we believe that the Marxian conception is dead? By no means, for proletarian violence comes upon the scene just at the moment when the conception of social peace is being held up as a means of moderating disputes; proletarian violence confines employers to their role of producers, and tends to restore the separation of the classes, just when they seemed on the point of intermingling in the democratic marsh.

Proletarian violence not only makes the future revolution certain, but it seems also to be the only means by which the European nations—at present stupefied by humanitarianism—can recover their former energy. This kind of violence compels capitalism to restrict its attentions solely to its material role and tends to restore to it the warlike qualities which it formerly possessed. A growing and solidly organised working class can compel the capitalist class to remain firm in the industrial war; if a united and revolutionary proletariat confronts a rich middle class, eager for conquest, capitalist society will have reached its historical perfection.

REFERENCES

1. This notion of *revolutionary preservation* is very important; I have pointed out something analogous in the passage from Judaism to Christianity (*Le Système historique de Renan*, pp. 72–73, 171–172, 467).
2. Cf. what I have said on the transformation which Marx wrought in Socialism, *Insegnamenti sociali*, pp. 179–186.
3. [The French is *sociétés de résistance*. What is meant is the syndicate, considered principally as a means of combining workmen against the employers.—*Trans. Note.*]
4. I will come back to this resemblance in Chapter VII. iii.
5. P. de Rousiers, *La Vie américaine, l'éducation et la société*, p. 19. "Fathers give very little advice to their children. and let them learn for themselves, as they say over there" (p. 14). "Not only does (the American) wish to be independent, but he wishes to be powerful" (*La Vie américaine: ranches, fermes et usines*, p. 6).
6. [This refers to the conduct of former syndicates which limited their ambitions to the interests of their own handicraft without concerning themselves with the general interests of the working classes.—*Trans. Note.*]
7. There is constant talk nowadays of organising labour. *i.e.* of utilising the corporative spirit by giving it over to the management of well-intentioned, *very serious* and responsible people, and liberating the workers from the yoke of *sophists*. The responsible people are de Mun, Charles Benoist (the amusing specialist in constitutional law), Arthur Fontaine, and the band of democratic *abbés*, . . . and lastly Gabriel Hanotaux!
8. Vilredo Pareto laughs at the simple middle class who are happy, because they are no longer threatened by intractible Marxians, and who have fallen into the snare of the conciliatory Marxians (*Systèmes socialistes*, tome ii. p. 453).
9. Cf. G. Sorel. *Insegnamenti sociali*, p. 53.
10. Mme. G. Renard has published in the *Suisse* of July 26, 1900, an article full of lofty psychological considerations about the workers' fete given by Millerand (Léon de Seilhac, *Le Monde socialiste*, pp. 307–309). Her husband has solved the grave question as to who will drink Clos-Vougeot in the society of the future (G. Renard, *Le Régime socialiste*, p. 175).
11. In an article written in September 1851 (the first of the series published under the title: *Revolution and Counter-revolution*), Marx established the following parallelism between the development of the middle class and of the proletariat: To a numerous, rich, concentrated, and powerful middle class corresponds a numerous, strong, concentrated and intelligent proletariat. Thus he seems to have thought that the intelligence of the proletariat depends on the historical conditions which secured power in society to the middle classes. He says, again, that the true characters of the class war only exist in countries where the middle class has recast the Government in conformity with its needs.

Conflict as Sociation * (*Simmel*)

The sociological significance of conflict (*Kampf*) has in principle never been disputed. Conflict is admitted to cause or modify interest groups, unifications, organizations. On the other hand, it may sound paradoxical in the common view if one asks whether irrespective of any phenomena that

* Reprinted from *Conflict* by Georg Simmel, translated by Kurt H. Wolff, pp. 13–17, by permission of the publisher, The Free Press, Glencoe, Ill. Copyright by The Free Press, A Corporation.

result from conflict or that accompany it, it itself is a form of sociation.[1] At first glance, this sounds like a rhetorical question. If every interaction among men is a sociation, conflict—after all one of the most vivid interactions, which, furthermore, cannot possibly be carried on by one individual alone—must certainly be considered as sociation. And in fact, *dissociating* factors—hate, envy, need, desire—are the *causes* of conflict; it breaks out because of them. Conflict is thus designed to resolve divergent dualisms; it is a way of achieving some kind of unity, even if it be through the annihilation of one of the conflicting parties. This is roughly parallel to the fact that it is the most violent symptom of a disease which represent the effort of the organism to free itself of disturbances and damages caused by them.

But this phenomenon means much more than the trivial *"si vis pacem para bellum"* [if you want peace, prepare for war]; it is something quite general, of which this maxim only describes a special case. Conflict itself resolves the tension between contrasts. The fact that it aims at peace is only one, an especially obvious, expression of its nature: the synthesis of elements that work both against and for one another. This nature appears more clearly when it is realized that both forms of relation—the antithetical and the convergent—are fundamentally distinguished from the mere indifference of two or more individuals or groups. Whether it implies the rejection or the termination of sociation, indifference is purely negative. In contrast to such pure negativity, conflict contains something positive. Its positive and negative aspects, however, are integrated; they can be separated conceptually, but not empirically.

THE SOCIOLOGICAL RELEVANCE OF CONFLICT

Social phenomena appear in a new light when seen from the angle of this sociologically positive character of conflict. It is at once evident then that if the relations among men (rather than what the individual is to himself and in his relations to objects) constitute the subject matter of a special science, sociology, then the traditional topics of that science cover only a subdivision of it: it is more comprehensive and is truly defined by a principle. At one time it appeared as if there were only two consistent subject matters of the science of man: the individual unit and the unit of individuals (society); any third seemed logically excluded. In this conception, conflict itself—irrespective of its contributions to these immediate social units—found no place for study. It was a phenomenon of its own, and its subsumption under the concept of unity would have been arbitrary as well as useless, since conflict meant the negation of unity.

A more comprehensive classification of the science of the relations of men should distinguish, it would appear, those relations which constitute a unit, that is, social relations in the strict sense, from those which counteract unity.[2] It must be realized, however, that both relations can usually be found in every historically real situation. The individual does not attain the unity of his personality exclusively by an exhaustive harmonization, according to logical, objective, religious, or ethical norms, of the contents of his personality. On the contrary, contradiction and conflict not only precede this unity but are operative in it at every moment of its existence. Just so, there probably exists no social unit in which convergent and divergent currents among its members are not inseparably interwoven. An absolutely centripetal and harmonious group, a pure "unification" (*"Vereinigung"*), not only is empirically unreal, it could show no real life process. The society of saints which Dante sees in the Rose of Paradise may be like such a group, but it is without any change and development; whereas the holy assembly of Church Fathers in Raphael's *Disputa* shows if not actual conflict, at least a considerable differentiation of moods and directions of thought, whence flow all the vitality and the really organic structure of that group. Just as the universe needs "love and hate," that is, attractive and repulsive forces, in order to have any form at all, so society, too, in order to attain a determinate shape, needs some quantitative ratio of harmony and disharmony, of association and competition, of favorable and unfavorable tendencies. But these discords are by no means mere sociological liabilities or negative instances. Definite, actual society does not result only from other social forces which are positive, and only to the extent that the negative factors do not hinder them. This common conception is quite superficial: society, as we know it, is the result of both categories of interaction, which thus both manifest themselves as wholly positive.[3]

Unity and Discord

There is a misunderstanding according to which one of these two kinds of interaction tears down what the other builds up, and what is eventually left standing is the result of the subtraction of the two (while in reality it must rather be designated as the result of their addition). This misunderstanding probably derives from the twofold meaning of the concept of unity. We designate as "unity" the consensus and concord of interacting individuals, as against their discords, separations, and disharmonies. But we also call "unity" the total group-synthesis of persons, energies, and forms, that is, the ultimate wholeness of that group, a wholeness which covers both strictly-speaking unitary relations and dualistic relations. We thus account for the group phenomenon which we feel to be "unitary" in terms of functional components considered *specifically* unitary; and in so doing, we disregard the other, larger meaning of the term.

This imprecision is increased by the corresponding twofold meaning of "discord" or "opposition." Since discord unfolds its negative, destructive character between particular individuals, we naively conclude that it must have the same effect on the total group. In reality, however, something which is negative and damaging between individuals if it is considered in isolation and as aiming in a particular direction, does not necessarily have the same effect within the total relationship of these individuals. For, a very different picture emerges when we view the conflict in conjunction with other inter-actions not affected by it. The negative and dualistic elements play an entirely positive role in this more comprehensive picture, despite the destruction they may work on particular relations. All this is very obvious in the competition of individuals within an economic unit.

REFERENCES

1. *"Vergesellschaftungsform." "Vergesellschaftung"* will be rendered as "sociation." On the term and its various translations, see *The Sociology of Georg Simmel, loc. cit.,* pp. lxiii–lxiv.—Tr.
2. "Einheit" is both "unit" and "unity," and Simmel uses the term promiscuously in both senses.—Tr.
3. This is the sociological instance of a contrast between two much more general con-ceptions of life. According to the common view, life always shows two parties in opposition. One of them represents the positive aspect of life, its content proper, if not its substance, while the very meaning of the other is non-being, which must be subtracted from the positive elements before they can constitute life. This is the common view of the relation between happiness and suffering, virtue and vice, strength and inadequacy, success and failure—between all possible contents and interruptions of the course of life. The highest conception indicated in respect to these contrasting pairs appears to me different: we must conceive of all these polar differentiations as of *one* life; we must sense the pulse of a central vitality even in that which, if seen from the standpoint of a particular ideal, ought not to be at all and is merely something negative; we must allow the total meaning of our existence to grow out of *both* parties. In the most comprehensive context of life, even that which as a single element is dis-turbing and destructive, is wholly positive; it is not a gap but the fulfillment of a role reserved for it alone. Perhaps it is not given to us to attain, much less always to maintain, the height from which all phenomena can be felt as making up the unity of life, even though from an objective or value standpoint, they appear to oppose one another as pluses and minuses, contradictions, and mutual eliminations. We are too inclined to think and feel that our essential being, our true, ultimate significance, is identical with one of these factions. According to our optimistic or pessimistic feeling of life, one of them appears to us as surface or accident, as something to be eliminated or subtracted, in order for the true and intrinsically consistent life to emerge. We are everywhere enmeshed in this dualism (which will presently be discussed in more detail in the text above)—in the most intimate as in the most comprehensive provinces of life, personal, objective, and social. We think we have, or are, a whole or unit which is composed of two logically and objectively opposed parties, and we identify this totality of ours with one of them, while we feel the other to be something alien

which does not properly belong and which denies our central and comprehensive being. Life constantly moves between these two tendencies. The one has just been described. The other lets the whole really *be* the whole. It makes the unity, which after all comprises both contrasts, alive in each of these contrasts and in their juncture. It is all the more necessary to assert the right of this second tendency in respect to the sociological phenomenon of conflict, because conflict impresses us with its socially destructive force as with an apparently indisputable fact.

The Peace in the Feud * (*Gluckman*)

Whenever an anthropological study is made of a whole society or of some smaller social group, it emphasizes the great complexity which develops in the relations between human beings. Some of this complexity arises from human nature itself, with its varied organic and personality needs. But the customs of each society exaggerate and complicate this complexity. Differences of age, sex, parentage, residence, and so on, have to be handled somehow. But customary forms for developing relations of kinship, for establishing friendships, for compelling the observance through ritual of right relations with the universe, and so forth—these customary forms first divide and then reunite men. One might expect that a small community, of just over a thousand souls, could reside together on an isolated Pacific island with a fairly simple social organization. In fact, such a community is always elaborately divided and cross-divided by customary allegiances; and the elaboration is aggravated by what is most specifically a production of man in society: his religion and his ritual. In his *Notes towards the Definition of Culture,* Mr. T. S. Eliot saw the importance of these divisions. He wrote: 'I . . . suggest that both class and region, by dividing the inhabitants of a country into two different kinds of groups, lead to a conflict favourable to creativeness and progress. And . . . these are only two of an indefinite number of conflicts and jealousies which should be profitable to society. Indeed, the more the better: so that everyone should be an ally of everyone else in some respects, and an opponent in several others, and no one conflict, envy or fear will predominate. . . .'

'I may put the idea of the importance of conflict within a nation more positively', he goes on, 'by insisting on the importance of various and sometimes conflicting loyalties.' This is the central theme of my lectures—how men quarrel in terms of certain of their customary allegiances, but are restrained from violence through other conflicting allegiances which are also enjoined on them by custom. The result is that conflicts in one set of rela-

* Reprinted from *Custom and Conflict in Africa* by Max Gluckman, pp. 1–4, by permission of the publishers, The Free Press, Glencoe, Ill., and Basil Blackwell, London.

tionships, over a wider range of society or through a longer period of time, lead to the re-establishment of social cohesion. Conflicts are a part of social life and custom appears to exacerbate these conflicts: but in doing so custom also restrains the conflicts from destroying the wider social order. I shall exhibit this process through the working of the feud, of hostility to authority, of estrangements within the elementary family, of witchcraft accusations and ritual, and even in the colour-bar, as anthropologists have studied these problems in Africa.

All over the world there are societies which have no governmental institutions. That is, they lack officers with established powers to judge on quarrels and to enforce their decisions, to legislate and take administrative action to meet emergencies, and to lead wars of offence and defence. Yet these societies have such well-established and well-known codes of morals and law, of convention and ritual, that even though they have no written histories, we may reasonably assume that they have persisted for many generations. They clearly do not live in unceasing fear of breaking up in lawlessness. We know that some of them have existed over long periods with some kind of internal law and order, and have successfully defended themselves against attacks by others. Indeed, they include turbulent warriors who raided and even terrorized their neighbours. Therefore when anthropologists came to study these societies, they were immediately confronted with the problem of where social order and cohesion lay.

I myself have not had the good fortune to study in detail such a society, in which private vengeance and self-help are the main overt sanctions against injury by others, and where this exercise of self-help is likely to lead to the waging of feuds. Both my own main fields of research have lain in powerful African kingdoms, where the processes of political control are akin to those patently observable in our own nation. But this lack of personal experience of a feuding society does enable me, without vanity, to bring to your attention what I consider to be one of the most significant contributions which social anthropological research has made to our understanding of social relations. Anthropologists have studied the threatened outbreak of feuds—I say 'threatened outbreak,' because nowadays the presence of European governments usually prevents open fighting. But these anthropologists have been able to see the situations which give rise to internecine fights, and, more importantly, to examine the mechanisms which lead to settlements. The critical result of their analysis is to show that these societies are so organized into a series of groups and relationships, that people who are friends on one basis are enemies on another. Herein lies social cohesion, rooted in the conflicts between men's different allegiances. I believe that it would be profitable to apply these analyses to those long-distant periods of European history when the feud was still apparently the main instrument for redress of injury.

But the analysis of feuding societies does not exhaust its interest when we see feud working as a specific institution where there is no government. As I have said, I myself have done research in African kingdoms; and I found it greatly illuminated my analyses of these kingdoms, when I sought in them the processes which my colleagues had disentangled from feuding. Underneath the patent framework of governmental control which organized the state, I found feud and the settlement of feud at work. Permanent states of hostility, like feuds, existed between sections of the nation. These hostilities were redressed by mechanisms similar to those which prevent feuds from breaking out in perpetual open fighting. The same processes go on around us within our own nation-state, and international relations.

The Functions of Social Conflict * (Coser)

Conflict within a group, we have seen, may help to establish unity or to re-establish unity and cohesion where it has been threatened by hostile and antagonistic feelings among the members. Yet, we noted that not *every* type of conflict is likely to benefit group structure, nor that conflict can subserve such functions for *all* groups: Whether social conflict is beneficial to internal adaptation or not depends on the type of issues over which it is fought as well as on the type of social structure within which it occurs. However, types of conflict and types of social structure are not independent variables.

Internal social conflicts which concern goals, values or interests that do not contradict the basic assumptions upon which the relationship is founded tend to be positively functional for the social structure. Such conflicts tend to make possible the readjustment of norms and power relations within groups in accordance with the felt needs of its individual members or subgroups.

Internal conflicts in which the contending parties no longer share the basic values upon which the legitimacy of the social system rests threaten to disrupt the structure.

One safeguard against conflict disrupting the consensual basis of the relationship, however, is contained in the social structure itself: it is provided by the institutionalization and tolerance of conflict. Whether internal conflict promises to be a means of equilibration of social relations or readjustment of rival claims, or whether it threatens to "tear apart," depends to a large extent on the social structure within which it occurs.

In every type of social structure there are occasions for conflict, since individuals and subgroups are likely to make from time to time rival claims to scarce resources, prestige or power positions. But social structures differ in the way in which they allow expression to antagonistic claims. Some show more tolerance of conflict than others.

Closely knit groups in which there exists a high frequency of interaction and high personality involvement of the members have a tendency to suppress conflict. While they provide frequent occasions for hostility (since both sentiments of love and hatred are intensified through frequency of interaction), the acting out of such feelings is sensed as a danger to such intimate relationships, and hence there is a tendency to suppress rather than to allow expression of hostile feelings. In close-knit groups, feelings of hostility tend, therefore, to accumulate and hence to intensify. If conflict breaks out in a group that has consistently tried to prevent expression of hostile feelings, it will be particularly intense for two reasons: First, because the conflict does not merely aim at resolving the immediate issue which led to its outbreak; all accumulated grievances which were denied expression previously are apt to emerge at this occasion. Second, because the total personality involvement of the group members makes for mobilization of all sentiments in the conduct of the struggle.

✓ Hence, the closer the group, the more intense the conflict. Where members participate with their total personality and conflicts are suppressed, the conflict, if it breaks out nevertheless, is likely to threaten the very root of the relationship.

In groups comprising individuals who participate only segmentally, conflict is less likely to be disruptive. Such groups are likely to experience a multiplicity of conflicts. This in itself tends to constitute a check against the breakdown of consensus: the energies of group members are mobilized in many directions and hence will not concentrate on one conflict cutting through the group. Moreover, where occasions for hostility are not permitted to accumulate and conflict is allowed to occur wherever a resolution of tension seems to be indicated, such a conflict is likely to remain focused primarily on the condition which led to its outbreak and not to revive blocked hostility; in this way, the conflict is limited to "the facts of the case."

One may venture to say that multiplicity of conflicts stands in inverse relation to their intensity.

So far we have been dealing with internal social conflict only. At this point we must turn to a consideration of external conflict, for the structure of the group is itself affected by conflicts with other groups in which it engages or which it prepares for. Groups which are engaged in continued struggle tend to lay claim on the total personality involvement of their member so that internal conflict would tend to mobilize all energies and affects of the members. Hence such groups are unlikely to tolerate more than limited departures from the group unity. In such groups there is a tendency to suppress conflict; where it occurs, it leads the group to break up through splits or through forced withdrawal of dissenters.

Groups which are not involved in continued struggle with the outside are less prone to make claims on total personality involvement of the membership and are more likely to exhibit flexibility of structure. The multiple internal conflicts which they tolerate may in turn have an equilibrating and stabilizing impact on the structure.

In flexible social structures, multiple conflicts crisscross each other and thereby prevent basic cleavages along one axis. The multiple group affiliations of individuals makes them participate in various group conflicts so that their total personalities are not involved in any single one of them. Thus segmental participation in a multiplicity of conflicts constitutes a balancing mechanism within the structure.

In loosely structure groups and open societies, conflict, which aims at a resolution of tension between antagonists, is likely to have stabilizing and integrative functions for the relationship. By permitting immediate and direct expression of rival claims, such social systems are able to readjust their structures by eliminating the sources of dissatisfaction. The multiple conflicts which they experience may serve to eliminate the causes for dissociation and to re-establish unity. These systems avail themselves, through the toleration and institutionalization of conflict, of an important stabilizing mechanism.

In addition, conflict within a group frequently helps to revitalize existent norms; or it contributes to the emergence of new norms. In this sense, social conflict is a mechanism for adjustment of norms adequate to new conditions. A flexible society benefits from conflict because such behavior, by helping to create and modify norms, assures its continuance under changed conditions. Such mechanism for readjustment of norms is hardly available to rigid systems: by suppressing conflict, the latter smother a useful warning signal, thereby maximizing the danger of catastrophic breakdown.

Internal conflict can also serve as a means for ascertaining the relative strength of antagonistic interests within the structure, and in this way constitute a mechanism for the maintenance or continual readjustment of the balance of power. Since the outbreak of the conflict indicates a rejection of a previous accommodation between parties, once the respective power of the contenders has been ascertained through conflict, a new equilibrium can be established and the relationship can proceed on this new basis. Consequently, a social structure in which there is room for conflict disposes of an important means for avoiding or redressing conditions of disequilibrium by modifying the terms of power relations.

Conflicts with some produce associations or coalitions with others. Conflicts through such associations or coalitions, by providing a bond between the members, help to reduce social isolation or to unite individuals and groups otherwise unrelated or antagonistic to each other. A social structure in which there can exist a multiplicity of conflicts contains a mechanism for bringing together otherwise isolated, apathetic or mutually hostile parties and for taking them into the field of public social activities. Moreover, such a structure fosters a multiplicity of associations and coalitions, whose diverse purposes crisscross each other, we recall, thereby preventing alliances along one major line of cleavage.

Once groups and associations have been formed through conflict with other groups, such conflict may further serve to maintain boundary lines between them and the surrounding social environment. In this way, social conflict helps to structure the larger social environment by assigning position to the various subgroups within the system and by helping to define the power relations between them.

Not all social systems in which individuals participate segmentally allow the free expression of antagonistic claims. Social systems tolerate or institutionalize conflict to different degrees. There is no society in which any and every antagonistic claim is allowed immediate expression. Societies dispose of mechanisms to channel discontent and hostility while keeping intact the relationship within which antagonism arises. Such mechanisms frequently operate through "safety-valve" institutions which provide substitute objects upon which to displace hostile sentiments as well as means of abreaction of aggressive tendencies.

Safety-valve institutions may serve to maintain both the social structure and the individual's security system, but they are incompletely functional for both of them. They prevent modification of relationships to meet changing conditions and hence the satisfaction they afford the individual can be only partially or momentarily adjustive. The hypothesis has been suggested that the need for safety-valve institutions increases with the rigidity of the social structure, i.e., with the degree to which it disallows direct expression of antagonistic claims.

Safety-valve institutions lead to a displacement of goal in the actor: he need no longer aim at reaching a solution of the unsatisfactory situation, but merely at releasing the tension which arose from it. Where safety-valve institutions provide substitute objects for the displacement of hostility, the conflict itself is channeled away from the original unsatisfactory relationship into one in which the actor's goal is no longer the attainment of specific results, but the release of tension.

PART II
Self–Other Concepts

7.

DEFINITION OF THE SITUATION

THAT THE STUDY of society can never attain the dignity of a science because human behavior is "free," and hence unpredictable, has been a perennial argument of the critics of social science. In an effort to answer this challenge, sociology has responded with two different methodological arguments.

Sociologists within one broad tradition have attempted to show that, no matter what the individual motives may be, it is possible to trace uniformities of behavior in human action. Emile Durkheim pointed out that rates of suicide varied in different types of group structures in relation to the degree of cohesion attained by these groups, and quite irrespective of the particular motives which led individuals to commit suicide. Other investigators have attempted to show that predictable uniformities exist in such diverse fields as birth rates, rates of narcotics addiction, of juvenile delinquency, and the like, which can be profitably investigated without recourse to an analysis of individual motivation.

In the first quarter of this century in the United States and somewhat earlier in Germany, the methodology underlying such studies was countered by an opposing school, which argued that social science deprived itself of its most precious tools if by a self-denying ordinance it abstained from examining the motivational structure of human action. The sociology of a chicken yard, they insisted, could indeed only be undertaken in terms of descriptions of the chicken's behavior, since we are forever barred from understanding the meanings that chickens attach to their activities. But the sociology of human beings could pursue a fundamentally different strategy, since it had the advantage of being able to probe beneath protocols of behavior into the subjective meanings of acting individuals.

This development was stimulated in Germany by such scholars as Wilhelm Dilthey (though certain of its roots can be traced to Hegel, Marx, and even to Vico), but was fully developed as a sociological mode of analysis by Max Weber. It was Weber's contention that the social sciences were concerned with the understanding, as distinct from simple behavioristic reporting, of human action, and that an essential element of the interpretation of human action was the effort to seize upon the subjectively intended meaning of the participants in it. At roughly the same time W. I. Thomas (1863–1947), one of the fathers of American sociology, advanced the theorem that it is essential in our study of man to find out how men define situations in which they find themselves and that "if men define situations as real, they are real in their consequences."

What Weber and Thomas set forth has by now become one of the axioms of sociological research. Stimulated by recent developments in Freudian and non-Freudian social psychology as well as by the trends outlined above, we have come to recognize the fact that men respond to outside stimuli in a selective manner and that such selection is powerfully influenced by the manner in which they define or interpret situations. Anticipatory definitions are likely to have enduring social consequences, even if these definitions seem to an outside observer to be completely devoid of an "objective" truth value. It may be especially relevant in these days to remind ourselves that if men believe in the existence of witches, such beliefs have powerful consequences in political and social relations.

But sociological, as distinct from psychological, analysis of definitions of situations does not rest its case with the study of individual meaning; it attempts to show that intersubjective understanding requires the acquisition of shared meanings. In their analysis of the functions of cultural norms in the rise of group structures, sociologists and anthropologists have emphasized that one of the essential functions of cultural norms is to provide members of a group or society with those shared definitions of the situation without which social living would be impossible.

If the scientific observer is able to penetrate to the typical definitions of the situation prevailing in particular groups, strata, or societies, he is able to make predictions as to the probable response of members of these groups in future situations. Hence the method here outlined, in addition to the method mentioned earlier, serves to validate the contention that sociology is a genuine science.

The further uses of the basic ideas of Weber and Thomas have been extensive and ramified—modern public opinion research, for example, is hardly conceivable without them—but we have limited ourselves to selections from some of the leading social theorists.

Professor Florian Znaniecki was associated with W. I. Thomas in the pioneering study of *The Polish Peasant* (1918–1921) in which the "definition of the situation" approach was first developed. He has since extensively developed the initial methodological approaches contained in that study, and our selection is from one of his major theoretical works. Professor MacIver, one of the masters of contemporary American sociology, has in his turn insisted upon the crucial significance of subjective interpretations, "dynamic assessments," as he calls them, in the understanding of human action. His *Social Causation,* from which we print a selection, may be counted among the very few sophisticated approaches to the field of sociological method to have appeared in the last quarter of a century. Professor Alfred Schuetz, a disciple of the German philosopher Edmund Husserl, whose phenomenological philosophy has deeply marked European social science, attempts in the last selection of this chapter, to combine phenomenological and sociological insights. His work strongly suggests that insistence on "subjective meaning" or "the definition of the situation" will from now on remain an essential feature of sociological theory.

The Definition of the Situation * (*Thomas*)

One of the most important powers gained during the evolution of animal life is the ability to make decisions from within instead of having them imposed from without. Very low forms of life do not make decisions, as we understand this term, but are pushed and pulled by chemical substances, heat, light, etc., much as iron filings are attracted or repelled by a magnet. They do tend to behave properly in given conditions—a group of small crustaceans will flee as in a panic if a bit of strychnia is placed in the basin containing them and will rush toward a drop of beef juice like hogs crowding around swill—but they do this as an expression of organic affinity for the one substance and repugnance for the other, and not as an expression of choice or "free will." There are, so to speak, rules of behavior but these represent a sort of fortunate mechanistic adjustment of the organism to typically recurring situations, and the organism cannot change the rule.

On the other hand, the higher animals, and above all man, have the power of refusing to obey a stimulation which they followed at an earlier time. Response to the earlier stimulation may have had painful consequences and so the rule or habit in this situation is changed. We call this ability the power of inhibition, and it is dependent on the fact that the nervous system carries memories or records of past experiences. At this point the determination of action no longer comes exclusively from outside sources but is located within the organism itself.

Preliminary to any self-determined act of behavior there is always a stage of examination and deliberation which we may call *the definition of the situation*. And actually not only concrete acts are dependent on the definition of the situation, but gradually a whole life-policy and the personality of the individual himself follow from a series of such definitions.

But the child is always born into a group of people among whom all the general types of situation which may arise have already been defined

* Reprinted from *The Unadjusted Girl* by William I. Thomas, pp. 41–44, with permission from The Social Science Research Council.

and corresponding rules of conduct developed, and where he has not the slightest chance of making his definitions and following his wishes without interference. Men have always lived together in groups. Whether mankind has a true herd instinct or whether groups are held together because this has worked out to advantage is of no importance. Certainly the wishes in general are such that they can be satisfied only in a society. But we have only to refer to the criminal code to appreciate the variety of ways in which the wishes of the individual may conflict with the wishes of society. And the criminal code takes no account of the many unsanctioned expressions of the wishes which society attempts to regulate by persuasion and gossip.

There is therefore always a rivalry between the spontaneous definitions of the situation made by the member of an organized society and the definitions which his society has provided for him. The individual tends to a hedonistic selection of activity, pleasure first; and society to a utilitarian selection, safety first. Society wishes its member to be laborious, dependable, regular, sober, orderly, self-sacrificing; while the individual wishes less of this and more of new experience. And organized society seeks also to regulate the conflict and competition inevitable between its members in the pursuit of their wishes. The desire to have wealth, for example, or any other socially sanctioned wish, may not be accomplished at the expense of another member of the society,—by murder, theft, lying, swindling, black mail, etc.

It is in this connection that a moral code arises, which is a set of rules or behavior norms, regulating the expression of the wishes, and which is built up by successive definitions of the situation. In practice the abuse arises first and the rule is made to prevent its recurrence. Morality is thus the generally accepted definition of the situation, whether expressed in public opinion and the unwritten law, in a formal legal code, or in religious commandments and prohibitions.

The family is the smallest social unit and the primary defining agency. As soon as the child has free motion and begins to pull, tear, pry, meddle, and prowl, the parents begin to define the situation through speech and other signs and pressures: "Be quiet", "Sit up straight", "Blow your nose", "Wash your face", "Mind your mother", "Be kind to sister", etc. This is the real significance of Wordsworth's phrase, "Shades of the prison house begin to close upon the growing child." His wishes and activities begin to be inhibited, and gradually, by definitions within the family, by playmates, in the school, in the Sunday school, in the community, through reading, by formal instruction, by informal signs of approval and disapproval, the growing member learns the code of his society.

In addition to the family we have the community as a defining agency. At present the community is so weak and vague that it gives us no idea of the former power of the local group in regulating behavior. Originally the community was practically the whole world of its members. It was composed of families related by blood and marriage and was not so large that all the members could not come together; it was a face-to-face group. I asked a Polish peasant what was the extent of an "*okolica*" or neighborhood—how far it reached. "It reaches," he said, "as far as the report of a man reaches— as far as a man is talked about." And it was in communities of this kind that the moral code which we now recognize as valid originated. The customs of the community are "folkways", and both state and church have in their more formal codes mainly recognized and incorporated these folkways.

The typical community is vanishing and it would be neither possible nor desirable to restore it in its old form. It does not correspond with the present direction of social evolution and it would now be a distressing condition in which to live. But in the immediacy of relationships and the participation of everybody in everything, it represents an element which we have lost and which we shall probably have to restore in some form of coöperation in order to secure a balanced and normal society,—some arrangement corresponding with human nature.

Subjective Meaning in the Social Situation I * (*Weber*)

1. Sociology (in the sense in which this highly ambiguous word is used here) is a science which attempts the interpretive understanding of social action in order thereby to arrive at a causal explanation of its course and effects. In 'action' is included all human behaviour when and in so far as the acting individual attaches a subjective meaning to it. Action in this sense may be either overt or purely inward or subjective; it may consist of positive intervention in a situation, or of deliberately refraining from such intervention or passively acquiescing in the situation. Action is social in so far as, by virtue of the subjective meaning attached to it by the acting individual (or individuals), it takes account of the behaviour of others and is thereby oriented in its course.[1]

* Reprinted from *Max Weber: The Theory of Social and Economic Organization*, translated by A. M. Henderson and Talcott Parsons, edited by Talcott Parsons, pp. 88–100, with permission of The Free Press, Glencoe, Ill., and William Hodge and Company Limited, London.

(A) THE METHODOLOGICAL FOUNDATIONS OF SOCIOLOGY [2]

1. 'Meaning' may be of two kinds. The term may refer first to the actual existing meaning in the given concrete case of a particular actor, or to the average or approximate meaning attributable to a given plurality of actors; or secondly to the theoretically conceived *pure type*[3] of subjective meaning attributed to the hypothetical actor or actors in a given type of action. In no case does it refer to an objectively 'correct' meaning or one which is 'true' in some metaphysical sense. It is this which distinguishes the empirical sciences of action, such as sociology and history, from the dogmatic disciplines in that area, such as jurisprudence, logic, ethics, and esthetics, which seek to ascertain the 'true' and 'valid' meanings associated with the objects of their investigation.

2. The line between meaningful action and merely reactive behaviour to which no subjective meaning is attached, cannot be sharply drawn empirically. A very considerable part of all sociologically relevant behaviour, especially purely traditional behaviour, is marginal between the two. In the case of many psychophysical processes, meaningful, i.e. subjectively understandable, action is not to be found at all; in others it is discernible only by the expert psychologist. Many mystical experiences which cannot be adequately communicated in words are, for a person who is not susceptible to such experiences, not fully understandable. At the same time the ability to imagine one's self performing a similar action is not a necessary prerequisite to understanding; 'one need not have been Caesar in order to understand Caesar.' For the verifiable accuracy[4] of interpretation of the meaning of a phenomenon, it is a great help to be able to put one's self imaginatively in the place of the actor and thus sympathetically to participate in his experiences, but this is not an essential condition of meaningful interpretation. Understandable and non-understandable components of a process are often intermingled and bound up together.

3. All interpretation of meaning, like all scientific observation, strives for clarity and verifiable accuracy of insight and comprehension (*Evidenz*). The basis for certainty in understanding can be either rational, which can be further subdivided into logical and mathematical, or it can be of an emotionally empathic or artistically appreciative quality. In the sphere of action things are rationally evident chiefly when we attain a completely clear intellectual grasp of the action-elements in their intended context of meaning. Empathic or appreciative accuracy is attained when, through sympathetic participation, we can adequately grasp the emotional context

in which the action took place. The highest degree of rational understanding is attained in cases involving the meanings of logically or mathematically related propositions; their meaning may be immediately and unambiguously intelligible. We have a perfectly clear understanding of what it means when somebody employs the proposition $2 \times 2 = 4$ or the Pythagorean theorem in reasoning or argument, or when someone correctly carries out a logical train of reasoning according to our accepted modes of thinking. In the same way we also understand what a person is doing when he tries to achieve certain ends by choosing appropriate means on the basis of the facts of the situation as experience has accustomed us to interpret them. Such an interpretation of this type of rationally purposeful action possesses, for the understanding of the choice of means, the highest degree of verifiable certainty. With a lower degree of certainty, which is, however, adequate for most purposes of explanation, we are able to understand errors, including confusion of problems of the sort that we ourselves are liable to, or the origin of which we can detect by sympathetic self-analysis.

On the other hand, many ultimate ends or values toward which experience shows that human action may be oriented, often cannot be understood completely, though sometimes we are able to grasp them intellectually. The more radically they differ from our own ultimate values, however, the more difficult it is for us to make them understandable by imaginatively participating in them. Depending upon the circumstances of the particular case we must be content either with a purely intellectual understanding of such values or when even that fails, sometimes we must simply accept them as given data. Then we can try to understand the action motivated by them on the basis of whatever opportunities for approximate emotional and intellectual interpretation seem to be available at different points in its course. These difficulties apply, for instance, for people not susceptible to the relevant values, to many unusual acts of religious and charitable zeal; also certain kinds of extreme rationalistic fanaticism of the type involved in some forms of the ideology of the 'rights of man' are in a similar position for people who radically repudiate such points of view.

The more we ourselves are susceptible to them the more readily can we imaginatively participate in such emotional reactions as anxiety, anger, ambition, envy, jealousy, love, enthusiasm, pride, vengefulness, loyalty, devotion, and appetites of all sorts, and thereby understand the irrational conduct which grows out of them. Such conduct is 'irrational,' that is, from the point of view of the rational pursuit of a given end. Even when such emotions are found in a degree of intensity of which the observer himself is completely incapable, he can still have a significant degree of emotional understanding of their meaning and can interpret intellectually their influence on the course of action and the selection of means.

For the purposes of a typological scientific analysis it is convenient to treat all irrational, affectually determined elements of behaviour as factors of deviation from a conceptually pure type of rational action. For example a panic on the stock exchange can be most conveniently analysed by attempting to determine first what the course of action would have been if it had not been influenced by irrational affects; it is then possible to introduce the irrational components as accounting for the observed deviations from this hypothetical course. Similarly, in analysing a political or military campaign it is convenient to determine in the first place what would have been a rational course, given the ends of the participants and adequate knowledge of all the circumstances. Only in this way is it possible to assess the causal significance of irrational factors as accounting for the deviations from this type. The construction of a purely rational course of action in such cases serves the sociologist as a type ('ideal type') which has the merit of clear understandability and lack of ambiguity. By comparison with this it is possible to understand the ways in which actual action is influenced by irrational factors of all sorts, such as affects[5] and errors, in that they account for the deviation from the line of conduct which would be expected on the hypothesis that the action were purely rational.

Only in this respect and for these reasons of methodological convenience, is the method of sociology 'rationalistic.' It is naturally not legitimate to interpret this procedure as involving a 'rationalistic bias' of sociology, but only as a methodological device. It certainly does not involve a belief in the actual predominance of rational elements in human life, for on the question of how far this predominance does or does not exist, nothing whatever has been said. That there is, however, a danger of rationalistic interpretations where they are out of place naturally cannot be denied. All experience unfortunately confirms the existence of this danger.

4. In all the sciences of human action, account must be taken of processes and phenomena which are devoid of subjective meaning,[6] in the role of stimuli, results, favouring or hindering circumstances. To be devoid of meaning is not identical with being lifeless or non-human; every artifact, such as for example a machine, can be understood only in terms of the meaning which its production and use have had or will have for human action; a meaning which may derive from a relation to exceedingly various purposes. Without reference to this meaning such an object remains wholly unintelligible.[7] That which is intelligible or understandable about it is thus its relation to human action in the role either of means or of end; a relation

of which the actor or actors can be said to have been aware and to which their action has been oriented. Only in terms of such categories is it possible to 'understand' objects of this kind. On the other hand processes or conditions, whether they are animate or inanimate, human or non-human, are in the present sense devoid of meaning in so far as they cannot be related to an intended purpose. That is to say they are devoid of meaning if they cannot be related to action in the role of means or ends but constitute only the stimulus, the favouring or hindering circumstances.[8] It may be that the incursion of the Dollart at the beginning of the twelfth century[9] had historical significance as a stimulus to the beginning of certain migrations of considerable importance. Human mortality, indeed the organic life cycle generally from the helplessness of infancy to that of old age, is naturally of the very greatest sociological importance through the various ways in which human action has been oriented to these facts. To still another category of facts devoid of meaning belong certain psychic or psychophysical phenomena such as fatigue, habituation, memory, etc.; also certain typical states of euphoria under some conditions of ascetic mortification; finally, typical variations in the reactions of individuals according to reaction-time, precision, and other modes. But in the last analysis the same principle applies to these as to other phenomena which are devoid of meaning. Both the actor and the sociologist must accept them as data to be taken into account.

It is altogether possible that future research may be able to discover non-understandable uniformities underlying what has appeared to be specifically meaningful action, though little has been accomplished in this direction thus far. Thus, for example, differences in hereditary biological constitution, as of 'races,' would have to be treated by sociology as given data in the same way as the physiological facts of the need of nutrition or the effect of senescence on action. This would be the case if, and in so far as, we had statistically conclusive proof of their influence on sociologically relevant behaviour. The recognition of the causal significance of such factors would naturally not in the least alter the specific task of sociological analysis or of that of the other sciences of action, which is the interpretation of action in terms of its subjective meaning. The effect would be only to introduce certain non-understandable data of the same order as others which, it has been noted above, are already present, into the complex of subjectively understandable motivation at certain points. Thus it may come to be known that there are typical relations between the frequency of certain types of teleological orientation of action or of the degree of certain kinds of rationality and the cephalic index or skin colour or any other biologically inherited characteristic.

5. Understanding may be of two kinds: the first is the direct observational understanding[10] of the subjective meaning of a given act as such, including verbal utterances. We thus understand by direct observation, in this sense, the meaning of the proposition $2 \times 2 = 4$ when we hear or read it. This is a case of the direct rational understanding of ideas. We also understand an outbreak of anger as manifested by facial expression, exclamations or irrational movements. This is direct observational understanding of irrational emotional reactions. We can understand in a similar observational way the action of a woodcutter or of somebody who reaches for the knob to shut a door or who aims a gun at an animal. This is rational observational understanding of actions.

Understanding may, however, be of another sort, namely explanatory understanding. Thus we understand in terms of *motive* the meaning an actor attaches to the proposition twice two equals four, when he states it or writes it down, in that we understand what makes him do this at precisely this moment and in these circumstances. Understanding in this sense is attained if we know that he is engaged in balancing a ledger or in making a scientific demonstration, or is engaged in some other task of which this particular act would be an appropriate part. This is rational understanding of motivation, which consists in placing the act in an intelligible and more inclusive context of meaning.[11] Thus we understand the chopping of wood or aiming of a gun in terms of motive in addition to direct observation if we know that the woodchopper is working for a wage or is chopping a supply of firewood for his own use or possibly is doing it for recreation. But he might also be 'working off' a fit of rage, an irrational case. Similarly we understand the motive of a person aiming a gun if we know that he has been commanded to shoot as a member of a firing squad, that he is fighting against an enemy, or that he is doing it for revenge. The last is affectually determined and thus in a certain sense irrational. Finally we have a motivational understanding of the outburst of anger if we know that it has been provoked by jealousy, injured pride, or an insult. The last examples are all affectually determined and hence derived from irrational motives. In all the above cases the particular act has been placed in an understandable sequence of motivation, the understanding of which can be treated as an explanation of the actual course of behaviour. Thus for a science which is concerned with the subjective meaning of action, explanation requires a grasp of the complex of meaning in which an actual course of understandable action thus interpreted belongs.[12] In all such cases, even where the processes are largely affectual, the subjective meaning of the action, including that also of the relevant meaning complexes, will be called the 'intended' meaning.[13] This involves a departure from ordinary usage, which speaks of intention in this sense only in the case of rationally purposive action.

6. In all these cases understanding involves the interpretive grasp of the meaning present in one of the following contexts: (a) as in the historical approach, the actually intended meaning for concrete individual action; or (b) as in cases of sociological mass phenomena the average of, or an approximation to, the actually intended meaning; or (c) the meaning appropriate to a scientifically formulated pure type (an ideal type) of a common phenomenon. The concepts and 'laws' of pure economic theory are examples of this kind of ideal type. They state what course a given type of human action would take if it were strictly rational, unaffected by errors or emotional factors and if, furthermore, it were completely and unequivocally directed to a single end, the maximization of economic advantage. In reality, action takes exactly this course only in unusual cases, as sometimes on the stock exchange; and even then there is usually only an approximation to the ideal type.[14]

Every interpretation attempts to attain clarity and certainty, but no matter how clear an interpretation as such appears to be from the point of view of meaning, it cannot on this account alone claim to be the causally valid interpretation. On this level it must remain only a peculiarly plausible hypothesis. In the first place the 'conscious motives' may well, even to the actor himself, conceal the various 'motives' and 'repressions' which constitute the real driving force of his action. Thus in such cases even subjectively honest self-analysis has only a relative value. Then it is the task of the sociologist to be aware of this motivational situation and to describe and analyse it, even though it has not actually been concretely part of the conscious 'intention' of the actor; possibly not at all, at least not fully. This is a borderline case of the interpretation of meaning. Secondly, processes of action which seem to an observer to be the same or similar may fit into exceedingly various complexes of motive in the case of the actual actor. Then even though the situations appear superficially to be very similar we must actually understand them or interpret them as very different, perhaps, in terms of meaning, directly opposed.[15] Third, the actors in any given situation are often subject to opposing and conflicting impulses, all of which we are able to understand. In a large number of cases we know from experience it is not possible to arrive at even an approximate estimate of the relative strength of conflicting motives and very often we cannot be certain of our interpretation. Only the actual outcome of the conflict gives a solid basis of judgment.

More generally, verification of subjective interpretation by comparison with the concrete course of events is, as in the case of all hypotheses, indispensable. Unfortunately this type of verification is feasible with relative accuracy only in the few very special cases susceptible of psychological experimentation. The approach to a satisfactory degree of accuracy is exceedingly various, even in the limited number of cases of mass phenomena which can be statistically described and unambiguously interpreted. For the rest there remains only the possibility of comparing the largest possible number of historical or contemporary processes which, while otherwise similar, differ in the one decisive point of their relation to the particular motive or factor the role of which is being investigated. This is a fundamental task of comparative sociology. Often, unfortunately, there is available only the dangerous and uncertain procedure of the 'imaginary experiment' which consists in thinking away certain elements of a chain of motivation and working out the course of action which would then probably ensue, thus arriving at a causal judgment.[16]

For example, the generalization called Gresham's Law is a rationally clear interpretation of human action under certain conditions and under the assumption that it will follow a purely rational course. How far any actual course of action corresponds to this can be verified only by the available statistical evidence for the actual disappearance of under-valued monetary units from circulation. In this case our information serves to demonstrate a high degree of accuracy. The facts of experience were known before the generalization, which was formulated afterwards; but without this successful interpretation our need for causal understanding would evidently be left unsatisfied. On the other hand, without the demonstration that what can here be assumed to be a theoretically adequate interpretation also is in some degree relevant to an actual course of action, a 'law,' no matter how fully demonstrated theoretically, would be worthless for the understanding of action in the real world. In this case the correspondence between the theoretical interpretation of motivation and its empirical verification is entirely satisfactory and the cases are numerous enough so that verification can be considered established. But to take another example, Eduard Meyer has advanced an ingenious theory of the causal significance of the battles of Marathon, Salamis, and Platea for the development of the cultural peculiarities of Greek, and hence, more generally, Western, civilization.[17] This is derived from a meaningful interpretation of certain symptomatic facts having to do with the attitudes of the Greek oracles and prophets towards the Persians. It can only be directly verified by reference to the examples of the conduct of the Persians in cases where they were victorious, as in Jerusalem, Egypt, and Asia Minor, and even this verification must neces-

sarily remain unsatisfactory in certain respects. The striking rational plausi-
bility of the hypothesis must here necessarily be relied on as a support. In
very many cases of historical interpretation which seem highly plausible,
however, there is not even a possibility of the order of verification which was
feasible in this case. Where this is true the interpretation must necessarily
remain a hypothesis.

7. A motive is a complex of subjective meaning which seems to the
actor himself or to the observer an adequate ground for the conduct in
question. We apply the term 'adequacy on the level of meaning' [18] to the
subjective interpretation of a coherent course of conduct when and in so
far as, according to our habitual modes of thought and feeling, its component
parts taken in their mutual relation are recognized to constitute a 'typical'
complex of meaning. It is more common to say 'correct.' The interpretation
of a sequence of events will on the other hand be called *causally* adequate
in so far as, according to established generalizations from experience, there
is a probability that it will always actually occur in the same way. An example of adequacy on the level of meaning in this sense is what is, according
to our current norms of calculation or thinking, the correct solution of an
arithmetical problem. On the other hand, a causally adequate interpretation
of the same phenomenon would concern the statistical probability that,
according to verified generalizations from experience, there would be a correct or an erroneous solution of the same problem. This also refers to currently accepted norms but includes taking account of typical errors or of
typical confusions. Thus causal explanation depends on being able to determine that there is a probability, which in the rare ideal case can be
numerically stated, but is always in some sense calculable, that a given
observable event (overt or subjective) will be followed or accompanied by
another event.

A correct causal interpretation of a concrete course of action is arrived
at when the overt action and the motives have both been correctly apprehended and at the same time their relation has become meaningfully comprehensible. A correct causal interpretation of typical action means that the
process which is claimed to be typical is shown to be both adequately grasped
on the level of meaning and at the same time the interpretation is to some
degree causally adequate. If adequacy in respect to meaning is lacking, then
no matter how high the degree of uniformity and how precisely its probability
can be numerically determined, it is still an incomprehensible statistical
probability, whether dealing with overt or subjective processes. On the other
hand, even the most perfect adequacy on the level of meaning has causal
significance from a sociological point of view only in so far as there is some

kind of proof for the existence of a probability[19] that action in fact normally takes the course which has been held to be meaningful. For this there must be some degree of determinable frequency of approximation to an average or a pure type.

Statistical uniformities constitute understandable types of action in the sense of this discussion, and thus constitute 'sociological generalizations,' only when they can be regarded as manifestations of the understandable subjective meaning of a course of social action. Conversely, formulations of a rational course of subjectively understandable action constitute sociological types of empirical process only when they can be empirically observed with a significant degree of approximation. It is unfortunately by no means the case that the actual likelihood of the occurrence of a given course of overt action is always directly proportional to the clarity of subjective interpretation. There are statistics of processes devoid of meaning such as death rates, phenomena of fatigue, the production rate of machines, the amount of rainfall, in exactly the same sense as there are statistics of meaningful phenomena. But only when the phenomena are meaningful is it convenient to speak of sociological statistics. Examples are such cases as crime rates, occupational distributions, price statistics, and statistics of crop acreage. Naturally there are many cases where both components are involved, as in crop statistics.

REFERENCES

1. In this series of definitions Weber employs several important terms which need discussion. In addition to *Verstehen,* which has already been commented upon, there are four important ones: *Deuten, Sinn, Handeln,* and *Verhalten. Deuten* has generally been translated as 'interpret.' As used by Weber in this context it refers to the interpretation of subjective states of mind and the meanings which can be imputed as intended by an actor. Any other meaning of the word 'interpretation' is irrelevant to Weber's discussion. The term *Sinn* has generally been translated as 'meaning'; and its variations, particularly the corresponding adjectives, *sinnhaft, sinnvoll, sinnfremd,* have been dealt with by appropriately modifying the term meaning. The reference here again is always to features of the content of subjective states of mind or of symbolic systems which are ultimately referable to such states of mind.

    The terms *Handeln* and *Verhalten* are directly related. *Verhalten* is the broader term referring to any mode of behaviour of human individuals, regardless of the frame of reference in terms of which it is analysed. 'Behaviour' has seemed to be the most appropriate English equivalent. *Handeln,* on the other hand, refers to the concrete phenomenon of human behaviour only in so far as it is capable of 'understanding,' in Weber's technical sense, in terms of subjective categories. The most appropriate English equivalent has seemed to be 'action.' This corresponds to the editor's usage in *The Structure of Social Action* and would seem to be fairly well established. 'Conduct' is also closely similar and has sometimes been used. *Deuten, Verstehen,* and *Sinn* are thus applicable to human behaviour only in so far as it constitutes action or conduct in this specific sense.—Ed.

2. Weber's text is organized in a somewhat unusual manner. He lays down certain fundamental definitions and then proceeds to comment upon them. The definitions themselves are in the original printed in large type, the subsidiary comments in

smaller type. For the purposes of this translation it has not seemed best to make a distinction in type form, but the reader should be aware that the numbered paragraphs which follow a definition or group of them are in the nature of comments, rather than the continuous development of a general line of argument. This fact accounts for what is sometimes a relatively fragmentary character of the development and for the abrupt transition from one subject to another. Weber apparently did not intend this material to be 'read' in the ordinary sense, but rather to serve as a reference work for the clarification and systematization of theoretical concepts and their implications. While the comments under most of the definitions are relatively brief, under the definitions of Sociology and of Social Action, Weber wrote what is essentially a methodological essay. This makes sec. 1 out of proportion to the other sections of this and the following chapters. It has, however, seemed best to retain Weber's own plan for the subdivision of the material.—Ed.

3. Weber means by 'pure type' what he himself generally called and what has come to be known in the literature about his methodology as the 'ideal type.' The reader may be referred for general orientation to Weber's own essay (to which he himself refers below), *Die Objektivität sozialwissenschaftlicher Erkenntnis*; to two works of Dr. Alexander von Schelting, 'Die logische Theorie der historischen Kulturwissenschaften von Max Weber' (*Archiv fuer Sozialwissenschaft*, vol. xlix), and *Max Webers Wissenschaftslehre*; and to the editor's *Structure of Social Action*, chap. xvi. A somewhat different interpretation is given in Theodore Abel, *Systematic Sociology in Germany*, chap. iv.—Ed.

4. This is an imperfect rendering of the German term *Evidenz*, for which, unfortunately, there is no good English equivalent. It has hence been rendered in a number of different ways, varying with the particular context in which it occurs. The primary meaning refers to the basis on which a scientist or thinker becomes satisfied of the certainty or acceptability of a proposition. As Weber himself points out, there are two primary aspects of this. On the one hand a conclusion can be 'seen' to follow from given premises by virtue of logical, mathematical, or possibly other modes of meaningful relation. In this sense one 'sees' the solution of an arithmetical problem or the correctness of the proof of a geometrical theorem. The other aspect is concerned with empirical observation. If an act of observation is competently performed, in a similar sense one 'sees' the truth of the relevant descriptive proposition. The term *Evidenz* does not refer to the process of observing, but to the quality of its result, by virtue of which the observer feels justified in affirming a given statement. Hence 'certainty' has seemed a suitable translation in some contexts, 'clarity' in others, 'accuracy' in still others. The term 'intuition' is not usable because it refers to the process rather than to the result.—Ed.

5. A term now much used in psychological literature, especially that of psychoanalysis. It is roughly equivalent to 'emotion' but more precise.—Ed.

6. The German term is *sinnfremd*. This should not be translated by 'meaningless,' but interpreted in the technical context of Weber's use of *Verstehen* and *Sinndeutung*. The essential criterion is the impossibility of placing the object in question in a complex of relations on the meaningful level.—Ed.

7. *Unverstehbar*.

8. Surely this passage states too narrow a conception of the scope of meaningful interpretation. It is certainly not *only* in terms such as those of the rational means-end schema, that it is possible to make action understandable in terms of subjective categories. This probably can actually be called a source of rationalistic bias in Weber's work. In practice he does not adhere at all rigorously to this methodological position. For certain possibilities in this broader field, see the editor's *Structure of Social Action*, chaps. vi and xi.—Ed.

9. A gulf of the North Sea which broke through the Netherlands coast, flooding an area.—Ed.

10. Weber here uses the term *aktuelles Verstehen*, which he contrasts with *erklärendes Verstehen*. The latter he also refers to as *motivationsmaessig*. 'Aktuell' in this context has been translated as 'observational.' It is clear from Weber's discussion that the primary criterion is the possibility of deriving the meaning of an act or symbolic

expression from immediate observation without reference to any broader context. In *erklärendes Verstehen,* on the other hand, the particular act must be placed in a broader context of meaning involving facts which cannot be derived from immediate observation of a particular act or expression.—Ed.

11. The German term is *Sinnzusammenhang.* It refers to a plurality of elements which form a coherent whole on the level of meaning. There are several possible modes of meaningful relation between such elements, such as logical consistency, the esthetic harmony of a style, or the appropriateness of means to an end. In any case, however, a *Sinnzusammenhang* must be distinguished from a system of elements which are causally interdependent. There seems to be no single English term or phrase which is always adequate. According to variations in the context, 'context of meaning,' 'complex of meaning,' and sometimes 'meaningful system' have been employed.—Ed.

12. On the significance of this type of explanation for causal relationship. See para. 6, pp. 96 ff. below in the present section.

13. The German is *gemeinter Sinn.* Weber departs from ordinary usage not only in broadening the meaning of this conception. As he states at the end of the present methodological discussion, he does not restrict the use of this concept to cases where a clear self-conscious awareness of such meaning can be reasonably attributed to every individual actor. Essentially, what Weber is doing is to formulate an operational concept. The question is not whether in a sense obvious to the ordinary person such an intended meaning 'really exists,' but whether the concept is capable of providing a logical framework within which scientifically important observations can be made. The test of validity of the observations is not whether their object is immediately clear to common sense, but whether the results of these technical observations can be satisfactorily organized and related to those of others in a systematic body of knowledge.—Ed.

14. The scientific functions of such construction have been discussed in the author's article in the *Archiv für Sozialwissenschaft,* vol. xix, p. 64 ff.

15. Simmel, in his *Probleme der Geschichtsphilosophie,* gives a number of examples.

16. The above passage is an exceedingly compact statement of Weber's theory of the logical conditions of proof of causal relationship. He developed this most fully in his essay *Die Objektivität sozialwissenschaftlicher Erkenntnis,* op. cit. It is also discussed in certain of the other essays which have been collected in the volume, *Gesammelte Aufsätze zur Wissenschaftslehre.* The best and fullest secondary discussion is to be found in Von Schelting's book, *Max Webers Wissenschaftslehre.* There is a briefer discussion in chap. xvi of the editor's *Structure of Social Action.*—Ed.

17. See Eduard Meyer, *Geschichte des Altertums,* Stuttgart, 1901, vol. iii, pp. 420, 444 ff.

18. The expression *sinnhafte Adäquanz* is one of the most difficult of Weber's technical terms to translate. In most places the cumbrous phrase 'adequacy on the level of meaning' has had to be employed. It should be clear from the progress of the discussion that what Weber refers to is a satisfying level of knowledge for the particular purposes of the subjective state of mind of the actor or actors. He is, however, careful to point out that *causal* adequacy involves in addition to this a satisfactory correspondence between the results of observations from the subjective point of view and from the objective; that is, observations of the overt course of action which can be described without reference to the state of mind of the actor. For a discussion of the methodological problem involved here, see *Structure of Social Action,* chaps. ii and v.—Ed.

19. This is the first occurrence in Weber's text of the term *Chance* which he uses very frequently. It is here translated by 'probability,' because he uses it as interchangeable with *Wahrscheinlichkeit.* As the term 'probability' is used in a technical mathematical and statistical sense, however, it implies the possibility of numerical statement. In most of the cases where Weber uses *Chance* this is out of the question. It is, however, possible to speak in terms of higher and lower degrees of probability. To avoid confusion with the technical mathematical concept, the term 'likelihood' will often be used in the translation. It is by means of this concept that Weber, in a highly ingenious way, has bridged the gap between the interpretation of meaning and the inevitably more complex facts of overt action.—Ed.

Subjective Meaning in the Social Situation II *(Znaniecki)

The primary empirical evidence about any cultural human action is the experience of the agent himself, supplemented by the experience of those who react to his action, reproduce it, or participate in it. The action of speaking a sentence, writing a poem, making a horseshoe, depositing money, proposing to a girl, electing an official, performing a religious rite, as empirical datum, is what it is in the experience of the speaker and his listeners, the poet and his readers, the blacksmith and the owner of the horse to be shod, the depositor and the banker, the proposing suitor and the courted girl, the voters and the official whom they elect, the religious believers who participate in the ritual. The scientist who wants to study these actions inductively must take them as they are in the human experience of those agents and reagents; they are his empirical data inasmuch and because they are theirs. I have expressed this elsewhere by saying that such data possess for the student *a humanistic coefficient*. The humanistic coefficient distinguishes cultural data from natural data, which the student assumes to be independent of the experience of human agents.

Every student of culture takes his data with a humanistic coefficient. The philologist studies a language as experienced by the people who speak it and understand it; the economist studies money and the active use of money as experienced by the people who use it; the student of art investigates actions of painting, composing or playing music, writing or reading a poem, as experienced by the artists and those aesthetically interested in their work; the political scientist studies elections as actively experienced by the electors, the politicians, and the candidates. There are various well-known techniques of finding out how other people experience the data which the student investigates: the investigator himself repeats, reproduces fully or vicariously, participates, observes, and supplements the direct information thus gained by whatever other people can tell him about their experiences. His data become finally as reliable as any data can be: nobody can doubt the data which a good philologist collects about speaking a language, or a good economist's data about the functioning of a bank, or a good art student's data about the work of artists.

Now, the orthodox behaviorist rejects this primary empirical evidence as a basis for inductive research. He does this first in studying the behavior

---

* Reprinted from *Social Actions* by Florian Znaniecki, pp. 11–17, with permission of the publisher, Rinehart & Company, Inc. Copyright, 1936, by Farrar & Rinehart, Inc.

of animals and infants, for obvious reasons: as a culturally educated observer, he cannot adequately reproduce their active experiences, nor can those experiences be made secondarily accessible to him by verbal communication. Moreover, the behavior itself at this stage shows to the observer such uniformities and causal relationships as to make the evidence of the agent's experience comparatively unimportant for the establishment of a number of valid theoretic generalizations.

When, however, the behaviorist continues to neglect this evidence in his approach to human activities at later stages of evolution, in spite of its being there fully accessible to him, and in spite of the fact that there are already in the various sciences of culture numerous valid inductive generalizations based upon this evidence, his attitude can be only explained, but not justified, partly by a desire to extend his theories beyond their original range at the cost of very little effort—which can be achieved most easily by avoiding the check of this new evidence; partly by the fear of introducing with the agent's "conscious" experience the old "mind" or "soul." Behavioristic studies do not take the gestures and words used by the agent with reference to the agent's own empirical reality as he experiences it, but reinterpret those words and gestures with reference to the agent's environment as the behavioristic observer views it. We shall have several occasions in later chapters to see how this metaphysical bias revenges itself in obstructing the progress of scientific analysis and generalization. Here we must mention only two essential characteristics of active human experiences which the orthodox behaviorist is prevented by this bias from taking into consideration.

The first of these characteristics belongs to all the experiences of human agents: it is the intrinsic objective meaningfulness of every datum with which the agent deals. Behaviorism reduces the problem of meaning to the meaning of symbols. But for the human agent not only symbols have a meaning, but every datum of his experience in which he is actively interested; every datum stands not only for itself, but for other data which it suggests. At an early stage of mental development this meaning is connected with the possibility of organic experiences suggested by the object; thus, food suggests certain experiences of the organs used in eating and digesting. At this stage it is still possible to substitute for it the concept of "incipient behavior." But gradually the meaning expands, includes suggestions of objects outside the organism, and becomes irreducible—even indirectly—to any definite incipient behavior. Steps heard in the next room to the hungry infant may indirectly mean the approach of food and provoke definite organic responses, but to the grown-up they mean the approach of a person toward whom the possible range of attitudes is almost unlimited. A painting suggests, on the one hand, a fragment of nature or a historical event which we never have and never can experience directly; on the other hand, a multiplicity of paintings in similar or different styles, in comparison with which we define its aesthetic characters.

No object as experienced by an active human individual can be defined merely by its sensory content, for on its meaning rather than on its sensory contact depends its practical significance for human activity. Not because of what it "is" as a natural datum, but because of what it "means" as a humanistic, cultural datum, does an object of activity appear to the agent as "useful" or "harmful," "good" or "bad," "beautiful" or "ugly," "pleasant" or "unpleasant." Since all meaningful objects are potential objects of activity and have a practical significance in somebody's experience, I have for twenty-five years been using the term *values* to distinguish logically meaningful objects as given to an agent from *things*, meaningless objects investigated by a student who takes them not as they are given to agents, but as they are supposed to exist "in themselves," as parts of nature. I call the *axiological significance* of a value that practical significance which it acquires when it is appreciated positively or negatively with reference to other values as a possible object of activity.

The second essential point that behaviorism leaves out of consideration in studying human actions is the existence in the experience of human agents of objects which are not only meaningful, but partly—often almost completely—*non-material* in content and irreducible to sensory perception. Such objects are, for instance, myths and other religious entities, political institutions, contents of literary works, scientific and philosophic concepts. Many words in civilized languages are not used to indicate objects given in sensory experience, but precisely to symbolize non-material, "spiritual" objects, to stabilize and communicate their contents.

The student of actions need not engage in philosophic speculation as to the "true essence" of these objects: in fact, it will be safest for him as a scientist to refrain from such speculations, whether his inclination be toward a radical Platonic "realism," affirming the absolute priority of a non-sensual world, or an equally radical "nominalism," reducing non-sensual objects to infinitely complex combinations of sensory data, or toward a more moderate position, like the "conceptualism" prevailing from the end of the Middle Ages to the end of the last century, or the sociologism of Durkheim's "collective representations."

He must be satisfied with the simple and obvious fact that human agents accept such objects as real and meaningful, ascribe to them a positive or a negative practical significance, are influenced by them and try to influence them, produce and reproduce them, cooperate and fight about them. Indeed, many of their cultural actions would never be performed, if such objects did not exist in their experience and were not regarded by them as real, though entirely different from the sensory data of their natural environment.

For the student of social actions this is a very important point. The primary objects of social actions are other human beings whom the agent tries to influence. This, as we have already said, is what distinguishes at first glance social actions from other actions such as technical production, economic consumption, aesthetic reproduction and creation, religious sanctification and purification, scientific thinking about nature—which do not bear upon human beings, but upon other objects, material or spiritual. We call therefore human beings, as objects of actions, *primary social values*. And a human being, as he appears to the agent for whom he is a social value, is not reducible to data of the agent's sensory experience. He is indeed a body, but he is also "something else"—"a conscious being," a being who has certain capacities and dispositions commonly called "psychological."

Now, it must be clearly understood that we, the sociologists, need not accept as "true" any ideas human agents may have about the "consciousness," "minds" or "souls," of those human beings with whom they deal actively as social values. From the scientific point of view, all we know and ever can know about human "consciousness" is the simple and obvious fact that other people, like ourselves, experience data and perform activities. In this limited and purely formal sense, we can say that every human individual is a "conscious subject," an "experiencing agent," provided we are aware that our task as scientists is not to speculate, as the metaphysicians with their own special methods do, about what conscious subjects "really are," whether their capacity to experience and to act is rooted in a "substance," a "mind," a "soul," an "organism," a "nervous system," or in a "function," an *"actus purus,"* a "transcendental ego," a specific kind of "energy," or what not. Ours is simply and unpretentiously to investigate the data which conscious agents experience and the activities which they perform.

But a "social agent," i.e., an agent who deals with a human being as a social value, is not a scientific sociologist: he is interested in this being not theoretically, but practically. And from his practical point of view the fact that this human being can experience and perform activities, just as the agent himself, appears as an exceedingly important, real characteristic of this human being, as essential as the fact that he has a body, or even more so. For there may be human beings whom a social agent never has experienced as bodies, whose bodily characteristics do not interest him, and yet whom he tries to influence as social values, and from whom he expects reactions—as when he mails a written request to a firm, an office, or a board of directors whose very names as individuals are unknown to him.

In so far, now, as social values appear to the agent to be "conscious realities," having a mental as well as a physical existence, they are to him values with a content partly material (like technical instruments) and partly non-material, spiritual (like myths, novels, or scientific concepts). This non-material content may predominate completely over the material content: thus, an institution like the treasury of a state is for the citizens primarily a number of active "minds" (if not a single "collective mind"), that may and do, if necessary, utilize human bodies, e.g., the bodies of policemen, to coerce citizens into paying taxes, but whose own bodily composition is of no importance to the tax-payer as compared with their "mental" capacities and dispositions.

It is impossible to take into account the empirical variety of social actions and to explain their changes, unless we realize this fundamental character of social values as they appear to the agents who deal with them. This is what orthodox behaviorists are afraid to do lest, by admitting that human beings appear to each other as psychological entities, they be led to admit that human beings are "in themselves" psychological entities. We shall see later on how unmotivated is this fear. Studying the origin and development of the social objectivation of men by men in the course of social actions, the sociologist can eliminate once and for ever the traditional assumption that psychological reality originally and irreducibly exists as the foundation of cultural life, by showing it to be a product of cultural activity, like religious myths or literary heroes.

Behaviorism as a theory of actions is thus inapplicable beyond its original range of animal and infant behavior (including incipient symbolization), and particularly inapplicable to social actions. This does not mean that all the monographic work it has done outside of this original range is worthless: on the contrary, some of it is really important. It is not the first time in the history of science that a wrong theory has stimulated valuable investigations. But the positive results of these investigations can be adequately utilized for general scientific purposes only after they are separated from the theory which they were meant to prove, and reinterpreted with reference to sounder theoretic hypotheses. Thus, some studies of the "symbolic process" throw a new light on the hitherto neglected problem of the use of symbols as instruments in social actions; but their true theoretic significance will become apparent only in connection with a better inductive theory of social actions than the one behaviorism now offers. The results of numerous investigations concerning the effects on human conduct of patho-logical organic changes or of environmental processes will be more valuable scientifically when the empirical characters of the original conduct itself are more thoroughly investigated, when cultural causality is better understood, and the effects of the changes are redefined more exactly than behavioristic preconceptions now permit.

Certain recent developments of behaviorism are already leading away from the narrowness of the theory of actions as organic responses to sensory stimuli. Behaviorism, as expressed by men like Read Bain, Kimball Young, L. L. Bernard, and E. Bogardus, ceases to be a particular doctrine or even a specific and exclusive method, and becomes an intellectual attitude which demands that human actions and their changes as empirical data be studied in the same spirit of scientific objectivity and inductive thoroughness and with the same elimination of useless traditions as chemical or biological data —which does not necessarily imply that they must be the same kind of data as the biologist's or the chemist's. We can but heartily agree with such an intellectual attitude, even though we believe that some of the methods in which it finds expression ought to be changed; but this is a later question.

Subjective Meaning in the Social Situation III * (*MacIver*)

1. A business man sits in his office. He has concluded an important deal. The tension under which he had been working is relaxed. He is back to the everyday routine and it has less savor than before. He is conscious of a vague restlessness. He wants a change of some sort. His days have been too slavishly devoted to the demands of business, he has been missing other things. He has been making money—why shouldn't he spend some, indulge himself a little? Why not take time off and go on a voyage? The business can get along without him for a few weeks. A steamship company's adver-tisement of a "luxury cruise," which he had read some days before, comes to his mind. "It is just the thing I need," he says to himself, "a complete change of scene." His wife has been warning him against overworking. His family will appreciate him more when he comes back after an absence. The air and sunshine will do him good. He will make new acquaintances. It will be pleasant to visit Rio and Buenos Aires and other places he has merely read about. The more he thinks of the idea the better he likes it. Before the

* Reprinted from *Social Causation* by R. M. MacIver, pp. 291–299, with permission of the publisher, Ginn and Company. Copyright, 1942, by Ginn and Company.

day is over he "makes up his mind" and telephones the steamship company for a reservation.

What has our business man been doing? He has been assessing a situation and arriving at a decision. He has had alternatives before him and has chosen between them. He is going to travel, for recreation or health or adventure. That is the way he puts it to others—or to himself. His statement of objective is necessarily incomplete and is probably a simplification. Anyhow he has reached a decision, probably without any meticulous calculation. He cannot really tell you how he arrived at it. *It is his dynamic assessment of a situation.* Let us take it at that for the present. In the process of making a decision, some desire, some valuation, simple or complex, has become dominant for the time being, as a determinant of action within the individual's scheme of values.

2. Having made his decision, our business man reorganizes his activities in order to attain his objective. He gives instructions for the conduct of his affairs during his absence. He makes arrangements for family needs. He foresees certain contingencies and provides against them. He cancels some engagements. He buys some travelling equipment. He turns resources hitherto neutral and undirected, such as the money he pays for his transportation, into specific means, the means for his new objective.

In all conscious behavior there is thus a twofold process of selective organization. On the one hand the value-system of the individual, his active cultural complex, his personality, is focussed in a particular direction, towards a particular objective. (Sometimes, as we previously pointed out, the incentive to the reorganization of activity may be a dominating motive that is not attached to a specific objective.) On the other hand certain aspects of external reality are selectively related to the controlling valuation, are distinguished from the rest of the external world, are in a sense withdrawn from it, since they now become themselves value factors, the means, obstacles, or conditions relevant to the value quest. The inner, or subjective, system is focussed by a dynamic valuation; and the outer, or external, system is "spotlighted" in that focus, the part within the spotlight being *transformed from mere externality into something also belonging to a world of values,* as vehicle, accessory, hindrance, and cost of the value attainment.

3. The traveller sets out on his voyage. He enters into a new system of social relations. He is subjected to new influences. He may be deflected thereby from his original objective, he may find new additional objectives, or he may pursue exclusively the first one. Even in the last event he may fail to attain his goal. The experience of adventure may fall flat, he may not improve his health, he may not achieve whatever other end he sought. His

assessment of the situation may have been faulty. He may have miscalculated the chances of success. He may have left out of the reckoning some important considerations. Or it may be that developments of an unforeseen character intervene and make his voyage nugatory.

In all conscious behavior we relate means to ends, but the process of establishing this relationship is contingent and involves an attribution of causality that may or may not be confirmed by experience. Before embarking on his ship our traveller had somehow assessed the situation. This assessment, whether superficial or thorough, involved a reckoning of alternatives. It contained, as do all decisions to act, a speculative element. A dynamic assessment weighs alternatives not yet actualized, sets what would be the consequences if this course were taken over against what would be the consequences if that course were taken. It is in this regard a causal judgment. We pointed out in a previous chapter that the attribution of social causation always contains a speculative factor of this sort. But the dynamic assessment, that is, the judgment that carries a decision to act, differs from the *post mortem* judgment of history or social science in that it is doubly contingent. In the historical attribution we imaginatively construct what would have happened if the historically presented event or act had not occurred, or at the least we postulate that certain happenings would not have occurred but for the event or act in question. One of the alternatives that must be weighed in the process of causal attribution is always imaginatively constructed. But in the practical judgment that unleashes action *both* of the final alternatives are constructs, for both refer to the future. The voyager chose what he thought likely to happen if he travelled in preference to what he thought likely to happen if he stayed at home.

4. Our traveller set out on his voyage without reckoning all the contingencies. No one does or could calculate all the possible combinations of circumstance that may conspire against—or in favor of—his enterprise. When a man decides to act he generally has two or three alternatives before him and he assesses these alternatives in the light of a few expectancies. These alone come within the focus of decision. But "there's many a slip 'twixt the cup and the lip." We can perhaps distinguish three types of contingency that may frustrate the attainment of an objective once decided upon. Two of these we have already suggested. The traveller may "change his mind" while he travels and be diverted to another quest. Or he may carry through his project and at the end find that he had miscalculated the means-end nexus—if he travels for health the voyage may not restore him. The first contingency occurs in the structure of the inner or subjective system; the second in the relationship of the inner and the outer—the relation

of means to ends was conceived to be such and such and it turned out to be different. But there is a third type of contingency which has reference to the dynamics of the external order alone. Our traveller probably did not consider the chance that his ship might strike a rock or founder in a storm. He certainly did not consider the chance that he might fall on a slippery deck and break his leg. He thought of the ship as an instrument of his ends and since most ships make the port they sail for he gave no consideration to the fact that the ship, as physical reality, is subjected to forces that are oblivious of its instrumental quality. It enters, like all instruments, into two causal systems, the means-end system of the conscious realm and the neutral system of physical nature. The adjustment of the dependent causality of the first system to the independent causality of the second is imperfect, and thus a new set of contingencies arises. Our traveller did not concern himself with these contingencies. He was content to assess a certain routine of experience that he expected would continue if he stayed at home and a certain alternative to that routine that he expected would occur if he took the voyage. He foresaw, under the impulse of the emotions congenial to his temperament, a preferable train of consequences as likely to occur if he decided to travel— and decided accordingly.

In all conscious behavior the situation we assess, as preliminary to action, is in no sense the total objective situation. In the first place it is obviously not the situation as it might appear to some omniscient and disinterested eye, viewing all its complex interdependences and all its endless contingencies. In the second place it is not the situation as inclusive of all the conditions and aspects observable, or even observed, by the participant himself. Many things of which he is aware he excludes from the focus of interest or attention. Many contingencies he ignores. The situation he assesses is one that he has selectively defined, in terms of his experience, his habit of response, his intellectual grasp, and his emotional engrossment. The dynamic assessment limits the situation by excluding all the numerous aspects that are not apprehended as relevant to the choice between alternatives. At the same time it includes in the situation various aspects that are not objectively given, that would not be listed in any merely physical inventory. For in the first place it envisages the situation as impregnated with values and susceptible of new potential values; and in the second place the envisagement is dependent on the ever-changing value-system of the individual, charged with memory of past experience, moulded by the impact of previous indoctrination, responsive to the processes of change within his whole psycho-organic being. Thus no two individuals envisage and define a situation in exactly the same way, even when they make a seemingly identical decision and even although social influences are always powerfully at work to merge individual assessments into a collective assessment.

Our simple instance of the traveller has brought out a number of points, which we recapitulate as follows:

1. A preliminary to conscious activity is a decision between alternatives —to do this or to do that, to do or not to do. In the process of decision-making the individual assesses a situation in the light of these alternatives. A choice between values congenial to the larger value-system of the individual is somehow reached.

2. The decision once taken, the other purposes or valuations of the individual are accommodated to it. Preparatory actions follow. In this orientation certain external factors are selectively reorganized and given subjective significance. They are construed as means, obstacles, conditions, and limitations, with reference to the attainment of the dominant desire or value. The dynamic assessment brings the external world selectively into the subjective realm, conferring on it subjective significance for the ends of action.

3. The dynamic assessment involves a type of causal judgment that differs from the *post factum* attribution of causality characteristic of the social sciences, in that it is doubly speculative. It rests always on a predictive judgment of the form: if this is done, this consequence will (is likely to) follow *and* if this is not done or if this other thing is done, this other consequence will (is likely to) follow. We may observe in passing that even the most simple-seeming choice may conceal a subtle and unfathomed subjective process.

4. The selectivity of the dynamic assessment, as it reviews the situation prior to decision and as it formulates the alternatives of action, makes it subject to several kinds of contingency and practical hazard. First, the dominant objective registered in the decision to act may not persist throughout the process leading to its attainment. Second, the means-ends nexus envisaged in the decision to act may be misapprehended. Third, the physical order assumed to be under control as the means and conditions of action may "erupt" into the situation in unanticipated ways. All conscious behaving is an implicit reckoning of probabilities, which may or may not be justified by the event.

Before we take leave of our simple case we may point out that the analysis of it contains already the clue to our main problem. What has particularly troubled us is that the various factors we causally relate to any socio-psychological phenomenon belong to different orders of reality. Yet they must somehow get together, they must somehow become comparable and co-ordinate, since they must operate with or against one another in the determination of the phenomenon. But how does, say, a moral conviction "co-operate" with an empty stomach in determining whether or not a man will steal? How does the prevalence of a particular religion combine with rural conditions in determining a high birthrate? How does the decline of religious authority combine with urban congestion and the improvement of contraceptives in the lowering of the birthrate? The suggested answer is that *in the dynamic assessment all the factors determining conscious behavior are brought into a single order.* The external factors enter not as such, but as considerations affecting or relative to the pursuit of ends. A change of religious attitudes and the expense of bringing up children both affect the value systems of the individuals concerned. At every moment of deliberation or decision the individual is faced with alternatives. He has not one desire but many, and they are not independent but interdependent. He seeks attainment not of one value but of a system of values, for that is what it means to have, or be, a personality. What choice he will make, what end he will here and now pursue, depends on the urgency of particular desires, the intensity of depth of particular valuations, relative to the variant conditions of attainment. The intensity and depth of particular valuations will in turn register a recognition of the different possibilities of attainment. The change in religious attitudes is not wholly independent of the conditions of urban living. In any event, it introduces a change in the individual's scheme of values. But so, indirectly, does the fact of urban congestion. It makes some values easier of attainment, and some harder. Values are values only as calling for attainment or for maintenance—there would be no values in a static world; conditions and means are such only as they make for or against the attaining or the maintaining of values.

Common-Sense and Scientific Interpretation of Human Action * (*Schuetz*)

I. INTRODUCTION: CONTENT OF EXPERIENCE AND THOUGHT OBJECTS

"Neither common sense nor science can proceed without departing from the strict consideration of what is actual in experience." This statement by A. N. Whitehead is at the foundation of his analysis of the Organization of Thought.[1] Even the thing perceived in everyday life is more than a simple sense presentation.[2] It is a thought object, a construct of a highly compli-

---

* Reprinted and abridged from *Philosophy and Phenomenological Research,* Vol. XIV, No. 1, September, 1953, with permission of the publisher and author.

cated nature, involving not only particular forms of time-successions in order to constitute it as an object of one single sense, say of sight,[3] and of space relations in order to constitute it as a sense-object of several senses, say of sight and touch,[4] but also a contribution of imagination of hypothetical sense presentations in order to complete it.[5] According to Whitehead, it is precisely the last-named factor, the imagination of hypothetical sense presentation, "which is the rock upon which the whole structure of common-sense thought is erected"[6] and it is the effort of reflective criticism "to construe our sense presentation as actual realization of the hypothetical thought object of perceptions."[7] In other words, the so-called concrete facts of common-sense perception are not so concrete as it seems. They already involve abstractions of a highly complicated nature, and we have to take account of this situation lest we commit the fallacy of misplaced concreteness.[8] . . .

All our knowledge of the world, in common-sense as well as in scientific thinking, involves constructs, namely, a set of abstractions, generalizations, formalizations, idealizations specific to the respective level of thought organization. Strictly speaking, there are no such things as facts, pure and simple. All facts are from the outset facts selected from a universal context by the activities of our mind. They are, therefore, always interpreted facts, namely, either facts looked at as detached from their context by an artificial abstraction or facts considered in their particular setting. In either case they carry along their interpretational inner and outer horizon. This does not mean that, in daily life or in science, we are unable to grasp the reality of the world. It just means that we grasp merely certain aspects of it, namely those which are relevant to us either for carrying on our business of living or from the point of view of a body of accepted rules of procedure of thinking called the method of science.

If, according to this view, all scientific constructs are designed to supersede the constructs of common-sense thought, then a principal difference between the natural and the social sciences becomes apparent. It is up to the natural scientists to determine which sector of the universe of nature, which facts and events therein, and which aspects of such facts and events are topically and interpretationally relevant to their specific purpose. These facts and events are neither preselected nor preinterpreted; they do not reveal intrinsic relevance structures. Relevance is not inherent in nature as such, it is the result of the selective and interpretative activity of man within nature or observing nature. The facts, data, and events with which the natural scientist has to deal are just facts, data, and events within his observational field but this field does not "mean" anything to the molecules, atoms, and electrons therein.

Yet the facts, events, and data before the social scientist are of an entirely different structure. His observational field, the social world, is not principally unstructurized. It has a particular meaning and relevance structure for the human beings living, thinking, and acting therein. They have preselected and preinterpreted this world by a series of common-sense constructs of the reality of daily life and it is these thought objects which determine their behavior, define the goal of their action, the means available for attaining them—in brief, which help them to find their bearing within their natural and socio-cultural environment and to come to terms with it. The thought objects constructed by the social scientists refer to and are founded upon the thought objects constructed by the common-sense thought of man living his everyday life among his fellowmen. Thus, the constructs used by the social scientist are, so to speak, constructs of the second degree, namely constructs of the constructs made by the actors on the social scene whose behavior the scientist observes and tries to explain in accordance with the procedural [9] rules of his science.

Modern social sciences find themselves faced with a serious dilemma. One school of thought feels that there is a basic difference in the structure of the social world and of the world of nature. This insight leads, however, to the erroneous conclusion that the social sciences are *toto coelo* different from the natural sciences, a view which disregards the fact that certain procedural rules relating to correct thought organization are common to all empirical sciences. The other school of thought tries to look at the behavior of man in the same way in which the natural scientist looks at the "behavior" of his thought objects, taking it for granted that the methods of the natural sciences (above all of mathematical physics) which have achieved such magnificent results, are the only scientific ones. On the other hand, it takes for granted that the very adoption of the methods of the natural sciences for establishing constructs will lead to reliable knowledge of social reality. Yet these two assumptions are incompatible with each other. An ideally refined and fully developed behavioristic system, for example, would lead far away from the constructs in terms of which men in the reality of daily life experience their own and their fellowmen's behavior.

To overcome this difficulty particular methodological devices are required, among them the constructs of patterns of rational action. For the purpose of further analysis of the specific nature of the thought objects of social sciences we have to characterize some of the common-sense constructs used by men in everyday life. It is upon the latter that the former are founded.

II. CONSTRUCTS OF THOUGHT OBJECTS IN COMMON-SENSE THINKING

Let us try to characterize the way in which the wide-awake [10] grown-up man looks at the intersubjective world of daily life within which and upon which he acts as a man amidst his fellowmen. This world existed before our birth, experienced and interpreted by others, our predecessors, as an organized world. Now it is given to our experience and interpretation. All interpretation of this world is based on a stock of previous experiences of it, our own or those handed down to us by parents or teachers, which experiences in the form of "knowledge at hand" function as a scheme of reference.

To this stock of knowledge at hand belongs our knowledge that the world we live in is a world of more or less well circumscribed objects with more or less definite qualities, objects among which we move, which resist us and upon which we may act. Yet none of these objects is perceived as insulated. From the outset it is an object within a horizon of familiarity and pre-acquaintanceship which is, as such, just taken for granted until further notice as the unquestioned, though at any time questionable stock of knowledge at hand. The unquestioned pre-experiences are, however, also from the outset, at hand as *typical* ones, that is, as carrying along open horizons of anticipated similar experiences. For example, the outer world is not experienced as an arrangement of individual unique objects, dispersed in space and time, but as "mountains," "trees," "animals," "fellowmen." I may have never seen an Irish setter but if I see one, I know that it is an animal and in particular a dog, showing all the familiar features and the typical behavior of a dog and not, say, of a cat. I may reasonably ask: "What kind of dog is this?" The question presupposes that the dissimilarity of this particular dog from all other kinds of dogs which I know stands out and becomes questionable merely by reference to the similarity it has to my unquestioned experiences of typical dogs. In the more technical language of Husserl, whose analysis of the typicality of the world of daily life we have tried to sum up,[11] what is experienced in the actual perception of an object is apperceptively transferred to any other similar object, perceived merely as to its type. Actual experience will or will not confirm my anticipation of the typical conformity with other objects. If confirmed, the content of the anticipated type will be enlarged; at the same time the type will be split up into sub-types; on the other hand the concrete real object will prove to have its individual characteristics, which, nevertheless, have a form of typicality.

Now, and this seems to be of special importance, I *may* take the typically apperceived object as an *exemplar* of the general type and allow myself to be led to this concept of the type, but I do not *need* by any means to think of the concrete dog as an exemplar of the general concept of "dog." "In general" my Irish setter Rover shows all the characteristics which the type "dog" according to my previous experience implies. Yet exactly what he has in common with other dogs is of no concern to me. I look at him as my friend and companion Rover, as such being distinguished from all the other Irish setters with which he shares certain typical characteristics of appearance and behavior. I am, without a special motive, not induced to look at Rover as a mammal, an animal, an object of the outer world, although I know that he is all this too.

Thus, in the natural attitude of daily life we are concerned merely with certain objects standing out over against the unquestioned field of pre-experienced other objects, and it is the outcome of the selecting activity of our mind to determine which particular characteristics of such an object are individual and which typical ones. More generally, we are merely concerned with some aspects of this particular typified object. Asserting of this object S that it has the characteristic property p in the form "S is p" is an elliptical statement. For S, taken without any question as it appears to me, is not merely p but also q and r and many other things. The full statement should read: "S is, among many other things, such as q and r, also p." If I assert with respect to an element of the world as taken for granted: "S is p," I do so because under the prevailing circumstances I am interested in the p-being of S, disregarding as not relevant its being also q and r.[12] . . .

Man finds himself at any moment of his daily life in a biographically determined situation, that is, in a physical and socio-cultural environment as defined by him,[13] within which he has his position, not merely his position in terms of physical space and outer time or of his status and role within the social system but also his moral and ideological position.[14] To say that this definition of the situation is biographically determined means to say that it has its history; it is the sedimentation of all of man's previous experiences, organized in the habitual possessions of his stock of knowledge, at hand, and as such his unique possession, given to him and to him alone. This biographically determined situation includes certain possibilities of future practical or theoretical activities which shall be briefly called the "purpose at hand." It is this purpose at hand which defines those elements among all the others contained in such a situation which are relevant for this purpose. This system of relevances in turn determines what elements have to be made a substratum of generalizing typification, what traits of these have to be selected as characteristically typical and what others as unique and individual, that is, how far we have to penetrate into the open horizon of typicality. To return to our previous example: A change in my purpose at hand and the system of relevances attached thereto, the shifting of the "context" within which S is interesting to me may induce me to become concerned with the q-being of S, its being also p having become irrelevant to me.

In analyzing the first constructs of common-sense thinking of everyday life we proceeded, however, as if the world were my private world and as if we were entitled to disregard the fact that it is from the outset an inter-subjective world of culture. It is intersubjective because we live in it as men among other men, bound to them through common influence and work, understanding others and being understood by them. It is a world of culture because, from the outset, the world of everyday life is a universe of significance to us, that is a texture of meaning which we have to interpret in order to find our bearings within it and to come to terms with it. This texture of meaning, however—and this distinguishes the realm of culture from that of nature—originates in and has been instituted by human actions, our own and our fellowmen's, contemporaries and predecessors. All cultural objects—tools, symbols, language systems, works of art, social institutions, etc.—point back by their very origin and meaning to the activities of human subjects. For this reason we are always conscious of the historicity of culture which we encounter in traditions and customs. This historicity is capable of being examined in its reference to human activities of which it is the sediment. For the same reason I cannot understand a cultural object without referring it to the human activity from which it originates. For example, I do not understand a tool, without knowing the purpose for which it was designed, a sign or symbol, without knowing for what it stands in the mind of the person who uses it, an institution, without understanding what it means for the individuals who orient their behavior on its existence. Here is the origin of the so-called postulate of subjective interpretation of the social sciences which will call for our attention later on.

Our next task is, however, to examine the additional constructs which emerge in common-sense thinking if we take into account that this world is not my private world but an intersubjective one and that, therefore, my knowledge of it is not my private affair but from the outset intersubjective or socialized. For our purpose we have briefly to consider three aspects of the problem of the socialization of knowledge, namely:

(*a*) *The reciprocity of perspectives.*

In the natural attitude of common-sense thinking of daily life I take it for granted that intelligent fellowmen exist. This implies that the objects of the world are, as a matter of principle, accessible to their knowledge, namely, either known to them or knowable by them. This I know and take for granted beyond question. But I know also and take for granted that, strictly speaking, the "same" object must mean something different to me and to any of my fellowmen. This is so because

(i) I, being "here," am at another distance from and experience other aspects as being typical of the objects than he, who is "there." For the same reason, certain objects are out of my reach (of my seeing, hearing, my manipulatory sphere, etc.) but within his and vice versa.

(ii) My and my fellowman's biographically determined situations, and therewith my and his purpose at hand and my and his system of relevances originating in such purposes, must needs differ, at least to a certain extent.

Common-sense thinking overcomes the differences in individual perspectives resulting from these factors by two basic idealizations:

(i) The idealization of the interchangeability of the standpoints: I take it for granted—and assume my fellowman does the same—that if I change places with him so that his "here" becomes mine, I would be at the same distance from things and see them in the same typicality as he actually does; moreover, the same things would be in my reach which are actually in his. (All this vice versa.)

(ii) The idealization of the congruency of the system of relevances: Until counter-evidence I take it for granted—and assume my fellowman does the same—that the differences in perspectives originating in my and his unique biographical situations are irrelevant for the purpose at hand of either of us and that he and I, that "We" assume that both of us have selected and interpreted the actually or potentially common objects and their features in an identical manner or at least an "empirically identical" manner, namely, sufficient for all practical purposes.

It is obvious that both idealizations, that of the interchangeability of the standpoints and that of the congruency of relevances—both together constituting the *general thesis of reciprocal perspectives*—are typifying constructs of objects of thought which supersede the thought objects of my and my fellowman's private experience. By the operation of these constructs of common-sense thinking it is assumed that the sector of the world taken for granted by me is also taken for granted by you, my individual fellowman, even more, that it is taken for granted by "Us," but this "We" does not merely include you and me but "everyone who belongs to us," namely, everyone whose system of relevances is substantially (sufficiently) in conformity with yours and mine. Thus, the general thesis of reciprocal perspectives leads to the apprehension of objects and their aspects actually known by me and potentially known by you as everyone's knowledge. Such knowledge is conceived to be objective and anonymous, namely detached from and independent of my and my fellowman's definition of the situation, my and his unique biographical circumstances and the actual and potential purposes at hand therein involved.

The terms "objects" and "aspect of objects" have to be interpreted in the broadest possible sense as objects of knowledge taken for granted. If we do so, we will discover the importance of the constructs of intersubjective thought objects originating in the structural socialization of knowledge just described, for many problems investigated, but not thoroughly analyzed, by eminent social scientists. What is supposed to be known in conformity by everyone who shares our system of relevances is the way of life considered to be the natural, the good, the right one by the members of the in-group";[15] as such it is at the origin of the many recipes for handling things and men in order to come to terms with typified situations, of the folkways and mores, of "traditional behavior," in the sense of Max Weber,[16] of their inconsistencies,[17] briefly of the "relative natural aspect of the world." [18] All these terms refer to constructs of a typified knowledge of a highly socialized structure which supersede the thought objects of my and my fellowman's private knowledge of the world as taken for granted. Yet this knowledge has its history, it is a part of our "social heritage." . . .

III. CONSTRUCTS OF THOUGHT OBJECTS BY THE SOCIAL SCIENCES

There will be hardly any issue among social scientists that the object of the social sciences is human behavior, its forms, its organization, and its products. There will be, however, different opinions whether this behavior should be studied in the same manner in which the natural scientist studies his object or whether the goal of the social sciences is the explanation of the "social reality" as experienced by man living his everyday life within the social world. The introductory section of the present paper attempted to show that both principles are incompatible with each other. In the following pages we take the position that the social sciences have to deal with human conduct and its common-sense interpretation in the social reality, involving the analysis of the whole system of projects and motives, of relevances and constructs dealt with in the preceding sections. Such an analysis refers by necessity to the subjective point of view, namely, to the interpretation of the action and its settings in terms of the actor. Since this postulate of the subjective interpretation is, as we have seen, a general principle of constructing course-of-action types in common-sense experience, any social science aspiring to grasp "social reality" has to adopt this principle also.

Yet, at first glance, it seems that this statement is in contradiction to the well-established method of even the most advanced social sciences. Take as an example modern economics. Is it not the "behavior of prices" rather than the behavior of men in the market situation which is studied by the economist, the "shape of demand curves" rather than the anticipations of economic subjects symbolized by such curves? Does not the economist investigate successfully subject matters such as "savings," "capital," "business cycle," "wages" and "unemployment," "multipliers" and "monopoly" as if these phenomena were entirely detached from any activity of the economic subjects, even less without entering into the subjective meaning structure such activities may have for them? The achievements of modern economic theories would make it preposterous to deny that an abstract conceptual scheme can be used very successfully for the solution of many problems. And similar examples could be given from the field of almost all the other social sciences. Closer investigation, however, reveals that this abstract conceptual scheme is nothing else than a kind of intellectual shorthand and that the underlying subjective elements of human actions involved are either taken for granted or deemed to be irrelevant with respect to the scientific purpose at hand—the problem under scrutiny—and are, therefore, disregarded. Correctly understood, the postulate of subjective interpretation as applied to economics as well as to all the other social sciences means merely that we always *can*—and for certain purposes *must*—refer to the activities of the subjects within the social world and their interpretation by the actors in terms of systems of projects, available means, motives, relevances and so on.[19]

But if this is true two other questions have to be answered. First we have seen from the previous analyses that the subjective meaning an action has for an actor is unique and individual because originating in the unique and individual biographical situation of the actor. How is it then possible to grasp subjective meaning scientifically?

We learned from Whitehead that all sciences have to construct thought objects of their own which supersede the thought objects of common-sense thinking.[20] The thought objects constructed by the social sciences do not refer to unique acts of unique individuals occurring within a unique situation. By particular methodological devices, the social scientist replaces the thought objects of common-sense thought relating to unique events and occurrences by constructing a model of a sector of the social world within which merely those typified events occur that are relevant to the scientist's particular problem under scrutiny. All the other happenings within the social world are considered as being irrelevant, as contingent "data," which have to be put beyond question by appropriate methodological techniques as, for instance, by the assumption "all other things being equal." [21] Nevertheless, it is possible to construct a model of a sector of the social world consisting of typical human interaction and to analyze this typical interaction pattern as to the meaning it might have for the personal types of actors who presumptively originated them.

The second question has to be faced. It is indeed the particular problem of the social sciences to develop methodological devices for attaining objective and verifiable knowledge of a subjective meaning structure. In order to make this clear we have to consider very briefly the particular attitude of the scientist to the social world.

This attitude of the social scientist is that of a mere disinterested observer of the social world. He is not involved in the observed situation, which is to him not of practical but merely of cognitive interest. It is not the theater of his activities but merely the object of his contemplation. He does not act within it, vitally interested in the outcome of his actions, hoping or fearing what their consequences might be but he looks at it with the same detached equanimity with which the natural scientist looks at the occurrences in his laboratory. . . .

By making up his mind to carry out a plan for scientific work governed by the disinterested quest for truth in accordance with pre-established rules, called the scientific method, the scientist has entered a field of pre-organized knowledge, called the corpus of his science.[22] He has either to accept what is considered by his fellow-scientist as established knowledge or to "show cause" why he cannot do so. Merely within this frame he may select his particular scientific problem and make his scientific decisions. This frame constitutes his "being in a scientific situation" which supersedes his biographical situation as a human being within the world. It is henceforth the scientific problem once established which determines alone what is and what is not relevant to its solution, therewith what has to be investigated and what can be taken for granted as a "datum," and, finally, the level of research in the broadest sense, that is, the abstractions, generalizations, formalizations, idealizations, briefly: the constructs required and admissible for considering the problem as being solved. In other words, the scientific problem is the "locus" of all possible constructs relevant to its solution, and each construct carries along—to borrow a mathematical term—a subscript referring to the problem for the sake of which it has been established. It follows that any shifting of the problem under scrutiny and the level of research involves a modification of the structures of relevance and of the constructs formed for the solution of another problem or on another level; a great many misunderstandings and controversies especially in the social sciences originate from disregarding this fact. . . .

Thus, adopting the scientific attitude, the social scientist observes human interaction patterns or their results insofar as they are accessible to his observation and open to his interpretation. These interaction patterns, however, he has to interpret in terms of their subjective meaning structure lest he abandon any hope of grasping "social reality."

In order to comply with this postulate the scientific observer proceeds in a similar way as the observer of a social interaction pattern in the world of everyday life, although guided by an entirely different system of relevances.

He begins to construct typical course-of-action patterns corresponding to the observed events. Thereupon he co-ordinates to these typical course-of-action patterns a personal type, namely, a model of an actor whom he imagines as being gifted with consciousness. Yet it is a consciousness restricted to containing nothing but all the elements relevant to the performance of the course-of-action patterns under observation and relevant, therewith, to the scientist's problem under scrutiny. He ascribes, thus, to this fictitious consciousness a set of typical in-order-to motives corresponding to the goals of the observed course-of-action patterns and typical because-motives upon which the in-order-to motives are founded. Both types of motives are assumed to be invariant in the mind of the imaginary actor-model.

Yet these models of actors are not human beings living within their biographical situation in the social world of everyday life. Strictly speaking, they do not have any biography or any history, and the situation into which they are placed is not a situation defined by them but defined by their creator, the social scientist. He has created these puppets or homunculi to manipulate them for his purpose. A merely specious consciousness is imputed to them by the scientist which is constructed in such a way that its presupposed stock of knowledge at hand (including the ascribed set of invariant motives), would make actions originating therefrom subjectively understandable, provided that these actions were performed by real actors within the social world. But the puppet and his artificial consciousness is not subjected to the ontological conditions of human beings. The homunculus was not born, he does not grow up, and he will not die. He has no hopes and no fears; he does not know anxiety as the chief motive of all his deeds. He is not free in the sense that his acting could transgress the limits his creator, the social scientist, has predetermined. He cannot, therefore, have other conflicts of interests and motives than those the social scientist has imputed to him. He cannot err, if to err is not his typical destiny. He cannot choose, except among the alternatives the social scientist has put before him as standing to his choice. Whereas man, as Simmel has clearly seen, enters any social relationship merely with a part of his self and is, at the same time, always within and outside of such a relationship, the homunculus, placed into a social relationship, is involved therein in his totality. He is nothing else but the originator of his typical functions because the artificial consciousness imputed to him contains merely those elements which are necessary to make such functions subjectively meaningful. . . .

If such a model of an actor is conceived as interrelated and interacting with others—they, too, being homunculi—then the general thesis of reciprocal perspectives, their interlocking, and, therewith, the correspondence of motives is determined by the constructor. The course-of-action and personal types supposedly formed by the puppet of his partners, including the definition of their systems of relevances, roles, motives, have not the character of a mere chance which will or will not be fulfilled by the supervening events. The homunculus is free from empty anticipations of the other's reactions to his own actions and also from self-typifications. He does not assume a role other than that attributed to him by the director of the puppet show, called the model of the social world. It is he, the social scientist, who sets the stage, who distributes the roles, who gives the cues, who defines when an "action" starts and when it ends and who determines, thus, the "span of projects" involved. All standards and institutions governing the behavioral pattern of the model are supplied from the outset by the constructs of the scientific observer. . . .

We said before that it is the main problem of the social sciences to develop a method in order to deal in an objective way with the subjective meaning of human action and that the thought objects of the social sciences have to remain consistent with the thought objects of common sense, formed by men in everyday life in order to come to terms with the social reality. The model constructs as described before fulfill these requirements if they are formed in accordance with the following postulates:

(1) THE POSTULATE OF LOGICAL CONSISTENCY

The system of typical constructs designed by the scientist has to be established with the highest degree of clarity and distinctness of the conceptual framework implied and must be fully compatible with the principles of formal logic. Fulfillment of this postulate warrants the objective validity of the thought objects constructed by the social scientist and their strictly logical character is one of the most important features by which scientific thought objects are distinguished from the thought objects constructed by common-sense thinking in daily life which they have to supersede.

(2) THE POSTULATE OF SUBJECTIVE INTERPRETATION

In order to explain human actions the scientist has to ask what model of an individual mind can be constructed and what typical contents must be attributed to it in order to explain the observed facts as the result of the activity of such a mind in an understandable relation. The compliance with this postulate warrants the possibility of referring all kinds of human action or their result to the subjective meaning such action or result of an action had for the actor.

(3) THE POSTULATE OF ADEQUACY

Each term in a scientific model of human action must be constructed in such a way that a human act performed within the life world by an individual actor in the way indicated by the typical construct would be understandable for the actor himself as well as for his fellowmen in terms of common-sense interpretation of everyday life. Compliance with this postulate warrants the consistency of the constructs of the social scientist with the constructs of common-sense experience of the social reality. . . .

REFERENCES

1. Alfred North Whitehead: *The Organization of Thought* (Williams and Norgate, London, 1917) now partially republished in *The Aims of Education* (Macmillan, New York, 1929), also as "Mentor-Book," New York, 1949. The quotations refer to this edition. For the first quotation see p. 110.
2. *Ibid.*, Chapter 9, "The Anatomy of Some Scientific Ideas, I Fact, II Objects."
3. *Ibid.*, p. 128 f. and 131.
4. *Ibid.*, p. 131 and 136.
5. *Ibid.*, p. 133.
6. *Ibid.*, p. 134.
7. *Ibid.*, p. 135.
8. Alfred North Whitehead: *Science and the Modern World* (Macmillan, New York 1925) reprinted as "Mentor-Book," New York, 1948, p. 52 ff.
9. As to the concept of procedural rules, see Felix Kaufmann, *Methodology of the Social Sciences* (Oxford University Press, New York, 1944), esp. Ch. III and IV; as to the divergent views of the relationship between the natural and the social sciences, ib., Ch. X.
10. As to the precise meaning of this term, see Alfred Schuetz: "On Multiple Realities," *Philosophy and Phaenomenological Research,* Vol. V, 1945, p. 537 f.
11. Edmund Husserl, *Erfahrung und Urteil,* Secs. 18–21 and 82–85; cf. also Alfred Schuetz: "Language, Language Disturbances and the Texture of Consciousness," *Social Research,* Vol. 17, September, 1950, esp. pp. 384–390.
12. See literature referred to in Footnote 11.
13. As to the concept of "Defining the Situation," see the various pertinent papers of W. I. Thomas, now collected in the volume, *Social Behavior and Personality, Contributions of W. I. Thomas to Theory and Social Research,* ed. by Edmund H. Volkart (Social Science Research Council, New York, 1951). Consult index and the valuable introductory essay by the editor.
14. Cf. Maurice Merleau-Ponty, *Phénoménologie de la Perception* (Paris, 1945).
15. William Graham Sumner, *Folkways, A Study of the Sociological Importance of Manners, Customs, Mores and Morals* (New York, Ginn, 1906).
16. Max Weber, *The Theory of Social and Economic Organization,* translated by A. M. Henderson and Talcott Parsons (Oxford University Press, New York, 1947), pp. 115ff; see also Talcott Parsons, *The Structure of Social Action* (McGraw-Hill, New York, 1937), Ch. XVI.
17. Robert S. Lynd, *Middletown in Transition* (New York, 1937), Ch. XII, and *Knowledge for What?* (Princeton, 1939), pp. 38–63.
18. Max Scheler, *Die Wissensformen und die Gesellschaft, Probleme einer Soziologie des Wissens* (Leipzig, 1926), pp. 58 ff. Cf. Howard Becker and Hellmuth Dahlke, "Max Scheler's Sociology of Knowledge," *Philosophy and Phen. Research,* II, 1942, pp. 310–22, esp. 315.
19. Ludwig Von Mises calls his "Treatise on Economics" rightly *Human Action* (New Haven, 1949). See also F. A. Hayek, *The Counter-Revolution of Science,* Glencoe, 1952, pp. 25–36.
20. See above, p. 3.
21. On this concept see Felix Kaufmann, *op. cit.,* p. 84 ff. and 213 ff., on the concept "scientific situation" p. 52 and 251.
22. *Ibid.*, pp. 42 and 232.

8.

ROLE-TAKING AND REFERENCE GROUP

EVER SINCE the major writings of William James appeared almost seventy years ago, American social psychologists have generally postulated the social origin of the individual's self-image. They have noted that the social self is, in James' terms, the recognition which one receives from his mates. The person's image of self, in other words, is taken over from the images of himself which others present to him, as indicated by their reaction of approval or disapproval. The individual learns to follow models of conduct which are suggested to him by others who are significant to him (see Chapter 4).

But anticipation of the response of "significant others" to himself is possible only if the maturing child learns to perceive the other person's point of view, "to take the role of the other." Hence, the ability imaginatively to enact the role of others is a precondition for the rational anticipation of the responses of others and for adequate perception of one's self. Our selection from George Herbert Mead, the eminent American social philosopher, is meant to illustrate the process sketched above.

Human beings do not act toward each other as isolated individuals; they are parts of larger communities and groups whose members have some common agreement about the various social roles and their "correct" performance. However, the *maturing* member of a society does not merely internalize random attitudes; rather he incorporates the typical and standardized role expectations as they are prevalent in the group or groups to which he belongs. Our selection from William Graham Sumner (1840–1910) is meant to indicate how attitudes to various types of situations are shaped to a large extent by the interiorization of the value-laden appraisals of the in-group.

So far we have still reasoned as if the "generalized other," the "conscience" of particular persons, incorporates the norms of the whole society of which they are a part. Yet recent research has made it clear that the individual incorporates only the norms of those segments of society which have become significant to him. The concept of "reference group" has been developed in recent years by a group of social psychologists and sociologists —as our selection from the social psychologist Muzafer Sherif is meant to show. It has helped to clarify the fact that the individual relates himself to selected groups of which he may not necessarily be a member. In other words, his identification may be with groups of which he is a member or with groups of which he would like to be a member. The work of Robert K. Merton and Alice Kitt on reference group theory indicates that many areas of social behavior in heterogeneous societies are illuminated once it is seen that men orient their behavior in terms of both membership and non-membership groups. Behavior which may be judged conformist from the viewpoint of a large organization such as the army may be considered deviant from the viewpoint of a sub-group with its own norms as distinct from those of the inclusive organization. Certain members of a sub-group may pattern their conduct according to the demands of the larger organization and its authoritative spokesmen. For them these men in authority, rather than their immediate associates, function as reference groups. Therefore, they are likely to exhibit conduct quite at variance with that of the in-group for whom the more specialized norms are a point of reference.

Our last selection, a very recent paper by Ralph Turner, represents an effort to clarify a number of theoretical issues that have arisen in the field under discussion, and to indicate the ways in which reference-group theory is related to, and possibly an extension of, those earlier types of theorizing about role-taking which stemmed directly from Mead's historic contribution.

Play, the Game, and the Generalized Other * (*Mead*)

We were speaking of the social conditions under which the self arises as an object. In addition to language we found two illustrations, one in play and the other in the game, and I wish to summarize and expand my account on these points. I have spoken of these from the point of view of children. We can, of course, refer also to the attitudes of more primitive people out of which our civilization has arisen. A striking illustration of play as distinct from the game is found in the myths and various of the plays which primitive people carry out, especially in religious pageants. The pure play attitude which we find in the case of little children may not be found here, since the participants are adults, and undoubtedly the relationship of these play processes to that which they interpret is more or less in the minds of even the most primitive people. In the process of interpretation of such rituals, there is an organization of play which perhaps might be compared to that which is taking place in the kindergarten in dealing with the plays of little children, where these are made into a set that will have a definite structure or relation-

* Reprinted from *Mind, Self and Society* by George H. Mead, pp. 152–164, by permission of The University of Chicago Press. Copyright 1934 by The University of Chicago.

ship. At least something of the same sort is found in the play of primitive people. This type of activity belongs, of course, not to the everyday life of the people in their dealing with the objects about them—there we have a more or less definitely developed self-consciousness—but in their attitudes toward the forces about them, the nature upon which they depend; in their attitude toward this nature which is vague and uncertain, there we have a much more primitive response; and that response finds its expression in taking the role of the other, playing at the expression of their gods and their heroes, going through certain rites which are the representation of what these individuals are supposed to be doing. The process is one which develops, to be sure, into a more or less definite technique and is controlled; and yet we can say that it has arisen out of situations similar to those in which little children play at being a parent, at being a teacher—vague personalities that are about them and which affect them and on which they depend. These are personalities which they take, roles they play, and in so far control the development of their own personality. This outcome is just what the kindergarten works toward. It takes the characters of these various vague beings and gets them into such an organized social relationship to each other that they build up the character of the little child.[1] The very introduction of organization from outside supposes a lack of organization at this period in the child's experience. Over against such a situation of the little child and primitive people, we have the game as such.

The fundamental difference between the game and play is that in the latter the child must have the attitude of all the others involved in that game. The attitudes of the other players which the participant assumes organize into a sort of unit, and it is that organization which controls the response of the individual. The illustration used was of a person playing baseball. Each one of his own acts is determined by his assumption of the action of the others who are playing the game. What he does is controlled by his being everyone else on that team, at least in so far as those attitudes affect his own particular response. We get then an "other" which is an organization of the attitudes of those involved in the same process.

The organized community or social group which gives to the individual his unity of self may be called "the generalized other." The attitude of the generalized other is the attitude of the whole community.[2] Thus, for example, in the case of such a social group as a ball team, the team is the generalized other in so far as it enters—as an organized process or social activity—into the experience of any one of the individual members of it.

If the given human individual is to develop a self in the fullest sense, it is not sufficient for him merely to take the attitudes of other human individuals toward himself and toward one another within the human social process, and to bring that social process as a whole into his individual experience merely in these terms: he must also, in the same way that he takes the attitudes of other individuals toward himself and toward one another, take their attitudes toward the various phases or aspects of the common social activity or set of social undertakings in which, as members of an organized society or social group, they are all engaged; and he must then, by generalizing these individual attitudes of that organized society or social group itself, as a whole, act toward different social projects which at any given time it is carrying out, or toward the various larger phases of the general social process which constitutes its life and of which these projects are specific manifestations. This getting of the broad activities of any given social whole or organized society as such within the experiential field of any one of the individuals involved or included in that whole is, in other words, the essential basis and prerequisite of the fullest development of that individual's self: only in so far as he takes the attitudes of the organized social group to which he belongs toward the organized, co-operative social activity or set of such activities in which that group as such is engaged, does he develop a complete self or possess the sort of complete self he has developed. And on the other hand, the complex co-operative processes and activities and institutional functionings of organized human society are also possible only in so far as every individual involved in them or belonging to that society can take the general attitudes of all other such individuals with reference to these processes and activities and institutional functionings, and to the organized social whole of experiential relations and interactions thereby constituted—and can direct his own behavior accordingly.

It is in the form of the generalized other that the social process influences the behavior of the individuals involved in it and carrying it on, i.e., that the community exercises control over the conduct of its individual members; for it is in this form that the social process or community enters as a determining factor into the individual's thinking. In abstract thought the individual takes the attitude of the generalized other [3] toward himself, without reference to its expression in any particular other individuals; and in concrete thought he takes that attitude in so far as it is expressed in the attitudes toward his behavior of those other individuals with whom he is involved in the given social situation or act. But only by taking the attitude of the generalized other toward himself, in one or another of these ways, can he think at all; for only thus can thinking—or the internalized conversation of gestures which constitutes thinking—occur. And only through the taking by individuals of the attitude or attitudes of the generalized other toward themselves is the existence of a universe of discourse, as that system of common or social meanings which thinking presupposes at its context, rendered possible.

The self-conscious human individual, then, takes or assumes the organized social attitudes of the given social group or community (or of some one section thereof) to which he belongs, toward the social problems of various kinds which confront that group or community at any given time, and which arise in connection with the correspondingly different social projects or organized co-operative enterprises in which that group or community as such is engaged; and as an individual participant in these social projects or co-operative enterprises, he governs his own conduct accordingly. In politics, for example, the individual identifies himself with an entire political party and takes the organized attitudes of that entire party toward the rest of the given social community and toward the problems which confront the party within the given social situation; and he consequently reacts or responds in terms of the organized attitudes of the party as a whole. He thus enters into a special set of social relations with all the other individuals who belong to that political party; and in the same way he enters into various other special sets of social relations, with various other classes of individuals respectively, the individuals of each of these classes being the other members of some one of the particular organized subgroups (determined in socially functional terms) of which he himself is a member within the entire given society or social community. In the most highly developed, organized, and complicated human social communities—those evolved by civilized man—these various socially functional classes or subgroups of individuals to which any given individual belongs (and with the other individual members of which he thus enters into a special set of social relations) are of two kinds. Some of them are concrete social classes or subgroups, such as political parties, clubs, corporations, which are all actually functional social units, in terms of which their individual members are directly related to one another. The others are abstract social classes or subgroups, such as the class of debtors and the class of creditors, in terms of which their individual members are related to one another only more or less indirectly, and which only more or less indirectly function as social units, but which afford or represent unlimited possibilities for the widening and ramifying and enriching of the social relations among all the individual members of the given society as an organized and unified whole. The given individual's membership in several of these abstract social classes or subgroups makes possible his entrance into definite social relations (however indirect) with an almost infinite number of other individuals who also belong to or are included within one or another of these abstract social classes or subgroups cutting across functional lines of demarcation which divide different human social communities from one another, and including individual members from several (in some cases from all) such communities. Of these abstract social classes or subgroups of human individuals the one which is most inclusive and extensive is, of course, the one defined by the logical universe of discourse (or system of universally significant symbols) determined by the participation and communicative interaction of individuals; for all such classes or subgroups, it is the one which claims the largest number of individual members, and which enables the largest conceivable number of human individuals to enter into some sort of social relation, however indirect or abstract it may be, with one another—a relation arising from the universal functioning of gestures as significant symbols in the general human social process of communication.

I have pointed out, then, that there are two general stages in the full development of the self. At the first of these stages, the individual's self is constituted simply by an organization of the particular attitudes of other individuals toward himself and toward one another in the specific social acts in which he participates with them. But at the second stage in the full development of the individual's self that self is constituted not only by an organization of these particular individual attitudes, but also by an organization of the social attitudes of the generalized other or the social group as a whole to which he belongs. These social or group attitudes are brought within the individual's field of direct experience, and are included as elements in the structure or constitution of his self, in the same way that the attitudes of particular other individuals are; and the individual arrives at them, or succeeds in taking them, by means of further organizing, and then generalizing, the attitudes of particular other individuals in terms of their organized social bearings and implications. So the self reaches its full development by organizing these individual attitudes of others into the organized social or group attitudes, and by thus becoming an individual reflection of the general systematic pattern of social or group behavior in which it and the others are all involved—a pattern which enters as a whole into the individual's experience in terms of these organized group attitudes which, through the mechanism of his central nervous system, he takes toward himself, just as he takes the individual attitudes of others.

The game has a logic, so that such an organization of the self is rendered possible: there is a definite end to be obtained; the actions of the different individuals are all related to each other with reference to that end so that they do not conflict; one is not in conflict with himself in the attitude of another man on the team. If one has the attitude of the person throwing the ball he can also have the response of catching the ball. The two are related so that they further the purpose of the game itself. They are interrelated in a unitary, organic fashion. There is a definite unity, then, which is introduced into the organization of other selves when we reach such a stage as that of the game, as over against the situation of play where there is a simple succession of one role after another, a situation which is, of course, characteristic of the child's own personality. The child is one thing at one time and another at another, and what he is at one moment does not determine what he is at another. That is both the charm of childhood as well as its inadequacy. You cannot count on the child; you cannot assume that all the things he does are going to determine what he will do at any moment. He is not organized into a whole. The child has no definite character, no definite personality.

The game is then an illustration of the situation out of which an organized personality arises. In so far as the child does take the attitude of the other and allows that attitude of the other to determine the thing he is going to do with reference to a common end, he is becoming an organic member of society. He is taking over the morale of that society and is becoming an essential member of it. He belongs to it in so far as he does allow the attitude of the other that he takes to control his own immediate expression. What is involved here is some sort of an organized process. That which is expressed in terms of the game is, of course, being continually expressed in the social life of the child, but this wider process goes beyond the immediate experience of the child himself. The importance of the game is that it lies entirely inside of the child's own experience, and the importance of our modern type of education is that it is brought as far as possible within this realm. The different attitudes that a child assumes are so organized that they exercise a definite control over his response, as the attitudes in a game control his own immediate response. In the game we get an organized other, a generalized other, which is found in the nature of the child itself, and finds its expression in the immediate experience of the child. And it is that organized activity in the child's own nature controlling the particular response which gives unity, and which builds up his own self.

What goes on in the game goes on in the life of the child all the time. He is continually taking the attitudes of those about him, especially the roles of those who in some sense control him and on whom he depends. He gets the function of the process in an abstract sort of a way at first. It goes over from the play into the game in a real sense. He has to play the game. The morale of the game takes hold of the child more than the larger morale of the whole community. The child passes into the game and the game expresses a social situation in which he can completely enter; its morale may have a greater hold on him than that of the family to which he belongs or the community in which he lives. There are all sorts of social organizations, some of which are fairly lasting, some temporary, into which the child is entering, and he is playing a sort of social game in them. It is a period in which he likes "to belong," and he gets into organizations which come into existence and pass out of existence. He becomes a something which can function in the organized whole, and thus tends to determine himself in his relationship with the group to which he belongs. That process is one which is a striking stage in the development of the child's morale. It constitutes him a self-conscious member of the community to which he belongs.

Such is the process by which a personality arises. I have spoken of this as a process in which a child takes the role of the other, and said that it takes place essentially through the use of language. Language is predominantly based on the vocal gesture by means of which co-operative activities in a community are carried out. Language in its significant sense is that vocal gesture which tends to arouse in the individual the attitude which it arouses in others, and it is this perfecting of the self by the gesture which mediates the social activities that gives rise to the process of taking the role of the other. The latter phrase is a little unfortunate because it suggests an actor's attitude which is actually more sophisticated than that which is involved in our own experience. To this degree it does not correctly describe that which I have in mind. We see the process most definitely in a primitive form in those situations where the child's play takes different roles. Here the very fact that he is ready to pay out money, for instance, arouses the attitude of the person who receives money; the very process is calling out in him the corresponding activities of the other person involved. The individual stimulates himself to the response which he is calling out in the other person, and then acts in some degree in response to that situation. In play the child does definitely act out the role which he himself has aroused in himself. It is that which gives, as I have said, a definite content in the individual which answers to the stimulus that affects him as it affects somebody else. The content of the other that enters into one personality is the response in the individual which his gesture calls out in the other.

We may illustrate our basic concept by a reference to the notion of property. If we say "This is my property, I shall control it," that affirmation calls out a certain set of responses which must be the same in any community in which property exists. It involves an organized attitude with reference to property which is common to all the members of the community. One must have a definite attitude of control of his own property and respect for the property of others. Those attitudes (as organized sets of responses) must be there on the part of all, so that when one says such a thing he calls out in himself the response of the others. He is calling out the response of what I have called a generalized other. That which makes society possible is such common responses, such organized attitudes, with reference to what we term property, the cults of religion, the process of education, and the relations of the family. Of course, the wider the society the more definitely universal these objects must be. In any case there must be a definite set of responses, which we may speak of as abstract, and which can belong to a very large group. Property is in itself a very abstract concept. It is that which the individual himself can control and nobody else can control. The attitude is different from that of a dog toward a bone. A dog will fight any other dog trying to take the bone. The dog is not taking the attitude of the other dog. A man who says "This is my property" is taking an attitude of the other person. The man is appealing to his rights because he is able to take the attitude which everybody else in the group has with reference to property, thus arousing in himself the attitude of others.

What goes to make up the organized self is the organization of the attitudes which are common to the group. A person is a personality because he belongs to a community, because he takes over the institutions of that community into his own conduct. He takes its language as a medium by which he gets his personality, and then through a process of taking the different roles that all the others furnish he comes to get the attitude of the members of the community. Such, in a certain sense, is the structure of a man's personality. There are certain common responses which each individual has toward certain common things, and in so far as those common responses are awakened in the individual when he is affecting other persons he arouses his own self. The structure, then, on which the self is built is this response which is common to all, for one has to be a member of a community to be a self. Such responses are abstract attitudes, but they constitute just what we term a man's character. They give him what we term his principles, the acknowledged attitudes of all members of the community toward what are the values of that community. He is putting himself in the place of the generalized other, which represents the organized responses of all the members of the group. It is that which guides conduct controlled by principles, and a person who has such an organized group of responses is a man whom we say has character, in the moral sense.

It is a structure of attitudes, then, which goes to make up a self, as distinct from a group of habits. We all of us have, for example, certain groups of habits, such as the particular intonations which a person uses in his speech. This is a set of habits of vocal expression which one has but which one does not know about. The sets of habits which we have of that sort mean nothing to us; we do not hear the intonations of our speech that others hear unless we are paying particular attention to them. The habits of emotional expression which belong to our speech are of the same sort. We may know that we have expressed ourselves in a joyous fashion but the detailed process is one which does not come back to our conscious selves. There are whole bundles of such habits which do not enter into a conscious self, but which help to make up what is termed the unconscious self.

After all, what we mean by self-consciousness is an awakening in ourselves of the group of attitudes which we are arousing in others, especially when it is an important set of responses which go to make up the members of the community. It is unfortunate to fuse or mix up consciousness, as we ordinarily use that term, and self-consciousness. Consciousness, as frequently used, simply has reference to the field of experience, but self-consciousness refers to the ability to call out in ourselves a set of definite responses which belong to the others of the group. Consciousness and self-consciousness are not on the same level. A man alone has, fortunately or unfortunately, access, to his own toothache, but that is not what we man by self-consciousness.

I have so far emphasized what I have called the structures upon which the self is constructed, the framework of the self, as it were. Of course we are not only what is common to all: each one of the selves is different from everyone else; but there has to be such a common structure as I have sketched in order that we may be members of a community at all. We cannot be ourselves unless we are also members in whom there is a community of attitudes which control the attitudes of all. We cannot have rights unless we have common attitudes. That which we have acquired as self-conscious persons makes us such members of society and gives us selves. Selves can only exist in definite relationships to other selves. No hard-and-fast line can be drawn between our own selves and the selves of others, since our own selves exist and enter as such into our experience only in so far as the selves of others exist and enter as such into our experience also. The individual possesses a self only in relation to the selves of the other members of his social group; and the structure of his self expresses or reflects the general behavior pattern of this social group to which he belongs, just as does the structure of the self of every other individual belonging to this social group.

REFERENCES

1. ["The Relation of Play to Education," *University of Chicago Record*, I (1896–97), 140 ff.]
2. It is possible for inanimate objects, no less than for other human organisms, to form parts of the generalized and organized—the completely socialized—other for any given human individual, in so far as he responds to such objects socially or in a social fashion (by means of the mechanism of thought, the internalized conversation of gestures). Any thing—any object or set of objects, whether animate or inanimate, human or animal, or merely physical—toward which he acts, or to which he responds, socially, is an element in what for him is the generalized other; by taking the attitudes of which toward himself he becomes conscious of himself as an object or individual, and thus develops a self or personality. Thus, for example, the cult, in its primitive form, is merely the social embodiment of the relation between the given social group or community and its physical environment—an organized social means, adopted by the individual members of that group or community, of entering into social relations with that environment, or (in a sense) of carrying on conversations with it; and in this way that environment becomes part of the total generalized other for each of the individual members of the given social group or community.
3. We have said that the internal conversation of the individual with himself in terms of words or significant gestures—the conversation which constitutes the process or activity of thinking—is carried on by the individual from the standpoint of the "generalized other." And the more abstract that conversation is, the more abstract thinking happens to be, the further removed is the generalized other from any connection with particular individuals. It is especially in abstract thinking, that is to say, that the conversation involved is carried on by the individual with the generalized other, rather than with any particular individuals. Thus it is, for example, that abstract concepts are concepts stated in terms of the attitudes of the entire social group or community; they are stated on the basis of the individual's consciousness of the attitudes of the generalized other toward them, as a result of his taking these attitudes of the generalized other and then responding to them. And thus it is also that abstract propositions are stated in a form which anyone—any other intelligent individual—will accept.

In-Groups and Out-Groups * (*Sumner*)

Tradition and Its Restraints. It is evident that the "ways" of the older and more experienced members of a society deserve great authority in any primitive group. We find that this rational authority leads to customs of deference and to etiquette in favor of the old. The old in turn cling stubbornly to tradition and to the example of their own predecessors. Thus tradition and custom become intertwined and are a strong coercion which directs the society upon fixed lines, and strangles liberty. Children see their parents always yield to the same custom and obey the same persons. They see that the elders are allowed to do all the talking, and that if an outsider enters, he is saluted by those who are at home according to rank and in fixed order.

* Reprinted from *Folkways* by William Graham Sumner, Ginn and Company, 1904, sections 12 and 13.

All this becomes rule for children, and helps to give to all primitive customs their stereotyped formality. "The fixed ways of looking at things which are inculcated by education and tribal discipline, are the precipitate of an old cultural development, and in their continued operation they are the moral anchor of the Indian, although they are also the fetters which restrain his individual will." [1]

The Concept of "Primitive Society"; We-Group and Others-Group. The conception of "primitive society" which we ought to form is that of small groups scattered over a territory. The size of the groups is determined by the conditions of the struggle for existence. The internal organization of each group corresponds to its size. A group of groups may have some relation to each other (kin, neighborhood, alliance, connubium and commercium) which draws them together and differentiates them from others. Thus a differentiation arises between ourselves, the we-group, or in-group, and everybody else, or the others-groups, out-groups. The insiders in a we-group are in a relation of peace, order, law, government, and industry, to each other. Their relation to all outsiders, or others-groups, is one of war and plunder, except so far as agreements have modified it. If a group is exogamic, the women in it were born abroad somewhere. Other foreigners who might be found in it are adopted persons, guest friends, and slaves.

REFERENCE
1. Globus, LXXXVII, 128.

Reference Groups in Human Relations * (*Sherif*)

Social psychology, on the whole, has been approached historically in contrasting ways. One approach starts with one or a few sovereign principles, such as imitation, suggestion, instinct, libido, etc. On the other hand, there have been attempts to study empirically every social psychological topic, every specific case of attitude in its own right, as though the results concerning the topic at hand are insulated from other facts in that general area.

The approaches which utilize one or a few sovereign concepts tended to start and end with premature formalizations, resulting in rather "closed-system" schools of social psychology, in spite of claims at being systematic

* By Muzafer Sherif (University of Oklahoma), reprinted from *Group Relations at the Crossroads*, The University of Oklahoma Lectures in Social Psychology, edited by Muzafer Sherif and M. O. Wilson, pp. 203–209, with permission of the publisher, Harper & Brothers, New York. Copyright, 1953, by Harper & Brothers.

and comprehensive. In view of the diverse problems that have to be considered, it has become evident that especially in social psychology we cannot just sit down and write off all the major principles and concepts in one or a few stretches.

On the other hand, approaches which claim that facts speak for themselves uncontaminated with theorizing end up, or rather scatter around, in almost endless discrete results, in lists, inventories, or unrelated social psychological syllabuses. The main trend of "public opinion" polling and attitude studies of diverse kinds have, on the whole, been of the latter sort until very recently.

Fortunately we do not have to be bound by either of these alternatives. There has been growing concern with attaining concepts which stem from serious preoccupation with persistent problems in social psychology, which are organically related to actual research (experimental and otherwise) and which can be utilized for pulling together in a comprehensive way seemingly unrelated facts in a major problem area. The concept of reference groups seems to be such a concept.

Even though this concept has started to spread only during the last four or five years, it has already received varied interpretations and usages. There are incipient signs of its becoming a magic term to explain anything and everything concerning group relations. It may more than pay if we spend some time at this early stage in clarifying our understanding of the concept in terms of the experimental work of which it is an extension, and in terms of its application to problems in group relations.

The general problem is obviously that of individual-group relationship. During the past decades the impact of vital events brought the problem of individual-group relationships into sharp focus, and this trend continues to gain momentum. The major character of this trend, as contrasted with the individualistic emphasis, is the realization that group situations generate differential effects of significant consequence. Group interaction is seen as the major determinant in attitude formation and attitude change, and other phenomena of vital consequence to the individual. During the last decades both sociologists and psychologists, with various approaches, contributed to an ever fuller realization of this trend. In several chapters of this volume, we have instructive surveys of this general trend.

Then what is the use of cluttering the already confusing inventory of concepts relative to the individual-group relationship with another? The necessity of the concept of reference group as differentiated from the more general term, group, needs justification. For concepts are not mere constructs which people, even scientists, can posit at will. Nor does consensus of opinion among professionals in an area make the use of a concept valid. As we look historically, consensus of opinion has been abandoned a good many times because, I suspect, it did not do justice to the understanding of events dealt with.

Two sets of events in particular have forced some such specified group concept as reference group to the foreground. One is related to socio-economic conditions; the other set is on the psychological side.

In a stable, integrated and relatively less differentiated society, there would probably be little necessity for the use of reference group as a separate concept. Modern man, especially in Western societies, is caught in the throes of vertical mobility, in the "dilemmas and contradictions of statuses," and the painful predicament of marginality created by the demands and goals orig-inating in diverse groups. He finds himself betwixt and between situations as he carries on the business of living in different roles in relation to diverse groups which not infrequently demand contradictory adjustment of his ex-perience and behavior. He is exposed through actual face-to-face contacts, through the mass media of communication, to pressures, demands, goals of diverse trends and ideologies. These are some of the many aspects of the setting in which he operates, through which he becomes indoctrinated, forms his identifications, faces a great variety of alternatives to choose from in line with his special needs, etc. If his psychological level of functioning were re-stricted largely to the impact of immediate stimulus situations and his behavior were regulated solely in terms of the immediate ups and downs of his biogenic motives and conditionings on that basis, he would probably not be troubled so much by the demands of overlapping and contradictory groups.

This leads to the second consideration, which relates to man's con-ceptual level of functioning. As he passes from one group situation to another from time to time, he reacts to the demands, pressures and appeals of new group situations in terms of the person he has come to consider himself to be and aspires to be. In other words, he reacts in terms of more or less consistent ties of belongingness in relation to his past and present identifications and his future goals for security of his identity, and also his status and prestige con-cerns. In short, this conceptual level of functioning makes possible regula-tion of experience and behavior in relation to values and norms that lie at times far beyond immediate group situations.

The conceptual level of functioning is, on the whole, taken too much for granted. We may be gaining a great deal if this conceptual level of functioning is deliberately brought into the discussion of motives and goals in relation to group situations. Of course, this idea is tied up with the notion of *levels* so cogently stressed by Schneirla, Lindesmith and Strauss, and others (35, 36, 26).

It is apparent, then, that the groups to which the individual relates himself need not always be the groups in which he is actually moving. His identifications need not always be with groups in which he is registered, is seen to be, or announced to be a member. The concept of reference groups forces itself through such facts. The concept becomes almost indispensable in dealing with the relation of individuals to groups in highly differentiated and poorly integrated societies, in societies in the process of acculturation and high tempo of transition.

With the above considerations in mind, reference groups can be characterized simply as *those groups to which the individual relates himself as a part or to which he aspires to relate himself psychologically*. It is apparent that the characterization of reference groups just presented is a psychological one, that is, it is made from the standpoint of the individual in the individual-group relationship.

In many cases, of course, the individual's reference groups are at the same time his membership groups.[1] However, in cases where the individual's membership groups are not his reference groups, it does not follow that the groups in which the individual actually interacts will not have an effect on him. On the contrary, this creates important psychological problems for him to which we shall have occasion to refer later when we deal with *marginality* as one instance of being caught between the positive attractions of one's reference group, which is not the membership group of the individual at the time, and demands and pressures of the membership group, which is not his reference group.

Numerous studies coming both from psychologists and from sociologists have shown that the major sources of the individual's weighty attitudes are the values or norms of the groups to which he relates himself, that is, of his reference groups. In fact, the values or norms of his reference groups constitute the major anchorages in relation to which his experience of self-identity is organized. This conception enables us to pull together a host of discrete data in various areas. At this point, we shall mention just one illustration. Textbooks on adolescence used to give rather lengthy lists of adolescent interests and attitudes which include some items that appear as oddities. All such lists of adolescent attitudes and interests can be pulled together under a unified conceptual scheme if they are related to the adolescent's reference groups. These are, on the whole, cliques spontaneously formed under the motivational stresses to which the youngsters are exposed, especially in societies in a high tempo of transition (7). Likewise, psychological problems of gang behavior, problems of marginality, problems of status regulation by individuals, etc., acquire conceptual unification when approached with some such concept as reference groups.

Of course, the various facts and problems which are brought to focus through the reference group concept historically pressed for consideration whether or not the term "reference group" was explicitly used. A number of investigators, especially sociologists, as we shall see, provided interesting and valuable analyses of these specific problems.

Among psychological studies, Chapman and Volkmann's 1939 experiment merits attention (6). The conception of this experiment, which served as a model for numerous others, derived explicitly from the general fact that judgments, perceptions, etc., take place within referential frameworks. Specifically, level of aspiration was conceived as an instance of "the effect upon a judgment of the frame of reference within which it is executed." Goals set in relation to the task in question were lowered or raised as the case might be, as determined by the position of experimentally introduced groups to the subject's own reference group. In short, the position of other groups relative to one's own reference group, which served as the major anchorage, determined the regulation of goals. The theoretical implications of this and related studies, especially Hyman's 1942 study on judgments of status, will be considered shortly.

More recently, the concept of reference group has come to the foreground with varying emphasis in the works of Hyman (15), Sherif and Cantril (40), Sherif (39), Newcomb (30), Lindesmith and Strauss (26), Merton and Kitt (28), Hartley (12), and Jahoda, Deutsch and Cook (16), among others. In spite of the short history of its use, the concept is already being utilized in somewhat different senses.

In studying the psychology of status, Hyman, who first used the term "reference group," found shifts in judgments of status with changes of the group or individual in terms of which judgment was made. This was seen as a specific case of an anchoring point in the frame of reference determining judgment, and was called "reference group" or "reference individual." Unfortunately, after the appearance of this important study in 1942, Hyman's contributions have not to date utilized the reference group concept.

In dealing with changing attitudes during adolescence, Sherif and Cantril (40), found the term most valuable. However, the characterization on the concept used in this paper was presented first in 1948 (39).

Newcomb demonstrated the usefulness of the reference group concept by recasting the previously reported results of his important Bennington

Study on attitude change in terms of the shifts or resistance to shifts in reference groups. In his *Social Psychology* (30), he characterized membership and reference groups in the sense they are used in this paper. However, he introduced the notions of positive and negative reference groups. A positive reference group, in Newcomb's terminology, "is one in which a person is motivated to be accepted and treated as a member (overtly or symbolically) whereas a negative reference group is one which the person is motivated to oppose or in which he does not want to be treated as a member." In addition, Newcomb speaks of one group being both a positive and negative reference group for the same person, in the sense that he may willingly conform to some of its norms and not to others.

In line with their stress on conceptual factors in human social behavior, so well expressed especially in their chapter "Men Without Symbols," Lindesmith and Strauss (26) emphasize that the individual's relatedness and identifications with groups need not be in terms of actual face-to-face relations. They found the concept of reference groups useful in dealing with such relatedness in particular. It seems, however, that "reference groups" refers specifically in their discussion to groups with which the individual identifies himself, but is not actually a member.

REFERENCES

1. To make this point clear, our previous treatment of membership and reference groups is introduced under the title "Effects of Membership and Other Reference Groups." (M. Sherif, *An Outline of Social Psychology*, Harper, 1948.)
6. Chapman, D. W., and Volkmann, J. A social determinant of the level of aspiration. *J. Abn. & Soc. Psychol.*, 1939, 34:225–238.
7. Davis, K. The sociology of parent-youth conflict. *Amer. Sociol. Rev.*, 1940, 5:523–535.
12. Hartley, E. L. Psychological problems of multiple group membership. In J. H. Rohrer, and M. Sherif (eds.), *Social Psychology at the Crossroads.* New York: Harper, 1951.
15. Hyman, H. H. The psychology of status. *Arch. Psychol.*, 1942, 269.
16. Jahoda, M., Deutsch, M., and Cook, S. W. *Research Methods in Social Relations.* New York: Dryden, 1951.
26. Lindesmith, A. R., and Strauss, A. L. *Social Psychology.* New York: Dryden, 1949.
28. Merton, R. K., and Kitt, A. S. Contributions to the theory of reference group behavior. In R. K. Merton and P. F. Lazarsfeld (eds.), *Continuities in Social Research: Studies in the Scope and Method of "The American Soldier."* Glencoe: The Free Press, 1950.
30. Newcomb, T. M. *Social Psychology.* New York: Dryden, 1950.
35. Schneirla, T. C. Problems in the biopsychology of social organization. *J. Abn. & Soc. Psychol.*, 1946, 41:385–402.
36. Schneirla, T. C. The "levels" concept in the study of social organization in animals. In J. H. Rohrer and M. Sherif (eds.), *Social Psychology at the Crossroads.* New York: Harper, 1951.
39. Sherif, M. *An Outline of Social Psychology.* New York: Harper, 1948.
40. Sherif, M., and Cantril, H. *The Psychology of Ego-Involvements.* New York: Wiley, 1947.

Reference Groups * (*Merton and Kitt*)

Theoretical Implications. In discussing this panel study, we want to bring into the open some of the connections between reference group theory and functional sociology which have remained implicit to this point, —an objective to which this study lends itself particularly well, since the findings of the study can be readily reformulated in terms of both kinds of theory, and are then seen to bear upon a range of behavior wider than that considered in the study itself.

The value of such reformulation for social theory is perhaps best seen in connection with the independent variable of "conformity." It is clear, when one thinks about it, that the type of attitude described as conformist in this study is at the polar extreme from what is ordinarily called "social conformity." For in the vocabulary of sociology, social conformity usually denotes conformity to the norms and expectations current in the individual's *own* membership-group. But in this study, conformity refers, not to the norms of the immediate primary group constituted by enlisted men but to the quite different norms contained in the official military mores. Indeed, as data in *The American Soldier* make clear, the norms of the in-groups of associated enlisted men and the official norms of the Army and of the stratum of officers were often at odds.[1] In the language of reference group theory, therefore, attitudes of conformity to the official mores can be described as a positive orientation to the norms of a non-membership group that is taken as a frame of reference. Such conformity to norms of an out-group is thus equivalent to what is ordinarily called nonconformity, that is, nonconformity to the norms of the in-group.[2]

This preliminary reformulation leads directly to two interrelated questions which we have until now implied rather than considered explicitly: what are the consequences, functional and dysfunctional, of positive orientation to the values of a group other than one's own? And further, which social processes initiate, sustain or curb such orientations?

Functions of positive orientation to non-membership reference groups. In considering, however briefly, the possible consequences of this pattern of conformity to non-membership group norms, it is advisable to distinguish between the consequences for the individuals exhibiting this behavior, the

* Reprinted from *Continuities in Social Research, Studies in the Scope and Method of "The American Soldier,"* edited by Robert K. Merton and Paul F. Lazarsfeld, pp. 86–95, by Robert K. Merton and Alice S. Kitt, with permission of the publisher, The Free Press, Glencoe, Ill.

sub-group in which they find themselves, and the social system comprising both of these.

For the individual who adopts the values of a group to which he aspires but does not belong, this orientation may serve the twin functions of aiding his rise into that group and of easing his adjustment after he has become part of it. That this first function was indeed served is the gist of the finding in *The American Soldier* that those privates who accepted the official values of the Army hierarchy were more likely than others to be promoted. The hypothesis regarding the second function still remains to be tested. But it would not, in principle, be difficult to discover empirically whether those men who, through a kind of *anticipatory socialization,* take on the values of the non-membership group to which they aspire, find readier acceptance by that group and make an easier adjustment to it. This would require the development of indices of group acceptance and adjustment, and a comparison, in terms of these indices, of those newcomers to a group who had previously oriented themselves to the group's values and those who had not. More concretely, in the present instance, it would have entailed a comparative study among the privates promoted to higher rank, of the subsequent group adjustment of those who had undergone the hypothesized preparation for status shifts and those who had previously held fast to the values of their in-group of enlisted men. Indices of later adjustment could be related to indices of prior value-orientation. This would constitute a systematic empirical test of a functional hypothesis.

It appears, further, that anticipatory socialization is functional for the individual only within a relatively open social structure providing for mobility. For only in such a structure would such attitudinal and behavior preparation for status shifts be followed by actual changes of status in a substantial proportion of cases. By the same token, the same pattern of anticipatory socialization would be dysfunctional for the individual in a relatively closed social structure, where he would not find acceptance by the group to which he aspires and would probably lose acceptance, because of his out-group orientation, by the group to which he belongs. This latter type of case will be recognized as that of the marginal man, poised on the edge of several groups but fully accepted by none of them.

Thus, the often-studied case of the marginal man [3] and the case of the enlisted man who takes the official military mores as a positive frame of reference can be identified, in a functional theory of reference group behavior, as special cases of anticipatory socialization. The marginal man pattern represents the special case in a relatively closed social system, in which the members of one group take as a positive frame of reference the norms of a group from which they are excluded in principle. Within such a social structure, anticipatory socialization becomes dysfunctional for the individual who becomes the victim of aspirations he cannot achieve and hopes he cannot satisfy. But, as the panel study seems to indicate, precisely the same kind of reference group behavior within a relatively open social system is functional for the individual at least to the degree of helping him to achieve the status to which he aspires. The same reference group behavior in different social structures has different consequences.

To this point, then, we find that positive orientation toward the norms of a non-membership group is precipitated by a passage between membership-groups, either in fact or in fantasy, and that the functional or dysfunctional consequences evidently depend upon the relatively open or closed character of the social structure in which this occurs. And what would, at first glance, seem entirely unrelated and disparate forms of behavior—the behavior of such marginal men as the Cape Coloured or the Eurasian, and of enlisted men adopting the values of military strata other than their own—are seen, after appropriate conceptualization, as special cases of reference group behavior.

Although anticipatory socialization may be functional for the *individual* in an open social system, it is apparently dysfunctional for the solidarity of the *group* or *stratum* to which he belongs. For allegiance to the contrasting mores of another group means defection from the mores of the in-group. And accordingly, as we shall presently see, the in-group responds by putting all manner of social restraints upon such positive orientations to certain out-group norms.

From the standpoint of the larger social system, the Army as a whole, positive orientation toward the official mores would appear to be functional in supporting the legitimacy of the structure and in keeping the structure of authority intact. (This is presumably what is meant when the text of *The American Soldier* refers to these conformist attitudes as "favorable from the Army's point of view.") But manifestly, much research needs to be done before one can say that this is indeed the case. It is possible, for example, that the secondary effects of such orientations may be so deleterious to the solidarity of the primary groups of enlisted men that their morale sags. A concrete research question might help clarify the problem: are outfits with relatively large minorities of men positively oriented to the official Army values more likely to exhibit signs of anomie and personal disorganization (*e.g.* non-battle casualties)? In such situations, does the personal "success" of conformists (promotion) only serve to depress the morale of the others by rewarding those who depart from the in-group mores?

In this panel study, as well as in several of the others we have reviewed here—for example, the study of soldiers' evaluations of the justification for their induction into the Army—reference group behavior is evidently related to the legitimacy ascribed to institutional arrangements. Thus, the older married soldier is less likely to think it "fair" that he was inducted; most enlisted men think it "unfair" that promotions are presumably based on "who you know, not what you know"; and so on. In part, this apparent emphasis on legitimacy is of course an artifact of the research: many of the questions put to soldiers had to do with their conception of the legitimate or illegitimate character of their situation or of prevailing institutional arrangements. But the researchers' own focus of interest was in turn the result of their having observed that soldiers were, to a significant degree, actually concerned with such issues of institutional legitimacy, as the spontaneous comments of enlisted men often indicate.[4]

This bears notice because imputations of legitimacy to social arrangements seem functionally related to reference group behavior. They apparently affect *the range of the inter-group or inter-individual comparisons* that will typically be made. If the structure of a rigid system of stratification, for example, is generally defined as legitimate, if the rights, perquisites and obligations of each stratum are generally held to be morally right, then the individuals within each stratum will be the less likely to take the situation of the other strata as a context for appraisal of their own lot. They will, presumably, tend to confine their comparisons to other members of their own or neighboring social stratum. If, however, the system of stratification is under wide dispute, then members of some strata are more likely to contrast their own situation with that of others, and shape their self-appraisals accordingly. This variation in the structure of systems and in the degree of legitimacy imputed to the rules of the game may help account for the often-noticed fact that the degree of dissatisfaction with their lot is often less among the people in severely depressed social strata in a relatively rigid social system, than among those strata who are apparently "better off" in a more mobile social system. At any rate, the *range of groups* taken as effective bases of comparison in different social systems may well turn out to be closely connected with the degree to which legitimacy is ascribed to the prevailing social structure.

Though much remains to be said, this is perhaps enough to suggest that the pattern of anticipatory socialization may have diverse consequences for the individuals manifesting it, the groups to which they belong, and the more inclusive social structure. And through such re-examination of this panel study on the personal rewards of conformity, it becomes possible to specify some additional types of problems involved in a more comprehensive functional analysis of such reference group behavior.

For example:

1. Since only a fraction of the in-group orient themselves positively toward the values of a non-membership group, it is necessary to discover the social position and personality types of those most likely to do so. For instance, are isolates in the group particularly ready to take up these alien values?
2. Much attention has been paid to the processes making for positive orientation to the norms of one's own group. But what are the processes making for such orientations to other groups or strata? Do relatively high rates of mobility serve to reinforce these latter orientations? (It will be remembered that *The American Soldier* provides data tangential to this point in the discussion of rates of promotion and assessment of promotion chances.) Suitably adapted, such data on actual rates of mobility, aspirations, and anticipatory socialization to the norms of a higher social stratum would extend a functional theory of conformist and deviant behavior.
3. What connections, if any, subsist between varying rates of mobility and acceptance of the legitimacy of the system of stratification by individuals diversely located in that system? Since it appears that systems with very low rates of mobility may achieve wide acceptance, what other interpretative variables need be included to account for the relationship between rates of mobility and imputations of legitimacy?
4. In civilian or military life, are the mobile individuals who are most ready to reaffirm the values of a power-holding or prestige-holding group the sooner accepted by that group? Does this operate effectively primarily as a latent function, in which the mobile individuals adopt these values because they experience them as superior, rather than deliberately adopting them only to gain acceptance? If such orientations are definitely motivated by the wish to belong, do they then become self-defeating, with the mobile individuals being characterized as strainers, strivers (or, in the Army, as brown-nosers bucking for promotion)?

Social processes sustaining and curbing positive orientations to non-membership groups. In the course of considering the functions of anticipatory socialization, we have made passing allusion to social processes which sustain or curb this pattern of behavior. Since it is precisely the data concerning such processes which are not easily caught up in the type of survey materials on attitudes primarily utilized in *The American Soldier,* and since these processes are central to any theory of reference group behavior, they merit further consideration.

As we have seen, what is anticipatory socialization from the standpoint of the individual is construed as defection and nonconformity by the group of which he is a member. To the degree that the individual identifies himself with another group, he alienates himself from his own group. Yet although the field of sociology has for generations been concerned with the determinants and consequences of group cohesion, it has given little *systematic* attention to the complementary subject of group alienation. When considered at all, it has been confined to such special cases as second-generation immigrants, conflict of loyalties between gang and family, *etc*. In large measure, the subject has been left to the literary observer, who could detect the drama inherent in the situation of the renegade, the traitor, the deserter. The value-laden connotations of these terms used to describe identification with groups other than one's own definitely suggest that these patterns of behavior have been typically regarded from the standpoint of the membership group. (Yet one group's renegade may be another group's convert.) Since the assumption that its members will be loyal is found in every group, else it would have no group character, no dependability of action, transfer of loyalty to another group (particularly a group operating in the same sphere of politics or economy), is regarded primarily in affective terms of sentiment rather than in detached terms of analysis. The renegade or traitor or climber —whatever the folk-phrase may be—more often becomes an object of vilification than an object for sociological study.

The framework of reference group theory, detached from the language of sentiment, enables the sociologist to identify and to locate renegadism, treason, the assimilation of immigrants, class mobility, social climbing, *etc.* as so many special forms of identification with what is at the time a non-membership group. In doing so, it affords the possibility of studying these, not as *wholly* particular and unconnected forms of behavior, but as different expressions of similar processes under significantly different conditions. The transfer of allegiance of upper class individuals from their own to a lower class—whether this be in the pre-revolutionary period of 18th century France or of 20th century Russia—belongs to the same family of sociological problems as the more familiar identification of lower class individuals with a higher class, a subject which has lately begun to absorb the attention of sociologists in a society where upward social mobility is an established value. Our cultural emphases notwithstanding, the phenomenon of topdogs adopting the values of the underdog is as much a reference group phenomenon lending itself to further inquiry as the underdogs seeking to become topdogs.

In such defections from the in-group, it may turn out, as has often been suggested, that it is the isolate, nominally in a group but only slightly incorporated in its network of social relations, who is most likely to become positively oriented toward non-membership groups. But, even if generally true, this is a static correlation and, therefore, only partly illuminating. What needs to be uncovered is the process through which this correlation comes to hold. Judging from some of the qualitative data in *The American Soldier* and from other studies of group defection, there is continued and cumulative interplay between a deterioration of *social relations* within the membership group and positive *attitudes* toward the norms of a non-membership group.

What the individual experiences as estrangement from a group of which he is a member tends to be experienced by his associates as repudiation of the group, and this ordinarily evokes a hostile response. As social relations between the individual and the rest of the group deteriorate, the norms of the group become less binding for him. For since he is progressively seceding from the group and being penalized by it, he is the less likely to experience rewards for adherence to the group's norms. Once initiated, this process seems to move toward a cumulative detachment from the group, in terms of attitudes and values as well as in terms of social relations. And to the degree that he orients himself toward out-group values, perhaps affirming them verbally and expressing them in action, he only widens the gap and reinforces the hostility between himself and his in-group associates. Through the interplay of dissociation and progressive alienation from the group values, he may become doubly motivated to orient himself toward the values of another group and to affiliate himself with it. There then remains the distinct question of the objective possibility of affiliating himself with his reference group. If the possibility is negligible or absent, then the alienated individual becomes socially rootless. But if the social system realistically allows for such change in group affiliations, then the individual estranged from the one group has all the more motivation to belong to the other.

This hypothetical account of dissociation and alienation, which of course only touches upon the processes which call for research in the field of reference group behavior, seems roughly in accord with qualitative data in *The American Soldier* on what was variously called brown-nosing, bucking for promotion, and sucking up. Excerpts from the diary of an enlisted man illustrate the interplay between dissociation and alienation: the outward-oriented man is too sedulous in abiding by the official mores—"But you're *supposed* to [work over there]. The lieutenant said you were supposed to."—this evokes group hostility expressed in epithets and ridicule—"Everybody is making sucking, kissing noises at K and S now"—followed by increasing dissociation within the group—"Ostracism was visible, but mild . . . few were friendly toward them . . . occasions arose where people avoided their company"—and more frequent association with men representing the non-membership reference group—"W, S and K sucked all afternoon; hung around lieutenants and asked bright questions." In this briefly summarized account, one sees the mechanisms of the in-group operating to curb positive orientation to the official mores [5] as well as the process through which this orientation develops among those who take these mores as their major frame of reference, considering their ties with the in-group as of only secondary importance.

Judging from implications of this panel research on conformity-and-mobility, then, there is room for study of the consequences of reference group behavior patterns as well as for study of their determinants. Moreover, the consequences pertinent for sociology are not merely those for the individuals engaging in this behavior, but for the groups of which they are a part. There develops also the possibility that the extent to which legitimacy is accorded the structure of these groups and the status of their members may affect the range of groups or strata which they ordinarily take as a frame of reference in assessing their own situation. And finally, this panel research calls attention to the need for close study of those processes in group life which sustain or curb positive orientations to non-membership groups, thus perhaps leading to a linking of reference group theory and current theories of social organization.

REFERENCES

1. Although the absolute percentages of men endorsing a given sentiment cannot of course be taken at face value since these percentages are affected by the sheer phrasing of the sentiment, it is nevertheless suggestive that data presented earlier in the volume (*e.g.,* I, 147 ff.) find only a small minority of the samples of enlisted men in this study adhering to the officially approved attitudes. By and large, a significantly larger proportion of officers abide by these attitudes.
2. There is nothing fixed about the boundaries separating in-groups from out-groups, membership-groups from non-membership-groups. These change with the changing situation. Vis-à-vis civilians or an alien group, men in the Army may regard themselves and be regarded as members of an in-group; yet, in another context, enlisted men may regard themselves and be regarded as an in-group in distinction to the out-group of officers. Since these concepts are relative to the situation, rather than absolute, there is no paradox in referring to the officers as an out-group for enlisted men in one context, and as members of the more inclusive in-group, in another context.
3. Qualitative descriptions of the behavior of marginal men, as summarized, for example, by E. V. Stonequist, *The Marginal Man* (New York, Scribner's, 1937), can be analytically recast as that special and restricted case of reference group behavior in which the individual seeks to abandon one membership-group for another to which he is socially forbidden access.
4. For example, in response to the question, "If you could talk with the President of the United States, what are the three most important questions you would want to ask him about war and your part in it?", a substantial proportion of both Negro and white troops evidently raised questions regarding the legitimacy of current practices and arrangements in the Army. The Negro troops of course centered on unjust practices of race discrimination, but 31 per cent of the white troops also introduced "questions and criticisms of Army life." (I, 504, *et passim.*)
5. An official War Department pamphlet given to new recruits attempted to give

"bucking" a blessing: " 'Bucking' implies all the things a soldier can honestly do to gain attention and promotion. The Army encourages individuals to put extra effort into drill, extra 'spit and polish' into personal appearance. At times this may make things uncomfortable for others who prefer to take things easier, but it stimulates a spirit of competition and improvement which makes ours a better Army." I, 264.

Role-Taking, Role Standpoint, and Reference-Group Behavior * (Turner) [1]

For decades sociologists have made reference to "taking the role of the other" ("role-taking" for short) as a basic explanatory concept in relating the acts of the individual to the social contexts of his actions. In general, the term has been employed as a broadly "sensitizing concept" [2] rather than with precise denotations suitable to empirical research. Some years after these terms had become commonplace in sociological literature a new school of social relations appropriated the term "role-taking" to describe the particular procedures involved in the psychodrama and sociodrama.[3] On top of this earlier vagueness have been superimposed recent discussions of "role-taking capacity" and "empathic ability." [4] Finally, a new concept of "reference group," which has achieved meteoric prominence, quite obviously overlaps in some respects the earlier role-taking.

In this paper we shall consider the value of the concept "role-taking" in its more traditional senses by an examination of some of the special variations in meaning which can be assigned to it. We shall suggest some conceptual distinctions which, by differentiating types of role-taking activity, can render use of the concept more specific and more precise. Based on this discussion, we can then suggest boundaries to forestall tendencies which broaden the concept beyond all usefulness. Finally, we shall note the light which our analysis of role-taking may shed upon the idea of reference group and attempt to designate the specific scope of each concept.

THE MEANING OF ROLE-TAKING

Role-taking in its most general form is a process of looking at or anticipating another's behavior by viewing it in the context of a role imputed to that other. It is thus always more than simply a reaction to another's behavior in terms of an arbitrarily understood symbol or gesture.

By *role* we mean a collection of patterns of behavior which are thought to constitute a meaningful unit and deemed appropriate to a person occupy-

* By Ralph H. Turner; reprinted from *The American Journal of Sociology*, January, 1956, pp. 316–328, by permission of the author and The University of Chicago Press.

ing a particular status in society (e.g., doctor or father), occupying an informally defined position in interpersonal relations (e.g., leader or compromiser), or identified with a particular value in society (e.g., honest man or patriot).[5] We shall stress the point that a role consists of behaviors which are regarded as making up a meaningful unit. The linkage of behaviors within roles is the source of our expectations that certain kinds of action will be found together. When people speak of trying to "make sense" of someone's behavior or to understand its meaning, they are typically attempting to find the role of which the observed actions are a part.

Role will be consistently distinguished from status or position or value type as referring to the whole of the behavior which is felt to belong intrinsically to those subdivisions. Role refers to behavior rather than position, so that one may *enact* a role but cannot *occupy* a role. However, role is a normative concept. It refers to expected or appropriate behavior and is distinguished from the manner in which the role is actually enacted in a specific situation, which is *role behavior* or *role performance*.[6] While a norm is a directive to action, a role is a *set of norms,* with the additional normative element that the individual is expected to be consistent. The role is made up of all those norms which are thought to apply to a person occupying a given position. Thus, we return to our initial emphasis that the crucial feature of the concept of role is its reference to the assumption that certain different norms are meaningfully related or "go together."

With only unimportant qualifications, we shall accept the delimited meaning of role-taking proposed by Walter Coutu,[7] which distinguishes the imaginative construction of the other's role (role-taking) from the overt enactment of what one conceives to be one's own appropriate role in a given situation (role-playing) and from the overt enactment of a role as a form of pretense ("playing-at" a role). Role-taking may proceed from identifying a position to inferring its role and in this manner anticipating the behavior of an individual. Or it may proceed from observing a segment of behavior to identifying the feelings or motives behind the behavior or to anticipating subsequent behavior. In either case certain actions are interpreted or anticipated upon the basis of the entire role of which they are assumed to be a part.

In the present discussion the manner in which an individual conceives the role of another will not be examined as an isolated form of behavior. The self-other relationship will be viewed as an aspect of a total social act.[8] The actor takes the role of another in carrying out some behavior of his own; role-taking is an adjunct to the determination or application of one's own role in a given situation. Accordingly, for present purposes we shall disregard the usage of role-taking as the enactment of roles in the sociodramatic setting when the usage detaches the roles from their specific implications for the way in which the actor will define his own role.[9] Furthermore, our purpose in understanding how the role-taking process shapes the actor's own behavior will determine the basis on which we shall distinguish types of role-taking activity. The critical differentiae for types of role-taking will revolve about the manner in which the self-other relationship affords a directive to the individual in the formulation of what his own behavior shall be.

ALTERNATIVE CLASSIFICATIONS OF ROLE-TAKING

It will help to convey the boundaries of the concept of role-taking as we are using it and clarify the major task of this paper if we first mention two alternative schemes for classifying role-taking behavior which we do not plan to emphasize, although we recognize their great importance. First, role-taking is frequently used to refer to an ability or capacity, and attention is accordingly centered about the accuracy with which the role of the other is inferred. Studies dealing with role-taking capacity or *empathic ability*[10] attempt to measure the degree to which the other-role as imaginatively constructed corresponds to the actual role as that other experiences it, and the individual is said to be taking the role of the other only when he accurately infers the other's feelings or anticipates his behavior.

From our standpoint, however, the process of role-taking is not inherently different when the inference is accurate from when it is inaccurate. Furthermore, once the actor formulates a conception of the role of the other, the manner in which that conception serves to shape his own behavior is unaffected by the accuracy or inaccuracy of the conception. Accordingly, we shall speak of the actor as taking the role of the other irrespective of whether his imputation is accurate or not.

Another important basis for classifying role-taking behavior which will not be elaborated here has to do with the criteria which are used to infer the role of the other. (*a*) As we have already noted, role-taking may be a matter of first observing some behavior of the other and then inferring the total role of which that behavior is assumed to be a part. In this sense one responds to the behavior of the other as a *gesture*, as an "incomplete act" which one completes in imagination by supplying the role of which it is an indication.[11] (*b*) Or role-taking may take place without any visible behavior on the part of the other, the role being inferred from a knowledge of the situation, from the supposed status or value. Role-taking of these two types undoubtedly calls upon somewhat different skills, so that the individual who has high facility in identifying the meanings of gestures may not be equally adept at supplying the role from a mere knowledge of the situation.

The criteria used to infer the role of the other may also be either projection or knowledge of the other. (*a*) In the case of projection, one constructs the other-role as he would if he himself were in the situation or had made the particular gesture. When role-taking proceeds in this manner, the particular identity of the other is immaterial to the role content, since the role conceptions of the actor are simply imputed to the other. (*b*) In contrast to projection one may interpret the other's gesture on the basis of prior experience with that individual or other individuals assumed to be like him. Or one infers the other's role from prior experience with that other's behavior in similar situations or from prior experience with the behavior of people like him in comparable situations.

Again, these distinctions are of considerable importance. But from our present standpoint the manner in which the role of the other is inferred must be distinguished from the manner in which the inferred other-role shapes the enactment of the self-role. In focusing upon the latter in this paper, we shall disregard the former. And we shall use the concept of role-taking to include these varied bases for inferring the other-role—whether from gesture or from situation and whether by projection or by knowledge of the other.

Distinctions which we shall discuss in greater detail have to do with the ways in which the imputed other-role is related to the choice or enactment of the self-role. We assume that two persons may identify and imaginatively construct the role of a relevant other in the same manner and yet themselves act in quite different ways. We shall emphasize two major axes for distinguishing types of other-determining-self relationships. The first of these is the *standpoint* which is adopted in the process of taking the role of the other.

STANDPOINT IN ROLE-TAKING

Taking the role of another may or may not include adopting the standpoint of the other as one's own. The role of the other may remain an object to the actor, so that he understands and interprets it without allowing its point of view to become his own, or the actor may allow the inferred attitudes of the other to become his own and to direct his behavior. Another way of stating the distinction is to note that an individual who is taking the role of another may identify with the role of that other, or else he may retain a clear separation of identity between the self-attitudes and the attitudes of the other. When role-taking includes adoption of the standpoint of the other, the role-taking process is an automatic determiner of behavior. One simply acts from the standpoint of the role. When the standpoint of the other is not adopted, some other factor must intervene to determine the kind of influence which the role imputed to the other will have on the actor.

An occasional confusion between taking the role of another and adopting the standpoint of another is partly responsible for the view that facility in role-taking necessarily results in altruistic or sympathetic behavior or eliminates divergence of purpose between opposing factions. Certain types of exploitation, for example, require elaborate role-taking behavior on the part of the exploiter. The "confidence man" frequently succeeds because of his ability to identify accurately the feelings and attitudes of the person with whom he is dealing while completely avoiding any involvement or identification with these feelings.

The standpoint is not, of course, something apart from the role. It is the core of the role. The difference to which we are referring concerns the ability to engage in an imaginative construction of the role of another while maintaining the separation of personal identities.

The early role-taking activity of the child does not make such a separation. To the degree to which he thinks or feels himself into a situation of another, he adopts as his own the attitudes appropriate to that situation. The more complex behavior in which the actor is able to see the other's role while maintaining a separation of identities appears to develop through two processes. First, the individual becomes concerned simultaneously with *multiple others*. As he takes the roles of two others simultaneously, he cannot simultaneously adopt the standpoints of each. Thus, in simultaneously taking the roles of his mother and his playmate, he cannot orient himself from each standpoint at the same time. Hence he may take the role of a playmate, but, in reacting to the imputed role, he may adopt the standpoint of his mother. The existence of conflicting standpoints in the varied roles which the individual has learned to take forces upon him a separation between taking the role and adopting its standpoint.

On the other hand, the presence of *stable purposes or needs* gradually leads the individual to engage in role-taking in an adaptive context. Such rudimentary understandings of the roles of others as the child may achieve are quite early put to use in the attempted pursuit of his own objectives. Role-taking makes possible both the manipulation of others and adjustment to them, becoming a means to a pre-existing end of some sort. The attitude and skill of role-taking which were learned in a relationship of identification become divorced from that relationship as it is discovered to be useful in promoting the individual's own purposes.

These two ways in which role-taking is divested of identification remain as two somewhat different kinds of standpoint which can be adopted toward the imputed role of the other. (1) In the former instance the standpoint adopted is that of a third party. The third-party standpoint indicates what behavior is expected of the actor, depending upon the inferences made concerning the role of the other. The point of view of the mother, for example, may be that her child should be friends with a neighbor only if that neighbor conceives his role as being a decent and respectable child. The role of the other, when divorced from adoption of its standpoint, becomes a datum in carrying out the standpoint of the third party.

The third-party standpoint may be recognized as that of a specific person or group, or it may be depersonalized into a norm. Such a norm provides the individual with a directive to action which is contingent upon his placing some construction on the role of the relevant other. In a study of college students' reactions toward a friend who had committed a hypothetical breach of the mores, for example, the majority volunteered some estimate of the role context in which the friend had committed the disapproved act. Some respondents found it appropriate not to report their friend's theft to the authorities when it could be assumed that the general role of the friend was still that of an honest, law-abiding person whose inconsistent behavior reflected unusual stress. For these respondents the norms defining their own responsibility were more dependent upon the role of the other than on any specific behavior in which he had engaged.[12] Whether the third-party standpoint is personalized or not, the actor engages in role-taking in order to determine how he *ought* to act toward the other.

(2) When role-taking is in the adaptive context, however, the standpoint consists of a purpose or objective rather than a specific directive. The actor must examine the probable interaction between the self-role and the other-role in terms of the promotion of a purpose. He lacks a specific or detailed directive supplied by the standpoint of a third party and consequently must shape his own role behavior according to what he judges to be the probable *effect of interaction* between his own role and the inferred role of the other.

This latter kind of role-taking behavior may be clarified with George Herbert Mead's classic distinction between "play" and the "game," as illustrated in baseball.[13] The skilful player in a game such as baseball cannot act solely according to a set of rules. The first baseman can learn in general when he is to field the ball, when to run to first base, etc. But, in order to play intelligently and to be prepared for less clearly defined incidents in the game, he must adjust his role performance to the roles of all the other players. This adjustment is in terms of the effect of interaction among roles toward the end of minimizing the score of the opposing team. Whether the first baseman fields the ball, runs to first, throws to home, etc., will depend upon what he thinks each of the other players will do and how his action will combine most effectively with theirs to keep the score down.

Mead has pointed out that in the "game" the actor must have in mind the roles of all the other players. However, there is more which is distinctive about this kind of role-taking than merely the simultaneous attention to multiple other-roles. The manner in which the actor relates his own role to the others is in terms of their *interactive effect* rather than simply in terms of accepting their direction. It is not so much what the pitcher wants him to do that determines the first baseman's action as what the first baseman judges will be the consequences if each acts in a particular way.[14]

This type of role-taking can be even more clearly illustrated in the case of exploitation or of salesmanship directed toward a reluctant buyer, in which cases the actor's purpose is not shared by the relevant other. In these instances the actor holds constantly in mind his imaginative construction of the role of the other and adjusts his own behavior so as to elicit and take advantage of behavior in the other which will enhance his own objectives. He sensitizes himself to the attitudes of the other while divesting himself of any identification with these attitudes. And these attitudes enter into determination of his own behavior through the criterion of effect in interaction with potential self-behavior.

Recapitulating this section, we have observed that an individual who in some sense puts himself in the position of another and imaginatively constructs that other's role may do so from one of three general standpoints. First, he may adopt the other's standpoint as his own, in which case he is identifying with the other-role and allowing it to become an automatic guide to his own behavior. Second, the role of the other may remain an object viewed from the standpoint of some personalized third party or depersonalized norm, in which case the role of the relevant other becomes a datum necessary in implementing the third-party directive. Third, the role of the relevant other may be viewed from the standpoint of its effect in interaction with potential self-behavior, as contributing toward some individual or shared purpose. The standpoint of the actor in role-taking may change in the course of a single act, or he may be plagued by alternative standpoints. But the manner in which the imagined other-role affects the actor's behavior will be different with each standpoint.

REFLEXIVENESS IN ROLE-TAKING

Borrowing a term from George Herbert Mead, we shall suggest that a second major distinction be made between reflexive and nonreflexive role-taking.[15] Mead uses the term "reflexive" in referring to the "characteristic of the self as an object to itself." When the role of the other is employed as a mirror, reflecting the expectations or evaluations of the self as seen in the other-role,[16] we may speak of *reflexive role-taking*.

While role-taking is a process of placing specific behaviors of the other in the context of his total role, the attention of the actor is never equally focused upon all the attitudes implied by that role. Rather, one's orientation determines that only certain attitudes of the other-role will be especially relevant to the determination of his own behavior. Role-taking in abstraction is importantly different from role-taking in a situation which calls for a determination of how the actor's role should be played, for the demands of the actor's role determine the selection of aspects of the other-role for emphasis. In one context one particular set of attitudes may be relevant to the determination of the actor's behavior; in another context the same set of attitudes may be irrelevant.

One of the most important distinctions which can be made among the kinds of other-attitudes is between those which are expectations or evaluations or images directed toward the self and those which are not. When the attention of the role-taker is focused upon the way in which he appears to the other, the role-taking is reflexive.

Reflexiveness is connected with what we popularly call "self-consciousness." When role-taking is reflexive, the individual is led not merely to consider the effects of his action or their compatibility with some standard or code but to picture himself specifically as an object of evaluation by someone else. An additional perspective is added to his conception of his own behavior.

The criteria of reflexiveness and standpoint placed in combination serve to delineate more sharply the different ways in which the self-other relationship can determine behavior. We shall examine role-taking from each of the three standpoints in order in its nonflexive and reflexive forms.

1. When the standpoint of the other-role is adopted, the other may serve as a model or standard which is accepted without self-consciousness either in the absence of alternative models or because of prestige or dependence in the relationship. Role-taking which is nonreflexive and identifying is probably the simplest and earliest form. The child's "playing-at" vari-

ous roles shifts fairly imperctibly into such role-taking in real-life situations. When confronted with situations like those in which he has seen a parent or older sibling enact a role, the child adopts as his own the attitudes of the role as he understands them. For example, a child of three or four who has been taught in a firm but kindly manner not to touch various objects will suddenly adopt as his own the entire role and standpoint of the parent when he finds himself in company with a younger and less responsible child. The behavior of the younger child calls up in the older the role which adults have taken toward him. Accordingly, he naïvely acts toward the younger child as he has learned to understand the role of the parent toward himself.

The same pattern of role-taking continues to be a major source of the values and attitudes of the individual. Whenever there is close attachment of one person to another, there is a tendency for the standpoint of the other to be adopted. Probably the attachment need not be positive in character. An attachment loaded with negative affect giving rise to intense rivalry leads each person to take the role of his rival and unwittingly adopt that rival's standpoint in many respects. Whenever prestige is accorded to someone, there is a tendency to take the role of the prestigeful person without disentangling that other's standpoint.

2. In contrast to this nonreflexive relationship a desire to conform to the other's expectations or to appear favorably in the other's eyes may shape the self-behavior into conformity with the other.

When role-taking involves identification and is reflexive, the self becomes specifically an object evaluated from the standpoint of the other. The attitudes of the other which are adopted as one's own are the attitudes toward one's self rather than toward external objects and values in the environment. At this stage a self-image is beginning to be formed, though it is not yet independent of the particular other whose role is being taken. From reflexive identifying role-taking the individual begins to develop an estimate of his own adequacy and worth. His own self-esteem is the adoption of the estimate of himself which he infers from the standpoint of the role of the other. The bonds of intimacy and prestige or the absence of alternative standpoints determine that the evaluations of relevant others will become the self-evaluations of the individual.

3. The distinction in self-consciousness is also important when the standpoint of a third party or norm is being adopted. Nonreflexive role-taking of this sort directs attention to attitudes in the role of the other whose recognition makes it possible to act according to a pre-existing directive. This pre-existing directive (incorporated in the third-party standpoint) may be of two sorts. It may, as already illustrated, make the appropriate self-

behavior conditional upon the role of the other. Or it may direct the actor to employ the roles of certain others as standards or models to compare with his own behavior. The third-party standpoint enables the actor to react discriminatingly toward the aspirations and attitudes of others in determining which shall be used as standards for his own aspirations and attitudes.

4. When role-taking from a third-party standpoint is reflexive, the standpoint enables the actor to react selectively to his audiences. His concern is not merely how he compares with the other but how he appears to the other. But his appearance to the other does not direct his own behavior in an automatic manner as in the case of identification. Instead, he can accept the evaluations of certain others as legitimate and reject the evaluations and expectations of different others as lacking legitimacy.[17]

As the third-party standpoint becomes stabilized and generalized so as to become a fairly consistent standpoint in the individual, it operates in reflexive role-taking as a fully evolved self-conception or self-image. Such a self-conception permits the actor to react selectively on two bases. First, it may tell the subject whose approval is worth seeking and whose is not. The parent tries to teach his child, for example, to seek the respect of his teachers and the children from "good" homes, while disregarding the opinions that children "without breeding" have of him. Second, it may designate the type of image one wishes to see reflected in the other's conception of one's self. The individual may wish to appear to all as an honest man, as an independent person, or as a good fellow. The self-conception directs the individual to behave in a manner which will evoke such an image of himself in the role of his audience. The two bases of selection may also operate together. Thus, the self-image (or third-party standpoint) may tell the actor that he should appear strong and distant to others in subordinate relations with himself, easy to get along with to others who are his peers and intimates, liked by others who are loyal citizens, and hated by others who are not loyal citizens.

5, 6. When role-taking occurs from the standpoint of interactive effect, it becomes reflexive when the reflected self-image is manipulated by the actor as a means of achieving his ends. The salesman who tries to create the impression that he would rather lose the sale than sell a person what he does not want, the propagandist attempting to appear "folksy," and the counselor responding nonevaluatively to his client are all trying to manipulate the image of themselves held by the other so as to foster their purposes. On the other hand, in baseball the role-taking is more concerned with the attitudes of the others toward the game than toward each other and is therefore nonflexive. The difference between reflexive and nonreflexive role-taking of this sort appears in two levels of playing a game such as poker. Each player will attempt to judge what other players are likely to do. But the superior player will also attempt by such techniques as bluffing, conspicuous misplay, randomized strategies, or the "poker face" to establish a false image of himself which will modify the play of others in anticipated directions.

SIGNIFICANCE OF THE TYPES

The types we have suggested are important because each finds the actor in a somewhat different relationship to the relevant other whose role he is attempting to infer. The types also differ in the complexity of the process and in the kind of discretion they permit the actor in shaping his own behavior. Though they are analytically distinguishable, however, the types are not characteristically found in complete empirical separation. They are importantly interrelated in the behavior of any individual in two ways: (a) hierarchically and (b) as alternative orientations to the other.

a) The fundamental source of social values appears to be the *standpoint of the other*. Accordingly, we may speak of role-taking which involves identification as being *derivative* with respect to the values of the individual. The person derives his values through adopting others' standpoints. In contrast, the other types of role-taking are implementive or validative with respect to values. They serve as means through which the values already acquired may be validated by reference to some standard or implemented in practice. Hence, these types are dependent upon role-taking with identification in two ways. They are dependent upon some prior role-taking as the source of values they express. And they are dependent upon prior learning of the skills of role-taking before the role-taking can be detached from adoption of the role standpoint.

Validation has to do with determining the personal relevance of values which one already accepts. One may adopt a value without making it a demand upon one's self. Or one may adopt a value with varying levels of aspiration regarding its achievement. Such validation—setting degrees of personal relevance and levels of aspiration—takes place in part through the simple laws of effect in learning theory and in part through role-taking. To the extent that it occurs through role-taking, it does so either via the reflexive attention to what others expect of the individual or through the comparison of the self with designated standards.

Part of the particular significance of reflexive role-taking lies in its validative function. When one adopts the other's standpoint in reflexive role-taking, he does more than simply adopt certain values; he adopts a definition of what is expected of him regarding that value. The child, for example, who identifies with the parent and adopts his attitudes toward others often does not see the personal relevance of these attitudes except in limited situations. The child is typically "hypocritical" and is distressed when the parent directs attention to his own behavior. At other times the child attempts to make every value a directive to his own behavior and must learn that what he admires in others is not necessarily required of himself.

The values derived in identification role-taking also point to certain groups or persons who serve as standards of comparison in performing the validation function. The individual takes the role of those to whom his attention is thus directed in order to judge what their attitudes are toward the values they profess, what their aspirations are, what effort they put forth, so that he may use these estimates comparatively in setting his own levels.

The *implementive function* of role-taking is carried out, as we have already described, either as demanded by a norm which makes the actor's behavior conditional upon the role of the relevant other or through the consideration of probable effects of the interaction of roles in promoting a given objective. Such implementation is dependent upon both the derivative and the validative functions. The individual must have both adopted values and formed some conception of their personal relevance before he proceeds to carry them out.

b) The hierarchical relationship among types of role-taking is important from the point of view of socialization or the genetic backgrounds of current attitudes. But, from the point of view of the act in process, the important relationship among types of role-taking lies in the fact that they are *alternative relationships* which the individual can establish to the role of the other which will make the effect of that other's attitudes quite different. In order to predict the behavior of a person, it is not sufficient to know that he will take the role of another or to know how accurately he will take that role. A small cue may change his relationship toward the perceived other-role. The high-pressure salesman who is exploiting the attitudes in the other-role to the full may suddenly begin to identify with the attitudes of that other and be rendered incapable of continuing his sales talk. Or an individual identifying with the role of another who is in misfortune may suddenly remember a social norm which leads him to detach himself and treat the other-role as an object.

The alternative relationships to the other-role may exist as recognized conflicts to the individual. The most frequently noted conflict between standpoints is between adopting the standpoint of the other and subjecting the role of the other to the scrutiny indicated by some norm. For example, a subject who inferred a set of attitudes in a friend which would account for his having committed a theft concluded that his obligation was to report the friend to the authorities. By adding that "he will probably hate me for it," he gave explicit recognition to the conflict.[18] Important also is the conflict between derivative and validative orientations, when the values adopted as part of a standpoint are not adequately supported in the indicated validating relationships. Conflicts also frequently exist between role-taking from the standpoint of interactive effect and the other types.

From the distinction among types of role-taking emerges a major theoretical problem for the study of role behavior. The problem is to isolate the variables which determine what kind of role-taking relationship the individual will assume with respect to any specific relevant other. We have already suggested that strong affect directed toward the other makes the more complex forms less likely to take place and that according prestige to the other has a similar effect. Another determinant is the degree to which the roles of different statuses receive normative sanction from the standpoint of a generalized other. For example, the tendency for a parent to identify with the role of his child when the latter has been hurt is reinforced by the fact that this is in keeping with the generalized standpoint in the society. Thus there is a more generalized imperative operating on the parent than the spontaneous identification arising out of affective involvement. There are also differences in the situational focus of attention which affect role-taking relationships.

BOUNDARIES TO ROLE-TAKING

The coexistence of different relationships in role-taking leads us to the further question of whether the concept has been so broadened in application as to lose its analytic utility. If we say, as some writers have, that, whenever an individual experiences an attitude toward some object, he is taking the role of some relevant other toward that object, then every action has been made into role-taking. On the other hand, if we limit role-taking to instances in which the subject recognizes and can conceptualize what he is doing, we make a dividing line which is indefensible in light of modern psychological understanding. The criterion of consciousness, then, is too narrow and the criterion of attitude source is too broad.

The key to a useful delimitation of the term becomes clear when we distinguish between a genetic or socialization framework in which we look into past experiences for the explanation of present behavior and an action framework in which we examine the dynamic interrelations among the elements contemporarily operating to determine action. The concept of role-taking belongs in the latter framework, designating a kind of relationship which may be contemporarily assumed toward a relevant other in the context of an act in process. Within the action framework we may say that a person is engaged in role-taking whenever the individual's conception or performance of his own role is altered by modifying his construction of the other-role.[19]

Even though we may suppose that all attitudes originate in some role-taking, the self-role can become autonomous; that is, it can become independent of the role-taking relationship which originally gave rise to it. Under the latter circumstance the self-role becomes stabilized so that the role-taking process is omitted or role-taking ceases to modify the self-role. One form of this autonomy is indicated when a person is said to have interiorized a social norm, meaning that an earlier process of role-taking has become truncated. The self-role may then persist unchanged even if the perceived attitudes of the relevant other change or if the affective relationship between self and other change.

A NOTE ON EMPATHY

Of the many senses in which *empathy* has been used, five can be particularly related to our current discussion. (1) By most traditional usage empathy refers to nonreflexive identifying role-taking, in which the individual unwittingly puts himself in the position of another and adopts his standpoint. (2) Sometimes empathy is presented as an ability that is desirable in personnel relations, in which case it designates the ability to understand the role of another while retaining one's personal detachment. According to this usage, empathy includes all role-taking except that in which the standpoint of the other is adopted as one's own. (3) Empathy is sometimes used to designate the process of seeing one's self as others see one, the ability to react to one's own behavior as others are reacting to it. This usage makes empathy identical with reflexive role-taking, regardless of standpoint. (4) Empathic capacity is sometimes used synonymously with role-taking capacity, to include all the forms of the process we have described. (5) When empathy is distinguished from projection, it refers to one criterion for inferring the other-role. In this usage all our types would be included so long as the role-taking is not based upon projection.

To make a choice among these usages by fiat would be an empty gesture. However, there are at least three implications of our present discussion for the current work dealing with empathy. First, the *tendency* to empathize, in whatever sense this is meant, is at least as important a variable as the *ability* to empathize. Under what circumstances will a person employ such empathic abilities as he has rather than merely enact a rigidly predetermined role or react to the other's gestures with standardized responses? Second, given the tendency and ability to empathize (using the term in its broader senses) what relationship to the inferred other-role will determine its effect on the individual's behavior? The tendency and ability in role-taking must be seen in combination with the tendency to assume certain kinds of relations with relevant others. Third, the standpoint in role-taking operates to focus attention selectively on the role being taken. Consequently, certain aspects of the other-role are seen more clearly or are more salient than others, depending upon the standpoint governing the empathic process. Since empathy or role-taking is not normally performed in a vacuum, the accuracy of empathic behavior will vary according to the focus of attention supplied by the governing standpoint. Consideration of empathic ability might profit from taking this observation into account. A quite tentative suggestion from one study of empathic ability that empathy is more accurate with respect to reflexive than nonreflexive aspects of the other-role may tell something about the focus of attention in the role-taking process within a clinical counseling situation.[20]

REFERENCE-GROUP BEHAVIOR

Two commentaries have recently pointed out different usages of the term "reference group." [21] Both have noted that a reference group may mean a group with which one compares himself in making a self-judgment. This usage prevails in the original work of Hyman and the more recent discussion by Merton and Kitt.[22] Both commentaries have also noted an alternative usage of reference group to mean the source of an individual's values (Kelley) or perspectives (Shibutani). Sherif, Newcomb, and Hartley have employed the concept chiefly in this sense.[23] A third usage suggested by Shibutani refers to a group whose acceptance one seeks. In the literature, however, the desire to be accepted is depicted as the mechanism which leads to the adoption of the values and perspectives of the reference group.[24] These are not, therefore, separate usages of the term but merely definitions, on the one hand, in terms of the effect of the reference group and, on the other hand, in terms of the mechanism of the reference group.

When a reference group is the source of values and perspectives, the identity of meaning with role-taking is apparent. One takes the role of a member of the group, which is synonymous with having "a psychologically functioning membership" [25] in the group, and one adopts the group's standpoint as one's own. Thus, except for emphasizing that the source of values need not be a group of which the individual is objectively a member, this use of reference group corresponds to one traditional usage of role-taking.

Reference group as a point of comparison corresponds partially to certain meanings of role-taking. The self-other relationship is essentially that which we have described as role-taking from a third-party standpoint. Merton and Kitt note the operation of a third-party standpoint in "the institutional definitions of the social structure which may focus the attention of members of a group or occupants of a social status upon certain *common* reference groups." [26] However, the actor may or may not take the role of a member of the reference group. So long as the actor is using the reference group only as a point of comparison in estimating his own social standing or in deciding whether to be satisfied or dissatisfied with his lot, external attributes of the other alone are involved. The role of the relevant other is not being taken. But when levels of aspiration, degrees of determination, and the like are being compared, the individual must necessarily take the role of the other in order to make a comparison.

In the preceding sense reference group as a point of comparison is a broader concept than role-taking from a third-party standpoint. However, in our discussion of role-taking we recognized that the standpoint of the third party might direct attention to the relevant other in more ways than simple comparison. Comparable relations of individual to group appear not to have been included in reference-group usages.

Dispute over the proper meaning of "reference group" seems to center about the acceptable generality of the concept. The limited usage which Sherif and Shibutani prefer, referring to the source of the individual's major perspectives and values, might well be named the *identification group*. The identification group is the source of values, since the individual takes the role of a member while adopting the member's standpoint as his own.

At the opposite extreme the individual's behavior is affected somewhat by groups whose members constitute merely conditions to his action. The groups are neutrally toned to the actor; he must merely take them into account in order to accomplish his purposes. The manner in which he takes them into account may or may not require role-taking, and they may or may not constitute his membership group. Such a group might well be designated by some such neutral term as *interaction group*.

In between are those groups which acquire value to the individual because the standpoint of his identification groups designates them as points of reference. Conforming to the standpoint of his identification group (or of an autonomous self-image which has become stabilized independently of the identification group from which it was derived), the individual compares himself with certain groups or notes the impression he is making on them or in some other way takes account of them. Again, whether this relationship does or does not involve role-taking will depend upon the directive supplied by the identification group or self-conception. These groups might be called *valuation groups,* since their effect upon the individual's behavior is determined by the valuation which his more basic orientations lead him to place upon them.

Finally, if reference-group theory is to encompass the ways in which individual-group relationships shape the roles and role behaviors of the individual, we should note a dichotomy cross-cutting the preceding distinctions. Certain reference groups within each of the preceding types might usefully be regarded as *audience groups* to the individual. These are the groups by whom the actor sees his role performance observed and evaluated, and he attends to the evaluations and expectations which members of the group hold toward him. The actor takes the role of his audience reflexively. An individual's relations with his identification groups may place the latter on some occasions as his audience and on other occasions not. The reaction to the audience may be that of uncritical acceptance of their evaluations and expectations toward him, or the responses of his audience may be interpreted in an interactive context or as directed by his identification group or self-conception.

In general, then, it appears that the concepts of reference group and role-taking are closely related. In the broadest sense reference-group behavior is somewhat more inclusive than role-taking, since one may take account of a reference group without taking the role of a member. The terms "reference group" and "relevant other" refer to essentially the same phenomena. The reference group is a *generalized other* which is viewed as possessing member roles and attributes independently of the specific individuals who compose it. The same general differentiations seem applicable on the bases of standpoint and reflexiveness (audience). Likewise, the same theoretical problems apply, and a similar principle regarding the boundaries of the concepts seems applicable.

REFERENCES

1. The author is indebted to Helen P. Beem for a critical reading of the manuscript.
2. Cf. Herbert Blumer, "What Is Wrong with Social Theory?" *American Sociological Review,* XIX (February, 1954), 3–9.
3. Cf. J. L. Moreno, *Psychodrama* (New York: Beacon House, 1946).
4. Cf. Leonard S. Cottrell, Jr., and Rosalind F. Dymond, "The Empathic Responses: A Neglected Field for Research," *Psychiatry,* XII (1949), 355–59; Rosalind F. Dymond, "A Scale for the Measurement of Empathic Ability," *Journal of Consulting*

Psychology, XIII (1949), 127–33; Harrison G. Gough, "A Sociological Theory of Psychopathy," *American Journal of Sociology*, LIII (March, 1948), 359–66.

5. Role is conceived more inclusively here than in Linton's famous definition (Ralph Linton, *The Study of Man* [New York: Appleton-Century Co., 1936], pp. 13 ff.). The term "appropriate" in the definition is purposely left without a further referent, since the particular content of the role (i.e., that which is regarded as appropriate) will vary depending upon the vantage point of the person or persons formulating the role conception. Cf. also Theodore R. Sarbin, "Role Theory," in *Handbook of Social Psychology*, ed. Gardner Lindzey (Cambridge, Mass.: Addison-Wesley Publishing Co., 1954), I, 223–58.

6. Cf. Theodore M. Newcomb, *Social Psychology* (New York: Dryden Press, 1950), p. 330.

7. "Role-playing vs. Role-taking: An Appeal for Clarification," *American Sociological Review*, XVI (April, 1951), 180–87. Coutu's reference to role-taking as "imagining what the other person 'thinks he is supposed to do' " (p. 181) corresponds to our usage if the word "supposed" is used in a broad sense. However, the distinction between attitude and role that Coutu mentions (p. 181) is well taken but need not be applied in the manner he suggests. If an attitude is a tendency to act toward a particular category of objects, a role is made up of attitudes. When one seeks to identify a particular attitude of some other person, he does so by placing himself in that other person's position, imaginatively reviewing that other's role until the attitude in question is indicated. Thus, taking the attitude of the other is part of a role-taking process, and Mead's usage does not do violence to contemporary use of the concept of role.

8. "Social act" is used in the sense indicated by Ellsworth Faris and George Herbert Mead. For a brief statement of this conception see Ellsworth Faris, *The Nature of Human Nature* (New York: McGraw-Hill Book Co., 1937), pp. 144 ff.

9. E.g., Theodore R. Sarbin, "The Concept of Role-taking," *Sociometry*, VI (August, 1943), 273–85.

10. Cottrell and Dymond, *op. cit.*; Dymond *op. cit.*; Gough, *op. cit.*

11. George Herbert Mead, *Mind, Self, and Society* (Chicago: University of Chicago Press, 1934), pp. 42 ff.

12. "Moral Judgment: A Study in Roles," *American Sociological Review*, XVII (January, 1954), 72–74.

13. *Op. cit.*, pp. 149 ff.

14. The anticipation of approval or disapproval from others may operate simultaneously with the mechanism being described here. However, the determination of a specific course of action to be followed at a particular instant in the game requires a more precise indication. This indication is afforded by viewing the consequences of particular combinations of roles involving self and others against the criterion of winning the game.

15. *Op. cit.*, pp. 136 ff.

16. The identity between reflexive role-taking and Cooley's "looking glass self" should be evident (Charles Horton Cooley, *Human Nature and the Social Order* [New York: Charles Scribner's Sons, 1922], p. 184).

17. "Legitimacy" in role-taking is discussed in Ralph H. Turner, "Self and Other in Moral Judgment," *American Sociological Review*, XIX (June, 1954), 254–55, 258.

18. To conceptualize such a situation as merely a conflict between norms or roles would be an oversimplification. The third-party standpoint is experienced as a fully sanctioned norm conveying obligation. It is opposed by the discomfort of having to think of one's self in a bad light to the degree to which one identifies with the other-role. The latter does not carry a sense of obligation such as the former.

19. Merton and Kitt point out that "individuals *unwittingly* respond to different frames of reference introduced by the experimenter" (Robert K. Merton and Alice Kitt, "Contributions to the Theory of Reference Group Behavior," in *Continuities in Social Research*, ed. Robert K. Merton and Paul F. Lazarsfeld [Glencoe, Ill., Free Press, 1950], p. 69).

20. Thomas G. Macfarlane, "Empathic Understanding in an Interpersonal Interview Situation" (unpublished Ph.D. dissertation, Department of Psychology, University of California, Los Angeles, 1952), pp. 115–16.

21. Harold H. Kelley, "Two Functions of Reference Groups," in *Readings in Social Psychology*, ed. Guy E. Swanson, Theodore M. Newcomb, and Eugene L. Hartley (New York: Henry Holt & Co., 1952), pp. 410–14; Tamotsu Shibutani, "Reference Groups as Perspectives," *American Journal of Sociology*, LX (May, 1955), 562–69.

22. Herbert Hyman, "The Psychology of Status," *Archives of Psychology*, No. 269, June, 1942; Merton and Kitt, *op. cit.*

23. Muzafer Sherif, *An Outline of Social Psychology* (New York: Harper & Bros., 1948), pp. 105–6, 123, *et passim;* Sherif, "The Concept of Reference Groups in Human Relations," in *Group Relations at the Crossroads*, ed. Muzafer Sherif and M. O. Wilson (New York: Harper & Bros., 1953), pp. 203–31; Newcomb, *op. cit.*, pp. 220–32; Eugene Hartley, "Psychological Problems of Multiple Group Membership," in *Social Psychology at the Crossroads*, ed. John H. Rohrer and Muzafer Sherif (New York: Harper & Bros., 1951), pp. 371–86.

24. "A fraternity or sorority to which you hope some day to belong is a reference group for you if your attitudes are in any way influenced by what you take to be its norms" (Newcomb, *op. cit.*, p. 226).

25. Newcomb, "Social Psychological Theory," in *Social Psychology at the Crossroads*, ed. Rohrer and Sherif, p. 48.

26. Merton and Kitt, *op. cit.*, pp. 64–65.

PART III

Structural Concepts

9.

PRIMARY GROUPS

THE TERM *primary group* was originally defined by Charles Horton Cooley (1864–1929), a pioneer American sociologist and social psychologist, and refers to a group characterized by intimate sympathetic face-to-face association and cooperation. Its *locus classicus* is the family, the play group, the neighborhood, or the village. Cooley believed that the primary group was nearly universal. He saw it as virtually the whole of social reality among preindustrial peoples and as of enduring importance even in urban industrial society.

Another great sociologist, the German writer Ferdinand Toennies (1855–1936), assumed that what he called the *Gemeinschaft*—quite like Cooley's primary group—was on the wane and would be superseded everywhere by the *Gesellschaft* or impersonal contractual type of relationship. Toennies' general point of view—briefly, that modern man is moving irreversibly away from the warmth of tribal life in small isolated communities to cold urban anonymity—was formulated in a dozen different ways by many acute observers. For instance, the superlatively gifted German sociologist, Max Weber, referred to the bureaucratization, depersonalization, and routinization that he saw all about him.

For two or three decades after Cooley's ideas had enjoyed their first vogue, they were usually ignored or dismissed as hopelessly dated. What seemed to matter in the twentieth century was the phenomenal growth of *secondary* groups (a term not even to be found in Cooley's lexicon), i.e., groups characterized by contractual rather than primary relationships, which were held to be the vestiges of a dying order. For the most part American sociologists disregarded primary-group theory, except to write an occasional critique of it. The objections stated in 1938 by the cultivated University of Chicago social scientist, Ellsworth Faris (1874–1953), are still telling and incisive, as the reader can judge for himself.

In the nineteen forties and fifties, however, a theoretical thread that had been broken for many years, was suddenly taken up again. Whereas the sociology between World Wars had been preoccupied with the decline in intimate interpersonal relationships, nearly a whole generation has recently rediscovered a countercurrent from the past. Its spokesmen postulate the universality and indestructibility of primary groups. They contend that man is affected by the family, the play group, and the neighborhood not only in

293

such sites as frontier America, but in modern "mass" society as well. Even such large apparently impersonal organizations as the United States Army or a manufacturing plant are seen, on analysis, to be composed of smaller and yet meaningful groups whose members experience the kind of association ordinarily imputed only to the primitive or agricultural past.

Primary groups are preeminently agencies of socialization. They transmit culture. How much of it they *create* is problematic. The two functions are clearly separate and distinct; failure to see the difference has led to extravagant claims of a monocausal character. To trace the rise and fall of civilizations, for example, to family stability, or revolutions and other political movements to parent-child relationships, is an oversimplification that neglects the fact that primary groups are representative of as well as creative of cultural configurations.

As a vehicle for the transmission of culture, such primary groups as the family or the peer group are irreplaceable. In this matter, from our present angle of vision Cooley would certainly appear to have been correct. Primary groups do change along what now seem to be fairly predictable lines (viz., the conjugal family replaces the consanguine family), but they persist as an integral part of the social order. No doubt metropolitan society itself could be subdivided into a multiplicity of affiliations based upon ethnic, class, occupational, and other ties which bind comparatively small groups of people in the center of an otherwise depersonalized environment.

On the positive side, then, contemporary theory has added to a considerable heritage the notion of "subcultures" acting upon and being acted upon the everarching culture itself. Complex modern social systems may be analyzed on the basis of how their segments differentially impinge on various groups. Very simply, to be an American is one thing; to be an American Negro in Harlem, or a member of the white underprivileged working class, or a midwestern businessman of the Episcopalian persuasion, is something else. We are conditioned by values common to the entire culture and unique to the subcultures that help to shape us.

The renewed interest in primary groups has been welcomed by many investigators who are able, for the first time, to transcend individual psychology and experiment with human material under controlled conditions. In their enthusiasm they have paved a one-way road, but there is traffic coming the other way on a much broader highway—the whole social heritage. A word of caution is in order: whatever laws of small-group behavior are adduced apply only to small groups. Independent verification is necessary to determine their applicability elsewhere. If we are mindful of this truism, it will be possible for us to avoid the dilemma that many social psychologists have had to face. Interest in small groups has generated several subdisciplines, such as those discussed by Edward A. Shils, a contemporary sociologist, in the reading that follows. In fact, interest is now so great that it threatens to eclipse our awareness of larger social forces. So long as the primary or small group is regarded as merely a part, and often a subsidiary part, of the total picture, social science will be the beneficiary. When a creative typology such as the one proposed by Fritz Redl, a brilliant clinical and social psychologist of our day, is added to small-group theory, then indeed, as he suggests in our selection, we have a powerful tool for combating "group-psychological mysticism, a too naive rationalism and psychiatric individualism."

Further encouragement comes not only from Everett C. Hughes' critique of the "rabble hypothesis" but from his positive idea of human relations as a "grid" of informal social groupings. With the sharpening of such conceptual tools to the point where they have a real cutting edge, some progress may certainly be discerned. For disentangling the fruitful from the sterile in this field, Edward A. Shils' judicious appraisal of both should stand for some time to come.

Primary Groups * (*Cooley*)

By primary groups I mean those characterized by intimate face-to-face association and cooperation. They are primary in several senses, but chiefly in that they are fundamental in forming the social nature and ideals of the individual. The result of intimate association, psychologically, is a certain fusion of individualities in a common whole, so that one's very self, for many purposes at least, is the common life and purpose of the group. Perhaps the simplest way of describing this wholeness is by saying that it is a "we"; it involves the sort of sympathy and mutual identification for which "we" is the natural expression. One lives in the feeling of the whole and finds the chief aims of his will in that feeling.

It is not to be supposed that the unity of the primary group is one of mere harmony and love. It is always a differentiated and usually a competitive unity, admitting of self-assertion and various appropriative passions; but these passions are socialized by sympathy, and come, or tend to come, under the discipline of a common spirit. The individual will be ambitious, but the chief object of his ambition will be some desired place in the thought of the others, and he will feel allegiance to common standards of service and fair play. So the boy will dispute with his fellows a place on the team, but above such disputes will place the common glory of his class and school.

The most important spheres of this intimate association and cooperation

—though by no means the only ones—are the family, the play-group of children, and the neighborhood or community group of elders. These are practically universal, belonging to all times and all stages of development; and are accordingly a chief basis of what is universal in human nature and human ideals. The best comparative studies of the family, such as those of Westermarck [1] or Howard,[2] show it to us as not only a universal institution, but as more alike the world over than the exaggeration of exceptional customs by an earlier school had led us to suppose. Nor can any one doubt the general prevalence of play-groups among children or of informal assemblies of various kinds among their elders. Such association is clearly the nursery of human nature in the world about us, and there is no apparent reason to suppose that the case has anywhere or at any time been essentially different.

As regards play, I might, were it not a matter of common observation, multiply illustrations of the universality and spontaneity of the group discussion and cooperation to which it gives rise. The general fact is that children, especially boys after about their twelfth year, live in fellowships in which their sympathy, ambition and honor are engaged even more, often, than they are in the family. Most of us can recall examples of the endurance by boys of injustice and even cruelty, rather than appeal from their fellows to parents or teachers—as, for instance, in the hazing so prevalent at schools, and so difficult, for this very reason, to repress. And how elaborate the discussion, how cogent the public opinion, how hot the ambitions in these fellowships.

Nor is this facility of juvenile association, as is sometimes supposed, a trait peculiar to English and American boys; since experience among our immigrant population seems to show that the offspring of the more restrictive civilizations of the continent of Europe form self-governing play-groups with almost equal readiness. Thus Miss Jane Addams, after pointing out that the "gang" is almost universal, speaks of the interminable discussion which every detail of the gang's activity receives, remarking that "in these social folk-motes, so to speak, the young citizen learns to act upon his own determination." [3]

Of the neighborhood group it may be said, in general, that from the time men formed permanent settlements upon the land, down, at least, to the rise of modern industrial cities, it has played a main part in the primary, heart-to-heart life of the people. Among our Teutonic forefathers the village community was apparently the chief sphere of sympathy and mutual aid for the commons all through the "dark" and middle ages, and for many purposes it remains so in rural districts at the present day. In some countries we still find it with all its ancient vitality, notably in Russia, where the mir, or self-governing village group, is the main theatre of life, along with the family, for perhaps fifty millions of peasants.

In our own life the intimacy of the neighborhood has been broken up by the growth of an intricate mesh of wider contacts which leaves us strangers to people who live in the same house. And even in the country the same principle is at work, though less obviously, diminishing our economic and spiritual community with our neighbors. How far this change is a healthy development, and how far a disease, is perhaps still uncertain.

Besides these almost universal kinds of primary association, there are many others whose form depends upon the particular state of civilization; the only essential thing, as I have said, being a certain intimacy and fusion of personalities. In our own society, being little bound by place, people easily form clubs, fraternal societies and the like, based on congeniality, which may give rise to real intimacy. Many such relations are formed at school and college, and among men and women brought together in the first instance by their occupations—as workmen in the same trade, or the like. Where there is a little common interest and activity, kindness grows like weeds by the roadside.

But the fact that the family and neighborhood groups are ascendant in the open and plastic time of childhood makes them even now incomparably more influential than all the rest.

Primary groups are primary in the sense that they give the individual his earliest and completest experience of social unity, and also in the sense that they do not change in the same degree as more elaborate relations, but form a comparatively permanent source out of which the latter are ever springing. Of course they are not independent of the larger society, but to some extent reflect its spirit; as the German family and the German school bear somewhat distinctly the print of German militarism. But this, after all, is like the tide setting back into creeks, and does not commonly go very far. Among the German, and still more among the Russian, peasantry are found habits of free cooperation and discussion almost uninfluenced by the character of the state; and it is a familiar and well-supported view that the village commune, self-governing as regards local affairs and habituated to discussion, is a very widespread institution in settled communities, and the continuator of a similar autonomy previously existing in the clan. "It is man who makes monarchies and establishes republics, but the commune seems to come directly from the hand of God." [4]

In our own cities the crowded tenements and the general economic and social confusion have sorely wounded the family and the neighborhood, but it is remarkable, in view of these conditions, what vitality they show; and there is nothing upon which the conscience of the time is more determined than upon restoring them to health.

These groups, then, are springs of life, not only for the individual but for social institutions. They are only in part moulded by special traditions, and, in larger degree, express a universal nature. The religion or government of other civilizations may seem alien to us, but the children or the family group wear the common life, and with them we can always make ourselves at home.

REFERENCES

1. The History of Human Marriage.
2. A History of Matrimonial Institutions.
3. Newer Ideals of Peace, 177.
4. De Tocqueville, Democracy in America, vol. i, chap. 5.

The Primary Group: Essence and Accident * (*Faris*)

The concept of primary group, while perhaps not the most important contribution of C. H. Cooley, may be the one for which he will be longest remembered. Others had spoken of the "we-group" and of the "in-group," but "primary group" is a happier phrase. In such groups, Cooley asserted, are to be found the very origins of human nature. The concept was coined at the right time and has been approved by the only effective authority, that of widespread quotation and continued use. The well-known passage reads:

> By primary groups I mean those characterized by intimate face-to-face association and cooperation. They are primary in several senses, but chiefly in that they are fundamental in forming the social nature and ideals of the individual. The result of intimate association, psychologically, is a certain fusion of individualities in a common whole, so that one's very self, for many purposes at least, is the common life and purpose of the group. Perhaps the simplest way of describing this wholeness is by saying that it is a "we"; it involves the sort of sympathy and mutual identification for which "we" is the natural expression. One lives in the feeling of the whole and finds the chief aims of his will in that feeling.[1]

There appear to be three properties of the primary group expressed or implied in this statement: the face-to-face relation, the temporal priority in experience, and the feeling of the whole as expressed by "we." The importance of the primary group, as he later shows, is that human nature arises

* By permission from *The Nature of Human Nature,* by Ellsworth Faris. Copyright, 1937, McGraw-Hill Book Company, Inc.

in it, and from it the human virtues of sympathy, kindness, justice, and fair play can be shown to originate.

The use of the conception raised certain difficulties. There was no terminology provided for the groups not primary; and many writers came to speak of "secondary groups," some authors actually putting these words into the mouth of Cooley though he nowhere uses the term.[2] The tendency has been to consider secondary groups as those which depend for communication on indirect media, such as newspapers.

A more serious question concerns the exact denotation of the concept. Attention was fixed on the face-to-face criterion to the neglect of the other differentia, and many now use the term as applying only to those who are physically present in the group relation. Implied has been the criterion of temporal priority which would limit primary groups to children, since adults have long ago lost connection with their first groups. The psychological criterion has received relatively little emphasis. There is value in a careful inquiry into the exact and definite qualities which mark off these groups from other groups.

The schoolmen made a distinction between the essence and the accident. The accident may define a concrete denoted object whose essence does not disappear when the accident is not present. Your table may be square and oaken, but being square and being made of oak are not essential to its being a table, and hence they are called accidents. It would be a table if round or oval or if made of maple or steel. The essential properties of a table can be stated in a careful definition, giving *genus* and *differentia*; but only error results from confusing accident and essence.

How essential to the definition of a primary group is the property face-to-face? Are all face-to-face groups primary groups? Are any groups primary groups where the relations are not face-to-face? Or is the face-to-face relation an accident? Similar questions arise concerning the temporal priority implied in the words, though in usage these have occasioned only minor difficulties.

There are groups to be described at the extreme of the series of which there appears to be no doubt. An American criminal court, with judge, jury, defendant, and counsel, are in a face-to-face nearness with none of the essential properties of the primary group as set forth in the quotation and the other passages in which Cooley uses his concept. For the court is externally controlled and governed by rules made by absent and ancient authorities. The actions are essentially institutional in character. A legislative body, even when small, or a board of directors with formal procedures, may be cited. A primary group may be as small as two, but an unwelcome bond salesman in your office does not necessarily mean that you and he form a primary group. Nor would a delinquent student summoned into the office of his dean form with that official such a group. Without multiplying instances it may, then, be assumed that not all face-to-face groups are in essence primary groups.

But do any groups not face-to-face have the properties of the primary group? There is reason to think so. A kinship group widely scattered in space, communicating only by letter, may be characterized by a common feeling of unity, exhibit "a certain fusion of individualities in a common whole," and be accurately classed as a primary group. A woman student has recorded an experience in which she "fell in love" with a woman author, wrote long letters to her, and was influenced by her profoundly and for many years, although the two had not ever seen each other at the time the account was written. Was not this a primary group? Historic friendships like that of Emerson and Carlyle did not rest on physical presence, nor indeed so originate. Comrades in a cause, if there is esprit de corps, often form primary groups independent of spatial separation. These seem to be genuine primary groups.

The problem, then, is whether primary group is a spatial concept or whether other criteria must be sought. This inquiry will lead us to a more fundamental question: the validity of the group concept itself. Is a group a mere aggregation of individuals and therefore a mere name, or does it denote specific sociological things to be defined, classified, and studied?

The differences of opinion on this issue are old and familiar, and no solution of the problem is attempted here. A clear statement of the point of view can be made and should be kept in mind by any who may wish to profit by this discussion. The word "group" is used by some writers to indicate merely the aggregate of the individuals which make it up. This is the proper usage which statistics employs. The ages of divorced persons can be grouped into classes, averages figured, and relations with other aspects calculated. Such a group is a mere collection of units, and the averages are abstract symbols denoting the generalized character of these units. But the *sociological* group involves consensus, concert, communication. The statistical group exists for the statistician; the sociological group exists for its members. In the former the individuals constitute the group; in the latter the group makes its members. The vigorous attack on the group concept which Allport and others have made seems to neglect this distinction. The reader will find a discussion of those opposing views easy of access.[3]

I should like to raise the further question of the degree to which a sociological group can be defined in strictly objective terms. To what extent is a group to be called objective, and to what degree must subjective attitudes and images be assumed as essential? Is the sociological group an experience, an organization of experiences? A primary group may, indeed, be described by an onlooker after observing movements and sounds; but he may be only interpreting the symptoms, leaving the very essence of the group life unnoticed, or else misinterpreting what he has seen and heard. Strictly behavioristic accounts of group life cannot take account of what the members of the group feel or think.

"The sort of mutual identification and sympathy for which 'we' is the natural expression," suggests that Cooley did not mean to make the face-to-face relation the essence and sine qua non of the primary group. And if the primary group is characterized by the "we-feeling," we must look to subjective criteria and cannot depend wholly on mere observation, externally attempted. The appeal must be to experience and not confined to behavior.

Behaviorism is professed by many who do not accept the extreme forms of the statement. There are left-wing behaviorists, right-wing behaviorists, and those who occupy the center. But it would be accurate to characterize all forms of behaviorism as motivated by a desire to be objective. There is a tendency to minimize and sometimes to deny the importance of the inner subjective aspects of experience. Left-wing behaviorists deny the very existence of consciousness, but even right-wing members of this school seek to phrase their facts in terms of movements that can be observed. Only thus, do they feel, can we have an objective science.

Cooley saw things differently. Since the movements of our muscles, when we glow with pride or long for friends, offer no set pattern, he insisted on the importance of the imagination and the feelings. When a man falls in love or "gets religion," the nervous currents are so inaccessible compared with the images and feelings and resultant attitudes that he considered these latter facts as basic and central. Those who know their Cooley will recall his bold statement that the solid facts of social life are the facts of the imagination. My friend is best defined as what I imagine he will do and say to me on occasion. Cooley taught that to understand human nature we must imagine imaginations. In his last book he quotes Holmes as saying that when John and Tom meet there are six persons present. There is John's real self (known only to his Maker), John's idea of himself, and John's idea of Tom, and, of course, three corresponding Toms. Cooley goes on to say that there are really twelve or more, including John's idea of Tom's idea of John's idea of Tom. And if this be thought a fanciful refinement, he insists that a misconception of this last type, when Germany made a fateful decision, was possibly the reason she lost the war. In these "echoes of echoes of echoes" of personality we have an a fortiori consideration of the importance of the subjective aspect of conduct.

Whether Cooley be correctly interpreted as meaning that the primary group is defined in essence as characterized by a certain kind of feeling is a matter of literary exegesis. The considerations advanced indicate this to be the logical conclusion. If there is group consciousness, esprit de corps—a feeling of "we"—then we have a primary group which will manifest attitudes and behavior appropriate and recognizable. The face-to-face position is a mere accident. Groups of friends and neighbors form primary groups, but the essential quality may be present in groups where spatial contiguity is lacking. The Woman's International League for Peace and Freedom has some hundreds of idealistic pacifists scattered over the world, most of whom have never seen each other. But they are comrades in the cause, are conscious of an enveloping sense of the whole group, think and speak and feel in terms of "we," and answer the definition of a primary group. We have shown, on the other hand, that many face-to-face groups lack this quality.

If our reasoning is sound, it follows that not every family is a primary group and that a school group may or may not be so defined. A domestic tyrant with commands, threats, and punishments may conceivably assemble his subjects around a table thrice daily in a group that lacks the essential qualities of the primary group. Likewise, a teacher may sometimes be the leader of a primary group; but one who has alienated the children may be hated or may be treated abstractly as a mere outsider and functionary in a company where there is no feeling of "we" and thus no primary group.

The correlative of the primary group is not a group whose members are separated or one where the communication is by indirect media. Rather is the primary group to be contrasted with the formal, the impersonal, the institutional. Its importance consists in the fact that the primary relations give rise to the essentially human experiences, so that human nature may be said to be created in primary group relations. The more completely the relations are mechanized, the more fractional the contacts become and the less effective in generating the sentiments which are distinctly human. If children in home and school are to be made to participate in the culture of their people, it is necessary that the home and school be primary groups, and the mere fact that they meet face-to-face with the members of the family or the school system is not sufficient to give it the essential character.

This is not to say that the primary group is a value concept and therefore superior to other types of groups. Human institutions are erected to meet human needs, and these needs may sometimes be better satisfied by institutions than by primary group relations. Indeed, primary group relations may intrude in a disorganizing manner, as when a police officer refuses to arrest a man because he is a friend. Here belong much of the corruption, bribery, nepotism, and "graft" of our modern life. Formal and institutional groups cannot perform their function unless the distinction between them and the primary group be kept with scrupulous clarity. Moreover, there is no sharp dividing line between the two clear types. There are marginal cases and transitional forms, and critical experiences can alter either or both of them; but there need be no vagueness if the essential qualities of each be accurately stated.

REFERENCES

1. Social Organization, 1909, p. 23.
2. Even von Wiese and Becker do this as late as 1932. See *Systematic Sociology*, p. 225.
3. See "Group and Institution," in Burgess, *Personality and the Social Group*, Chicago, 1929, pp. 102–180.

Ten Types of Group Formation * (*Redl*)

All the *Ten Types* presented deal with group formation "around" a central person. The difference between the ten types lies in the different role of the central person for the basic processes of group formation. The method which has been used to present these ten types is somewhat involved. Its peculiarity for the whole problem will become a topic of discussion later. Let it suffice at this point to say that an attempt has been made to present each type by describing one or more "illustrative examples." The explanation and formula which is thought to differentiate the type from others is then given. This summarizes the nature of the constituent group formative processes at work.

The "examples" are not necessarily identical with clinical material, nor are they to be used as "proof" for the formula which follows them. The examples are intended as illustrations for the purpose of introduction and explanation of each type. In condensing many observations into a composite picture, a host of practically irrelevant items were discarded in order to isolate one process. These illustrative examples will be best understood if they are taken as graphic slides. They all claim to be based on concrete reality experiences, but none of them pretends to be a photograph. Problems of frequency and actuality—for example—will be taken up in "discussion" of the ten types immediately following their presentation.

* Reprinted by special permission of The William Alanson White Psychiatric Foundation, Inc., from "Group Emotion and Leadership," by Fritz Redl, *Psychiatry*, Vol. V, No. 4, November, 1942, pp. 575–585. Copyright, 1942, by The William Alanson White Psychiatric Foundation, Inc.

TYPE 1: "THE PATRIARCHAL SOVEREIGN"

Illustrative example: This group is composed of approximately ten-year-old children, most of whom are just at that point in their development where they most fully represent the end states of "childhood" immediately before the outbreak of preadolescent symptoms. In charge of them is a teacher who fits the following description: "He is an elderly gentleman of stern but not unfriendly exterior, decided but fundamentally mild in his manner. He stands for "order and discipline" but they are values so deeply ingrained in him that he hardly thinks of them explicitly, nor does it occur to anyone to doubt them in his presence. He believes in good and thorough work, knows very clearly what he expects and leaves no doubt about it in the minds of his students." The atmosphere of the classroom may be easily described. The children accept his values without question. Their emotions about him are a mixture of love and adoration, with an element of anxiety in all those instances in which they are not quite sure of his approval. As long as they behave according to his code they feel happily secure—sheltered. Thoughts and imaginations which do not comply with his code are suppressed in his presence. The jokes he makes, or acknowledges, are funny. If one youngster is not quite so ready as the others to concentrate his filial adoration upon this type of a teacher, makes unfitting remarks, unruly gestures, or shows lack of submission, the others will experience a deep feeling of moral indignation—even though they may have enjoyed this youngster's jokes a few minutes previously during the recreation period. They all love their teacher and trust him infinitely, but certain thoughts must never enter their minds in his presence. When questioned or doubted by this teacher, tears come more easily than words; behind the happy security felt in his presence there is a nagging fear of its loss which streams into awareness every once in a while without apparent cause.

Explanation: These youngsters love their teacher, but that is not all that occurs. Their love is of a type which leads to "identification." It would be absurd to say that they want to be like their teacher, but they want to behave so that their teacher will approve of them.

Formula: These children became a group because they incorporate the "super-ego"—conscience—of the central person, into their own. On the basis of this similarity between them, they develop group emotions toward each other.

TYPE 2: "THE LEADER"

Illustrative example: This group of boys are between fifteen and seventeen years of age. Most of them are far beyond their preadolescence—at the verge of transition from earlier adolescence into later adolescence. The teacher in charge of them is, or has the appearance of being, very young. He has an attractive exterior. He is somewhat juvenile but not too unpleasantly so in his views and behavior. He also stands for "work and discipline," and gets his youngsters to comply without much outward pressure. However, the basis on which he gets them to accept has authority is a little different. He differs from the patriarch mainly in that he strongly sympathizes with the drives of the children. They are clearly aware of it. He plays a dual role in his teaching. In his own super-ego, he is identified with the order and the demands of the school which he represents; but he is keenly aware of the instinctual demands of the youngsters. In order to combine both he has to display considerable technical skill. If he succeeds, he makes his class feel secure and happy; if he fails, they are frightened either of him or of their own drives. The children adore him, but they also accept what he stands for without much question. The boy who misbehaves is not the greatest danger to the emotional equilibrium of the group. He elicits moral pity rather than indignation from the others. The danger is the boy who tries to get a more intensive emotional counter response from the teacher than the others, while less ready to pay for it by conscientious output of work. He is hated and despised by them. A single youngster in that group, feeling negatively viewed by the teacher, is unhappy rather than frightened. Undesirable thoughts and actions still remain confessable. To be "understood"—accepted—is the minimum requirement of group happiness in this class.

Explanation: A central person of this kind appeals to the love emotions as well as to the narcissistic tendencies in the children. However, it would be difficult to say that they put the teacher in the place of their "conscience." Rather they place him in the other part of their super-ego, in what is usually called their "ego-idea," which means that they start wishing to become the type of person he is.

Formula: The children become a group because they incorporate the teacher's personality into their ego-ideal. On the basis of this similarity they develop group emotions toward each other. This formula coincides most closely with that of Freud in *Group Psychology and the Analysis of the Ego*.

Type 3: "The Tyrant"

Illustrative example: This is a class of children approximately ten years old, near the verge of preadolescence. In charge of them is an elderly, or middle-aged teacher, among whose motives for teaching were one or both of the following: He is compulsively bound to repeat a certain pattern of "discipline" against the children because this is the only way he can prove late obedience to some of the demands of his own parents; or, his most intensive drive satisfactions lie in the direction of sadism, and he has to use the children as objects for that purpose. This teacher will not "stand for" anything, but has to "impose" some kind of capricious "order" or "discipline" all the time. Nor will he be satisfied to do so quietly. He will require a noisy machinery of special tricks, rules, and revenge techniques. His concept of discipline, too, will be of the most compulsive, unrealistic sort; the way he works it out is as "unchild-minded" as possible. In short, there is a "regular tyrant" in charge of this class. Everyday psychology might tempt one to expect children to hate the teacher and fight him as much as they dared. Indeed, this does happen in a few examples, which I will describe later. The entirely different reaction from the youngsters is surprising. These children submit easily. They rebel against the silly pedantry of this tyrant less vehemently than other groups do against the reasonable demands of their beloved leader. Nor do they submit only temporarily. What they show is genuine "identification." How strong is this identification? This is illustrated by the youngster who does dare to rebel in such a class. He has a difficult time. He has everyone against him, the teacher, the other youngsters, and himself. The others show intensive signs of moral indignation, eventually becoming afraid of the child.

However, one difference seems obvious. The emotional relations these youngsters develop among themselves seem less intensive than in the other illustrations. Children of such classes develop little "comradeship"—unlike those who just hate their teacher without identifying with him—and they seem to be afraid of each other, and distrustful. They seem to fear that too much intimacy might endanger the successful repression of their hostility and might force them to realize what cowards they are.

Explanation: Doubtless, the identification of these children with their tyrant is genuine. He is the central person for that group. Unlike the two previous illustrations, this identification occurs from a different motive. It is not love which causes them to identify, but fear. Of course, not all fear leads into identification, but it does in the type just described.

Formula: These children incorporate the super-ego of the central person into their own by way of identification, the outgrowth of fear of the aggressor, and on this basis establish group emotions between each other.

TYPE 4: THE CENTRAL PERSON AS LOVE OBJECT

Freud mentioned an example of group formation which he exempted from the leadership type. It fits into the pattern according to the broadened concept of the *central person* I have introduced.

Imagine a number of women who are in love with a singer or pianist and crowd around him after his performance. Certainly each of them would prefer to be jealous of all the others. However, considering their large number and how impossible it is for them to reach the aim of their infatuation, they resign and instead of pulling each other's hair, they act like a uniform group. They bring ovations to their idol in common actions and would be glad to divide his locks among themselves.[1]

The life in the school class furnishes two similar examples for illustration.

Illustrative example, 1: There is a group of sixteen-year-old girls in a class of a girls' high school. In charge of them is a male teacher—young, attractive, but narcissistic enough so that they are not too greatly frightened sexually from the outset. It is known that in some such cases "the whole class falls in love with him." From that moment on, they will act like a group in many ways along the line of Freud's example. Despite their infatuation for him, it would not be surprising if the teacher complained that he had trouble with discipline—that these girls did not obey him or follow his wishes without pressure. It seems that this kind of "being in love" with the central person does not make for "identification" described in *Type 2*.

Illustrative example, 2: In a co-educational class of approximately sixteen-year-old children, there is one especially pretty girl, rather narcissistic. In similar situations one frequently finds a whole cluster of boys loving and adoring her in various ways, but equally unsuccessful insofar as their wish for exclusive possession goes. The girl is equipped with special skill for keeping them all equidistant and yet equally near. Symptoms of dense group formation may sometimes be observed among these boys. They seem very close to each other, and yet their relationship is not genuine friendship. It is on a group emotional basis. This becomes evident when the girl ultimately decides in favor of one of her suitors. The other boys then begin to hate him as their rival, with the exception perhaps of the one or two who may move even closer to the successful colleague and, thus, enjoy some of the satisfactions denied to them *via* the mechanism of *altruistic concession.*[2]

Explanation: There is no doubt that the group emotional symptoms are genuine and that the teacher in *Example 1* and the girl in *Example 2* are playing the role of the central person without whose presence this type of group formative process would not have been evoked. However, it is also evident that these central persons could not be called "leaders" by any interpretation of the term—that the other children do not "identify" with them. Nor do they incorporate their central person's standards. The central person remains "outside" but does call out a display of group emotional symptoms in these children.

Formula: The children choose one and the same person as an object of their love, and on the basis of this similarity they develop group emotions between each other.

TYPE 5: THE CENTRAL PERSON AS OBJECT OF AGGRESSIVE DRIVES

Illustrative example, 1: A type of teacher similar to the one described under the heading of "tyrant" is less intensive in his sadism, less superior in the rest of his personality traits. He is in charge of a group of rather problematic adolescents in a school setup which is so well regimented through an established system of suppressive rules that no one dares to rebel, because it would be too futile. These children obey their teacher under the constant application of pressure. They behave sufficiently well to keep out of trouble, but they do so grudgingly. They neither identify with the teacher nor with what he represents. Their relationship toward him—with the possible exception of a "sissy" in the class—is one of intensive hatred, of piled-up aggression which is kept from exploding only by their reality-insight. And yet, although they do not identify with the teacher, the emotions they develop toward each other will be truly positive and strong. The amount of 'comradeship' these children display is enormous—greater than in any of the other groups. He who dares to identify with the hatred oppressor is an outcast—arouses a lynching attitude in the rest of the class. Their feeling toward him is one of moral indignation, but its content is different from the other examples. It is moral indignation "from beneath," to use one of Nietzsche's terms.

Illustrative example, 2: Here is a group of children who have developed no special group structure. There is no person in charge of them with a sufficiently outspoken personality to encourage any of the previously mentioned types of group formation. A new youngster suddenly enters the class who differs from them in that he is a very outspoken type. This new youngster is especially narcissistic, defiant, lofty, and unskilled in handling other people's weaknesses. If he is intellectually superior, he need not even be of a different ethnic group. Everyone's aggression is immediately turned against him. At the same time one may observe that his entrance into the class has indirectly influenced group formative processes. They move closer together; their common aggression against him seems to "bind" them, and they become more of a "group" than they were before.

Explanation: This new youngster cannot be called a "leader." The others neither like him nor "identify" with him. They do quite the contrary; and yet, he does apparently become the focal point of their group formative procedures, much as the teacher did in *Example 1*.

Formula: The children choose one and the same person as an object of their aggressive drives and through this similarity develop group emotions about each other.

Type 6: The Organizer

Illustrative example: In a class of approximately thirteen-year-old boys there are five who find clandestine enjoyment of the cigarette as a symbol of adulthood. And yet, all five are of the type who have decided worries about how they can obtain cigarettes. They have neither the money to buy them, the courage to do so, nor the impudence to steal them from their fathers. Pre-adolescent revolt against adult concepts of what a good child should be has not progressed far enough. A new boy, for whom smoking is no great problem, enters the class. He neither invites, instigates nor encourages the others in this enterprise. They all know that he can get the desired cigarettes for them if they but ask. I have seen cases where hardly any other factor was involved. The boys neither loved nor admired this youngster; on the contrary, he was rather looked down upon as socially inferior. They did not fear him nor did he use any direct or indirect pressure upon them. Yet, by the mere fact of getting them the cigarettes, they suddenly eventuated into a regular "group," held together on the basis of their participation in the same forbidden pleasure.

Explanation: Perhaps this example seems more complicated—less credible—than the others, being unaccustomed to finding this function of the organizer isolated. Usually, it is coupled with other roles which the central person assumes for the potential group members. Although there are not many clear examples of this type, they cannot be reduced to any of the other types because neither love, hatred, nor identification is involved.

Formula: The central person renders an important service to the ego of the potential group members. He does so by providing the means for the satisfaction of common undesirable drives and thus prevents guilt feelings, anxieties, and conflicts which otherwise would be involved in that process for them. On the basis of this service, the latent undesirable drives of these youngsters can manifest openly. Through this common conflict-solution, group emotions develop in the interpersonal situation.

TYPE 7: THE SEDUCER

Illustrative example, 1: In a group of thirteen-year-old boys, six involved in "group masturbation," are apprehended. The first superficial examination by school authorities reveals apparent, unequal participation. Some were on-lookers, none were mutually active; all agreed that one of them was the "leader" of the gang. After thorough investigation the following situation was revealed. The obvious "culprit" was most "actively" engaged in masturbation. He was the "first to start it." However, he was not at all active in encouraging the others to join or to perform likewise. He was a little more developed than any of them; he masturbated freely at home without special guilt feelings. Masturbation meant something entirely different for him than for them, nor did he need the group from the standpoint of sex satisfaction. He gained nothing from the group situation, except prestige. He was not homosexual in the usual sense of the term; more surprising, perhaps, is the fact that the others neither especially loved nor feared him. They were more infantile than he. They had sufficiently conquered their anxieties about sex curiosity to take the first step in active experimentation on a highly pregenital level. However, they might not have done so alone, since that would have made them feel guilty about it. Actually, they used this boy for the purpose of "seduction." They needed him and the group situation allowed them to overcome their restrictions. Only after he was the "first one to do it" were they ready and able to join.

Illustrative example, 2: A class of fifteen-year-old children, in high spirits towards the end of their morning sessions, wait for their teacher to arrive. He is somewhat late. He is the "leader" type, with a slight patriarchial tendency. Recently, at an examination period, a considerable amount of tension and dissatisfaction was extant. The relationship between them and their teacher was rather strained. He now enters the room. They stand at attention as was expected. Suddenly, one youngster, neither much liked, respected, nor feared by the others, starts yelling aggressively in a much more rebellious manner than anyone would have expected, especially toward this teacher. There is a moment of surprise. Before the teacher can react manifestly, they all join in. The whole class is in an uproar, more intensively so than any of them can afterwards "understand."

Explanation: Both examples beyond doubt represent group formation through the existence of a central person. In both cases the potential group members had much in common before the group formative processes began. It is also evident that they did not start before the central person committed the 'first act.' Apparently what evoked the group emotional reactions was the fact that these central persons committed an "initiatory" act. Through this act, the satisfaction of undesirable drives became possible in others, who would otherwise not have openly expressed them. This concept of the "initiatory act" is not an invention but the description of a procedure observed so frequently in school and adult life that it does not require proof. It needs, however, to be explained. Thus far, I do not attempt to show why the "first act" may have such magical power over other people's suppressed drives. I simply allude to the fact here and keep its explanation for a later presentation.

What occurred in these children is here described. There is a strong increase in the intensity of undesirable drives—sex, in *Example 1*, aggressions, in *Example 2*. The personal super-ego of these children remains strong enough to suppress any possibility of the drives becoming overt. The ego of these children is in a predicament. Pressed with equal strength from oppressed drives and super-ego demands, it knows not what to do. Anxiety and uneasiness are the usual emotional accompaniments of such disturbances to balance. It is on the basis of such a situation that the effect of an "initiatory act" seems to take place.

Formula: The central person renders a service to the ego of the potential group members. He does this by committing the "initiatory act" and thus prevents guilt feelings, anxieties, and conflicts. On the basis of this service, the latent drives of these children manifest openly. Through this common conflict-solution, they develop group emotions.

Type 8: The Hero

Illustrative example: This is the same tyrant-group described under *Type 3* —where all the children were fully identified with their oppressor—at a later interval. These children have developed further into preadolescent rebelliousness. Their reality insight begins to fade in important issues: yet sufficiently frightened, they keep their defensive identification against rebellious wishes. The tyrant now begins to make deplorable mistakes. He chooses, for example, one child as the preferable object of his sadism and persecutes him more and more persistently. The others almost pity the child, but pity would imply criticism of their tyrant, and that would tend to revive their own dangerously rebellious feelings against him. So, they hold as tightly to their protective identification with the oppressor as they can. However, one of them has more courage. Something in his history makes him less able to endure this—or, perhaps, his insight into the real dangers implied by rebellion dwindles more rapidly. In any event, he is one day unable to tolerate the teacher's attack upon his victim. This boy defends his colleague and is considered "fresh" and reckless. The whole class gasps with surprise. They expect something fearful to happen. Surely the teacher will kill that child, or lightning will strike out of the clear sky. But no avenging stroke of lightning descends to quell the rebellion. The teacher is evidently too surprised or frightened momentarily to know what to do. When he demonstrates his fury, it is too late. The "hero" has worked his miracle. All the youngsters have altered their sentiments, at least secretly. Now they adore him and even start identifying with him. He takes his punishment, but remains victorious.

Explanation: The situation is similar to the one previously described, but events now move in the opposite direction. These youngsters suffer similarly from a number of suppressed tendencies—such as just rebellion in favor of a suffering colleague—however, they are too fearful of the realistic consequences of such feelings. Their personal cowardice hinders them from doing what they feel is right, but what would have awful consequences for them. Again the hero commits the "initiatory act." Through his demonstration of courage the others suddenly discard anxieties and dare—if not to act, then, at least—to feel what their own standard of justice has long wanted them to experience.

Formula: The central person renders a service to the ego of the potential group members. He does so by committing the 'initiatory act' and thus saves them anxieties and conflicts. The "initiatory act," however, leads in the direction of moral values *versus* cowardly self-protection this time. On the basis of this service the undesirable tendencies toward cowardly submission in these children are conquered. Through this common conflict-solution group psychological emotions are evoked.

Type 9: The "Bad Influence"

There are children in many classes who are constantly being accused of being "undesirable elements" by all teachers, parents, and by the other children, too. And yet, they can scarcely be accused of "having an evil" influence. Usually what they are accused of is unclear but it is assumed that their mere presence in the classroom affects the others badly—"brings out the worst in them." And yet it would be embarrassing to say how they do this. Accusations made against them often have to be withdrawn, because no definite basis exists in fact. Nothing can be proved. Sometimes, admittedly, these children are not so difficult to manage; they are better than the influence they are accused of having on the others. Fundamentally, this is an accusation of seduction through magic. Apparently belief in the infectiousness of something within these children seems absurd, and yet, it is not. The background upon which the accusations are made is usually true. These children do affect the others, not overtly—quite in contrast to the "seducer type"—but, by their presence in the same room, something happens to these youngsters which makes them unruly, full of "dirty" ideas, or just difficult to manage. What supports this?

Illustrative example: In a botany class of eleven-year-old children, a word is mentioned which reminds those who "know" of a sex situation. About a dozen are preoccupied with associations of this sort. When the word is mentioned, they all look at one boy, then at each other. They grin. He grins back. The whole room at this moment, is divided in two. The threads of this little clique are spread like a net over it. Next day a nearly identical situation recurs. However, that boy happens to be absent from class. Nothing happens. The children fail to make the same association as the day before. Their little "gang" remains submerged in the group without interruption.

Explanation: This type again is very similar to that of the "seducer"; the difference, however, rests in the technique used for "seduction." Nothing like the "initiatory act" is implied here. The explanation has to be reduced to a more descriptive statement to show how the "bad influence" works. The dynamic explanation must be considered later.

With the inner constellation of the potential group members similar to that described in the seduction type, it can apparently be said that they possess a number of undesirable drives which seek expression; their super-ego is in command of the situation, so that satisfaction of these undesirable drives is impossible without the penalty of remorse and anxiety; and, the ego of these children is in a "bad jam," squeezed between the urges of their drives and the demands of a strong super-ego.

The inner constellation of the "bad influence" type of a central person is different from that of the group members. In him there is no conflict. His drives in the same direction do not set loose conflicts and problems for him. He faces them and does not care. Alertness, on the part of the others to this event seems sufficient encouragement for the expression of what they had just been trying to suppress. This really means the assumption of a definite process which might best be described by saying that the "unconflicted" personality constellation has an infectious influence on the conflicted whenever they meet. This again is the description of an easily observable fact, which by itself provides no understanding of the process. However, it is enough to explain the group formative processes in these cases. It is important to realize that these examples of so-called "bad influence" are usually group psychological procedures.

Formula: The central person renders a service to the ego of the potential group members. He does so by virtue of the "infectiousness of the unconflicted personality constellation upon the conflicted one." Through this, he saves them the expense of guilt feelings, anxieties, and conflicts. On the basis of this service, the latent undesirable drives of these children can manifest openly. Through this common conflict solution, these children develop group emotions in relationship with each other.

TYPE 10: THE "GOOD EXAMPLE"

Illustrative example: The same class as the one mentioned in the previous example contains another group of boys who "gang up" with each other even more intensively than do the undesirable ones. Nevertheless, the teacher would hesitate to call them a "gang" or even a group. They are just a bunch of very good friends, he would say. However, one of them is the obvious center, and he "has a marvelous influence" upon the others. They are much nicer when he is around. If pressed, the teacher could hardly explain how that boy manages to influence them for he obviously does nothing. In looking at this group more closely, the following situation is discovered. These children are not "friends" in the personal meaning of this term. All are at that stage where they are full of new curiosities of which they are afraid, because they would feel guilty in satisfying them. This one boy, however, is far removed from any undesirable thought or act.

Explanation: The inner constellation in the potential group members shows a number of undesirable drives seeking expression, the super-ego is decidedly against this but scarcely able to maintain its position for long, and the ego is in a "bad jam" about how to maintain balance in such a situation. The inner constellation of the central boy in this situation contains no conflict of this kind. The mere idea of expressing undesirable thoughts in his presence is impossible. So, the group moves closer to him; in his presence they feel secure. What they fear is their own drives; what they look for is some support for their endangered super-ego. The situation is the exact reverse of the *Bad Influence* example.

Formula: The central person renders a service to the ego of the potential group members. He does so by virtue of the "infectiousness of the unconflicted personality constellation upon the conflicted one." Through this, he saves them the necessity to face their own drives of which they are afraid, and conflicts resulting from this. This time, however, the solution leads in the direction of moral values instead of undesirable drives. On the basis of this service, the children can suppress their undesirable drives according to the command of their own super-ego. Through this common conflict solution they develop group emotions in the relationship with each other.

SUMMARY

For the purpose of rapid summary, these ten types can be grouped into three main categories and tabulated.

THE ROLE OF THE CENTRAL PERSON FOR THE GROUP FORMATIVE PROCESS

The Central Person as an Object of Identification
On the Basis of Love
    Incorporation into conscience ....Type 1
    Incorporation into the "ego ideal" ....Type 2
On the basis of Fear
    Identification with the aggressor ....Type 3

The Central Person as an Object of Drives
  As an object of love drives ....Type 4
  As an object of aggressive drives ....Type 5

The Central Person as an Ego Support
  Providing means for drive satisfaction ....Type 6
  Dissolving conflict situations through guilt-anxiety assuagement.
    Through the technique of the initiatory act in the service
    of drive satisfaction ....Type 7
    and in the service of drive defense ....Type 8
    Through the "infectiousness of the unconflicted personality
    constellation over the conflicted one" in the service of
    drive satisfaction ....Type 9
    and in the service of drive defense ....Type 10

DISCUSSION OF THE 10 TYPES

GROUP PSYCHOLOGICAL SPECULATIONS

The description of 10 different group psychological patterns under "type" headings does not effect a compulsively logical separation between them. In fact, they are not rigid "types" of groups so much as they are typical *trends* in group formative processes. Simplification and abbreviation may have made the types seem much more final and exclusive than they are meant to be. The 10 "types" are *auxiliary concepts for exploratory pur-*

poses only. Holding them toward practical life situations should help to show certain trends in them that might not otherwise have been discovered. That is all they are good for. Nothing could be more wrong than to extrapolate practical group experience into any one of these "types," as though any one real group situation would ever be a clear exemplification of them.

Example: The "organizer" of a group usually combines "leader" or "seducer" functions, and *vice versa*—there is rarely a leader, tyrant, or seducer situation without some organizing activity linked up with it. Yet, there will usually be differences as to the degree to which the one or other type of relationship of central person to group is *basic,* or *secondary* to group formation. Also, a person may start out by being the "hero," "seducer," or what not, and on the basis of this group formation he may, later, enter leader-organizer and other relationships, or even transform himself entirely from one to the other role. This seems to be the case where a person suddenly becomes central by a "hero" situation, then, on that basis, develops more pervading leadership functions for his group.

In establishing the "10 types," as auxiliary concepts for exploration, the question of their application to *historical, political and educational reality* was neglected. This question is certainly a big temptation. For, no doubt, it would be interesting to know which type of group formation—or which mixture of them—is more frequently represented in any one cultural situation, or at any one time in history, or at any one socio-economic, national, "racial" place.

However, I am convinced that it would be premature to try such speculations at the moment. There are two main handicaps. First, any decision about *frequency* and reality distribution of types or type mixtures can *never be the result of speculation but only of very specific research.* Such research, done on the basis of the conceptual equipment suggested here, has not been undertaken yet. Therefore, it might be interesting to play with analogies, but scientific statements on such questions would be definitely out of place. Second, the real, psychoanalytic structure of any one group situation is very hard to ascertain. It definitely *need not be identical* with the terminology which that group chooses to express its allegiances. Nor can it always be guessed easily from a surface study of expressions of group life. In fact, the distance between the actual underlying group emotional constellation and the surface manifestations of overt group verbiage and group behavior, may be as great, at times, as the distance between the conscious dream content and the latent dream thoughts. . . .

While a positive application of my typology to any actual political or historical situation seems premature, I believe that I am ready to make one negative suggestion: the picture I have portrayed would make one highly suspicious of all attempts at *group psychological mysticism,* of a *too naive rationalism,* and would also warn against what could be called *psychiatric individualism.*

REFERENCES

1. Freud, Sigmund, *Group Psychology and the Analysis of the Ego*; London, Hogarth Press, 1922 (134 pp.).
2. Freud, Anna, *The Ego and the Mechanisms of Defense*; London, Hogarth Press, 1922 (-x and 196 pp.).

The Knitting of Racial Groups in Industry * (*Hughes*)

Elton Mayo has recently given the name "rabble hypothesis" [1] to the assumptions which, he claims, still guide not merely many managements in dealing with workers, but also many of those who investigate industrial behavior. He refers to the belief that an industrial organization is an aggregation of individuals each seeking his own gain without reference to other persons, and consequently each capable of being induced to greater effort by devices focused upon this desire for advantage. To this assumption Mayo opposes the view that a working force normally consists of social groups, whose members are highly responsive to each other's social gestures and identify their fates with those of their fellows; social groups which, further, are related to others in the larger system of social relations in and about industry. Mayo argues that a state of good cooperation is dependent upon the existence of such groups, even though one of their functions may be some restriction of individual production. He believes, finally, that the "solitary," the person who does not feel himself part of any such group, is actually somewhat disorganized, and not likely to function well in the long run.

The theme of my remarks is that a fruitful way of analyzing race relations in industry is to look at them against whatever grid of informal social groupings and of relations within and between such groups exists in the industries, departments and jobs in which Negroes or other new kinds of employees are put to work. Recent experience suggests that this grid of

* Address given before American Sociological Society at the 40th Annual Meeting, March 1–3, 1946, Cleveland, Ohio, by Everett Cherrington Hughes (University of Chicago). Reprinted from *American Sociological Review*, Vol. 11, No. 5, October, 1946, pp. 512–515, with permission of the publisher, The American Sociological Society, and the author.

relationships, and the manner in which Negroes are introduced into it, are more significant in the success of a policy of hiring Negroes than are the generalized racial attitudes of the white workers concerned.

Polling of white workers to find whether they favor the hiring of Negroes as their equal and close fellow-workers would almost anywhere result in an emphatic "No." Workers generally prefer not to have any new kinds of workers introduced among and equal to themselves. But Negroes have been successfully employed among white workers; and many other new kinds of workers have been introduced among older kinds of workers who were not enthusiastic about them. Polling of attitudes, on this simple basis, gives little clue to the probable behavior of the old workers to the new. The simple "No" of the workers to many proposals of management is not to be taken at face value; for industry has not been run by majority vote of the workers, and a "No" is often no more than a demonstration of protest. In fact, workers more or less expect each other to object to changes proposed by management.

It does not follow that racial preferences and dislikes have no bearing on the question whether the races will work well together. Racial attitudes themselves take on new dimensions when looked at in the framework of the human relations prevailing in industry. It is characteristic of industry that groups of workers who have knit themselves into some kind of organization in and about their work develop some set of expectations, considered little short of rights, that their jobs and their work-fellowship should be limited to persons of some certain kind—as to age, sex, race, ethnic qualities, education and social class. Mr. Orvis Collins, in a recent paper,[2] shows how the management of a New England factory got itself into an impasse by violating the expectation that certain kinds of jobs should belong to Irishmen. We could do with a good deal more investigation of what workers in various jobs and industries consider the proper kind of fellow-worker, what they think are their own rights in the matter, and of the devices which they use the expel newcomers not of the kind they want and of those which management and unions have used to get the newcomers accepted. Such expectations are not likely to be stated formally; they may not even be admitted informally. Defense of the breach of them is likely, as in the case reported by Mr. Collins, to be hidden by indirection of various kinds. It is also probable that some of the so-called non-economic behavior attributed to people new to industry—erratic changing of jobs, failure to respond to wage incentives, quitting industrial work entirely and returning home to farms—may be due not merely to unfamiliarity with the ways of industry. It may be a reaction to rejection by those among whom they have been put to work.

I used the expression "grid of informal relations." By this I mean simply the pattern of grouping which prevails in a place of work. The factory cafeteria exhibits such a grid; this is the pattern which renews itself every day at noon, when there are the most and the greatest variety of people there. The employees sort themselves according to their rank, sex, and race, and to their places in the office or out in the plant. The observers found also, that while it was seldom possible for all of the workers who belonged to a given close circle to come to the cafeteria and find places at the same table, they did— so far as possible—eat together.

The individual thus finds his table in a grid of rank, sex, race, and personal relations. At a union picnic the unit of the pattern was the table, each serving as headquarters for one or two family parties. The management families were in one corner of the grounds; the mass of the Negro families were concentrated toward the opposite corner. In the middle zone were some tables at which a Negro family party and a white family party sat, but so grouped that Negro faced Negro and white faced white. Near the platform used for announcements, dancing and contests, were the only tables with racially mixed parties. These were the union leaders in charge of the picnic. Thus, in this grid, the family—which is by American definition not racially mixed—and rank within the factory worked together to form a pattern, which the union slightly disturbed by drawing a few people away from the family and away from factory rank to form a small nucleus based on special function.

I mention these examples first, not because of the inherent significance of seating arrangements in cafeterias and at picnics, but because they illustrate so vividly what I mean by a grid of relationships. Incidentally, in both cases the Negroes—with the exception of the few union committeemen at the picnic—fitted into that space in the pattern whose occupants were most numerous and of the lowest rank. None of them had characteristics which would set up any expectation that they might fit anywhere else.

On the job itself, the patterns of relationship are subject in varying measure to the physical lay-out of the shop, the distribution of workers of different races among the various kinds of jobs, by the degree of dependence of one worker upon others for successful performance of his work, as well as by the social atmosphere created by management, supervision, the union and the workers themselves. Furthermore, the informal relations among workers are not always so immediately visible as in the cafeteria and at the picnic. But generally such relations are there, although not all workers are part of any network of groups of people who cooperate in some special way to control what goes on with reference to work or other matters.

THE FIXING ROOM

A department called the Fixing Room in a certain plant illustrates one kind of grid or grouping at work and its consequences for race relations. The work is done by teams of three men. The members of a team meet and exchange tools and materials without a word and without even a direct look at each other. In fact, there is something of a cult of silence among them. The bonus, which is a large part of their income, is based upon the product of a team. The skills are learned on the job from the other members of the team to which one is assigned. The men are nearly all Poles, past middle age, bound together by kinship and neighborhood. The teams and the whole group together are notoriously and successfully impervious to management's attempts to control their relations, and even the choice of new employees. They pick their own fellows. The labor shortage of the war dried up the sources of new men of their kind and management tried to get new help—Negroes. Several Negro men were hired, but all left after a few days. Interviews with these Negro men revealed that they were subjected to a not very subtle, but very effective torture by the other members of the teams to which they were assigned. Later, the management tried the device of hiring a whole Negro team, which complicated the matter of learning the job; they stayed for some time, achieved a very creditable rate of production, and recently quit in a group. We have not yet found out what happened, but I venture to say that it was fundamentally a case of rejection by the older workers. In this shop there is no place for the solitary individual. One must be integrated into a team-clique to work at all. The homogeneity and traditional solidarity and autonomy of the whole department conspired to make the men unwilling to accept new kinds of workers and make management impotent to bring about change against their will.

The power of resistance was probably increased by connivance of the foremen. Many of the foremen in this plant are old-timers, who worked for the father of the present manager. They have a sort of proprietary interest in the departments they supervise; their idiosyncrasies are rather affectionately tolerated. The foremen can thus be, in effect, leaders of departmental cliques. A change of policy thus meets a very dense and intricate resisting structure. In their efforts to hire Negroes in the Fixing Room, management did not succeed in penetrating it. . . .

REFERENCES

1. *The Social Problems of an Industrial Civilization.* Boston, 1945. Chapter II, and passim.
2. "Ethnic Behavior in Industry." *American Journal of Sociology.* LI (January, 1946), 293–298.

The Primary Group in Current Research * (*Shils*)

As a result of the convergence of the underlying themes which were only implicit in a wide variety of concrete research interests, most of which had a distinctly practical orientation and were quite independent of one another, the study of small groups has now become a major field of American socio-logical research. The degree of theoretical self-consciousness is still not great among sociologists, and there has not yet come forth a common body of hypotheses concerning behavior in primary groups, the conditions of pri-mary-group formation, maintenance, and change, or the consequences of primary-group structure for other parts of social structure. A large amount of research has been done along the lines laid down by the leading figures whose work has been briefly described in the preceding sections. There has been some convergence of techniques—the sociometric technique has been widely adopted—and the range of subject matter to which certain techniques have been applied has been extended (e.g., the students of Lewin who pre-viously had concentrated their special techniques largely on children's and youth groups have broadened their interest to industrial and administrative groups). Here and there, too, the possibilities of the theoretical unification of primary-group analysis on a more general level have been perceived.[1] In this section we shall review some representative investigations which carry on the work of renovators of the study of the primary group and illustrate the most recent trend.

The two leading problems which engage the students of small groups in American sociology are (a) the function of the primary group in formal organizations, and (b) the internal dynamics of the primary group. In studies of both problems the conditions of the development of solidarity among the members, the emergence of certain types of relations with leaders, the formation of subgroups and of cleavage within groups, the conditions of the effective incorporation of new members, and the consequences of the techniques of leadership for relations among the rank and file are dealt with. In studies of the former problem, however, attention is concentrated on the influence of the internal working of the primary group on the patterns of group relations which have been formally prescribed by bureaucratic authority. It is thus a problem of the relationship between the primary group

* Reprinted from Chapter III, "The Study of the Primary Group" by Edward A. Shils in *The Policy Sciences* edited by Daniel Lerner and Harold D. Lasswell with permission of the publishers, Stanford University Press. Copyright 1951 by the Board of Trustees of Leland Stanford Junior University. Publication assisted by a grant from the Carnegie Corporation of New York.

and the commanding authority, be it person, symbol, or institution, outside the primary group itself. In studies of the latter problem, less attention is paid to context and more to the group's endogenous elements deriving from the personal characteristics and roles of the members and the nature of the tasks they confront. The problems are closely related and the same investigations frequently deal with both of them.

The studies of the functioning of primary groups in formal organizations have mostly been conducted in the field of industrial organization. Here the example of Mayo's researches has determined the principal lines of development. The efflorescence of the study of industrial relations in American universities following the Second World War derives mostly from Mayo's inspiration; and, although there have been many divergences and outspoken criticisms (particularly of the failure of Mayo to appreciate the limits of primary-group formation and effectiveness in a modern industrial system), still the predominant themes of interpretation are easy to trace to him. Among sociologists, Warner, in the fourth volume of his "Yankee City" series,[2] has applied Mayo's hypothesis in his attempted explanation of a long strike in a factory in Newburyport. According to Warner, the strike was the result of the disintegration of primary-group ties between various ranks in the technical and managerial hierarchy within the factory and their replacement by a formalized bureaucratic authority, the main seat of which was physically far distant from the town itself.

Warner, following Mayo, contends that under these conditions primary-group solidarity could not be realized. The resultant divergences of expectation and evaluation generated hostility to a degree which might have been avoided if the relations of mutual trust characteristic of a primary group or quasi-primary group had existed. The same fundamental hypothesis is pursued in a variety of concrete studies undertaken by Everett Hughes and other members of the Committee on Human Relations in Industry (University of Chicago) [3] with special attention to the influences of ethnic characteristics on cleavages and solidarity within the factory.

Large-scale studies of industrial group-solidarity and *anomie* have also been undertaken by social psychologists whose intellectual backgrounds have little in common with that of Mayo and his school. We refer here to the investigations of industrial morale through the extensive analysis of wide samples, using standardized methods of interview; and to the intensive group-behavior investigations using the methods of observation developed in the study of children's and youth groups and making experimental modifications in the situation to discover the role of primary-group factors in determining the degree and rate of acceptance of heteronomous norms. The first (use of an analysis of wide samples) is an extension of the particular form of public opinion polling developed by Rensis Likert on behalf of the Department of Agriculture before and during World War II. It was used in a series of studies conducted by Likert and by Daniel Katz and Herbert Hyman [4] in war production industries (munitions and ship building). Although the techniques are different from those of Mayo, the studies revealed the operation of variables resembling those discovered by him. Hostile relations with management, unsatisfactory work relations, and other factors indicative of poor primary-group relations had a negative effect on morale and kept output at a low level. Where stability of the working force and primary-group formation could be achieved, morale was higher and productivity correspondingly higher.

In the Likert-Katz studies, samples of the entire factory population were used instead of the combination of intensive interviewing and prolonged concrete observation of one or a very few actual small working groups in the factory in the style of Mayo. The desideratum of direct clinical observation of the group in action has been sacrificed in these studies for the other desiderata of statistical representativeness and reliability of observations. But this choice is not an ineluctable one; these are not mutually exclusive alternatives in the study of the primary group, and the possibility of fusing them both has been shown by the procedures adopted by the second of the groups of social psychologists referred to above. The combination of Mayo's intensive interviews and clinical observation with more adequate concern for rigorous statistical standards—both in the selection of the cases to be observed and in the methods of observation and recording which are characteristic of the Lewin circle—has helped to raise the level of primary-group studies. Lewin's group has in the last few years gone beyond the studies of children's and adolescent groups in schools and clubs to the study of adults in large organizations. This new trend is well represented in the study of French and Coch.[5] The role of the small group in the making of a decision to modify a given technique of work was shown to be related to the rate with which the working group achieved a managerially established norm of efficiency. In cases in which a small body of workers was simply informed that they were to use a new technique which had been decided on by the management, adoption of the new technique was accompanied by a persistent decline in productive efficiency. In an experimental group, the decision was conveyed from management to the group of workers, who then were given the opportunity to discuss the new technique and arrive at some understanding of the justification for the innovation. Through representatives whom they chose, the workers then developed the procedure by which the new technique was to be introduced; the rate of remuneration was worked out in the same way; and the representatives then trained their group companions. In this group, efficiency was soon regained on a fairly high level. In two other experimental groups, the same procedure as in the first experimental group was used, except that the groups were smaller and all the workers participated in elaborating and deciding on the method of introducing the change in technique, the method of remuneration, etc. In these groups, which had more widespread initiative and participation in the making of the decisions which the group had to execute, productive efficiency was regained more quickly and on a higher level than in either the control or the experimental groups.[6]

Bavelas,[7] in the same factory, also studied the influence of primary-group solidarity and a democratic relationship with the extra-primary-group authority (i.e., management) in determining the attainment of certain production goals. Where exhortations by management were used to obtain acceptance of the goals, there were small immediate rises with rapid regressions to the old level. Where, on the other hand, the workers met with a skilled discussion leader in a conference room to discuss work problems, to decide whether they were to set a group production goal, and to determine the content and level of that goal, productivity underwent a very marked increase which was then sustained over a long period.

For some time there had been an awareness among American social scientists that output restrictions among industrial workers were being practiced as defensive measures against some anticipated hostile actions of management (e.g., a "speed-up" when a given output norm was reached). On the whole, these social scientists had imputed the restrictive practices to deliberate decisions of trade-union functionaries. One of the discoveries resulting from Roethlisberger and Dickson's study of the Bank Wiring group had been the proposition that restrictive practices are autonomously generated defensive devices of alienated primary groups. A study by Orvis Collins, Melville Dalton, and Donald Wray[8] has shown in concrete form the powerful pressures that arise from primary-group membership to direct the behavior of the individual toward conformity with the informal requirements of the primary group for defense against the "enemy" outside the group, whether the enemy is the unincorporated "rate busting" worker or the rate-raising agent of management.

Studies of informal primary-group structure as a restraint on output have been made largely by the Mayo circle. They have therefore been concrete and impressionistic, on the whole, in their mode of observation— like that just referred to—although they have often attempted to overcome the limitations of unclear categories associated with their clinical method by using diagrams presenting the spatial relationships of the group members.[9] Attempts to escape from the vagueness of previous studies of the *alienated* primary group, i.e., the primary group which resists effective incorporation into the formal authority system (of the factory, for example) has been made by some of the members of the "applied anthropology" circle,[10] whose background goes beyond the boundaries of Mayo's doctrine. The most significant of these efforts is that by Horsfall and Arensberg[11] in which they attempt to describe with minute accuracy and in a standardized schema the process of interaction characteristic of an alienated primary group. It should perhaps be said of this investigation that precision is not the equivalent of accuracy. Like the prodigious effort of Roethlisberger and Dickson to record all the topics mentioned by the workers in interviews, which they then classified under an utterly haphazard, *ad hoc* set of rubrics unrelated to the categories appropriate to the description or analysis of group organization, this study by Horsfall and Arensberg, which attempts to demonstrate concretely the existence of an alienated primary group and which has no causal hypothesis of any sort to test, is satisfied simply to classify all actions regardless of their content as "interactions" and distinguishes them primarily by origin inside or outside the primary group. Thus, because of the contentlessness of the categories,[12] the painstaking recording and tabulation carried out by the investigators tell us much less than their impressionistic clinical observations and are far less valuable scientifically than the much more differentiated, much more relevant, and equally precise categories of observation and recording used by Lewin in his classic studies.

One of the most original studies in recent industrial sociology is Dalton's examination[13] of the characteristics of the "rate buster," the individual who refuses to conform with the restrictive practice informally established and required in the informal working primary group. The rate buster is shown to be an individual who is generally resistant to primary-group incorporation and has a highly individualistic, aggressive orientation. This investigation raises important new questions concerning the personality factors in primary-group formation; it helps us to see that certain kinds of personality qualities prevent incorporation into either incorporated or alienated primary groups.

Several studies of the foreman[14] (the agent of authority in closest contact with the mass of the factory workers) have provided concrete insight into the conditions under which industrial primary groups are incorporated with or alienated from the authority system of the factory. The results, although impressionistic (continuing the technique of investigation used by Mayo) have corresponded to the more rigorously controlled results of the recent investigations into industrial sociology made by Lewin's group at the Research Center on Group Dynamics.[15]

The function of the primary group in formal structures has also been investigated by sociologists concerned with military organization. The elaborate studies conducted by Samuel Stouffer[16] and his colleagues for the United States Army during the Second World War have shown the great importance of primary-group loyalty for military morale and hence for efficiency in combat. These studies have shown the relative unimportance of direct identification with the total symbols of the military organization as a whole, of the state, or of the political cause in the name of which a war is fought, as contrasted with the feelings of strength and security in the military primary group and of loyalty to one's immediate comrades. The soldier's motivation to fight is not derived from his perceiving and striving toward any strategic or political goals; it is a function of his need to protect his primary group and to conform with its expectations. The military machine thus obtains its inner cohesion not simply by a series of commands controlling the behavior of soldiers disciplined to respect the symbols of formal authority, but rather through a system of overlapping primary groups. The effective transmission and execution of commands along the formal line of authority can be successful only when it coincides with this system of informal groups. Using less rigorous methods of observation—the Stouffer team made great innovations in the scientific study of attitudes during the war—but with a more elaborate conceptual scheme derived from psychoanalytic and sociological theory, the same results were obtained by Dicks and Shils in the study of the German army during the war.[17] This study, made on the basis of a great number of interviews with German soldiers, showed that the main motivation of the German soldier derived from his loyalty to an authoritarian primary group, the protective leader of which was the noncommissioned officer and, to a lesser extent, the junior officer. The larger structure of the army was significant as a system of supply which enabled the junior officers and noncommissioned officers to maintain their protective and nutritive roles, and as a source of strategic and tactical directives which did not place too much strain on the protective role of the officer as the leading figure of the primary group. Direct identifications and loyalties to higher authorities played little part in this structure; and the system broke down only when primary groups could not be formed because of initial incorporation difficulties (e.g., linguistic and other barriers) and when the primary-group leader could no longer fulfill his protection functions.[18]

A number of studies in other contexts have called attention to the importance, for the efficiency of large organizations, of the correspondence between the formal chain of command in the larger organization and the informal primary group network. Leighton,[19] in his investigation of the War Relocation Center for Japanese in Arizona, has shown that communications between the United States government authorities formally charged with the conduct of the center and the Japanese inhabitants were effective only when the persons formally empowered by camp administrators to receive the communications and decisions were also the informally selected leaders of the primary groups spontaneously chosen by the Japanese inhabitants of the center. The same phenomenon has been reported in investigations of situations in which the decisions of centralized formal authority could penetrate the community only through the network of primary groups, the leaders of which served as intermediaries in the communication system.[20] In these cases, community solidarity and effectiveness in the implementation of the decisions of the authority were achieved only when the agents for the execution of the decisions were also the informally chosen leaders of the primary groups of the community.

Thus, since the publication of Mayo's first book, *The Human Problems of an Industrial Civilization*, in 1933, the study of the relationship between primary groups and the larger, formally organized structures in which they exist has undergone a notable substantive development. The main hypotheses have become somewhat more differentiated, and the range of their application has increased. Somewhat less progress has been made in studying the formation and internal dynamics of primary groups since the fundamental work of Lewin and his students in the late 1930's. No subsequent research in this field has reached the level of this classic with respect either to the exact construction of hypotheses or the rigorous mode of testing them.

The new developments in the study of small groups have largely occurred in the improvement of techniques of observation. A recording system which permits the satisfactory synchronous notation of ongoing group behavior in a large number of refined and pertinent categories has been developed by Bales.[21] Steinzor[22] has also attempted to cope with the difficult problem of recording the rich material of small-group action reliably and in categories which will be relevant to theoretically significant analyses. The emergence of relatively low-cost sound-recording instruments in the United States since the war has given an impetus to the accurate observation of verbally expressed interaction. The drive for accuracy in recording has been greatly stimulated by the emergence of content analysis[23] as a research technique. Content analysis was originally used by Lasswell for the analysis of psychoanalytic interview material but subsequently was developed chiefly in the study of mass communications. It is now being brought back to its original use in the analysis (classification) of the content of verbatim records of verbal productions in group situations. The use of sound-recording devices together with content analysis permits the avoidance of impressionism in estimating the frequency of various types of actions and relationships. Also, when combined with the action and group-structure records which have been described by Bales and others, sound recordings make it possible to describe more accurately—in categories which are relevant to the testing of hypotheses concerning group solidarity—cleavage, extent of participation, role played in group decision, and other important variables central to the study of the primary group.[24] Among the few new trends in the study of the internal dynamics which elaborate an important direction of Lewin's own interests are the studies in group decision-making conducted by Bavelas.[25] A closely related development is the systematic study of the process of group discussion which is also being carried on by Lewin's circle.[26] Here the internal group conditions and the characteristics of the task affecting the attainment of agreement are being examined by the same exact procedures as have been used in their studies of group action.

Other studies of the obstructing or facilitating influence of primary-group situations on the making of decisions by group members have increased our understanding of political behavior. In their study of electoral behavior, Lazarsfeld and Berelson[27] discovered the importance of familial and extra-familial primary-group situations in facilitating or inhibiting electoral choice. Having begun with a number of the conventional variables in the public sphere such as religion, class, residence, and exposure to campaign propaganda, they discovered that an independent role is played by the degree of agreement or disagreement on political issues within the primary group. This study also indicates that the public variables themselves are in some sense mediated through primary-group relations. Since that time Merton[28] and others have gone on to examine the structure of influence through which the primary-group leader acts in influencing the political opinions, consumption standards, and tastes of those who are associated with him.

These latter studies show in a very definite way, the overlap between studies of internal group dynamics and the studies of the function of primary groups in the larger social structures. Lewin's and Merton's studies, like the studies on the American and German armies mentioned earlier, strengthen the argument that clear insight into the functioning of primary groups is crucial for understanding the integration of the larger social structure. In both cases we have seen that individuals who are members of larger social structures make their decisions and concert their actions within those structures, not by the direct focus of attention on the central authority, but rather by identification with some individual with whom they have primary-group relationships and who serves to transmit to them ideas from and concerning the larger structure.

As we have intimated above, the work on group dynamics has suffered through lack of explicit connection with a causal theory of human behavior. Lewin's contribution to theory did not go beyond a complex system of descriptive terms which were to a large extent metaphorical in nature. It did not derive from a series of basic postulates regarding the motivation of behavior, and this deficiency has not been overcome by the heirs of Lewin's approach. Indeed, the deficiency becomes less likely to be repaired as the disciples of Lewin come to take the foundations which he laid more and more for granted, and to concentrate their efforts on the improvement of their research techniques and on the public diffusion of the lessons which they learned from the master.[29] Nor has the deficiency been remedied by the concrete clinical work of the industrial sociologists who have sprung from Mayo.

There is, however, gradually emerging from that other major current of small-group analysis, a series of insights which are still inchoate and unformulated in any explicit fashion. These are the insights which have arisen from psychoanalytically oriented group-psychotherapy. The cautious description of group processes to be found in the tentative and preliminary articles of Wilfred R. Bion gives some clew to the possibility of extending psychoanalytic hypotheses regarding the working of personality to the highly differentiated and subtle interplay of personalities in the group situation. The most important attempts made in the United States to analyze group structure on the basis of psychoanalytic interpretation of directly observed group action have been made by Fritz Redl.[30] In a series of articles which are based on and which describe his work with delinquent boys in Detroit, Redl, following the leads in Freud's *Group Psychology and Analysis of the Ego,* has shown the function of the group leader in reinforcing or weakening tendencies within the id and the superego. The person who takes the initiative in the performance of aggressive action against authority facilitates through identification with him the release of similar tendencies, otherwise repressed, in the other members of the group. Likewise, a leader who confirms the authority or who himself is an authority, strengthens (through the identification process) the superego tendencies in the members of the group and thus maintains order within the group. Redl has continued his work with a very sensitive analysis of the nature of the relations between leaders and members in the primary group, in which his courageous adaptation of psychoanalytic hypotheses concerning love and identification have enabled him to throw light on the conditions under which leaders can transform the behavior of their followers both within the group and apart from it. Through his work (and Bion's in England) it is now becoming possible to see in its most incipient form the possibility of unifying psycho-analytic theory, in a reformulated version, with the empirical regularities observed in the clinical and experimental studies of group behavior.

Earlier we referred to the convergence of various trends in American social research toward the study of the primary group. It is important, how-ever, not to overestimate the extent to which it has already occurred. The process of convergence is still in its very preliminary stages. Only a small proportion of the investigators whose work contributes to the analysis of the primary group are aware that they are doing so. Most of them are interested first of all in certain particular problems, such as employer-employee rela-tions, military morale, and social mobility. Often they proceed on such a concrete level with the end of explaining what has happened (e.g., in a single firm) that they do not find it necessary to use general categories or general hypotheses. Few investigators have undertaken simultaneously to utilize systematic theoretical hypotheses relating to a general theory of behavior and to observe data in a systematic and rigorous way.[31]

Nonetheless, signs of convergence, especially in the domain of research technique and choice of subject matters, are already visible: we may cite illustratively the combination of content-analysis technique with exact observational and recording techniques, the use of experimental techniques on industrial subject matters, the application of public-opinion polling tech-niques to the study of group processes previously observed only clinically or experimentally, and the assimilation into experimental work of the socio-metric technique. The different schools which work with varying degrees of self-consciousness on primary-group problems are gradually interpene-trating one another. The most important convergence from the scientific point of view—that is, unification of systematic empirical work with sub-stantive theoretical hypotheses—has not yet gone as far as scientific and practical developments require. However, we may with moderate optimism predict that in the not-too-distant future experimental techniques and psy-choanalytic hypotheses will be fused as a result of the close cooperation between the two leading circles of investigators into primary-group problems —a fusion of the experimental and the exact observational process developed by Lewin and his followers with the psychoanalytic interpretations in use among members of the Tavistock Institute in London.[32]

The increasingly high importance which sociologists and administrators are now according to the primary group must not, of course, blind sociologists to the significance of extra-primary-group determinants of behavior both within the primary groups themselves and beyond their boundaries. In the study of the determinants of primary-group formation and distintegration, the tendency, owing perhaps to the recruitment of the investigators from laboratory and clinical psychology and from psychoanalysis, has been to disregard the wider structural conditions of primary-group formation, maintenance, or disintegration and to concentrate only on those variables within the primary-group situation itself or in its immediate environment. The failure to perceive the relevance of variables which are involved in the economic-ecological system has already led to a reaction against industrial sociology among some students of industrial relations in the United States —this despite Mayo's own derivation from Durkheim, who saw primary-group disintegration as a function of changes in the larger social structure. The primary group will be adequately understood scientifically only when its interconnections with the ecological and corporate context have been perceived and given proper emphasis alongside the variables which the newer analyses have rendered visible to our eyes. The significance of primary groups in the social structure will be more properly appreciated when their influence on behavior has been traced not merely to the actions which occur within the primary groups themselves but also into the personality structure of their members and into the remoter areas in the behavior of individual members (their behavior in political situations, in corporate bodies such as the church, in unorganized interclass and intraclass relations, and in other primary groups). Despite the possible danger of overestimation of the significance of primary groups, there can be no doubt that the renaissance of the study of primary groups in American society is leading to a new and more realistic awareness of the dynamic components of social life which operate in all spheres, those which are informally organized as well as those which are formally organized, those which are individuated as well as those which are consensual in their integration. This renaissance is pushing us toward a more exact and elaborate understanding of the nature of the situation and, in doing so, it aids our comprehension of the co-ordination of the social structure as a whole.

REFERENCES

1. A. Bavelas, "A Mathematical Model for Group Structures," *Applied Anthropology*, VII (1948), 16–30.
2. W. L. Warner and J. O. Low, *The Social System of the Modern Factory* ("Yankee City Series," Vol. IV [1947]).
3. E. C. Hughes, "The Knitting of Ethnic Groups in Industry," *American Sociological Review*, XI (1946), 512–19; W. F. Whyte (ed.), *Industry and Society* (1946), esp. chap. ii by B. B. Gardner ("The Factory as a Social System"), chap. iv by Chester

Barnard ("Functions and Pathology of Status Systems in Formal Organizations"), and chap. vi by E. C. Hughes ("Race Relations in Industry"). See also W. F. Whyte, *Human Relations in the Restaurant Industry* (1948).

4. Daniel Katz and Herbert Hyman, "Morale in War Industries," in T. Newcomb and E. Hartley (eds.), *Readings in Social Psychology* (1947), pp. 437–47.

5. J. R. P. French and Lester Coch, "Overcoming Resistance to Change," *Human Relations,* I, No. 4 (1948), 512–32.

6. This is an instance of the overlapping, to which we have already referred, between (1) the interest in the relations between primary groups and formal authority within the structure but outside the primary group; and (2) the interest of the Lewinian social psychologists in the internal dynamics of group structure. The Lewinians had in their earlier studies concentrated on intra-group authority and the responses thereto. In the later studies they have extended their interests to the responses to external authority, with a consequent gain of clarification beyond the point reached by Mayo.

7. A. Bavelas, unpublished manuscript referred to in K. Lewin, "Frontiers in Group Dynamics," Part I, *Human Relations,* I, No. 1 (1947), pp. 25–26.

8. "Restriction of Output and Social Cleavage in Industry," *Applied Anthropology,* V, No. 3 (1946), 1–14.

9. F. J. Roethlisberger and W. J. Dickson, *Management and the Worker: Technical vs. Social Organization in an Industrial Plant* (1934), pp. 501, 503–7; W. F. Whyte, *Street Corner Society* (1943), pp. 95, 184.

10. "The Society for Applied Anthropology" consists of psychologists, anthropologists, and sociologists interested in the application of the theory of informal primary groups in the solution of governmental and industrial administrative problems. It draws its membership from a variety of intellectual circles—from the Mayo, the Moreno, and the Lewin circles, from rural sociologists who apply the cartographic techniques developed by Galpin from psychoanalytic anthropology, and from other sources.

11. Alexander Horsfall and Conrad M. Arsenberg, "Teamwork and Productivity in a Shoe Factory," *Human Organization,* VIII, No. 1 (1949), 13–25.

12. One may perhaps add the comment at this point that much of the quantitative refinement achieved by the sociometrists in their study of small groups is nothing more than the result of an exploratory combination of the measurements of a very small set of variables of uncertain meaning.

13. Melville Dalton, "Worker Response and Social Background," *Journal of Political Economy,* LV, No. 4 (1947), 323–32.

14. Burleigh B. Gardner and W. F. Whyte, "The Man in the Middle: Position and Problems of the Foreman," *Applied Anthropology,* IV, No. 2 (1945), 1–28; F. J. Roethlisberger, "The Foreman: Master and Victim of Double Talk," *Harvard Business Review,* XXIII, No. 3 (1945), 283–98. Interesting parallels between the position of the foreman and the noncommissioned officer can be derived from S. A. Stouffer *et al., The American Soldier: Adjustment During Army Life (Studies in Social Psychology in World War II,* Vol. I [1949]), pp. 401–10.

15. For a general summary of these, see Ronald Lippitt, "A Program of Experimentation on Group Functioning and Group Productivity," in W. Dennis *et al., Current Trends in Social Psychology* (1947), pp. 14–49; see also, the *Second Annual Report* (1949) of the Survey Research Center, University of Michigan.

16. S. A. Stouffer *et al., The American Soldier: Combat and Its Aftermath (Studies in Social Psychology in World War II,* Vol. II [1949]), pp. 130–49.

17. Henry V. Dicks, *Psychological Foundations of the Wehrmacht* (War Office: Directorate of Army Psychiatry [London, 1944]); and E. A. Shils and M. Janowitz, "Cohesion and Disintegration of the *Wehrmacht* in World War II," *Public Opinion Quarterly,* XII (1948), 280–315. The same conclusions are indicated in their study of the United States Air Force by R. Grinker and J. Speigel, *Men Under Stress* (1945).

18. The studies of Shils and Dicks showed that authoritarian leadership can indeed be a crucial component in primary groups composed of persons with personality needs which can best be satisfied by authoritative protection or in primary groups operating

in situations which bring these needs for paternal protection to the fore. This hypothesis should be borne in mind in considering the extrapolation of the results of the Lewin-Lippitt-White researches into all other types of authority situations. With certain types of personalities or in certain types of situations (tasks and threats) primary-group solidarity might well be disintegrated by democratic leadership. This hypothesis certainly is compatible with the conclusions of the Iowa research.

19. Alexander Leighton, *The Governing of Men* (1945).
20. Charles P. Loomis, *Studies of Rural Social Organization in the United States, Latin America and Germany* (1945), pp. 151–72; W. F. Whyte, "The Social Role of the Settlement House," *Applied Anthropology*, VI, No. 1 (1945), 18–19; F. L. W. Richardson, "First Principles of Rural Rehabilitation," *Applied Anthropology*, IV, No. 3 (1945), 16–31.
21. Robert F. Bales and H. Gerbrands, "The Interaction Recorder," *Human Relations*, I, No. 4 (1948), 456–63.
22. Bernard Steinzor, "The Development and Evaluation of a Measure of Social Interaction," *Human Relations*, II, No. 2 (1949), 103–22.
23. B. Berelson and P. F. Lazarsfeld, *The Analysis of Communication Content* (1948); H. D. Lasswell and Nathan Leites, *The Language of Politics* (1949); Ernst Kris and Hans Speier, *German Radio Propaganda* (1944).
24. The sociometric technique has scarcely been improved since it was first applied by Moreno. The elaborate combinations of observations made by Helen Jennings have not been connected in any way with increased possibilities for observing categories of behavior previously not observable by sociometric techniques. What Jennings has done has been to increase the number of computations made from the same elementary observations of individual choices and rejections, being chosen and being rejected (e.g., "number chosen by subject and number choosing him," "number chosen by subject and number reciprocating him," "number choosing subject and number reciprocating him," "number rejected by subject and number rejecting him," etc.). The extensions of the "sociometric" technique by Loomis and others have shifted the sociometric technique from the observation of preferences to the observation of actual association in specific activities. (See C. P. Loomis, "Political and Occupational Cleavages in a Hanoverian Village, Germany: A Sociometric Study," *Sociometry*, IX, No. 4 [1946], 316–33.) The purer sociometrists still restrict themselves to elementary choices and rejections, while the "extension" made by Loomis represents really an adaptation of the sociogram for depicting actual rather than preferred associations.
25. Currently in progress at the Massachusetts Institute of Technology.
26. Leland P. Bradford and John R. P. French (eds.), "The Dynamics of the Discussion Group: A Symposium," *Journal of Social Issues*, IV, No. 2 (1948), 1–75; see also Elliot Jacques, "Interpretative Group Discussion as a Method of Facilitating Social Change," *Human Relations*, I, No. 4 (1948), 533–49. Elaborate studies of discussion are now under way at the Research Center for Group Dynamics at the University of Michigan.
27. P. F. Lazarsfeld, B. Berelson, and H. Gaudet, *The People's Choice* (1944).
28. Robert K. Merton, "Patterns of Interpersonal Influence and of Communications Behavior in a Local Community," in P. F. Lazarsfeld and Frank Stanton (eds.), *Communications Research* (1948–49); Frank Stewart, "A Sociometric Study of Influence in Southtown," *Sociometry*, X, No. 1 (1947), 11–31, and X, No. 3 (1947), 273–86.
29. Some of the important work of this group in communicating its knowledge and skill to nonscientific audiences is described in Ronald Lippitt. *Training in Community Relations: A Research Exploration Toward New Group Skills* (1949).
30. Fritz Redl, "Group Emotion and Leadership," *Psychiatry*, V (1942), 513–96; "Resistance in Therapy Groups," *Human Relations*, I, No. 3 (1948), 307–13; "Group Psychological Elements in Discipline Problems," *American Journal of Orthopsychiatry*, XIII (1943), 77–82; "Discipline and Group Psychology," *Journal of the National Association of Deans of Women*, XI (1947), 3–15; *Group Psychological Problems in Classroom Teaching* (American Council on Education, 1939); "The

Psychology of Gang Formation and the Treatment of Juvenile Delinquents," *The Psychoanalytic Study of the Child,* I (1945), 367–77.

31. Actually, since the death of Lewin, such methods have become a little less frequent.

32. This fusion is being greatly facilitated by the collaboration of these two groups in the journal *Human Relations* and in the seminars at Bethel, Maine, and in England during the summer of 1949.

10.

STATUS

THE CONCEPT of "status," once referred only to *inherited* status, a fixed, usually hereditary, position within the social order. Such was the usage of writers like the distinguished nineteenth century English evolutionist, Sir Henry Maine (1822–1888) and two vastly important American sociologists, Robert E. Park (1864–1944) and Ernest W. Burgess, who in 1921 coauthored the still valuable, if somewhat dated, *Introduction to the Science of Sociology*. Maine had written of the transition from status to contract; many other writers, even in our own time, have elaborated the dichotomy. For Park and Burgess, as our reading makes clear, the relevant contrast was that between status and competition, the latter being evident even in primitive societies, but eventually eclipsing the former altogether.

With the development of modern anthropology and sociology, status has been broadened to encompass all culturally prescribed rights and duties inherent in social positions, whatever their origin. The individual is now viewed as having a total status which generally combines a large number of subsidiary statuses. The eminent American anthropologist, Ralph Linton (1893–1953) distinguished between ascribed (or inherited) status—which would have been a redundancy to earlier theorists—and achieved status, which results from personal attainment of goals set forth by the culture. This distinction has been all but universally accepted in social science. As such there are certain irreducible bases for the determination of status, among them those mentioned by Linton: age, sex, and occupation. Furthermore, status, whether the by-product of effort or the result of birth, carries with it an image of exemplary behavior, a model of collective expectations. The concept of status is related to the concept of "role," i.e., what Linton calls the more dynamic aspect of status which we shall discuss both in this context and in relation to reference groups (see Section 8). It is impossible fully to dissociate them.

All of the foregoing applies in equal measure to simple nonliterate societies and to complex civilizations. However, the growth of modern industrial society produces a tremendous differentiation of functions. While age and sex continue to be relevant factors in status ascription, the occupa-

335

tional determination of status and the occupational definition of role assumed unprecedented importance. In the status-role situation there are always meaningful "others" whose approval is sought by conformity to their shared understandings and who in turn provide a variety of gratifications for the well socialized individual. This is the meaning of an omnipresent process that Talcott Parsons has termed "the complimentarity of expectations." Znaniecki, in his subtle analysis of role and status, refers to the same phenomenon in speaking of "social circles," each of which has its own set of values. These are ever-widening circles which in the modern world have tended to produce a bewildering multiplicity of differential standards.

We have chosen to include the more abstract observations contained in Znaniecki's *The Social Role of the Man of Knowledge,* and to let Robert K. Merton's appreciative and creative review speak for some of the theoretical implications suggested by this work. Park and Burgess in the twenties had inspired a whole series of substantive studies focused upon various occupations, and Znaniecki, in considering the savant, picked up a thread that had long been neglected. At present, the sociology of professions, occasionally integrated with the sociology of knowledge, as in Znaniecki and Merton, is enjoying a new resurgence.

Although the way a man earns his living will decisively affect his status, it does not necessarily *clarify* all his rights and responsibilities. Indeed, the rapidity of social change so typical of our age may create doubt and confusion about appropriate (socially acceptable) conduct in areas where virtual certainty previously obtained. In general, status is problematic when roles are vaguely or ambiguously defined. Thus, women, mothers-in-law, adolescents, and the aged are suspended in a painful and doubtful position across the American social scene. Robert Park, concerned with race mixture, discussed the half-breed, born of two cultures, but not fully accepted by either. He labeled this type of person "the marginal man." Many students of sociology have found Park's phrase suggestive, not the least of them Everett C. Hughes, who has illuminated certain dilemmas and contradictions of status by applying the phrase not so much to racial as to professional relations. His essay is indicative of a productive trend in sociological theory.

Personal Competition, Social Selection, and Status * [1] (*Park and Burgess*)

The function of personal competition, considered as a part of the social system, is to assign to each individual his place in that system. If "all the world's a stage," this is a process that distributes the parts among the players. It may do it well or ill, but after some fashion it does it. Some may be cast in parts unsuited to them; good actors may be discharged altogether and worse ones retained; but nevertheless the thing is arranged in some way and the play goes on.

That such a process must exist can hardly, it seems to me, admit of question; in fact, I believe that those who speak of doing away with competition use the word in another sense than is here intended. Within the course of the longest human life there is necessarily a complete renewal of the persons whose communication and cooperation make up the life of society. The new members come into the world without any legible sign to indicate what they are fit for, a mystery to others from the first and to themselves as soon as they are capable of reflection: the young man does not know for what he is adapted, and no one else can tell him. The only possible way to get light upon the matter is to adopt the method of experiment. By trying one thing and another and by reflecting upon his experience, he begins to find out about himself, and the world begins to find out about him. His field of investigation is of course restricted, and his own judgment and that of others liable to error, but the tendency of it all can hardly be other than to guide his choice to that one of the available careers in which he is best adapted to hold his own. I may say this much, perhaps, without assuming anything regarding the efficiency or justice of competition as a distributor of social functions, a matter regarding which I shall offer some suggestions later. All I wish to say here is that the necessity of some selective process is inherent in the conditions of social life.

It will be apparent that, in the sense in which I use the term, competition is not necessarily a hostile contention, nor even something of which the competing individual is always conscious. From our infancy onward throughout life judgments are daily forming regarding us of which we are unaware, but which go to determine our careers. "The world is full of judgment days." A and B, for instance, are under consideration for some appointment; the experience and personal qualifications of each are duly weighed by those having the appointment to make, and A, we will say, is chosen. Neither of the two need know anything about the matter until the selection is made. It is eligibility to perform some social function that makes a man a competitor, and he may or may not be aware of it, or, if aware of it, he may or may not be consciously opposed to others. I trust that the reader will bear in mind that I always use the word competition in the sense here explained.

There is but one alternative to competition as a means of determining the place of the individual in the social system, and that is some form of status, some fixed, mechanical rule, usually a rule of inheritance, which decides the function of the individual without reference to his personal traits, and thus dispenses with any process of comparison. It is possible to conceive of a society organized entirely upon the basis of the inheritance of functions, and indeed societies exist which may be said to approach this condition. In India, for example, the prevalent idea regarding the social function of the individual is that it is unalterably determined by his parentage, and the village blacksmith, shoemaker, accountant, or priest has his place assigned to him by a rule of descent as rigid as that which governs the transmission of one of the crowns of Europe. If all functions were handed down in this way, if there were never any deficiency or surplus of children to take the place of their parents, if there were no progress or decay in the social system making necessary new activities or dispensing with old ones, then there would be no use for a selective process. But precisely in the measure that a society departs from this condition, that individual traits are recognized and made available, or social change of any sort comes to pass, in that measure must there be competition.

Status is not an active process, as competition is; it is simply a rule of conservation, a makeshift to avoid the inconveniences of continual readjustment in the social structure. Competition or selection is the only constructive principle, and everything worthy the name of organization had at some time or other a competitive origin. At the present day the eldest son of a peer may succeed to a seat in the House of Lords simply by right of birth; but his ancestor got the seat by competition, by some exercise of personal qualities that made him valued or loved or feared by a king or a minister.

Sir Henry Maine has pointed out that increase of competition is a characteristic trait of modern life, and that the powerful ancient societies of the old world were for the most part non-competitive in their structure. While this is true, it would be a mistake to draw the inference that status is a peculiarly natural or primitive principle of organization and competition a comparatively recent discovery. On the contrary the spontaneous relations among men, as we see in the case of children, and as we may infer from the life of the lower animals, are highly competitive, personal prowess and ascendency being everything and little regard being paid to descent simply as such. The regime of inherited status, on the other hand, is a comparatively complex and artificial product, necessarily of later growth, whose very general prevalence among the successful societies of the old world is doubtless to be explained by the stability and consequently the power which it was calculated to give to the social system. It survived because under certain conditions it was the fittest. It was not and is not universally predominant among savages or barbarous peoples. With the American Indians, for example, the definiteness and authority of status were comparatively small, personal prowess and initiative being correspondingly important. The interesting monograph on Omaha sociology, by Dorsey, published by the United States Bureau of Ethnology, contains many facts showing that the life of this people was highly competitive. When the tribe was at war any brave could organize an expedition against the enemy, if he could induce enough others to join him, and this organizer usually assumed the command. In a similar way the managers of the hunt were chosen because of personal skill; and, in general, "any man can win a name and rank in the state by becoming 'wacuce' or brave, either in war or by the bestowal of gifts and the frequent giving of feasts."

Throughout history there has been a struggle between the principles of status and competition regarding the part that each should play in the social system. Generally speaking the advantage of status is in its power to give order and continuity. As Gibbon informs us, "The superior prerogative of birth, when it has obtained the sanction of time and popular opinion, is the plainest and least invidious of all distinctions among mankind," and he is doubtless right in ascribing the confusion of the later Roman Empire largely to the lack of an established rule for the transmission of imperial authority. The chief danger of status is that of suppressing personal development, and so of causing social enfeeblement, rigidity, and ultimate decay. On the other hand, competition develops the individual and gives flexibility and animation to the social order, its danger being chiefly that of distintegration in some form or other. The general tendency in modern times has been toward the relative increase of the free or competitive principle, owing to the fact that the rise of other means of securing stability has diminished the need for status. The latter persists, however, even in the freest countries, as the method by which wealth is transmitted, and also in social classes, which, so far as they exist at all, are based chiefly upon inherited wealth and the culture and opportunities that go with it. The ultimate reason for this persistence—without very serious opposition—in the face of the obvious inequalities and limitations upon liberty that it perpetuates is perhaps the fact that no other method of transmission has arisen that has shown itself capable of giving continuity and order to the control of wealth.

2. PERSONAL COMPETITION AND THE EVOLUTION OF INDIVIDUAL TYPES [2]

The ancient city was primarily a fortress, a place of refuge in time of war. The modern city, on the contrary, is primarily a convenience of commerce and owes its existence to the market place around which it sprang up. Industrial competition and the division of labor, which have probably done most to develop the latent powers of mankind, are possible only upon condition of the existence of markets, of money and other devices for the facilitation of trade and commerce.

The old adage which describes the city as the natural environment of the free man still holds so far as the individual man finds in the chances, the diversity of interests and tasks, and in the vast unconscious co-operation of city life, the opportunity to choose his own vocation and develop his peculiar individual talents. The city offers a market for the special talents of individual men. Personal competition tends to select for each special task the individual who is best suited to perform it.

The difference of natural talents in different men is, in reality, much less than we are aware of; and the very different genius which appears to distinguish men of different professions, when grown up to maturity, is not upon many occasions so much the cause, as the effect of the division of labour. The difference between the most dissimilar characters, between a philosopher and a common street porter, for example, seems to arise not so much from nature, as from habit, custom and education. When they came into the world, and for the first six or eight years of their existence, they were perhaps very much alike, and neither their parents nor playfellows could perceive any remarkable difference. About that age, or soon after, they come to be employed in different occupations. The difference of talents comes then to be taken notice of, and widens by degrees, till at last the vanity of the philosopher is willing to acknowledge scarce any resemblance. But without the disposition to truck, barter, and exchange, every man must have procured to himself every necessary and conveniency of life which he wanted. All must have had the same duties to perform, and the same work to do, and there could have been no such difference of employment as could alone give occasion to any great difference of talent.

As it is the power of exchanging that gives occasion to the division of labour, so the extent of this division must always be limited by the extent of that power, or, in other words, by the extent of the market. . . . There are some sorts of industry, even of the lowest kind, which can be carried on nowhere but in a great town.

Success, under conditions of personal competition, depends upon concentration, upon some single task, and this concentration stimulates the demand for rational methods, technical devices, and exceptional skill. Exceptional skill, while based on natural talent, requires special preparation, and it has called into existence the trade and professional schools, and finally bureaus for vocational guidance. All of these, either directly or indirectly, serve at once to select and emphasize individual differences.

Every device which facilitates trade and industry prepares the way for a further division of labor and so tends further to specialize the tasks in which men find their vocations.

The outcome of this process is to break down or modify the older organization of society, which was based on family ties, on local associations, on culture, caste, and status, and to substitute for it an organization based on vocational interests.

In the city every vocation, even that of a beggar, tends to assume the character of a profession, and the discipline which success in any vocation imposes, together with the associations that it enforces, emphasizes this tendency.

The effect of the vocations and the division of labor is to produce, in the first instance, not social groups but vocational types—the actor, the plumber, and the lumber-jack. The organizations, like the trade and labor unions, which men of the same trade or profession form are based on common interests. In this respect they differ from forms of association like the neighborhood, which are based on contiguity, personal association, and the common ties of humanity. The different trades and professions seem disposed to group themselves in classes, that is to say, the artisan, business, and professional classes. But in the modern democratic state the classes have as yet attained no effective organization. Socialism, founded on an effort to create an organization based on "class consciousness," has never succeeded in creating more than a political party.

The effects of the division of labor as a discipline may therefore be best studied in the vocational types it has produced. Among the types which it would be interesting to study are: the shopgirl, the policeman, the peddler, the cabman, the night watchman, the clairvoyant, the vaudeville performer, the quack doctor, the bartender, the ward boss, the strike-breaker, the labor agitator, the school teacher, the reporter, the stockbroker, the pawnbroker; all of these are characteristic products of the conditions of city life; each with its special experience, insight, and point of view determines for each vocational group and for the city as a whole its individuality.

REFERENCES

1. Adapted from Charles H. Cooley, "Personal Competition," in *Economic Studies*, IV (1899), No. 2, 78–86.
2. From Robert E. Park, "The City," in the *American Journal of Sociology*, XX (1915), 584–86.

Status and Role * (*Linton*)

In the preceding chapter we discussed the nature of society and pointed out that the functioning of societies depends upon the presence of patterns for reciprocal behavior between individuals or groups of individuals. The polar positions in such patterns of reciprocal behavior are technically known as *statuses.* The term *status,* like the term *culture,* has come to be used with a double significance. A *status,* in the abstract, is a position in a particular pattern. It is thus quite correct to speak of each individual as having many statuses, since each individual participates in the expression of a number of patterns. However, unless the term is qualified in some way, the *status* of any individual means the sum total of all the statuses which he occupies. It represents his position with relation to the total society. Thus the status of Mr. Jones as a member of his community derives from a combination of all the statuses which he holds as a citizen, as an attorney, as a Mason, as a Methodist, as Mrs. Jones's husband, and so on.

A status, as distinct from the individual who may occupy it, is simply a collection of rights and duties. Since these rights and duties can find expression only through the medium of individuals, it is extremely hard for us to maintain a distinction in our thinking between statuses and the people who hold them and exercise the rights and duties which constitute them. The relation between any individual and any status he holds is somewhat like that between the driver of an automobile and the driver's place in the machine. The driver's seat with its steering wheel, accelerator, and other controls is a constant with ever-present potentialities for action and control, while the driver may be any member of the family and may exercise these potentialities very well or very badly.

A *role* represents the dynamic aspect of a status. The individual is socially assigned to a status and occupies it with relation to other statuses. When he puts the rights and duties which constitute the status into effect, he is performing a role. Role and status are quite inseparable, and the distinction between them is of only academic interest. There are no roles without statuses or statuses without roles. Just as in the case of *status,* the term *role* is used with a double significance. Every individual has a series of roles deriving from the various patterns in which he participates and at the same time a *role* in general, which represents the sum total of these roles and determines what he does for his society and what he can expect from it.

* Reprinted from *The Study of Man* by Ralph Linton, pp. 113–119, with permission of the publisher, Appleton-Century-Crofts, Inc. Copyright, 1936, by Appleton-Century-Crofts, Inc.

Although all statuses and roles derive from social patterns and are integral parts of patterns, they have an independent function with relation to the individuals who occupy particular statuses and exercise their roles. To such individuals the combined status and role represent the minimum of attitudes and behavior which he must assume if he is to participate in the overt expression of the pattern. Status and role serve to reduce the ideal patterns for social life to individual terms. They become models for organizing the attitudes and behavior of the individual so that these will be congruous with those of the other individuals participating in the expression of the pattern. Thus if we are studying football teams in the abstract, the position of quarter-back is meaningless except in relation to the other positions. From the point of view of the quarter-back himself it is a distinct and important entity. It determines where he shall take his place in the line-up and what he shall do in various plays. His assignment to this position at once limits and defines his activities and establishes a minimum of things which he must learn. Similarly, in a social pattern such as that for the employer-employee relationship the statuses of employer and employee define what each has to know and do to put the pattern into operation. The employer does not need to know the techniques involved in the employee's labor, and the employee does not need to know the techniques for marketing or accounting.

It is obvious that, as long as there is no interference from external sources, the more perfectly the members of any society are adjusted to their statuses and roles the more smoothly the society will function. In its attempts to bring about such adjustments every society finds itself caught on the horns of a dilemma. The individual's formation of habits and attitudes begins at birth, and, other things being equal, the earlier his training for a status can begin the more successful it is likely to be. At the same time, no two individuals are alike, and a status which will be congenial to one may be quite uncongenial to another. Also, there are in all social systems certain roles which require more than training for their successful performance. Perfect technique does not make a great violinist, nor a thorough book knowledge of tactics an efficient general. The utilization of the special gifts of individuals may be highly important to society, as in the case of the general, yet these gifts usually show themselves rather late, and to wait upon their manifestation for the assignment of statuses would be to forfeit the advantages to be derived from commencing training early.

Fortunately, human beings are so mutable that almost any normal individual can be trained to the adequate performance of almost any role. Most of the business of living can be conducted on a basis of habit, with little need for intelligence and none for special gifts. Societies have met the dilemma by developing two types of statuses, the *ascribed* and the *achieved*. *Ascribed* statuses are those which are assigned to individuals without reference to their innate differences or abilities. They can be predicted and trained for from the moment of birth. The *achieved* statuses are, as a minimum, those requiring special qualities, although they are not necessarily limited to these. They are not assigned to individuals from birth but are left open to be filled through competition and individual effort. The majority of the statuses in all social systems are of the ascribed type and those which take care of the ordinary day-to-day business of living are practically always of this type.

In all societies certain things are selected as reference points for the ascription of status. The things chosen for this purpose are always of such a nature that they are ascertainable at birth, making it possible to begin the training of the individual for his potential statuses and roles at once. The simplest and most universally used of these reference points is sex. Age is used with nearly equal frequency, since all individuals pass through the same cycle of growth, maturity, and decline, and the statuses whose occupation will be determined by age can be forecast and trained for with accuracy. Family relationships, the simplest and most obvious being that of the child to its mother, are also used in all societies as reference points for the establishment of a whole series of statuses. Lastly, there is the matter of birth into a particular socially established group, such as a class or caste. The use of this type of reference is common but not universal. In all societies the actual ascription of statuses to the individual is controlled by a series of these reference points which together serve to delimit the field of his future participation in the life of the group.

The division and ascription of statuses with relation to sex seems to be basic in all social systems. All societies prescribe different attitudes and activities to men and to women. Most of them try to rationalize these prescriptions in terms of the physiological differences between the sexes or their different roles in reproduction. However, a comparative study of the statuses ascribed to women and men in different cultures seems to show that while such factors may have served as a starting point for the development of a division the actual ascriptions are almost entirely determined by culture. Even the psychological characteristics ascribed to men and women in different societies vary so much that they can have little physiological basis. Our own idea of women as ministering angels contrasts sharply with the ingenuity of women as torturers among the Iroquois and the sadistic delight they took in the process. Even the last two generations have seen a sharp change in the psychological patterns for women in our own society. The delicate, fainting lady of the middle eighteen-hundreds is as extinct as the dodo.

When it comes to the ascription of occupations, which is after all an integral part of status, we find the differences in various societies even more marked. Arapesh women regularly carry heavier loads than men "because their heads are so much harder and stronger." In some societies women do most of the manual labor; in others, as in the Marquesas, even cooking, housekeeping, and baby-tending are proper male occupations, and women spend most of their time primping. Even the general rule that women's handicap through pregnancy and nursing indicates the more active occupations as male and the less active ones as female has many exceptions. Thus among the Tasmanians seal-hunting was women's work. They swam out to the seal rocks, stalked the animals, and clubbed them. Tasmanian women also hunted opossums, which required the climbing of large trees.

Although the actual ascription of occupations along sex lines is highly variable, the pattern of sex division is constant. There are very few societies in which every important activity has not been definitely assigned to men or to women. Even when the two sexes cooperate in a particular occupation, the field of each is usually clearly delimited. Thus in Madagascar rice culture the men make the seed beds and terraces and prepare the fields for transplanting. The women do the work of transplanting, which is hard and back-breaking. The women weed the crop, but the men harvest it. The women then carry it to the threshing floors, where the men thresh it while the women winnow it. Lastly, the women pound the grain in mortars and cook it.

When a society takes over a new industry, there is often a period of uncertainty during which the work may be done by either sex, but it soon falls into the province of one or the other. In Madagascar, pottery is made by men in some tribes and by women in others. The only tribe in which it is made by both men and women is one into which the art has been introduced within the last sixty years. I was told that during the fifteen years preceding my visit there had been a marked decrease in the number of male potters, many men who had once practised the art having given it up. The factor of lowered wages, usually advanced as the reason for men leaving one of our own occupations when women enter it in force, certainly was not operative here. The field was not overcrowded, and the prices for men's and women's products were the same. Most of the men who had given up the trade were vague as to their reasons, but a few said frankly that they did not like to compete with women. Apparently the entry of women into the occupation had robbed it of a certain amount of prestige. It was no longer quite the thing for a man to be a potter, even though he was a very good one.

The use of age as a reference point for establishing status is as universal as the use of sex. All societies recognize three age groupings as a minimum: child, adult, and old. Certain societies have emphasized age as a basis for assigning status and have greatly amplified the divisions. Thus in certain African tribes the whole male population is divided into units composed of those born in the same years or within two- or three-year intervals. However, such extreme attention to age is unusual, and we need not discuss it here.

The physical differences between child and adult are easily recognizable, and the passage from childhood to maturity is marked by physiological events which make it possible to date it exactly for girls and within a few weeks or months for boys. However, the physical passage from childhood to maturity does not necessarily coincide with the social transfer of the individual from one category to the other. Thus in our own society both men and women remain legally children until long after they are physically adult. In most societies this difference between the physical and social transfer is more clearly marked than in our own. The child becomes a man not when he is physically mature but when he is formally recognized as a man by his society. This recognition is almost always given ceremonial expression in what are technically known as puberty rites. The most important element in these rites is not the determination of physical maturity but that of social maturity. Whether a boy is able to breed is less vital to his society than whether he is able to do a man's work and has a man's knowledge. Actually, most puberty ceremonies include tests of the boy's learning and fortitude, and if the aspirants are unable to pass these they are left in the child status until they can. For those who pass the tests, the ceremonies usually culminate in the transfer to them of certain secrets which the men guard from women and children.

The passage of individuals from adult to aged is harder to perceive. There is no clear physiological line for men, while even women may retain their full physical vigor and their ability to carry on all the activities of the adult status for several years after the menopause. The social transfer of men from the adult to the aged group is given ceremonial recognition in a few cultures, as when a father formally surrenders his official position and titles to his son, but such recognition is rare. As for women, there appears to be no society in which the menopause is given ceremonial recognition, although there are a few societies in which it does alter the individual's status. Thus Comanche women, after the menopause, were released from their disabilities with regard to the supernatural. They could handle sacred objects, obtain power through dreams and practise as shamans, all things forbidden to women of bearing age.

The general tendency for societies to emphasize the individual's first change in age status and largely ignore the second is no doubt due in part to the difficulty of determining the onset of old age. However, there are also psychological factors involved. The boy or girl is usually anxious to grow up, and this eagerness is heightened by the exclusion of children from certain activities and knowledge. Also, society welcomes new additions to the most active division of the group, that which contributes most to its perpetuation and well-being. Conversely, the individual who enjoys the thought of growing old is atypical in all societies. Even when age brings respect and a new measure of influence, it means the relinquishment of much that is pleasant. We can see among ourselves that the aging usually refuse to recognize the change until long after it has happened.

The Social Role and the Social Circle * (*Znaniecki*)

In recent years the term "social role" has been used by many sociologists to denote the phenomena in question.[1] We say that a priest, a lawyer, a politician, a banker, a merchant, a physician, a farmer, a workman, a soldier, a housewife, a teacher performs a specific social role. Furthermore, the concept (with certain variations) has proved applicable not only to individuals who specialize in certain activities but also to individuals as members of certain groups: thus, an American, a Frenchman, a Methodist, a Catholic, a Communist, a Fascist, a club member, a member of the family (child, father, mother, grandparent) plays a certain social role.[2] An individual in the course of his life performs a number of different roles, successively or simultaneously; the synthesis of all the social roles he has ever performed from birth to death constitutes his social personality.

Every social role presupposes that between the individual performing the role, who may thus be called a "social person," and a smaller or larger set of people who participate in his performance and may be termed his "social circle" there is a common bond constituted by a complex of values which all of them appreciate positively. These are economic values in the case of a merchant or a banker and the circle formed by his clients; hygienic values for the physician and his patients; political values for a king and his subjects; religious values for the priest and his circle of lay believers;

* Reprinted from *The Social Role of the Man of Knowledge* by Florian Znaniecki, pp. 13–19, with permission of the publisher, Columbia University Press. Copyright, 1940, by Columbia University Press.

aesthetic values for the artist and the circle of his admirers and critics; a combination of various values which fill the content of family life between the child and his family circle. The person is an object of positive valuation on the part of his circle because they believe that they all need his cooperation for the realization of certain tendencies connected with these values. The banker's cooperation is presumably needed by those who tend to invest or borrow money; the physician's cooperation by those who wish to regain or to preserve their own health and the health of the people in whom they are interested; the child's cooperation by other family members for the maintenance of family life. On the other hand, the person obviously cannot perform his role without the cooperation of his circle—though not necessarily the cooperation of any particular individual within the circle. There can be no active banker without clients, no practicing physician without patients, no reigning king without subjects, no child-in-the-family without other family members.

The person is conceived by his circle as an organic and psychological entity who is a "self," conscious of his own existence as a body and a soul and aware of how others regard him. If he is to be the kind of person his social circle needs, his "self" must possess in the opinion of the circle certain qualities, physical and mental, and not possess certain other qualities. For instance, organic "health" or "sickness" affects his supposed capacity to perform most roles, but particularly occupational roles, such as the farmer's, the workman's, the soldier's, and the housewife's, which require certain bodily skills; while lack of training in the "proper" ways of moving and eating may exclude an individual from roles which require "society" manners. Some roles are limited to men, others to women; there are upper or lower age limits for every role; the majority of roles imply certain somatic racial characteristics and definite, though variable, standards of external appearance.

The psychological qualities ascribed to persons performing social roles are enormously diversified: in every Western language there are hundreds of words denoting supposed traits of "intelligence" and "character"; and almost every such trait has, or had in the past, an axiological significance, that is, is positively or negatively valued, either in all persons or in persons performing certain kinds of role. In naive popular reflection, such psychological traits are real qualities of a substantial "mind" or "soul," whose existence is manifested by specific acts (including verbal statements) of the individual.

A person who is needed by a social circle and whose self possesses the qualities required for the role for which he is needed has a definite social *status,* that is, his circle grants him certain rights and enforces those rights, when necessary, against individual participants of the circle or outsiders. Some of those rights concern his bodily existence. For instance, he has an ecological position, the right to occupy a definite space (as home, room, office, seat) where he is safe from bodily injury, and the right to move safely over given territories. His economic position includes rights to use certain material values regarded as necessary for his subsistence on a level commensurate with his role. Other rights involve his "spiritual welfare": he has a fixed moral standing, can claim some recognition, social response, and participation in the nonmaterial values of his circle.

He, in turn, has a social *function* to fulfill; he is regarded as obliged to achieve certain tasks by which the supposed needs of his circle will be satisfied and to behave toward other individuals in his circle in a way that shows his positive valuation of them.

Such are the essential components which we believe, on the basis of previous studies, to be found in all social roles, although of course the specific composition of different kinds of social role varies considerably. But our knowledge of a social role is not complete if we know only its composition, for a role is a dynamic system and its components may be variously interconnected in the course of its performance. There are many different ways of performing a role, according to the dominant active tendencies of the performer. He may, for instance, be mainly interested in one of the components of his role—the social circle, his own self, the status, or the function—and tend to subordinate other components to it. And, whatever his main interest, he may tend to conform with the demands of his circle or else try to innovate, to become independent of those demands. And, again, in either case he may be optimistically confident in the opportunities offered by his role and tend to expand it or else he may mistrust its possibilities and tend to restrict it to a perfectly secure minimum.

The possibility of reaching such general conclusions about all social roles and more specific, though still widely applicable, generalizations about social roles of a certain kind—such as the role of peasant, priest, merchant, factory worker, or artist—points obviously to the existence of essential uniformities and also of important variations among these social phenomena. Social roles constitute one general class of social system, and this class may be subdivided into less general classes, these into subclasses, and so on; for instance, within the specific class of factory worker there are hundreds of subclasses of workers employed in particular trades and there is another line of differentiation according to the economic organization of the factories in which they are employed. Systematic sociology stands before a task similar to that of systematic biology with its still greater complication of classes and subclasses of living organisms; and here, as there, only uniformities of specific systems make possible a further search for static and dynamic laws. But, manifestly, the source of uniformities in the social field is different from that in the field of biology.

Although in both fields differentiation is due to variations of individual systems, biological uniformities are due in the main to heredity; whereas uniformities of social systems, like those of all cultural systems, are chiefly the result of a reflective or unreflective use of the same *cultural patterns* in many particular cases. There is obviously a fundamental and universal, though unreflective, cultural pattern in accordance with which all kinds of lasting relationships between individuals and their social milieus are normatively organized and which we denote by the term "social role." The genesis of this pattern is lost in an inaccessible past, and so are the origins of what are probably its earliest variations, that is, those which everywhere differentiate individual roles according to sex and age.

But most of the patterns which have evolved during the history of mankind can be studied in the course of their becoming and duration. They originated usually by differentiation from older undifferentiated patterns, more seldom by entirely original, though gradual, invention. Many of these new patterns were short-lived or applied only within small collectivities, but some have lasted for thousands of years and spread over whole continents. In modern American society we find a number of patterns of social roles which can be traced back to prehistoric times, some still very vital, like the pattern of the rural housewife, others probably mere survivals destined soon to disappear, such as the patterns of the magician and the fortune teller.

REFERENCES

1. Some sociologists prefer the term "personal role." The concept may be traced back to C. H. Cooley's *Human Nature and the Social Order* (1902). R. E. Park, E. W. Burgess, G. H. Mead, E. T. Hiller, and others have developed it since then. In the form here presented, it has been utilized in a series of monographic investigations based on firsthand materials and carried on for a number of years by myself and my assistants. These investigations covered the following classes of social role: peasant, peasant housewife, farm laborer, industrial worker, unemployed worker, child in family, pupil in school, youthful member of playgroup, soldier, teacher, artist. Materials have been drawn in each case from several national societies. Some of these studies have been published, mostly in Polish. The first outline of the present study was published in the *Polish Sociological Review*, 1937.
2. Cf. the author's "Social Groups as Products of Cooperating Individuals," *American Journal of Sociology*, May, 1939.

The Social Role of the Man of Knowledge.
By Florian Znaniecki: *A Review* * (*Merton*)

Znaniecki sets himself two main types of problems in this study of specialists in knowledge. (Throughout this book, the terms scientist, savant, and man of knowledge are used synonymously and broadly to designate such specialists.) The first of these problems is taxonomic: what is the composition and structure of the various types of scientists' social roles; what are their interrelations; their lines of development? Secondly, how, if at all, are the systems of knowledge and methods of savants influenced by the normative patterns which define their behavior in a social order? The very formulation of these questions is clear evidence that Znaniecki has not confused problems in the sociology of knowledge with a sociological theory of knowledge, that is, with a special epistemology. This is a study in substantive *Wissenssoziologie,* not an essay on the foundations of valid knowledge.

Znaniecki conceives a social role as a dynamic social system involving four interacting components: (1) the *social circle*: a set of persons who interact with the actor and estimate his performance (*i.e.,* the effective audience); (2) the actor's *self*: the physical and psychological characteristics attributed to him by virtue of his position; (3) the actor's *social status*: the permissions and immunities assigned to him as inherent in his position; (4) the actor's *social functions*: his contributions to his social circle. This paradigm defines the minimal elements which must be examined in the systematic comparison of social roles.

A scant outline of Znaniecki's typology of scientists' roles will not, of course, set forth the analytical uses to which this typology is put. It will, however, indicate the classificatory framework within which his analyses are expressed. Znaniecki's reconstructions of the presumable lines of development of one role into another are not included in this outline.

TYPES OF SOCIAL ROLES OF MEN OF KNOWLEDGE

A. TECHNOLOGY ADVISERS
   1. *Technological expert*: the diagnostician who defines the relevant data in the situation, their essential components and interrelations and the theoretic foundations for planned collective tasks; he performs the "staff" or advisory function.

* By Robert K. Merton, reprinted from *American Sociological Review*, Vol. VI, No. 1, 1941, pp. 111–115, with permission of the publisher, The American Sociological Society, and the author.

2. *Technological leader*: the executive-director who devises the plan and selects the instrumentalities for its execution on the basis of a complex of practically-oriented, heterogeneous knowledge.

B. SAGES [1] (provide intellectual justification of collective tendencies of their party, sect, stratum).

	Apologists for existing tendencies	Idealists with norms not contained in the existing order or in the opposition-party
1. *Conservative*:	(a) "Standpatter"	(b) Meliorist
2. *Novationist*:	(a) Oppositionist	(b) Revolutionary

C. SCHOLARS (i.e., Schoolmen)
1. *Sacred scholar*: perpetuates sacred truths through exact and faithful reproduction of their symbolic expressions; he is charged with the maintenance of a self-contained stable, unchallengeable, sacred system of unchanging truths.
2. *Secular scholar*: with the following subtypes:
   (a) *discoverer of truth*: initiates a "school of thought" with a claim to "absolute truth" validated by the certainty of rational evidence.
   (b) *systematizer*: tests and organizes the total existing knowledge in certain fields into a coherent system by means of deduction from the self-evident first principles established by the discoverer.
   (c) *contributor*: furnishes new findings which are implicitly or explicitly expected to furnish new proof that experience accords with the master's system; revises "unsatisfactory" inductive evidence until it is so integrated or is "justifiably" rejected.
   (d) *fighter for truth*: ensures the logical victory of one school over another by convincing scholars in a polemical situation that his school has a truth-claim validated by rationalistic evidence. (Differs from tendentious partisan sage by confining polemics to a closed arena accessible only to those who hold truth as dominant value.)
   (e) *disseminator of knowledge*
      (1) *popularizer*: cultivates amateur interests among adults, thus aiding popular support of learning, especially in democratized society.
      (2) *educating teacher*: imparts theoretic knowledge to youth as part of their non-occupational education.

D. CREATORS OF KNOWLEDGE (Explorers)
1. *Discoverer of facts* (*fact-finder*): discovers hitherto unknown and unanticipated empirical data, largely as a basis for modifications in existing systems of knowledge.
2. *Discoverer of problems* (*inductive theorist*): discovers new and unfore-

seen theoretic problems which are to be solved by new theoretical constructions.

It should be noted at once that this is a classification of social *roles* and not of persons, and that individual men of knowledge may incorporate several of these analytically distinguishable roles. A further development of Znaniecki's analysis would lead to a statement of the circumstances under which shifts from one role to another occur.

Znaniecki skilfully traces a variety of relations between the components of these classified roles; relations between role-definitions and types of knowledge cultivated; types of knowledge and bases of positive estimation of the scientist by members of the society; normative role-definitions and attitudes toward practical and theoretical knowledge; etc. These relations are examined genetically and functionally. A brief review cannot even list these relations, but one or two instances will serve to illustrate the systematic findings.

A convincing demonstration of the value of Znaniecki's approach is found in his suggestive though brief resume of the various attitudes toward "new unanticipated facts" of those who perform different intellectual roles. It should be noted that *these divers attitudes can be "understood" (or "derived") from the particular role-systems in which the men of knowledge participate;* it is, in other words, an analysis of the ways in which various social structures exert pressures for the adoption of certain attitudes toward new empirical data. The *specialized interest* in the finding of new facts is construed as a revolt against established systems of thought which have persisted largely because they have not been confronted with fresh stubborn facts. Later, to be sure, even this "rebellious" activity becomes institutionalized, but it arises initially in opposition to established and vested intellectual systems. The technological leader regards genuinely new facts with suspicion, for they may destroy belief in the rationality of his established plans, or show the inefficiency of his plans, or disclose undesirable consequences of his program. New facts within the compass of his activity threaten his status. The technological expert, under the control of the leader, is circumscribed in new fact-finding lest he discover facts which are unwelcome to the powers that be. (See, for example, the suppression of new but "unwanted" inventions.) The sage, with his predetermined conclusions, has no use for the impartial observer of new facts which might embarrass his tendentious views. Scholars have positive or negative attitudes toward genuinely new facts, depending upon the extent to which the schools' system is established: in the initial stages new facts are at least acceptable, but once the system is fully formulated the intellectual commitment of the school precludes a favorable attitude toward novel findings. Thus, "a discoverer of facts, freely roaming in search of the unexpected, has no place in a milieu of scientists with well-regulated traditional roles." Znaniecki provides a pioneering analysis of the kind of intellectual neophobia which Pareto largely treated as given rather than problematical.

In similar fashion, Znaniecki shows how rivalry between schools of sacred thought leads to secularization. The most general theorem holds that conflict, as a type of social interaction, leads to the partial secularization of sacred knowledge in at least three ways. First, the usual appeal to sacred authority cannot function in the conflict situation, inasmuch as the rival schools either accept different sacred traditions or interpret the same tradition diversely. "Rational analysis" is adopted as an impartial arbiter. Secondly, members of the out-group (non-believers) must be persuaded that their own faiths are suspect and that another faith has more to commend it. This again involves rational or pseudo-rational argument, since there is no other common unchallenged authority. Finally, the battle of the sacred schools awakens skepticism on the part of intellectual onlookers, and such skepticism must be curbed lest it subvert the authority of the sacred school among the "public." One such safeguard is again rational persuasion. A body of empirical data to which this analysis is peculiarly appropriate, though Znaniecki does not explicitly deal with it, is the situation of the contending Protestant sects during the 16th and 17th centuries. These, in the process of validating their claims to sacred authority for their conflicting views, gradually adopted an elaborate set of rationalistic and empirical bases for legitimacy.[2] The forces conducing to the secularization of sacred knowledge in this historical period are readily conceptualized in Znaniecki's terms. When, however, it becomes manifest that the multiplicity of schools, dogmas and power-structures precludes dominance by any one school, a *modus vivendi* is found in a doctrine of mutual toleration.

In summary, then, this little book presents a conceptual framework for organizing varied materials in one sphere of the sociology of knowledge. It contributes a rich store of hypotheses which often derive from Znaniecki's earlier work, and so have a measure of empirical confirmation at the outset. It should be said, however, as Znaniecki would doubtlessly be the first to acknowledge, that this book is simply a prolegomenon to the sociology of men of knowledge; an introduction, moreover, liable to several criticisms. It includes no systematic documentation, although it may be inferred from the text that a considerable body of empirical data was the basis for much of the work. It would have been especially desirable to include systematic evidence in the generalized account of the ways in which the various roles presumably developed from earlier structures. At present, Znaniecki's account is simply a plausible reconstruction, with all the liabilities to which such developmental schemes are subject. His leading hypothesis that these roles develop by successive differentiation is amenable to empirical test; until it is so tested it can be considered only conjectural. The value of the work would have been considerably enhanced, also, if the role-paradigm (social circle, self, status, function) had been more fully exploited in the analysis of each of the roles actually discussed. As it is, most attention is devoted to the functions of each role and not enough to the structural relations between the other components. Perhaps this is only tantamount to saying that Znaniecki's conceptions are so fertile that he has found it possible to gather only the ripest of the first-fruits. Such forthcoming empirical studies as Logan Wilson's *Academic Man* will doubtless profit by the conceptual framework which Znaniecki has built for handling such subjects. His classification is of course provisional and lends itself to necessary modifications. In short, this is a prospectus which no future student of the subject dare neglect; it is a promise of things to come and a promise which is in part its own fulfillment.

REFERENCES

1. Attention should be called to the instructive comparison between these roles and Mannheim's concepts of ideologists and utopianists. The four-fold table and resultant types, supplied by the reviewer, are clearly implicit in Znaniecki's text (pp. 72–77).
2. *Cf.* Richard Baxter, *Christian Directory,* London, 1825, I, 171, in a passage written in 1665: "They that believe, and know not why, or know no sufficient reason to warrant their faith, do take a fancy, or opinion, or a dream for faith." Or, Henry More, *Brief Discourse of the True Grounds of the Certainty of Faith in Point of Religion,* London, 1688, 578: ". . . to take away all the certainty of sense rightly circumstantiated, is to take away all the certainty of belief in the main points of our religion."

Dilemmas and Contradictions of Status * (*Hughes*)

It is doubtful whether any society ever had so great a variety of statuses or recognized such a large number of status-determining characteristics as does ours. The combinations of the latter are, of course, times over more numerous than the characteristics themselves. In societies where statuses [1] are well defined and are entered chiefly by birth or a few well-established sequences of training or achievement, the particular personal attributes proper to each

* By Everett Cherrington Hughes, reprinted from *The American Journal of Sociology* Vol. L., July 1944–May 1945, pp. 353–359, by permission of The University of Chicago Press, and the author.

status are woven into a whole. They are not thought of as separate entities. Even in our society, certain statuses have developed characteristic patterns of expected personal attributes and a way of life. To such, in the German language, is applied the term *Stand*.

Few of the positions in our society, however, have remained fixed long enough for such an elaboration to occur. We put emphasis on change in the system of positions which make up our social organization and upon mobility of the individual by achievement. In the struggle for achievement, individual traits of the person stand out as separate entities. And they occur in peculiar combinations which make for confusion, contradictions, and dilemmas of status.

I shall, in this paper, elaborate the notion of contradictions and dilemmas of status. Illustrations will be taken from professional and other occupational positions. The idea was put into a suggestive phrase by Robert E. Park when he wrote of the "marginal man." He applied the term to a special kind of case—the racial hybrid—who, as a consequence of the fact that races have become defined as status groups, finds himself in a status dilemma.

Now there may be, for a given status or social position, one or more specifically determining characteristics of the person. Some of them are formal, or even legal. No one, for example, has the status of physician unless he be duly licensed. A foreman is not such until appointed by proper authority. The heavy soprano is not a prima donna in more than temperament until formally cast for the part by the director of the opera. For each of these particular positions there is also an expected technical competence. Neither the formal nor the technical qualifications are, in all cases, so clear. Many statuses, such as membership in a social class, are not determined in a formal way. Other statuses are ill-defined both as to the characteristics which determine identification with them and as to their duties and rights.

There tends to grow up about a status, in addition to its specifically determining traits, a complex of auxiliary characteristics which come to be expected of its incumbents. It seems entirely natural to Roman Catholics that all priests should be men, although piety seems more common among women. In this case the expectation is supported by formal rule. Most doctors, engineers, lawyers, professors, managers, and supervisors in industrial plants are men, although no law requires that they be so. If one takes a series of characteristics, other than medical skill and a license to practice it, which individuals in our society may have, and then thinks of physicians possessing them in various combinations, it becomes apparent that some of the combinations seem more natural and are more acceptable than others to the great body of potential patients. Thus a white, male, Protestant physician of old American stock and of a family of at least moderate social standing would be acceptable to patients of almost any social category in this country. To be sure, a Catholic might prefer a physician of his own faith for reasons of spiritual comfort. A few ardent feminists, a few race-conscious Negroes, a few militant sectarians, might follow their principles to the extent of seeking a physician of their own category. On the other hand, patients who identify themselves with the "old stock" may, in an emergency, take the first physician who turns up.[2]

If the case is serious, patients may seek a specialist of some strange or disliked social category, letting the reputation for special skill override other traits. The line may be crossed also when some physician acquires such renown that his office becomes something of a shrine, a place of wonderful, last-resort cures. Even the color line is not a complete bar to such a reputation. On the contrary, it may add piquancy to the treatment of a particularly enjoyed malady or lend hope to the quest for a cure of an "incurable" ailment. Allowing for such exceptions, it remains probably true that the white, male, Protestant physician of old American stock, although he may easily fail to get a clientele at all, is categorically acceptable to a greater variety of patients than is he who departs, in one or more particulars, from this type.

It is more exact to say that, if one were to imagine patients of the various possible combinations of these same characteristics (race, sex, religion, ethnic background, family standing), such a physician could treat patients of any of the resulting categories without a feeling by the physician, patient, or the surrounding social circle that the situation was unusual or shocking. One has only to make a sixteen-box table showing physicians of the possible combinations of race (white and Negro) and sex with patients of the possible combinations to see that the white male is the only resulting kind of physician to whom patients of all the kinds are completely accessible in our society (see Table I).

One might apply a similar analysis to situations involving other positions, such as the foreman and the worker, the teacher and the pupil. Each case may be complicated by adding other categories of persons with whom the person of the given position has to deal. The teacher, in practice, has dealings not only with pupils but with parents, school boards, other public functionaries, and, finally, his own colleagues. Immediately one tries to make this analysis, it becomes clear that a characteristic which might not interfere with some of the situations of a given position may interfere with others.

I do not maintain that any considerable proportion of people do con-

TABLE I *

Patient	Physician			
	White Male	*White Female*	*Negro Male*	*Negro Female*
White male				
White female				
Negro male				
Negro female				

* I have not used this table in any study of preferences but should be glad if anyone interested were to do so with selected groups of people.

sciously put together in a systematic way their expectations of persons of given positions. I suggest, rather, that people carry in their minds a set of expectations concerning the auxiliary traits properly associated with many of the specific positions available in our society. These expectations appear as advantages or disadvantages to persons who, in keeping with American social belief and practice, aspire to positions new to persons of their kind.

The expected or "natural" combinations of auxiliary characteristics become embodied in the stereotypes of ordinary talk, cartoons, fiction, the radio, and the motion picture. Thus, the American Catholic priest, according to a popular stereotype, is Irish, athletic, and a good sort who with difficulty refrains from profanity in the presence of evil and who may punch someone in the nose if the work of the Lord demands it. Nothing could be farther from the French or French-Canadian stereotype of the good priest. The surgeon, as he appears in advertisements for insurance and pharmaceutical products, is handsome, socially poised, and young of face but gray about the temples. These public, or publicity, stereotypes—while they do not necessarily correspond to the facts or determine peoples expectations— are at least significant in that they rarely let the person in the given position have any strikes against him. Positively, they represent someone's ideal conception; negatively, they take care not to shock, astonish, or put doubts into the mind of a public whose confidence is sought.

If we think especially of occupational status, it is in the colleague-group or fellow-worker group that the expectations concerning appropriate auxiliary characteristics are worked most intricately into sentiment and conduct. They become, in fact, the basis of the colleague-group's definition of its common interests, of its informal code, and of selection of those who become the inner fraternity—three aspects of occupational life so closely related that few people separate them in thought or talk.

The epithets "hen doctor," "boy wonder," "bright young men," and "brain trust" express the hostility of colleagues to persons who deviate from the expected type. The members of a colleague-group have a common interest in the whole configuration of things which control the number of potential candidates for their occupation. Colleagues, be it remembered, are also competitors. A rational demonstration that an individual's chances for continued success are not jeopardized by an extension of the recruiting field for the position he has or hopes to attain, or by some short-cutting of usual lines of promotion, does not, as a rule, liquidate the fear and hostility aroused by such a case. Oswald Hall found that physicians do not like one of their number to become a consultant too soon.[3] Consulting is something for the crowning, easing-off years of a career; something to intervene briefly between high power and high blood-pressure. He who pushes for such practice too early shows an "aggressiveness" which is almost certain to be punished. It is a threat to an order of things which physicians—at least, those of the fraternity of successful men—count upon. Many of the specific rules of the game of an occupation become comprehensible only when viewed as the almost instinctive attempts of a group of people to cushion themselves against the hazards of their careers. The advent of colleague-competitors of some new and peculiar type, or by some new route, is likely to arouse anxieties. For one thing, one cannot be quite sure how "new people"—new in kind—will act in the various contingencies which arise to test the solidarity of the group.[4]

How the expectations of which we are thinking become embodied in codes may be illustrated by the dilemma of a young woman who became a member of that virile profession, engineering. The designer of an airplane is expected to go up on the maiden flight of the first plane built according to the design. He (*sic*) then gives a dinner to the engineers and workmen who worked on the new plane. The dinner is naturally a stag party. The young woman in question designed a plane. Her co-workers urged her not to take the risk—for which, presumably, men only are fit—of the maiden voyage. They were, in effect, asking her to be a lady rather than an engineer. She chose to be an engineer. She then gave the party and paid for it like a man. After food and the first round of toasts, she left like a lady.

Part of the working code of a position is discretion; it allows the colleagues to exchange confidences concerning their relations to other people. Among these confidences one finds expressions of cynicism concerning their mission, their competence, and the foibles of their superiors, themselves, their clients, their subordinates, and the public at large. Such expressions take the burden from one's shoulders and serve as a defense as well. The unspoken mutual confidence necessary to them rests on two assumptions concerning one's fellows. The first is that the colleague will not misunderstand; the second is that he will not repeat to uninitiated ears. To be sure that a new fellow will not misunderstand requires a sparring match of social gestures. The zealot who turns the sparring match into a real battle, who takes a friendly initiation too seriously, is not likely to be trusted with the lighter sort of comment on one's work or with doubts and misgivings; nor can he learn those parts of the working code which are communicated only by hint and gesture. He is not to be trusted, for though he is not fit for stratagems, he is suspected of being prone to treason. In order that men may communicate freely and confidentially, they must be able to take a good deal of each other's sentiments for granted. They must feel easy about their silences as well as about their utterances. These factors conspire to make colleagues, with a large body of unspoken understandings, uncomfortable in the presence of what they consider odd kinds of fellows. The person who is the first of his kind to attain a certain status is often not drawn into the informal brotherhood in which experiences are exchanged, competence built up, and the formal code elaborated and enforced. He thus remains forever a marginal man.

Now it is a necessary consequence of the high degree of individual mobility in America that there should be large numbers of people of new kinds turning up in various positions. In spite of this and in spite of American heterogeneity, this remains a white, Anglo-Saxon, male, Protestant culture in many respects. These are the expected characteristics for many favored statuses and positions. When we speak of racial, religious, sex, and ethnic prejudices, we generally assume that people with these favored qualities are not the objects thereof. In the stereotyped prejudices concerning others, there is usually contained the assumption that these other people are peculiarly adapted to the particular places which they have held up to the present time; it is a corollary implication that they are not quite fit for new positions to which they may aspire. In general, advance of a new group —women, Negroes, some ethnic groups, etc.—to a new level of positions is not accompanied by complete disappearance of such stereotypes but only by some modification of them. Thus, in Quebec the idea that French-Canadians were good only for unskilled industrial work was followed by the notion that they were especially good at certain kinds of skilled work but were not fit to repair machines or to supervise the work of others. In this series of modifications the structure of qualities expected for the most-favored positions remains intact. But the forces which make for mobility continue to create marginal people on new frontiers.

Technical changes also break up configurations of expected status characteristics by altering the occupations about which they grow up. A new machine or a new managerial device—such as the assembly line—may create new positions or break old ones up into numbers of new ones. The length of training may be changed thereby and, with it, the whole traditional method of forming the person to the social demands of a colleague-group. Thus, a snip of a girl is trained in a few weeks to be a "machinist" on a practically foolproof lathe; thereby the old foolproof machinist, who was initiated slowly into the skills and attitudes of the trade, is himself made a fool of in his own eyes or—worse—in the eyes of his wife, who hears that a neighbor's daughter is a machinist who makes nearly as much money as he. The new positions created by technical changes may, for a time, lack definition as a status. Both the technical and the auxiliary qualifications may be slow in taking form. The personnel man offers a good example. His title is perhaps twenty years old, but the expectations concerning his qualities and functions are still in flux.[5]

Suppose we leave aside the problems which arise from technical changes, as such, and devote the rest of this discussion to the consequences of the appearance of new kinds of people in established positions. Every such occurrence produces, in some measure, a status contradiction. It may also create a status dilemma for the individual concerned and for other people who have to deal with him.

The most striking illustration in our society is offered by the Negro who qualifies for one of the traditional professions. Membership in the Negro race, as defined in American mores and/or law, may be called a master status-determining trait. It tends to overpower, in most crucial situations, any other characteristics which might run counter to it. But professional standing is also a powerful characteristic—most so in the specific relationships of professional practice, less so in the general intercourse of people. In the person of the professionally qualified Negro these two powerful characteristics clash. The dilemma, for those whites who meet such a person, is that of having to choose whether to treat him as a Negro or as a member of his profession.

The white person in need of professional services, especially medical, might allow him to act as doctor in an emergency. Or it may be allowed that a Negro physician is endowed with some uncanny skill. In either case, the white client of ordinary American social views would probably avoid any nonprofessional contacts with the Negro physician.[6] In fact, one way of reducing status conflict is to keep the relationship formal and specific. This is best done by walking through a door into a place designed for the specific relationship, a door which can be firmly closed when one leaves. A common scene in fiction depicts a lady of degree seeking, veiled and alone, the address of the fortuneteller or the midwife of doubtful practice in an obscure corner of the city. The anonymity of certain sections of cities allows people to seek specialized services, legitimate but embarrassing as well as illegitimate, from persons with whom they would not want to be seen by members of their own social circle.

Some professional situations lend themselves more than others to such quarantine. The family physician and the pediatrician cannot be so easily isolated as some other specialists. Certain legal services can be sought indirectly by being delegated to some queer and unacceptable person by the family lawyer. At the other extreme is school teaching, which is done in full view of the community and is generally expected to be accompanied by an active role in community activities. The teacher, unlike the lawyer, is expected to be an example to her charges.

For the white colleagues of the Negro professional man the dilemma is even more severe. The colleague-group is ideally a brotherhood; to have within it people who cannot, given one's other attitudes, be accepted as brothers is very uncomfortable. Furthermore, professional men are much more sensitive than they like to admit about the company in which non-professionals see them. The dilemma arises from the fact that, while it is bad for the profession to let laymen see rifts in their ranks, it may be bad for the individual to be associated in the eyes of his actual or potential patients with persons, even colleagues, of so despised a group as the Negro. The favored way of avoiding the dilemma is to shun contacts with the Negro professional. The white physician or surgeon of assured reputation may solve the problem by acting as consultant to Negro colleagues in Negro clinics and hospitals.

For the Negro professional man there is also a dilemma. If he accepts the role of Negro to the extent of appearing content with less than full equality and intimacy with his white colleagues, for the sake of such security and advantage as can be so got, he himself and others may accuse him of sacrificing his race. Given the tendency of whites to say that any Negro who rises to a special position is an exception, there is a strong temptation for such a Negro to seek advantage by fostering the idea that he is unlike others of his race. The devil who specializes in this temptation is a very insinuating fellow; he keeps a mailing list of "marginal men" of all kinds and origins. Incidentally, one of the by-products of American mores is the heavy moral burden which this temptation puts upon the host of Americans who have by great effort risen from (sic) groups which are the objects of prejudice.

There may be cases in which the appearance in a position of one or a few individuals of a kind not expected there immediately dissolves the auxiliary expectations which make him appear odd. This is not, however, the usual consequence. The expectations usually continue to exist, with modifications and with exceptions allowed.

A common solution is some elaboration of social segregation. The woman lawyer may become a lawyer to women clients, or she may specialize in some kind of legal service in keeping with woman's role as guardian of the home and of morals. Women physicians may find a place in those specialties of which only women and children have need. A female electrical engineer was urged by the dean of the school from which she had just been graduated to accept a job whose function was to give the "woman's angle" to design of household electrical appliances. The Negro professional man finds his clients among Negroes. The Negro sociologist generally studies race relations and teaches in a Negro college. A new figure on the American scene is the Negro personnel man in industries which have started employing Negro workers. His functions are to adjust difficulties of Negro workers, settle minor clashes between the races, and to interpret management's policies to the Negro as well as to present and explain the Negro's point of view to management. It is a difficult job. Our interest for the moment, however, is in the fact that the Negro, promoted to this position, acts only with reference to Negro employees. Many industries have had women personnel officials to act with reference to women. In one sense, this is an extension of the earlier and still existing practice of hiring from among a new ethnic group in industry a "straw boss" to look after them. The "straw boss" is the liaison officer reduced to lowest terms.

Another solution, which also results in a kind of isolation if not in segregation, is that of putting the new people in the library or laboratory, where they get the prestige of research people but are out of the way of patients and the public. Recently, industries have hired a good many Negro chemists to work in their testing and research laboratories. The chemist has few contacts with the production organization. Promotion within the laboratory will put the Negro in charge of relatively few people, and those few will be of his own profession. Such positions do not ordinarily lead to the positions of corresponding importance in the production organization. They offer a career line apart from the main streams of promotion to power and prestige.

These solutions reduce the force of status contradiction by keeping the new person apart from the most troublesome situations. One of the consequences is that it adds new stories to the superstructure of segregation. The

Negro hospital and medical school are the formal side of this. The Negro personnel man and foreman show it within the structure of existing institutions. There are evidences that physicians of various ethnic groups are being drawn into a separate medical system of hospitals, clinics, and schools, partly because of the interest of the Roman Catholic church in developing separate institutions but also partly because of the factors here discussed. It is doubtful whether women will develop corresponding separate systems to any great extent. In all of these cases, it looks as if the highest point which a member of these odd groups may attain is determined largely by the number of people of his own group who are in a position to seek his services or in a position such that he may be assigned by other authority to act professionally with reference to them. On the other hand, the kind of segregation involved may lead professional people, or others advanced to special positions, to seek— as compensation—monopoly over such functions with reference to their own group.

Many questions are raised by the order of things here discussed. One is that of the place of these common solutions of status conflict in the evolution of the relations between the sexes, the races, and the ethnic groups of our society. In what circumstances can the person who is accepted formally into a new status, and then informally kept within the limits of the kind mentioned, step out of these limits and become simply a lawyer, foreman, or whatever? Under what circumstances, if ever, is the "hen doctor" simply a doctor? And who are the first to accept her as such—her colleagues or her patients? Will the growth of a separate superstructure over each of the segregated bottom groups of our society tend to perpetuate indefinitely the racial and ethnic division already existing, or will these superstructures lose their identity in the general organization of society? These are the larger questions.

The purpose of the paper, however, is not to answer these large questions. It is rather to call attention to this characteristic phenomenon of our heterogeneous and changing society and to suggest that it become part of the frame of reference of those who are observing special parts of the American social structure.

REFERENCES

1. "Status" is here taken in its strict sense as a defined social position for whose incumbents there are defined rights, limitations of rights, and duties. See the *Oxford Dictionary* and any standard Latin lexicon. Since statuses tend to form a hierarchy, the term itself has—since Roman times—had the additional meaning of rank.
2. A Negro physician, driving through northern Indiana, came upon a crowd standing around a man just badly injured in a road accident. The physician tended the man and followed the ambulance which took him to the hospital. The hospital authorities

tried to prevent the physician from entering the hospital for even long enough to report to staff physicians what he had done for the patient. The same physician, in answer to a Sunday phone call asking him to visit a supposedly very sick woman, went to a house. When the person who answered the door saw that the physician was a Negro, she insisted that they had not called for a doctor and that no one in the house was sick. When he insisted on being paid, the people in the house did so, thereby revealing their lie. In the first instance, an apparently hostile crowd accepted the Negro as a physician because of urgency. In the second, he was refused presumably because the emergency was not great enough.

3. Oswald Hall, "The Informal Organization of Medical Practice" (unpublished Ph.D. dissertation, University of Chicago, 1944).

4. It may be that those whose positions are insecure and whose hopes for the higher goals are already fading express more violent hostility to "new people." Even if so, it must be remembered that those who are secure and successful have the power to exclude or check the careers of such people by merely failing to notice them.

5. The personnel man also illustrates another problem which I do not propose to discuss in this paper. It is that of an essential contradiction between the various functions which are united in one position. The personnel man is expected to communicate the mind of the workers to management and then to interpret management to the workers. This is a difficult assignment. The problem is well stated by William F. Whyte, in "Pity the Personnel Man," *Advanced Management*, October–December, 1944, pp. 154–58. The Webbs analyzed the similar dilemma of the official of a successful trade-union in their *History of Trade-Unionism* (rev. ed.; London: Longmans, Green, 1920).

6. The Negro artist can be treated as a celebrity. It is within the code of social tuft-hunting that one may entertain, with a kind of affected Bohemian intimacy, celebrities who, on all counts other than their artistic accomplishments, would be beyond the pale.

11.
CLASS

"CLASS" IS AN ambiguous term which has been used loosely in everyday parlance and not much more rigorously in some of the technical literature. There is nevertheless a common understanding that class pertains to hierarchical position in the social order and differential distribution of prestige based on that position. It refers to one form of stratification by contrast with another major form, usually called "caste." Class implies mobility, i.e., the possibility of movement up and down the social scale, whereas the mark of caste is a hereditary relationship to other castes which is in principle incapable of change. Caste exists by the Weberian criteria (*connubium* and *commensality*) when intermarriage and intimate social intercourse are prohibited. Class permits, if it does not encourage, these relationships. About this much in the realm of social stratification general agreement could be achieved. The rest would probably give rise to divergent views.

In the final paragraphs of the third volume of his *chef d'oeuvre*, Karl Marx (1818–1883) undertook, too late, to define the word "class." We reproduce that tantalizing passage from *Capital* for two reasons: (1) there is no other attempt known to us in all of Marx's writing to be so explicit about class; (2) the fragment from an unfinished classic indicates that whatever inferential meaning one may impute to a concept that is the very cornerstone of Marxism, Marx himself fully understood its complexity.

It should be said that there are many "Marxes"—and unresolved difficulties or "residual categories," to use Talcott Parsons' term, in all of them. We ought to be aware of at least four incarnations: the young Marx, the mature one, the scholar, and the agitator. As the author of *Capital*, he is also the mature scholar, and something less than that as coauthor of *The German Ideology.* Yet our selection from the earlier work foreshadows that conception of class which we fairly associate with Marx. For him class is much more often than not a condition generated by the economic division of labor and shaped thereafter according to what he called the relations of production. There is much more. There are shadings and nuances. There is above all class conflict. *The Communist Manifesto,* promulgated in 1848 by Marx and

Friedrich Engels (1820–1895), asserts that, "The history of all hitherto exist-ing society is the history of class struggles . . . Freeman and slave, patrician and plebian, lord and serf, guildmaster and journeyman, in a word oppressor and oppressed, stood in constant opposition to one another. . . ."

It is not, however, for formulating and fostering the class struggle that sociological theory owes so much to Marx, but rather for his pointing sharply to the objective reality of social stratification. Marx spoke of *class conscious-ness* as well as class. He recognized the difference between them, but thought that in time one would inevitably come to "reflect" the other. Max Weber, the titan of German sociology, had a somewhat different definition of class, although it was perhaps not so great a departure from Marx as he supposed. Albert Salomon, a profound German-American sociologist who studied with Weber, has said that his teacher whom he has named "the bourgeois Marx" was engaged in a lifelong dialogue with the ghost of Marx. Weber held that class could be defined in exclusively economic or market terms, and in this there is no basic disagreement with Marx. However, it was his merit carefully to have distinguished class, so defined, from other closely related levels of stratification. The subjective or attitudinal side of this phenomenon Weber calls status and it connotes everything that clusters around honor. For him, as for Thorstein Veblen (1857–1929), status sug-gests the consumption of goods rather than their production.

Until recently, with the major exception of Thorstein Veblen, Amer-ican theory touched but fleetingly and superficially on the subject of class. Pitirim Sorokin wrote a useful textbook called *Social Mobility* thirty years ago, but its roots were European. From Italy came the powerful challenge of Gaetano Mosca (1858–1941) and Vilfredo Pareto (1848–1923) to whom stratification was a central and ineradicable fact, and from Germany there emerged a great deal of richly suggestive speculation. Of the latter we have a representative sampling from the essays of Josef Schumpeter (1883–1950) and Hans Speier.

In the United States no one has treated class with such mastery as Veblen who not only used it as the basis for twelve remarkable books but inseminated the thought of nearly all who later discussed the subject. That influence is particularly evident in the earliest and still most valuable com-munity study, the *Middletown* of Robert and Helen M. Lynd.

The literature has lately been enlivened by an ongoing intramural battle between members of the same sociological school. It turns chiefly on the question of whether existing class inequality is positively functional. We will let the principals speak for themselves. The discussion on both sides deserves respectful attention. It promises to take us one step forward in an area of the greatest theoretical importance that has been static or retrograde for far too long.

The Definition of Class * (*Marx*)

The owners of mere labor-power, the owners of capital, and the landlords, whose respective sources of income are wages, profit and ground-rent, in other words, wage laborers, capitalists and landlords, form the three great classes of modern society resting upon the capitalist mode of production.

In England, modern society is indisputably developed most highly and classically in its economic structure. Nevertheless the stratification of classes does not appear in its pure form, even there. Middle and transition stages obliterate even here all definite boundaries, although much less in the rural districts than in the cities. However, this is immaterial for our analysis. We have seen that the continual tendency and law of development of capitalist production is to separate the means of production more and more from labor, and to concentrate the scattered means of production more and more in large groups, thereby transforming labor into wage labor and the means of production into capital. In keeping with this tendency we have, on the other hand, the independent separation of private land from capital and labor,[1] or the transformation of all property in land into a form of landed property corresponding to the capitalist mode of production.

The first question to be answered is this: What constitutes a class? And this follows naturally from another question, namely: What constitutes wage laborers, capitalists and landlords into three great social classes?

At first glance it might seem that the identity of their revenues and their sources of revenue does that. They are three great social groups, whose component elements, the individuals forming them, live on wages, profit and ground-rent, or by the utilization of their labor-power, their capital, and their private land.

However, from this point of view physicians and officials would also form two classes, for they belong to the two distinct social groups, and the revenues of their members flow from the same common source. The same would also be true of the infinite dissipation of interests and positions created by the social division of labor among laborers, capitalists and landlords. For instance, the landlords are divided into owners of vineyards, farms, forest, mines, fisheries.

* Reprinted from *Capital,* Vol. III, by Karl Marx, edited by Frederick Engels, translated from the first German edition by Ernest Untermann, pp. 1031–1032, Charles H. Kerr & Company, Chicago, Ill., 1909.

REFERENCE

1. F. List remarks correctly: "Prevalence of self-management in the case of large estates proves only a lack of civilization, of means of communication, of home industries and rich cities. For this reason it is found everywhere in Russia, Poland, Hungary, Mecklenburg. Formerly it prevailed also in England. But with the rise of commerce and industry came their division into medium-sized farms and their occupancy by tenants." (*The Agrarian Constitution, the Petty Farm, and Emigration,* 1842, p. 10.)

Class and the Division of Labor *
(Marx and Engels)

The relations of different nations among themselves depend upon the extent to which each has developed its productive forces, the division of labour and internal intercourse. This statement is generally recognized. But not only the relation of one nation to others, but also the whole internal structure of the nation itself depends on the stage of development reached by its production and its internal and external intercourse. How far the productive forces of a nation are developed is shown most manifestly by the degree to which the division of labour has been carried. Each new productive force, in so far as it is not merely a quantitative extension of productive forces already known (for instance the bringing into cultivation of fresh land) brings about a further development of the division of labour.

The division of labour inside a nation leads at first to the separation of industrial and commercial from agricultural labour, and hence to the separation of town and country and a clash of interests between them. Its further development leads to the separation of commercial from industrial labour. At the same time through the division of labour there develop further, inside these various branches, various divisions among the individuals co-operating in definite kinds of labour. The relative position of these individual groups is determined by the methods employed in agriculture, industry and commerce (patriarchalism, slavery, estates, classes.) These same conditions are to be seen (given a more developed intercourse) in the relations of different nations to one another.

The various stages of development in the division of labour are just so many different forms of ownership; i.e., the existing stage in the division of labour determines also the relations of individuals to one another with reference to the material, instrument, and product of labour.

* Reprinted from *The German Ideology* by Karl Marx and Friedrich Engels, New York, 1939, pp. 8–12.

The first form of ownership is tribal ownership. It corresponds to the undeveloped stage of production, at which a people lives by hunting and fishing, by the rearing of beasts or, in the highest stage, agriculture. In the latter case it presupposes a great mass of uncultivated stretches of land. The division of labour is at this stage still very elementary and is confined to a further extension of the natural division of labour imposed by the family. The social structure is therefore limited to an extension of the family; patriarchal family chieftains; below them the members of the tribe; finally slaves. The slavery latent in the family only develops gradually with the increase of population, the growth of wants, and with the extension of external relations, of war or of trade.

The second form is the ancient communal and State ownership which proceeds especially from the union of several tribes into a city by agreement or by conquest, and which is still accompanied by slavery. Beside communal ownership we already find movable, and later also immovable, private property developing, but as an abnormal form subordinate to communal ownership. It is only as a community that the citizens hold power over their labouring slaves, and on this account alone, therefore, they are bound to the form of communal ownership. It is the communal private property which compels the active citizens to remain in this natural form of association over against their slaves. For this reason the whole structure of society based on this communal ownership, and with it the power of the people, decays in the same measure as immovable private property evolves. The division of labour is already more developed. We already find the antagonism of town and country; later the antagonism between those states which represent town interests and those which represent country, and inside the towns themselves the antagonism between industry and maritime commerce. The class relation between citizens and slaves is now completely developed.

This whole interpretation of history appears to be contradicted by the fact of conquest. Up till now violence, war, pillage, rape and slaughter, etc., have been accepted as the driving force of history. Here we must limit ourselves to the chief points and take therefore only a striking example—the destruction of an old civilization by a barbarous people and the resulting formation of an entirely new organization of society. (Rome and the barbarians; Feudalism and Gaul; the Byzantine Empire and the Turks.) With the conquering barbarian people war itself is still, as hinted above, a regular form of intercourse, which is the more eagerly exploited as the population increases, involving the necessity of new means of production to supersede the traditional and, for it, the only possible, crude mode of production. In Italy it was, however, otherwise. The concentration of landed property (caused not only by buying-up and indebtedness but also by inheritance, since loose living being rife and marriage rare, the old families died out and their possessions fell into the hands of a few) and its conversion into grazing-land (caused not only by economic forces still operative to-day but by the importation of plundered and tribute-corn and the resultant lack of demand for Italian corn) brought about the almost total disappearance of the free population. The very slaves died out again and again, and had constantly to be replaced by new ones. Slavery remained the basis of the whole productive system. The plebeians, mid-way between freemen and slaves, never succeeded in becoming more than a proletarian rabble. Rome indeed never became more than a city; its connection with the provinces was almost exclusively political and could therefore easily be broken again by political events.

With the development of private property, we find here for the first time the same conditions which we shall find again, only on a more extensive scale, with modern private property. On the one hand the concentration of private property, which began very early in Rome (as the Licinian agrarian law proves) and proceeded very rapidly from the time of the civil wars and especially under the Emperors; on the other hand, coupled with this, the transformation of the plebeian small peasantry into a proletariat, which, however, owing to its intermediate position between propertied citizens and slaves, never achieved an independent development.

The third form of ownership is feudal or estate-property. If antiquity started out from the town and its little territory, the Middle Ages started out from the country. This different starting-point was determined by the sparseness of the population at that time, which was scattered over a large area and which received no large increase from the conquerors. In contrast to Greece and Rome, feudal development therefore extends over a much wider field, prepared by the Roman conquests and the spread of agriculture at first associated with it. The last centuries of the declining Roman Empire and its conquest by the barbarians destroyed a number of productive forces; agriculture had declined, industry had decayed for want of a market, trade had died out or been violently suspended, the rural and urban population had decreased. From these conditions and the mode of organization of the conquest determined by them, feudal property developed under the influence of the Germanic military constitution. Like tribal and communal ownership, it is based again on a community; but the directly producing class standing over against it is not, as in the case of the ancient community, the slaves, but the enserfed small peasantry. As soon as feudalism is fully developed, there also arises antagonism to the towns. The hierarchical system of land ownership, and the armed bodies of retainers associated with it, gave the nobility power over the serfs. This feudal organization was, just as much as the ancient communal ownership, an association against a subjected producing class; but the form of association and the relation to the direct producers were different because of the different conditions of production.

This feudal organization of land-ownership had its counterpart in the towns in the shape of corporative property, the feudal organization of trades. Here property consisted chiefly in the labour of each individual person. The necessity for association against the organized robber-nobility, the need for communal covered markets in an age when the industrialist was at the same time a merchant, the growing competition of the escaped serfs swarming into the rising towns, the feudal structure of the whole country: these combined to bring about the guilds. Further, the gradually accumulated capital of individual craftsmen and their stable numbers, as against the growing population, evolved the relation of journeyman and apprentice, which brought into being in the towns a hierarchy similar to that in the country.

Thus the chief form of property during the feudal epoch consisted on the one hand of landed property with serf-labour chained to it, and on the other of individual labour with small capital commanding the labour of journeymen. The organization of both was determined by the restricted conditions of production—the small-scale and primitive cultivation of the land, and the craft type of industry. There was little division of labour in the heyday of feudalism. Each land bore in itself the conflict of town and country and the division into estates was certainly strongly marked; but apart from the differentiation of princes, nobility, clergy and peasants in the country, and masters, journeymen, apprentices and soon also the rabble of casual labourers in the towns, no division of importance took place. In agriculture it was rendered difficult by the strip-system, beside which the cottage industry of the peasants themselves emerged as another factor. In industry there was no division of labour at all in the individual trades themselves, and very little between them. The separation of industry and commerce was found already in existence in older towns; in the newer it only developed later, when the towns entered into mutual relations.

The grouping of larger territories into feudal kingdoms was a necessity for the landed nobility as for the towns. The organization of the ruling class, the nobility, had, therefore, everywhere a monarch at its head.

The fact is, therefore, that definite individuals who are productively active in a definite way enter into these definite social and political relations. Empirical observation must in each separate instance bring out empirically, and without any mystification and speculation, the connection of the social and political structure with production. The social structure and the State are continually evolving out of the life-process of definite individuals, but of individuals, not as they may appear in their own or other people's imagination, but as they really are; i.e., as they are effective, produce materially, and are active under definite material limits, presuppositions and conditions independent of their will.

Are the Peasants a Class? * (*Marx*)

The small peasants form a vast mass, the members of which live in similar conditions, but without entering into manifold relations with one another. Their mode of production isolates them from one another, instead of bringing them into mutual intercourse. The isolation is increased by France's bad means of communication and by the poverty of the peasants. Their field of production, the small holding, admits of no division of labour in its cultivation, no application of science and, therefore, no multiplicity of development, no diversity of talents, no wealth of social relationships. Each individual peasant family is almost self-sufficient; it itself directly produces the major part of its consumption and thus acquires its means of life more through exchange with nature than in intercourse with society. The small holding, the peasant and his family; alongside them another small holding, another peasant and another family. A few score of these make up a village, and a few score of villages make up a Department. In this way, the great mass of the French nation is formed by simple addition of homologous magnitudes, much as potatoes in a sack form a sackful of potatoes. In so far as millions of families live under economic conditions of existence that divide their mode of life, their interests and their culture from those of the other classes and put them in hostile contrast to the latter, they form a class. In so far as there is merely a local interconnection among these small peasants, and the identity of their interests begets no unity, no national union and no political organisation, they do not form a class. They are consequently incapable of enforcing their class interest in their own name, whether through

* Reprinted from *The Eighteenth Brumaire of Louis Napoleon*, by Karl Marx. English translation, 1898.

a parliament or through a convention. They cannot represent themselves, they must be represented. Their representative must at the same time appear as their master, as an authority over them, as an unlimited governmental power, that protects them against the other classes and sends them the rain and the sunshine from above. The political influence of the small peasants, therefore finds its final expression in the executive power subordinating society to itself.

*   *   *

After the first Revolution had transformed the peasants form semi-villeins into freeholders, Napoleon confirmed and regulated the conditions on which they could exploit undisturbed the soil of France which had only just come into their possession and slake their youthful passion for property. But what is now causing the ruin of the French peasant is his dwarf holding itself, the division of the land, the form of property which Napoleon consolidated in France. It is precisely the material conditions which made the feudal peasant into a small peasant and Napoleon into an emperor. Two generations have sufficed to produce the inevitable result : progressive deterioration of agriculture, progressive indebtedness of the agriculturist. The "Napoleonic" form of property, which at the beginning of the nineteenth century was the condition for the liberation and enrichment of the French country folk, has developed in the course of this century as the law of their enslavement and pauperisation. And it is just this law which is the first of the "*idées napoléoniennes*" which the second Bonaparte has to uphold. If he still shares with the peasants the illusion that the cause of their ruin is to be sought not in this small holding property itself but outside it in the influence of secondary causes, then his experiments will burst like soap bubbles when they come into contact with the relations of production.

The economic development of this small holding property has turned the relation of the peasants to the remaining classes of society completely upside down. Under Napoleon, the fragmentation of the land in the countryside supplemented free competition and the beginning of big industry in the towns. [Even the favouring of the peasant class was in the interest of the new bourgeois order. This newly-created class was the many-sided extension of the bourgeois regime beyond the gates of the towns, its realisation on a national scale.] This class was the ubiquitous protest against the landed aristocracy which had just been overthrown.

[If it was favoured above all, it, above all, offered the point of attack for the restoration of the feudal lands.]

The roots that this small holding property struck in French soil deprived feudalism of all nutriment. Its landmarks formed the natural fortifications of the bourgeoisie against any *coup de main* on the part of its old overlords. But in the course of the nineteenth century the feudal lords were replaced by urban usurers; the feudal obligation that went with the land was replaced by the mortgage; aristocratic landed property was replaced by bourgeois capital. The small holding of the peasant is now only the pretext that allows the capitalist to draw profits, interest and rent from the soil, while leaving it to the tiller of the soil himself to see how he can extract his wages. The mortgage debt burdening the soil of France imposes on the French peasantry payment of an amount of interest equal to the annual interest on the entire British national debt. Small holding property, in this enslavement by capital to which its development inevitably pushes forward, has transformed the mass of the French nation into troglodytes. Sixteen million peasants (including women and children) dwell in hovels, a large number of which have but one opening, others only two and the most favoured only three. And windows are to a house what the five senses are to the head. The bourgeois order, which at the beginning of the century set the state to stand guard over the newly arisen small holding and manured it with laurels, has become a vampire that sucks out its blood and marrow and throws them into the alchemistic cauldron of capital. The *Code Napoléon* is now nothing but a *codex* of distraints, forced sales and compulsory auctions. To the four million (including children, etc.) officially recognised paupers, vagabonds, criminals and prostitutes in France, must be added five millions who hover on the margin of existence and either have their haunts in the countryside itself or, with their rags and their children, continually desert the countryside for the towns and the towns for the countryside. The interests of the peasants, therefore, are no longer, as under Napoleon, in accord with, but in opposition to the interests of the bourgeoisie, to capital. Hence the peasants find their natural ally and leader in the *urban proletariat* whose task is the overthrow of the bourgeois order. But *strong and unlimited government*—and this is the second *"idée napoléonienne,"* which the second Napoleon has to carry out—is called upon to defend by force this "material" order. This "material order" also serves as the catchword in all Bonaparte's proclamations against the rebellious peasants.

Class and Status * (*Weber*)

1: ECONOMICALLY DETERMINED POWER AND THE SOCIAL ORDER

Law exists when there is a probability that an order will be upheld by a specific staff of men who will use physical or psychical compulsion with the intention of obtaining conformity with the order, or of inflicting sanctions for infringement of it.[1] The structure of every legal order directly influences the distribution of power, economic or otherwise, within its respective community. This is true of all legal orders and not only that of the state. In general, we understand by 'power' the chance of a man or of a number of men to realize their own will in a communal action even against the resistance of others who are participating in the action.

'Economically conditioned' power is not, of course, identical with 'power' as such. On the contrary, the emergence of economic power may be the consequence of power existing on other grounds. Man does not strive for power only in order to enrich himself economically. Power, including economic power, may be valued 'for its own sake.' Very frequently the striving for power is also conditioned by the social 'honor' it entails. Not all power, however, entails social honor: The typical American Boss, as well as the typical big speculator, deliberately relinquishes social honor. Quite generally, 'mere economic' power, and especially 'naked' money power, is by no means a recognized basis of social honor. Nor is power the only basis of social honor. Indeed, social honor, or prestige, may even be the basis of political or economic power, and very frequently has been. Power, as well as honor, may be guaranteed by the legal order, but, at least normally, it is not their primary source. The legal order is rather an additional factor that enhances the chance to hold power or honor; but it cannot always secure them.

The way in which social honor is distributed in a community between typical groups participating in this distribution we may call the 'social order.' The social order and the economic order are, of course, similarly related to the 'legal order.' However, the social and the economic order are not identical. The economic order is for us merely the way in which economic goods and services are distributed and used. The social order is of course

---

* From *From Max Weber: Essays in Sociology,* pp. 180–184, edited by H. H. Gerth and C. Wright Mills, copyright, 1946, by Oxford University Press, New York. Reprinted by permission.

conditioned by the economic order to a high degree, and in its turn reacts upon it.

Now: 'classes,' 'status groups,' and 'parties' are phenomena of the distribution of power within a community.

2: DETERMINATION OF CLASS-SITUATION BY MARKET-SITUATION

In our terminology, 'classes' are not communities; they merely represent possible, and frequent, bases for communal action. We may speak of a 'class' when (1) a number of people have in common a specific causal component of their life chances, in so far as (2) this component is represented exclusively by economic interests in the possession of goods and opportunities for income, and (3) is represented under the conditions of the commodity or labor markets. [These points refer to 'class situation,' which we may express more briefly as the typical chance for a supply of goods, external living conditions, and personal life experiences, in so far as this chance is determined by the amount and kind of power, or lack of such, to dispose of goods or skills for the sake of income in a given economic order. The term 'class' refers to any group of people that is found in the same class situation.]

It is the most elemental economic fact that the way in which the disposition over material property is distributed among a plurality of people, meeting competitively in the market for the purpose of exchange, itself creates specific life chances. According to the law of marginal utility this mode of distribution excludes the non-owners from competing for highly valued goods; it favors the owners and, in fact, gives to them a monopoly to acquire such goods. Other things being equal, this mode of distribution monopolizes the opportunities for profitable deals for all those who, provided with goods, do not necessarily have to exchange them. It increases, at least generally, their power in price wars with those who, being propertyless, have nothing to offer but their services in native form or goods in a form constituted through their own labor, and who above all are compelled to get rid of these products in order barely to subsist. This mode of distribution gives to the propertied a monopoly on the possibility of transferring property from the sphere of use as a 'fortune,' to the sphere of 'capital goods'; that is, it gives them the entrepreneurial function and all chances to share directly or indirectly in returns on capital. All this holds true within the area in which pure market conditions prevail. 'Property' and 'lack of property' are, therefore, the basic categories of all class situations. It does not matter whether these two categories become effective in price wars or in competitive struggles.

Within these categories, however, class situations are further differentiated : on the one hand, according to the kind of property that is usable for returns; and, on the other hand, according to the kind of services that can be offered in the market. Ownership of domestic buildings, productive establishments; warehouses; stores; argriculturally usable land, large and small holdings—quantitative differences with possibly qualitative consequences—; ownership of mines; cattle; men (slaves) ; disposition over mobile instruments of production, or capital goods of all sorts, especially money or objects that can be exchanged for money easily and at any time; disposition over products of one's own labor or of others' labor differing according to their various distances from consumability; disposition over transferable monopolies of any kind—all these distinctions differentiate the class situations of the propertied just as does the 'meaning' which they can and do give to the utilization of property, especially to property which has money equivalence. Accordingly, the propertied, for instance, may belong to the class of rentiers or to the class of entrepreneurs.

Those who have no property but who offer services are differentiated just as much according to their kinds of services as according to the way in which they make use of these services, in a continuous or discontinuous relation to a recipient. But always this is the generic connotation of the concept of class : that the kind of chance in the *market* is the decisive moment which presents a common condition for the individual's fate. 'Class situation' is, in this sense, ultimately 'market situation.' The effect of naked possession *per se*, which among cattle breeders gives the non-owning slave or serf into the power of the cattle owner, is only a forerunner of real 'class' formation. However, in the cattle loan and in the naked severity of the law of debts in such communities, for the first time mere 'possession' as such emerges as decisive for the fate of the individual. This is very much in contrast to the agricultural communities based on labor. The creditor-debtor relation becomes the basis of 'class situations' only in those cities where a 'credit market,' however primitive, with rates interest increasing according to the extent of dearth and a factual monopolization of credits, is developed by a plutocracy. Therewith 'class struggles' begin.

Those men whose fate is not determined by the chance of using goods or services for themselves on the market, e.g., slaves, are not, however, a 'class' in the technical sense of the term. They are, rather, a 'status group.'

3: COMMUNAL ACTION FLOWING FROM CLASS INTEREST

According to our terminology, the factor that creates 'class' is unambiguously economic interest, and indeed, only those interests involved in the existence of the 'market.' Nevertheless, the concept of 'class-interest' is an ambiguous one: even as an empirical concept it is ambiguous as soon as one understands by it something other than the factual direction of interests following with a certain probability from the class situation for a certain 'average' of those people subjected to the class situation. The class situation and other circumstances remaining the same, the direction in which the individual worker, for instance, is likely to pursue his interests may vary widely, according to whether he is constitutionally qualified for the task at hand to a high, to an average, or to a low degree. In the same way, the direction of interests may vary according to whether or not a *communal* action of a larger or smaller portion of those commonly affected by the 'class situation,' or even an association among them, e.g., a 'trade union,' has grown out of the class situation from which the individual may or may not expect promising results. [Communal action refers to that action which is oriented to the feeling of the actors that they belong together. Societal action, on the other hand, is oriented to a rationally motivated adjustment of interests.] The rise of societal or even of communal action from a common class situation is by no means a universal phenomenon.

The class situation may be restricted in its effects to the generation of essentially *similar* reactions, that is to say, within our terminology, of 'mass actions.' However, it may not have even this result. Furthermore, often merely an amorphous communal action emerges. For example, the 'murmuring' of the workers known in ancient oriental ethics: the moral disapproval of the work-master's conduct, which in its practical significance was probably equivalent to an increasingly typical phenomenon of precisely the latest industrial development, namely, the 'slow down' (the deliberate limiting of work effort) of laborers by virtue of tacit agreement. The degree in which 'communal action' and possibly 'societal action,' emerges from the 'mass actions' of the members of a class is linked to general cultural conditions, especially to those of an intellectual sort. It is also linked to the extent of the contrasts that have already evolved, and is especially linked to the *transparency* of the connections between the causes and the consequences of the 'class situation.' For however different life chances may be, this fact in itself, according to all experience, by no means gives birth to 'class action' (communal action by the members of a class). The fact of being conditioned and the results of the class situation must be distinctly recognizable. For only then the contrast of life chances can be felt not as an absolutely given fact to be accepted, but as a resultant from either (1) the given distribution of property, or (2) the structure of the concrete economic order. It is only then that people may react against the class structure not only through acts of an intermittent and irrational protest, but in the form of rational association. There have been 'class situations' of the first category (1), of a specifically naked and transparent sort, in the urban centers of Antiquity and during the Middle Ages; especially then, when great fortunes were accumulated by factually monopolized trading in industrial products of these localities or in foodstuffs. Furthermore, under certain circumstances, in the rural economy of the most diverse periods, when agriculture was increasingly exploited in a profit-making manner. The most important historical example of the second category (2) is the class situation of the modern 'proletariat.'

REFERENCE

1. *Wirtschaft und Gesellschaft,* part III, chap. 4, pp. 631–40. The first sentence in paragraph one and the several definitions in this chapter which are in brackets do not appear in the original text. They have been taken from other contexts of *Wirtschaft und Gesellschaft.*

Conspicuous Consumption * (*Veblen*)

In what has been said of the evolution of the vicarious leisure class and its differentiation from the general body of the working classes, reference has been made to a further division of labor—that between different servant classes. One portion of the servant class, chiefly those persons whose occupation is vicarious leisure, come to undertake a new, subsidiary range of duties —the vicarious consumption of goods. The most obvious form in which this consumption occurs is seen in the wearing of liveries and the occupation of spacious servants' quarters. Another, scarcely less obtrusive or less effective form of vicarious consumption, and a much more widely prevalent one, is the consumption of food, clothing, dwelling, and furniture by the lady and the rest of the domestic establishment.

But already at a point in economic evolution far antedating the emergence of the lady, specialized consumption of goods as an evidence of pecuniary strength had begun to work out in a more or less elaborate system. The beginning of a differentiation in consumption even antedates the appearance of anything that can fairly be called pecuniary strength. It is traceable back to the initial phase of predatory culture, and there is even a suggestion that an incipient differentiation in this respect lies back of the beginnings of the predatory life. This most primitive differentiation in the consumption of goods is like the later differentiation with which we are all so intimately familiar, in that it is largely of a ceremonial character, but unlike the latter it does not rest on a difference in accumulated wealth. The utility of consumption as an evidence of wealth is to be classed as a derivative growth. It is an adaptation to a new end, by a selective process, of a distinction previously existing and well established in men's habits of thought.

In the earlier phases of the predatory culture the only economic differentiation is a broad distinction between an honorable superior class made up of the able-bodied men on the one side, and a base inferior class of laboring women on the other. According to the ideal scheme of life in force at that time it is the office of the men to consume what the women produce. Such consumption as falls to the women is merely incidental to their work; it is a means to their continued labor, and not a consumption directed to their own comfort and fullness of life. Unproductive consumption of goods is honorable, primarily as a mark of prowess and a perquisite of human dignity; secondarily it becomes substantially honorable in itself, especially the consumption of the more desirable things. The consumption of choice articles of food, and frequently also of rare articles of adornment, becomes tabu to the women and children; and if there is a base (servile) class of men, the tabu holds also for them. With a further advance in culture this tabu may change into simple custom of a more or less rigorous character; but whatever be the theoretical basis of the distinction which is maintained, whether it be a tabu or a larger conventionality, the features of the conventional scheme of consumption do not change easily. When the quasi-peaceable stage of industry is reached, with its fundamental institution of chattel slavery, the general principle, more or less rigorously applied, is that the base, industrious class should consume only what may be necessary to their subsistence. In the nature of things, luxuries and the comforts of life belong to the leisure class. Under the tabu, certain victuals, and more particularly certain beverages, are strictly reserved for the use of the superior class.

The ceremonial differentiation of the dietary is best seen in the use of intoxicating beverages and narcotics. If these articles of consumption are costly, they are felt to be noble and honorific. Therefore the base classes, primarily the women, practice an enforced continence with respect to these stimulants, except in countries where they are obtainable at a very low cost. From archaic times down through all the length of the patriarchal regime it has been the office of the women to prepare and administer these luxuries, and it has been the perquisite of the men of gentle birth and breeding to consume them. Drunkenness and the other pathological consequences of the free use of stimulants therefore tend in their turn to become honorific, as being a mark, at the second remove, of the superior status of those who are able to afford the indulgence. Infirmities induced by over-indulgence are among some peoples freely recognized as manly attributes. It has even happened that the name for certain diseased conditions of the body arising from such an origin has passed into everyday speech as a synonym for "noble" or "gentle." It is only at a relatively early stage of culture that the symptoms of expensive vice are conventionally accepted as marks of a superior status, and so tend to become virtues and command the deference of the community; but the reputability that attaches to certain expensive vices long retains so much of its force as to appreciably lessen the disapprobation visited upon the men of the wealthy or noble class for any excessive indulgence. The same invidious distinction adds force to the current disapproval of any indulgence of this kind on the part of women, minors, and inferiors. This invidious traditional distinction has not lost its force even among the more advanced peoples of today. Where the example set by the leisure class retains its imperative force in the regulation of the conventionalities, it is observable that the women still in great measure practice the same traditional continence with regard to stimulants.

This characterization of the greater continence in the use of stimulants practiced by the women of the reputable classes may seem an excessive refinement of logic at the expense of common sense. But facts within easy reach of anyone who cares to know them go to say that the greater abstinence of women is in some part due to an imperative conventionality; and this conventionality is, in a general way, strongest where the patriarchal tradition—the tradition that the woman is a chattel—has retained its hold in greatest vigor. In a sense which has been greatly qualified in scope and rigor, but which has by no means lost its meaning even yet, this tradition says that the woman, being a chattel, should consume only what is necessary to her sustenance—except so far as her further consumption contributes to the comfort or the good repute of her master. The consumption of luxuries, in the true sense, is a consumption directed to the comfort of the consumer himself, and is, therefore, a mark of the master. Any such consumption by others can take place only on a basis of sufferance. In communities where the popular habits of thought have been profoundly shaped by the patriarchal tradition we may accordingly look for survivals of the tabu on luxuries at least to the extent of a conventional deprecation of their use by the unfree and dependent class. This is more particularly true as regards certain luxuries, the use of which by the dependent class would detract sensibly from the comfort or pleasure of their masters, or which are held to be of doubtful legitimacy on other grounds. In the apprehension of the great conservative middle class of Western civilization the use of these various stimulants is obnoxious to at least one, if not both, of these objections; and it is a fact too significant to be passed over that it is precisely among these middle classes of the Germanic culture, with their strong surviving sense of the patriarchal proprieties, that the women are to the greatest extent subject to a qualified tabu on narcotics and alcoholic beverages. With many qualifications—with more qualifications as the patriarchal tradition has gradually weakened—the general rule is felt to be right and binding that women should consume only for the benefit of their masters. The objection of course presents itself that expenditure on women's dress and household paraphernalia is an obvious exception to this rule; but it will appear in the sequel that this exception is much more obvious than substantial.

During the earlier stages of economic development, consumption of goods without stint, especially consumption of the better grades of goods—ideally all consumption in excess of the subsistence minimum—pertains normally to the leisure class. This restriction tends to disappear, at least formally, after the later peaceable stage has been reached, with private ownership of goods and an industrial system based on wage labor or on the petty household economy. But during the earlier quasi-peaceable stage, when so many of the traditions through which the institution of a leisure class has affected the economic life of later times were taking form and consistency, this principle has had the force of a conventional law. It has served as the norm to which consumption has tended to conform, and any appreciable departure from it is to be regarded as an aberrant form, sure to be eliminated sooner or later in the further course of development.

The quasi-peaceable gentleman of leisure, then, not only consumes, of the staff of life beyond the minimum required for subsistence and physical efficiency, but his consumption also undergoes a specialization as regards the quality of the goods consumed. He consumes freely and of the best, in food, drink, narcotics, shelter, services, ornaments, apparel, weapons and accoutrements, amusements, amulets, and idols or divinities. In the process of gradual amelioration which takes place in the articles of his consumption, the motive principle and the proximate aim of innovation is no doubt the higher efficiency of the improved and more elaborate products for personal comfort and well-being. But that does not remain the sole purpose of their consumption. The canon of reputability is at hand and seizes upon such innovations as are, according to its standard, fit to survive. Since the consumption of these more excellent goods is an evidence of wealth, it becomes honorific; and conversely, the failure to consume in due quantity and quality becomes a mark of inferiority and demerit.

This growth of punctilious discrimination as to qualitative excellence in eating, drinking, etc., presently affects not only the manner of life, but also the training and intellectual activity of the gentleman of leisure. He is no longer simply the successful, aggressive male—the man of strength, resource, and intrepidity. In order to avoid stultification he must also cultivate his tastes, for it now becomes incumbent on him to discriminate with some nicety between the noble and the ignoble in consumable goods. He becomes a connoisseur in creditable viands of various degrees of merit, in manly beverages and trinkets, in seemly apparel and architecture, in weapons, games, dances, and the narcotics. This cultivation of the æsthetic faculty requires time and application, and the demands made upon the gentleman in this direction therefore tend to change his life of leisure into a more or less arduous application to the business of learning how to live a life of ostensible leisure in a becoming way. Closely related to the requirement that the gentleman must consume freely and of the right kind of goods, there is the requirement that he must know how to consume them in a seemly manner. His life of leisure must be conducted in due form. Hence arise good manners in the way pointed out in an earlier chapter. High-bred manners and ways of living are items of conformity to the norm of conspicuous leisure and conspicuous consumption.

Conspicuous consumption of valuable goods is a means of reputability to the gentleman of leisure. As wealth accumulates on his hands, his own unaided effort will not avail to sufficiently put his opulence in evidence by this method. The aid of friends and competitors is therefore brought in by resorting to the giving of valuable presents and expensive feasts and entertainments. Presents and feasts had probably another origin than that of naïve ostentation, but they acquired their utility for this purpose very early, and they have retained that character to the present; so that their utility in this respect has now long been the substantial ground on which these usages rest. Costly entertainments, such as the potlatch or the ball, are peculiarly adapted to serve this end. The competitor with whom the entertainer wishes to institute a comparison is, by this method, made to serve as a means to the end. He consumes vicariously for his host at the same time that he is a witness to the consumption of that excess of good things which his host is unable to dispose of singlehanded, and he is also made to witness his host's facility in etiquette.

In the giving of costly entertainments other motives, of a more genial kind, are of course also present. The custom of festive gatherings probably originated in motives of conviviality and religion; these motives are also present in the later development, but they do not continue to be the sole motives. The latter-day leisure-class festivities and entertainments may continue in some slight degree to serve the religious need and in a higher degree the needs of recreation and conviviality, but they also serve an invidious purpose; and they serve it none the less effectually for having a colorable non-invidious ground in these more avowable motives. But the economic effect of these social amenities is not therefore lessened, either in the vicarious consumption of goods or in the exhibition of difficult and costly achievements in etiquette.

As wealth accumulates, the leisure class develops further in function and structure, and there arises a differentiation within the class. There is a more or less elaborate system of rank and grades. This differentiation is furthered by the inheritance of wealth and the consequent inheritance of gentility. With the inheritance of gentility goes the inheritance of obligatory leisure; and gentility of a sufficient potency to entail a life of leisure may be inherited without the complement of wealth required to maintain a dignified leisure. Gentle blood may be transmitted without goods enough to afford a reputably free consumption at one's ease. Hence results a class of impecunious gentlemen of leisure, incidentally referred to already. These half-caste gentlemen of leisure fall into a system of hierarchical gradations. Those who stand near the higher and the highest grades of the wealthy leisure class, in point of birth, or in point of wealth, or both, outrank the remoter-born and the pecuniarily weaker. These lower grades, especially the impecunious, or marginal, gentlemen of leisure, affiliate themselves by a system of dependence or fealty to the great ones; by so doing they gain an increment of repute, or of the means with which to lead a life of leisure, from their patron. They become his courtiers or retainers, servants; and being fed and countenanced by their patron they are indices of his rank and vicarious consumers of his superfluous wealth. Many of these affiliated gentlemen of leisure are at the same time lesser men of substance in their own right; so that some of them are scarcely at all, others only partially, to be rated as vicarious consumers. So many of them, however, as make up the retainers and hangers-on of the patron may be classed as vicarious consumers without qualification. Many of these again, and also many of the other aristocracy of less degree, have in turn attached to their persons a more or less comprehensive group of vicarious consumers in the persons of their wives and children, their servants, retainers, etc.

Throughout this graduated scheme of vicarious leisure and vicarious consumption the rule holds that these offices must be perfomed in some such manner, or under some such circumstance or insignia, as shall point plainly to the master to whom this leisure or consumption pertains, and to whom therefore the resulting increment of good repute of right inures. The consumption and leisure executed by these persons for their master or patron represents an investment on his part with a view to an increase of good fame. As regards feasts and largesses this is obvious enough, and the imputation of repute to the host or patron here takes place immediately, on the ground of common notoriety. Where leisure and consumption is performed vicariously by henchmen and retainers, imputation of the resulting repute to the patron is effected by their residing near his person so that it may be plain to all men from what source they draw. As the group whose good esteem is to be secured in this way grows larger, more patent means are required to indicate the imputation of merit for the leisure performed, and to this end uniforms, badges, and liveries come into vogue. The wearing of uniforms or liveries implies a considerable degree of dependence, and may even be said to be a mark of servitude, real or ostensible. The wearers of uniforms and liveries may be roughly divided into two classes—the free and the servile, or the noble and the ignoble. The services performed by them are likewise divisible into noble and ignoble. Of course the distinction is not observed with strict consistency in practice; the less debasing of the base services and the less honorific of the noble functions are not infrequently merged in the same person. But the general distinction is not on that account to be overlooked. What may add some perplexity is the fact that this fundamental distinction between noble and ignoble, which rests on the nature of the ostensible service performed, is traversed by a secondary distinction into honorific and humiliating, resting on the rank of the person for whom the service is performed or whose livery is worn. So, those offices which are by right the proper employment of the leisure class are noble; such as government, fighting, hunting, the care of arms and accoutrements, and the like— in short, those which may be classed as ostensibly predatory employments. On the other hand, those employments which properly fall to the industrious class are ignoble; such as handicraft or other productive labor, menial services and the like. But a base service performed for a person of very high degree may become a very honorific office; as for instance the office of a Maid of Honor or of a Lady in Waiting to the Queen, or the King's Master of the Horse or his Keeper of the Hounds. The two offices last named suggest a principle of some general bearing. Whenever, as in these cases, the menial service in question has to do directly with the primary leisure employments of fighting and hunting, it easily acquires a reflected honorific character. In this way great honor may come to attach to an employment which in its own nature belongs to the baser sort.

In the later development of peaceable industry, the usage of employing an idle corps of uniformed men-at-arms gradually lapses. Vicarious consumption by dependents bearing the insignia of their patron or master narrows down to a corps of liveried menials. In a heightened degree, therefore, the livery comes to be a badge of servitude, or rather of servility. Something of an honorific character always attached to the livery of the armed retainer, but this honorific character disappears when the livery becomes the exclusive badge of the menial. The livery becomes obnoxious to nearly all who are required to wear it. We are yet so little removed from a state of effective slavery as still to be fully sensitive to the sting of any imputation of servility. This antipathy asserts itself even in the case of the liveries or uniforms which some corporations prescribe as the distinctive dress of their employees. In this country the aversion even goes the length of discrediting—in a mild and uncertain way—those government employments, military and civil, which require the wearing of a livery or uniform.

With the disappearance of servitude, the number of vicarious consumers attached to any one gentleman tends, on the whole, to decrease. The like is of course true, and perhaps in a still higher degree, of the number of dependents who perform vicarious leisure for him. In a general way, though not wholly nor consistently, these two groups coincide. The dependent who was first delegated for these duties was the wife, or the chief wife; and, as would be expected, in the later development of the institution, when the number of persons by whom these duties are customarily performed gradually narrows, the wife remains the last. In the higher grades of society a large volume of both these kinds of service is required; and here the wife is of course still assisted in the work by a more or less numerous corps of menials. But as we descend the social scale, the point is presently reached where the duties of vicarious leisure and consumption devolve upon the wife alone. In the communities of the Western culture, this point is at present found among the lower middle class.

And here occurs a curious inversion. It is a fact of common observance that in this lower middle class there is no pretense of leisure on the part of the head of the household. Through force of circumstances it has fallen into disuse. But the middle-class wife still carries on the business of vicarious leisure, for the good name of the household and its master. In descending the social scale in any modern industrial community, the primary fact—the conspicuous leisure of the master of the household—disappears at a relatively high point. The head of the middle-class household has been reduced by economic circumstances to turn his hand to gaining a livelihood by occupations which often partake largely of the character of industry, as in the case of the ordinary business man of today. But the derivative fact— the vicarious leisure and consumption rendered by the wife, and the auxiliary vicarious performance of leisure by menials—remains in vogue as a conventionality which the demands of reputability will not suffer to be slighted. It is by no means an uncommon spectacle to find a man applying himself to work with the utmost assiduity, in order that his wife may in due form render for him that degree of vicarious leisure which the common sense of the time demands.

The leisure rendered by the wife in such cases is, of course, not a simple manifestation of idleness or indolence. It almost invariably occurs disguised under some form of work or household duties or social amenities, which prove on analysis to serve little or no ulterior end beyond showing that she does not occupy herself with anything that is gainful or that is of substantial use. As has already been noticed under the head of manners, the greater part of the customary round of domestic cares to which the middle-class housewife gives her time and effort is of this character. Not that the results of her attention to household matters, of a decorative and mundificatory character, are not pleasing to the sense of men trained in middle-class proprieties; but the taste to which these effects of household adornment and tidiness appeal is a taste which has been formed under the selective guidance of a canon of propriety that demands just these evidences of wasted effort. The effects are pleasing to us chiefly because we have been taught to find them pleasing. There goes into these domestic duties much solicitude for a proper combination of form and color, and for other ends that are to be classed as æsthetic in the proper sense of the term; and it is not denied that effects having some substantial æsthetic value are sometimes attained. Pretty much all that is here insisted on is that, as regards these amenities of life, the housewife's efforts are under the guidance of traditions that have been shaped by the law of conspicuously wasteful expenditure of time and substance. If beauty or comfort is achieved—and it is a more or less fortuitous circumstance if they are—they must be achieved by means and methods that commend themselves to the great economic law of wasted effort. The more reputable, "presentable" portion of middle-class household paraphernalia are, on the one hand, items of conspicuous consumption, and on the other hand, apparatus for putting in evidence the vicarious leisure rendered by the housewife.

The requirement of vicarious consumption at the hands of the wife continues in force even at a lower point in the pecuniary scale than the requirement of vicarious leisure. At a point below which little if any pretense of wasted effort, in ceremonial cleanness and the like, is observable, and where there is assuredly no conscious attempt at ostensible leisure, decency still requires the wife to consume some goods conspicuously for the reputability of the household and its head. So that, as the latter-day outcome of this evolution of an archaic institution, the wife, who was at the outset the drudge and chattel of the man, both in fact and in theory—the producer of goods for him to consume—has become the ceremonial consumer of goods which he produces. But she still quite unmistakably remains his chattel in theory; for the habitual rendering of vicarious leisure and consumption is the abiding mark of the unfree servant.

This vicarious consumption practiced by the household of the middle and lower classes can not be counted as a direct expression of the leisure-class scheme of life, since the household of this pecuniary grade does not belong within the leisure class. It is rather that the leisure-class scheme of life here comes to an expression at the second remove. The leisure class stands at the head of the social structure in point of reputability; and its manner of life and its standards of worth therefore afford the norm of reputability for the community. The observance of these standards, in some degree of approximation, becomes incumbent upon all classes lower in the scale. In modern civilized communities the lines of demarcation between social classes have grown vague and transient, and wherever this happens the norm of reputability imposed by the upper class extends its coercive influence with but slight hindrance down through the social structure to the lowest strata. The result is that the members of each stratum accept as their ideal of decency the scheme of life in vogue in the next higher stratum, and bend their energies to live up to that ideal. On pain of forfeiting their good name and their self-respect in case of failure, they must conform to the accepted code, at least in appearance.

The basis on which good repute in any highly organized industrial community ultimately rests is pecuniary strength; and the means of showing pecuniary strength, and so gaining or retaining a good name, are leisure and a conspicuous consumption of goods. Accordingly, both of these methods are in vogue as far down the scale as it remains possible; and in the lower strata in which the two methods are employed, both offices are in great part delegated to the wife and children of the household. Lower still, where any degree of leisure, even ostensible, has become impracticable for the wife, the conspicuous consumption of goods remains and is carried on by the wife and children. The man of the household also can do something in this direction, and indeed, he commonly does; but with a still lower descent into the levels of indigence—along the margin of the slums—the man, and presently also the children, virtually cease to consume valuable goods for appearances, and the woman remains virtually the sole exponent of the household's pecuniary decency. No class of society, not even the most abjectly poor, forgoes all customary conspicuous consumption. The last items of this category of consumption are not given up except under stress of the direst necessity. Very much of squalor and discomfort will be endured before the last trinket or the last pretense of pecuniary decency is put away. There is no class and no country that has yielded so abjectly before the pressure of physical want as to deny themselves all gratification of this higher or spiritual need.

Aptitude, Class and Leadership * (*Schumpeter*)

Shifts of family position within a class are seen to take place everywhere, without exception. They cannot be explained by the operation of chance, nor by automatic mechanisms relating to outward position, but only as the consequences of the different degree to which families are qualified to solve the problems with which their social environment confronts them.

Class barriers are always, without exception, surmountable and are, in fact, surmounted, by virtue of the same qualifications and modes of behavior that bring about shifts of family position within the class.

The process by which the individual family crosses class barriers is the same process by which the family content of classes is formed in the first instance, and this family content is determined in no other way.

Classes themselves rise and fall according to the nature and success with which they—meaning here, their members—fulfill their characteristic function, and according to the rise and fall in the social significance of this function, or of those functions which the class members are willing and able to accept instead—the relative social significance of a function always being determined by the degree of social leadership which its fulfillment implies or creates.

These circumstances explain the evolution of individual families and

* Reprinted from *Imperialism and Social Classes* by Joseph A. Schumpeter, pp. 159–168, Noonday Press, 1951, with permission of Imrie de Vegh, as Trustee u/w Elizabeth Boody Schumpeter. Translated from the original publication, *Die Sozialen Klassen im Ethnisch Homogenen Milieu* which appeared in the Archiv für Sozialwissenschaft und Sozial-politik in 1927 (Vol. 57, pp. 1–67). This text is taken from a reprint of the original English translation. Coyright 1951 by the trustees under the will of Elizabeth Boody Schumpeter.

the evolution of classes as such. They also explain why social classes exist
at all.

We draw the following conclusions from these statements:

The ultimate foundation on which the class phenomenon rests consists
of individual differences in aptitude. What is meant is not differences in an
absolute sense, but differences in aptitude with respect to those functions
which the environment makes "socially necessary"—in our sense—at any
given time; and with respect to leadership, along lines that are in keeping
with those functions. The differences, moreover, do not relate to the physical
individual, but to the clan or family.

Class structure is the ranking of such individual families by their
social value in accordance, ultimately, with their differing aptitudes. Actually this is more a matter of social value, once achieved, becoming firmly
established. This process of entrenchment and its perpetuation constitutes a
special problem that must be specifically explained—at bottom this is the
immediate and specific "class problem." Yet even this entrenched position,
which endures in group terms, offering the picture of a class made secure
above and beyond the individual, ultimately rests on individual differences
in aptitude. Entrenched positions, which constitute the class stratification of
society, are attained or created by behavior which in turn is conditioned
by differential aptitudes.[1]

From other points of view—some of them still in the field of sociology,
others beyond it and even beyond the field of science altogether—the essence
of social classes may appear in a different light. They may seem organs of
society, legal or cultural entities, conspiracies against the rest of the nation.
From the explanatory viewpoint they are merely what we have described
them to be. And all that is left for us to do is to particularize, illustrate, and
supplement our own result in certain points.

First, as to aptitude, differences in aptitude, family aptitude: Insofar as
"aptitude" is something that shows itself immediately in the physical individual—much like the color of hair or eyes—our line of reasoning, as already
indicated, comes back to the physical individual. Insofar as, first, relevant
"aptitudes" are not merely physical and, second, "aptitude" can be considered only the basis for "behavior," our argument also comes back to the
individual psyche. In our presentation we have endeavored to emphasize
that this implies neither the errors of individualism nor a process of "psycho-
logization" that loses itself in surface phenomena. We cannot help those
who are unable to see that the individual is a *social* fact, the psychological
an *objective* fact, who cannot give up toying with the empty contrasts of
the individual *vs.* the social, the subjective *vs.* the objective. But it is more

important to guard against tautological confusion between "aptitude" and "success" in which only the latter is taken to be susceptible to empirical observation, while the former becomes a mere word like the *vis soporifica* of opium. We contend that both can be empirically investigated, independently of each other. In the Goths under Teja, we recognize "aptitude" for the function of a military master class, even though history shows that they were not blessed with "successs" when they encountered Narses.

To establish the presence of such an "aptitude" does not confer any laurels, nor does it testify to moral worth. From many points of view—religious, esthetic, moral—it may have to be evaluated in a negative sense. It may, in particular, be antisocial—and this is not necessarily a value judgment, but may be a judgment based on facts. Success for the individual, the family, the class does not necessarily mean success for other segments of the population or for the nation as a whole; indeed, it may mean the very opposite. The extent to which this is true is, of course, of considerable importance, not only for our evaluation of the class phenomenon and of certain historical classes, but also for our scientific knowledge of social cause and effect. Even from the examples cited in this study it is evident that in some cases success in establishing class position does represent "social achievement"—in other words, that it enhances the position of others, as well as of those responsible for the success. In other cases this is not true, while in still others the ultimate judgment must depend on a deeper analysis, based on theoretical economics, of the consequences for which the behavior in question is responsible. Finally, a distinction must always be made *between the social significance of a given mode of behavior and the social significance of the qualities that make such behavior possible.* It is not enough merely to have a moral defect in order to become a bandit or a tyrant. As a rule, the person in question must also "have what it takes." In other words, the process of social rise or decline can be described in terms of "natural selection" only in a very restricted sense. But important as these matters are, enlightening as studies concerning them may be, this aspect of the case does not concern us here.

"Aptitude" may be "natural" or acquired. In the latter case it may be acquired individually or by family background. The relevance of these distinctions to our problem is obvious. The greater the role played by natural and family-acquired aptitude, the firmer will class position be. Its firmness will also be inversely proportional to the degree to which an acquired aptitude—of itself or by its effect on the mode and goals of life—prevents the acquisition of other aptitudes, and directly proportional to the degree of significance which outward achievements flowing from an already elevated position carry with respect to the acquisition of new aptitudes. These matters merely have to be mentioned for it to be seen that they hold a good part of class history. But for the first step which our investigation takes they are of no particular importance. Even acquired aptitude is a datum at any given time.

Aptitude determines a quality or a system of qualities only with respect to certain definite functions. The relationship is similar to that between biological adaptation and survival in a given physical environment. There are, for example, specific predispositions—those having to do with music and mathematics have been most exhaustively investigated—which have virtually no relationship to other natural endowments. Yet there are other talents that apply to a multiplicity of functions—the capacity for intellectual analysis, for example. Will power in its various manifestations is an important element in this respect, and there is, of course, the well-known phenomenon of all-around capacity which is equally effective in the face of most of the practical demands of life. Spearman's studies of this quality have given rise to the theory of a "central factor," but actually this is no more than a word for something already empirically confirmed. From the viewpoint of class history and class theory, we are concerned, first, with the fact that class functions and their relative social necessity change only slowly. Secondly, we find that the socially necessary functions that succeed one another in historical time are related in important respects—administrative skill, resoluteness, and the ability to command are vital in any leading position. Thirdly, the functions relevant to our study all have to do with the same factor, namely, social leadership. Over and above this, however, the two cited facts are of the greatest importance to an understanding of class evolution and to any "interpretive" history of class structure. The fact of the special aptitude—especially the acquired kind—emerges with particular clarity when we compare, for example, the type of the warlord of the early Middle Ages with that of the modern stock-exchange speculator. It is a fact that serves to explain why the same class does not always retain leadership— something that is by no means explained by the mere circumstance that the relative importance of functions changes. For the function alone is not the essence of the class. And the facts brought out in the central-factor theory do sometimes explain, in whole or in part, why a class often maintains its social position so well, despite a decline in the function peculiar to it, over a long period of time.

In an ethnically homogeneous environment, special and general aptitudes, physical and mental, those of will and of intellect, are probably distributed according to the normal curve. This has been carefully demonstrated with physical characteristics that are most readily susceptible to measurement, notably body height and weight. Beyond this, we have extensive experimental material only for school children. As for the capacity of adults to measure up to the tasks of daily life, we have only our general impression to go by.[2] Further investigations would be very important in advancing class research, but our present purpose is served well enough by the fact, scarcely disputed, that individual differences in aptitude do exist and that individual aptitudes do not fall into sharply marked categories, separated by empty space, but shade by imperceptible nuances from high to low. The situation is different only when there are sharp ethnical differences, such as between Mongols and Slavs, whites or Arabs and Negroes.

If it were true that individual aptitudes bear no relationship to the aptitudes of ancestors and progeny—if none were inherited and all individuals were simply sports—then the elements of position and acquired aptitude would still be capable of forming relatively stable groups, though the course of history would have been different. If aptitudes were never inherited and always distributed according to the laws of chance, the position of classes and of families within them would manifestly be far less stable than it actually is. There can scarcely be any doubt of the inheritance of physical characteristics. As for mental characteristics, we have as yet only data in the field of defects, though these are in a state of fruitful evolution. For obvious reasons, it is difficult and dangerous to go beyond them, in the field of statistics as well as of genealogy.[3] Again, therefore, we emphasize that while it may be hopeless to pass considered judgment on the cultural significance of a class—and, incidentally, on most other basic questions of the social order, past or future—until this point has been settled, the basic idea of the class theory here presented is quite independent of it.

As to the question of leadership, if we are to be properly understood, all the romance and gibberish surrounding this term must be discarded. We are not concerned with the individual leadership of the creative mind or of the genius. We do not care whether this phenomenon is of big or small importance in social science or whether it is irrelevant; whether it plays a causal role, direct or indirect; whether such individuals function autonomously or by their own laws. In short, the entire problem of the "great man" has no bearing on our subject. Nor do we by any means insist that group leadership, which alone concerns us here, necessarily "leads" in the direction where it desires to go of its own free will, or that it creates the realm of possibility into which it leads—a realm realized only under its leadership. We are content to say that social leadership means to decide, to command, to prevail, to advance. As such it is a special function, always clearly discernible in the actions of the individual and within the social whole. It emerges only with respect to ever new individual and social situations and would never exist if individual and national life always ran its course in the same way and by the same routine. Yet by its very nature it almost never occurs in the "pure" state. It is virtually always linked to certain other functions and offices, by virtue of which it is exercised and from which it receives its peculiar coloration and direction. But whatever the trend and the form may be, leadership always remains leadership. Ordinarily individuals differ in their capacity for it, much as they differ in their ability to sing, though it must be added that both the attainment and the practice of leadership are aided by a tradition of leadership. And, as is the case with other aptitudes, the aptitude for leadership is not necessarily strongly marked in a few individuals and nonexistent in the rest. Most individuals possess it to a modest degree, sufficient for the simplest tasks of everyday life, while one minority has it to a stronger, another to a lesser degree. The absolute extent of aptitude for leadership in a given nation (or the qualities on which it is based) largely determines the history of that nation; and within it individual families are ranked by social value in the order in which they possess this aptitude and these qualities. It is because this aptitude is distributed continuously throughout a nation, without gaps and discontinuities, that class barriers are characteristically in a state of flux. Classes particularly deficient or altogether lacking in it secure it through talented individuals who become renegades or declassed. If such classes are already on the rise, they may be led by those of their members who would otherwise ascend to higher classes but instead now devote themselves to the task of leadership within the class. Such ranking by degree of aptitude for leadership is, immediately, one of physical individuals and can owe any supra-individual constancy only to the fact of the inheritance of characteristics. It leads to objectively defined family position and, by extension and entrenchment, to class position of those families that, by our criterion, are approximately coordinate.

As for the process of entrenchment, the kind of success that is the basis for the individual's rise normally tends to repeat itself, simply because as a rule the individual manages to carry out the same kind of task again and again and because success generally paves the way for further success. Even so, success, once achieved, exerts a continuing effect, without further accomplishment, for two reasons: First of all, the prestige it engenders assumes a life of its own. It does not necessarily disappear when its basis disappears— nor, for that matter, does its basis readily disappear. *This is the very heart and soul of the independent organic existence of "class."* In the second place, in the vast majority of cases success brings in its wake important functional positions and other powers over material resources. The position of the physical individual becomes entrenched, and with it that of the family. This opens up further opportunities to the family, often to an even greater degree than to the successful individual himself, though these positive factors are to some extent offset by the deadening effect on the original impetus of exalted position and security, by the diversion and complication of interests, and perhaps also by the sheer exhaustion of energies which everyday experience shows to be not uncommon. *Coordinate families then merge into a social class, welded together by a bond, the substance and effect of which we now understand. This relationship assumes a life of its own and is then able to grant protection and confer prestige.* In addition to the natural endowment of the class members, there are other factors that determine the course and the firmness of class structure and class position—factors that have little or no connection with aptitude. Among those that have no such connection is the outward course of history. There are times of quietude, for example, their tranquillity stemming from causes that have nothing to do with the qualities of the ruling classes, times during which class position is long maintained without effort, times during which only such events occur as the ruling classes are well able to master; and when it is otherwise, events may be entirely beyond control. Another such factor is the character of the economic base of a class. From the viewpoint of the German nobility, for example, it was pure chance that the opportunity existed for large-scale agricultural production which proved to be a very durable and relatively easily managed source of capitalist income. Thirdly, it may likewise be mostly chance, for better or for worse, whether a suitable new function can be found at the time the old one enters into a decline. But this already passes into the other group of factors. It does have some slight connection with the capacities of the families in the class—whether, for example, the class propagates itself or withers by inbreeding. The connection with class aptitude is somewhat closer —whether or not the attainable function is a suitable basis for general leadership. The warlord was automatically the leader of his people in virtually every respect. The modern industrialist is anything but such a leader. And this explains a great deal about the stability of the former's position and the instability of the latter's. Even closer is the connection between class efficiency and adaptability to altered circumstances. There is the aristocrat, for example, who hurls himself into an election campaign as his ancestors rode into battle; and there is the aristocrat who says to himself: "I can't very well ask my valet to vote for me." Here, in fact, is the measure of two radically different types of European aristocrat. The class situation may so specialize members of the class that adaptation to new situations becomes all but impossible. From the viewpoint of this and similar factors, we can see in proper perspective why members of the ruling classes in present-day Europe so often seem to make a bad joke of our theory that class position and capacity go together. Finally, there is but a slight connection between the endowment of a class and the facility with which it grasps and handles growing power. Highly competent classes are often quite blind to the vital importance of this factor, for themselves as well as for the destiny of their people. Yet that importance is unmistakable. It is the ease with which English industrial families in the nineteenth century managed to rise into "society," by way of financial success and politics,[4] that gave England its unique leadership class. This, after all, was true even of rising intellectual talent—and the life stories of two "physical individuals," Disraeli and Lassalle, give symbolic expression to a segment of two national destinies.

REFERENCES

1. It is only this process of entrenchment that creates a special cultural background, a greater or lesser degree of promptness in concerted action, one aspect of which is expressed in the concept of the class struggle. We refrain here from passing any judgment on the actual significance of this factor.
2. The impression is not entirely a general one, for we do have concrete instances to go by, notably studies of relatively homogeneous bodies of civil servants.
3. This becomes clear in its full significance when we compare Goddard's study of the Kallikak family, for example, with Galton's *Hereditary Genius*. But both material and methods are steadily improving. Even today, we can agree that K. Pearson's pithy statement, "ability runs in stocks," is far truer than its opposite, especially since everyday experience confirms it. But should not then class position, once established, endure *ad infinitum* in every case? Before we embarked on our study, this might have been a reasonable question. But I have no answer for those who put it at this point.
4. A noteworthy feature of this system is the elaborate "ordeal" which the rising family as a rule had to endure.

Social Stratification * (*Speier*)

Any discussion of social stratification has to cope with the difficulty that the term "social class" is not definitely fixed and uniformly understood in sociological literature. How can we rid it of ambiguities?

(1) The term should not be used as a synonym for related concepts which have assumed a univocal meaning. Income classes, occupational strata, races, interest groups or other clearly definable groupings should not be called social classes. It is true that for merely technical reasons these groupings may serve as a convenient point of departure for an analysis of

* Condensed from *American Sociological Review*, April, 1936. Reprinted from *Social Order and the Risks of War* by Hans Speier, pp. 19–26, with permission of the publisher, George W. Stewart, Publisher, Inc., New York.

particular aspects of social stratification; the analyst who tries to measure the size of social classes or the degree of mobility among their members must use these concepts, since they are offered to him by census reports and similar statistics. He should be aware, however, that they are only auxiliary terms, and that their identification with social classes is inadvisable and confusing.

(2) The theory of social stratification should not refer to a specific society, but should be general enough to apply to various social structures. We know of societies in which high social rank is conferred by age, and others where it is conferred by physical strength. There are systems in which the social classes tend to coincide with occupational groups, others where they conform rather with the income pyramid, cutting across all occupations. No theory which proceeds from a particular objective criterion or set of criteria can do more than describe social stratification in a particular system; it must fail to explain the phenomenon of social class as such.

The Marxian concept of social class may stand as an illustration of this kind of theory. According to the Marxian analysis, social class depends on similarity of economic interest. The individual's relation to the means of production determines his decisive economic interests, and these are held to influence political behavior, create struggle and result in a historic trend toward freedom, provided that the unpropertied class pursues its interest. If, for the sake of argument, we disregard the fact that actually the individual identifies himself with various interest groups, there still remains the objection that this view is invalid for societies which are not predominantly capitalistic in character. Suggestions that the primary determination of behavior by economic interests is a historically limited phenomenon, not a general characteristic of man's social nature, may be found even in the writings of Engels and Marx. But neither they nor their disciples, with the single exception of Georg Lukacs,[1] have taken these considerations as a challenge to test the applicability of the theory to other than capitalist societies.

(3) A theory of social stratification should define its objective, in order that it may be distinguished from a general theory of the influence of society on human behavior. All theories of stratification hold that similarity of behavior and of social relationship is a criterion of social class, much as opinions differ as to the forces which make for this similarity. Yet almost all of these analyses fail to dissociate the general theory of behavior from the special theory of social stratification. The frame of reference which consists in behavior in general is too wide for a definition of class. *The specific characteristic of the relation between social classes is hierarchy*. The idea of hierarchy is implicit in everyday language in such phrases as upper and

lower classes, high social rank, social climbing, and the like.[2] Similarity of behavior should be regarded as relevant in describing class affiliation, only in so far as it pertains to social superiority or inferiority within the given social structure. Social equality, in other words, exists only within the class. This does not, of course, exclude the possibility of distinguishing subclasses on the basis of refined criteria of class.

The superiority of one class implies its recognition by an inferior class; the inferiority of another class implies the actual acceptance of this status by its members. Thus the relationship between classes is never merely imposed; it must be understood in terms of a reciprocal evaluation.[3] This evaluation can be explicit; more important, however, is its implicit expression in the existing order of ranks. The position on the social scale of any individual is but the objective manifestation of social evaluations which are implied in the way the individual and his external qualities are typically treated by men of different positions, and in the way that men of different positions are typically treated by him.[4] It is only this typical behavior that gives quasi-objectivity to such observable facts as the positive and negative privileges of various classes, the customary limitations of relationship and career, class-attitudes, even the exercise of power and the acquiescence to it. This objectivity allows us to study any class-system without getting immediately involved in the problem of evaluation. To neglect the basic phenomenon of evaluation, however, would prevent us from understanding the significance of the facts under analysis. The significance of these facts is revealed only through interpretation of implicit values. If we disregard them, we ascribe to social reality qualities of the physical world which it does not possess. Social stratification is a trait of non-material rather than of material culture.

In general the theories of social class do not center around the problem of recognition of values. Either they take for granted that a particular class is high or low on the social scale, thus confining themselves to description; or they emphasize a particular objective basis upon which the hierarchy rests, which again is taken as a matter of fact. None of the objective bases used by this second group of theories implies a solution of the problem of hierarchy: whether occupation or interest, education or race be taken as the basis of class formation, such objective criteria are incapable of suggesting the social value of particular occupations, special interest groups, specific kinds of education or a particular race. They can do no more than suggest that certain differences exist in society, with respect to any particular criterion. The criterion of wealth or income is especially deceptive; since differences in wealth or income are capable of quantitative measurement, they suggest a corresponding hierarchy of qualitatively different classes. We know of many social structures, which we have no right to regard as exceptions, where wealth does not confer high social status, and of others in which its influence is at least outweighed by other factors. The possibility of quantitative gradation only blurs the problem and cannot solve it.

Thus, there are two difficulties in any attempt to find an objective basis for social differentiation. First, there is no empirical evidence that any such basis can be true of all societies, since social history teaches us that occupational or economic differences, or whatever set of factors we find as the basis of hierarchy in one social structure, is insignificant or irrelevant in another. Second, such an objective basis can only indicate differences; it cannot furnish any principle to explain the alignment of these differences in hierarchies.

Two solutions of the problem stand out. First, it may be argued that social status results from functional authority. Hierarchical differences arise whenever there is a division of functions into managerial and executive work, since such a division necessitates disciplined cooperation and requires gradations of authority. Thus a similar degree of functional authority seems a possible criterion of class similarity.

Certainly there is always some interconnection between functional authority and social status. But the nature of this connection is not immutable. It is dependent on social and technological change and is the object of social conflict and struggle. It is true that the surgeon will always be functionally superior to the nurse, the foreman to the workers, the bank president to his clerks. But it does not follow that they will always be socially superior. There are officers and privates in all organized armies, no matter whether the army is military or civil, whether the social order is capitalistic, communistic, or otherwise. In times of rapid social transformation the difference between functional authority and social status becomes conspicuous. Bolshevist Russia, attempting to build up an industrial economy, has as much need of trained specialists and skilled workers as any other society pursuing this purpose, regardless of its particular structure. The substitution of party membership for capitalist control as a basis for social recognition does not eliminate the functional authority. It does, however, affect the social distance between the specialists and the bulk of the workers, since it means that the specialists are not given superior social status which is granted to them in varying degrees in capitalist societies. With enough imagination one may even conceive of a system of social recognition that is planned by the state and adjusted to the changing objectives of society. C. C. North [5] alludes to this possibility of shifting social appreciation from one group to another in a democratic society. Whether this be feasible or not, it would not necessarily affect functional differences of any kind.

In capitalist societies, the degrees of functional authority are tied up with social distinctions as long as those who are functionally superior derive their authority from the social power and prestige of the class that owns the means of production. But the trend of modern management in plants and offices is toward the depersonalization of control. This is accomplished partly by mechanical devices like conveyors, partly by impersonal departmental control, which may be mutual. There are even possibilities of controlling the superior by functionally inferior workers; the typist, who is paid not according to time but according to the number of letters written in a time-unit tends to increase the efficiency of the correspondent whose function it is to dictate the letters. Thus the hierarchical relation between the two employees is reversed in this particular respect. Because of this depersonalization of control and its dissociation from ownership, the "capitalist" of the Marxian theory no longer has any personal reality in modern enterprise. He appears in the form of methods of management and of numerous proxies who in the lower grades may be poor, dependent, and exceedingly "anti-capitalistic"—functionaries; their chance of seeing a capitalist is in a moving picture which presents the present in terms of the past.

This functional division is most highly developed in large, non-agricultural enterprises in big cities. The trend toward depersonalization of control neutralizes personal dominance, typical of earlier stages of capitalist development, and permits of a less personal discussion of deficiencies in the economic set-up. Thus the relation between functional authority and social status becomes looser as functional authority loses its personal quality.

The second theory that attempts to explain social stratification, without resort to an objective basis, uses as a criterion social needs or wants. According to this analysis the class which ranks highest satisfies the most important wants of society, while the lower reaches of the social hierarchy are occupied by those who are of no social use. The argument has been frequently used both in scientific literature and in popular writings. Adam Ferguson in England, Holbach in France, and Garve in Germany alluded to it when they suggested that the emphasis placed on certain virtues corresponds to the predominant wants of society: in other words, that a system primarily engaged in civil pursuits would appreciate honesty and thrift, while one trading little, but regularly threatened by war, would award its honors to martial prowess. According to Gumplowicz, the general law of class formation is that every general need, be it religious, military, commercial, or otherwise, brings about classes that satisfy it. Unfortunately, however, the argument does not carry much weight as far as the problem of hierarchy is concerned, for it gives no clue as to the relative importance of the wants to be satisfied. It requires an arbitrary evaluation to declare that the slaves in antiquity were less important than the free citizens, many of whom bore the character of rentiers, or that the clergy of the Middle Ages and the intelligentsia of ancient China were more useful than the peasantry, which occupied a far lower social status.

The argument is quite different, however, if it takes the formulation that a class is based on its members' contribution to *what is considered to be useful*. Thus, class is considered not in terms of its social usefulness as such, but in terms of its contribution according to a scale of values peculiar to a specific social structure. With this formulation it can be understood that certain social wants, say religious wants, are accorded less importance than others, say economic wants, and their satisfaction treated as less useful. In this form the argument has been one of the most powerful social ideas of modern times, helping to disintegrate feudal relationships and to buttress the claims for social recognition of the modern middle classes. The demand that rank should correspond to usefulness meant a revaluation of the existing social order, which was regarded as unjust by the middle classes. Jean Bodin seems to have been the first philosopher who justified the social recognition of commercial activities in these terms; not much later, in 1623, Emeric Crucé elaborated the argument in his *Nouveau Cynée*. Neither of them referred to usefulness in general, but to *economic* usefulness, thus foreshadowing the polemic possibilities of the concept which was so effective when the middle classes were eager to demonstrate the uselessness of groups primarily engaged in military, political, or religious activities.

In the history of Western society the argument from economic usefulness has been most effectively tied up with the appreciation of work. It is Christian and urban in origin and is still powerful in contemporary society.

As Henri Pirenne has lucidly demonstrated, it was in the urban communities of the Middle Ages, beginning in the 11th century, that work was liberated from both the disgrace and the compulsion to which it was subject in feudal economy. The craftsman in the town was free from the serfdom which pressed upon labor in ancient and feudal economic relations. In antiquity and in feudal society, the principles of social evaluation were primarily political and military, not primarily economic in character.[6] But with the revival of trade and urban life work rather than power began to be socially honored, and correspondingly leisure rather than labor began to be socially despised. The institutionalization of these values in the first stages of urban economy meant a complete reversal of the feudal stratification in which those who worked were held inferior to those who did not. Moreover, within the towns the class conflict which has been typical of capitalism in all its stages began to manifest itself. There was increasing antagonism between the poorer classes and the new plutocracy of the merchants of wool and cloth; and in this struggle, which reached its climax in the 14th century, the poorer classes formulated their rebellion in terms of the very forces which had made urban economy and its social system possible. The rich and powerful families were now reproached for not performing a useful function in the community. Even the term "leisure class" was a common slogan among the rebellious poor. The egalitarian evaluations have always been characteristic of the lower classes, even though not all lower classes have been egalitarian; and down to twentieth century communism this argument of the value and utility of work as against the unproductivity of the powerful has been in the arsenal of social radicalism.

The implications of the argument from usefulness need not be further elaborated. What has been said may illustrate how far even the fundamental concepts for an analysis of social stratification are influenced by ultra-scientific evaluations, which are the harder to escape in the degree to which they are an intrinsic part of the personal cultural equation of the analyst. The search for a single causative force for the evaluations which manifest themselves in social stratifications must be futile; its success would mean "the revelation of the laws of history." The sociologist, in analyzing social stratification, should try to elucidate the operation and interactions of the various forces that make for the integration and disintegration of the class system. His primary task in interpreting a particular social stratification is to define its implicit principles of evaluation. In doing this, it is possible to distinguish primary, secondary, and subordinate principles of evaluation and their relative significance in the formation of classes and subclasses. In American society, for example, the principles of wealth and race are outstanding, while nationality, denomination, and family tradition are among the subordinate principles; their significance varies in the various classes. In Germany nationality plays a minor role and racial discrimination is a new phenomenon, while noble birth, state service, and education are more important than in this country; among whole classes they may well outweigh economic handicaps. In this pluralism of evaluations are reflected both the natural conditions and the history of a society.

The class at the top of the social hierarchy sets standards for the whole system. The very fact of superiority implies its recognition as such, and thus the superior classes represent images [7] to be imitated by the inferior classes. The process of imitation operates at a different speed in different social structures and in different domains of life. The Lynds have observed that the working classes in Middletown today employ the habits of the business class of roughly a generation ago. Principles of social evaluation which were once of primary significance may continue as of secondary or tertiary importance, and thus qualify the new primary principle. An upper class which owes its rank primarily to the evaluation of capitalistic wealth may be hierarchized according to a secondary principle dominant in the preceding social structure, which gives preference to immobile wealth. Thus capitalists who owe their wealth to mining may enjoy higher social esteem than equally wealthy capitalists in the textile industry. If yesterday's images happened to be military officers and Junkers, as in Germany, both the business class and the dependent classes of today will be under the spell of this heritage. They will be equally under its spell whether their attitude be one of submissiveness or of resentment.

In American society, on the other hand, the lack of an influential aristocratic tradition is an important factor in stratification; it is one reason for the middle-class character of skilled labor and also for the conspicuous unwillingness of the American middle classes to believe in social fate. Their social image has too long been represented by the successful self-made man.

In a word, the social stratification of the present can never be fully explained without reference to the past.

It may be objected that a lower class may refuse to participate in the evaluations which are implied in a class system, that it may reject standards and repudiate social images offered from above, developing standards of its own. In such a case we have the phenomenon of social *revaluation*,[8] typical of dynamic social structures. The revaluation may be the potential nucleus of a new stratification. It should be noted, however, that the revaluation lacks institutional sanction, and that even the class which most violently disapproves of the valuations implied in a system in which it is inferior does implicitly consent to the system in many inescapable conformities. Thus "reality" may assume an insidious power to discredit the loftiest revaluation.

REFERENCES

1. Georg Lukacs, *Geschichte und Klassenbewusstsein*, Berlin, 1923, pp. 229–260.
2. Pitirim Sorokin, *Social Mobility*, New York, 1927, p. 3.
3. A necessary qualification of this statement is given on p. 26.
4. T. H. Marshall, "Social Class," *Sociological Review*, 1934, p. 60.
5. Cecil C. North, *Social Differentiation*, Chapel Hill, 1926, p. 325.
6. This has been emphasized by Max Weber.
7. For the concept of "social image," see chapter 4.
8. This term is used, though in a slightly different sense, by Thomas and Znaniecki, *The Polish Peasant*, vol. 1, pp. 128 ff.

The Working Class and the Business Class *
(*Lynd and Lynd*)

At first glance it is difficult to see any semblance of pattern in the workaday life of a community exhibiting a crazy-quilt array of nearly four hundred ways of getting its living—such diverse things as being abstractors, accountants, auditors, bank cashiers, bank tellers, bookkeepers, cashiers, checkers, core makers, crane operators, craters, crushers, cupola tenders, dye-workers, efficiency engineers, electricians, electrical engineers, embalmers, entomologists, estimating engineers, illuminating engineers, linotypists, mechanical engineers, metallurgists, meteorologists, riggers, riveters, rivet makers, and so on indefinitely. On closer scrutiny, however, this welter may be resolved into two kinds of activities. The people who engage in them will be referred to throughout the report as the Working Class and the Business Class.[1] Members of the first group, by and large, address their activities in getting their living primarily to *things,* utilizing material tools in the making of things and the performance of services, while the members of the second group address their activities predominantly to *people* in the selling or promotion of things, services, and ideas. This second group supplies to Middletown the multitude of non-material institutional activities such as "credit," "legal contract," "education," "sale for a price," "management," and "city government" by which Middletown people negotiate with each other in converting the narrowly specialized product of their workaday lives into "a comfortable evening at home," "a Sunday afternoon out in the car," "fire protection," "a new go-cart for the baby," and all the other things that constitute living in Middletown. If the Federal Census distribution of those gainfully employed in Middletown in 1920 is reclassified according to this grouping we find that there are two and one-half times as many in the working class as in the business class—seventy-one in each 100 as against twenty-nine.[2]

No such classification is entirely satisfactory. The aerial photographer inevitably sacrifices minor contours as he ascends high enough to view a total terrain. Within these two major groups there is an infinite number of gradations—all the way from the roughest day laborer to the foreman, the foundry molder, and the linotype operator in the one group, and from the retail clerk and cashier to the factory owner and professional man in the

* Reprinted from *Middletown,* by Robert Lynd and Helen Merrill Lynd, pp. 22–24, copyright, 1928, by Harcourt, Brace and Company, Inc. Published in Great Britain by Constable and Company Ltd. Reprinted by permission of the publishers.

other. There is naturally, too, a twilight belt in which some members of the two groups overlap or merge.

Were a minute structural diagram the aim of this study, it would be necessary to decipher in much greater detail the multitude of overlapping groupings observable in Middletown. Since what is sought, however, is an understanding of the major functional characteristics of this changing culture, it is important that significant outlines be not lost in detail, and the groups in the city which exhibit the dominant characteristics most clearly must, therefore, form the foci of the report. While an effort will be made to make clear at certain points variant behavior within these two groups, it is after all this division into working class and business class that constitutes the outstanding cleavage in Middletown. The mere fact of being born upon one or the other side of the watershed roughly formed by these two groups is the most significant single cultural factor tending to influence what one does all day long throughout one's life; whom one marries; when one gets up in the morning; whether one belongs to the Holy Roller or Presbyterian church; or drives a Ford or a Buick; whether or not one's daughter makes the desirable high school Violet Club; or one's wife meets with the Sew We Do Club or with the Art Students' League; whether one belongs to the Odd Fellows or to the Masonic Shrine; whether one sits about evenings with one's necktie off; and so on indefinitely throughout the daily comings and goings of a Middletown man, woman, or child.

Wherever throughout the report either Middletown or any group within the city is referred to as a unit, such a mode of expression must be regarded as simply a shorthand symbol. Any discussions of characteristics of groups are of necessity approximations only and the fact that the behavior of individuals is the basis of social behavior must never be lost sight of.

REFERENCES

1. Other terms which might be utilized to differentiate these two groups by their vocational activities are: people who address their activities to things and people who address their activities to persons; those who work with their hands and those who work with their tongues; those who make things and those who sell or promote things and ideas; those who use material tools and those who use various non-material institutional devices.
2. Four of the twenty-nine in each 100 grouped with the business class belong to a group of users of highly-skilled techniques—architects, surgeons, chemists, and so on—who, though addressing their activities in getting a living more to things than to people, are not here grouped with the working class because all their other activities would place them with the business class. It should be borne in mind throughout that the term business class, as here used, includes these and other professional workers. Since it is the business interests of the city that dominate and give their tone, in the main, to the lawyer, chemist, architect, engineer, teacher, and even to some extent preacher and doctor, such a grouping by and large accurately represents the facts.

Careful consideration was given to the applicability for the purposes of this study of the conventional tripartite division into Lower Class, Middle Class, and Upper Class. This was rejected, however, for the following reasons: (1) Since the dominance of the local getting-a-living activities impresses upon the group a pattern of social stratification based primarily upon vocational activity, it seemed advisable to utilize terms that hold this vocational cleavage to the fore. (2) In so far as the traditional threefold classification might be applied to Middletown today, the city would have to be regarded as having only a lower and a middle class; eight or nine households might conceivably be considered as an upper class, but these families are not a group apart but are merged in the life of the mass of businessfolk. R. H. Gretton, while pointing out the difficulty of separating out any group in present-day industrial society as "Middle Class," defines it as precisely that group here called the business class: "The Middle Class is that portion of the community to which money is the primary condition and the primary instrument of life. . . . It . . . includes merchant and capitalist manufacturer . . . [and the] professional class." *The English Middle Class* (London; Bell, 1917), pp. 1–13.

Some Principles of Stratification *
(*Davis and Moore*)

In a previous paper some concepts for handling the phenomena of social inequality were presented.[1] In the present paper a further step in stratification theory is undertaken—an attempt to show the relationship between stratification and the rest of the social order.[2] Starting from the proposition that no society is "classless," or unstratified, an effort is made to explain, in functional terms, the universal necessity which calls forth stratification in any social system. Next, an attempt is made to explain the roughly uniform distribution of prestige as between the major types of positions in every society. Since, however, there occur between one society and another great differences in the degree and kind of stratification, some attention is also given to the varieties of social inequality and the variable factors that give rise to them.

Clearly, the present task requires two different lines of analysis—one to understand the universal, the other to understand the variable features of stratification. Naturally each line of inquiry aids the other and is indispensable, and in the treatment that follows the two will be interwoven, although, because of space limitations, the emphasis will be on the universals.

Throughout, it will be necessary to keep in mind one thing—namely, that the discussion relates to the system of positions, not to the individuals occupying those positions. It is one thing to ask why different positions carry different degrees of prestige, and quite another to ask how certain individuals get into those positions. Although, as the argument will try to show, both

* By Kingsley Davis and Wilbert E. Moore, reprinted from *American Sociological Review*, Vol. X, 1945, No. 2, pp. 242–249, with permission of The American Sociological Society and the authors.

questions are related, it is essential to keep them separate in our thinking. Most of the literature on stratification has tried to answer the second question (particularly with regard to the ease or difficulty of mobility between strata) without tackling the first. The first question, however, is logically prior and, in the case of any particular individual or group, factually prior.

THE FUNCTIONAL NECESSITY OF STRATIFICATION

Curiously, however, the main functional necessity explaining the universal presence of stratification is precisely the requirement faced by any society of placing and motivating individuals in the social structure. As a functioning mechanism a society must somehow distribute its members in social positions and induce them to perform the duties of these positions. It must thus concern itself with motivation at two different levels: to instill in the proper individuals the desire to fill certain positions, and, once in these positions, the desire to perform the duties attached to them. Even though the social order may be relatively static in form, there is a continuous process of metabolism as new individuals are born into it, shift with age, and die off. Their absorption into the positional system must somehow be arranged and motivated. This is true whether the system is competitive or non-competitive. A competitive system gives greater importance to the motivation to achieve positions, whereas a non-competitive system gives perhaps greater importance to the motivation to perform the duties of the positions; but in any system both types of motivation are required.

If the duties associated with the various positions were all equally pleasant to the human organism, all equally important to societal survival, and all equally in need of the same ability or talent, it would make no difference who got into which positions, and the problem of social placement would be greatly reduced. But actually it does make a great deal of difference who gets into which positions, not only because some positions are inherently more agreeable than others, but also because some require special talents or training and some are functionally more important than others. Also, it is essential that the duties of the positions be performed with the diligence that their importance requires. Inevitably, then, a society must have, first, some kind of rewards that it can use as inducements, and, second, some way of distributing these rewards differentially according to positions. The rewards and their distribution become a part of the social order, and thus give rise to stratification.

One may ask what kind of rewards a society has at its disposal in distributing its personnel and securing essential services. It has, first of all, the things that contribute to sustenance and comfort. It has, second, the things that contribute to humor and diversion. And it has, finally, the things that contribute to self-respect and ego expansion. The last, because of the peculiarly social character of the self, is largerly a function of the opinion of others, but it nonetheless ranks in importance with the first two. In any social system all three kinds of rewards must be dispensed differentially according to positions.

In a sense the rewards are "built into" the position. They consist in the "rights" associated with the position, plus what may be called its accompaniments or perquisites. Often the rights, and sometimes the accompaniments, are functionally related to the duties of the position. (Rights as viewed by the incumbent are usually duties as viewed by cther members of the community.) However, there may be a host of subsidiary rights and perquisites that are not essential to the function of the position and have only an indirect and symbolic connection with its duties, but which still may be of considerable importance in inducing people to seek the positions and fulfil the essential duties.

If the rights and perquisites of different positions in a society must be unequal, then the society must be stratified, because that is precisely what stratification means. Social inequality is thus an unconsciously evolved device by which societies insure that the most important positions are conscientiously filled by the most qualified persons. Hence every society, no matter how simple or complex, must differentiate persons in terms of both prestige and esteem, and must therefore possess a certain amount of institutionalized inequality.

It does not follow that the amount or type of inequality need be the same in all societies. This is largely a function of factors that will be discussed presently.

THE TWO DETERMINANTS OF POSITIONAL RANK

Granting the general function that inequality subserves, one can specify the two factors that determine the relative rank of different positions. In general those positions convey the best reward, and hence have the highest rank, which (a) have the greatest importance for the society and (b) require the greatest training or talent. The first factor concerns function and is a matter of relative significance; the second concerns means and is a matter of scarcity.

Differential Functional Importance. Actually a society does not need to reward positions in proportion to their functional importance. It merely needs to give sufficient reward to them to insure that they will be filled competently. In other words, it must see that less essential positions do not compete successfully with more essential ones. If a position is easily filled, it need not be heavily rewarded, even though important. On the other hand, if it is important but hard to fill, the reward must be high enough to get it filled anyway. Functional importance is therefore a necessary but not a sufficient cause of high rank being assigned to a position.[3]

Differential Scarcity of Personnel. Practically all positions, no matter how acquired, require some form of skill or capacity for performance. This is implicit in the very notion of position, which implies that the incumbent must, by virtue of his incumbency, accomplish certain things.

There are, ultimately, only two ways in which a person's qualifications come about: through inherent capacity or through training. Obviously, in concrete activities both are always necessary, but from a practical standpoint the scarcity may lie primarily in one or the other, as well as in both. Some positions require innate talents of such high degree that the persons who fill them are bound to be rare. In many cases, however, talent is fairly abundant in the population but the training process is so long, costly, and elaborate that relatively few can qualify. Modern medicine, for example, is within the mental capacity of most individuals, but a medical education is so burdensome and expensive that virtually none would undertake it if the position of the M.D. did not carry a reward commensurate with the sacrifice.

If the talents required for a position are abundant and the training easy, the method of acquiring the position may have little to do with its duties. There may be, in fact, a virtually accidental relationship. But if the skills required are scarce by reason of the rarity of talent or the costliness of training, the position, if functionally important, must have an attractive power that will draw the necessary skills in competition with other positions. This means, in effect, that the position must be high in the social scale—must command great prestige, high salary, ample leisure, and the like.

How Variations Are to Be Understood. In so far as there is a difference between one system of stratification and another, it is attributable to whatever factors affect the two determinants of differential reward—namely, functional importance and scarcity of personnel. Positions important in one society may not be important in another, because the conditions faced by the societies, or their degree of internal development, may be different. The same conditions, in turn, may affect the question of scarcity; for in some societies the stage of development, or the external situation, may wholly obviate the necessity of certain kinds of skill or talent. Any particular system of stratification, then, can be understood as a product of the special conditions affecting the two aforementioned grounds of differential reward.

MAJOR SOCIETAL FUNCTIONS AND STRATIFICATION

Religion. The reason why religion is necessary is apparently to be found in the fact that human society achieves its unity primarily through the possession by its members of certain ultimate values and ends in common. Although these values and ends are subjective, they influence behavior, and their integration enables the society to operate as a system. Derived neither from inherited nor from external nature, they have evolved as a part of culture by communication and moral pressure. They must, however, appear to the members of the society to have some reality, and it is the role of religious belief and ritual to supply and reinforce this appearance of reality. Through belief and ritual the common ends and values are connected with an imaginary world symbolized by concrete sacred objects, which world in turn is related in a meaningful way to the facts and trials of the individual's life. Through the worship of the sacred objects and the beings they symbolize, and the acceptance of supernatural prescriptions that are at the same time codes of behavior, a powerful control over human conduct is exercised, guiding it along lines sustaining the institutional structure and conforming to the ultimate ends and values.

If this conception of the role of religion is true, one can understand why in every known society the religious activities tend to be under the charge of particular persons, who tend thereby to enjoy greater rewards than the ordinary societal member. Certain of the rewards and special privileges may attach to only the highest religious functionaries, but others usually apply, if such exists, to the entire sacerdotal class.

Moreover, there is a peculiar relation between the duties of the religious official and the special privileges he enjoys. If the supernatural world governs the destinies of men more ultimately than does the real world, its earthly representative, the person through whom one may communicate with the supernatural, must be a powerful individual. He is a keeper of sacred tradition, a skilled performer of the ritual, and an interpreter of lore and myth. He is in such close contact with the gods that he is viewed as possessing some of their characteristics. He is, in short, a bit sacred, and hence free from some of the more vulgar necessities and controls.

It is no accident, therefore, that religious functionaries have been associated with the very highest positions of power, as in theocratic regimes.

Indeed, looking at it from this point of view, one may wonder why it is that they do not get *entire* control over their societies. The factors that prevent this are worthy of note.

In the first place, the amount of technical competence necessary for the performance of religious duties is small. Scientific or artistic capacity is not required. Anyone can set himself up as enjoying an intimate relation with deities, and nobody can successfully dispute him. Therefore, the factor of scarcity of personnel does not operate in the technical sense.

One may assert, on the other hand, that religious ritual is often elaborate and religious lore abstruse, and that priestly ministrations require tact, if not intelligence. This is true, but the technical requirements of the profession are for the most part adventitious, not related to the end in the same way that science is related to air travel. The priest can never be free from competition, since the criteria of whether or not one has genuine contact with the supernatural are never strictly clear. It is this competition that debases the priestly position below what might be expected at first glance. That is why priestly prestige is highest in those societies where membership in the profession is rigidly controlled by the priestly guild itself. That is why, in part at least, elaborate devices are utilized to stress the identification of the person with his office—spectacular costume, abnormal conduct, special diet, segregated residence, celibacy, conspicuous leisure, and the like. In fact, the priest is always in danger of becoming somewhat discredited—as happens in a secularized society—because in a world of stubborn fact, ritual and sacred knowledge alone will not grow crops or build houses. Furthermore, unless he is protected by a professional guild, the priest's identification with the supernatural tends to preclude his acquisition of abundant worldly goods.

As between one society and another it seems that the highest general position awarded the priest occurs in the medieval type of social order. Here there is enough economic production to afford a surplus, which can be used to support a numerous and highly organized priesthood; and yet the populace is unlettered and therefore credulous to a high degree. Perhaps the most extreme example is to be found in the Buddhism of Tibet, but others are encountered in the Catholicism of feudal Europe, the Inca regime of Peru, the Brahminism of India, and the Mayan priesthood of Yucatan. On the other hand, if the society is so crude as to have no surplus and little differentiation, so that every priest must be also a cultivator or hunter, the separation of the priestly status from the others has hardly gone far enough for priestly prestige to mean much. When the priest actually has high prestige under these circumstances, it is because he also performs other important functions (usually political and medical).

In an extremely advanced society built on scientific technology, the priesthood tends to lose status, because sacred tradition and supernaturalism drop into the background. The ultimate values and common ends of the society tend to be expressed in less anthropomorphic ways, by officials who occupy fundamentally political, economic, or educational rather than religious positions. Nevertheless, it is easily possible for intellectuals to exaggerate the degree to which the priesthood in a presumably secular milieu has lost prestige. When the matter is closely examined the urban proletariat, as well as the rural citizenry, proves to be surprisingly god-fearing and priest-ridden. No society has become so completely secularized as to liquidate entirely the belief in transcendental ends and supernatural entities. Even in a secularized society some system must exist for the integration of ultimate values, for their ritualistic expression, and for the emotional adjustments required by disappointment, death, and disaster.

Government. Like religion, government plays a unique and indispensable part in society. But in contrast to religion, which provides integration in terms of sentiments, beliefs, and rituals, it organizes the society in terms of law and authority. Furthermore, it orients the society to the actual rather than the unseen world.

The main functions of government are, internally, the ultimate enforcement of norms, the final arbitration of conflicting interests, and the overall planning and direction of society; and externally, the handling of war and diplomacy. To carry out these functions it acts as the agent of the entire people, enjoys a monopoly of force, and controls all individuals within its territory.

Political action, by definition, implies authority. An official can command because he has authority, and the citizen must obey because he is subject to that authority. For this reason stratification is inherent in the nature of political relationships.

So clear is the power embodied in political position that political inequality is sometimes thought to comprise all inequality. But it can be shown that there are other bases of stratification, that the following controls operate in practice to keep political power from becoming complete: (a) The fact that the actual holders of political office, and especially those determining top policy must necessarily be few in number compared to the total population. (b) The fact that the rulers represent the interest of the group rather than of themselves, and are therefore restricted in their behavior by rules and mores designed to enforce this limitation of interest. (c) The fact that the holder of political office has his authority by virtue of his office and nothing else, and therefore any special knowledge, talent, or capacity he may claim is purely incidental, so that he often has to depend upon others for technical assistance.

In view of these limiting factors, it is not strange that the rulers often have less power and prestige than a literal enumeration of their formal rights would lead one to expect.

Wealth, Property, and Labor. Every position that secures for its incumbent a livelihood is, by definition, economically rewarded. For this reason there is an economic aspect to those positions (e.g., political and religious) the main function of which is not economic. It therefore becomes convenient for the society to use unequal economic returns as a principal means of controlling the entrance of persons into positions and stimulating the performance of their duties. The amount of the economic return therefore becomes one of the main indices of social status.

It should be stressed, however, that a position does not bring power and prestige *because* it draws a high income. Rather, it draws a high income because it is functionally important and the available personnel is for one reason or another scarce. It is therefore superficial and erroneous to regard high income as the cause of a man's power and prestige, just as it is erroneous to think that a man's fever is the cause of his disease.[4]

The economic source of power and prestige is not income primarily, but the ownership of capital goods (including patents, good will, and professional reputation). Such ownership should be distinguished from the possession of consumers' goods, which is an index rather than a cause of social standing. In other words, the ownership of producers' goods is, properly speaking, a source of income like other positions, the income itself remaining an index. Even in situations where social values are widely commercialized and earnings are the readiest method of judging social position, income does not confer prestige on a position so much as it induces people to compete for the position. It is true that a man who has a high income as a result of one position may find this money helpful in climbing into another position as well, but this again reflects the effect of his initial, economically advantageous status, which exercises its influence through the medium of money.

In a system of private property in productive enterprise, an income above what an individual spends can give rise to possession of capital wealth. Presumably such possession is a reward for the proper management of one's finances originally and of the productive enterprise later. But as social differentiation becomes highly advanced and yet the institution of inheritance persists, the phenomenon of pure ownership, and reward for pure ownership, emerges. In such a case it is difficult to prove that the position is functionally important or that the scarcity involved is anything other than extrinsic and accidental. It is for this reason, doubtless, that the institution of private property in productive goods becomes more subject to criticism as social development proceeds toward industrialization. It is only this pure, that is, strictly legal and functionless ownership, however, that is open to attack; for some form of active ownership, whether private or public, is indispensable.

One kind of ownership of production goods consists in rights over the labor of others. The most extremely concentrated and exclusive of such rights are found in slavery, but the essential principle remains in serfdom, peonage, encomienda, and indenture. Naturally this kind of ownership has the greatest significance for stratification, because it necessarily entails an unequal relationship.

But property in capital goods inevitably introduces a compulsive element even into the nominally free contractual relationship. Indeed, in some respects the authority of the contractual employer is greater than that of the feudal landlord, inasmuch as the latter is more limited by traditional reciprocities. Even the classical economics recognized that competitors would fare unequally, but it did not pursue this fact to its necessary conclusion that, however it might be acquired, unequal control of goods and services must give unequal advantage to the parties to a contract.

Technical Knowledge. The function of finding means to single goals, without any concern with the choice between goals, is the exclusively technical sphere. The explanation of why positions requiring great technical skill receive fairly high rewards is easy to see, for it is the simplest case of the rewards being so distributed as to draw talent and motivate training. Why they seldom if ever receive the highest rewards is also clear: the importance of technical knowledge from a societal point of view is never so great as the integration of goals, which takes place on the religious, political, and economic levels. Since the technological level is concerned solely with means, a purely technical position must ultimately be subordinate to other positions that are religious, political, or economic in character.

Nevertheless, the distinction between expert and layman in any social order is fundamental, and cannot be entirely reduced to other terms. Methods of recruitment, as well as of reward, sometimes lead to the erroneous interpretation that technical positions are economically determined. Actually, however, the acquisition of knowledge and skill cannot be accomplished by purchase, although the opportunity to learn may be. The control of the avenues of training may inhere as a sort of property right in certain families or classes, giving them power and prestige in consequence. Such a situation adds an artificial scarcity to the natural scarcity of skills and talents. On the other hand, it is possible for an opposite situation to arise. The rewards of technical position may be so great that a condition of excess supply is created, leading to at least temporary devaluation of the rewards. Thus "unemployment in the learned professions" may result in a debasement of the prestige of those positions. Such adjustments and readjustments are constantly occurring in changing societies; and it is always well to bear in mind that the efficiency of a stratified structure may be affected by the modes of recruitment for positions. The social order itself, however, sets limits to the inflation or deflation of the prestige of experts: an over-supply tends to debase the rewards and discourage recruitment or produce revolution, whereas an under-supply tends to increase the reward or weaken the society in competition with other societies.

Particular systems of stratification show a wide range with respect to the exact position of technically competent persons. This range is perhaps most evident in the degree of specialization. Extreme division of labor tends to create many specialists without high prestige since the training is short and the required native capacity relatively small. On the other hand it also tends to accentuate the high position of the true experts—scientists, engineers, and administrators—by increasing their authority relative to other functionally important positions. But the idea of a technocratic social order or a government or priesthood of engineers or social scientists neglects the limitations of knowledge and skills as a basic for performing social functions. To the extent that the social structure is truly specialized the prestige of the technical person must also be circumscribed.

VARIATION IN STRATIFIED SYSTEMS

The generalized principles of stratification here suggested form a necessary preliminary to a consideration of types of stratified systems, because it is in terms of these principles that the types must be described. This can be seen by trying to delineate types according to certain modes of variation. For instance, some of the most important modes (together with the polar types in terms of them) seem to be as follows:

(a) *The Degree of Specialization.* The degree of specialization affects the fineness and multiplicity of the gradations in power and prestige. It also influences the extent to which particular functions may be emphasized in the invidious system, since a given function cannot receive much emphasis in the hierarchy until it has achieved structural separation from the other functions. Finally, the amount of specialization influences the bases of selection. Polar types: *Specialized, Unspecialized.*

(b) *The Nature of the Functional Emphasis*. In general when emphasis is put on sacred matters, a rigidity is introduced that tends to limit specialization and hence the development of technology. In addition, a brake is placed on social mobility, and on the development of bureaucracy. When the preoccupation with the sacred is withdrawn, leaving greater scope for purely secular preoccupations, a great development, and rise in status, of economic and technological positions seemingly takes place. Curiously, a concomitant rise in political position is not likely, because it has usually been allied with the religious and stands to gain little by the decline of the latter. It is also possible for a society to emphasize family functions—as in relatively undifferentiated societies where high mortality requires high fertility and kinship forms the main basis of social organization. Main types: *Familistic, Authoritarian (Theocratic* or sacred, and *Totalitarian* or secular), *Capitalistic*.

(c) *The Magnitude of Invidious Differences*. What may be called the amount of social distance between positions, taking into account the entire scale, is something that should lend itself to quantitative measurement. Considerable differences apparently exist between different societies in this regard, and also between parts of the same society. Polar types: *Equalitarian, Inequalitarian*.

(d) *The Degree of Opportunity*. The familiar question of the amount of mobility is different from the question of the comparative equality or inequality of rewards posed above, because the two criteria may vary independently up to a point. For instance, the tremendous divergences in monetary income in the United States are far greater than those found in primitive societies, yet the equality of opportunity to move from one rung to the other in the social scale may also be greater in the United States than in a hereditary tribal kingdom. Polar types: *Mobile* (open), *Immobile* (closed).

(e) *The Degree of Stratum Solidarity*. Again, the degree of "class solidarity" (or the presence of specific organizations to promote class interests) may vary to some extent independently of the other criteria, and hence is an important principle in classifying systems of stratification. Polar types: *Class organized, Class unorganized*.

EXTERNAL CONDITIONS

What state any particular system of stratification is in with reference to each of these modes of variation depends on two things: (1) its state with reference to the other ranges of variation, and (2) the conditions outside the system of stratification which nevertheless influence that system. Among the latter are the following:

(a) *The Stage of Cultural Development.* As the cultural heritage grows, increased specialization becomes necessary, which in turn contributes to the enhancement of mobility, a decline of stratum solidarity, and a change of functional emphasis.

(b) *Situation with Respect to Other Societies.* The presence or absence of open conflict with other societies, of free trade relations or cultural diffusion, all influence the class structure to some extent. A chronic state of warfare tends to place emphasis upon the military functions, especially when the opponents are more or less equal. Free trade, on the other hand, strengthens the hand of the trader at the expense of the warrior and priest. Free movement of ideas generally has an equalitarian effect. Migration and conquest create special circumstances.

(c) *Size of the Society.* A small society limits the degree to which functional specialization can go, the degree of segregation of different strata, and the magnitude of inequality.

COMPOSITE TYPES

Much of the literature on stratification has attempted to classify concrete systems into a certain number of types. This task is deceptively simple, however, and should come at the end of an analysis of elements and principles, rather than at the beginning. If the preceding discussion has any validity, it indicates that there are a number of modes of variation between different systems, and that any one system is a composite of the society's status with reference to all these modes of variation. The danger of trying to classify whole societies under such rubrics as *caste, feudal,* or *open class* is that one or two criteria are selected and others ignored, the result being an unsatisfactory solution to the problem posed. The present discussion has been offered as a possible approach to the more systematic classification of composite types.

REFERENCES

1. Kingsley Davis, "A Conceptual Analysis of Stratification." *American Sociological Review.* 7: 309–32, June, 1942.
2. The writers regret (and beg indulgence) that the present essay, a condensation of a longer study, covers so much in such short space that adequate evidence and qualification cannot be given and that as a result what is actually very tentative is presented in an unfortunately dogmatic manner.
3. Unfortunately, functional importance is difficult to establish. To use the position's prestige to establish it, as is often unconsciously done, constitutes circular reasoning from our point of view. There are, however, two independent clues: (a) the degree to which a position is functionally unique, there being no other positions that can perform the same function satisfactorily; (b) the degree to which other positions are

dependent on the one in question. Both clues are best exemplified in organized systems of positions built around one major function. Thus, in most complex societies the religious, political, economic, and educational functions are handled by distinct structures not easily interchangeable. In addition, each structure possesses many different positions, some clearly dependent on, if not subordinate to, others. In sum, when an institutional nucleus becomes differentiated around one main function, and at the same time organizes a large portion of the population into its relationships, the *key* positions in it are of the highest functional importance. The absence of such specialization does not prove functional unimportance, for the whole society may be relatively unspecialized; but it is safe to assume that the more important functions receive the first and clearest structural differentiation.

4. The symbolic rather than intrinsic role of income in social stratification has been succinctly summarized by Talcott Parsons, "An Analytical Approach to the Theory of Social Stratification," *American Journal of Sociology.* 45: 841–862, May, 1940.

Some Principles of Stratification: A Critical Analysis * (*Tumin*) †

The fact of social inequality in human society is marked by its ubiquity and its antiquity. Every known society, past and present, distributes its scarce and demanded goods and services unequally. And there are attached to the positions which command unequal amounts of such goods and services certain highly morally-toned evaluations of their importance for the society.

The ubiquity and the antiquity of such inequality has given rise to the assumption that there must be something both inevitable and positively functional about such social arrangements.

Clearly, the truth or falsity of such an assumption is a strategic question for any general theory of social organization. It is therefore most curious that the basic premises and implications of the assumption have only been most casually explored by American sociologists.

The most systematic treatment is to be found in the well-known article by Kingsley Davis and Wilbert Moore, entitled "Some Principles of Stratification." [1] More than twelve years have passed since its publication, and though it is one of the very few treatments of stratification on a high level of generalization, it is difficult to locate a single systematic analysis of its reasoning. It will be the principal concern of this paper to present the beginnings of such an analysis.

    * By Melvin W. Tumin reprinted from *American Sociological Review,* Vol. 18, 1953, No. 4, with permission of The American Sociological Society and the author.
    † The writer has had the benefit of a most helpful criticism of the main portions of this paper by Professor W. J. Goode of Columbia University. In addition, he has had the opportunity to expose this paper to criticism by the Staff Seminar of the Sociology Section at Princeton. In deference to a possible rejoinder by Professors Moore and Davis, the writer has not revised the paper to meet the criticisms which Moore has already offered personally.

The central argument advanced by Davis and Moore can be stated in a number of sequential propositions, as follows:

(1) Certain positions in any society are functionally more important than others, and require special skills for their performance.

(2) Only a limited number of individuals in any society have the talents which can be trained into the skills appropriate to these positions.

(3) The conversion of talents into skills involves a training period during which sacrifices of one kind or another are made by those undergoing the training.

(4) In order to induce the talented persons to undergo these sacrifices and acquire the training, their future positions must carry an inducement value in the form of differential, i.e., privileged and disproportionate access to the scarce and desired rewards which the society has to offer.[2]

(5) These scarce and desired goods consist of the rights and perquisites attached to, or built into, the positions, and can be classified into those things which contribute to (a) sustenance and comfort, (b) humor and diversion, (c) self-respect and ego expansion.

(6) This differential access to the basic rewards of the society has as a consequence the differentiation of the prestige and esteem which various strata acquire. This may be said, along with the rights and perquisites, to constitute institutionalized social inequality, i.e., stratification.

(7) Therefore, social inequality among different strata in the amounts of scarce and desired goods, and the amounts of prestige and esteem which they receive, is both positively functional and inevitable in any society.

Let us take these propositions and examine them *seriatim.*[3]

(1) Certain positions in any society are more functionally important than others and require special skills for their performance.

The key term here is "functionally important." The functionalist theory of social organization is by no means clear and explicit about this term. The minimum common referent is to something known as the "survival value" of a social structure.[4] This concept immediately involves a number of perplexing questions. Among these are: (a) the issue of minimum vs. maximum survival, and the possible empirical referents which can be given to those terms; (b) whether such a proposition is a useless tautology since any *status quo* at any given moment is nothing more and nothing less than everything present in the *status quo*. In these terms, all acts and structures must be judged positively functional in that they constitute essential portions of the *status quo*; (c) what kind of calculus of functionality exists which will enable us, at this point in our development, to add and subtract long and short range consequences, with their mixed qualities, and arrive at some summative judgment regarding the rating an act or structure should receive on a scale of greater or lesser functionality? At best, we tend to make primarily intuitive judgments. Often enough, these judgments involve the use of value-laden criteria, or, at least, criteria which are chosen in preference to others not for any sociologically systematic reasons but by reason of certain implicit value preferences.

Thus, to judge that the engineers in a factory are functionally more important to the factory than the unskilled workmen involves a notion regarding the dispensability of the unskilled workmen, or their replaceability, relative to that of the engineers. But this is not a process of choice with infinite time dimensions. For at some point along the line one must face the problem of adequate motivation for *all* workers at all levels of skill in the factory. In the long run, *some* labor force of unskilled workmen is as important and as indispensable to the factory as *some* labor force of engineers. Often enough, the labor force situation is such that this fact is brought home sharply to the entrepreneur in the short run rather than in the long run.

Moreover, the judgment as to the relative indispensability and replaceability of a particular segment of skills in the population involves a prior judgment about the bargaining-power of that segment. But this power is itself a culturally shaped *consequence* of the existing system of rating, rather than something inevitable in the nature of social organization. At least the contrary of this has never been demonstrated, but only assumed.

A generalized theory of social stratification must recognize that the prevailing system of inducements and rewards is only one of many variants in the whole range of possible systems of motivation which, at least theoretically, are capable of working in human society. It is quite conceivable, of course, that a system of norms could be institutionalized in which the idea of threatened withdrawal of services, except under the most extreme circumstances, would be considered as absolute moral anathema. In such a case, the whole notion of relative functionality, as advanced by Davis and Moore, would have to be radically revised.

(2) *Only a limited number of individuals in any society have the talents which can be trained into the skills appropriate to these positions (i.e., the more functionally important positions).*

The truth of this proposition depends at least in part on the truth of proposition 1 above. It is, therefore, subject to all the limitations indicated above. But for the moment, let us assume the validity of the first proposition and concentrate on the question of the rarity of appropriate talent.

If all that is meant is that in every society there is a *range* of talent, and that some members of any society are by nature more talented than others, no sensible contradiction can be offered, but a question must be raised here regarding the amount of sound knowledge present in any society concerning the presence of talent in the population.

For, in every society there is some demonstrable ignorance regarding the amount of talent present in the population. *And the more rigidly stratified a society is, the less chance does that society have of discovering any new facts about the talents of its members.* Smoothly working and stable systems of stratification, wherever found, tend to build-in obstacles to the further exploration of the range of available talent. This is especially true in those societies where the opportunity to discover talent in any one generation varies with the differential resources of the parent generation. Where, for instance, access to education depends upon the wealth of one's parents, and where wealth is differentially distributed, large segments of the population are likely to be deprived of the chance even to *discover* what are their talents.

Whether or not differential rewards and opportunities are functional in any one generation, it is clear that if those differentials are allowed to be socially inherited by the next generation, then, the stratification system is specifically dysfunctional for the discovery of talents in the next generation. In this fashion, systems of social stratification tend to limit the chances available to maximize the efficiency of discovery, recruitment and training of "functionally important talent." [5]

Additionally, the unequal distribution of rewards in one generation tends to result in the unequal distribution of motivation in the succeeding generation. Since motivation to succeed is clearly an important element in the entire process of education, the unequal distribution of motivation tends to set limits on the possible extensions of the educational system, and hence, upon the efficient recruitment and training of the widest body of skills available in the population.[6]

Lastly, in this context, it may be asserted that there is some noticeable tendency for elites to restrict further access to their privileged positions, once they have sufficient power to enforce such restrictions. This is especially true in a culture where it is possible for an elite to contrive a high demand and a proportionately higher reward for its work by restricting the numbers of the elite available to do the work. The recruitment and training of doctors in modern United States is at least partly a case in point.

Here, then, are three ways, among others which could be cited, in which stratification systems, once operative, tend to reduce the survival value of a society by limiting the search, recruitment and training of functionally important personnel far more sharply than the facts of available talent would appear to justify. It is only when there is genuinely equal access to recruitment and training for all potentially talented persons that differential rewards can conceivably be justified as functional. And stratification systems are apparently *inherently antagonistic* to the development of such full equality of opportunity.

(3) *The conversion of talents into skills involves a training period during which sacrifices of one kind or another are made by those undergoing the training.*

Davis and Moore introduce here a concept, "sacrifice" which comes closer than any of the rest of their vocabulary of analysis to being a direct reflection of the rationalizations, offered by the more fortunate members of a society, of the rightness of their occupancy of privileged positions. It is the least critically thought-out concept in the repertoire, and can also be shown to be least supported by the actual facts.

In our present society, for example, what are the sacrifices which talented persons undergo in the training period? The possibly serious losses involve the surrender of earning power and the cost of the training. The latter is generally borne by the parents of the talented youth undergoing training, and not by the trainees themselves. But this cost tends to be paid out of income which the parents were able to earn generally by virtue of *their* privileged positions in the hierarchy of stratification. That is to say, the parents' ability to pay for the training of their children is part of the differential *reward* they, the parents, received for their privileged positions in the society. And to charge this sum up against sacrifices made by the youth is falsely to perpetuate a bill or a debt already paid by the society to the parents.

So far as the sacrifice of earning power by the trainees themselves is concerned, the loss may be measured relative to what they might have earned had they gone into the labor market instead of into advanced training for the "important" skills. There are several ways to judge this. One way is to take all the average earnings of age peers who did go into the labor market for a period equal to the average length of the training period. The total income, so calculated, roughly equals an amount which the elite can, on the average, earn back in the first decade of professional work, over and above the earnings of his age peers who are not trained. Ten years is probably the maximum amount needed to equalize the differential.[7] There remains, on the average, twenty years of work during each of which the skilled person then goes on to earn far more than his unskilled age peers. And, what is often forgotten, there is then still another ten or fifteen year period during which the skilled person continues to work and earn when his unskilled age peer is either totally or partially out of the labor market by virtue of the attrition of his strength and capabilities.

One might say that the first ten years of differential pay is perhaps justified, in order to regain for the trained person what he lost during his training period. But it is difficult to imagine what would justify continuing such differential rewards beyond that period.

Another and probably sounder way to measure how much is lost during the training period is to compare the per capita income available to the trainee with the per capita income of the age peer on the untrained labor market during the so-called sacrificial period. If one takes into account the earlier marriage of untrained persons, and the earlier acquisition of family dependents, it is highly dubious that the per capita income of the wage worker is significantly larger than that of the trainee. Even assuming, for the moment, that there is a difference, the amount is by no means sufficient to justify a lifetime of continuing differentials.

What tends to be completely overlooked, in addition, are the psychic and spiritual rewards which are available to the elite trainees by comparison with their age peers in the labor force. There is, first, the much higher prestige enjoyed by the college student and the professional-school student as compared with persons in shops and offices. There is, second, the extremely highly valued privilege of having greater opportunity for self-development. There is, third, all the psychic gain involved in being allowed to delay the assumption of adult responsibilities such as earning a living and supporting a family. There is, fourth, the access to leisure and freedom of a kind not likely to be experienced by the persons already at work.

If these are never taken into account as rewards of the training period it is not because they are not concretely present, but because the emphasis in American concepts of reward is almost exclusively placed on the material returns of positions. The emphases on enjoyment, entertainment, ego enhancement, prestige and esteem are introduced only when the differentials in these which accrue to the skilled positions need to be justified. If these other rewards were taken into account, it would be much more difficult to demonstrate that the training period, as presently operative, is really sacrificial. Indeed, it might turn out to be the case that even at this point in their careers, the elite trainees were being differentially rewarded relative to their age peers in the labor force.

All of the foregoing concerns the quality of the training period under our present system of motivation and rewards. Whatever may turn out to be the factual case about the present system—and the factual case is moot—the more important theoretical question concerns the assumption that the training period under *any* system must be sacrificial.

There seem to be no good theoretical grounds for insisting on this assumption. For, while under any system certain costs will be involved in training persons for skilled positions, these costs could easily be assumed by the society-at-large. Under these circumstances, there would be no need to compensate anyone in terms of differential rewards once the skilled positions were staffed. In short, there would be no need or justification for stratifying social positions on *these* grounds.

(4) *In order to induce the talented persons to undergo these sacrifices and acquire the training, their future positions must carry an inducement value in the form of differential, i.e., privileged and disproportionate access to the scarce and desired rewards which the society has to offer.*

Let us assume, for the purposes of the discussion, that the training period is sacrificial and the talent is rare in every conceivable human society. There is still the basic problem as to whether the allocation of differential rewards in scarce and desired goods and services is the only or the most efficient way of recruiting the appropriate talent to these positions.

For there are a number of alternative motivational schemes whose efficiency and adequacy ought at least to be considered in this context. What can be said, for instance, on behalf of the motivation which De Man called "joy in work," Veblen termed "instinct for workmanship" and which we latterly have come to identify as "intrinsic work satisfaction"? Or, to what extent could the motivation of "social duty" be institutionalized in such a fashion that self interest and social interest come closely to coincide? Or, how much prospective confidence can be placed in the possibilities of institutionalizing "social service" as a widespread motivation for seeking one's appropriate position and fulfilling it conscientiously?

Are not these types of motivations, we may ask, likely to prove most appropriate for precisely the "most functionally important positions"? Especially in a mass industrial society, where the vast majority of positions become standardized and routinized, it is the skilled jobs which are likely to retain most of the quality of "intrinsic job satisfaction" and be most readily identifiable as socially serviceable. Is it indeed impossible then to build these motivations into the socialization pattern to which we expose our talented youth?

To deny that such motivations could be institutionalized would be to overclaim our present knowledge. In part, also, such a claim would seem to derive from an assumption that what has not been institutionalized yet in human affairs is incapable of institutionalization. Admittedly, historical experience affords us evidence we cannot afford to ignore. But such evidence cannot legitimately be used to deny absolutely the possibility of heretofore untried alternatives. Social innovation is as important a feature of human societies as social stability.

On the basis of these observations, it seems that Davis and Moore have stated the case much too strongly when they insist that a "functionally important position" which requires skills that are scarce, "must command great prestige, high salary, ample leisure, and the like," if the appropriate talents are to be attracted to the position. Here, clearly, the authors are postulating the unavoidability of very specific types of rewards and, by implication, denying the possibility of others.

(5) *These scarce and desired goods consist of rights and perquisites attached to, or built into, the positions and can be classified into those things which contribute to (a) sustenance and comfort; (b) humor and diversion; (c) self-respect and ego expansion.*

(6) *This differential access to the basic rewards of the society has as a consequence the differentiation of the prestige and esteem which various strata acquire. This may be said, along with the rights and perquisites, to constitute institutionalized social inequality, i.e., stratification.*

With the classification of the rewards offered by Davis and Moore there need be little argument. Some question must be raised, however, as to whether any reward system, built into a general stratification system, must allocate equal amounts of all three types of reward in order to function effectively, or whether one type of reward may be emphasized to the virtual neglect of others. This raises the further question regarding which type of emphasis is likely to prove most effective as a differential inducer. Nothing in the known facts about human motivation impels us to favor one type of reward over the other, or to insist that all three types of reward must be built into the positions in comparable amounts if the position is to have an inducement value.

It is well known, of course, that societies differ considerably in the kinds of rewards they emphasize in their efforts to maintain a reasonable balance between responsibility and reward. There are, for instance, numerous societies in which the conspicuous display of differential economic advantage is considered extremely bad taste. In short, our present knowledge commends to us the possibility of considerable plasticity in the way in which different types of rewards can be structured into a functioning society. This is to say, it cannot yet be demonstrated that it is *unavoidable* that differential prestige and esteem shall accrue to positions which command differential rewards in power and property.

What does seem to be unavoidable is that differential prestige shall be given to those in any society who conform to the normative order as against those who deviate from that order in a way judged immoral and detrimental. On the assumption that the continuity of a society depends on the continuity and stability of its normative order, some such distinction between conformists and deviants seems inescapable.

It also seems to be unavoidable that in any society, no matter how literate its tradition, the older, wiser and more experienced individuals who are charged with the enculturation and socialization of the young must have more power than the young, on the assumption that the task of effective socialization demands such differential power.

But this differentiation in prestige between the conformist and the deviant is by no means the same distinction as that between strata of individuals each of which operates *within* the normative order, and is composed of adults. The *latter* distinction, in the form of differentiated rewards and prestige between social strata is what Davis and Moore, and most sociologists, consider the structure of a stratification system. The *former* distinctions have nothing necessarily to do with the workings of such a system nor with the efficiency of motivation and recruitment of functionally important personnel.

Nor does the differentiation of power between young and old necessarily create differentially valued strata. For no society rates its young as less morally worthy than its older persons, no matter how much differential power the older ones may temporarily enjoy.

(7) *Therefore, social inequality among different strata in the amounts of scarce and desired goods, and the amounts of prestige and esteem which they receive, is both positively functional and inevitable in any society.*

If the objections which have heretofore been raised are taken as reasonable, then it may be stated that the only items which any society *must* distribute unequally are the power and property necessary for the performance of different tasks. If such differential power and property are viewed by all as commensurate with the differential responsibilities, and if they are culturally defined as *resources* and not as rewards, then no differentials in prestige and esteem need follow.

Historically, the evidence seems to be that every time power and property are distributed unequally, no matter what the cultural definition, prestige and esteem differentiations have tended to result as well. Historically, however, no systematic effort has ever been made, under propitious circumstances, to develop the tradition that each man is as socially worthy as all other men so long as he performs his appropriate tasks conscientiously. While such a tradition seems utterly utopian, no known facts in psychological or social science have yet demonstrated its impossibility or its dysfunctionality for the continuity of a society. The achievement of a full institutionalization of such a tradition seems far too remote to contemplate. Some successive approximations at such a tradition, however, are not out of the range of prospective social innovation.

What, then, of the "positive functionality" of social stratification? Are there other, negative, functions of institutionalized social inequality which can be identified, if only tentatively? Some such dysfunctions of stratification have already been suggested in the body of this paper. Along with others they may now be stated, in the form of provisional assertions, as follows:

(1) Social stratification systems function to limit the possibility of discovery of the full range of talent available in a society. This results from the fact of unequal access to appropriate motivation, channels of recruitment and centers of training.

(2) In foreshortening the range of available talent, social stratification systems function to set limits upon the possibility of expanding the productive resources of the society, at least relative to what might be the case under conditions of greater equality of opportunity.

(3) Social stratification systems function to provide the elite with the political power necessary to procure acceptance and dominance of an ideology which rationalizes the *status quo,* whatever it may be, as "logical," "natural" and "morally right." In this manner, social stratification systems function as essentially conservative influences in the societies in which they are found.

(4) Social stratification systems function to distribute favorable self-images unequally throughout a population. To the extent that such favorable self-images are requisite to the development of the creative potential inherent in men, to that extent stratification systems function to limit the development of this creative potential.

(5) To the extent that inequalities in social rewards cannot be made fully acceptable to the less privileged in a society, social stratification systems function to encourage hostility, suspicion and distrust among the various segments of a society and thus to limit the possibilities of extensive social integration.

(6) To the extent that the sense of significant membership in a society depends on one's place on the prestige ladder of the society,

social stratification systems function to distribute unequally the sense of significant membership in the population.

(7) To the extent that loyalty to a society depends on a sense of significant membership in the society, social stratification systems function to distribute loyalty unequally in the population.

(8) To the extent that participation and apathy depend upon the sense of significant membership in the society, social stratification systems function to distribute the motivation to participate unequally in a population.

Each of the eight foregoing propositions contains implicit hypotheses regarding the consequences of unequal distribution of rewards in a society in accordance with some notion of the functional importance of various positions. These are empirical hypotheses, subject to test. They are offered here only as exemplary of the kinds of consequences of social stratification which are not often taken into account in dealing with the problem. They should also serve to reinforce the doubt that social inequality is a device which is uniformly functional for the role of guaranteeing that the most important tasks in a society will be performed conscientiously by the most competent persons.

The obviously mixed character of the functions of social inequality should come as no surprise to anyone. If sociology is sophisticated in any sense, it is certainly with regard to its awareness of the mixed nature of any social arrangement, when the observer takes into account long as well as short range consequences and latent as well as manifest dimensions.

SUMMARY

In this paper, an effort has been made to raise questions regarding the inevitability and positive functionality of stratification, or institutionalized social inequality in rewards, allocated in accordance with some notion of the greater and lesser functional importance of various positions. The possible alternative meanings of the concept "functional importance" has been shown to be one difficulty. The question of the scarcity or abundance of available talent has been indicated as a principal source of possible variation. The extent to which the period of training for skilled positions may reasonably be viewed as sacrificial has been called into question. The possibility has been suggested that very different types of motivational schemes might conceivably be made to function. The separability of differentials in power and property considered as resources appropriate to a task from such differentials considered as rewards for the performance of a task has also been suggested. It has also been maintained that differentials in prestige and esteem do not necessarily follow upon differentials in power and property when the latter are considered as appropriate resources rather than rewards. Finally, some negative functions, or dysfunctions, of institutionalized social inequality have been tentatively identified revealing the mixed character of the outcome of social stratification, and casting doubt on the contention that

> Social inequality is thus an unconsciously evolved device by which societies insure that the most important positions are conscientiously filled by the most qualified persons.[8]

REFERENCES

1. *American Sociological Review*, X (April, 1945), pp. 242–249. An earlier article by Kingsley Davis, entitled, "A Conceptual Analysis of Stratification," *American Sociological Review*, VII (June, 1942), pp. 309–321, is devoted primarily to setting forth a vocabulary for stratification analysis. A still earlier article by Talcott Parsons, "An Analytical Approach to the Theory of Social Stratification," *American Journal of Sociology*, XLV (November, 1940), pp. 849–862, approaches the problem in terms of why "differential ranking is considered a really fundamental phenomenon of social systems and what are the respects in which such ranking is important." The principal line of integration asserted by Parsons is with the fact of the normative orientation of any society. Certain crucial lines of connection are left unexplained, however, in this article, and in the Davis and Moore article of 1945 only some of these lines are made explicit.
2. The "scarcity and demand" qualities of goods and services are never explicitly mentioned by Davis and Moore. But it seems to the writer that the argument makes no sense unless the goods and services are so characterized. For if rewards are to function as differential inducements they must not only be differentially distributed but they must be both scarce and demanded as well. Neither the scarcity of an item by itself nor the fact of its being in demand is sufficient to allow it to function as a differential inducement in a system of unequal rewards. Leprosy is scarce and oxygen is highly demanded.
3. The arguments to be advanced here are condensed versions of a much longer analysis entitled, *An Essay on Social Stratification*. Perforce, all the reasoning necessary to support some of the contentions cannot be offered within the space limits of this article.
4. Davis and Moore are explicitly aware of the difficulties involved here and suggest two "independent clues" other than survival value. See footnote 3 on p. 244 of their article.
5. Davis and Moore state this point briefly on p. 248 but do not elaborate it.
6. In the United States, for instance, we are only now becoming aware of the amount of productivity we, as a society, lose by allocating inferior opportunities and rewards, and hence, inferior motivation, to our Negro population. The actual amount of loss is difficult to specify precisely. Some rough estimate can be made, however, on the assumption that there is present in the Negro population about the same range of talent that is found in the white population.
7. These are only very rough estimates, of course, and it is certain that there is considerable income variation within the so-called elite group, so that the proposition holds only relatively more or less.
8. Davis and Moore, *op. cit.*, p. 243.

12.

BUREAUCRACY

BUREAUCRACY MAY BE DEFINED as that type of hierarchical organization which is designed rationally to coordinate the work of many individuals in the pursuit of large-scale administrative tasks. The sociologist uses the term "bureaucracy" in order to designate a certain type of structure, a particular organization of rationally coordinated unequals, and he rejects a popular usage of the term which equates bureaucracy with "red tape," inefficiency, and the like.

The nineteenth century produced a number of brilliantly descriptive and literary accounts of modern bureaucracies. Among the most perceptive were the work of the German sociologist Lorenz von Stein (1815–1890), Balzac's splendid novel, *The Functionaries,* and Dickens' *Bleak House.* All of these teach us much about the origins and working of bureaucracy, but it was Max Weber who began the systematic study of this area. Weber attempted to define a "pure type" of bureaucratic organization by abstracting what he considered the most characteristic features of bureaucracy. He hoped thus to furnish a kind of "measuring rod" which could direct and guide future investigators of specific bureaucratic structures. By providing an ideal construct of the pure form of bureaucracy, Weber sought to permit subsequent research to measure departures from the model. We have chosen two selections from his work. The first is meant to acquaint the reader with the main characteristics of Weber's ideal-type, the second illustrates his more general views about the progressive rationalization and disenchantment of the world which finds the trend toward increasing bureaucratization one of its central manifestations.

Though Weber's work has been seminal, it has frequently been misunderstood. It was often mistakenly assumed that he provided a description of concrete bureaucracies rather than an abstract conceptual scheme. Thus misunderstood, Weber's work of course did not lead to further investigations; it was either accepted or rejected and was not applied to research. Only in the last twenty or so years have his ideas begun to bear fruit in American research. Weber's theory is now neither accepted nor rejected, but it is put to use. Before we consider its influence on younger American theorists, we must turn to that other father of the modern theory of bureaucracy, Robert Michels.

Robert Michels (1876–1936) was a German-Italian sociologist who, though active in many fields of sociological theorizing, will be best remembered for his *Political Parties,* which has exerted considerable influence on both sociological and political theory. While Weber had in the main focused on bureaucratic structures in public and private administration, Michels was concerned with voluntary associations. *Political Parties* was based primarily on the history of European socialist and trade-union organizations before the First World War. If Weber's work was, as we have seen, often unduly simplified by his immediate successors, Michels himself tended to certain oversimplifications. Thus, when he stated his alleged "iron law of oligarchy," i.e., the "law" that all organizations necessarily assume an oligarchical character in the course of their development, his evidence seemed to support only the more moderate view that all organizations have a tendency to develop in the oligarchical forms if this tendency is not counterbalanced by other forces. But Michels' classic analysis of oligarchical tendencies in voluntary associations has, in conjunction with Weber's work, continued to provide the starting point for the bulk of recent investigations into bureaucratic processes.

Robert K. Merton's study of *Bureaucratic Structure and Personality* is a fruitful extension of certain insights provided by Max Weber. Merton's analysis of the ritualistic elements in the role-personality of the bureaucrat has exerted a considerable influence on recent research in the field. While Weber tended to emphasize the positive functions of bureaucracy, Merton allows us to see its dysfunctions as well.

Philip Selznick's book, *T.V.A. and the Grass Roots,* is one of the most important recent works in the empirical analysis of bureaucratic structures. Our selection is taken from a somewhat earlier essay in which Selznick attempted to fuse elements derived from both Weber and Michels into a consistent theory of bureaucracy.

Our last two selections are intended to acquaint the reader with some aspects of recent theorizing in the area. The pages from Alvin Gouldner's analysis of bureaucratic processes in a gypsum mine and Peter Blau's study of work and interpersonal relations in two different government agencies indicate the extent to which recent research and theorizing, while indebted to Weber and Michels, has significantly extended and modified their findings. In this area of research it appears that we have indeed begun to witness a most rewarding trend of cumulation of findings and genuine continuity of theory.

Characteristics of Bureaucracy * (Weber)

Modern officialdom functions in the following specific manner:

I. There is the principle of fixed and official jurisdictional areas, which are generally ordered by rules, that is, by laws or administrative regulations

1. The regular activities required for the purposes of the bureaucratically governed structure are distributed in a fixed way as official duties.

2. The authority to give the commands required for the discharge of these duties is distributed in a stable way and is strictly delimited by rules concerning the coercive means, physical, sacerdotal, or otherwise, which may be placed at the disposal of officials.

3. Methodical provision is made for the regular and continuous fulfilment of these duties and for the execution of the corresponding rights; only persons who have the generally regulated qualifications to serve are employed.

In public and lawful government these three elements constitute 'bureaucratic authority.' In private economic domination, they constitute bureaucratic 'management.' Bureaucracy, thus understood, is fully developed in political and ecclesiastical communities only in the modern state, and, in the private economy, only in the most advanced institutions of capitalism. Permanent and public office authority, with fixed jurisdiction, is not the historical rule but rather the exception. This is so even in large political structures such as those of the ancient Orient, the Germanic and Mongolian empires of conquest, or of many feudal structures of state. In all these cases, the ruler executes the most important measures through personal trustees, table-companions, or court-servants. Their commissions and authority are not precisely delimited and are temporarily called into being for each case.

II. The principles of office hierarchy and of levels of graded authority mean a firmly ordered system of super- and subordination in which there is a supervision of the lower offices by the higher ones. Such a system offers the governed the possibility of appealing the decision of a lower office to its higher authority, in a definitely regulated manner. With the full development of the bureaucratic type, the office hierarchy is monocratically organized. The principle of hierarchical office authority is found in all bureaucratic structures: in state and ecclesiastical structures as well as in large party organizations and private enterprises. It does not matter for the character of bureaucracy whether its authority is called 'private' or 'public.'

* From From Max Weber: Essays in Sociology, pp. 196–204, edited by H. H. Gerth and C. Wright Mills, copyright 1946, by Oxford University Press. Reprinted by permission.

When the principle of jurisdictional 'competency' is fully carried through, hierarchical subordination—at least in public office—does not mean that the 'higher' authority is simply authorized to take over the business of the 'lower.' Indeed, the opposite is the rule. Once established and having fulfilled its task, an office tends to continue in existence and be held by another incumbent.

III. The management of the modern office is based upon written documents ('the files'), which are preserved in their original or draught form. There is, therefore, a staff of subaltern officials and scribes of all sorts. The body of officials actively engaged in a 'public' office, along with the respective apparatus of material implements and the files, make up a 'bureau.' In private enterprise, 'the bureau' is often called 'the office.'

In principle, the modern organization of the civil service separates the bureau from the private domicile of the official, and, in general, bureaucracy segregates official activity as something distinct from the sphere of private life. Public monies and equipment are divorced from the private property of the official. This condition is everywhere the product of a long development. Nowadays, it is found in public as well as in private enterprises; in the latter, the principle extends even to the leading entrepreneur. In principle, the executive office is separated from the household, business from private correspondence, and business assets from private fortunes. The more consistently the modern type of business management has been carried through the more are these separations the case. The beginnings of this process are to be found as early as the Middle Ages.

It is the peculiarity of the modern entrepreneur that he conducts himself as the 'first official' of his enterprise, in the very same way in which the ruler of a specifically modern bureaucratic state spoke of himself as 'the first servant' of the state.[1] The idea that the bureau activities of the state are intrinsically different in character from the management of private economic offices is a continental European notion and, by way of contrast, is totally foreign to the American way.

IV. Office management, at least all specialized office management—and such management is distinctly modern—usually presupposes thorough and expert training. This increasingly holds for the modern executive and employee of private enterprises, in the same manner as it holds for the state official.

V. When the office is fully developed, official activity demands the full working capacity of the official, irrespective of the fact that his obligatory time in the bureau may be firmly delimited. In the normal case, this is only the product of a long development, in the public as well as in the private office. Formerly, in all cases, the normal state of affairs was reversed: official business was discharged as a secondary activity.

VI. The management of the office follows general rules, which are more or less stable, more or less exhaustive, and which can be learned. Knowledge of these rules represents a special technical learning which the officials possess. It involves jurisprudence, or administrative or business management.

The reduction of modern office management to rules is deeply embedded in its very nature. The theory of modern public administration, for instance, assumes that the authority to order certain matters by decree—which has been legally granted to public authorities—does not entitle the bureau to regulate the matter by commands given for each case, but only to regulate the matter abstractly. This stands in extreme contrast to the regulation of all relationships through individual privileges and bestowals of favor, which is absolutely dominant in patrimonialism, at least in so far as such relationships are not fixed by sacred tradition.

THE POSITION OF THE OFFICIAL

All this results in the following for the internal and external position of the official:

I. Office holding is a 'vocation.' This is shown, first, in the requirement of a firmly prescribed course of training, which demands the entire capacity for work for a long period of time, and in the generally prescribed and special examinations which are prerequisites of employment. Furthermore, the position of the official is in the nature of a duty. This determines the internal structure of his relations, in the following manner: Legally and actually, office holding is not considered a source to be exploited for rents or emoluments, as was normally the case during the Middle Ages and frequently up to the threshold of recent times. Nor is office holding considered a usual exchange of services for equivalents, as is the case with free labor contracts. Entrance into an office, including one in the private economy, is considered an acceptance of a specific obligation of faithful management in return for a secure existence. It is decisive for the specific nature of modern loyalty to an office that, in the pure type, it does not establish a relationship to a *person,* like the vassal's or disciple's faith in feudal or in patrimonial relations of authority. Modern loyalty is devoted to impersonal and functional purposes. Behind the functional purposes, of course, 'ideas of culture-values' usually stand. These are *ersatz* for the earthly or supra-mundane personal master: ideas such as 'state,' 'church,' 'community,' 'party,' or 'enterprise' are thought of as being realized in a community; they provide an ideological halo for the master.

The political official—at least in the fully developed modern state—is not considered the personal servant of a ruler. Today, the bishop, the priest, and the preacher are in fact no longer, as in early Christian times, holders of purely personal charisma. The supra-mundane and sacred values which they offer are given to everybody who seems to be worthy of them and who asks for them. In former times, such leaders acted upon the personal command of their master; in principle, they were responsible only to him. Nowadays, in spite of the partial survival of the old theory, such religious leaders are officials in the service of a functional purpose, which in the present-day 'church' has become routinized and, in turn, ideologically hallowed.

II. The personal position of the official is patterned in the following way:

1. Whether he is in a private office or a public bureau, the modern official always strives and usually enjoys a distinct *social esteem* as compared with the governed. His social position is guaranteed by the prescriptive rules of rank order and, for the political official, by special definitions of the criminal code against 'insults of officials' and 'contempt' of state and church authorities.

The actual social position of the official is normally highest where, as in old civilized countries, the following conditions prevail: a strong demand for administration by trained experts; a strong and stable social differentiation, where the official predominantly derives from socially and economically privileged strata because of the social distribution of power; or where the costliness of the required training and status conventions are binding upon him. The possession of educational certificates—to be discussed elsewhere [2]— are usually linked with qualification for office. Naturally, such certificates or patents enhance the 'status element' in the social position of the official. For the rest this status factor in individual cases is explicitly and impassively acknowledged; for example, in the prescription that the acceptance or rejection of an aspirant to an official career depends upon the consent ('election') of the members of the official body. This is the case in the German army with the officer corps. Similar phenomena, which promote this guild-like closure of officialdom, are typically found in patrimonial and, particularly, in prebendal officialdoms of the past. The desire to resurrect such phenomena in changed forms is by no means infrequent among modern bureaucrats. For instance, they have played a role among the demands of the quite proletarian and expert officials (the *tretyj* element) during the Russian revolution.

Usually the social esteem of the officials as such is especially low where the demand for expert administration and the dominance of status conventions are weak. This is especially the case in the United States; it is often the case in new settlements by virtue of their wide fields for profitmaking and the great instability of their social stratification.

2. The pure type of bureaucratic official is *appointed* by a superior authority. An official elected by the governed is not a purely bureaucratic figure. Of course, the formal existence of an election does not by itself mean that no appointment hides behind the election—in the state, especially, appointment by party chiefs. Whether or not this is the case does not depend upon legal statutes but upon the way in which the party mechanism functions. Once firmly organized, the parties can turn a formally free election into the mere acclamation of a candidate designated by the party chief. As a rule, however, a formally free election is turned into a fight, conducted according to definite rules, for votes in favor of one of two designated candidates.

In all circumstances, the designation of officials by means of an election among the governed modifies the strictness of hierarchical subordination. In principle, an official who is so elected has an autonomous position opposite the superordinate official. The elected official does not derive his position 'from above' but 'from below,' or at least not from a superior authority of the official hierarchy but from powerful party men ('bosses'), who also determine his further career. The career of the elected official is not, or at least not primarily, dependent upon his chief in the administration. The official who is not elected but appointed by a chief normally functions more exactly, from a technical point of view, because, all other circumstances being equal, it is more likely that purely functional points of consideration and qualities will determine his selection and career. As laymen, the governed can become acquainted with the extent to which a candidate is expertly qualified for office only in terms of experience, and hence only after his service. Moreover, in every sort of selection of officials by election, parties quite naturally give decisive weight not to expert considerations but to the services a follower renders to the party boss. This holds for all kinds of procurement of officials by elections, for the designation of formally free, elected officials by party bosses when they determine the slate of candidates, or the free appointment by a chief who has himself been elected. The contrast, however, is relative: substantially similar conditions hold where legitimate monarchs and their subordinates appoint officials, except that the influence of the followings are then less controllable.

Where the demand for administration by trained experts is considerable, and the party followings have to recognize an intellectually developed, educated, and freely moving 'public opinion,' the use of unqualified officials falls back upon the party in power at the next election. Naturally, this is more likely to happen when the officials are appointed by the chief. The demand for a trained administration now exists in the United States, but in the large cities, where immigrant votes are 'corraled,' there is, of course, no educated public opinion. Therefore, popular elections of the administrative chief and also of his subordinate officials usually endanger the expert qualification of the official as well as the precise functioning of the bureaucratic mechanism. It also weakens the dependence of the officials upon the hierarchy. This holds at least for the large administrative bodies that are difficult to supervise. The superior qualification and integrity of federal judges, appointed by the President, as over against elected judges in the United States is well known, although both types of officials have been selected primarily in terms of party considerations. The great changes in American metropolitan administrations demanded by reformers have proceeded essentially from elected mayors working with an apparatus of officials who were appointed by them. These reforms have thus come about in a 'Caesarist' fashion. Viewed technically, as an organized form of authority, the efficiency of 'Caesarism,' which often grows out of democracy, rests in general upon the position of the 'Caesar' as a free trustee of the masses (of the army or of the citizenry), who is unfettered by tradition. The 'Caesar' is thus the unrestrained master of a body of highly qualified military officers and officials whom he selects freely and personally without regard to tradition or to any other considerations. This 'rule of the personal genius,' however, stands in contradiction to the formally 'democratic' principle of a universally elected officialdom.

3. Normally, the position of the official is held for life, at least in public bureaucracies; and this is increasingly the case for all similar structures. As a factual rule, *tenure for life* is presupposed, even where the giving of notice or periodic reappointment occurs. In contrast to the worker in a private enterprise, the official normally holds tenure. Legal or actual life-tenure, however, is not recognized as the official's right to the possession of office, as was the case with many structures of authority in the past. Where legal guarantees against arbitrary dismissal or transfer are developed, they merely serve to guarantee a strictly objective discharge of specific office duties free from all personal considerations. In Germany, this is the case for all juridical and, increasingly, for all administrative officials.

Within the bureaucracy, therefore, the measure of 'independence,' legally guaranteed by tenure, is not always a source of increased status for the official whose position is thus secured. Indeed, often the reverse holds, especially in old cultures and communities that are highly differentiated. In such communities, the stricter the subordination under the arbitrary rule of the master, the more it guarantees the maintenance of the conventional seigneurial style of living for the official. Because of the very absence of these legal guarantees of tenure, the conventional esteem for the official may rise in the same way as, during the Middle Ages, the esteem of the nobility of office [3] rose at the expense of esteem for the freemen and as the king's judge surpassed that of the people's judge. In Germany, the military officer or the administrative official can be removed from office at any time, or at least far more readily than the 'independent judge,' who never pays with loss of his office for even the grossest offense against the 'code of honor' or against social conventions of the salon. For this very reason, if other things are equal, in the eyes of the master stratum the judge is considered less qualified for social intercourse than are officers and administrative officials, whose greater dependence on the master is a greater guarantee of their conformity with status conventions. Of course, the average official strives for a civil-service law, which would materially secure his old age and provide increased guarantees against his arbitrary removal from office. This striving, however, has its limits. A very strong development of the 'right to the office' naturally makes it more difficult to staff them with regard to technical efficiency, for such a development decreases the career-opportunities of ambitious candidates for office. This makes for the fact that officials, on the whole, do not feel their dependency upon those at the top. This lack of a feeling of dependency, however, rests primarily upon the inclination to depend upon one's equals rather than upon the socially inferior and governed strata. The present conservative movement among the Badenia clergy, occasioned by the anxiety of a presumably threatening separation of church and state, has been expressly determined by the desire not to be turned 'from a master into a servant of the parish.' [4]

4. The official receives the regular *pecuniary* compensation of a normally fixed *salary* and the old age security provided by a pension. The salary is not measured like a wage in terms of work done, but according to 'status,' that is, according to the length of service. The relatively great security of the official's income, as well as the rewards of social esteem, make the office a sought-after position, especially in countries which no longer provide opportunities for colonial profits. In such countries, this situation permits relatively low salaries for officials.

5. The official is set for a '*career*' within the hierarchical order of the public service. He moves from the lower, less important, and lower paid to the higher positions. The average official naturally desires a mechanical

fixing of the conditions of promotion: if not of the offices, at least of the salary levels. He wants these conditions fixed in terms of 'seniority,' or possibly according to grades achieved in a developed system of expert examinations. Here and there, such examinations actually form a character *indelebilis* of the official and have lifelong effects on his career. To this is joined the desire to qualify the right to office and the increasing tendency toward status group closure and economic security. All of this makes for a tendency to consider the offices as 'prebends' of those who are qualified by educational certificates. The necessity of taking general personal and intellectual qualifications into consideration, irrespective of the often subaltern character of the educational certificate, has led to a condition in which the highest political offices, especially the positions of 'ministers,' are principally filled without reference to such certificates.

REFERENCES

1. Frederick II of Prussia.
2. Cf. *Wirtschaft und Gesellschaft,* pp. 73 ff. and part II. (German Editor.)
3. 'Ministerialen.'
4. Written before 1914. (German editor's note.)

Some Consequences of Bureaucratization * (*Weber*)

Imagine the consequences of that comprehensive bureaucratization and rationalization which already to-day we see approaching. Already now, throughout private enterprise in wholesale manufacture, as well as in all other economic enterprises run on modern lines, *Rechenhaftigkeit,* rational calculation, is manifest at every stage. By it, the performance of each individual worker is mathematically measured, each man becomes a little cog in the machine and, aware of this, his one preoccupation is whether he can become a bigger cog. Take as an extreme example the authoritative power of the State or of the municipality in a monarchical constitution: it is strikingly reminiscent of the ancient kingdom of Egypt, in which the system of the 'minor official' prevailed at all levels. To this day there has never existed a bureaucracy which could compare with that of Egypt. This is known to everyone who knows the social history of ancient times; and it is equally apparent that to-day we are proceeding towards an evolution which resembles that system in every detail, except that it is built on other foundations, on technically more perfect, more rationalized, and therefore much more

* Abridged from Max Weber, *Gesammelte Aufsaetze zur Soziologie und Sozialpolitik,* pp. 412 ff. English translation in J. P. Mayer, *Max Weber and German Politics,* 2nd ed., pp. 126–128. Copyright, 1956, by Faber and Faber, Ltd. Reprinted by permission.

mechanized foundations. The problem which besets us now is not: how can this evolution be changed?—for that is impossible, but: what will come of it? We willingly admit that there are honourable and talented men at the top of our administration; that in spite of all the exceptions such people have opportunities to rise in the official hierarchy, just as the universities, for instance, claim that, in spite of all the exceptions, they constitute a chance of selection for talent. But horrible as the thought is that the world may one day be peopled with professors (laughter)—we would retire on to a desert island if such a thing were to happen (laughter)—it is still more horrible to think that the world could one day be filled with nothing but those little cogs, little men clinging to little jobs and striving towards bigger ones—a state of affairs which is to be seen once more, as in the Egyptian records, playing an ever-increasing part in the spirit of our present administrative system, and specially of its offspring, the students. This passion for bureaucracy, as we have heard it expressed here, is enough to drive one to despair. It is as if in politics the spectre of timidity—which has in any case always been rather a good standby for the German—were to stand alone at the helm; as if we were deliberately to become men who need 'order' and nothing but order, who become nervous and cowardly if for one moment this order wavers, and helpless if they are torn away from their total incorporation in it. That the world should know no men but these: it is in such an evolution that we are already caught up, and the great question is therefore not how we can promote and hasten it, but what can we oppose to this machinery in order to keep a portion of mankind free from this parcelling-out of the soul, from this supreme mastery of the bureaucratic way of life. The answer to this question to-day clearly does not lie here.

Bureaucracy and Political Parties * (*Michels*)

The organization of the state needs a numerous and complicated bureaucracy. This is an important factor in the complex of forces of which the politically dominant classes avail themselves to secure their dominion and to enable themselves to keep their hands upon the rudder.

The instinct of self-preservation leads the modern state to assemble and to attach to itself the greatest possible number of interests. This need of the organism of the state increases *pari passu* with an increase among the multitude, of the conviction that the contemporary social order is defective and even irrational—in a word, with the increase of what the authorities are

* Reprinted from *Political Parties* by Robert Michels, pp. 185–188, with permission of the publisher, The Free Press, Glencoe, Ill. Copyright, 1915, by The Free Press, A Corporation.

accustomed to term discontent. The state best fulfils the need for securing a large number of defenders by constituting a numerous caste of officials, of persons directly dependent upon the state. This tendency is powerfully reinforced by the tendencies of modern political economy. On the one hand, from the side of the state, there is an enormous supply of official positions. On the other hand, among the citizens, there is an even more extensive demand. This demand is stimulated by the ever-increasing precariousness in the position of the middle classes (the smaller manufacturers and traders, independent artisans, farmers, etc.) since there have come into existence expropriative capitalism on the grand scale, on the one hand, and the organized working classes on the other—for both these movements, whether they wish it or not, combine to injure the middle classes. All those whose material existence is thus threatened by modern economic developments endeavour to find safe situations for their sons, to secure for these a social position which shall shelter them from the play of economic forces. Employment under the state, with the important right to a pension which attaches to such employment, seems created expressly for their needs. The immeasurable demand for situations which results from these conditions, a demand which is always greater than the supply, creates the so-called "intellectual proletariat." The numbers of this body are subject to great fluctuations. From time to time the state, embarrassed by the increasing demand for positions in its service, is forced to open the sluices of its bureaucratic canals in order to admit thousands of new postulants and thus to transform these from dangerous adversaries into zealous defenders and partisans. There are two classes of intellectuals. One consists of those who have succeeded in securing a post at the manger of the state, whilst the other consists of those who, as Scipio Sighele puts it, have assaulted the fortress without being able to force their way in.[1] The former may be compared to an army of slaves who are always ready, in part from class egoism, in part for personal motives (the fear of losing their own situations), to undertake the defence of the state which provides them with bread. They do this whatever may be the question concerning which the state has been attacked and must therefore be regarded as the most faithful of its supporters. The latter, on the other hand, are sworn enemies of the state. They are those eternally restless spirits who lead the bourgeois opposition and in part also assume the leadership of the revolutionary parties of the proletariat. It is true that the state bureaucracy does not in general expand as rapidly as do the discontented elements of the middle class. None the less, the bureaucracy continually increases. It comes to assume the form of an endless screw. It grows ever less and less compatible with the general welfare. And yet this bureaucratic machinery remains essential. Through it alone can be satisfied the claim of the educated members of the population for secure positions. It is further a means of self-defence for the state. As the late Amilcare Puviani of the University of Perugia, the political economist to whom we are indebted for an important work upon the legend of the state, expresses it, the mechanism of bureaucracy is the outcome of a protective reaction of a right of property whose legal basis is weak, and is an antidote to the awakening of the public conscience.[2]

The political party possesses many of these traits in common with the state. Thus the party in which the circle of the *élite* is unduly restricted, or in which, in other words, the oligarchy is composed of too small a number of individuals, runs the risk of being swept away by the masses in a moment of democratic effervescence. Hence the modern party, like the modern state, endeavors to give to its own organization the widest possible base, and to attach to itself in financial bonds the largest possible number of individuals.[3] Thus arises the need for a strong bureaucracy and these tendencies are reinforced by the increase in the tasks [4] imposed by modern organization.[5]

As the party bureaucracy increases, two elements which constitute the essential pillars of every socialist conception undergo an inevitable weakening: an understanding of the wider and more ideal cultural aims of socialism, and an understanding of the international multiplicity of its manifestations. Mechanism becomes an end in itself. The capacity for an accurate grasp of the peculiarities and the conditions of existence of the labour movement in other countries diminishes in proportion as the individual national organizations are fully developed. This is plain from a study of the mutual international criticisms of the socialist press. In the days of the so-called "socialism of the émigrés," the socialists devoted themselves to an elevated policy of principles, inspired by the classical criteria of internationalism. Almost every one of them was, if the term may be used, a specialist in this more general and comprehensive domain. The whole course of their lives, the brisk exchange of ideas on unoccupied evenings, the continued rubbing of shoulders between men of the most different tongues, the enforced isolation from the bourgeois world of their respective countries, and the utter impossibility of any "practical" action, all contributed to this result. But in proportion as, in their own country, paths of activity were opened for the socialists, at first for agitation and soon afterwards for positive and constructive work, the more did a recognition of the demands of the everyday life of the party divert their attention from immortal principles. Their vision gained in precision but lost in extent. The more cotton-spinners, boot and shoe operatives, or brushmakers the labour leader could gain each month for his union, the better versed he was in the tedious subtleties of insurance against accident and illness, the greater the industry he could display in the specialized questions of factory inspection and of arbitration in trade disputes, the better acquainted he might be with the system of checking the amount of individual purchases in co-operative stores and with the methods for the control of the consumption of municipal gas, the more difficult was it for him to retain a general interest in the labour movement, even in the narrowest sense of this term. As the outcome of inevitable psychophysiological laws, he could find little time and was likely to have little inclination for the study of the great problems of the philosophy of history, and all the more falsified consequently would become his judgment of international questions. At the same time he would incline more and more to regard every one as an "incompetent," an "outsider," an "unprofessional," who might wish to judge questions from some higher outlook than the purely technical; he would incline to deny the good sense and even the socialism of all who might desire to fight upon another ground and by other means than those familiar to him within his narrow sphere as a specialist. This tendency towards an exclusive and all-absorbing specialization, towards the renunciation of all far-reaching outlooks, is a general characteristic of modern evolution. With the continuous increase in the acquirements of scientific research, the polyhistor is becoming extinct. His place is taken by the writer of monographs. The universal zoologist no longer exists, and we have instead ornithologists and entomologists; and indeed the last become further subdivided into lepidopterists, coleopterists, myrmecologists.

REFERENCES

1. Scipio Sighele, *L'Intelligenza della Folla,* Bocca, Turin, 1903, p. 160.
2. Amilcare Puviani, *Teoria della Illusione finanziaria,* R. Sandron, Milan-Naples-Palermo, 1903, pp. 258 et seq.
3. The governing body of Tammany in New York consists of four hundred persons. The influence of this political association is concentrated in a sub-commitee of thirty persons, the so-called Organization Committee (Ostrogorsky, *La Démocratie etc.,* ed. cit., vol. ii, p. 199).
4. Cf. pp. 33 et seq.
5. Inquiries made by Lask have shown how deeply rooted in the psychology of the workers is the desire to enter the class of those who receive pensions. A very large number of proletarians, when asked what they wished to do with their sons, replied: "To find them employment which would give right to a pension." Doubtless this longing is the outcome of the serious lack of stability characteristic of the social and economic conditions of the workers (Georg v. Schulze-Gaevernitz, *Nochmals: "Marx oder Kant?,"* "Archiv für Sozialwiss.," xxx, fasc. 2, p. 520).

An Approach to a Theory of Bureaucracy * (*Selznick*)

This analysis will consider bureaucracy as a special case of the general theory of purposive organization. Recent sociological research has made explicit several conceptions which must serve as essential background for any analysis such as that to follow. Based upon that research, three hypotheses may be introduced here:

A. *Every organization creates an informal structure.*

B. *In every organization, the goals of the organization are modified (abandoned, deflected, or elaborated) by processes within it.*

C. *The process of modification is effected through the informal structure.*

Three recent sociological studies have elucidated these hypotheses.

(1) In an intensive examination of a shop department, Roethlisberger and Dickson found clear evidences of an informal structure. This structure consisted of a set of procedures (binging, sarcasm, ridicule) by means of which control over members of the group was exercised, the formation of cliques which functioned as instruments of control, and the establishment of informal leadership. "The men had elaborated, spontaneously and quite unconsciously, an intricate social organization around their collective beliefs and sentiments." [1]

The informal structure of the worker group grew up out of the day-to-day practices of the men as they groped for ways of taking care of their own felt needs. There was no series of conscious acts by which these procedures were instituted, but they were no less binding on that account. These needs largely arose from the way in which the men defined their situation within the organization. The informal organization served a triple *function*: (a) it served to control the behavior of the members of the worker group; (b) within the context of the larger organization (the plant), it was an attempt on the part of the particular group to control the conditions of its existence; (c) it acted as a mechanism for the expression of personal relationships for which the formal organization did not provide. Thus the informal structure provided those avenues of aggression, solidarity, and prestige-construction required by individual members.

The *consequence* of the activity of the men through the informal organization was a deleterious effect upon the professed goal of the organization as a whole: it resulted in the restriction of output. In asserting its control over the conditions of the job, the group wanted above all to protect itself from outside interference, exhibiting a strong resistance to change.

Thus the facts in this empirical investigation illustrate the hypotheses noted

* By Philip Selznick, reprinted from *American Sociological Review*, Vol. VIII, 1943, No. 1, pp. 47–54, with permission of The American Sociological Society and the author.

above: the creation of an informal organization, the modification of the professed goal (maximum output), and the effectuation of this modification through the informal structure. In addition, three important characteristics of the informal structure were observed in the study: (a) it arises spontaneously; (b) the bases of the relationships are personal, involving factors of prestige, acceptance within the group, friendship ties, etc.; and (c) the relationships are *power* relationships, oriented toward techniques of *control*. These characteristics are general, and they are important for conceiving of the theory of bureaucratic behavior as a special case of the general theory of organization.

(2) C. I. Barnard, in his theoretical analysis of organizational structure, concerned mainly with the problems of the executive discusses explicitly the character and function of informal structures which arise out of the attempts to solve those problems. By informal structures he means "the aggregate of the personal contacts and interactions and the associated groupings of people" which do not have common or joint purposes, and which are, in fact, "indefinite and rather structureless." [2] He says, further, that "though common or joint purposes are excluded by definition, common or joint results of an important character nevertheless come from such organization." [3]

Barnard lists three functions of informal structures as they operate in formal organizations: (a) as a means of communication, establishing norms of conduct between superordinates and subordinates; (b) "maintenance of cohesiveness in formal organizations through regulating the willingness to serve and the stability of objective authority"; (c) "the maintenance of the feeling of personal integrity, of self-respect, of independent choice." [4] The last mentioned function means simply that the individual's "integrity" is protected by the *appearance* of choice, at the same time that subtle group pressures guarantee control of his actions. Barnard's view of the functions of the informal structure is primarily in terms of the needs of the executive (control through friendship ties, personal authority, a "grape-vine" system, etc.), but it is clear that his analysis agrees with the hypothesis that the informal organization is oriented essentially toward the techniques of control. In the Roethlisberger and Dickson study, it was the worker group which was attempting to control the conditions of its existence; in this case, it is the executive who is doing the same thing.

(3) A discussion by Waller and Henderson [5] based on the study of institutions of segregative care, gives further evidence for the theses presented here. The general hypotheses about organizational processes are confirmed by the examination of such structures as private schools, transient camps, prisons, flophouses, reformatories and military organizations. The authors set the problem in this way:

> Each of our institutions has an idea or purpose—most of them have several purposes more or less compatible with one another—and this idea or purpose gives rise to an institutional structure. The institutional structure consists of a system of organized groups. The interaction of these elements is a principal clue to the understanding of institutions of segregative care. Without a structure, the purpose of an institution would be an empty form of words, and yet the process of translating the purpose into an institutional structure always somehow deflects and distorts it.

It is thus the iron necessity of an organizational structure for the achievement of group goals which creates the paradox to which we have referred. The ideals of those who construct the organization are one thing; the "facts of life" operating independently of and often against those ideals are something else again.

Professed and Operational Goals. Running an organization, as a specialized and essential activity, generates problems which have no necessary (and often an opposed) relationship to the professed or "original" goals of the organization. The day-to-day behavior of the group becomes centered around specific problems and proximate goals which have primarily an internal relevance. Then, since these activities come to consume an increasing proportion of the time and thoughts of the participants, they are—from the point of view of actual behavior—*substituted* for the professed goals.

The day-to-day activity of men is ordered by those specific problems which have a direct relevance to the materials with which they have to deal. "Ultimate" issues and highly abstract ideas which do not specify any concrete behavior have therefore little direct influence on the bulk of human activities. (The general ideas, of course, may influence action by setting its context and, often, defining its limits.) This is true not because men are evil or unintelligent, but because the "ultimate" formulations are not *helpful* in the constant effort to achieve that series of equilibria which represent behavioral solutions to the specific problems which day-to-day living poses. Besides those professed goals which do not specify any concrete behavior, which are analogous to non-procedural formulations in science, there are other professed goals which require actions which conflict with what must be done in the daily business of running an organization. In that conflict the professed goals will tend to go down in defeat, usually through the process of being extensively ignored. This phenomenon may be introduced as a fourth hypothesis in the general theory of organization:

> D. *The actual procedures of every organization tend to be molded by action toward those goals which provide operationally relevant solutions for the daily problems of the organization as such.*

This hypothesis does not deny that operational goals may be, and very often are, specified in the formulation of the professed goals of the organization. But in any case it is the operational goals which must be looked to for an understanding of the conduct of the organization.

What is meant by the "daily problems"? Consider a boys' reformatory.[6] The institution is organized on the basis of progressive ideals as specified in social work literature. But the processes of constructing and operating the organization create problems and demands, effective daily, to which the general ideals give no adequate answer. Since, however, the existence of the organization depends upon such answers, and since the way of life of everyone concerned depends on the continued existence of the organization, a set of procedural rules is worked out which *is helpful* in solving these problems. These rules are, in practice, substituted for the professed ideals. "The social work ideals are fine, but how can we do otherwise than use techniques of discipline, regimentation, spying, etc.?" This is the cry of those who must meet daily crises in the institutions of segregative care. "Holiday speech," "lip-service," "we've got to be practical" are expressions which confirm from ordinary experience, repeated over and over again, the validity of this hypothesis.

The "Tragedy of Organization." Beyond such specific sociological investigations as have been mentioned, it is necessary only to point to the fact of organizational frustration as a persistent characteristic of the age of relative democracy. The tragedy of organization is evident precisely in the fact and in the consequences of increased participation in associational endeavour.

There have been many critics of democracy, but relatively few have ventured to support the sweeping judgment of Robert Michels that democracy leads inevitably to oligarchy.[7] It must be admitted, however, that in this discussion the thesis of Michels finds much comfort. For this theory (taken in its sociological rather than in it psychological context) stands or falls, in terms of its lasting significance, with the possibility of establishing that there are processes inherent in and internal to organization as such which tend to frustrate action toward professed goals. The burden of research, on the plane of organizations in general, indicates quite clearly that such is the case.

Bearing in mind the hypotheses stated above, and the specified character of the informal structure (spontaneity, network of personal relationships, orientation toward control), we may turn to the problem of bureaucracy itself.

The Term Bureaucracy. If the ideas developed above have been clear, it will be readily evident that the approach which identifies bureaucracy with any administrative system based on professionalization and on hierarchical subordination is not accepted here. Such a point of view is maintained in the work of Friedrich and Cole [8] on the Swiss Civil Service; the interest of the authors is clearly in the *formal* structure of the administrative apparatus as a mechanism of, in this case, popular government. The structure is related to the asserted, professed purposes of the administration; and *bureaucratiza-*

tion is conceived of as the tendency toward the complete achievement of the formal system.

The same point of view is evident in Max Weber's long and careful essay on bureaucracy—the outstanding work in the literature we have at present: [9] The main burden of Weber's work is devoted to an examination of the roots, conditions, and dominant features of the formal organization of an administrative hierarchy. The development of this structure with its dominant features of authoritative jurisdiction, hierarchy of office, specialized training and general abstract rules of procedure, is a process of the *depersonalization* of administrative relationships. Weber's main interest was in the development of rational bureaucratic behaviour as a break from the ties of seignorial leadership set up under the feudal system. The development of centralized hierarchical administration did in fact involve a tendency to vitiate that particular kind of personal influence. But what Weber seems to have only partly understood is that the dynamics of the administrative apparatus itself created new personal influences—those of the administrators themselves seeking their own ends and engaging, as newly powerful participants, in power relationships. That Weber did not overlook the facts of the case is clear from his final pages, in which he discusses the power-role of the bureaucracy. Although recognizing them, he seems to have neglected their theoretical importance.

The use of the term bureaucracy, not as designating an administrative organization as such, but rather some special characteristics of that organization, is common in the literature. Thus Laski's [10] definition of bureaucracy emphasizes the *de facto* power relationships and their consequences. Again, although Dimock and Hyde [11] *define* bureaucracy in terms of the subdivision of jurisdiction, hierarchy and professionalization of personnel, their *use* of the term indicates an interest in such phenomena as "organizational resistance," with the formal structure operating as simply the environment of the bureaucratic tendencies.

The idea of bureaucracy proposed here is consonant although not identical with the usage of Laski and Dimock-Hyde. It will be considered in terms of the hypotheses suggested above. "Bureaucratic behaviour" will designate that behavior of *agents in social action* which:

(1) tends to create the organization-paradox, that is, the modification of the professed aims of the organization—aims toward which the agent is formally supposed to strive; this process obtains

(2) through such behavior patterns in the informal organization as are centered primarily around the ties of influence among the functionaries,

and as tend to concentrate the locus of power in the hands of the officials; and

(3) through such patterns as develop through the displacement of the functionaries' motives on the habit level, e.g., routinization.

This does not mean that every situation in which the organization-paradox is found is a bureaucratic one. Bureaucracy is concerned with the behavior of officials, while the action of, say, worker groups, may also lead to deflection of an organization. It is clear from this definition that the emphasis is on the *informal* structure as the mechanism or manifestation of bureaucratic patterns; it does not follow, of course, that those patterns are uninfluenced by the character of the formal organization.

A final point is the question of size. For the most part, the existence of bureaucracy in any sense is associated with large organizations. For Dimock and Hyde, for example, "The broadest structural cause of bureaucracy, whether in business or in government, is the tremendous size of the organization." [12] Indeed, there seems to be little doubt that the factor of sheer size is a very important element in concrete bureaucratic structures. However, because of the patterns exhibited in the behavior of agents in small organized groups and because of the implications for greater generality, the formulation used here does not make the factor of size crucial for the existence of bureaucratic behavior patterns.

Bureaucratization: A General Formulation. A brief analytical formula stating the general character of the process of bureaucratization may here be introduced:

(1) Co-operative effort, under the conditions of increasing number and complexity of functions, requires the *delegation of functions*. Thus action which seeks more than limited, individual results becomes *action through agents*. It is the activity of officials acting as agents with which the discussion of bureaucracy is concerned.

(2) The use of intermediaries creates a tendency toward a *bifurcation of interest* between the initiator of the action and the agent employed. This is due to the creation of two sets of problems: for the initiator, the achievement of the goal which spurred him to action, and for the intermediary, problems which are concerned chiefly with his social position as agent. The character of the agent's new values are such as to generate actions whose objective consequences undermine the professed aims of the organization. This conflict need not be between the employer as a person or a group and the agent, for the latter may be able to manipulate the ideas of the former, but between the actual course of the organization and those aims formally asserted, whether the employer recognizes the conflict or not.

(3) This bifurcation of interest makes dominant, for initiator and agent alike, the issue of *control*. What is at stake for each is the control of the conditions (the organizational mechanism) which each group will want to manipulate (not necessarily consciously) toward solving its special problems. In this struggle for control, an *informal structure* is created, based largely on relationships involving personal influences rather than formal rules.

(4) Because of the concentration of skill and the control of the organizational mechanism in the hands of the intermediaries, it becomes possible for the problems of the officials as such to become those which operate *for the organization*. The action of the officials tends to have an increasingly *internal relevance,* which may result in the deflection of the organization from its original path, which, however, usually remains as the formally professed aim of the organization.

The Bureaucratic Leader vs. the Rank and File Which Employs Him. Utilizing the scheme outlined above, let us examine a concrete type of bureaucratic situation, that which opposes a bureaucratic leader to the rank and file for which he is formally an agent. This situation tends to arise whenever a group of people organize for the attainment of shared objectives, with the additional aim of conducting their organization along democratic lines. Common examples are political parties, trade unions, a national political democracy.

(1) The need for the delegation of functions to a leader arises from the pressure of the wide range of problems, with which every individual must deal in his social existence, against strictly limited time and ability as well as against the social pressures which limit the exercise of certain functions to only some personality types and to members of only some classes. Even in the small group, individual differences in terms of aptitude for the various functions of organized effort (speaker, writer, record-keeper, etc.) play an important role in creating a leader-ranks relationship.

(2) Another bifurcation of problems arises from the fact that the problems and interests which impel men to organization are of a quite different kind from those which occur in running the organization. Whenever the ranks are needed to carry out the work of the organization, this gap becomes of real importance. Spurts in organizational effort on the part of the members occur when a direct connection can be seen between this organizational work and the reason for allegiance to the organization. Thus a political party can get "activity" when it carries on direct political propaganda—but the day-to-day task of keeping the party together, shaping its character, and strengthening its roots in various centers of power are tasks too far divorced from the original problems to stir most people from their ordinary way of living. In a political democracy, too, only heated contests over broad issues can really "bring out the vote," while the

day-to-day changes which in the long run are decisive remain uninfluenced by the mass.

(3) There is a hierarchy of values attached to *kinds of work*. Thus even equality between a worker in a unionized plant and the union organizer, in terms of money, does not alter the situation. It is the kind of work involved which is valued above the work of the ordinary members. Not only is there the fact of being well-known (the prestige of bare celebrity), but the facts of having certain powers, however small, of being associated with the incumbent leadership and of being acquainted with the "mysteries" of organization are important. There are always men who *want* to be officials.

(4) Positive valuation of the office as such raises new problems for the bureaucrat. His interest in the ultimate purpose of the organization, or in the "common good," becomes subordinate to his preoccupation with the problems involved in the *maintenance* of his post. This is not the same thing as the attempt to hold on to an official sinecure; for in this case, the post is primarily a source of social prestige and power. In many cases, the leaders could obtain better positions financially in another field. The leader of a women's club who, *because she has a following,* is treated with respect by political or other socially important forces, has more than a merely well-paid position. A. J. Muste, in his discussion of factional fights in trades unions [13] deals with the problem of why a leadership seeks to maintain its status. He points to reasons such as those already mentioned: the positions are pleasant, the return to the shop is humiliating, the official tends to become less efficient in his old trade. In addition there are motives connected with what they honestly consider to be the good of the union. They feel that they are better (more competent, have a better policy) than the opposition and that they have given more to the union and deserve to be left in power. This is often quite sincere and even *objectively a correct appraisal.* For our purposes that changes nothing: whether honest or corrupt, the tendency is for leaders, to use the same general procedures for the maintenance of their power. This ought not to be surprising: if the question of organizational dominance as such becomes directive in action, and the available means are limited, it is to be expected that the characters of their procedures would converge toward a common type, regardless of their ultimate reasons for desiring dominance.

(5) The delegation of functions introduces a relation of *dependence*. This is enforced by and perhaps directly dependent upon the *professionalization* of the work of the officialdom. To the extent that the necessary knowledge and skill are increased, the possibilities for replacement of the leadership are diminished. The existence of the organization itself becomes dependent on the continued functioning of the incumbent leadership. And so long as this is true, and the ranks still require the organization (or think they require it), their dependence upon the leaders become firmly established. This has nothing to do with the existence of formal (*e.g.*, constitutional) procedures for replacing leaders; these may continue to exist, but they are relatively harmless to the intrenched leaders (because functionless) so long as the ranks fear the consequences of using them.

(6) In order to be secure in his position, the leader-bureaucrat must strive

to make himself as independent as possible from the ranks. He must seek a power-base which is not controlled by them. He may attempt to derive his strength from an electorate more general than the party or union membership. Thus he will be able to follow independent policies by claiming that he has a responsibility to a broader base than the party ranks; and the ranks cannot do without his influence on outside groups. In a nation, an independent politician tends to cultivate those forces, such as a ruling economic group, which control the instruments which shape mass opinion as well as the electoral machinery, but which are not themselves controlled by the mass. It is a well-established political principle that a politician reacts most sensitively to those forces to which he owes the maintenance of his position; to the extent that forces can be developed apart from the electorate, he can—and often must, because he becomes dependent upon the new force—assert his independence from his formal constituency.

(7) The leader-bureaucrat must seek a personal base *within* a group itself: some mechanism directly dependent on, devoted to, or in alliance with him which can be used to maintain his organizational fences. A class base in a nation, a political faction in a trade union, paid gangsters, an elite guard, a secret police force, protégés and confidants—these are the weapons which he must use in order to be independent of the shifting sands of public favor.

(8) Because of this series of problems which the bureaucrat must face, his action in the name of the group, that is, that activity carried on to further its professed purposes, comes to have more and more a chiefly *internal relevance*. Actions are taken, policies adopted, with an eye more to the effect of the action or policy on the power-relations *inside* the organization than to the achievement of its professed goals. An organization drive in a trade union, party activity, legislative action, even the "activities program" of a club—all come to be oriented toward the problem of self-maintenance before possible onslaughts from the membership. Factors of "morale"—the condition wherein the ranks support the incumbent leadership—become dominant. *Bureaucratization is in a sense the process of transforming this set of procedures from a minor aspect of organization into a leading consideration in the behavior of the leadership.*

(9) Struggles within a group tend to become exclusively struggles *between leaders*. The masses (rank and file) play the role of manipulable weapons in the conflict between the controlling groups. The struggle for control between the initiators and the agent-officials is a very complex problem. The rank and file as a group (and in an important sense the leader, too, because he has to build an apparatus which creates new problems for him) cannot exercise *direct* control. Even a struggle against an incumbent leadership must be carried on through intermediaries. When a faction is formed, it being an organization too, the relations which operated for the organization as a whole come to be effective within the faction. The faction leaders assert their dominance over their groups and come to grips with one another as leaders whose strength is measured by the forces they can deploy. There are, however, three ways in which the influence of the rank and file is felt in a democratic organization: (a) the threat of spontaneous rank and file action and of a consequent internal revolt makes the construction of bureaucratic power-relationships necessary as a preventive

measure; (b) opposing faction leaders tend to champion the professed aim of the organization against the leaders who abandoned it, thus expressing, if temporarily, the desires of the rank and file; and (c) pressure groups, often spontaneous, which do not seek the seizure of the organizational reins, may influence the course of the leadership in directions desired by the mass. This last, however, has usually a limited measure of success precisely because no direct threat to the power of the leadership is offered. It is significant that tolerance of these groups is a function of the extent to which they are interested in "new leadership."

(10) The bureaucrats, like every other social type with a power-position to maintain, *construct an ideology* peculiar to their social position. The following general characteristics may be noted.

(a) By the identification of the particular administration with the group as a whole: playing upon the known desire of the ranks for the maintenance of the organization (national, state, party, union, etc.), the leadership attempts to spread the idea that any opposition immediately places the very existence of the organization in jeopardy. In defending itself from attack, it tends to identify its opposition with enemies of the group as such. Thus opponents are "disrupters," "foreign agents," "agents of an alien class," etc.

(b) An incumbent leadership tends to adopt the ideology of *centralization*, while those out of office call for *autonomy*. The opposition wants to retain its dominance over the local groups or factions which it controls and in general desires to avoid increasing the power of the central authority; the concentration of the control of the organizational mechanism (jobs, equipment, finances) is especially to be avoided, although the minority may not object to that within its own domain. For the ruling group, on the other hand, it is convenient that its power, *especially* over the organizational mechanism, be increased; it is also desirable that the central powers have the right to step into the affairs of a local group dominated by the opposition, in order to be able to take the offensive against it within the center of its own power. Each side attempts to defend its view by appealing to the professed aims of the group as a whole. In an action organization, the leadership will stress the military aspect and the importance of centralization for discipline action; the opposition will stress the importance of democracy. Although this rule is often broken, there is a tendency for *neither* side to discuss the matter on the basis of the power-motives involved, either in defense of their own view or in criticism of their opponents. This is not surprising, for that would create the danger of exposing the irrelevance of the struggle to the overt aims of the group, which would inevitably result in alienating some of the ranks from both. They therefore sometimes form a pact of silence on these matters, carrying the discussion forward on the level of general principles, at the same time waging furious battle in the shadow-land of informal maneuver.

(c) The leadership creates the ideology of the "collective submission to the collective will." [14] The obvious necessity for the delegation of certain functions is generalized, and democracy is interpreted sufficiently broadly to include the notion that the group has the democratic right to abdicate its power. The leader, it is proclaimed, represents the "general will," and every action that he takes is justifiable on the ground that he is merely exercising the desires of the collective. Thus the symbol of democracy itself becomes an ideological bulwark of autocracy within the group.

(d) An existing leadership tends to don the mantle of *conservatism,* with its many variant expressions justifying the maintenance of existing conditions. Since, having the power they are responsible for the exercise of the basic functions of the group or state, they must abandon slogans which are characteristic of irresponsible minorities. The latter need not be considered merely a term of opprobrium; the fact is that a minority *can* be irresponsible because its function as an opposition is radically different from its function as an administrative leadership, manning and responsible for the conduct of the chief posts of a party or a state. In small groups too, the function of the critic may change, and with that his ideas as well, when he is faced with the *new* problem of carrying out a program.[15] It is also important to note that a party can be deeply conservative in some aspects and revolutionary in others: thus in the Marxist parties, factors in conservative ideology such as dependence on tradition, depreciation of youth, and rigidity in organizational procedure may go hand in hand with a thoroughly revolutionary program with respect to *outside* political events. Needless to say, the internal character of such an organization plays an important rôle if that organization achieves any great social influence.

The above discussion emphasizes certain characteristic tendencies in the organization process. These tendencies are, however, analytical: they represent abstractions from concrete organizational patterns. To state these tendencies is merely to *set* a problem, for although they ascribe to organizations in general an *initial presumption of bureaucratic consequence,* it always remains to be determined to what degree the bureaucratic tendencies have become dominant. It may be said, indeed, that this is the way organizations will develop if they are permitted to follow the line of least resistance. That is what does happen, often enough. But in the real world of living organizations there is always the possibility of counter-pressure, of devising techniques for blocking the bureaucratic drift. The study of these techniques, which must be based on a clear understanding of the general nature of the problem involved, is one of the most pressing intellectual tasks of our time.

REFERENCES

1. F. J. Roethlisberger, and W. J. Dickson, *Management and the Worker,* Cambridge: Harvard University Press, 1941, p. 524.
2. C. I. Barnard, *The Functions of the Executive,* Cambridge: Harvard University Press, 1940, p. 115.
3. *Ibid.*
4. *Loc. cit.,* pp. 122–123.
5. W. Waller and W. Henderson, "Institutions of Segregative Care and the Organized Group" (unpublished manuscript), 1941.
6. From a description by Mr. F. E. Robin.
7. *Political Parties,* Hearst's International Library Co., New York, 1915.

8. C. J. Friedrich, and T. Cole, *Responsible Bureaucracy*, Cambridge: Harvard University Press, 1932, p. 84.
9. Max Weber, "Bürokratie," Ch. 7, Pt. 3 of *Wirtschaft und Gesellschaft*. Since translated in *The Theory of Economic and Social Organization*.
10. H. J. Laski, "Bureaucracy" in *Encyclopedia of the Social Sciences*, v. 3, p. 70.
11. M. E. Dimock, and H. Hyde, *Bureaucracy and Trusteeship in Large Corporations*, TNEC Monograph No. 11, p. 31.
12. *Ibid.*, p. 36.
13. "Factional Fights in Trade Unions," *American Labor Dynamics*, ed. by J. B. S. Hardman, New York, Harcourt, Brace, 1928.
14. See Robert Michels' excellent chapter on "Bonapartist Ideology" in his *Political Parties*.
15. For material on the metamorphosis of leaders see Michels, *op. cit.*, and J. B. S. Hardman, "Problems of a Labor Union Somewhere in the U.S.," pp. 163–6, in his *American Labor Dynamics*.

Bureaucratic Structure and Personality * (*Merton*)

A formal, rationally organized social structure involves clearly defined patterns of activity in which, ideally, every series of actions is functionally related to the purposes of the organization.[1] In such an organization there is integrated a series of offices, of hierarchized statuses, in which inhere a number of obligations and privileges closely defined by limited and specific rules. Each of these offices contains an area of imputed competence and responsibility. Authority, the power of control which derives from an acknowledged status, inheres in the office and not in the particular person who performs the official role. Official action ordinarily occurs within the framework of preexisting rules of the organization. The system of prescribed relations between the various offices involves a considerable degree of formality and clearly defined social distance between the occupants of these positions. Formality is manifested by means of a more or less complicated social ritual which symbolizes and supports the "pecking order" of the various offices. Such formality, which is integrated with the distribution of authority within the system, serves to minimize friction by largely restricting (official) contact to modes which are previously defined by the rules of the organization. Ready calculability of others' behavior and a stable set of mutual expectations is thus built up. Moreover, formality facilitates the interaction of the occupants of offices despite their (possibly hostile) private attitudes toward one another. In this way, the subordinate is protected from the arbitrary action of his superior, since the actions of both are constrained by a mutually recognized set of rules. Specific procedural devices foster objectivity and restrain the "quick passage of impulse into action." [2]

* Reprinted from *Social Theory and Social Structure* by Robert K. Merton, pp. 151–160, with permission of the publisher, The Free Press, Glencoe, Ill. Copyright, 1949, by The Free Press, A Corporation.

THE STRUCTURE OF BUREAUCRACY

The ideal type of such formal organization is bureaucracy and, in many respects, the classical analysis of bureaucracy is that by Max Weber.[3] As Weber indicates, bureaucracy involves a clear-cut division of integrated activities which are regarded as duties inherent in the office. A system of differentiated controls and sanctions is stated in the regulations. The assignment of roles occurs on the basis of technical qualifications which are ascertained through formalized, impersonal procedures (e.g., examinations). Within the structure of hierarchically arranged authority, the activities of "trained and salaried experts" are governed by general, abstract, clearly defined rules which preclude the necessity for the issuance of specific instructions for each specific case. The generality of the rules requires the constant use of *categorization*, whereby individual problems and cases are classified on the basis of designated criteria and are treated accordingly. The pure type of bureaucratic official is appointed, either by a superior or through the exercise of impersonal competition; he is not elected. A measure of flexibility in the bureaucracy is attained by electing higher functionaries who presumably express the will of the electorate (e.g., a body of citizens or a board of directors). The election of higher officials is designed to affect the purposes of the organization, but the technical procedures for attaining these ends are carried out by a continuous bureaucratic personnel.[4]

Most bureaucratic offices involve the expectation of life-long tenure, in the absence of disturbing factors which may decrease the size of the organization. Bureaucracy maximizes vocational security.[5] The function of security of tenure, pensions, incremental salaries and regularized procedures for promotion is to ensure the devoted performance of official duties, without regard for extraneous pressures.[6] The chief merit of bureaucracy is its technical efficiency, with a premium placed on precision, speed, expert control, continuity, discretion, and optimal returns on input. The structure is one which approaches the complete elimination of personalized relationships and non-rational considerations (hostility, anxiety, affectual involvements, etc.).

With increasing bureaucratization, it becomes plain to all who would see that man is to a very important degree controlled by his social relations to the instruments of production. This can no longer seem only a tenet of Marxism, but a stubborn fact to be acknowledged by all, quite apart from their ideological persuasion. Bureaucratization makes readily visible what was previously dim and obscure. More and more people discover that to work, they must be employed. For to work, one must have tools and equipment. And the tools and equipment are increasingly available only in bureaucracies, private or public. Consequently, one must be employed by the bureaucracies in order to have access to tools in order to work in order to live. It is in this sense that bureaucratization entails separation of individuals from the instruments of production, as in modern capitalistic enterprise or in state communistic enterprise (of the 1949 variety), just as in the post-feudal army, bureaucratization entailed complete separation from the instruments of destruction. Typically, the worker no longer owns his tools nor the soldier, his weapons. And in this special sense, more and more people become workers, either blue collar or white collar or stiff shirt. So develops, for example, the new type of the scientific worker, as the scientist is "separated" from his technical equipment—after all, the physicist does not ordinarily own his cyclotron. To work at his research, he must be employed by a bureaucracy with laboratory resources.

Bureaucracy is administration which almost completely avoids public discussion of its techniques, although there may occur public discussion of its policies.[7] This secrecy is confined neither to public nor to private bureaucracies. It is held to be necessary to keep valuable information from private economic competitors or from foreign and potentially hostile political groups. And though it is not often so called, espionage among competitors is perhaps as common, if not as intricately organized, in systems of private economic enterprise as in systems of national states. Cost figures, lists of clients, new technical processes, plans for production—all these are typically regarded as essential secrets of private economic bureaucracies which might be revealed if the bases of all decisions and policies had to be publicly defended.

THE DYSFUNCTIONS OF BUREAUCRACY

In these bold outlines, the positive attainments and functions of bureaucratic organization are emphasized and the internal stresses and strains of such structures are almost wholly neglected. The community at large, however, evidently emphasizes the imperfections of bureaucracy, as is suggested by the fact that the "horrid hybrid," bureaucrat, has become an epithet, a *Schimpfwort*.

The transition to a study of the negative aspects of bureaucracy is afforded by the application of Veblen's concept of "trained incapacity," Dewey's notion of "occupational psychosis" or Warnotte's view of "professional deformation." Trained incapacity refers to that state of affairs in which one's abilities function as inadequacies or blind spots. Actions based upon training and skills which have been successfully applied in the past may result in inappropriate responses *under changed conditions*. An inadequate flexibility in the application of skills, will, in a changing milieu, result in more or less serious maladjustments.[8] Thus, to adopt a barnyard illustration used in this connection by Burke, chickens may be readily conditioned to interpret the sound of a bell as a signal for food. The same bell may now be used to summon the "trained chickens" to their doom as they are assembled to suffer decapitation. In general, one adopts measures in keeping with his past training and, under new conditions which are not recognized as *significantly* different, the very soundness of this training may lead to the adoption of the wrong procedures. Again, in Burke's almost echolalic phrase, "people may be unfitted by being fit in an unfit fitness"; their training may become an incapacity.

Dewey's concept of occupational psychosis rests upon much the same observations. As a result of their day to day routines, people develop special preferences, antipathies, discriminations and emphases.[9] (The term psychosis is used by Dewey to denote a "pronounced character of the mind.") These psychoses develop through demands put upon the individual by the particular organization of his occupational role.

The concepts of both Veblen and Dewey refer to a fundamental ambivalence. Any action can be considered in terms of what it attains or what it fails to attain. "A way of seeing is also a way of not seeing—a focus upon object A involves a neglect of object B." [10] In his discussion, Weber is almost exclusively concerned with what the bureaucratic structure attains: precision, reliability, efficiency. This same structure may be examined from another perspective provided by the ambivalence. What are the limitations of the organizations designed to attain these goals?

For reasons which we have already noted, the bureaucratic structure exerts a constant pressure upon the official to be "methodical, prudent, disciplined." If the bureaucracy is to operate successfully, it must attain a high degree of reliability of behavior, an unusual degree of conformity with prescribed patterns of action. Hence, the fundamental importance of discipline which may be as highly developed in a religious or economic bureaucracy as in the army. Discipline can be effective only if the ideal patterns are buttressed by strong sentiments which entail devotion to one's duties, a keen sense of the limitation of one's authority and competence, and methodical performance of routine activities. The efficacy of social structure depends ultimately upon infusing group participants with appropriate attitudes and sentiments. As we shall see, there are definite arrangements in the bureaucracy for inculcating and reinforcing these sentiments.

At the moment, it suffices to observe that in order to ensure discipline (the necessary reliability of response), these sentiments are often more intense than is technically necessary. There is a margin of safety, so to speak, in the pressure exerted by these sentiments upon the bureaucrat to conform to his patterned obligations, in much the same sense that added allowances (precautionary overestimations) are made by the engineer in designing the supports for a bridge. But this very emphasis leads to a transference of the sentiments from the *aims* of the organization onto the particular details of behavior required by the rules. Adherence to the rules, originally conceived as a means, becomes transformed into an end-in-itself; there occurs the familiar process of *displacement of goals* whereby "an instrumental value becomes a terminal value." [11] Discipline, readily interpreted as conformance with regulations, whatever the situation, is seen not as a measure designed for specific purposes but becomes an immediate value in the life-organization of the bureaucrat. This emphasis, resulting from the displacement of the original goals, develops into rigidities and an inability to adjust readily. Formalism, even ritualism, ensues with an unchallenged insistence upon punctilious adherence to formalized procedures.[12] This may be exaggerated to the point where primary concern with conformity to the rules interferes with the achievement of the purposes of the organization, in which case we have the familiar phenomenon of the technicism or red tape of the official. An extreme product of this process of displacement of goals is the bureaucratic virtuoso, who never forgets a single rule binding his action and hence is unable to assist many of his clients.[13] A case in point, where strict recognition of the limits of authority and literal adherence to rules produced this result, is the pathetic plight of Bernt Balchen, Admiral Byrd's pilot in the flight over the South Pole.

According to a ruling of the department of labor Bernt Balchen . . . cannot receive his citizenship papers. Balchen, a native of Norway, declared his intention in 1927. It is held that he has failed to meet the condition of five years' continuous residence in the United States. The Byrd antarctic voyage took him out of the country, although he was on a ship carrying the American flag, was an invaluable member of the American expedition, and in a region to which there is an American claim because of the exploration and occupation of it by Americans, this region being Little America.

The bureau of naturalization explains that it cannot proceed on the assumption that Little America is American soil. That would be *trespass on international questions* where it has no sanction. So far as the bureau is concerned, Balchen was out of the country and *technically* has not complied with the law of naturalization.[14]

STRUCTURAL SOURCES OF OVERCONFORMITY

Such inadequacies in orientation which involve trained incapacity clearly derive from structural sources. The process may be briefly recapitulated. (1) An effective bureaucracy demands reliability of response and strict devotion to regulations. (2) Such devotion to the rules leads to their transformation into absolutes; they are no longer conceived as relative to a given set of purposes. (3) This interferes with ready adaptation under special conditions not clearly envisaged by those who drew up the general rules. (4) Thus, the very elements which conduce toward efficiency in general produce inefficiency in specific instances. Full realization of the inadequacy is seldom attained by members of the group who have not divorced themselves from the "meanings" which the rules have for them. These rules in time become symbolic in cast, rather than strictly utilitarian.

Thus far, we have treated the ingrained sentiments making for rigorous discipline simply as data, as given. However, definite features of the bureaucratic structure may be seen to conduce to these sentiments. The bureaucrat's official life is planned for him in terms of a graded career, through the organizational devices of promotion by seniority, pensions, incremental salaries, *etc.*, all of which are designed to provide incentives for disciplined action and conformity to the official regulations.[15] The official is tacitly expected to and largely does adapt his thoughts, feelings and actions to the prospect of this career. But *these very devices* which increase the probability of conformance also lead to an over-concern with strict adherence to regulations which induces timidity, conservatism, and technicism. Displacement of sentiments from goals onto means is fostered by the tremendous symbolic significance of the means (rules).

Another feature of the bureaucratic structure tends to produce much the same result. Functionaries have the sense of a common destiny for all those who work together. They share the same interests, especially since there is relatively little competition insofar as promotion is in terms of seniority. In-group aggression is thus minimized and this arrangement is therefore conceived to be positively functional for the bureaucracy. However, the esprit de corps and informal social organization which typically develops in such situations often leads the personnel to defend their entrenched interests rather than to assist their clientele and elected higher officials. As President Lowell reports, if the bureaucrats believe that their status is not adequately recognized by an incoming elected official, detailed information will be withheld from him, leading him to errors for which he is held responsible. Or, if he seeks to dominate fully, and thus violates the sentiment of self-integrity of the bureaucrats, he may have documents brought to him in such numbers that he cannot manage to sign them all, let alone read them.[16] This illustrates the defensive informal organization which tends to arise whenever there is an apparent threat to the integrity of the group.[17]

It would be much too facile and partly erroneous to attribute such resistance by bureaucrats simply to vested interests. Vested interests oppose any new order which either eliminates or at least makes uncertain their differential advantage deriving from the current arrangements. This is undoubtedly involved in part in bureaucratic resistance to change but another process is perhaps more significant. As we have seen, bureaucratic officials affectively identify themselves with their way of life. They have a pride of craft which leads them to resist change in established routines; at least, those changes which are felt to be imposed by co-workers. This nonlogical pride of craft is a familiar pattern found even, to judge from Sutherland's *Professional Thief,* among pickpockets who, despite the risk, delight in mastering the prestige-bearing feat of "beating a left breech" (picking the left front trousers pocket).

In a stimulating paper, Hughes has applied the concepts of "secular" and "sacred" to various types of division of labor; "the sacredness" of caste and *Stände* prerogatives contrasts sharply with the increasing secularism of occupational differentiation in our mobile society.[18] However, as our discussion suggests, there may ensue, in particular vocations and in particular types of organization, the *process of sanctification* (viewed as the counterpart of the process of secularization). This is to say that through sentiment-formation, emotional dependence upon bureaucratic symbols and status, and affective involvement in spheres of competence and authority, there develop prerogatives involving attitudes of moral legitimacy which are established as values in their own right, and are no longer viewed as merely technical means for expediting administration. One may note a tendency for certain bureaucratic norms, originally introduced for technical reasons, to become rigidified and sacred, although, as Durkheim would say, they are *laïque en apparence*.[19] Durkheim has touched on this general process in his description of the attitudes and values which persist in the organic solidarity of a highly differentiated society.

PRIMARY VS. SECONDARY RELATIONS

Another feature of the bureaucratic structure, the stress on depersonalization of relationships, also plays its part in the bureaucrat's trained incapacity. The personality pattern of the bureaucrat is nucleated about this norm of impersonality. Both this and the categorizing tendency, which develops from the dominant role of general, abstract rules, tend to produce conflict in the bureaucrat's contacts with the public or clientele. Since functionaries minimize personal relations and resort to categorization, the peculiarities of individual cases are often ignored. But the client who, quite understandably, is convinced of the "special features" of *his* own problem often objects to such categorical treatment. Stereotyped behavior is not adapted to the exigencies of individual problems. The impersonal treatment of affairs which are at times of great personal significance to the client gives rise to the charge of "arrogance" and "haughtiness" of the bureaucrat. Thus, at the Greenwich Employment Exchange, the unemployed worker who is securing his insurance payment resents what he deems to be "the impersonality and, at times, the apparent abruptness and even harshness of his treatment by the clerks. . . . Some men complain of the superior attitude which the clerks have." [20]

Still another source of conflict with the public derives from the bureaucratic structure. The bureaucrat, in part irrespective of his position with*in* the hierarchy, acts as a representative of the power and prestige of the entire structure. In his official role he is vested with definite authority. This often leads to an actually or apparently domineering attitude, which may only be exaggerated by a discrepancy between his position within the hierarchy and his position with reference to the public.[21] Protest and recourse to other officials on the part of the client are often ineffective or largely precluded by the previously mentioned esprit de corps which joins the officials into a more or less solidary in-group. This source of conflict *may* be minimized in private enterprise since the client can register an effective protest by transferring his trade to another organization within the competitive system. But with the monopolistic nature of the public organization, no such alternative is possible. Moreover, in this case, tension is increased because of a discrepancy between ideology and fact: the governmental personnel are held to be "servants of the people," but in fact they are usually superordinate, and release of tension can seldom be afforded by turning to other agencies for the necessary service.[22] This tension is in part attributable to the confusion of the status of bureaucrat and client; the client may consider himself socially superior to the official who is at the moment dominant.[23]

Thus, with respect to the relations between officials and clientele, one structural source of conflict is the pressure for formal and impersonal treatment when individual, personalized consideration is desired by the client. The conflict may be viewed, then, as deriving from the introduction of inappropriate attitudes and relationships. Conflict with*in* the bureaucratic structure arises from the converse situation, namely, when personalized relationships are substituted for the structurally required impersonal relationships. This type of conflict may be characterized as follows.

The bureaucracy, as we have seen, is organized as a secondary, formal group. The normal responses involved in this organized network of social expectations are supported by affective attitudes of members of the group. Since the group is oriented toward secondary norms of impersonality, any failure to conform to these norms will arouse antagonism from those who have identified themselves with the legitimacy of these rules. Hence, the substitution of personal for impersonal treatment within the structure is met with widespread disapproval and is characterized by such epithets as graft, favoritism, nepotism, apple-polishing, etc. These epithets are clearly manifestations of injured sentiments.[24] The function of such "automatic resentment" can be clearly seen in terms of the requirements of bureaucratic structure.

Bureaucracy is a secondary group structure designed to carry on certain activities which cannot be satisfactorily performed on the basis of primary group criteria.[25] Hence behavior which runs counter to these formalized norms becomes the object of emotionalized disapproval. This constitutes a functionally significant defence set up against tendencies which jeopardize the performance of socially necessary activities. To be sure, these reactions are not rationally determined practices explicitly designed for the fulfillment of this function. Rather, viewed in terms of the individual's interpretation of the situation, such resentment is simply an immediate response opposing the "dishonesty" of those who violate the rules of the game. However, this subjective frame of reference notwithstanding, these reactions serve the latent function of maintaining the essential structural elements of bureaucracy by reaffirming the necessity for formalized, secondary relations and by helping to prevent the disintegration of the bureaucratic structure which would occur should these be supplanted by personalized relations. This type of conflict may be generically described as the intrusion of primary group attitudes when secondary group attitudes are institutionally demanded, just as the bureaucrat-client conflict often derives from interaction on impersonal terms when personal treatment is individually demanded.[26]

PROBLEMS FOR RESEARCH

The trend towards increasing bureaucratization in Western Society, which Weber had long since foreseen, is not the sole reason for sociologists to turn their attention to this field. Empirical studies of the interaction of bureaucracy and personality should especially increase our understanding of social structure. A large number of specific questions invite our attention. To what extent are particular personality types selected and modified by the various bureaucracies (private enterprise, public service, the quasi-legal political machine, religious orders)? Inasmuch as ascendancy and submission are held to be traits of personality, despite their variability in different stimulus-situations, do bureaucracies select personalities of particularly submissive or ascendant tendencies? And since various studies have shown that these traits can be modified, does participation in bureaucratic office tend to increase ascendant tendencies? Do various systems of recruitment (e.g., patronage, open competition involving specialized knowledge or "general mental capacity," practical experience) select different personality types? Does promotion through seniority lessen competitive anxieties and enhance administrative efficiency? A detailed examination of mechanisms for imbuing the bureaucratic codes with affect would be instructive both sociologically and psychologically. Does the general anonymity of civil service decisions tend to restrict the area of prestige-symbols to a narrowly defined inner circle? Is there a tendency for differential association to be especially marked among bureaucrats?

The range of theoretically significant and practically important questions would seem to be limited only by the accessibility of the concrete data. Studies of religious, educational, military, economic, and political bureaucracies dealing with the interdependence of social organization and personality formation should constitute an avenue for fruitful research. On that avenue, the functional analysis of concrete structures may yet build a Solomon's House for sociologists.

REFERENCES

1. For a development of the concept of "rational organization," see Karl Mannheim, *Mensch und Gesellschaft im Zeitalter des Umbaus* (Leiden: A. W. Sijthoff, 1935), esp. pp. 28 ff.
2. H. D. Lasswell, *Politics* (New York: McGraw-Hill, 1936), pp. 120–21.
3. Max Weber, *Wirtschaft und Gesellschaft* (Tübingen: J. C. B. Mohr, 1922), Pt. III, chap. 6; pp. 650–678. For a brief summary of Weber's discussion, see Talcott Parsons, *The Structure of Social Action* (Glencoe: The Free Press, 1949), esp. pp. 506 ff. For a description, which is not a caricature, of the bureaucrat as a personality type, see C. Rabany, "Les types sociaux: le fonctionnaire," *Revue générale d'administration*, LXXXVIII (1907), 5–28.
4. Karl Mannheim, *Ideology and Utopia* (New York: Harcourt, Brace, 1936), pp. 18n., 105 ff. See also Ramsay Muir, *Peers and Bureaucrats* (London: Constable, 1910), pp. 12–13.
5. E. G. Cahen-Salvador suggests that the personnel of bureaucracies is largely constituted of those who value security above all else. See his "La situation matérielle et morale des fonctionnaires," *Revue politique et parlementaire* (1926), p. 319.

6. H. J. Laski, "Bureaucracy," *Encyclopedia of the Social Sciences.* This article is written primarily from the standpoint of the political scientist rather than that of the sociologist.

7. Weber, *op. cit.,* p. 671.

8. For a stimulating discussion and application of these concepts, see Kenneth Burke, *Permanence and Change* (New York: New Republic, 1935), pp. 50 ff.; Daniel Warnotte, "Bureaucratie et Fonctionnarisme," *Revue de l'Institut de Sociologie,* XVII (1937), 245.

9. *Ibid.,* pp. 58–59.

10. *Ibid.,* p. 70.

11. This process has often been observed in various connections. Wundt's *heterogony of ends* is a case in point; Max Weber's *Paradoxie der Folgen* is another. See also MacIver's observations on the transformation of civilization into culture and Lasswell's remark that "the human animal distinguishes himself by his infinite capacity for making ends of his means." See R. K. Merton, "The Unanticipated Consequences of Purposive Social Action," *American Sociological Review,* I (1936), 894–904. In terms of the psychological mechanisms involved, this process has been analyzed most fully by Gordon W. Allport, in his discussion of what he calls "the functional autonomy of motives." Allport emends the earlier formulations of Woodworth, Tolman, and William Stern, and arrives at a statement of the process from the standpoint of individual motivation. He does not consider those phases of the social structure which conduce toward the "transformation of motives." The formulation adopted in this paper is thus complementary to Allport's analysis; the one stressing the psychological mechanisms involved, the other considering the constraints of the social structure. The convergence of psychology and sociology toward this central concept suggests that it may well constitute one of the conceptual bridges between the two disciplines. See Gordon W. Allport, *Personality* (New York: Henry Holt & Co., 1937), chap. 7.

12. See E. C. Hughes, "Institutional Office and the Person," *American Journal of Sociology,* XLIII (1937), 404–413; R. K. Merton, "Social Structure and Anomie," *American Sociological Review,* III (1938), 6720681; E. T. Hiller, "Social Structure in Relation to the Person," *Social Forces,* XVI (1937), 34–44.

13. Mannheim, *Ideology and Utopia,* p. 106.

14. Quoted from the *Chicago Tribune* (June 24, 1931, p. 10) by Thurman Arnold, *The Symbols of Government* (New Haven: Yale University Press, 1935), pp. 201–2. (My italics.)

15. Mannheim, *Mensch und Gesellschaft,* pp. 32–33. Mannheim stresses the importance of the "Lebensplan" and the "Amtskarriere." See the comments by Hughes, *op. cit.,* 413.

16. A. L. Lowell, *The Government of England* (New York, 1908), I, 189 ff.

17. For an instructive description of the development of such a defensive organization in a group of workers, see F. J. Roethlisberger and W. J. Dickson, *Management and the Worker* (Boston: Harvard School of Business Administration, 1934).

18. E. C. Hughes, "Personality Types and the Division of Labor," *American Journal of Sociology,* XXXIII (1928), 754–768. Much the same distinction is drawn by Leopold von Wiese and Howard Becker, *Systematic Sociology* (New York: John Wiley & Sons, 1932), pp. 222–25 *et passim.*

19. Hughes recognizes one phase of this process of sanctification when he writes that professional training "carries with it as a by-product assimilation of the candidate to a set of professional attitudes and controls, *a professional conscience and solidarity. The profession claims and aims to become a moral unit.*" Hughes, *op. cit.,* p. 762, (italics inserted). In this same connection, Sumner's concept of *pathos,* as the halo of sentiment which protects a social value from criticism, is particularly relevant, inasmuch as it affords a clue to the mechanism involved in the process of sanctification. See his *Folkways* (Boston: Ginn & Co., 1906), pp. 180–181.

20. " 'They treat you like a lump of dirt they do. I see a navvy reach across the counter and shake one of them by the collar the other day. The rest of us felt like cheering. Of course he lost his benefit over it. . . . But the clerk deserved it for his sassy

way.' " (E. W. Bakke, *The Unemployed Man*, New York: Dutton, 1934, pp. 79–80). Note that the domineering attitude was *imputed* by the unemployed client who is in a state of tension due to his loss of status and self-esteem in a society where the ideology is still current that an "able man" can always find a job. That the imputation of arrogance stems largely from the client's state of mind is seen from Bakke's own observation that "the clerks were rushed, and had no time for pleasantries, but there was little sign of harshness or a superiority feeling in their treatment of the men." Insofar as there is an objective basis for the imputation of arrogant behavior to bureaucrats, it may possibly be explained by the following juxtaposed statements. "Auch der moderne, sei es öffentliche, sei es private, Beamte erstrebt immer und geniesst meist den Beherrschten gegenüber eine spezifisch gehobene, 'ständische' soziale Schätzung." (Weber, *op. cit.*, 652.) "In persons in whom the craving for prestige is uppermost, hostility usually takes the form of a desire to humiliate others." (K. Horney, *The Neurotic Personality of Our Time*, New York: Norton, 1937, pp. 178–79).

21. In this connection, note the relevance of Koffka's comments on certain features of the pecking-order of birds. "If one compares the behavior of the bird at the top of the pecking list, the despot, with that of one very far down, the second or third from the last, then one finds the latter much more cruel to the few others whom he lords it than the former in his treatment of all members. As soon as one removes from the group all members above the penultimate, his behavior becomes milder and may even become very friendly. . . . It is not difficult to find analogies to this in human societies, and therefore one side of such behavior must be primarily the effects of the social groupings, and not of individual characteristics." K. Koffka, *Principles of Gestalt Psychology* (New York: Harcourt, Brace, 1935), pp. 668–9.

22. At this point the political machine often becomes functionally significant. As Steffens and others have shown, highly personalized relations and the abrogation of formal rules (red tape) by the machine often satisfy the needs of individual "clients" more fully than the formalized mechanism of governmental bureaucracy. See the slight elaboration of this as set forth in Chapter I.

23. As one of the unemployed men remarked about the clerks at the Greenwich Employment Exchange: " 'And the bloody blokes wouldn't have their jobs if it wasn't for us men out of a job either. That's what gets me about their holding their noses up.' " Bakke, *op. cit.*, p. 80.

24. The diagnostic significance of such linguistic indices as epithets has scarcely been explored by the sociologist. Sumner properly observes that epithets produce "summary criticisms" and definitions of social situations. Dollard also notes that "epithets frequently define the central issues in a society," and Sapir has rightly emphasized the importance of context of situations in appraising the significance of epithets. Of equal relevance is Linton's observation that "in case histories the way in which the community felt about a particular episode is, if anything, more important to our study than the actual behavior. . . ." A sociological study of "vocabularies of encomium and opprobrium" should lead to valuable findings.

25. *Cf.* Ellsworth Faris, *The Nature of Human Nature* (New York: McGraw-Hill, 1937), pp. 41 ff.

26. Community disapproval of many forms of behavior may be analyzed in terms of one or the other of these patterns of substitution of culturally inappropriate types of relationship. Thus, prostitution constitutes a type-case where coitus, a form of intimacy which is institutionally defined as symbolic of the most "sacred" primary group relationship, is placed within a contractual context, symbolized by the exchange of that most impersonal of all symbols, money. See Kingsley Davis, "The Sociology of Prostitution," *American Sociological Review*, II (1937), 744–55.

Two Types of Bureaucracy * (*Gouldner*)

Inevitably, there were certain obscurities in Weber's work which, if clarified, may enable it to be put to better use. Several of these can be noted in Weber's discussion of the factors which make a bureaucracy "effective." He wrote:

"The effectiveness of legal (in the present context, "bureaucratic"—A.W.G.) authority rests on the acceptance of the validity of the following . . . 1. That any given legal norm may be established by agreement or imposition, on the grounds of expediency or rational values, or both, with a claim to obedience at least on the part of the members of the corporate group." [1]

Here a critical problem is disposed of in a surprisingly cavalier manner, for Weber fails to weigh the possibility that a bureaucracy's effectiveness, or other of its characteristics, might vary with the manner in which rules are initiated, whether by imposition or agreement. Tacitly, he seems to have assumed that the cultural setting of a specific bureaucracy would be neutral toward different methods of initiating bureaucratic rules. Since, however, our culture is not neutral but prefers agreed-upon, rather than imposed rules, these two cannot be fused together without blurring the dynamics of bureaucratic organization. It is partly for this reason that the present study will not talk about factory rules in general, but instead will consider different concrete rules, those dealing with absenteeism, safety, smoking, promotions and transfers, and will attempt to discriminate differences in pattern associated with different methods of installing the rules.

Weber was silent on several other questions: First, to *whom* did the rules have to be useful, if bureaucratic authority was to be effective? Secondly, in terms of *whose* goals were the rules a rational device? Whose end did they have to realize if the bureaucracy was to operate effectively? Weber tended to assume that the ends of different strata within a bureaucracy were identical, or at least highly similar, and hence was not compelled to distinguish them from each other. This appears to have derived partly from his use of the seemingly solidary government bureaucracy as an implicit model. Had he focused on the factory bureaucracy with its more evident tensions between supervisor and supervised, as this study shall, he would have been immediately aware that a given rule could be rational or expedient for achieving the ends of one stratum, say management, but might be neither rational nor expedient for workers.[2]

* Reprinted from *Patterns of Industrial Bureaucracy*, by Alvin W. Gouldner, pp. 19–24, with permission of the publisher, The Free Press, Glencoe, Ill. Copyright, 1954, by The Free Press, A Corporation.

A "bureaucracy" can be said to have "ends" only in a metaphorical sense. To be precise, however, it is necessary to specify the ends of different people, or the typical ends of different strata within the organization. Such a refocusing suggests these ends may vary, are not necessarily identical or salient for all personnel, and, may in fact, be contradictory, a conclusion which will in no way startle students of industry, however much some students of administration have systematically neglected it.

Weber's abortive distinction between imposed and agreed-upon rules is indicative of two broader strands which are woven together in his theory. There is, first, his emphasis on bureaucracy as administration by the "expert" or the technically trained. Weber conceived of our epoch as one in which the dilettante was fast disappearing, and held modern modes of administration to be characterized by the prominence attached to specialized skills. In this vein he asserted:

"The choice is only between bureaucracy and dilettantism in the field of administration. The primary source of bureaucratic administration lies in the role of technical knowledge . . . [3] The question is always who controls the existing machinery and such control is possible only in a very limited degree to persons who are not technical specialists . . . [4] Bureaucratic administration means fundamentally the exercise of control on the basis of knowledge. This is the feature of it which makes it specifically rational . . . [5] Bureaucracy is superior in knowledge, including both technical knowledge and knowledge of the concrete fact within its own sphere of interest." [6]

There was, however, another ingredient in Weber's conception of bureaucracy; this had to do with the role of *discipline,* an element that parallels his emphasis on "imposition" as a source of bureaucratic rules. According to Weber, bureaucracy is the "most rational offspring" of discipline.[7]

"The content of discipline," wrote Weber, "is nothing but the consistently rationalized, methodically trained and exact execution of the received order, in which all personal criticism is unconditionally suspended and the actor is unswervingly and exclusively set for carrying out the command." [8]

Talcott Parsons, one of the most perceptive commentators on Weber's theory, has stressed that, "*Above all* bureaucracy involves discipline . . . It is the fitting of individual actions into a complicated pattern in such a way that the character of each and its relation to the rest can be accurately controlled . . ." [9] Thus bureaucracy involves an emphasis on obedience; and by "obedience" Weber meant that the content of a command becomes "the basis of action for its own sake." [10]

Weber, then, thought of bureaucracy as a Janus-faced organization, looking two ways at once. On the one side, it was administration based on expertise; while on the other, it was administration based on discipline. In the first emphasis, obedience is invoked as a means to an end; an individual obeys because the rule or order is felt to be the best known method of realizing some goal.

In his second conception, Weber held that bureaucracy was a mode of administration in which obedience was an end in itself. The individual obeys the order, setting aside judgments either of its rationality or morality, primarily because of the *position* occupied by the person commanding. The content of the order is not examinable. In this vein, the Nazi guards in concentration camps justified their unspeakable atrocities because, as they said, "We were given orders." In the first pattern, then, the individual obeys, in part, because of his feelings about the rule or order; in the second, he obeys *regardless* of his feelings.

Talcott Parsons has pointed up this equivocal character of Weber's theory of bureaucracy in an astute but all too brief footnote. He suggests that Weber had confused two distinct types of authority: (a) authority which rest on "incumbency of a legally defined office," and (b) that which is based on "technical competence." [11] Parsons uses the medical relationship as the archtype of authority which is based on technical competence. He states that the doctor's "authority rests fundamentally on the belief on the part of the patient that the physician has and will employ *for his benefit* a technical competence adequate to help him in his illness." [12] (Our emphasis —A.W.G.) The critical phrase here is, "for his (i.e., the patient's) benefit." In other words, sheer technical competence by itself may not elicit the patient's consent to the doctor's prescriptions.

The patient may reject the doctor's authority if he feels his own needs are being violated in their relationship. He may, for example, feel that the doctor is financially exploiting him. Again, the inmates of Nazi concentration camps did not accept the authority of the doctors who were "experimenting" on them, even though they may have had no doubts concerning the doctors' medical skills. Along similar lines, Parsons states that this form of authority, that based on technical competence, "depends entirely on securing . . . voluntary consent . . ." [13]

It seems clear, therefore, that Weber's conception of bureaucracy as the "rule of the expert," as in Parsons' telescoped analysis of this pattern, is a form of authority not legitimated solely by the presence or use of technical skills. Apparently, it takes something more than this to elicit voluntary consent.

The conclusion to which this excursion has led is this: Weber seems to have been describing implicitly not one but two types of bureaucracy. One of these may be termed the "representative" form of bureaucracy, based on rules established by agreement, rules which are technically justified and administered by specially qualified personnel, and to which consent is given voluntarily. In examining factory patterns which exemplify this type, closer attention deserves to be paid to the role of "consent" and to the diversity of sources from which it springs. A second pattern which may be called the "punishment-centered" bureaucracy, is based on the imposition of rules, and on obedience for its own sake. Here, too, the pattern must be examined in its relation to the flow or withdrawal of consent. At an appropriate point it will be necessary to see whether this crude distinction can illuminate our empirical materials and, conversely, whether the data can help to refine and develop these conceptual starting-points.

REFERENCES

1. Henderson and Parsons, Ibid., p. 329.
2. This is considered more generally in our discussion of Wilbert E. Moore's, "Industrial Sociology: Status and Prospects," *American Sociological Review*, Vol. XIII, No. 4, Aug., 1948, pp. 396–400.
3. Henderson and Parsons, Ibid., p. 337.
4. Ibid., p. 337.
5. Ibid., p. 339.
6. Ibid., p. 339.
7. Mills and Gerth, Ibid., p. 254.
8. Mills and Gerth, Ibid., p. 254.
9. Talcott Parsons, *The Structure of Social Action*, McGraw-Hill Book Co., 1937, New York, p. 507.
10. Henderson and Parsons, Ibid., p. 327.
11. Henderson and Parsons, Ibid., p. 59.
12. Ibid.
13. Ibid.

The Dynamics of Bureaucracy * (*Blau*)

Weber conceived of bureaucracy as the social mechanism that maximizes efficiency in administration and also as a form of social organization with specific characteristics. Both these criteria cannot be part of the definition, since the relationship between the attributes of social institution and its consequences is a question for empirical verification and not a matter of definition. Weber's discussion may be interpreted in one of two ways. Either he defined bureaucracy by specifying formal characteristics and hypothesized its superior operating efficiency; or he intended to define it as any adminis-

* Reprinted from *The Dynamics of Bureaucracy* by Peter M. Blau, pp. 202–206, by permission of The University of Chicago Press. Copyright, 1955, by The University of Chicago.

trative apparatus that maximizes efficiency and advanced hypotheses about organizational attributes that would typically have this effect.[1]

In terms of the second alternative, bureaucracies can be looked upon as institutionalized strategies for the achievement of administrative objectives by the concerted effort of many officials. They are methods of organizing social conduct in order to transform exceptional problems into routine duties of experts [2] and to effect the co-ordination of specialized tasks. In different cultures, different social arrangements will prove most suitable for these purposes. When an authoritarian orientation toward social relationships prevails in the family and in the society generally and when lack of education limits the qualification of subaltern officials, as in Germany at Weber's time, strict hierarchical control may be the most efficient method of bureaucratic operation. However, when equality in social relationships is highly valued and when a much higher level of popular education has been reached, as in the United States today, permitting junior officials considerable discretion in discharging their responsibilities may be a more efficient system of administration. Similarly, in a culture where people are oriented toward century-old traditions, bureaucratic efficiency probably requires less change in organization than in a young culture where progress is a central value.

Internal as well as external forces made change a recurrent phenomenon in the two organizations studied [by this author] and efficient operations depended on such readiness to reorganize. The concept of organizational need has been helpful in the analysis of these processes of bureaucratic development, since it indicates the relationship between the consequences of established practices and the emergence of new ones. Many social patterns that served important functions for operations also had some dysfunctions, that is, they produced conditions that impeded the effective attainment of organizational objectives. These emergent needs often gave rise to new practices which met them. The introduction of statistical records in the employment agency, for instance, effected needed improvements in placement operations, but it also engendered competitiveness, which interfered with service to handicapped clients and with productivity in general. In response to these two organizational needs, social innovations developed that restored operating efficiency. First, special interviewers for handicapped clients assumed duties that obligated other interviewers to help them find jobs for their clients. Second, one group of regular interviewers devised methods for discouraging competitive tendencies, and this increased productivity, as indicated by the fact that this group was more productive than the other group of regular interviewers, where competitive practices prevailed.

Contacts with clients furnish another illustration of adjustments that had dysfunctions necessitating further adjustments. Interviewers concerned with making many placements were frustrated by refusals of benefit clients to accept low-paying jobs. They often tried, therefore, to discourage such refusals by the more or less implicit threat that unemployment benefits would be discontinued. This practice, although adequate for its purpose, created conflicts with clients, which were particularly disturbing for these service-oriented interviewers. The resulting tensions constituted new obstacles to the effective performance of duties. In response to this emergent need, a custom developed that restored equanimity, namely, complaining and joking about clients in conversations with colleagues. This new pattern, in turn, had a dysfunction. It facilitated the interviewer's work, not by eliminating conflicts with clients, but by immunizing him against their disturbing effects, and consequently made inconsiderate treatment of clients more likely. Since this dysfunction, which did not directly interfere with operations, did not give rise to an organizational need, it persisted, to the detriment of clients.

Consultations in the federal agency reveal a different aspect of the same process of change in the structure. Agents, anxious to assure the accuracy of their decisions without exposing their difficulties to the supervisor, were in need of advice from another source. The practice of consulting colleagues met this need. It reduced the anxiety about making decisions which interfered with operations, and it generated social cohesion. However, it also produced needs that led to new patterns of interpersonal relationships.

To consult peers was easier than to consult the superior in the department, but if they were approached for help too often, they ceased to be peers, and this made consulting them more difficult. As the advice of some agents was in constant demand, while others recurrently requested assistance with solving their problems, status differences emerged in the group. Agents hesitated to consult expert colleagues too frequently, lest their unofficial position suffer, just as they were reluctant to ask the supervisor too many questions for fear of endangering their official position. In either case, hierarchical relations prevented free access to consultants. The resurgent need for advice from actual peers induced most agents to establish partnerships of mutual consultation and to reserve consultations with experts for their most perplexing problems.

Peer relationships rest on reciprocity in social exchange. Unilateral services engender obligations which destroy equality of status and erect barriers to the free flow of communication. This interference with egalitarian social interaction is dysfunctional for work groups. The emerging status distinctions in Department Y not only restricted the choice of consultant but even threatened the integrated position of the less competent agents.

As all were attracted to popular experts, the others felt left out of group life and experienced a need for better interpersonal relationships. This need was also met by new patterns of interaction. The less competent agents tended to cultivate extensive informal relations with colleagues during the lunch period. Since this improved their popularity, it constituted an equalizing force. Although some status differences persisted, alternative mechanisms for becoming integrated in this group re-created equivalence of status in fundamental respects.

Social cohesion depends on basic equality of status. Co-operative interaction, such as the pattern of consultation, therefore affects it in two opposite ways. Co-operation is a major source of cohesion in work groups, because it unites members in the voluntary exchange of valued assistance, but it simultaneously weakens cohesion by giving rise to status distinctions which inhibit social intercourse and thus limit feelings of fellowship. As a result of these conflicting forces, cohesiveness is not a stable condition. It requires constant effort to renew the fundamental equality that makes the members of the group fully accessible to one another and permits them to become interested in one another as distinctive persons. Treatment of associates as unique individuals rather than as social types develops primarily among peers, and such an approach is a prerequisite for social interaction that is intrinsically gratifying and thereby produces strong social ties. To perpetuate group cohesion, the orientation in interpersonal relations should disallow quantitative differentiation of status but stress qualitative differentiation of persons. This orientation toward equals whose particular qualities merit consideration is also likely to enhance identification with the purposes of the group and its standards of behavior, at least in a culture where submission to authoritarian commands is negatively valued.

The significance of an egalitarian approach is not restricted to the internal structure of the work group but extends to the larger bureaucratic organization. Rational operations require the expeditious removal of obstructions to efficient performance. Effective communication in the hierarchy of authority, without which needed official innovations would not be made, is a necessary condition for this adjustment, but not a sufficient one. No system of rules and supervision can be so finely spun that it anticipates all exigencies that may arise. Moreover, some impediments to efficiency, such as the feelings of anxiety and other emotional tensions which often develop in the course of operations, cannot be eradicated by official decree. Maximum rationality in the organization, therefore, depends on the ability of operating officials to assume the initiative in establishing informal relations and instituting unofficial practices that eliminate operational difficulties as they occur. This ability, in turn, presupposes the absence of acute feelings of inequality among the members of the bureaucracy.

To be sure, the status distinctions inherent in the exercise of authority are necessary for the effective administration of a large organization, where officials in central positions must be able to direct and co-ordinate the work of specialized groups. However, since bureaucratic authority rests on social consensus that issuing certain directives is just as much the duty of the superior as compliance with these directives is that of subordinates, such compliance is not experienced as subjugation, while obedience to arbitrary commands of a superior would be. Hence bureaucratic authority itself does not create profound feelings of inequality, although it involves some status differences, but it often gives rise to additional hierarchical distinctions, which are not essential for systematic administration and which destroy all feelings of equality. If subaltern officials are treated as inferiors whose sole duty is to obey detailed orders of their superior, they have neither sufficient security nor incentive to cope with problems of their work on their own initiative. To supply the confidence and motivation needed for such efforts, junior officials must be considered as collaborators of administrators in the pursuit of common professional objectives. This limited type of egalitarian treatment, which is not too dissimilar from that which actually prevailed in the federal agency, is not incompatible with the exercise of bureaucratic authority. Of course, the absence of fundamental inequalities is not the only bureaucratic condition that must be met for work groups to take the initiative in making improvements when obstructions to efficient operations arise.

REFERENCES

1. A basic shortcoming of the ideal-type construct is that it contains both definitions of concepts and hypotheses about empirical relationships but fails to make a distinction between these two fundamentally different scientific tools. For other criticisms of Weber's ideal type see Schelting (1922), Parsons (1937), pp. 601–24, and Friedrich (1952).
2. See Hughes (1951), who shows that the emergencies of other people become the daily routine of professional experts.

13.

ANOMIE

ANOMIE MEANS a condition of normlessness, a moral vacuum, the suspension of rules, a state sometimes referred to as de-regulation. *Anomie* presupposes a prior condition in which behavior is normatively determined. A painful social crisis upsets that equilibrium, disturbs large numbers of people, greatly attenuates the regulative force of tradition, and produces widespread *anomie.*

It is unlikely that anyone has enriched sociological thought more than the incomparable French theorist, Emile Durkheim and among his many contributions, this concept looms large. It was he who early in his work introduced the term *anomie.* Later he developed it as an explanatory concept in analyzing several concrete social problems. Since then references to *anomie* have gained wide currency.

Durkheim witnessed a major phase of what many observers have since called moral anarchy as it enveloped large sectors of the French Republic. Economic distress and social dislocation, which were to grow even more acute, had already shaken the Western world. One manifestation of the malaise that particularly fascinated Durkheim was a steadily rising suicide rate. He addressed himself to the subject in a classic study that, after more than half a century, still remains a touchstone for all further work. In addition to egoistic or individualistic suicide, the familiar form of self-destruction, and altruistic suicide, a less common inclination to sacrifice one's own life for some higher cause, Durkheim singled out *anomic suicide* for reasons largely explained in the pages reprinted here.

It is not always easy to fructify social science, and although Durkheim supplied a useful lead, it lay dormant for many years. Hence, it is necessary to move forward to the late nineteen thirties, in order to locate a point in American thought at which *anomie* again becomes a vital concept. That point is the famous essay of an eminent American sociologist, Robert K. Merton, entitled "Social Structure and Anomie." Durkheim had theorized that an abrupt and unforeseen growth or diminution of an individual's power and wealth tended to produce *anomie*, and also that in the sphere of business and trade it was a regular, therefore statistically normal, factor. Similarly,

Merton defines his aim as that of discovering how "some social structures exert a definite pressure upon certain persons in the society to engage in non-conformist rather than conformist conduct." By refining the analysis of *anomie*, Merton emphasizes the differential impact of culturally defined goals and acceptable modes of obtaining those goals in different segments of the population. *Anomie* with respect to the means used is quite different from *anomie* with respect to the ends in view; it may exist in either one, in neither, or in both means *and* ends. This four-fold division makes it possible to construct the kind of typology which has become Merton's trademark, and as such, opens up new avenues of research.

Talcott Parsons, whose name for at least two decades has been synonomous with sociological theory and who in *The Structure of Social Action* awakened American interest in his towering European predecessors, took up the question of *anomie* in his second comprehensive work, *The Social System*. We have excerpted one relevant portion. There are others. It is perhaps worth quoting one passage from the second chapter of his book: "The polar antithesis of full institutionalization is . . . *anomie*, the absence of structured complementarity of the interaction process or, what is the same thing, the complete breakdown of normative order . . . This is, however, a limiting concept which is never descriptive of a concrete social system. Just as there are degrees of institutionalization so are there also degrees of *anomie*. The one is the obverse of the other." In short, *anomie* is a construct which, with its polar opposite, full institutionalization, may be the basis for a continuum from within which real social predicaments can be usefully studied.

Anomie and Suicide * (*Durkheim*)

No living being can be happy or even exist unless his needs are sufficiently proportioned to his means. In other words, if his needs require more than can be granted, or even merely something of a different sort, they will be under continual friction and can only function painfully. Movements incapable of production without pain tend not to be reproduced. Unsatisfied tendencies atrophy, and as the impulse to live is merely the result of all the rest, it is bound to weaken as the others relax.

In the animal, at least in a normal condition, this equilibrium is established with automatic spontaneity because the animal depends on purely material conditions. All the organism needs is that the supplies of substance

* Reprinted from *Suicide: A Study in Sociology*, by Emile Durkheim, translated by George Simpson, pp. 246–257, with permission of the publishers, The Free Press, Glencoe, Ill., and Routledge & Kegan Paul Ltd., London. Copyright 1951 by The Free Press, A Corporation.

and energy constantly employed in the vital process should be periodically renewed by equivalent quantities; that replacement be equivalent to use. When the void created by existence in its own resources is filled, the animal, satisfied, asks nothing further. Its power of reflection is not sufficiently developed to imagine other ends than those implicit in its physical nature. On the other hand, as the work demanded of each organ itself depends on the general state of vital energy and the needs of organic equilibrium, use is regulated in turn by replacement and the balance is automatic. The limits of one are those of the other; both are fundamental to the constitution of the existence in question, which cannot exceed them.

This is not the case with man, because most of his needs are not dependent on his body or not to the same degree. Strictly speaking, we may consider that the quantity of material supplies necessary to the physical maintenance of a human life is subject to computation, though this be less exact than in the preceding case and a wider margin left for the free combinations of the will; for beyond the indispensable minimum which satisfies nature when instinctive, a more awakened reflection suggests better conditions, seemingly desirable ends craving fulfillment. Such appetites, however, admittedly sooner or later reach a limit which they cannot pass. But how determine the quantity of well-being, comfort or luxury legitimately to be craved by a human being? Nothing appears in man's organic nor in his psychological constitution which sets a limit to such tendencies. The functioning of individual life does not require them to cease at one point rather than at another; the proof being that they have constantly increased since the beginnings of history, receiving more and more complete satisfaction, yet with no weakening of average health. Above all, how establish their proper variation with different conditions of life, occupations, relative importance of services, etc.? In no society are they equally satisfied in the different stages of the social hierarchy. Yet human nature is substantially the same among all men, in its essential qualities. It is not human nature which can assign the variable limits necessary to our needs. They are thus unlimited so far as they depend on the individual alone. Irrespective of any external regulatory force, our capacity for feeling is in itself an insatiable and bottomless abyss.

But if nothing external can restrain this capacity, it can only be a source of torment to itself. Unlimited desires are insatiable by definition and insatiability is rightly considered a sign of morbidity. Being unlimited, they constantly and infinitely surpass the means at their command; they cannot be quenched. Inextinguishable thirst is constantly renewed torture. It has been claimed, indeed, that human activity naturally aspires beyond assignable limits and sets itself unattainable goals. But how can such a undetermined state be any more reconciled with the conditions of mental life than with the demands of physical life? All man's pleasure in acting, moving and exerting himself implies the sense that his efforts are not in vain and that by walking he has advanced. However, one does not advance when one walks toward no goal, or—which is the same thing—when his goal is infinity. Since the distance between us and it is always the same, whatever road we take, we might as well have made the motions without progress from the spot. Even our glances behind and our feeling of pride at the distance covered can cause only deceptive satisfaction, since the remaining distance is not proportionately reduced. To pursue a goal which is by definition unattainable is to condemn oneself to a state of perpetual unhappiness. Of course, man may hope contrary to all reason, and hope has its pleasures even when unreasonable. It may sustain him for a time; but it cannot survive the repeated disappointments of experience indefinitely. What more can the future offer him than the past, since he can never reach a tenable condition nor even approach the glimpsed ideal? Thus, the more one has, the more one wants, since satisfactions received only stimulate instead of filling needs. Shall action as such be considered agreeable? First, only on condition of blindness to its uselessness. Secondly, for this pleasure to be felt and to temper and half veil the accompanying painful unrest, such unending motion must at least always be easy and unhampered. If it is interfered with only restlessness is left, with the lack of ease which it, itself, entails. But it would be a miracle if no insurmountable obstacle were never encountered. Our thread of life on these conditions is pretty thin, breakable at any instant.

To achieve any other result, the passions first must be limited. Only then can they be harmonized with the faculties and satisfied. But since the individual has no way of limiting them, this must be done by some force exterior to him. A regulative force must play the same role for moral needs which the organism plays for physical needs. This means that the force can only be moral. The awakening of conscience interrupted the state of equilibrium of the animal's dormant existence; only conscience, therefore, can furnish the means to re-establish it. Physical restraint would be ineffective; hearts cannot be touched by physio-chemical forces. So far as the appetites are not automatically restrained by physiological mechanisms, they can be halted only by a limit that they recognize as just. Men would never consent to restrict their desires if they felt justified in passing the assigned limit. But, for reasons given above, they cannot assign themselves this law of justice. So they must receive it from an authority which they respect, to which they yield spontaneously. Either directly and as a whole, or through the agency of one of its organs, society alone can play this moderating role; for it is the only moral power superior to the individual, the authority of which he accepts. It alone has the power necessary to stipulate law and to set the point beyond which the passions must not go. Finally, it alone can estimate the reward to be prospectively offered to every class of human functionary, in the name of the common interest.

As a matter of fact, at every moment of history there is a dim perception, in the moral consciousness of societies, of the respective value of different social services, the relative reward due to each, and the consequent degree of comfort appropriate on the average to workers in each occupation. The different functions are graded in public opinion and a certain coefficient of well-being assigned to each, according to its place in the hierarchy. According to accepted ideas, for example, a certain way of living is considered the upper limit to which a workman may aspire in his efforts to improve his existence, and there is another limit below which he is not willingly permitted to fall unless he has seriously demeaned himself. Both differ for city and country workers, for the domestic servant and the day-laborer, for the business clerk and the official, etc. Likewise the man of wealth is reproved if he lives the life of a poor man, but also if he seeks the refinements of luxury overmuch. Economists may protest in vain; public feeling will always be scandalized if an individual spends too much wealth for wholly superfluous use, and it even seems that this severity relaxes only in times of moral disturbance.[1] A genuine regimen exists, therefore, although not always legally formulated, which fixes with relative precision the maximum degree of ease of living to which each social class may legitimately aspire. However, there is nothing immutable about such a scale. It changes with the increase or decrease of collective revenue and the changes occurring in the moral ideas of society. Thus what appears luxury to one period no longer does so to another; and the well-being which for long periods was granted to a class only by exception and supererogation, finally appears strictly necessary and equitable.

Under this pressure, each in his sphere vaguely realizes the extreme limit set to his ambitions and aspires to nothing beyond. At least if he respects regulations and is docile to collective authority, that is, has a wholesome moral constitution, he feels that it is not well to ask more. Thus, an end and goal are set to the passions. Truly, there is nothing rigid nor absolute about such determination. The economic ideal assigned each class of citizens is itself confined to certain limits, within which the desires have free range. But it is not infinite. This relative limitation and the moderation it involves, make men contented with their lot while stimulating them moderately to improve it; and this average contentment causes the feeling of calm, active happiness, the pleasure in existing and living which characterizes health for societies as well as for individuals. Each person is then at least, generally speaking, in harmony with his condition, and desires only what he may legitimately hope for as the normal reward of his activity. Besides, this does not condemn man to a sort of immobility. He may seek to give beauty to his life; but his attempts in this direction may fail without causing him to despair. For, loving what he has and not fixing his desire solely on what he lacks, his wishes and hopes may fail of what he has happened to aspire to, without his being wholly destitute. He has the essentials. The equilibrium of his happiness is secure because it is defined, and a few mishaps cannot disconcert him.

But it would be of little use for everyone to recognize the justice of the hierarchy of functions established by public opinion, if he did not also consider the distribution of these functions just. The workman is not in harmony with his social position if he is not convinced that he has his desserts. If he feels justified in occupying another, what he has would not satisfy him. So it is not enough for the average level of needs for each social condition to be regulated by public opinion, but another, more precise rule, must fix the way in which these conditions are open to individuals. There is no society in which such regulation does not exist. It varies with times and places. Once it regarded birth as the almost exclusive principle of social classification; today it recognizes no other inherent inequality than hereditary fortune and merit. But in all these various forms its object is unchanged. It is also only possible, everywhere, as a restriction upon individuals imposed by superior authority, that is, by collective authority. For it can be established only by requiring of one or another group of men, usually of all, sacrifices and concessions in the name of the public interest.

Some, to be sure, have thought that this moral pressure would become unnecessary if men's economic circumstances were only no longer determined by heredity. If inheritance were abolished, the argument runs, if everyone began life with equal resources and if the competitive struggle were fought out on a basis of perfect equality, no one could think its results unjust. Each would instinctively feel that things are as they should be.

Truly, the nearer this ideal equality were approached, the less social restraint will be necessary. But it is only a matter of degree. One sort of heredity will always exist, that of natural talent. Intelligence, taste, scientific, artistic, literary or industrial ability, courage and manual dexterity are gifts received by each of us at birth, as the heir to wealth receives his capital or as the nobleman formerly received his title and function. A moral discipline will therefore still be required to make those less favored by nature accept the lesser advantages which they owe to the chance of birth. Shall it be demanded that all have an equal share and that no advantage be given those more useful and deserving? But then there would have to be a discipline far stronger to make these accept a treatment merely equal to that of the mediocre and incapable.

But like the one first mentioned, this discipline can be useful only if considered just by the peoples subject to it. When it is maintained only by custom and force, peace and harmony are illusory; the spirit of unrest and discontent are latent; appetites superficially restrained are ready to revolt. This happened in Rome and Greece when the faiths underlying the old organization of the patricians and plebeians were shaken, and in our modern societies when aristocratic prejudices began to lose their old ascendancy. But this state of upheaval is exceptional; it occurs only when society is passing through some abnormal crisis. In normal conditions the collective order is regarded as just by the great majority of persons. Therefore, when we say that an authority is necessary to impose this order on individuals, we certainly do not mean that violence is the only means of establishing it. Since this regulation is meant to restrain individual passions, it must come from a power which dominates individuals; but this power must also be obeyed through respect, not fear.

It is not true, then, that human activity can be released from all restraint. Nothing in the world can enjoy such a privilege. All existence being a part of the universe is relative to the remainder; its nature and method of manifestation accordingly depend not only on itself but on other beings, who consequently restrain and regulate it. Here there are only differences of degree and form between the mineral realm and the thinking person. Man's characteristic privilege is that the bond he accepts is not physical but moral; that is, social. He is governed not by a material environment brutally imposed on him, but by a conscience superior to his own, the superiority of which he feels. Because the greater, better part of his existence transcends the body, he escapes the body's yoke, but is subject to that of society.

But when society is disturbed by some painful crisis or by beneficent but abrupt transitions, it is momentarily incapable of exercising this influence; thence come the sudden rises in the curve of suicides which we have pointed out above.

In the case of economic disaster, indeed, something like a declassification occurs which suddenly casts certain individuals into a lower state than their previous one. Then they must reduce their requirements, restrain their needs, learn greater self-control. All the advantages of social influence are lost so far as they are concerned; their moral education has to be recommenced. But society cannot adjust them instantaneously to this new life and teach them to practice the increased self-repression to which they are unaccustomed. So they are not adjusted to the condition forced on them, and its very prospect is intolerable; hence the suffering which detaches them from a reduced existence even before they have made trial of it.

It is the same if the source of the crisis is an abrupt growth of power and wealth. Then, truly, as the conditions of life are changed, the standard according to which needs were regulated can no longer remain the same; for it varies with social resources, since it largely determines the share of each class of producers. The scale is upset; but a new scale cannot be immediately improvised. Time is required for the public conscience to reclassify men and things. So long as the social forces thus freed have not regained equilibrium, their respective values are unknown and so all regulation is lacking for a time. The limits are unknown between the possible and the impossible, what is just and what is unjust, legitimate claims and hopes and those which are immoderate. Consequently, there is no restraint upon aspirations. If the disturbance is profound, it affects even the principles controlling the distribution of men among various occupations. Since the relations between various parts of society are necessarily modified, the ideas expressing these relations must change. Some particular class especially favored by the crisis is no longer resigned to its former lot, and, on the other hand, the example of its greater good fortune arouses all sorts of jealousy below and about it. Appetites, not being controlled by a public opinion become disoriented, no longer recognize the limits proper to them. Besides, they are at the same time seized by a sort of natural erethism simply by the greater intensity of public life. With increased prosperity desires increase. At the very moment when traditional rules have lost their authority, the richer prize offered these appetites stimulates them and makes them more exigent and impatient of control. The state of de-regulation or *anomie* is thus further heightened by passions being less disciplined, precisely when they need more disciplining.

But then their very demands make fulfillment impossible. Over-weening ambition always exceeds the results obtained, great as they may be, since there is no warning to pause here. Nothing gives satisfaction and all this agitation is uninterruptedly maintained without appeasement. Above all, since this race for an unattainable goal can give no other pleasure but that of the race itself, if it is one, once it is interrupted the participants are left empty-handed. At the same time the struggle grows more violent and painful, both from being less controlled and because competition is greater. All classes contend among themselves because no established classification any longer exists. Effort grows, just when it becomes less productive. How could the desire to live not be weakened under such conditions?

This explanation is confirmed by the remarkable immunity of poor countries. Poverty protects against suicide because it is a restraint in itself. No matter how one acts, desires have to depend upon resources to some extent; actual possessions are partly the criterion of those aspired to. So the less one has the less he is tempted to extend the range of his needs indefinitely. Lack of power, compelling moderation, accustoms men to it, while nothing excites envy if no one has superfluity. Wealth, on the other hand, by the power it bestows, deceives us into believing that we depend on ourselves only. Reducing the resistance we encounter from objects, it suggests the possibility of unlimited success against them. The less limited one feels, the more intolerable all limitation appears. Not without reason, therefore, have so many religions dwelt on the advantages and moral value of poverty. It is actually the best school for teaching self-restraint. Forcing us to constant self-discipline, it prepares us to accept collective discipline with equanimity, while wealth, exalting the individual, may always arouse the spirit of rebellion which is the very source of immorality. This, of course, is no reason why humanity should not improve its material condition. But though the moral danger involved in every growth of prosperity is not irremediable, it should not be forgotten.

III

If *anomie* never appeared except, as in the above instances, in intermittent spurts and acute crisis, it might cause the social suicide-rate to vary from time to time, but it would not be a regular, constant factor. In one sphere of social life, however—the sphere of trade and industry—it is actually in a chronic state.

For a whole century, economic progress has mainly consisted in freeing industrial relations from all regulation. Until very recently, it was the function of a whole system of moral forces to exert this discipline. First, the influence of religion was felt alike by workers and masters, the poor and the rich. It consoled the former and taught them contentment with their lot by informing them of the providential nature of the social order, that the share of each class was assigned by God Himself, and by holding out the hope for just compensation in a world to come in return for the inequalities of this world. It governed the latter, recalling that worldly interests are not man's entire lot, that they must be subordinate to other and higher interests, and that they should therefore not be pursued without rule or measure. Temporal power, in turn, restrained the scope of economic functions by its supremacy over them and by the relatively subordinate role it assigned them. Finally, within the business world proper, the occupational groups by regulating salaries, the price of products and production itself, indirectly fixed the average level of income on which needs are partially based by the very force of circumstances. However, we do not mean to propose this organization as a model. Clearly it would be inadequate to existing societies without great changes. What we stress is its existence, the fact of its useful influence, and that nothing today has come to take its place.

Actually, religion has lost most of its power. And government, instead of regulating economic life, has become its tool and servant. The most opposite schools, orthodox economists and extreme socialists, unite to reduce government to the role of a more or less passive intermediary among the various social functions. The former wish to make it simply the guardian of individual contracts; the latter leave it the task of doing the collective bookkeeping, that is, of recording the demands of consumers, transmitting them to producers, inventorying the total revenue and distributing it according to a fixed formula. But both refuse it any power to subordinate other social organs to itself and to make them converge toward one dominant aim. On both sides nations are declared to have the single or chief purpose of achieving industrial prosperity; such is the implication of the dogma of economic materialism, the basis of both apparently opposed systems. And as these theories merely express the state of opinion, industry, instead of being still regarded as a means to an end transcending itself, has become the supreme end of individuals and societies alike. Thereupon the appetites thus excited have become freed of any limiting authority. By sanctifying them, to so speak, this apotheosis of well-being has placed them above all human law. Their restraint seems like a sort of sacrilege. For this reason, even the purely utilitarian regulation of them exercised by the industrial world itself through the medium of occupational groups has been unable to persist. Ultimately, this liberation of desires has been made worse by the very development of industry and the almost infinite extension of the market. So long as the producer could gain his profits only in his immediate neighborhood, the restricted amount of possible gain could not much overexcite ambition. Now that he may assume to have almost the entire world as his customer, how could passions accept their former confinement in the face of such limitless prospects?

Such is the source of the excitement predominating in this part of society, and which has thence extended to the other parts. There, the state of crisis and *anomie* is constant and, so to speak, normal. From top to bottom of the ladder, greed is aroused without knowing where to find an ultimate foothold. Nothing can calm it, since its goal is far beyond all it can attain. Reality seems valueless by comparison with the dreams of fevered imaginations; reality is therefore abandoned, but so too is possibility abandoned when it in turn becomes reality. A thirst arises for novelties, unfamiliar pleasures, nameless sensations, all of which lose their savor once known. Henceforth one has no strength to endure the least reverse. The whole fever subsides and the sterility of all the tumult is apparent, and it is seen that all these new sensations in their infinite quantity cannot form a solid foundation of happiness to support one during days of trial. The wise man, knowing how to enjoy achieved results without having constantly to replace them with others, finds in them an attachment to life in the hour of difficulty. But the man who has always pinned all his hopes on the future and lived with his eyes fixed upon it, has nothing in the past as a comfort against the present's afflictions, for the past was nothing to him but a series of hastily experienced stages. What blinded him to himself was his expectation always to find further on the happiness he had so far missed. Now he is stopped in his tracks; from now on nothing remains behind or ahead of him to fix his gaze upon. Weariness alone, moreover, is enough to bring disillusionment, for he cannot in the end escape the futility of an endless pursuit.

We may even wonder if this moral state is not principally what makes economic catastrophes of our day so fertile in suicides. In societies where a man is subjected to a healthy discipline, he submits more readily to the blows of chance. The necessary effort for sustaining a little more discomfort costs him relatively little, since he is used to discomfort and constraint. But when every constraint is hateful in itself, how can closer constraint not seem intolerable? There is no tendency to resignation in the feverish impatience of men's lives. When there is no other aim but to outstrip constantly the point arrived at, how painful to be thrown back! Now this very lack of organization characterizing our economic condition throws the door wide to every sort of adventure. Since imagination is hungry for novelty, and ungoverned, it gropes at random. Setbacks necessarily increase with risks and thus crises multiply, just when they are becoming more destructive.

Yet these dispositions are so inbred that society has grown to accept them and is accustomed to think them normal. It is everlastingly repeated that it is man's nature to be eternally dissatisfied, constantly to advance, without relief or rest, toward an indefinite goal. The longing for infinity is daily represented as a mark of moral distinction, whereas it can only appear within unregulated consciences which elevate to a rule the lack of rule from which they suffer. The doctrine of the most ruthless and swift progress has become an article of faith. But other theories appear parallel with those praising the advantages of instability, which, generalizing the situation that gives them birth, declare life evil, claim that it is richer in grief than in pleasure and that it attracts men only by false claims. Since this disorder is greatest in the economic world, it has most victims there.

Industrial and commercial functions are really among the occupations which furnish the greatest number of suicides. Almost on a level with the liberal professions, they sometimes surpass them; they are especially more afflicted than agriculture, where the old regulative forces still make their appearance felt most and where the fever of business has least penetrated. Here is best recalled what was once the general constitution of the economic order. And the divergence would be yet greater if, among the suicides of industry, employers were distinguished from workmen, for the former are probably most stricken by the state of *anomie*. The enormous rate of those with independent means (720 per million) sufficiently shows that the possessors of most comfort suffer most. Everything that enforces subordination attenuates the effects of this state. At least the horizon of the lower classes is limited by those above them, and for this same reason their desires are more modest. Those who have only empty space above them are almost inevitably lost in it, if no force restrains them.

REFERENCE

1. Actually, this is a purely moral reprobation and can hardly be judicially implemented. We do not consider any reestablishing of sumptuary laws desirable or even possible.

Social Structure and Anomie * (*Merton*)

A decade ago, and all the more so before then, one could speak of a marked tendency in psychological and sociological theory to attribute the faulty operation of social structures to failures of social control over man's imperious biological drives. The imagery of the relations between man and society implied by this doctrine is as clear as it is questionable. In the beginning, there are man's biological impulses which seek full expression. And then, there is the social order, essentially an apparatus for the management of impulses, for the social processing of tensions, for the "renunciation of instinctual gratifications," in the words of Freud. Nonconformity with the demands of a social structure is thus assumed to be anchored in original nature.[1] It is the biologically rooted impulses which from time to time break

* Reprinted from *Social Theory and Social Structure* by Robert K. Merton, pp. 125–133, with permission of the publisher, The Free Press, Glencoe, Ill. Copyright, 1949, by The Free Press, A Corporation.

through social control. And by implication, conformity is the result of an utilitarian calculus or of unreasoned conditioning.

With the more recent advancement of social science, this set of conceptions has undergone basic modification. For one thing, it no longer appears so obvious that man is set against society in an unceasing war between biological impulse and social restraint. The image of man as an untamed bundle of impulses begins to look more like a caricature than a portrait. For another, sociological perspectives have increasingly entered into the analysis of behavior deviating from prescribed patterns of conduct. For whatever the role of biological impulses, there still remains the further question of why it is that the frequency of deviant behavior varies within different social structures and how it happens that the deviations have different shapes and patterns in different social structures. Today, as a decade ago, we have still much to learn about the processes through which social structures generate the circumstances in which infringement of social codes constitutes a "normal" (that is to say, an expectable) response.[2] This paper is an essay seeking clarification of the problem.

The framework set out in this essay is designed to provide one systematic approach to the analysis of social and cultural sources of deviant behavior. Our primary aim is to discover how some *social structures exert a definite pressure upon certain persons in the society to engage in noncomformist rather than conformist conduct.* If we can locate groups peculiarly subject to such pressures, we should expect to find fairly high rates of deviant behavior in these groups, not because the human beings comprising them are compounded of distinctive biological tendencies but because they are responding normally to the social situation in which they find themselves. Our perspective is sociological. We look at variations in the *rates* of deviant behavior, not at its incidence.[3] Should our quest be at all successful, some forms of deviant behavior will be found to be as psychologically normal as conformist behavior, and the equation of deviation and abnormality will be put in question.

PATTERNS OF CULTURAL GOALS AND INSTITUTIONAL NORMS

Among the several elements of social and cultural structures, two are of immediate importance. These are analytically separable although they merge in concrete situations. The first consists of culturally defined goals, purposes and interests, held out as legitimate objectives for all or for diversely located members of the society. The goals are more or less integrated—the degree is a question of empirical fact—and roughly ordered in some hierarchy of value. Involving various degrees of sentiment and significance, the prevailing goals comprise a frame of aspirational reference. They are the things "worth striving for." They are a basic, though not the exclusive, component of what Linton has called "designs for group living." And though some, not all, of these cultural goals are directly related to the biological drives of man, they are not determined by them.

A second element of the cultural structure defines, regulates and controls the acceptable modes of reaching out for these goals. Every social group invariably couples its cultural objectives with regulations, rooted in the mores or institutions, of allowable procedures for moving toward these objectives. These regulatory norms are not necessarily identical with technical or efficiency norms. Many procedures which from the standpoint of particular individuals would be most efficient in securing desired values— the exercise of force, fraud, power—are ruled out of the institutional area of permitted conduct. At times, the disallowed procedures include some which would be efficient for the group itself—*e.g.*, historic taboos on vivisection, on medical experimentation, on the sociological analysis of "sacred" norms—since the criterion of acceptability is not technical efficiency but value-laden sentiments (supported by most members of the group or by those able to promote these sentiments through the composite use of power and propaganda). In all instances, the choice of expedients for striving toward cultural goals is limited by institutionalized norms.

Sociologists often speak of these controls as being "in the mores" or as operating through social institutions. Such elliptical statements are true enough, but they obscure the fact that culturally standardized practices are not all of a piece. They are subject to a wide gamut of control. They may represent definitely prescribed or preferential or permissive or proscribed patterns of behavior. In assessing the operation of social controls, these variations—roughly indicated by the terms *prescription, preference, permission* and *proscription*—must of course be taken into account.

To say, moreover, that cultural goals and institutionalized norms operate jointly to shape prevailing practices is not to say that they bear a constant relation to one another. The cultural emphasis placed upon certain goals varies independently of the degree of emphasis upon institutionalized means. There may develop a very heavy, at times a virtually exclusive, stress upon the value of given goals, involving comparatively little concern with the institutionally prescribed means of striving toward these goals. The limiting case of this type is reached when the range of alternative procedures is governed only by technical rather than by institutional norms. Any and all procedures which promise attainment of the all-important goal would be permitted in this hypothetical polar case. This constitutes one type of mal-integrated culture. A second polar type is found in groups where activities originally conceived as instrumental are transmuted into self-contained practices, lacking further objectives. The original purposes are forgotten and close adherence to institutionally prescribed conduct becomes a matter of ritual.[4] Sheer conformity becomes a central value. For a time, social stability is ensured—at the expense of flexibility. Since the range of alternative behaviors permitted by the culture is severely limited, there is little basis for adapting to new conditions. There develops a tradition-bound, 'sacred' society marked by neophobia. Between these extreme types are societies which maintain a rough balance between emphases upon cultural goals and institutionalized practices, and these constitute the integrated and relatively stable, though changing, societies.

An effective equilibrium between these two phases of the social structure is maintained so long as satisfactions accrue to individuals conforming to both cultural constraints, *viz.*, satisfactions from the achievement of goals and satisfactions emerging directly from the institutionally canalized modes of striving to attain them. It is reckoned in terms of the product and in terms of the process, in terms of the outcome and in terms of the activities. Thus continuing satisfactions must derive from sheer participation in a competitive order as well as from eclipsing one's competitors if the order itself is to be sustained. If concern shifts exclusively to the outcome of competition, then those who perennially suffer defeat will, understandably enough, work for a change in the rules of the game. The sacrifices occasionally—not, as Freud assumed, invariably—entailed by conformity to institutional norms must be compensated by socialized rewards. The distribution of statuses through competition must be so organized that positive incentives for adherence to status obligations are provided *for every position* within the distributive order. Otherwise, as will soon become plain, aberrant behavior ensues. It is, indeed, my central hypothesis that aberrant behavior may be regarded sociologically as a symptom of dissociation between culturally prescribed aspirations and socially structured avenues for realizing these aspirations.

Of the types of societies which result from independent variation of cultural goals and institutionalized means, we shall be primarily concerned with the first—a society in which there is an exceptionally strong emphasis upon specific goals without a corresponding emphasis upon institutional procedures. If it is not to be misunderstood, this statement must be elaborated. No society lacks norms governing conduct. But societies do differ in the degree to which the folkways, mores and institutional controls are effectively integrated with the goals which stand high in the hierarchy of cultural values. The culture may be such as to lead individuals to center their emotional convictions about the complex of culturally acclaimed ends, with far less emotional support for prescribed methods of reaching out for these ends. With such differential emphases upon goals and institutional procedures, the latter may be so vitiated by the stress on goals as to have the behavior of many individuals limited only by considerations of technical expediency. In this context, the sole significant question becomes: Which of the available procedures is most efficient in netting the culturally approved value? [5] The technically most effective procedure, whether culturally legitimate or not, becomes typically preferred to institutionally prescribed conduct. As this process of attenuation continues, the society becomes unstable and there develops what Durkheim called "anomie" (or normlessness). [6]

The working of this process eventuating in anomie can be easily glimpsed in a series of familiar and instructive, though perhaps trivial, episodes. Thus, in competitive athletics, when the aim of victory is shorn of its institutional trappings and success becomes construed as "winning the game" rather than "winning under the rules of the game," a premium is implicitly set upon the use of illegitimate but technically efficient means. The star of the opposing football team is surreptitiously slugged; the wrestler incapacitates his opponent through ingenious but illicit techniques; university alumni covertly subsidize "students" whose talents are confined to the athletic field. The emphasis on the goal has so attenuated the satisfactions deriving from sheer participation in the competitive activity that only a successful outcome provides gratification. Through the same process, tension generated by the desire to win in a poker game is relieved by successfully dealing one's self four aces or, when the cult of success has truly flowered, by sagaciously shuffling the cards in a game of solitaire. The faint twinge of uneasiness in the last instance and the surreptitious nature of public delicts indicate clearly that the institutional rules of the game are *known* to those who evade them. But cultural (or idiosyncratic) exaggeration of the success-goal leads men to withdraw emotional support from the rules. [7]

This process is of course not restricted to the realm of competitive sport, which has simply provided us with microcosmic images of the social macrocosm. The process whereby exaltation of the end generates a literal *demoralization, i.e.,* a deinstitutionalization, of the means occurs in many [8] groups where the two components of the social structure are not highly integrated.

Contemporary American culture appears to approximate the polar type in which great emphasis upon certain success-goals occurs without equivalent emphasis upon institutional means. It would of course be fanciful to assert that accumulated wealth stands alone as a symbol of success just as it would be fanciful to deny that Americans assign it a place high in their scale of values. In some large measure, money has been consecrated as a value in itself, over and above its expenditure for articles of consumption or its use for the enhancement of power. "Money" is peculiarly well adapted to become a symbol of prestige. As Simmel emphasized, money is highly abstract and impersonal. However acquired, fraudulently or institutionally, it can be used to purchase the same goods and services. The anonymity of an urban society, in conjunction with these peculiarities of money, permits wealth, the sources of which may be unknown to the community in which the plutocrat lives or, if known, to become purified in the course of time, to serve as a symbol of high status. Moreover, in the American Dream there is no final stopping point. The measure of "monetary success" is conveniently indefinite and relative. At each income level, as H. F. Clark has found, Americans want just about twenty-five per cent more (but of course this "just a bit more" continues to operate once it is obtained). In this flux of shifting standards, there is no stable resting point, or rather, it is the point which manages always to be "just ahead." An observer of a community in which annual salaries in six figures are not uncommon reports the anguished words of one victim of the American Dream: "In this town, I'm snubbed socially because I only get a thousand a week. That hurts." [9]

To say that the goal of monetary success is entrenched in American culture is only to say that Americans are bombarded on every side by precepts which affirm the right or, often, the duty of retaining the goal even in the face of repeated frustration. Prestigeful representatives of the society reinforce the cultural emphasis. The family, the school and the workplace— the major agencies shaping the personality structure and goal formation of Americans—join to provide the intensive disciplining required if an individual is to retain intact a goal that remains elusively beyond reach, if he is to be motivated by the promise of a gratification which is not redeemed. As we shall presently see, parents serve as a transmission belt for the values and goals of the groups of which they are a part—above all, of their social class or of the class with which they identify themselves. And the schools are of course the official agency for the passing on of the prevailing values, with a large proportion of the textbooks used in city schools implying or stating explicitly "that education leads to intelligence and consequently to job and money success." [10] Central to this process of disciplining people to maintain their unfulfilled aspirations are the cultural prototypes of success, the living documents testifying that the American Dream can be realized if one but has the requisite abilities. Consider in this connection the following excerpt from the business journal, *Nation's Business,* drawn from a large mass of comparable materials found in mass communications setting forth the values of business class culture.

The Document (*Nation's Business* *Vol. 27, No. 8, p. 7*)	*Its Sociological Implications*
" 'You have to be born to those jobs, buddy, or else have a good pull.'	Here is an heretical opinion, possibly born of continued frustration, which rejects the worth of retaining an apparently unrealizable goal and, moreover, questions the legitimacy of a social structure which provides differential access to this goal.
"That's an old sedative to ambition.	The counter-attack, explicitly asserting the cultural value of retaining one's aspirations intact, of not losing "ambition."
"Before listening to its seduction, ask these men:	A clear statement of the function to be served by the ensuing list of "successes." These men are living testimony that the social structure is such as to permit these aspirations to be achieved, *if one is worthy.* And correlatively, failure to reach these goals testifies only to one's own personal shortcomings. Aggression provoked by failure should therefore be directed inward and not outward, against oneself and not against a social structure which provides free and equal access to opportunity.
"Elmer R. Jones, president of Wells-Fargo and Co., who began life as a poor boy and left school at the fifth grade to take his first job.	Success prototype I: *All* may properly have the *same* lofty ambitions, for however lowly the starting-point, true talent can reach the very heights. Aspirations must be retained intact.
"Frank C. Ball, the Mason fruit jar king of America, who rode from Buffalo to Muncie, Indiana, in a boxcar along with his brother George's	Success prototype II: Whatever the present results of one's strivings, the future is large with promise; for the common man may yet become a king.

horse, to start a little business in Muncie that became the biggest of its kind.

"J. L. Bevan, president of the Illinois Central Railroad, who at twelve was a messenger boy in the freight office at New Orleans."

Gratifications may seem forever deferred, but they will finally be realized as one's enterprise becomes "the biggest of its kind."

Success prototype III: If the secular trends of our economy seem to give little scope to small business, then one may rise within the giant bureaucracies of private enterprise. If one can no longer be a "king" in a realm of his own creation, he may at least become a "president" in one of the economic democracies. No matter what one's present station, messenger boy or clerk, one's gaze should be fixed at the top.

From divers sources there flows a continuing pressure to retain high ambition. The exhortational literature is immense, and one can choose only at the risk of seeming invidious. Consider only these: The Reverend Russell H. Conwell, with his *Acres of Diamonds* address heard and read by hundreds of thousands and his subsequent book, *The New Day, or Fresh Opportunities: A Book for Young Men*; Elbert Hubbard, who delivered the famous *Message to Garcia* at Chautauqua forums throughout the land; Orison Swett Marden, who, in a stream of books, first set forth *The Secret of Achievement,* praised by college presidents, then explained the process of *Pushing to the Front,* eulogized by President McKinley and finally, these democratic testimonials notwithstanding, mapped the road to make *Every Man a King.* The symbolism of a commoner rising to the estate of economic royalty is woven deep in the texture of the American culture pattern, finding what is perhaps its ultimate expression in the words of one who knew whereof he spoke, Andrew Carnegie: "Be a king in your dreams. Say to yourself, 'My place is at the top.' " [11]

Coupled with this positive emphasis upon the obligation to maintain lofty goals is a correlative emphasis upon the penalizing of those who draw in their ambitions. Americans are admonished "not to be a quitter" for in the dictionary of American culture, as in the lexicon of youth, "there is no such as word 'fail.' " The cultural manifesto is clear: one must not quit, must not cease striving, must not lessen his goals, for "not failure, but low aim, is crime."

Thus the culture enjoins the acceptance of three cultural axioms: First, all should strive for the same lofty goals since these are open to all;

second, present seeming failure is but a way-station to ultimate success; and third, genuine failure consists only in the lessening or withdrawal of ambition.

In rough psychological paraphrase, these axioms represent, first, a symbolic "secondary reinforcement" of incentive; second, curbing the threatened extinction of a response through an associated stimulus; third, increasing the motive-strength to evoke continued responses despite the continued absence of reward.

In sociological paraphrase, these axioms represent, first, the deflection of criticism of the social structure onto one's self among those so situated in the society that they do not have full and equal access to opportunity; second, the preservation of a given structure of social power by having individuals in the lower social strata identify themselves, not with their compeers, but with those at the top (whom they will ultimately join); and third, providing pressures for conformity with the cultural dictates of unslackened ambition by the threat of less than full membership in the society for those who fail to conform.

It is in these terms and through these processes that contemporary American culture continues to be characterized by a heavy emphasis on wealth as a basic symbol of success, without a corresponding emphasis upon the legitimate avenues on which to march toward this goal. How do individuals living in this cultural context respond? And how do our observations bear upon the doctrine that deviant behavior typically derives from biological impulses breaking through the restraints imposed by culture? What, in short, are the consequences for the behavior of people variously situated in a social structure of a culture in which the emphasis on dominant success-goals has become increasingly separated from an equivalent emphasis on institutionalized procedures for seeking these goals?

REFERENCES

1. See, for example, S. Freud, *Civilization and Its Discontents* (*passim,* and esp. at p. 63); Ernest Jones, *Social Aspects of Psychoanalysis* (London, 1924) p. 28. If the Freudian notion is a variety of the "original sin" doctrine, then the interpretation advanced in this paper is a doctrine of "socially derived sin."
2. "Normal" in the sense of the psychologically expectable, if not culturally approved, response to determinate social conditions. This statement does not, of course, deny the role of biological and personality differences in fixing the *incidence* of deviant behavior. It is simply that *this* is not the problem considered here. It is in the same sense as our own, I take it, that James S. Plant speaks of the "normal reaction of normal people to abnormal conditions." See his *Personality and the Cultural Pattern* (New York, 1937), p. 248.
3. The position taken here has been perceptively described by Edward Sapir. ". . . problems of social science differ from problems of individual behavior in degree of specificity, not in kind. Every statement about behavior which throws the emphasis, explicitly or implicitly, on the actual, integral experiences of defined personalities

or types of personalities is a datum of psychology or psychiatry rather than of social science. Every statement about behavior which aims, not to be accurate about the behavior of an actual individual or individuals or about the expected behavior of a physically and psychologically defined type of individual, but which abstracts from such behavior in order to bring out in clear relief certain expectancies with regard to those aspects of individual behavior which various people share, as an interpersonal or 'social' pattern, is a datum, however crudely expressed, of social science." I have here chosen the second perspective; although I shall have occasion to speak of attitudes, values and function, it will be from the standpoint of how the social structure promotes or inhibits their appearance in specified types of situations. See Sapir, "Why Cultural Anthropology Needs the Psychiatrist," *Psychiatry*, 1938, 1, 7–12.

4. This ritualism may be associated with a mythology which rationalizes these practices so that they appear to retain their status as means, but the dominant pressure is toward strict ritualistic conformity, irrespective of the mythology. Ritualism is thus most complete when such rationalizations are not even called forth.

5. In this connection, one sees the relevance of Elton Mayo's paraphrase of the title of Tawney's well-known book. "Actually the problem is *not that of the sickness of an acquisitive society; it is that of the acquisitiveness of a sick society.*" *Human Problems of an Industrial Civilization* (New York, 1933), p. 153. Mayo deals with the process through which wealth comes to be the basic symbol of social achievement and sees this as arising from a state of anomie. My major concern here is with the social consequences of a heavy emphasis upon monetary success as a goal in a society which has not adapted its structure to the implications of this emphasis. A complete analysis would require the simultaneous examination of both processes.

6. Durkheim's resurrection of the term "anomie" which, so far as I know, first appears in approximately the same sense in the late sixteenth century, might well become the object of an investigation by a student interested in the historical filiation of ideas. Like the term "climate of opinion" brought into academic and political popularity by A. N. Whitehead three centuries after it was coined by Joseph Glanvill, the word "anomie" (or anomy or anomia) has lately come into frequent use, once it was reintroduced by Durkheim. Why the resonance in contemporary society? For a magnificent model of the type of research required by questions of this order, see Leo Spitzer, *"Milieu and Ambiance*: An Essay in Historical Semantics," *Philosophy and Phenomenological Research,* 1942, 3, 1–42, 169–218.

7. It appears unlikely that cultural norms, once interiorized, are wholly eliminated. Whatever residuum persists will induce personality tensions and conflict, with some measure of ambivalence. A manifest rejection of the once-incorporated institutional norms will be coupled with some latent retention of their emotional correlates. "Guilt feelings," "a sense of sin," "pangs of conscience" are diverse terms referring to this unrelieved tension. Symbolic adherence to the nominally repudiated values or rationalizations for the rejection of these values constitute a more subtle expression of these tensions.

8. "Many," not all, unintegrated groups, for the reason mentioned earlier. In groups where the primary emphasis shifts to institutional means, the outcome is normally a type of ritualism rather than anomie.

9. Leo C. Rosten, *Hollywood* (New York, 1940), p. 40.

10. Malcolm S. MacLean, *Scholars, Workers and Gentlemen* (Harvard University Press, 1938), p. 29.

11. *Cf.* A. W. Griswold, *The American Cult of Success* (Yale University doctoral dissertation, 1933); R. O. Carlson, *"Personality Schools": A Sociological Analysis,* (Columbia University Master's Essay, 1948).

Institutionalization and Anomie * (*Parsons*)

It should immediately be evident on general grounds that the most fundamental mechanisms of social control are to be found in the normal processes
of interaction in an institutionally integrated social system. The essentials
of these processes have been analyzed and illustrated throughout the earlier
chapters of this work. Hence it is necessary here only to add a few points.
The central phenomena are to be found in the institutional integration of
motivation and the reciprocal reinforcement of the attitudes and actions of
the different individual actors involved in an institutionalized social structure. These considerations apply to any one pattern of role-expectations. But
institutionalization has integrative functions on various levels, both with
reference to the different roles in which any one actor is involved, and to the
coordination of the behavior of different individuals. The latter has been
dealt with in a number of contexts.

A few remarks are, however, in order in the former context. The individual engages in a wide variety of different activities and becomes involved
in social relationships with a large number of different people whose relations to him vary greatly. One of the primary functions of institutionalization is to help order these different activities and relationships so that they
constitute a sufficiently coordinated system, to be manageable by the actor
and to minimize conflicts on the social level. There are two particularly interesting aspects of this ordering. One is the establishment of a time schedule
so that different times are "set aside" for different activities, with different
people. "Time off" from occupational obligations on Sundays, holidays,
vacations, etc., is one example. The fact that there is a time for each of many
different activities—and also a place—keeps the claims of each from interfering with those of the others. In fact a society so complex as ours probably
could not function without relatively rigid time scheduling, and the problem
of the cultural values and psychological need-disposition structure of such a
time organization is of great importance. We know that in many societies the
motivational prerequisites for fitting into such a time-orientation do not
exist.

A second major area is the establishment of institutionalized priorities.
Especially in a relatively free and mobile society it is inevitable that people
should become involved in situations where conflicting demands are made

upon them. It is quite obvious that such situations are sources of serious potential conflict. This can be minimized if there is a legitimized priority scale so that in choosing one obligation above the other the individual can in general be backed by the sentiments of a common value system. It is indeed in areas where this scheme of priorities is indefinite or not well integrated that loopholes for deviance are most common. One example of such a potential conflict may be cited. A physician has peculiarly sharply emphasized obligations to his patients. But he also has important obligations to his family. Far more than in most occupations he is often called away at times when the family has important claims on him—meal times, evenings when social engagements may be scheduled, etc. The institutionalized expectation of the priority of the claims of patients is indispensable to the physician in dealing with his wife on such an occasion. As Merton has so well analyzed, the exposure to situations of such conflict without clearly institutionalized priorities of obligations is a very important aspect of *anomie*.

The above considerations do not however concern mechanisms of social control in a strict sense though they describe essential aspects of the background on which we must understand the operation of such mechanisms. When we turn to the consideration of normal social interaction within such an institutionalized framework as a process of mutually influenced and contingent action we see that a process of social control is continually going on. Actors are continually doing and saying things which are more or less "out of line," such as by insinuation impugning someone's motives, or presuming too much. Careful observation will show that others in the situation often without being aware of it, tend to react to these minor deviances in such a way as to bring the deviant back "into line," by tactfully disagreeing with him, by a silence which underlines the fact that what he said was not acceptable, or very often by humor as a tension-release, as a result of which he comes to see himself more nearly as others see him. These minor control mechanisms are, it may be maintained, the way in which the institutionalized values are implemented in behavior. They are, on a certain level, the most fundamental mechanisms of all, and only when they break down does it become necessary for more elaborate and specialized mechanisms to come into play.

Beyond the scope of such mechanisms there are points in the social system at which people are exposed to rather special strains. In a good many such cases we find special phenomena which have been interpreted to function at least in part as mechanisms for "coping" with such strains with a minimum of disruptive consequences for the social system. Two types may be briefly discussed. One is the type of situation where because of uncertainty factors or specially acute adjustment problems there is exposure to what, for the persons concerned, is an unusual strain. In general the field of religion and magic yields many examples of this. The problem of uncertainty in the health field and of bereavement are good examples. The reactions which such unusual strains tend to produce are of the character noted above. They both include potentially disruptive components and are unstructured in relation to the social system. In the case of uncertainty, as in gardening in the Trobriands, one of these may be discouragement, a general tendency to withdrawal. Similarly in the case of bereavement, there may be a loss of incentive to keep on going. Ritual on such occasions serves to organize the reaction system in a positive manner and to put a check on the disruptive tendencies.[1]

One aspect of such ritual patterns is always the permissive one of giving an opportunity for "acting out" symbolically the wishes and emotional tensions associated with the situation of strain. It provides opportunities for a permissive relaxation of some of the disciplines of everyday life which are characterized in part by a relatively strict pressure to reality-orientation. But at the same time it is by no means a completely free and untrammeled opportunity for expression. Action is on the contrary strictly channeled into culturally prescribed forms, which prevent "wandering all over the lot." It is a conspicuous feature of such rituals that they are communally prescribed and thus give the support of emphasizing group concern with the situation. They also symbolically assert the dominant value attitudes, thus in the case of death for instance the importance of the survivors going on living in terms of that value system, redefining the solidarity with the deceased in these terms: it is "what he would have wished." [2]

A slightly different type of structuring of behavior which is certainly in part significant as a mechanism of control is what may be called the "secondary institution." The American youth culture is a good example. Like ritual it has its conspicuous permissive aspect, so much so that it shades over into explicit deviance. In this permissive aspect it also may be regarded as primarily a "safety valve" of the social system in that attempting to keep youth completely in line with adult disciplines would probably greatly increase the strains of their position. But it also has more positive control aspects. One of these is the integration of the youth culture with major institutional structures, mainly in the field of formal education. This not only brings it under direct adult supervision, but it legitimizes some of the patterns, for example athletics and dances. In spite of the deviant fringe, the existence of such a legitimized core undoubtedly keeps down the total amount of deviance.

Finally there are certain "self-liquidating" features of the youth culture which are relatively hard to identify but probably quite important. In a variety of ways, through the experience of youth culture activities and relationships the individual in the optimum case goes through a process of emotional development to the point where he ceases to need youth culture and "graduates" into full adult status. Of course in this as in many features of our social control system there are innumerable "miscarriages." But broadly speaking it is extremely probable that on the whole the net effect tends to be emotionally "maturing." For example, the very insistence on independence from adult control accustoms the individual to take more and more responsibility on his own. In the youth culture phase he tends to substitute dependency on his peer group for that on the parents, but gradually he becomes emancipated from even this dependency. Similarly in the relations of the sexes the youth culture offers opportunities and mechanisms for emotional maturation. The element of rebelliousness against the adult world helps to emancipate from more immature object-attachments, while certain features of the "rating and dating" complex protect the individual during the process of this emancipation from deeper emotional involvements than he is yet able to accept. The very publicity of such relationships within the peer group serves as such a protection. Thus the youth culture is not only projective but also exposes the individual passing through it to positively adjustive influences.[3]

It will be noted that the above mechanisms operate within the framework of socially legitimated interaction. Within the normal processes of nipping of minor deviances in the bud of course no differentiated social structures are involved at all. In the case of "safety-valve" mechanisms like ritual, and of secondary institutional patterns, there are special social structures. These entail a limited permissiveness for modes of behavior and types of emotional expression which would be tabooed in ordinary everyday life, e.g., the display of "grief" at funeral ceremonies. But this permissiveness is rather narrowly limited, and it is of the greatest importance that it operates within a system of interaction which is continuous with the main institutionalized social structure, differing from it only with respect to occasion, or as in the case of the youth culture, to stage in the socialization process. The behavior is emphatically not stigmatized as deviant, but is legitimized for people in the relevant situations. They are treated in the present context because of their relevance to the control of *potentially* deviant motivational elements.

Thus it is clear that some balance of permissiveness and its restriction is maintained. Support is clearly given through the institutionalized legitimation of the patterns in question and the resulting solidarity. Generally speaking, however, there is little conscious manipulation of sanctions.

REFERENCES

1. Almost the classic analysis of this type of function of ritual is Malinowski's analysis of funeral ceremonies in *Magic, Science and Religion*. As Kroeber, *op. cit.*, notes, however, there are still important problems of the universality of the relationship between such strains and ritual which must be further studied.

2. We shall discuss in the next two chapters some of the ways in which the religious orientation of a society can be of the first importance with reference to its general system of values in the secular sphere. The control mechanisms in certain areas of special strain tend in turn to be integrated with both. This is the essential difference between the view of religion taken here and that of Kardiner in *The Individual and His Society*. The latter tends to treat it overwhelmingly as a "projective system" which expresses motivational elements which are blocked by the disciplines of secular life. This is undoubtedly *one* major aspect of the matter, but only one.

3. Suggestive evidence of the importance of the youth culture in this connection is given in Demareth's study of a sample of schizophrenics. An early "maturity" of interests combined with lack of participation in youth culture activities was highly characteristic of the group. Not one of the 20 had established satisfactory heterosexual relationships on a youth culture level. It may well be that without the youth culture there would be many more schizophrenic breakdowns. See N. J. Demareth, *Adolescent Status and the Individual*, unpublished Ph.D. dissertation, Harvard University, 1942. It is also suggestive that one element of alcoholism for men may be connected with over-involvement in the youth culture and failure to become emancipated from it at the proper time. The alcoholic may be in part an adolescent who is unsuccessfully trying to be an adult.

14.

STRUCTURE AND FUNCTION

SOCIOLOGICAL THEORIZING in the last few decades has been profoundly influenced by a group of thinkers who have emphasized the so-called "functionalist" or "structural-functional" approach. As some of our selections will illustrate, by no means all of the social scientists who have worked in this tradition are agreed upon the precise denotations or connotations of these terms. We might nevertheless suggest as a point of departure that "structure" in their usage generally refers to a set of relatively stable and patterned relationships of social units, while by "function" they mean those consequences of any social activity which make for the adaptation or adjustment of a given structure or its component parts. In other words, "structure" refers to a system with relatively enduring patterns, and "function" refers to the dynamic process within the structure.

This type of analysis arose out of the need felt by sociologists and anthropologists to develop theoretical and methodological tools adequate for dealing with the interrelatedness of various "traits," institutions, groups, etc., within a total social system, and to overcome certain atomistic and descriptive methods which had prevailed in the nineteenth century.

Functionalism was brought into sociological thought by borrowing directly and developing analogies for concepts in the biological sciences. Biology since the middle of the last century frequently referred to the "structure" of an organism, meaning a relatively stable arrangement of relationships between the different cells, and referred to the consequences of the activity of the various organs in the life process of the organism as their "function." As our excerpt from Herbert Spencer (1820–1903), the great British evolutionary sociologist, will make clear, structure-function theory in sociology was at first conceived not only as pointing to many analogies and similarities between the body social and the biological organism, but as revealing that the same principles, the same "definition of life," applied to both. This early *organicism* has long since been abandoned in sociology. Yet Spencer's contribution, that of having introduced functional types of analysis into sociology, should not be forgotten—as it so often has been.

The first systematic formulation of the logic of a functionalist approach in sociology can be found in the work of Emile Durkheim. Durkheim was no longer intent upon illustrating alleged correspondences between biological and sociological processes, but he made it his task to explore systematically the contributions that particular social factors, such as ritual, crime, punishment, and role differentiation, make to the maintenance or change of given social structures. Our selection from Durkheim illustrates the distinctions he suggests between causal and functional types of analysis and indicates that these two methods, far from being antithetical, are in fact complementary.

Functional analysis in this country was crucially influenced by the work of two British anthropologists, A. R. Radcliffe-Brown and Bronislaw Malinowski. Though an Englishman, trained at Cambridge, Radcliffe-Brown closely followed in the footsteps of Durkheim and his school. Like Durkheim, he was often led, as our selection makes clear, to utilize analogical models imported from biology to illustrate his conceptualization of social function. This tendency probably accounted for his propensity to devote his attention mainly to the function of each element in the maintenance and development of a *total* structure and to neglect the functional consequences of specific elements for differentiated parts of such structures or for their individual components. It is this last distinction, above all, which led Bronislaw Malinowski to distinguish his type of functionalism from that of his eminent colleague. To Malinowski the Durkheimian bent in the work of Radcliffe-Brown led to "a tendency to ignore completely the individual and to eliminate the biological element from the functional analysis of culture." Malinowski proposed "to link up functionally the various types of cultural responses, such as economic, legal, educational, scientific, magic and religious" and then to show that they were all related to the biological needs of individuals. But, whatever the differences between the two eminent anthropologists, and they should not be minimized, it remains true that their life work in anthropological research provides us with splendid illustrations of the fruitfulness of an approach that focuses attention upon the functional interrelatedness of the parts that make a cultural and structural whole. Their work enables one to perceive cultures as single functioning systems interrelated in their component parts, rather than as a patchwork of culture traits, institutions, customs, and norms.

Vilfredo Pareto (1848–1923), the distinguished Italian sociologist, developed a system of analysis which, though it cannot be called "functionalist," nevertheless incorporates many features of functional analysis. Pareto, who had done distinguished work in mathematical economics before he developed an interest in sociological theory, abandoned the biological analogies still so pronounced in the thinkers discussed above in favor of an attempt to build a generalized theory of social systems on the model of mechanics. He saw society as essentially a system in equilibrium, consisting of parts so interdependent that every change in each part will necessarily affect all other parts as well as the system as a whole. While Pareto's world view is now generally considered to be of relatively limited usefulness, there are elements in it, such as the classification of logical and non-logical actions and the differentiation between objective end and subjective purpose, that seem to present fruitful leads for functional analysis. In fact, Merton's later distinction between latent and manifest functions would seem to be fore-shadowed in these pages.

Our final selection, from the work of Robert K. Merton, is part of a larger study in which the whole functionalist school, its assumptions and its shortcomings, are discussed in detail. This seems to us the most sophisticated treatment of the functionalist approach now available. Merton introduces a number of important new concepts into functional analysis, such as the concept of *functional alternatives* and the distinction between *latent* and *manifest* functions. In addition, he provides us with a tentative codification for functional analysis which is as invaluable for the judgment of past theory as it is for the development of future research and theory.

Space does not permit us to present samples of the work of other significant contributors to functional theory in contemporary sociology. We can merely mention the names of Talcott Parsons, Marion J. Levy, Jr., and Kingsley Davis. Yet many of the selections in other parts of this book reflect, directly or indirectly, a functionalist orientation, and thus may be said to supplement the selections in this section.

Social Structure and Social Function * (*Spencer*)

SOCIAL STRUCTURES

In societies, as in living bodies, increase of mass is habitually accompanied by increase of structure. Along with that integration which is the primary trait of evolution, both exhibit in high degrees the secondary trait, differentiation.

The association of these two characters in animals was described in the *Principles of Biology*. . . .

So, too, is it with societies. As we progress from small groups to larger; from simple groups to compound groups; from compound groups to doubly compound ones; the unlikenesses of parts increase. The social aggregate, homogeneous when minute, habitually gains in heterogeneity along with each increment of growth; and to reach great size must acquire great complexity. Let us glance at the leading stages.

Naturally in a state like that of the Cayaguas or Wood Indians of South

* Abridged from Herbert Spencer, *The Principles of Sociology*, Vol. I, pp. 471–489. New York, Appleton-Century-Crofts, Inc., 1897.

America, so little social that "one family lives at a distance from another," social organization is impossible; and even where there is some slight association of families, organization does not arise while they are few and wandering. Groups of Esquimaux, of Australians, of Bushmen, of Fuegians, are without even that primary contrast of parts implied by settled chieftainship. Their members are subject to no control but such as is temporarily acquired by the stronger, or more cunning, or more experienced: not even a permanent nucleus is present. Habitually where larger simple groups exist, we find some kind of head. Though not a uniform rule (for, as we shall hereafter see, the genesis of a controlling agency depends on the nature of the social activities), this is a general rule. The headless clusters, wholly ungoverned, are incoherent, and separate before they acquire considerable sizes; but along with maintenance of an aggregate approaching to, or exceeding, a hundred, we ordinarily find a simple or compound ruling agency—one or more men claiming and exercising authority that is natural, or supernatural, or both. This is the first social differentiation. Soon after it there frequently comes another, tending to form a division between regulative and operative parts. In the lowest tribes this is rudely represented only by the contrast in status between the sexes: the men, having unchecked control, carry on such external activities as the tribe shows us, chiefly in war; while the women are made drudges who perform the less skilled parts of the process of sustentation. But that tribal growth, and establishment of chieftainship, which gives military superiority, presently causes enlargement of the operative part by adding captives to it. This begins unobtrusively. While in battle the men are killed, and often afterwards eaten, the non-combatants are enslaved. Patagonians, for example, make slaves of women and children taken in war. Later, and especially when cannibalism ceases, comes the enslavement of male captives; whence results, in some cases, an operative part clearly marked off from the regulative part. Among the Chinooks, "slaves do all the laborious work." We read that the Beluchi, avoiding the hard labour of cultivation, impose it on the Jutts, the ancient inhabitants whom they have subjugated. Beecham says it is usual on the Gold Coast to make the slaves clear the ground for cultivation. And among the Felathahs "slaves are numerous: the males are employed in weaving, collecting wood or grass, or on any other kind of work; some of the women are engaged in spinning . . . in preparing the yarn for the loom, others in pounding and grinding corn, etc."

Along with that increase of mass caused by union of primary social aggregates into a secondary one, a further unlikeness of parts arises. The holding together of the compound cluster implies a head of the whole as well as heads of the parts; and a differentiation analogous to that which originally produced a chief, now produces a chief of chiefs. Sometimes the combination is made for defence against a common foe, and sometimes it results from conquest by one tribe of the rest. In this last case the predominant tribe, in maintaining its supremacy, develops more highly its military character: thus becoming unlike the others.

After such clusters of clusters have been so consolidated that their united powers can be wielded by one governing agency, there come alliances with, or subjugations of, other clusters of clusters, ending from time to time in coalescence. When this happens there results still greater complexity in the governing agency, with its king, local rulers, and petty chiefs; and at the same time, there arise more marked divisions of classes—military, priestly, slave, etc. Clearly, then, complication of structure accompanies increase of mass.

This increase of heterogeneity, which in both classes of aggregates goes along with growth, presents another trait in common. Beyond unlikenesses of parts due to development of the co-ordinating agencies, there presently follow unlikenesses among the agencies co-ordinated—the organs of alimentation, etc., in the one case, and the industrial structures in the other.

When animal-aggregates of the lowest order unite to form one of a higher order, and when, again, these secondary aggregates are compounded into tertiary aggregates, each component is at first similar to the other components; but in the course of evolution dissimilarities arise and become more and more decided . . . It is thus with the minor social groups combined into a major social group. Each tribe originally had within itself such feebly-marked industrial divisions as sufficed for its low kind of life; and those were like those of each other tribe. But union facilitates exchange of commodities; and if, as mostly happens, the component tribes severally occupy localities favourable to unlike kinds of production, unlike occupations are initiated, and there result unlikenesses of industrial structure. Even between tribes not united, as those of Australia, barter of products furnished by their respective habitats goes on so long as war does not hinder. And evidently when there is reached such a stage of integration as in Madagascar, or as in the chief Negro states of Africa, the internal peace that follows subordination to one government makes commercial intercourse easy. The like parts being permanently held together, mutual dependence becomes possible; and along with growing mutual dependence the parts grow unlike.

The advance of organization which thus follows the advance of aggregation, alike in individual organisms and in social organisms, conforms in both cases to the same general law: differentiations proceed from the more general to the more special. First broad and simple contrasts of parts; then within each of the parts primarily contrasted, changes which make unlike divisions of them; then within each of these unlike divisions, minor unlikenesses; and so on continually.

The successive stages in the development of a vertebrate column, illustrate this law in animals . . . During social evolution analogous metamorphoses may everywhere be traced. The rise of the structure exercising religious control will serve as an example. In simple tribes, and in clusters of tribes during their early stages of aggregation, we find men who are at once sorcerers, priests, diviners, exorcists, doctors,—men who deal with supposed supernatural beings in all the various possible ways: propitiating them, seeking knowledge and aid from them, commanding them, subduing them. Along with advance in social integration, there come both differences of function and differences of rank. In Tanna "there are rain-makers . . . and a host of other 'sacred men;' " in Fiji there are not only priests, but seers; among the Sandwich Islanders there are diviners as well as priests; among the New Zealanders, Thomson distinguishes between priests and sorcerers; and among the Kaffirs, besides diviners and rain-makers, there are two classes of doctors who respectively rely on supernatural and on natural agents in curing their patients. More advanced societies, as those of ancient America, show us still greater multiformity of this once-uniform group. In Mexico, for example, the medical class, descending from a class of sorcerers who dealt antagonistically with the supernatural agents supposed to cause disease, were distinct from the priests, whose dealings with supernatural agents were propitiatory. Further, the sacerdotal class included several kinds, dividing the religious offices among them—sacrificers, diviners, singers, composers of hymns, instructors of youth; and then there were also gradations of rank in each. This progress from general to special in priesthoods, has, in the higher nations, led to such marked distinctions that the original kinships are forgotten. The priest-astrologers of ancient races were initiators of the scientific class, now variously specialized; from the priest-doctors of old have come the medical class with its chief division and minor divisions; while within the clerical class proper, have arisen not only various ranks from Pope down to acolyte, but various kinds of functionaries—dean, priest, deacon, chorister, as well as others classed as curates and chaplains. Similarly if we trace the genesis of any industrial structure; as that which from primitive blacksmiths who smelt their own iron as well as make implements from it, brings us to our iron-manufacturing districts, where preparation of the metal is separated into smelting, refining, puddling, rolling, and where turning this metal into implements is divided into various businesses.

The transformation here illustrated is, indeed, an aspect of that transformation of the homogeneous into the heterogeneous which everywhere characterizes evolution; but the truth to be noted is that it characterizes the evolution of individual organisms and of social organisms in especially high degrees. . . .

SOCIAL FUNCTIONS

Changes of structures cannot occur without changes of functions. Much that was said in the last chapter might, therefore, be said here with substituted terms. Indeed, as in societies many changes of structure are more indicated by changes of function than directly seen, it may be said that these last have been already described by implication.

There are, however, certain functional traits not manifestly implied by traits of structure. To these a few pages must be devoted.

If organization consists in such a construction of the whole that its parts can carry on mutually-dependent actions, then in proportion as organization is high there must go a dependence of each part upon the rest so great that separation is fatal; and conversely. This truth is equally well shown in the individual organism and in the social organism.

The lowest animal-aggregates are so constituted that each portion, similar to every other in appearance, carries on similar actions; and here spontaneous or artificial separation interferes scarcely at all with the life of either separated portion. When the faintly-differentiated speck of protoplasm forming a Rhizopod is accidentally divided, each division goes on as before. . . . The like happens for the like reason with the lowest social aggregates. A headless wandering group of primitive men divides without any inconvenience. Each man, at once warrior, hunter, and maker of his own weapons, hut, etc., with a squaw who has in every case the like drudgeries to carry on, needs concert with his fellows only in war and to some extent in the chase; and, except for fighting, concert with half the tribe is as good as concert with the whole. Even where the slight differentiation implied by chieftainship exists, little inconvenience results from voluntary or enforced separation. Either before or after a part of the tribe migrates, some man becomes head, and such low social life as is possible recommences.

With highly-organized aggregates of either kind it is very different. We cannot cut a mammal in two without causing immediate death. Twisting off the head of a fowl is fatal. Not even a reptile, though it may survive the loss of its tail, can live when its body is divided. And among annulose creatures it similarly happens that though in some inferior genera, bisection does not kill either half, it kills both in an insect, an arachnid, or a crustacean. If in high societies the effect of mutilation is less than in high animals, still it is great. Middlesex separated from its surroundings would in a few days have all its social processes stopped by lack of supplies. Cut off the cotton-district from Liverpool and other ports, and there would come arrest of its industry followed by mortality of its people. Let a division be made between the coal-mining populations and adjacent populations which smelt metals or make broadcloth by machinery, and both, forthwith dying socially by arrest of their actions, would begin to die individually. Though when a civilized society is so divided that part of it is left without a central controlling agency, it may presently evolve one; yet there is meanwhile much risk of dissolution, and before re-organization is efficient, a long period of disorder and weakness must be passed through.

So that the consensus of functions becomes closer as evolution advances. In low aggregates, both individual and social, the actions of the parts are but little dependent on one another; whereas in developed aggregates of both kinds, that combination of actions which constitutes the life of the whole, makes possible the component actions which constitute the lives of the parts.

Another corollary, manifest a priori and proved a posteriori, must be named. Where parts are little differentiated, they can readily perform one another's functions; but where much differentiated they can perform one another's functions very imperfectly, or not at all . . .

In social organisms, low and high, we find these relatively great and relatively small powers of substitution. Of course, where each member of the tribe repeats every other in his mode of life, there are no unlike functions to be exchanged; and where there has arisen only that small differentiation implied by the barter of weapons for other articles, between one member of the tribe skilled in weapon-making and others less skilled, the destruction of this specially-skilled member entails no great evil; since the rest can severally do for themselves that which he did for them, though not quite so well. Even in settled societies of considerable sizes, we find the like holds to a great degree. Of the ancient Mexicans, Zurita says—"Every Indian knows all handicrafts which do not require great skill or delicate instruments;" and in Peru each man "was expected to be acquainted with the various handi-crafts essential to domestic comfort:" the parts of the societies were so slightly differentiated in their occupations, that assumption of one another's occupations remained practicable. But in societies like our own, specialized industrially and otherwise in high degrees, the actions of one part which fails in its function cannot be assumed by other parts. Even the rela-tively-unskilled farm labourers, were they to strike, would have their duties very inadequately performed by the urban population; and our iron manufactures would be stopped if their trained artisans, refusing to work, had to be replaced by peasants or hands from cotton factories. Still less could the higher functions, legislative, judicial, etc., be effectually performed by coal-miners and navvies.

Evidently the same reason for this contrast holds in the two cases. In proportion as the units forming any part of an individual organism are limited to one kind of action, as that of absorbing, or secreting, or contracting, or conveying an impulse, and become adapted to that action, they lose adaptation to other actions; and in the social organism the discipline required for effectually discharging a special duty, causes unfitness for discharging special duties widely unlike it.

Beyond these two chief functional analogies between individual organisms and social organisms, that when they are little evolved, division or mutilation causes small inconvenience, but when they are much evolved it causes great perturbation or death, and that in low types of either kind the parts can assume one another's functions, but cannot in high types; sundry consequent functional analogies might be enlarged on did space permit.

There is the truth that in both kinds of organisms the vitality increases as fast as the functions become specialized. In either case, before there exist structures severally adapted for the unlike actions, these are ill-performed; and in the absence of developed appliances for furthering it, the utilization of one another's services is but slight. But along with advance of organization, every part, more limited in its office, performs its office better; the means of exchanging benefits become greater; each aids all, and all aid each with increasing efficiency; and the total activity we call life, individual or national, augments.

Causal and Functional Analysis * (*Durkheim*)

Most sociologists think they have accounted for phenomena once they have shown how they are useful, what role they play, reasoning as if facts existed only from the point of view of this role and with no other determining cause than the sentiment, clear or confused, of the services they are called to render. That is why they think they have said all that is necessary, to render them intelligible, when they have established the reality of these services and have shown what social needs they satisfy.

* Reprinted from *The Rules of Sociological Method* by Emile Durkheim, pp. 89–97, with permission of the publisher, The Free Press, Glencoe, Ill. Copyright, 1938, by The Free Press, A Corporation.

Thus Comte traces the entire progressive force of the human species to this fundamental tendency "which directly impels man constantly to ameliorate his condition, whatever it may be, under all circumstances," [1] and Spencer relates this force to the need for greater happiness. It is in accordance with this principle that Spencer explains the formation of society by the alleged advantages which result from co-operation; the institution of government, by the utility of the regularization of military co-operation; [2] the transformations through which the family has passed, by the need for reconciling more and more perfectly the interests of parents, children, and society.

But this method confuses two very different questions. To show how a fact is useful is not to explain how it originated or why it is what it is. The uses which it serves presuppose the specific properties characterizing it but do not create them. The need we have of things cannot give them existence, nor can it confer their specific nature upon them. It is to causes of another sort that they owe their existence. The idea we have of their utility may indeed motivate us to put these forces to work and to elicit from them their characteristic effects, but it will not enable us to produce these effects out of nothing. This proposition is evident so long as it is a question only of material, or even psychological, phenomena. It would be equally evident in sociology if social facts, because of their extreme intangibility, did not wrongly appear to us as without all intrinsic reality. Since we usually see them as a product purely of mental effort, it seems to us that they may be produced at will whenever we find it necessary. But since each one of them is a force, superior to that of the individual, and since it has a separate existence, it is not true that merely by willing to do so may one call them into being. No force can be engendered except by an antecedent force. To revive the spirit of the family, where it has become weakened, it is not enough that everyone understand its advantages; the causes which alone can engender it must be made to act directly. To give a government the authority necessary for it, it is not enough to feel the need for this authority; we must have recourse to the only sources from which all authority is derived. We must, namely, establish traditions, a common spirit, etc.; and for this it is necessary again to go back along the chain of causes and effects until we find a point where the action of man may be effectively brought to bear.

What shows plainly the dualism of these two orders of research is that a fact can exist without being at all useful, either because it has never been adjusted to any vital end or because, after having been useful, it has lost all utility while continuing to exist by the inertia of habit alone. There are, indeed, more survivals in society than in biological organisms. There are even cases where a practice or a social institution changes its function without thereby changing its nature. The rule, *Is pater quem justae nuptiae declar-ant*,[3] has remained in our code essentially the same as it was in the old Roman law. While its purpose then was to safeguard the property rights of a father over children born to the legitimate wife, it is rather the rights of children that it protects today. The custom of taking an oath began by being a sort of judiciary test and has become today simply a solemn and imposing formality. The religious dogmas of Christianity have not changed for centuries, but the role which they play is not the same in our modern societies as in the Middle Ages. Thus, the same words may serve to express new ideas. It is, moreover, a proposition true in sociology, as in biology, that the organ is independent of the function—in other words, while remaining the same, it can serve different ends. The causes of its existence are, then, independent of the ends it serves.

Nevertheless, we do not mean to say that the impulses, needs, and desires of men never intervene actively in social evolution. On the contrary, it is certain that they can hasten or retard its development, according to the circumstances which determine the social phenomena. Apart from the fact that they cannot, in any case, make something out of nothing, their actual intervention, whatever may be its effects, can take place only by means of efficient causes. A deliberate intention can contribute, even in this limited way, to the production of a new phenomenon only if it has itself been newly formed or if it is itself a result of some transformation of a previous intention. For, unless we postulate a truly providential and pre-established harmony, we cannot admit that man has carried with him from the beginning—potentially ready to be awakened at the call of circumstances—all the intentions which conditions were destined to demand in the course of human evolution. It must further be recognized that a deliberate intention is itself something objectively real; it can, then, neither be created nor modified by the mere fact that we judge it useful. It is a force having a nature of its own; for that nature to be given existence or altered, it is not enough that we should find this advantageous. In order to bring about such changes, there must be a sufficient cause.

For example, we have explained the constant development of the division of labor by showing that it is necessary in order that man may maintain himself in the new conditions of existence as he advances in history. We have attributed to this tendency, which is rather improperly named the "instinct of self-preservation," an important role in our explanations. But, in the first place, this instinct alone could not account for even the most rudimentary specialization. It can do nothing if the conditions on which the division of labor depends do not already exist, i.e., if individual differences have not increased sufficiently as a consequence of the progressive disintegration of the common consciousness and of hereditary influences.[4] It was even necessary that division of labor should have already begun to exist for its usefulness to be seen and for the need of it to make itself felt. The very development of individual differences, necessarily accompanied by a greater diversity of tastes and aptitudes, produced this first result. Further, the instinct of self-preservation did not, of itself and without cause, come to fertilize this first germ of specialization. We were started in this new direction, first, because the course we previously followed was now barred and because the greater intensity of the struggle, owing to the more extensive consolidation of societies, made more and more difficult the survival of individuals who continued to devote themselves to unspecialized tasks. For such reasons it became necessary for us to change our mode of living. Moreover, if our activity has been turned toward a constantly more developed division of labor, it is because this was also the direction of least resistance. The other possible solutions were emigration, suicide, and crime. Now, in the average case, the ties attaching us to life and country and the sympathy we have for our fellows are sentiments stronger and more resistant than the habits which could deflect us from narrower specialization. These habits, then, had inevitably to yield to each impulse that arose. Thus the fact that we allow a place for human needs in sociological explanations does not mean that we even partially revert to teleology. These needs can influence social evolution only on condition that they themselves, and the changes they undergo, can be explained solely by causes that are deterministic and not at all purposive.

But what is even more convincing than the preceding considerations is a study of actual social behavior. Where purpose reigns, there reigns also a more or less wide contingency; for there are no ends, and even fewer means, which necessarily control all men, even when it is assumed that they are placed in the same circumstances. Given the same environment, each individual adapts himself to it according to his own disposition and in his own way, which he prefers to all other ways. One person will seek to change it and make it conform to his needs; another will prefer to change himself and moderate his desires. To arrive at the same goal, many different ways can be and actually are followed. If, then, it were true that historic development took place in terms of ends clearly or obscurely felt, social facts should present the most infinite diversity; and all comparison should be almost impossible.

To be sure, the external events which constitute the superficial part of social life vary from one people to another, just as each individual has his own history, although the bases of physical and moral organization are the same for all. But when one comes in contact with social phenomena, one is, on the contrary, surprised by the astonishing regularity with which they occur under the same circumstances. Even the most minute and the most trivial practices recur with the most astonishing uniformity. A certain nuptial ceremony, purely symbolical in appearance, such as the carrying-off of the betrothed, is found to be exactly the same wherever a certain family type exists; and again this family type itself is linked to a whole social organization. The most bizarre customs, such as the couvade, the levirate, exogamy, etc., are observed among the most diverse peoples and are symptomatic of a certain social state. The right to make one's will appears at a certain phase of history, and the more or less important restrictions limiting it offer a fairly exact clue to the particular stage of social evolution. It would be easy to multiply examples. This wide diffusion of collective forms would be inexplicable if purpose or final causes had the predominant place in sociology that is attributed to them.

When, then, the explanation of a social phenomenon is undertaken, we must seek separately the efficient cause which produces it and the function it fulfils. We use the word "function," in preference to "end" or "purpose," precisely because social phenomena do not generally exist for the useful results they produce. We must determine whether there is a correspondence between the fact under consideration and the general needs of the social organism, and in what this correspondence consists, without occupying ourselves with whether it has been intentional or not. All these questions of intention are too subjective to allow scientific treatment.

Not only must these two types of problems be separated, but it is proper, in general, to treat the former before the latter. This sequence, indeed, corresponds to that of experience. It is natural to seek the causes of a phenomenon before trying to determine its effects. This method is all the more logical since the first question, once answered, will often help to answer the second. Indeed, the bond which units the cause to the effect is reciprocal to an extent which has not been sufficiently recognized. The effect can doubtless not exist without its cause; but the latter, in turn, needs its effect. It is from the cause that the effect draws its energy; but it also restores it to the cause on occasion, and consequently it cannot disappear without the cause showing the effects of its disappearance.[5]

For example, the social reaction that we call "punishment" is due to the intensity of the collective sentiments which the crime offends; but, from another angle, it has the useful function of maintaining these sentiments at the same degree of intensity, for they would soon diminish if offenses against them were not punished.[6] Similarly, in proportion as the social milieu becomes more complex and more unstable, traditions and conventional beliefs are shaken, become more indeterminate and more unsteady, and reflective powers are developed. Such rationality is indispensable to societies and individuals in adapting themselves to a more mobile and more complex environment.[7] And again, in proportion as men are obliged to furnish more highly specialized work, the products of this work are multiplied and are of better quality; but this increase in products and improvement in quality are necessary to compensate for the expense which this more considerable work entails.[8] Thus, instead of the cause of social phenomena consisting of a mental anticipation of the function they are called to fill, this function, on the contrary, at least in a number of cases, serves to maintain the pre-existent cause from which they are derived. We shall, then, find the function more easily if the cause is already known.

If the determination of function is thus to be delayed, it is still no less necessary for the complete explanation of the phenomena. Indeed, if the usefulness of a fact is not the cause of its existence, it is generally necessary that it be useful in order that it may maintain itself. For the fact that it is not useful suffices to make it harmful, since in that case it costs effort without bringing in any returns. If, then, the majority of social phenomena had this parasitic character, the budget of the organism would have a deficit and social life would be impossible. Consequently, to have a satisfactory understanding of the latter, it is necessary to show how the phenomena comprising it combine in such a way as to put society in harmony with itself and with the environment external to it. No doubt, the current formula, which defines social life as a correspondence between the internal and the external milieu, is only an approximation; however, it is in general true. Consequently, to explain a social fact it is not enough to show the cause on which it depends; we must also, at least in most cases, show its function in the establishment of social order.

REFERENCES

1. *Cours de philosophie positive*, IV, 262.
2. *Principles of Sociology*, II, 247.
3. Legal marriage with the mother establishes the father's rights over the children.
4. *Division du travail*, Book II, chaps. iii and iv.
5. We do not wish to raise here questions of general philosophy, which would not be in place. Let us say, however, that, if more profoundly analyzed, this reciprocity of cause and effect might furnish a means of reconciling scientific mechanism with the teleology which the existence, and especially the persistence, of life implies.
6. *Division du travail social*, Book II, chap. ii, notably pp. 105 ff.
7. *Ibid.*, pp. 52–53.
8. *Ibid.*, pp. 301 ff.

Functionalism in Anthropology * (*Malinowski*)

The Functional Analysis of Culture.—This type of theory aims at the explanation of anthropological facts at all levels of development by their function, by the part which they play within the integral system of culture, by the manner in which they are related to each other within the system, and by the manner in which this system is related to the physical surroundings. It aims at the understanding of the nature of culture, rather than at conjectural reconstructions of its evolution or of past historical events.

Two factors contribute toward the development of the functional point of view. The modern specialist field-worker soon recognises that in order to *see* the facts of savage life, it is necessary to understand the nature of the cultural process. Description cannot be separated from explanation, since in the words of a great physicist, "explanation is nothing but condensed description." Every observer should ruthlessly banish from his work conjecture, preconceived assumptions and hypothetical schemes, but not theory.

Modern field work thus regards a theory as purely empirical, never going beyond inductive evidence, serving only to gain an insight into the mechanism of culture in its various phases: social organisation, belief and material outfit. The field-worker who lives among savages soon discards the antiquarian outlook. He sees every implement constantly used; every custom backed up by strong feeling and cogent ideas; every detail of social organisation active and effective. He perceives that culture, above all, provides primitive man with the means of satisfying his wants, and of mastering his surroundings. The functional view of culture insists therefore upon the principle that in every type of civilisation, every custom, material object, idea and belief fulfils some vital function, has some task to accomplish, represents an indispensable part within a working whole.

It keeps always in mind the biological basis of human civilisation, the correlation of culture to human wants, hence to human instincts and emotional dispositions. Instincts, emotions and ideas cannot, however, be treated by biology alone but must be approached through the study of mental process. Psychology, therefore, is indispensable for due understanding of culture.

At the same time the functional view teaches that man in the very fact of culture transcends his biological outfit. In his implements, weapons, clothes and ornaments he extends his anatomical endowment, whether to protect his life, to charm his fellow-beings or to procure his nourishment. Knowledge

* By Bronislaw Malinowski, reprinted from "Anthropology," *Encyclopaedia Britannica,* first supplementary volume, 1936, pp. 132–139, with permission of the publisher.

supplies man with responses which go far beyond anything implied in instinct. In dogmatic belief we have a new type of mental attitude not observed in animals. Biology is therefore not enough to explain human adjustments through culture. Psychology again is not sufficient, for man does all important business in common, while every individual contribution has to be translated into cultural fact, imprinted upon material objects and linked with social organisation. The other approach to the functional method is from the evolutionary point of view, nowadays generally discredited and discarded, yet fundamentally sound when correctly set forth. The development of culture consists in the gradual crystallisation of well-defined institutions out of mixed and non-specialised behaviour. The essential features of each institution remain permanent while the less relevant ones change considerably. In order to understand, however, what is essential and what is not, it is necessary to define each institution and custom by its function. Again since the essence of evolution consists not in a sequence of different forms changing one into another, but in a better adaptation of an institution to its function, the more precise way of posing the evolutionary problem leads inevitably to the functional point of view.

The functional view of culture can be traced back to the inchoate but stimulating writings of A. Bastian, to the suggestions of Lazarus and Steinthal, to the work of E. B. Tylor and W. Robertson Smith. It is implied in the best achievements of modern field-work (notably of the American anthropologists, F. Boas; J. W. Fewkes; C. Wissler; A. Fletcher and La Flèche; A. E. Jenks; A. L. Kroeber; Elsie C. Parsons; J. R. Swanton; P. E. Goddard; J. O. and G. A. Dorsey; R. H. Lowie; F. C. Cole; P. Radin; E. Sapir; Ruth Benedict). It has been active in the work of the French school, where it is constantly gaining ground (compare the latest publications of MM. Davy, Fauconnet, Granet, Mauss and Rivet). Functional interpretations will be found predominant among the soundest theories of the comparative school (Brinton; H. Schurtz; W. Wundt; J. G. Frazer; H. Webster; E. A. Crawley; Westermarck; Van Gennep; Marett). The comparative school however has allowed the evolutionary view to overshadow the functional method, while most American anthropologists have failed to disentangle the empirical interpretation of culture in terms of function from reconstruction in terms of conjectural history. They have thus lapsed into a type of explanation which at its best belongs to archaeology, and thus have greatly sterilised their otherwise splendid field-work and stimulating theory.

Recently, however, and among a small number of anthropologists only, the functional method has been applied systematically and exclusively in field-work and theory (W. Hoernlé; B. Malinowski; A. Radcliffe-Brown; Richard Thurnwald).

The functional method, by showing what culture does for a primitive community, establishes its value and thus utters a warning against too hasty interference with native belief and institution and too wasteful an exploitation of native labour and resources. By demonstrating how primitive custom and law work, it furnishes the administrator with practical hints of how to frame and administer native regulations. By inquiring into savage economic organisation, the functional method can teach how to manage indigenous labour and how to trade with the natives. By a sympathetic study of early belief and ritual, it can instruct the missionary how to graft a new creed upon the old one without destroying what is good and sound in it.

The functional method, concerned as it is with the actual working and mechanism of primitive culture, supplies the right theoretical foundation for the practical application of anthropology (*see* ANTHROPOLOGY, APPLIED), for which mere antiquarian reconstructions, whether historical or evolutionary, are irrelevant.

The following analysis of concrete problems is carried out from a functional point of view.

THE CULTURAL FUNCTION OF MARRIAGE AND FAMILY

This is perhaps the most debated and the most instructive of all anthropological problems.

The Institutions of Marriage and Family.—Careful inductive comparison reveals one important indication: marriage and family are almost universal, and can be traced through all types and levels of culture. Their universality can be accounted for by the functional analysis of these institutions. Two functions of paramount importance are fulfilled by any institution which regulates mating and propagation; the maintenance of racial quality and the maintenance of the continuity of culture. Sociological considerations prove that the individual family based on monogamous marriage provides the best opportunities for effective sexual selection. It also supplies the best training for the future cultural work and sociological orientation of the young individual (Lowie, Kroeber, E. C. Parsons). The importance of the family as the early social and cultural pattern for later life has been independently established by anthropology and psychoanalysis (A. Radcliffe-Brown, J. C. Flügel). The family is the link between instinctive endowment and the acquisition of cultural inheritance, in that it permits the biological bonds between parent and infant gradually to ripen into social ties. It also eliminates a number of dangers due to the disruptive factors of the sexual instinct.

Regulated Licence.—This phenomenon does not allow of a simple and satisfactory solution. As culture advances and larger numbers of men and women come into contact, the experimental component of the sexual instinct drives people to indiscriminate mating. Freedom in pre-nuptial intercourse, festive licence, religious prostitution, lewd marriage ceremonies are the rule in savage and barbarous communities, with the exception perhaps of those on the lowest level (Schmidt and Koppers). Again, in some tribes the institution of marriage suffers temporary obliteration in the form of wife-lending or exchange, *jus primae noctis,* sexual over-rights of chiefs and magicians and similar relaxations of the matrimonial type. These customs have been explained as "survivals of primitive promiscuity." That such an explanation is untenable has been convincingly shown by Westermarck. There are two ways of regulating the intercourse between the sexes: either by suppressing all irregular mating, or by allowing a well-defined and limited licence. Biology and psycho-analytic theory teach that stern repression and rigid sex morals are not a complete solution of the problems here involved. Anthropology, moreover, shows that this problem is especially present at low levels of culture. According to some authorities, a regulated and limited licence should be considered as an imperfect but effective way of dealing with the disruptive forces of sex. Such regulation, moreover, is in no savage tribe found to be subversive to the fundamental institutions of marriage and the family which exist in spite of it everywhere.

At the same time, there is not one single tribe where sexual licence is found untrammelled, where anything approaching promiscuity obtains. Two forms of regulation are found everywhere: the strict prohibition of the wife's adultery safeguards the bonds of marriage and is only now and then over-ruled by exceptional customs; the prohibition of incest within the household safeguards the integrity of the family. This is very often extended to exogamy which embraces the whole clan.

The Clan.—The clan and the classificatory principle of kinship appear on a closer sociological analysis not to be substitutes for the family and household, but the outcome of more extended co-operation in matters other than sexual mating and the rearing of children (A. Radcliffe-Brown, A. L. Kroeber, Thurnwald). The clan functions principally in economic, legal, and above all, in ceremonial matters. It is also closely connected with age-grades, secret societies and men's clubs wherever these exist; with the ceremonial distributions of wealth (the *kula*, the *potlatch* or the *hakari*), with magical specialisation and co-operation. Thus, in its functional definition, the clan represents the non-sexual and non-genetic extension of the kinship principle beyond the household and above the natural function of the family. Exogamy again appears as an additional bond of solidarity—a natural extension of the principle of incest running side by side with the extension of the kinship principle. As the link between the individual family and the wider groupings of local and political type, the clan is of special importance.

The clan is always due to the over-emphasis of one side of kinship—an over-emphasis necessary to eliminate any ambiguity in the transmissions of heredity rights and obligations. This has been aptly summed up by Dr. Lowie in his terminology of bilateral and unilateral kinship. The clan appears therefore as the natural result of the two influences which come into the foreground as culture advances: the continuity of tradition on the one hand and the extension of co-operation on the other. The clan allows of the establishment of greater cohesion within each generation and across succeeding generations. The explanation here given accounts for the institution, neither by an accident nor by specific ideas, nor by a hypothetical primitive communism in sexual matters, but by reference to certain deep-seated influences of cultural progress working before our very eyes. With all this, although the clan is of great benefit for society and culture, it never becomes an absolute necessity like the family. It is rather a symptom of advancing social differentiation than its inevitable effect. Thus, although the family and marriage are found to be universal, there exist tribes without any subdivisions into clans, moieties or matrimonial classes. Further, since the clan is associated with the general scheme of development, it cannot be regarded as a fortuitous index of this or that culture.

Mother-right and Father-right.—The correlated phenomenon of unilateral kinship also plays a very important part in diffusionist schemes. Mother-right and father-right respectively have been taken by Ankermann, Graebner, Rivers, W. Schmidt and Koppers as principal indices in their classification of cultures. But the question arises, is either mother-right or father-right an independent element, or are they both always correlated? It seems, however, that mother-right and father-right are never found in isolation, but always co-exist—one of them emphasised by the tribal law and the economic arrangements, the other, though subordinate, never completely absent. Until the problem thus raised has been solved, until the proof is given that mother-right and father-right can exist as exclusive, sharply defined stages or sociological principles, their use as indices of culture, and evidence of its spread must remain meaningless. Here again, functional analysis of the methods of reckoning descent leads to a clear definition of such concepts, indispensable for their use in any speculative constructions.

Problem of Sex.—Thus the family, the clan, sexual restrictions, as well as sexual liberties, are not the stages of a transformation nor fortuitous indices of cultural type or cultural stratum, but correlated, component parts of one big institution: the institution which controls the mating of sexes, the procreation of offspring and the education of the young, and fulfils the integral function of racial and cultural continuity. The nature of its component elements is explained by the part which they play within this integral scheme. The functional method might also be extended to all the other aspects of organisation—territorial, political, legal and economic. Each is related to an essential need of human society and culture, distribution over its locality, defence, maintenance of order, and the production of necessaries and values.

ECONOMIC ORGANISATION

Until the researches of anthropologists in Melanesia, in New Zealand, in North-West America, in Africa, and in Micronesia revealed a wealth of material, and theoretical students laid stress on the cultural importance of primitive economics, there reigned in anthropology the simple, occupational view of primitive husbandry. Schemes of occupational stages or types, the collecting of food, hunting, fishing, the tending of herds, the raising of crops and industrial production were set forward as the only subject matter of descriptive or analytical economics, as it is called.

In all such views, primitive man is regarded as having but simple elementary needs, and proceeding reasonably and naturally to satisfy them. The little spare time he has left over he devotes to the casual production of superfluities, and to the satisfaction of his hobbies, which latter activities, however, are usually placed outside the domain of economics. Thus we read in an authoritative work, *Notes and Queries in Anthropology:* "The first essential of maintenance is a supply of food; and in many simple communities the actual food quest and operations arising from it . . . . occupy by far the greater part of the people's time and energy, leaving little opportunity for the satisfaction of any lesser needs." And again, we are told by another writer (Buxton) that generally the savage "has no means to acquire more wealth than he can carry about on his person or on the persons of his family." The main questions cut short by such *a priori* assumptions are those of the incentives to production, of the organisation of labour and of the primitive forms of the apportionment of wealth.

The Economic Motive.—Is it true then that primitives work only to satisfy their primary needs? In the lowest stages of culture people are ready to endure thirst and hunger, but bent upon stimulants or narcotics. We know of tribes without clothing, but of none without ornaments. There are natives without fixed habitations, yet keen on the display of such wealth as they possess. At higher levels, under more favourable conditions, certain commodities are actually produced far in excess of actual needs. And this is not done "in exchange for food or for the means of obtaining it," as runs the usual opinion (*Notes and Queries*).

Nor is it carried out through economic foresight. Large quantities of accumulated food and wealth are employed instead for festive display, for ceremonial yet useless donations, sometimes even for mere destruction, often on a gigantic scale. All such customs serve merely for the manifestation of the wealth of the owner, of his generosity, of his economic power. In the South Seas, the accumulated food is employed for the production of objects of value by the feeding of artisans, who devote themselves to the polishing of axe-blades, to carving, to the making of shell ornaments or of mats (Thurnwald, Müller-Wissmar). Some of these early forms of valuable tokens of wealth have a distinctly religious character, serve in ritual ceremonies, are associated with belief and possess elaborate mythical pedigrees (Mauss). Finally, there is one very important fact which contradicts the merely utilitarian view of primitive economic incentives: the products of savage industries in general, far from being made with the minimum of effort required for their utility, show a lavishness of artistic detail, of decoration and pedantic finish, which often put to shame any civilised artisan. The joy in the work, the satisfaction of perfect craftsmanship, the artistic passion for the general appearance of the finished product dominate savage industries and enterprise.

It is clear from this evidence that the "first essentials of maintenance," the primary needs and the requirements of practical utility, do not exclusively control the economic effort of primitive man. Nor is their aim always to achieve the utilitarian maximum of effect by the minimum of effort. To understand the driving forces of early production, it is, therefore, not sufficient to make reference to man's animal needs. It is necessary to realise also the native ideas of value: their pleasure in the integral effect of their work in which artistic, sporting, social and even religious motives are mixed with those of pure utility.

The Character of Early Production.—The well-known scheme of K. Buecher, who would place the whole range of primitive husbandry within the limits of the "individual search for food" and of "closed household economy" is the clearest expression of the view that primitive man works for himself and his family alone, and that he knows no production on a wider, a communal or tribal scale.

A fuller insight into the nature of primitive labour reveals the existence of organisation. Even in the lowest cultures there are tasks which transcend the forces of one individual or of one family—the felling of trees, drive-hunting, the very collecting of food. At higher stages, such pursuits as communal hunting and fishing, the making of gardens, the construction of houses and canoes require some type of organised labour. This points to a definite specialisation, distribution and synchronisation in time, a division of functions, an integration of the individual contributions to the common end. If we enquire what are the elements of the economic organisation, it soon becomes clear that we must distinguish between moral or persuasive, and social or coercive factors. K. Buecher in a later work (*Arbeit und Rhythmus*) has drawn attention to the great importance of rhythm for successful work. Many other stimulants and incentives could be mentioned, the most efficient of which is unquestionably work in company. Conversation, jokes, mutual assistance and interest relieve the tedium of solitary labour, while emulation, example and the satisfaction of pride are under primitive conditions possible only in communal work. The best worker is always recognised as such among savages, and his leadership is followed. Much more important, however, is the moral prestige enjoyed by supernatural expert knowledge which, in the form of magic, always controls vital and difficult economic pursuits. Marking the dates, inaugurating the successive stages, imposing periods of rest and setting the time limits, it acts as an organising, co-ordinating influence.

Social coercion is the other important force of economic organisation. As soon as distinctions of rank and power arise they are used as means of extorting labour, while, on the other hand, economic inequalities function as indices of social status.

Primitive Ownership.—This economic problem has been discussed with some detail by anthropology. But while, on the one hand, the writers, who, like Buecher, assume an atomised economic production, admit only of individual or personal ownership, those following Morgan, and influenced by a strong socialistic bent, Engels, Bebel, Cunow, make the savage into a communist. As a matter of fact, property, which is but one form of legal relationship, is neither purely individualistic nor communal, but always mixed (*cf. Nature,* Supplement, Feb. 1926, on "Law and Order").

The misuse of such conceptions as "communism," associated with an incorrect application of the concept of "money" may be exemplified on a scheme recently put forward by the late Dr. Rivers. Dr. Rivers designates certain forms of valuables found in Melanesia, such as mats, arrows, pigs' jawbones and, above all, shell discs, as "money," following the usage of white traders, missionaries and planters. Dr. Rivers, to justify the use of this word, insists that these objects "are used for no other purpose" and "have a very definite scale of value," but he gives in other contexts a definite and concrete account of several ways in which these objects are used "for other purposes," and thus stultifies his first criterion. The second criterion is obviously insufficient for identifying a commodity as "money." All objects have in our economy "a very definite scale of value," yet we do not apply the word money to a pair of slippers, a motor-car or a picture by Raphael, nor use these things as such.

Now the taking of terminological liberties with well-defined concepts has its dangers. "Money" has no sooner been introduced into the argument than communism crops up and the two are related by a remarkable piece of reasoning:

The subject of communism in property is closely connected with that of money. A thoroughly communistic people can have no use for money among themselves. If they possess anything which can be regarded as currency, it can only be used in transactions with other peoples. The use of money should therefore be associated with the disappearance of communism; if it can be shown that Melanesian money is due to immigrant influence, and especially to that of the Kava people, we shall have gone far to establish the conclusions already suggested. (*History of Melanesian Society*, vol. 2, p. 385.)

And again:

A thoroughly communistic people would have no need for money, and any explanation of the communism of Polynesia will therefore furnish also the explanation of the absence of money (p. 392).

And as an "historical explanation" of these facts:

The explanation of the absence of money in Polynesia and of the communism of its people is to be found in the special mode of settlement of the Kava people (p. 393).

These passages furnish a conspicuous example of how ill-defined concepts lead to far-fetched schemes and unsound constructions.

Summary.—To sum up briefly, it is incorrect to assume that man for a long time has lived in a semi-natural primitive stage of individual acquisition of food and primary utilities. Equally untrue is the correlated assumption that he lifted himself out of this condition by the gradual application of the economic principle of maximum of effect for the minimum of effort. Instead, from the outset, artificial, cultural, non-instinctive aims have been indispensable to him and his culture. Early types of value and symbols of wealth have spurred him from the outset to economic effort. This effort is organised and standardised by tradition. The real problem, therefore, consists in gaining insight into the primitive forms of condensed wealth, into the mixture of motives and impulses which drive man; and in studying the manner in which these primitive incentives control organised effective effort. All the conclusions arrived at show that for the discussion of economic problems it is necessary to consider the relation of early wealth to religion and to magic as well as its function in primitive social structure.

The borderland questions—the influence of economics on social structure; the problem of wealth as the foundation of rank, power and status; the rule of give-and-take in social obligations; ceremonial distribution of goods and its economic importance—are gradually coming into the forefront of anthropological interest, and open up entirely new horizons in theory and observances. They bring it into close contact with the disciplines of economics, history and sociology (Buecher, Schwiedland, M. Weber, K. Lamprecht).

The relation between the various larger aspects of culture opens a new type of problem. Social organisation is largely dependent upon economic foundations, while economics cannot be studied without a knowledge of the various groups within the tribe. Religion and magic are not independent, but are intimately associated with economic pursuits, with power and prestige, with domestic life and everyday necessities.

THE SUPERNATURAL

Here the functional view is put to its acid test. What can be the function of primitive belief and superstition, of animism considered as valueless, crude and mistaken, of magic, regarded as a spurious and fallacious pseudo-science, of totemism, of barbarous burial ceremonies and of cruel initiation rites? And yet the method here set forth stands and falls with the possibility of defining the whole of the supernatural. It is bound to show in what way belief and ritual work for social integration, technical and economic efficiency, for culture as a whole—indirectly therefore for the biological and mental welfare of each individual member.

The Current Theories.—Most modern theories in fact come near to the posing of this problem and to its solution. It is implied in the whole structure of Frazer's *Golden Bough,* in the contributions of Westermarck to the moral side of religion, in Durkheim's analysis of the integrative function of public ceremonial, in the additions of Hubert and Mauss to his theories, in Marett's analysis of magic, in Crawley's vitalistic view of religion, above all, in the analysis of Andaman belief and ceremonial by A. Radcliffe-Brown. But too often the functional view is still smothered by evolutionary or historical discussions—as to whether magic preceded religion, as to what was the primitive form of religion, and so on.

Magic.—The great number of modern theories dealing with magic range between two apparently opposed views, which label magic as primitive science or primitive stupidity (*Urdummheit*) respectively. We must reject the implication of the first theory, that magic preceded science, and that it once did fulfill that function. It must be placed to the credit of this theory, however, that it does full justice to the practical context of magic. The second theory emphasising the central conception of impersonal ubiquitous force—*mana, orenda, wakan* rightly appreciates the difference between belief and knowledge; and brings out the mystical character of magic (Marett, Hubert and Mauss, Preuss).

The functional theory reconciles both points of view. Let us start from the close association of magic with practical activities. First, every practical pursuit amongst savages is always primarily based upon knowledge and is never exclusively controlled by magic. There are in all savage cultures certain activities in which technical ability, guided by knowledge, completely suffices. In others, the help of magic is also invoked. What are the respective contributions of knowledge and of magic to such a mixed activity? In its essentials the division of function between the two is very simple: as far as his knowledge goes, as far as he can safely rely on experience, reason and technical ability, the native—whether in his gardening or fishing, in the building of craft, in warfare or sailing—does not use magic. No savage has ever been observed to select the tree for his dug-out by divination, to bring forth seedlings by formulae without having planted them. Only where, in spite of knowledge and effort, the results still turn unaccountably against him, only when forces completely beyond his mental grasp and practical control baffle him—in dealing with garden pests, with the supply of fish and animals, in securing wind or weather, in preventing disaster at sea or in war, above all, in dealing with bodily decay, disease or personal accidents—does the savage resort to supernatural means of filling the lacunae in his practical power.

The type of belief met in magic is always an affirmation of man's power to deal with the situation by a rite or spell. This belief simply repeats in a standardised manner, what hope all the time has whispered within the individual's own mind. Again, the rite repeats in a fixed, definite form what the natural expression of emotions already contains, only, as a rite, it is carried out with a purpose and with the conviction that it is a means to an end.

When we compare the forms of the fixed magical ritual, they are remarkably akin to the response of upset equilibrium occurring under similar conditions. Black magic, which corresponds to the sentiment of hate, and which replaces the outbursts of impotent rage, contains in its most typical ritual of stabbing, pointing the bone, mimic destruction, in the text of its formulae, a reproduction of the various gestures, words and types of behaviour, which we can watch in the natural vent of the emotions. Exorcism of evil powers repeats in word and deed the reactions of fear.

In all practical activities, the successful ends, which hope vividly brings before the mental vision at moments of uncertainty and suspense, are connected in such ritual, which bridges over the fateful moments. Sir J. Frazer's apposite term of "imitative magic" and his exhaustive illustrations of his point of view illustrate also the present theory. Here it is only suggested that the association of "ideas," designated by Frazer as the cause of "imitative magic," can only be accounted for by our theory of imperfect biological adjustment induced by culture. Baffled instinct arouses emotional tension as well as a conflict of ideas and an impasse in conduct. Through magic, culture prescribes the adequate ideas, standardises the valuable emotional tone and establishes a line of conduct which carries man over the dangerous moment.

This new type of explanation, based on the functional method, shows how cultural behaviour, in the very act of bestowing immense benefits and advantages on man, also opens up new problems and creates new needs. To satisfy these a new type of behaviour, ritual practices and a new mental adjustment, faith or mystical outlook, come into being, thus providing an answer to the question which is always essential: What actual benefit does magic confer upon man, what is its positive contribution to culture? It is a remedy for specific maladjustments and mental conflicts, which culture creates in allowing man to transcend his biological equipment.

Social Consequences.—In its traditional aspect, magic leads to important social consequences. It is the essence of magical lore that every word of a formula must be spoken correctly without omission or alteration, every detail of the rite performed. Since magical knowledge can live only in man's memory, the correct transmission, the legitimate filiation of magic are essential to man's confidence in its efficiency. The inheritance of magic is always one of the most important problems of descent and of the modes of reckoning kinship. As a rule, magic is handed on within the family circle.

In this connection it is important to stress that *all* forms of magic usually perform an important social rôle. No magic can be regarded as anti-social in the sense in which Durkheim and his school attempt to define it. Even sorcery or black magic functions as a legitimate though dangerous weapon, of which one of the main uses is in the enforcing of an established power and the biddings of law. The actual manner in which magic is connected with practical activities makes it, as we have seen, into the very skeleton of economic organisation. It supplies most of the co-ordinating and driving forces of labour, it develops the qualities of forethought, of order, of steadiness and punctuality, which are essential to all successful enterprise. Thus magic fulfils an indispensable function within culture. It satisfies a definite need which cannot be satisfied by any other factor of primitive civilisation.

Totemism.—Totemism is a belief which affirms an intimate bond between a group of men and an animal or vegetable species, sometimes a class of objects. It raises therefore two problems, the first as to the nature of the belief, the second as to the social organisation with which it is linked.

Most theories saw its origin in some small or accidental detail of social organisation or belief, as in nicknames, guardian spirits, transmigration of souls and, recently, in the Freudian theory of parricide. To the functional theory the real problem, however, is : what is the function of a type of belief which affirms the affinity between man and animal, is correlated with clan organisation and leads to moral and ritual rules associated with the multiplication, killing and eating of animals?

Man's interest in his surroundings is primarily practical. He has to collect food, construct his dwelling, roam about his district to hunt or fish. In the forefront of importance are the animals in his territory—those which feed him, those whose skins clothe him, whose feathers, teeth and claws supply him with ornaments and those which threaten his safety or comfort. Hence the whole of animal life has an intense interest and significance for him.

Now in dealing with the animal kingdom, in obtaining the useful species to eat, in defending himself against the dangerous or repulsive ones, primitive man, where his natural means fail him, has recourse to supernatural ones. The magical claims over any aspect of nature lead always to an assertion of a sort of affinity or kinship between the magician and the object controlled. Indeed most magic implies mythological descent from animals or affiliation to them. Thus we see that the native's practical interest in the animal or vegetable kingdom leads through magic directly to the assertion of a mutual bond.

Magic has a tendency to become specialised and departmental, exclusive and hereditary in a kinship group or clan. The subdivision of the tribe into totemic clans seems to be best explained, therefore, by the hypothesis that such clans were originally magical bodies engaged in controlling, through spell and rite, certain animal or vegetable species for the welfare of the tribe.

Thus is assigned to totemism a definite cultural function. Selective interest in vitally relevant factors of the environment, man's capacity to control it, are embodied in a system of beliefs which standardise, enhance and sacralise these culturally valuable mental states. By endorsing man's confidence and his hopes of effective control, by making these tendencies substantial in an explicit mythological dogma, totemism contributes to individual happiness, to social cohesion and to the general efficiency of culture.

Summary.—In recent work (Frazer, Crawley, Van Gennep, Miss Jane Harrison) much stress has been laid upon the association of religion with the crises of life. In fact in most religions, savage or civilised, the main phases of human life history—conception and pregnancy, birth and puberty, marriage and death—are associated with belief, ritual and mythological stories. Religion therefore fulfils at vital crises an indispensable function in the scheme of human culture.

Culture entails a transformation of direct instinctive response into a mode of behaviour governed by purposive ends, that is, by cultural values. The super-instinctive type of behaviour leads man into impasses and difficulties out of which he can be extricated only by rules of thought and of behaviour which also have to be supplied by culture. In practical pursuits magic helps man over the difficulties. The rôle of Religion consists in the establishment of spiritual ends, dogmatic realities and moral rules of conduct. In totemism, which sacralises important factors of the environment; in the belief in immortality and in the associated ideas about communion with spirits and their influence on human fate; in the consecration of food and of indispensable elements of culture, such as fire, standard implements, tokens of wealth; in surrounding tribal tradition and order by the halo of sanctity, religion is the source of social and cultural values.

PRIMITIVE KNOWLEDGE

Reason, the capacity to know, to invent and to evolve theories, has been regarded as the distinctive mark of man, dividing Homo Sapiens from other living beings. Perhaps over-confident exaggeration of this has led to the recent reaction which denies to the primitive mind any power of reasoning and of observation.

But had primitive technique been studied not as a self-contained object, but in its functional dependence upon knowledge on the one hand and magic on the other, the theory of a primitive mystical and prelogical mentality could never have been erected. Primitive man shows a rational behaviour, an unimpeachable logic and a definite power of empirical observation, not only in his technology, but also in his major economic pursuits and in his sociological behaviour.

Language.—This subject has been so far but imperfectly studied by anthropologists, and its cultural theory is as yet hardly outlined. The study of dead languages by grammarians and philologists has caused speech to be regarded as a self-contained phenomenon governed by special laws of its own. It was a considerable step forward when, some time ago, the study of language was taken up by psychologists, who began to treat it in correlation with thought and other phenomena (Lazarus, Steinthal, Wundt). The structural features of language were explained as an adequate expression of reasoning, of emotional states, of aesthetic needs and of the characteristics of the human will. Even this, however, is not sufficient.

Recent developments in linguistics, as well as in the philosophy of language, have set forth the view that language cannot at any stage of development be regarded as an adequate expression of logical, metaphysical, aesthetic or scientific categories (J. Dewey, Jespersen, Ogden and Richards). Language, in all societies and at all stages of development, is an essential part of human action (Dewey). Communication by spoken word is indispensable for any concerted activity and enters into all aspects of culture as a working element.

From the functional point of view, a word which designates an implement is as much an essential manner of using that implement as is any type of bodily skill required to handle it. The master of a craft, however primitive, must be able to give his orders in case of emergency in a technically adequate and theoretically correct manner, and the bodily reactions of his vocal apparatus are as essential to the practical issue as the manual dexterity of his crew. Language plays a similar part in warfare, in economic pursuits, in ceremonial activities. In religious and magical ritual, the spoken word is conceived and felt by man to be a creative act which produces a definite practical effect.

But if speech, in its primitive forms, is an indispensable instrument of cultural behaviour, its structure must be correlated to pragmatic needs and to the requirements of action rather than to logical, reflective or oratorical necessities. Hence the categories of primitive speech must be a compromise between logical and rational conditions, sociological and practical needs, and certain limitations imposed by material culture.

The problem of meaning cannot be treated by the study of language, torn out of its cultural context. The classical philologist has already summoned the archaeologist to his assistance. The study of living languages of the primitive type, helped out by the study of living cultures, would, no doubt, reveal to us infinitely more than can be reached by the study of dead speech. A word is as sterile without the knowledge of how it is used in live context, as behaviour remains mysterious without its accompanying flow of speech. Life is neither mere verbiage nor a pantomime. Speech has been given man for action, and as mere loquacity it is a disease of culture.

Mythology as Primitive Science.—In order to vindicate the autonomy of knowledge within primitive culture, it is still necessary to deal with the view that, at low levels of culture, myth is a substitute for science. We read in an authoritative handbook:—

Myths are stories which, however marvellous and improbable to us, are nevertheless related in all good faith, because they are intended, or believed by the teller, to explain by means of something concrete and intelligible, an abstract idea, or such vague and difficult conceptions as creation, death, distinctions of race or animal species, the different occupations of men and women; the origins of rites and customs, or striking natural objects or prehistoric monuments; the meaning of the names of persons or places. Such stories are sometimes described as *aetiological,* because their purpose is to explain why something exists or happens (*Notes and Queries,* pp. 210 and 211).

We are thus told that primitive man evolves stories and believes in them, in order to explain abstract ideas. As a matter of fact myth is not a form of primitive science, but an aspect of religion, magic and morality; its function is not to explain queries nor to illuminate abstract or obscure points, but to strengthen belief, to substantiate morals and to enhance tradition, in short to bring home to primitive man all that has to be believed, obeyed and accepted.

To establish our point, we have to place myth within the scheme of primitive culture and to show its pragmatic function. Myth is a part of folklore in the narrower sense of the word, that is, of oral tradition. Man in all ages and all climes possesses a body of concrete stories which can readily be divided into several classes.

Of these, the first serves predominantly for amusement and recreation. Stories of this class describe more or less dramatic or funny adventures of men and animals, ogres and hobgoblins, all of which are not regarded as real. Such tales, when studied within their cultural context and regarded from the native point of view, are found to play an important part in native life, in that they enhance sociability, fill out seasons of enforced idleness or make up the substance of amicable gatherings.

Another class of stories, taken more seriously, refer to important exploits and heroic deeds of past generations and are considered to be true. The sociological function of such stories is that they develop family pride, knit the kinship bonds and serve to increase communal or tribal solidarity.

There are finally stories which are regarded as sacred and connected in a specific manner with magical and religious cult, with social organisation and with the body of tribal custom and moral rules. These and these only could be regarded as "explanatory" stories, in that, among other subjects, they account for the origins of the world, give the reasons for death, furnish revelations of future existence, and promise immortality, narrate the beginnings of magic, and so on. The explanatory character, however, is prominent only as long as the story is considered without its cultural context. In all cases where the associated ideas and feelings have been observed; where we know the conditions under which the myth is recited or enacted; above all where the practical influence of the myth has been studied—we are able to assign a definite cultural function to it. Thus, in connection with magic, we find stories which are not intended to *explain* the ritual or the phenomenon governed by magic, but are meant to substantiate the belief in magical efficiency. All such stories give us an account of an extremely successful, miraculous precedent. Around the various religious rites and ceremonies, there cluster stories which vouch for the efficiency of the religious acts in obtaining the desired effect.

Again, we have a class of myths which confirm the existence of privileges, give the antecedents of rank and power, or enforce duties and which, in general, strengthen traditional law and order. Wherever myth, that is a sacred story, has been studied in connection with the sources of its sanctity as well as with its sacralising results, it can be shown that it has served to strengthen faith by reference to an original Golden Age, to miraculous precedents in the dim past. The study of myth in conjunction with ritual and institution has been carried out only in limited areas, for instance in the Andaman Is. (A. Radcliffe-Brown), in Central Australia (Spencer and Gillen), in Melanesia (B. Malinowski), in Northwestern America (Boas and others), in Polynesia (Elsdon Best). All the facts we know, however, prove that myth is in no way comparable to primitive science, but that instead it functions as a religious warrant, vouching for the truth of belief, the efficacy of ritual, and the fitness and justice of moral or social duty.

THE IDENTIFICATION OF CULTURE

The functional method seems at first sight to be of especially easy application to artifacts, to material objects fashioned by man for his cultural uses. Food stuffs ready for consumption, man's equipment in protective shelter and clothing, his tools and his weapons, are all obviously means to an end.

The Place of Artifacts in Culture.—But this very facility has its dangers. The purposive character of most artifacts has made the *implement* into the typical representative of material objects: hence, all these have generally been regarded as representing the *technique* of culture. It is deemed sufficient to state how these objects are *made* and how they are *handled*. In *Notes and Queries* one-third of the space is devoted to "technology," the description of manual production and of the handling of artifacts. In the *Handbook of Folklore,* this study is defined as an anthropology with technological considerations cut out. All this is incorrect, since "material culture" is not an autonomous, self-contained province of culture, such as religion, law or economics, each of which fulfils a specific function. Material culture is an indispensable accessory of every single aspect, every pursuit and institution and thus fulfils a general function.

On the other hand, the bald technological treatment is not sufficient to do justice to any class of artifacts. The objects of immediate consumption or use, as well as tools and implements, are essentially correlated to economics and must be studied within its context. The same applies to a weapon, the proper analysis of which immediately leads to the description of the manner in which it is wielded, thus to the methods of warfare and war magic and, finally, to the political organisation of the tribe.

There is no single type of human activity without its material accessories. There is not one artifact, however practical or simple, which could be properly understood without its context of living culture, including belief as well as technique, social organisation and traditional knowledge.

Any general theories of culture or of progress which ascribe all driving power to either the material or the moral aspect of culture alone are guilty of one-sided exaggerations. Philosophy of history without a scientific basis is of little value. Functional anthropology on the other hand finds great help in the conception of culture as a form of biological adaptation on a gigantic scale, which empirically analyses the concepts of progress and of cultural reality and seeks to place the study of culture within the scheme of other sciences. Modern empirical philosophy has also been in turn greatly influenced by anthropological work, above all, by the theories about primitive knowledge, its relation to faith and to practical activities (W. Wundt, L. T. Hobhouse, K. Lamprecht,

M. Weber; above all, J. Dewey and the Columbia School of Culture Philosophy).

The Criteria of Cultural Identity.—The other danger which the study of material culture harbours for the anthropologist is the fallacy of *fixed form*. The strict determination of shape imposed upon many artifacts, especially tools, by their use, has made many objects appear perfectly defined by their form. An axe-blade, a knife, a bow and arrow, a spoon, a walking stick, "will be, as a rule, recognised at once as such" (Graebner, p. 56). Again we are told that the concepts and means of identification "are so much matters of everyday use to the ethnologist that the activity of the intellect, as it compares the objects, remains below the threshold of consciousness" (p. 57). These statements contain a very serious fallacy, obvious when it is remembered that nothing of any scientific value can be achieved by the study of isolated aspects, or, worse still, of isolated objects. And any definition by form treats an object as a self-contained isolated entity. As soon as an object is defined by relation and by function it has to be considered as a part of a larger whole, and it is the form of the whole which becomes the relevant factor in our definition.

The criteria of form and of quantity, as defined by Ratzel, Graebner, Schmidt and others constitute the foundation of the historical method. When studying the problem of the identification of cultural objects and the complexes of such objects, writers of this school seek to show to what extent similarities and ideas found in different parts of the world can be explained by diffusion, by the hypothesis that they "have been developed at a single culture centre in the far distant past and have been disseminated thence over the whole world" (Kroeber, *Anthropology,* p. 200). They have thus not only to prove the identity of two objects, but to prove it so that their genealogical kinship, their identical birth in a parent culture, is established.

In order to do that, the "infallible and objective criteria" of form and quantity have been elaborated. We are told that two things belonging to two different cultures can be regarded as the same, "when identities appear, which are not founded in the essence of the object or, speaking of material goods, in its material" (Graebner, p. 98; *ibid.,* p. 108; Schmidt and Koppers, p. 68; Kroeber, p. 199). A classical example is the identification of West African and Melanesian bows, made by Ratzel on account of the similarity of their section, means of attachment of the cord and the material (lawyer cane) of which the cord is made. Not one of these features, we are told, can be explained by its function or by the limitations imposed through material or purpose.

On this example, we may also observe the second criterion, that of quantity. The bow in the two regions shows not one, but a number of features apparently not related to each other.

> If a trait is composed of several elements which stand in no necessary relation to each other, and these several elements recur among distinct or remote peoples in the same combination . . . one can be reasonably sure of the real identity of common origin of the complex trait,

says Kroeber summarising the diffusionist point of view (*Anthropology*, pp. 199–200).

The "quantity" criterion applies not only to details found on one object, but to objects, customs and institutions, provided these are not related to one another. Such an *ensemble* is then usually called "a cultural complex," such as the cultural complex consisting of the bow already mentioned as well as shields, houses, masks, drums and clothing. This, Frobenius believes, forms a really identical stratum of culture both in West Africa and Melanesia.

When the two criteria are carefully examined, the functional anthropologist perceives that the assumption of wide occurrence of meaningless and irrelevant objects and unrelated complexes rests primarily upon a mere deficiency of knowledge. An object, or a detail of it, appears to us "inessential," "arbitrary," "devoid of function" only as long as we do not understand the function of that detailed feature or object. Since the study at first hand of savage races has been conducted mostly in an amateurish manner, and our collections are crammed with unlabelled, undefined, misunderstood specimens, the argument from irrelevance, *i.e.*, from our ignorance, has no value in anthropology. The fact is that the more we know about the culture of a region, the fewer features appear to us "extrinsic" or "arbitrary," the more all is revealed correlated, determined, provided with a function. And this brings us to the crux of the argument: form without function is an empty concept in the science of culture.

A pointed stick can be used as a spear in war or in the hunt, as a digging or punting pole, as a ceremonial staff or magical wand, as well as for many other purposes. The details of its form are adapted to the function and defined by it. And this holds good with regard to every item of material culture.

Once we begin to define form by function, both criteria, that of *meaningless form* and of *fortuitous coincidence*, break down completely. An object can be defined and identified only by its use, the study of use leads us again to connect the object with the pursuit, the institution, the aspect.

The real identities of culture appear to lie in the organic connection of its parts, in the function which a detail fulfils within its scheme, in the relation between the scheme, the environment and the human needs. Meaningless details disappear, shape becomes alive with meaning and with function, and a testimony of irrelevant form falls away as worthless. The method of formal treatment breaks down even more completely in the study of primitive sociology, economics and supernaturalism than in that of material culture.

And this entails a partial qualification of the criticism of the historical method. First of all, many students in mapping out distributions apply functional identifications of culture instead of formal ones (especially Wissler, Kroeber and Lowie). In the second, it is always possible to profess a bad method and to use a good one. The coincidence of details in an object or simultaneous appearance of objects is an important fact, whether we try to find out its organic relations or rest satisfied with denying them. The distribution of such objects or complexes does raise a problem. The objection is that in the opinion of the upholders of the historical doctrine, the problem is solved. For to them a distribution of such similar traits or complexes is a proof of common origin, a proof just because they affirm the absence of any inner relation or function. To the functional school, on the other hand, who cannot rest satisfied with dogmatically abiding by a gap in our knowledge, distribution raises a series of problems. In the first place how far we can regard the complex as an organic unity; secondly, what is the function of this coherent whole; thirdly, in view of this function, have we to assume independent development along similar lines, convergence along dissimilar lines or mechanical transmission? The real explanation, however, underlying any of these hypotheses, lies in the discovery of correlations and of permanence through function.

Summary.—The outer framework of material culture is correlated in a clear and direct manner to the satisfaction of man's biological needs. It constitutes the *milieu* which man evolves to interpose between himself and the rigours, dangers and insufficiencies of his physical surroundings. But this material apparatus has to be operated by men collectively, organised and controlled by the body of tradition, scientific as well as religious and magical. Thus indirectly most elements of social cohesion as well as certain beliefs and ideas can be correlated with man's primary needs, and explained by the biological function which they fulfil and the survival value which they possess. But this is not sufficient, and here an extremely important addition has to be made: the facts of social organisation impose certain conditions upon human behaviour, imply restrictions and create new wants, which again call forth specific cultural arrangements. Thus, higher forms of organised labour need some compulsion, supplied by political inequalities, and some moral framework, supplied by certain forms of magic.

Mental development running side by side with higher technical ability brings about fear, thought and reflection which make man anticipate his destiny and probe into the past and future of his world. The beliefs of primitive man about future life, the beginnings of the world and spiritual powers have to be correlated with his increasing mental outlook as well as with the widening social horizon and the development of cultural values. Social cohesion requires some means of enforcing the various rules imposed upon the individual for the common good, and this brings about the sanctions and inducements, which constitute the essence of primitive law. In all this the functional view avoids the error of attributing any priority to one or the other aspect of culture. Material objects, social grouping, traditional and moral values, as well as knowledge, are all welded into a functional system. To explain any item of culture, material or moral, means to indicate its functional place within an institution, which has to be thus explained with reference to its aspect and this again has to be placed within the system of culture.

Finally, anthropology hopes, with the help of her sister sciences, to state the place of culture in the scheme of organic evolution; to show how it is correlated to the instinctive animal equipment of the human species; to demonstrate how it has allowed man to rise above the brute level, to control his surroundings, to develop his knowledge, his faith and his conscience.

Objective End and Subjective Purpose * (*Pareto*)

Every social phenomenon may be considered under two aspects: as it is in reality, and as it presents itself to the mind of this or that human being. The first aspect we shall call *objective*, the second *subjective*. Such a division is necessary, for we cannot put in one same class the operations performed by a chemist in his laboratory and the operations performed by a person practising magic; the conduct of Greek sailors in plying their oars to drive their ship over the water and the sacrifices they offered to Poseidon to make sure of a safe and rapid voyage. In Rome the Laws of the XII Tables punished

* Reprinted from *The Mind and Society* by Vilfredo Pareto, Vol. I, pp. 76–79, copyright, 1935, by Harcourt, Brace and Company, Inc. Reprinted by permission of the publishers.

anyone casting a spell on a harvest. We choose to distinguish such an act from the act of burning a field of grain.

We must not be misled by the names we give to the two classes. In reality both are subjective, for all human knowledge is subjective. They are to be distinguished not so much by any difference in nature as in view of the greater or lesser fund of factual knowledge that we ourselves have. We know, or think we know, that sacrifices to Poseidon have no affect whatsoever upon a voyage. We therefore distinguish them from other acts which (to our best knowledge, at least) are capable of having such effect. If at some future time we were to discover that we have been mistaken, that sacrifices to Poseidon are very influential in securing a favourable voyage, we should have to reclassify them with actions capable of such influence. All that of course is pleonastic. It amounts to saying that when a person makes a classification, he does so according to the knowledge he has. One cannot imagine how things could be otherwise.

There are actions that use means appropriate to ends and which logically link means with ends. There are other actions in which those traits are missing. The two sorts of conduct are very different according as they are considered under their objective or their subjective aspect. From the subjective point of view nearly all human actions belong to the logical class. In the eyes of the Greek mariners sacrifices to Poseidon and rowing with oars were equally logical means of navigation. To avoid verbosities which could only prove annoying, we had better give names to these types of conduct.[1] Suppose we apply the term *logical actions* to actions that logically conjoin means to ends not only from the standpoint of the subject performing them, but from the standpoint of other persons who have a more extensive knowledge—in other words, to actions that are logical both subjectively and objectively in the sense just explained. Other actions we shall call *nonlogical* (by no means the same as "illogical"). This latter class we shall subdivide into a number of varieties.

A synoptic picture of the classification will prove useful:

The ends and purposes here in question are immediate ends and purposes. We choose to disregard the indirect. The objective end is a real one, located within the field of observation and experience, and not an imaginary end, located outside that field. An imaginary end may, on the other hand, constitute a subjective purpose.

Logical actions are very numerous among civilized peoples. Actions connected with the arts and sciences belong to that class, at least for artists and scientists. For those who physically perform them in mere execution of

GENERA AND SPECIES
HAVE THE ACTIONS LOGICAL ENDS AND PURPOSES:

	Objectivity?	*Subjectivity?*
CLASS I: LOGICAL ACTIONS (The objective end and the subjective purpose are identical.)		
	Yes	Yes
CLASS II: NON-LOGICAL ACTIONS (The objective end differs from the subjective purpose.)		
Genus 1	No	No
Genus 2	No	Yes
Genus 3	Yes	No
Genus 4	Yes	Yes

SPECIES OF THE GENERA 3 AND 4

3a, 4a	The objective end would be accepted by the subject if he knew it.
3b, 4b	The objective end would be rejected by the subject if he knew it.

orders from superiors, there may be among them non-logical actions of our II-4 type. The actions dealt with in political economy also belong in very great part in the class of logical actions. In the same class must be located, further, a certain number of actions connected with military, political, legal, and similar activities.

So at the very first glance induction leads to the discovery that non-logical actions play an important part in society. Let us therefore proceed with our examination of them.

First of all, in order to get better acquainted with these non-logical actions, suppose we look at a few examples. Many others will find their proper places in chapters to follow. Here are some illustrations of actions of Class II:

Genera 1 and 3, which have no subjective purpose, are of scant importance to the human race. Human beings have a very conspicuous tendency to paint a varnish of logic over their conduct. Nearly all human actions therefore work their way into genera 2 and 4. Many actions performed in deference to courtesy and custom might be put in genus 1. But very very often people give some reason or other to justify such conduct, and that transfers it to genus 2. Ignoring the indirect motive involved in the fact that a person violating common usages incurs criticism and dislike, we might find a certain number of actions to place in genera 1 and 3.

Says Hesiod: [2] "Do not make water at the mouth of a river emptying into the sea, nor into a spring. You must avoid that. Do not lighten your bowels there, for it is not good to do so." The precept not to befoul rivers at their mouths belongs to genus 1. No objective or subjective end or purpose is apparent in the avoidance of such pollution. The precept not to befoul drinking-water belongs to genus 3. It has an objective purpose that Hesiod may not have known, but which is familiar to moderns: to prevent contagion from certain diseases.

It is probable that not a few actions of genera 1 and 3 are common among savages and primitive peoples. But travellers are bent on learning at all costs the reasons for the conduct they observe. So in one way or another they finally obtain answers that transfer the conduct to genera 2 and 4.

REFERENCES

1. As we have already said (sections 116 f.), it would perhaps be better to use designations that have no meanings in themselves, such as letters of the alphabet. On the other hand, such a system would impair the clarity of our argument. We must therefore resign ourselves to using terms of ordinary speech; but the reader must bear in mind that such words, or their etymologies, in no way serve to describe the things they stand for. Things have to be examined directly. Names are just labels to help us keep track of them (section 119).
2. *Opera et dies,* vv. 757–58.

A Paradigm for Functional Analysis in Sociology * (*Merton*)

As an initial and admittedly tentative step in the direction of codifying functional analysis in sociology, we set forth a paradigm of the concepts and problems central to this approach. As will become at once evident, the chief components of this paradigm have progressively emerged in the foregoing pages as we have critically examined the vocabularies, postulates, concepts and ideological imputations now current in the field. The paradigm brings these together in compact form, thus permitting simultaneous inspection of the major requirements of functional analysis and serving as an aid to self-correction of provisional interpretations, a result difficult to achieve when

* Reprinted from *Social Theory and Social Structure* by Robert K. Merton, pp. 49–61, with permission of the publisher, The Free Press, Glencoe, Ill. Copyright, 1949, by The Free Press, A Corporation.

concepts are scattered and hidden in page after page of discursive exposition.[1] The paradigm presents the hard core of concept, procedure and inference in functional analysis.

Above all, it should be noted that the paradigm does not represent a set of categories introduced *de novo,* but rather a *codification* of those concepts and problems which have been forced upon our attention by critical scrutiny of current research and theory in functional analysis. (Reference to the preceding sections of this chapter will show that the groundwork has been prepared for every one of the categories embodied in the paradigm.)

PARADIGM FOR FUNCTIONAL ANALYSIS IN SOCIOLOGY

1. THE ITEM(S) TO WHICH FUNCTIONS ARE IMPUTED
   The entire range of sociological data can be, and much of it has been, subjected to functional analysis. The basic requirement is that the object of analysis represent a *standardized* (*i.e.* patterned and repetitive) item, such as social roles, institutional patterns, social processes, cultural pattern, culturally patterned emotions, social norms, group organization, social structure, devices for social control, *etc.*
   > Basic query: what must enter into the protocol of observation of the given item if it is to be amenable to systematic functional analysis?

2. CONCEPTS OF SUBJECTIVE DISPOSITIONS (MOTIVES, PURPOSES)
   At some point, functional analysis invariably assumes or explicitly operates with some conception of the motivation of individuals involved in a social system. As the foregoing discussion has shown, these concepts of subjective disposition are often and erroneously merged with the related, but different, concepts of objective consequences of attitude, belief and behavior.
   > Basic query: in which types of analysis is it sufficient to take observed motivations as *data,* as givens, and in which are they properly considered as *problematical,* as derivable from other data?

3. CONCEPTS OF OBJECTIVE CONSEQUENCES (FUNCTIONS, DYSFUNCTIONS)
   We have observed two prevailing types of confusion enveloping the several current conceptions of "function":
   (1) the tendency to confine sociological observations to the *positive* contributions of a sociological item to the social or cultural system in which it is implicated; and
   (2) the tendency to confuse the subjective category of *motive* with the objective category of *function.*
   Appropriate conceptual distinctions are required to eliminate these confusions. The first problem calls for a concept of *multiple consequences* and *a net balance of an aggregate of consequences.*
   Functions are those observed consequences which make for the adaptation or adjustment of a given system; and *dysfunctions,* those observed consequences which lessen the adaptation or adjustment of the system.

There is also the empirical possibility of *non-functional* consequences, which are simply irrelevant to the system under consideration.

In any given instances, an item may have both functional and dysfunctional consequences, giving rise to the difficult and important problem of evolving canons for assessing the net balance of the aggregate of consequences. (This is, of course, most important in the use of functional analysis for guiding the formation and enactment of policy.)

The second problem (of confusion between motives and functions) requires us to introduce a conceptual distinction between the cases in which the subjective aim-in-view coincides with the objective consequence, and the cases in which they diverge.

Manifest functions are those objective consequences contributing to the adjustment or adaptation of the system which are intended and recognized by participants in the system;

Latent functions, correlatively, being those which are neither intended nor recognized.[2]

> Basic query: what are the effects of seeking to transform a previously latent function into a manifest function (involving the problem of the role of knowledge in human behavior and the problems of "manipulation" of human behavior)?

4. CONCEPTS OF THE UNIT SUBSERVED BY THE FUNCTION

We have observed the difficulties entailed in *confining* analysis to functions fulfilled for "the society," since items may be functional for some individuals and subgroups and dysfunctional for others. It is necessary, therefore, to consider a *range* of units affected by the given item: individuals in diverse statuses, subgroups, the larger social system and culture systems. (Terminologically, this implies the concepts of psychological function, group function, societal function, cultural function, *etc.*)

5. CONCEPTS OF FUNCTIONAL REQUIREMENTS (NEEDS, PREREQUISITES)

Embedded in every functional analysis is some conception, tacit or expressed, of functional requirements of the system under observation. As noted elsewhere,[3] this remains one of the cloudiest and empirically most debatable concepts in functional theory. As utilized by sociologists, the concept of functional requirement tends to be tautological or *ex post facto;* it tends to be confined to conditions of "survival" of a given system; it tends, as in the work of Malinowski, to include biological as well as social "needs." This involves the difficult problem of establishing types of functional requirements (universal vs. highly specific); procedures for validating the assumption of these requirements; *etc.*

> Basic query: what is required to establish the validity of such an intervening variable as "functional requirement" in situations where rigorous experimentation is impracticable?

6. CONCEPTS OF THE MECHANISMS THROUGH WHICH FUNCTIONS ARE FULFILLED

Functional analysis in sociology, as in other disciplines like physiology and psychology, calls for a "concrete and detailed" account of the mechanisms which operate to perform a given function. This refers, not to psychological, but to social, mechanisms (*e.g.,* role-segmentation, insulation of institutional demands, hierarchic ordering of values, social division of labor, ritual and ceremonial enactments, *etc.*).

> Basic query: what is the presently available inventory of social mechanisms corresponding, say, to the large inventory of psychological mechanisms? What are the methodological problems entailed in discerning the operation of these social mechanisms?

7. CONCEPTS OF FUNCTIONAL ALTERNATIVES (FUNCTIONAL EQUIVALENTS OR SUBSTITUTES)

As we have seen, once we abandon the gratuitous assumption of the functional indispensability of given social structures, there is immediately required some concept of functional alternatives, equivalents, or substitutes. This focusses attention on the *range of possible variation* in the items which can, in the given instance, subserve a functional requirement. It unfreezes the identity of the existent and the inevitable.

> Basic query: since scientific proof of the equivalence of an alleged functional alternative ideally requires rigorous experimentation, and since this is not often practicable in large-scale sociological situations, which practicable procedures of inquiry most nearly approximate the logic of experiment?

8. CONCEPTS OF STRUCTURAL CONTEXT (OR STRUCTURAL CONSTRAINT)

The range of variation in the items which *can* fulfill designated functions within a given instance is not unlimited (and this has been repeatedly noted in our foregoing discussion). The interdependence of the elements of a social structure limit the effective possibilities of change or functional alternatives. The concept of structural constraint corresponds, in the area of social structure, to Goldenweiser's "principle of limited possibilities" in a broader sphere. Failure to recognize the relevance of interdependence and attendant structural restraints leads to utopian thought in which it is tacitly assumed that certain elements of a social system can be eliminated without affecting the rest of that system. This consideration is recognized by both Marxist social scientists (*e.g.* Karl Marx) and by non-Marxists (*e.g.* Malinowski).[4]

> Basic query: how narrowly does a given structural context limit the range of variation in the items which can effectively satisfy functional requirements? Do we find, under conditions yet to be determined, an area of indifference, in which any one of a wide range of alternatives may fulfill the function?

9. CONCEPTS OF DYNAMICS AND CHANGE

We have noted that functional analysts *tend* to focus on the statics of social structure and to neglect the study of structural change. The concept of dysfunction, which implies the concept of strain, stress and tension on the structural level, provides an analytical approach to the study of dynamics and change. How are observed dysfunctions contained within a given structure, so that they do not produce instability? Does the accumulation of stresses and strains produce pressure for change in such directions as are likely to lead to their reduction?

  Basic query: does the prevailing concern among functional analysts with the concept of *social equilibrium* divert attention from the phenomena of *social disequilibrium?* Which available procedures will permit the sociologist most adequately to gauge the accumulation of stresses and strains in a given social system? To what extent does the structural context permit the sociologist to anticipate the most probable directions of social change?

10. PROBLEMS OF VALIDATION OF FUNCTIONAL ANALYSIS
  Throughout the paradigm, attention has been called repeatedly to the *specific* points at which assumptions, imputations and observations must be validated.[5] This requires, above all, a rigorous statement of the sociological procedures of analysis which most nearly approximate the *logic* of experimentation. It requires a systematic review of the possibilities and limitations of *comparative* (cross-cultural and cross-group) *analysis.*

  Basic query: to what extent is functional analysis limited by the difficulty of locating adequate *samples of social systems* which can be subjected to comparative (quasi-experimental) study? [6]

11. PROBLEMS OF THE IDEOLOGICAL' IMPLICATIONS OF FUNCTIONAL ANALYSIS
  It has been emphasized in a preceding section, that functional analysis has no intrinsic commitment to a given ideological position. This does not gainsay the fact that *particular* functional analyses and *particular* hypotheses advanced by functionalists may have an identifiable ideological role. This, then, becomes a specific problem for the sociology of knowledge: to what extent does the social position of the functional sociologist (*e.g., vis-à-vis* a particular "client" who has authorized a given research) evoke one rather than another formulation of a problem, affect his assumptions and concepts, and limit the range of inferences drawn from his data?

  Basic query: how does one detect the ideological tinge of a given functional analysis and to what degree does a particular ideology stem from the basic assumptions adopted by the sociologist? Is the incidence of these assumptions related to the status and research role of the sociologist?

Before proceeding to a more intensive study of some parts of this paradigm, let us be clear about the uses to which it is supposed the paradigm can be put. After all, taxonomies of concepts may be multiplied endlessly without materially advancing the tasks of sociological analysis. What, then, are the purposes of the paradigm and how might it be used?

PURPOSES OF THE PARADIGM

  The first and foremost purpose is to supply a provisional codified guide for adequate and fruitful functional analysis. This objective evidently implies that the paradigm contains the minimum set of concepts with which the sociologist must operate in order to carry through an adequate functional analysis and, as a corollary, that it can be used here and now as a guide for the critical study of existing analyses. It is thus intended as an all-too-compact and elliptical guide to the formulation of researches in functional analysis and as an aid in locating the distinctive contributions and deficiencies of earlier researches. Limitations of space will permit us to apply only limited sections of the paradigm to a critical appraisal of a selected list of cases in point.

Secondly, the paradigm is intended to lead directly to the postulates and (often tacit) assumptions underlying functional analysis. As we have found in earlier parts of this chapter, some of these assumptions are of central importance, others insignificant and dispensable, and still others, dubious and even misleading.

In the third place, the paradigm seeks to sensitize the sociologist not only to the narrowly scientific implications of various types of functional analysis, but also to their political and sometimes ideological implications. The points at which a given functional analysis presupposes an implicit political outlook and the points at which it has bearing on "social engineering" are concerns which find an integral place in the paradigm.

It is obviously beyond the limits of this chapter to explore in detail the large and inclusive problems involved in the paradigm. This must await fuller exposition in a volume devoted to this purpose. We shall, therefore, confine the remainder of the present discussion to brief applications of only the first parts of the paradigm to a severely limited number of cases of functional analysis in sociology. And, from time to time, these few cases will be used as a springboard for discussion of special problems which are only imperfectly illustrated by the cases in hand.

ITEMS SUBJECTED TO FUNCTIONAL ANALYSIS

At first glance, it would appear that the sheer *description* of the item to be analyzed functionally entails few, if any, problems. Presumably, one should describe the item "as fully and as accurately" as possible. Yet, at second thought, it is evident that this maxim provides next to no guidance for the observer. Consider the plight of a functionally oriented neophyte armed only with this dictum as an aid to answering the question: *what* am I to observe, *what* am I to incorporate into my field notes, and *what* may I safely omit?

Without assuming that a detailed and circumstantial answer can now be supplied to the field worker, we can nevertheless note that the question itself is legitimate and that *implicit* answers have been partly developed. To tease out these implicit answers and to codify them, it is necessary to approach cases of functional analysis with the query: *what kinds of data have been consistently included, no matter what the item undergoing analysis, and why have these rather than any other data been included?*

It soon becomes apparent that the functionalist orientation largely determines what is included in the description of the item to be interpreted. Thus, the description of a magical performance or a ceremonial is not confined to an account of the spell or formula, the rite and the performers. It systematically includes a systematic account of the people participating and the onlookers, of the types and rates of interaction among performers and audience, of changes in these patterns of interaction in the course of the ceremonial. Thus, describing Hopi rain ceremonials, for example, entails describing more than the actions seemingly oriented toward the intervention of the gods in meteorological phenomena. It involves a report of *who* is variously involved in the pattern of behavior. And the description of the participants (and onlookers) is in *structural terms,* that is, in terms of locating these people in their inter-connected social statuses.

Brief excerpts will illustrate how functional analyses begin with a systematic inclusion (and, preferably, charting) of the statuses and social interrelations of those engaging in the behavior under scrutiny.

Chiricahua puberty ceremonial for girls: the extended domestic family (parents and relatives financially able to help) bear the expense of this four-day ceremony. The parents select the time and place for the ceremonial. "All the members of the *girl's encampment* attend and nearly all the *members of the local group.* A goodly sprinkling of visitors from *other local groups* and some *travelers from outside bands* are to be seen, and their numbers increase as the day wears on." The *leader of the local group* to which the girl's family belongs speaks, welcoming all visitors. In short, this account explicitly calls attention to the following statuses and groups variously involved in the ceremonial: the girl; her parents and immediate family; the local group, especially through its leader; the band represented by members of outside local groups, and the "tribe by members of other bands." [7]

As we shall see in due course, but it bears stating at this point, *the sheer description* of the ceremony (partly) in terms of the statuses and group affiliations of those variously involved *provides a major clue to the functions* performed by this ceremonial. In a word, we suggest that structural description of participants in the activity under analysis provides hypotheses for subsequent functional interpretations.

Another illustration will again indicate the nature of such descriptions in terms of role, status, group affiliation and the interrelations among these.

Patterned responses to mirriri (hearing obscenity directed at one's sister) among the Australian Murngin: the standardized pattern must be all too briefly described: when a husband swears at his wife in the presence of her brother, the brother engages in the seemingly anomalous behavior of throwing spears at the wife (not the husband) and her sisters. The description of this pattern goes on to include status descriptions of the participants. The *sisters* are members of the brother's *clan*; the husband comes from another clan.

Note again that participants are *located* within social structures and this location is basic to the subsequent functional analysis of this behavior.[8]

But these are cases drawn from non-literate society, and it may be assumed that this and other requirements for description are peculiar to non-literate materials. Turning to other instances of functional analyses of patterns found in modern Western society, we shall find this same requirement as well as additional guides to "needed descriptive data."

The "romantic love complex" in American society: although all societies recognize "occasional violent emotional attachments," contemporary American society is among the few which capitalize upon romantic attachments and in popular belief, at least, makes these the basis for choice of a marriage partner. This characteristic pattern of choice minimizes or eliminates the selection of one's mate by parents or the wider kinship group.[9]

Note that the emphasis upon one pattern of choice of mates thereby excludes alternative patterns of choice known to occur elsewhere. This case suggests a *second* desideratum for a type of data to be included in the account of the item subjected to functional analysis. In describing the characteristic (modal) pattern for handling a standardized problem (choice of marriage-partner), the observer, wherever possible, indicates the alternatives which are thereby excluded. This, as we shall see, provides direct clues to the structural context of the pattern and, by suggesting pertinent comparative materials, points toward the validation of the functional analysis.

A *third* integral element of the description of the problematical item preparatory to the actual functional analysis—a further requirement for preparing the specimen for analysis, so to speak—is to include the *"meanings"* (or cognitive and affective significance) of the activity or pattern for members of the group. In fact, as will become evident, a fully circumstantial account of the meanings attached to the item goes far toward suggesting appropriate lines of functional analysis. A case drawn from Veblen's many functional analyses serves to illustrate the general thesis:

The cultural pattern of conspicuous consumption: the conspicuous consumption of relatively expensive commodities "means" (symbolizes) sufficient wealth to "afford" such expenditures and wealth in turn is honorific. Persons engaging in conspicuous consumption not only derive gratification from the direct consumption but also from the heightened status reflected in the attitudes and opinions of others who observe this consumption. This pattern is most notable among the leisure class, *i.e.,* those who can and largely do refrain from productive labor [this is the status or role component of the description]. However, it diffuses to other strata who seek to emulate the pattern and who likewise experience pride in "wasteful" expenditures. Finally, consumption in conspicuous terms tends to crowd out other criteria for consumption (*e.g.* "efficient" expenditure of funds)—[This is an explicit reference to alternative modes of consumption obscured from view by the cultural emphasis on the pattern under scrutiny.] [10]

As is well known, Veblen goes on to impute a variety of functions to the pattern of conspicuous consumption—functions of aggrandizement of status, of validation of status, of "good repute," of display of pecuniary strength (p. 84)—which go far toward explaining the continuance of the pattern. *The clues to the imputed functions are provided almost wholly by the description of the pattern itself* which includes explicit references to (1) status of those differentially exhibiting the pattern, (2) known alternatives to the pattern of consuming in terms of display and "wastefulness" rather than in terms of private and "intrinsic" enjoyment of the item of consumption; and (3) the divers meanings culturally ascribed to the behavior of conspicuous consumption by participants in and observers of the pattern.

These three prerequisites for the description of the specimen to be analyzed are by no means exhaustive. A full descriptive protocol, adequate for subsequent functional analysis, will inevitably spill over into a range of immediate psychological and social consequences of the behavior. But these may be more profitably examined in connection with the concepts of function. It is here only necessary to repeat that the description of the item does not proceed according to whim or intuition, but must include at least these three characteristics of the item, if the preanalytical descriptive protocol is to be of optimum value for functional analysis. Though much remains to be learned concerning desiderata for the descriptive phase of the total analysis, this brief presentation of models for descriptive content may serve to indicate that procedures for functional analysis *can* be codified—ultimately to the point where the sociological field worker will have a chart of observation.

Another case illustrates a further desideratum for the description of the item to be analyzed.

Taboo on out-marriage: the greater the degree of group solidarity, the more marked the sentiment adverse to marriage with people outside the group. "It makes no difference what is the cause of the desire for group solidarity . . ." Out-marriage *means* either losing one's group-member to another group or incorporation in one's own group of individuals who have not been thoroughly socialized in the values, sentiments and practices of the in-group.[11]

This suggests a *fourth* type of datum to be included in the description of the social or cultural specimen, prior to functional analysis. Inevitably, participants in the practice under scrutiny have *some* array of motives for conformity or for deviation. *The descriptive account should, so far as possible, include an account of these motivations, but these motives must not be confused, as we have seen, with (a) the objective pattern of behavior or (b) with the social functions of that pattern.* Inclusion of motives in the descriptive account helps explain the *psychological* functions subserved by the pattern and often proves suggestive with respect to the social functions.

Thus far, we have been considering items which are clearly patterned practices or beliefs, patterns recognized as such by participants in the society. Thus, members of the given society can, in varying degrees, describe the contours of the Chiricahua puberty ceremony, of the Murngin mirriri pattern, the choice of mates on the basis of romantic attachments, the concern with consuming conspicuously and the taboos on out-marriage. These are all parts of the overt culture and, as such, are more or less fully known to those who share in this culture. The social scientist, however, does not confine himself to these overt patterns. From time to time, he uncovers a covert cultural pattern, a set of practices or beliefs which is as consistently patterned as overt patterns, but which is not regarded as a normatively regulated pattern by the participants. Examples of this are plentiful. Thus, statistics show that in a quasi-caste situation such as that governing Negro-white relations in this country, the prevailing pattern of interracial marriage (when it occurs) is between white females and Negro males (rather than between Negro females and white males). This pattern, which we may call caste hypogamy, is not institutionalized but it is persistent and remarkably stable.[12]

Or, to take another instance of a fixed but apparently unrecognized pattern. Malinowski reports that Trobrianders cooperatively engaged in the technological task of building a canoe are engaged not only in that explicit technical task but also in establishing and reinforcing interpersonal relations among themselves in the process. Much of the recent data on those primary groups called "informal organizations," deals with these patterns of relations which are observed by the social scientist but unrecognized, at least in their full implications, by the participants.[13]

All this points to a *fifth* desideratum for the descriptive protocol: regularities of behavior *associated* with the nominally central activity (although not part of an explicit culture pattern) should be included in the protocols of the field worker, since these *unwitting regularities* often provide basic clues to distinctive functions of the total pattern. As we shall see, the inclusion of these "unwitting" regularities in the descriptive protocol directs the investigator almost at once to analysis of the pattern in terms of what we have called latent functions.

In summary, then, the descriptive protocol should, so far as possible, include:

1) location of participants in the pattern within the social structure—differential participation;
2) consideration of alternative modes of behavior excluded by emphasis on the observed pattern (*i.e.* attention not only to what occurs but also to what is omitted by virtue of the existing pattern);
3) the emotive and cognitive meanings attached by participants to the pattern;
4) a distinction between the motivations for participating in the pattern and the objective behavior involved in the pattern;
5) regularities of behavior not recognized by participants but which are none-theless associated with the central pattern of behavior.

That these desiderata for the observer's protocol are far from complete is altogether likely. But they do provide a tentative step in the direction of *specifying* points of observation which facilitate subsequent functional analysis. They are intended to be somewhat more specific than is ordinarily found in such general statements of procedure as those advising the observer to be sensitive to the "context of situation."

REFERENCES

1. For a brief statement of the purpose of analytical paradigms such as this, see the note on paradigms elsewhere in *Social Theory and Social Structure*.
2. The relations between the "unanticipated consequences" of action and "latent functions" can be clearly defined, since they are implicit in the foregoing section of the paradigm. The unintended consequences of action are of three types:
    (1) those which are functional for a given system, and these comprise the latent functions;
    (2) those which are dysfunctional for a given system, and these comprise the latent dysfunctions; and
    (3) those which are irrelevant to the system which they affect neither functionally nor dysfunctionally, *i.e.*, the pragmatically unimportant class of non-functional consequences.

For a preliminary and now-outmoded statement, see R. K. Merton, "The unantici-pated consequences of purposive social action," *American Sociological Review,* 1936, 1, 894–904.

3. R. K. Merton, "Discussion of Parsons' 'Position of Sociological Theory,'" *American Sociological Review,* 1949, 13:164–168.

4. Previously cited excerpts from Marx document this statement, but these are, of course, only a few out of many places in which Marx in effect stresses the impor-tance of taking account of the structural context. In *A Contribution to the Critique of Political Economy* (appearing in 1859 and republished in Karl Marx, *Selected Works, op. cit.,* I, 354–371), he observes for example: "No social order ever dis-appears before all the productive forces for which there is room in it have been de-veloped; and new higher relations of production never appear before the material conditions of their existence have matured in the womb of the old society itself. Therefore, mankind always sets itself only such tasks as it can solve; since, looking at the matter more closely, we will always find that the task itself arises only when the material conditions necessary for its solution already exist or are at least in the process of formation." (p. 357) Perhaps the most famous of his many references to the con-straining influence of a given social structure is found in the second paragraph of *The Eighteenth Brumaire of Louis Napoleon:* "Man makes his own history, but he does not make it out of whole cloth: he does not make it out of conditions chosen by himself, but out of such conditions as he finds close at hand." (From the paraphrase of the original as published in Marx, *Selected Works,* II, 315.) To my knowledge, A. D. Lindsay is the most perceptive among the commentators who have noted the theoretic implications of statements such as these. See his little book, *Karl Marx's Capital: An Introductory Essay* (Oxford University Press, 1931), esp. at 27–52.

And for other language with quite different ideological import and essentially similar theoretic implications, see B. Malinowski, "Given a definite cultural need, the means of its satisfaction are small in number, and therefore the cultural arrange-ment which comes into being in response to the need is determined within narrow limits." "Culture," *Encyclopedia of the Social Sciences, op. cit.,* 626.

5. By this point, it is evident that we are considering functional analysis as a method for the *interpretation* of sociological data. This is not to gainsay the important role of the functional orientation in sensitizing sociologists to the *collection of* types of data which might otherwise be neglected. It is perhaps unnecessary to reiterate the axiom that one's concepts *do* determine the inclusion or exclusion of data, that, despite the etymology of the term, *data* are not "given" but are "contrived" with the inevitable help of concepts. In the process of evolving a functional interpretation, the socio-logical analyst invariably finds it necessary to obtain data other than those initially contemplated. Interpretation and the collection of data are thus inextricably bound up in the array of concepts and propositions relating these concepts. For an extension of these remarks, see my paper on "Sociological Theory" in the present volume.

6. Inspection of the book by George P. Murdock, *Social Structure* (New York, Macmil-lan, 1949), is enough to show that procedures such as those involved in the cross-cultural survey hold large promise for dealing with certain methodological problems of functional analysis.

7. Morris E. Opler, "An Outline of Chiricahua Apache Social Organization," in Fred Eggan ed. *Social Anthropology of North American Tribes* (Chicago, University of Chicago Press, 1937), 173–239, esp. at 226–230 [italics supplied].

8. W. L. Warner, *A Black Civilization—A Social Study of an Australian Tribe* (New York, Harper & Bros., 1937), 112–113.

9. For various approaches to a functional analysis of the "romantic love complex," see Ralph Linton, *Study of Man* (New York. D. Appleton-Century Co., 1936). 174–5; T. Parsons, "Age and Sex in the Social Structure of the United States," *American Sociological Review,* Oct. 1942, 7, 604–616, esp. at 614–15: T. Parsons. "The Kinship System of the Contemporary United States." *American Anthropologist,* 1943, 45, 22–38. esp. at 31–32. 36–37, both reprinted in his *Essays in Sociological Theory, op. cit.;* T. Parsons, "The Social Structure of the Family," in Ruth N.

Anshen ed., *The Family: Its Function and Destiny* (New York, Harper, 1949), 173–201; R. K. Merton, "Intermarriage and the Social Structure," *Psychiatry,* 1941, 4, 361–74, esp. at 367–8; and Isidor Thorner, "Sociological Aspects of Affectional Frustration," *Psychiatry,* 1943, 6, 157–173, esp. at 169–172.

10. Thorstein Veblen, *The Theory of the Leisure Class* (New York, Vanguard Press, 1928), esp. chapters 2–4.
11. Romanzo Adams, *Interracial Marriage in Hawaii,* esp. at 197–204; Merton, "Intermarriage . . . ," *op. cit.,* esp. at 368–9; K. Davis "Intermarriage in Caste Societies," *American Anthropologist,* 1941, 43, 376–395.
12. *Cf.* Merton, "Intermarriage . . . ," *op. cit.*; Otto Klineberg ed. *Characteristics of the American Negro* (New York, Harper, 1943).
13. The rediscovery of the primary group by those engaged in sociological studies of industry has been one of the chief fillips to the functional approach in recent sociological research. Reference is had here to the work of Elton Mayo, Roethlisberger and Dickson, William Whyte, and Burleigh Gardner, among many others. There remain, of course, the interesting differences in *interpretation* to which these data lend themselves.

15.

SOCIOLOGY OF KNOWLEDGE

THE SOCIOLOGY OF KNOWLEDGE may be broadly defined as that branch of sociology which studies the relationships between thought and society. Far from being restricted to the sociological analysis of scientific and certified knowledge, as the term would seem to imply, its practitioners have concerned themselves with practically the entire range of intellectual products— from philosophies to ideologies, from political doctrines to theological thought. In all these fields the sociology of knowledge attempts to relate the ideas it studies to the socio-historical settings in which they are produced and received.

Almost since its inception the sociology of knowledge has been entangled in discussions involving the epistemological consequences of some of its assertions, especially with regard to questions of the truth and validity of the ideas under study. Would not attempts, for example, to uncover the roots of particular propositions in the social position of their originators lead to a total relativism? Such discussions are consequential and intellectually exciting, but for the most part we shall have to bypass them here, since we are convinced that the genesis of an idea can never establish its validity or invalidity. We shall be concerned mainly with the assertion that there are functional relationships between social structures and both the categories of thought and the ideas operative within such structures.

Though, as we shall see, systematic sociology of knowledge originated in nineteenth century European thought, its antecedents go back considerably farther. Thus when Bacon wrote: "Of much like kind are those impressions of nature, which are imposed upon the mind by the sex, by the age, by the region, by health and sickness, by beauty and deformity and the like, which are inherent and not extern; and again those which are caused by extern fortune; as sovereignty, nobility, obscure birth, riches, want, magistracy, privateness, prosperity, adversity, constant fortune, variable fortune, rising per saltum, per gradus, and the like," [1] he had already outlined the general territory which later systematic sociology of knowledge would claim as its province.

Though similar insights can be shown to have occurred not infrequently among European thinkers of the seventeenth and eighteenth centuries, it nevertheless remains true that systematic sociology of knowledge received its main impetus from two trends in nineteenth century European sociological thought: the Marxian tradition in Germany and the Durkheimian tradition in France. Although these two main streams, as well as their later tributaries by no means converge in all of their fundamental assumptions, they are at the starting point of most theorizing in the field. A third significant strain of influence on the development of the sociology of knowledge, American Pragmatism and Social Behaviorism, will also have to be considered here, since recent American thinking in the field may be considered as an attempted synthesis of these earlier European traditions with this native strain of thought.

MARXISM AND GERMAN SOCIOLOGY OF KNOWLEDGE

In his attempt to dissociate himself from the pan-logical system of his former master Hegel as well as from the "critical philosophy" of his former "Young Hegelian" friends, Karl Marx attempted in his early writings to establish a connection between philosophies and the concrete social structures in which they emerged. "It has not occurred to any of these philosophers," writes the young Marx in *The German Ideology*, "to inquire into the connection of German philosophy with German reality, the relation of their criticism to their own material surroundings." [2] This programmatic orientation once established, Marx was naturally led to move away from his earlier concern with the intrinsic problems of philosophy toward a consideration of relationships between philosophy and society. More specifically, he was now concerned with analyzing the ways in which systems of ideas appeared to be dependent on the social position, more particularly the class position, of their proponents.

In his struggle against the dominant ideas of his time, Marx was led to a resolute relativization of these ideas. The eternal verities of dominant thought appear to him upon analysis to be but the expression of the class interests of their exponents:

Your ideas are themselves the outcome of bourgeois methods of production and of bourgeois property relations; just as your "right" is only the will of your class writ large as law—a will whose trends are determined by the material conditions under which your class lives. Your interests lead you to think that your methods of production, your property relations, are eternal laws of natural reason, instead of transient outcomes of the course of production. Earlier ruling classes, now fallen from power, shared this delusion. You understand that it was a delusion as regards the property of classical days, and as regards the property of feudal days, but you cannot see that it is no less a delusion as regards bourgeois property. [3]

Marx thus attempted to functionalize ideas systematically, i.e., to relate the ideas of individuals to their social roles and to the class positions they occupy in society: "The mode of production in material life determines the general character of the social, political and intellectual process of life. It is not the consciousness of men that determines their existence, but on the contrary their social existence determines their consciousness." [4]

While most of Marx's analysis concerned the relationship of middle-class ideas to the middle-class interests and ways of life, he stated quite specifically that the same relationship also held true with regard to the emergence of new dissident and revolutionary ideas. These also could only emerge if shifting class structures produced a new revolutionary class: "The existence of revolutionary ideas presupposes the existence of a revolutionary class . . . When changes occur in people's modes of life, in their social relations or social systems, there will also be changes in their ideas, and outlooks and conceptions . . . What does the history of ideas prove, if not that mental production changes concomitantly with material production?" [5]

In their writings of a later period Marx and Engels were to qualify and refine the somewhat sweeping statements which they had initially made— often in a polemical context. They were thus led to grant a certain degree of intrinsic autonomy to the concrete development of legal, political, religious, literary, artistic and, especially, scientific ideas, and to stress that these, far from being simple reflections of the economic and class substructures, did in themselves react upon these structures: "It is not that the economic position is the cause and alone active, while everything else has only a passive effect. There is rather, interaction on the basis of economic necessity, which *ultimately* always asserts itself." [6]

But while the original Marxian thesis so interpreted became a considerably more flexible instrument, it also lost some of its distinctive qualities. Interpreted rigidly, it tended to lend itself as a rather crude tool for "debunking" all adverse thought; interpreted flexibly, it became difficult to distinguish from non-Marxian attempts at functionalizing thought. In addition, as Robert K. Merton has pointed out, when it is stated in so flexible a manner, it becomes so indistinct that it is impossible to invalidate it at all, since any set of data may be so interpreted as to fit it. [7]

Marxian methods of analysis in this area, as in so many others, exerted a powerful if often subterranean influence on subsequent German social thought. Even the most determined adversaries of the system were impelled to take up the challenge it presented and were thus forced to relate themselves to it. even if only in order to reject it. The work of Werner Sombart or Max Weber is intimately related to the challenges of Marx.

Though contributions to what might loosely be called sociology of knowledge can be found in the works of many an academic sociologist in

Germany in the early twentieth century, and though orthodox Marxists, especially the Hungarian thinker Georg Lukacs [8] also contributed significant clarifications, it remained for two German scholars, Max Scheler and Karl Mannheim, to develop a corpus of theory which represents the first systematic elaboration of a sociology of knowledge as a new scientific discipline. We will deal with Karl Mannheim first, since his contribution is more directly tied to the main themes of Marxian thought previously considered.

Mannheim, deeply influenced by the Marxian tradition, though not part of it, undertook so to generalize the Marxian interpretation as to divest it of all those polemical elements which had been conspicuous in the writing of its originators: "Nothing was to prevent the opponents of Marxism," Mannheim wrote, "from availing themselves of the weapon and applying it to Marxism itself." [9] Mannheim attempted to transform what for Marx had been primarily a means of attack against the thought of opponents into a more general tool of analysis. "What was once the intellectual armament of a party is transformed into a method of research in social and intellectual history generally . . . the thought of every group is seen as arising out of its life conditions." [10]

While in the Marxian formulations attention was focused on unmasking ideological pretensions, on calling attention to the uses of ideology in the defense of class privileges, and on pointing to the distortions and falsifications of ideas, Mannheim's widened orientation allowed for the probability that all ideas, even "truths," were related to and hence influenced by the social and historical situation in which they emerged: The very fact that each thinker is affiliated with particular groups in society, that he occupies a certain status and enacts a social role, colors his intellectual outlook. Thus it is "not men in general who think, or even isolated individuals who do the thinking, but men in certain groups who have developed a particular style of thought in an endless series of responses to certain typical situations characterizing their common position . . . Men living in groups do not merely coexist physically as discrete individuals. They do not confront the objects of the world from the abstract level of contemplating mind as such, nor do they do so exclusively as solitary beings. On the contrary they act with and against one another in diversely organized groups, and while doing so they think with and against one another." [11]

Mannheim was thus led to define the sociology of knowledge as a theory of the social or existential determination of thinking. He explained:

The existential determination of thought may be regarded as a demonstrated fact in those realms of thought in which we can show (a) that the process of knowing does not actually develop historically in accordance with immanent laws, that it does not follow only from the "nature of things" or from "pure logical possibilities" and that it is not driven by an "inner dialectic." On the contrary, the emergence and the crystallization of actual thought are influenced at many decisive points by extra-theoretical factors, existential factors. This existential determination of thought will also have to be regarded as a fact (b) if the influence of these existential factors on the concrete content of knowledge is of more than peripheral importance, if they are relevant not only to the genesis of ideas, but penetrate into their forms and content and if, furthermore, they decisively determine the scope and the intensity of our experience and observation, i.e., that which we formerly referred to as the "perspective" of the subject." [12]

To Mannheim, then, all knowledge, all ideas are "bound to a location" within the social process. At particular times a particular group can have fuller access to the understanding of a social phenomenon than other groups, but no group can claim to have total access to it. (At times, though, Mannheim expressed the hope that "detached intellectuals" might in our age achieve a "unified perspective" free of existential determination.) Mannheim thus rejects the claim of Marxian thought that "adequate knowledge" can be achieved by the proletarian class; no class can be said to have a monopoly on truth, each standpoint falls short of complete truth. "There is an existentially determined truth content in human thought at every stage of its development." [13] The various standpoints or perspectives express the aspirations of different concrete groups, and the task of the new discipline is to ascertain the empirical correlations between standpoints and structural and historical positions. Mannheim did not claim, of course, that such relating of ideas to the social structure can ever replace an intrinsic consideration of these ideas. Just as the sociology of art, since it furnishes no esthetic criteria, cannot possibly distinguish between good and bad works of art, but can enhance our understanding of both, so the sociology of knowledge, while unable to furnish valid evidence of truth, enlarges our comprehension of a system of ideas by permitting us to understand it within the context of the social situation in which it is immersed.

Many of Mannheim's critics have drawn attention to what they consider an element of self-contradiction in Mannheim's thesis. To quote only one of them, H. Otto Dahlke, "The notion of relativism or relationism . . . is self-contradictory, for it must presuppose its own absoluteness. The sociology of knowledge . . . must assume its own validity, if it is to have any meaning." [14] Mannheim, especially in his earlier writings, did indeed lay himself open to such attacks, yet it would seem clear that he never meant to assert that "existential determination" was a kind of total determination leaving no room for an examination of the ideas under discussion in other terms. He writes: "It is, of course, true that in the social sciences, as elsewhere, the ultimate criterion of truth and falsity is to be found in the investigation of the object, and the sociology of knowledge is no substitute for this." [15] Mannheim, in his mature view, considered the sociology of knowledge as *one* sociological discipline, but not as a panacea which eliminated the need for using all other methods of investigation. By considering the social perspectives of individuals and groups, i.e., "the manner in which one views an object, what one perceives in it, and how one construes it in his thinking," Mannheim felt that one reaches a point where he is engaged in more than sociological description and where this procedure "becomes a critique by redefining the scope and the limits of the perspective implicit in given assertions." The procedure is thus by no means irrelevant for the determination of the truth of a statement; yet it can only be a "first preparatory step leading to direct discussion." [16] "A new type of objectivity in the social sciences is attainable not through the exclusion of evaluations but through the critical awareness and control of them," [17] which the sociology of knowledge may make possible.

No matter what the imprecisions and methodological shortcomings of Mannheim's theoretical statements are judged to be, he has given us a number of concrete studies such as "Conservative Thought" [18] and "Competition as a Cultural Phenomenon," [19] which have been recognized as important contributions to the field even by those who have rejected or criticized Mannheim's theoretical apparatus.

Marx laid primary stress on economic and class factors in the determination of ideas; Mannheim expanded this conception to include a variety of other social factors such as generations, status groups, occupational groups, etc. Max Scheler went still further in widening the range of factors which influence thought forms.[20] There is no constant independent variable which determines the emergence of ideas, Scheler claimed, but in the course of history there occurs a definite sequence of "real factors"; in non-literate groups there is a domination of blood and kinship ties which constitute the independent variable; later, political factors and, finally, in the modern world, economic factors are to be considered the independent variables to which thought structures have to be related. Furthermore, Scheler rejected what he considered the "naturalism" and relativism of previous sociological theorizing in order to assert that there existed an a-temporal, absolute order of values and ideas, a realm of eternal essences, which is totally distinct from social and historical reality. It depends then, Scheler taught, on the predominance of different "real factors," those particular parts of the eternal realm of ideas and essences can be grasped at particular points in time. The real factor "opens and closes, in determinate way and order, the sluice gates of the stream of thought."

It cannot be the purpose of this essay to determine the validity of any of the systems of thought under discussion, but we might simply state that Scheler's theory of eternal essences depends on a certain number of metaphysical assumptions which are clearly not susceptible to scientific validation. His proposal, on the other hand, to widen the range of existential factors that may be related to particular systems of ideas is testable and provides fruitful hypotheses for research. In sum, Scheler made a number of significant efforts to establish relations between particular types of group structures and different types of knowledge and ideas. He attempted to show, for example, the interrelations between the hierarchical medieval world of communal estates and the medieval conception of the world as a hierarchy culminating in God, between the content of Plato's theory of ideas and the organization of the Platonic academy, and between the rise of mechanistic models of thought and the rise of bourgeois *Gesellschaft* types of society. Unfortunately little of the sociological work of Max Scheler has as yet been translated into English and his influence has therefore remained quite peripheral in the English speaking world.

FRENCH CONTRIBUTIONS TO THE SOCIOLOGY OF KNOWLEDGE

Though Emile Durkheim's contributions to the sociology of knowledge form only a relatively small part of his total work and though some of his statements in this area are mixed with epistemological speculation of a somewhat dubious character, they must be considered as part of the most vital pioneering work in the field.

In his attempt to establish the social origin and function of morals, values, and religion, and in explaining these as different forms of "collective representations," Durkheim was led to consider a similar explanation of the basic forms of logical classification and of the fundamental categories of thought itself.

In a paper written in collaboration with the anthropologist Marcel Mauss,[21] he attempted to account for the origins of spatial, temporal, and other classifications among non-literate peoples and was led to assert that these classifications closely approximate the social organization of the tribe. The first "classes" were classes of men, he asserts, and the classification of other objects was simply an extension of the social classifications already established. All animals and objects were classified as belonging to this or that clan, phratry or other kinship group. Durkheim contended that though scientific classification has become largely divorced from these social origins, the very manner in which we express logical relations today—when, for example, we refer to things which "belong to the same family"—still reveals their social origins.

In a later work Durkheim returned to these ideas and extended them to develop, though in sketchy and somewhat tentative form, a sociological explanation of all the fundamental categories of human thought, especially the concepts of time and space. He now claimed that these fundamental categories are not only transmitted by society, but that they are social creations. Society is decisive in the genesis of logical thought by forming the concepts of which that thought is made.

There are societies in Australia and North America where space is conceived in the form of an immense circle, because the camp has a circular form; and this spatial circle is divided up exactly like the tribal circle, and is in its image. There are as many regions distinguished as there are clans in the tribe, and it is the place occupied by the clans inside the encampment which had determined the orientation of these regions. Each region is defined by the totem of the clan to which it is assigned. Among the Zuni, for example, the pueblo contains seven quarters; . . . . Now their space also contains seven quarters, and each of these seven quarters of the world is in intimate connection with a quarter of the pueblo. . . . Thus the social organization has been the model for the spatial organization and a reproduction of it.[22]

Similarly with the category *time*:

Try to represent what the notion of time would be without the processes by which we divide it, measure it or express it with objective signs . . . We cannot conceive of time, except on condition of distinguishing its different moments. Now what is the origin of this differentiation? . . . . It is not *my time* that is thus arranged; it is time in general, such as it is objectively thought of by everybody in a single civilization. . . . These indispensable guide lines, in relation to which all things are temporally located, are taken from social life. The divisions into days, weeks, months, years etc. correspond to the periodical recurrence of rites, feasts, and public ceremonies. A calendar expresses the rhythm of the collective activities, while at the same time its function is to assure their regularity.[23]

These Durkheimian notions have often been challenged. Pitirim Sorokin, for example, has pointed out that geographical and cosmic factors were too easily discarded by Durkheim and his followers. Thus if the division of time into days, weeks, months, etc., expresses the rhythm of collective activity, it even more clearly expresses the rhythm of natural phenomena, the daily alternation of light and darkness, the sequence of the seasons, etc. Similarly with regard to space: The natural milieu is not something so formless as to lack coordination, "to the right of the hill," "below the mountain," etc., are spatial coordinations quite well known to non-literate peoples. This is corroborated, as Sorokin notes, by the fact of relatively uniform representations of space and time in a great many social groups with the most different social and political organizations.[24]

Perhaps a more fundamental criticism is advanced by Claude Lévi-Strauss, who has written that "Society cannot exist without symbolism, but instead of showing how the appearance of symbolic thought makes social life altogether possible and necessary, Durkheim tries the reverse, i.e. to make symbolism grow out of society. . . . Sociology cannot explain the genesis of symbolic thought, but has just to take it for granted in man." [25]

While one may grant that Durkheim thus failed to establish the social origin of all categories of thought, one may still consider that his was a crucial contribution in that it indicated a way of relating variations in systems of concepts to variations in social organization. It is this latter part of Durkheim's contribution, rather than some of his more debatable epistemological positions, that has deeply influenced later developments in the sociology of knowledge. Thus Marcel Granet, the eminent sinologist, used a Durkheimian frame of reference in relating the typical conceptions of time and space of ancient Chinese thought to such social factors as feudal organization and the rhythmic alternations of concentrated and dispersed group activities, while he traced the lack of abstract ideas and Aristotelean categories of logic in Chinese culture to Chinese language, the structure of which he in turn related to Chinese social structure.[26]

Durkheimian conceptions have also been fruitful in classical studies. Thus Jane Harrison [27] traces a number of Greek religious notions to the ceremonies of tribal initiation in conjunction with certain seasonal tribal festivities, and Francis Cornford [28] relates Greek philosophical ideas to prior religious notions and ultimately to the clan structure of the Greek tribes.

Finally Maurice Halbwachs, perhaps the most brilliant of Durkheim's successors, attempted to establish how even such private and intimate mental activities as dreams and memory need for their organization a stable reference in the group life in which the individual participates.[29]

AMERICAN ANTECEDENTS OF THE SOCIOLOGY OF KNOWLEDGE

The work of the major philosophers of American Pragmatism, Peirce, James, and Dewey, abounds with suggestive leads for the sociology of knowledge. To the extent that Pragmatism stressed the organic process by which every act of thought is linked to human conduct, and thus rejected the radical distinction between thinking and acting which had informed most classical philosophies, it prepared the ground for consideration of the more specifically sociological links between the social process and the thought process. Insofar as the Pragmatists stressed that thought is in its very nature bound to the social situation in which it arises they set the stage for efforts to inquire into the relations between a thinker and his audience. American pragmatists tended to reject the traditional view according to which an "object" of thought was to be sharply distinguished from the thinking "subject"; they posited instead an intimate connection between the object and the perceiving subject, a transaction between them. They thus dealt with ideas which, in a very different intellectual tradition, were later investigated by Karl Mannheim. Like Mannheim, they stressed that, to quote Louis Wirth, "in the realm of the social, particularly, truth is not merely a matter of simple correspondence between thought and existence, but is tinged with the investigator's interest in his subject matter, his standpoint, his evaluations, in short the definition of his object of attention." [30]

Space does not permit an extended examination of these thinkers here. Let us therefore quote a few ideas propounded by John Dewey as an illustration of the ways in which American pragmatism can be regarded as a force in the development of the sociology of knowledge. Dewey in his *Quest for Certainty* asked why Greek philosophy glorified the invariant at the expense of the changing, theoretical thought at the expense of practical activity, rational and necessary knowledge at the expense of probability. He answered:

It would be possible to argue (and, I think, with much justice) that failure to make action central in the search for such security as is humanly possible is a survival of the impotency of man in those stages of civilization when he had few means of regulating and utilizing the conditions upon which the occurrence of consequences depends. As long as man was unable by means of the arts of practice to direct the course of events, it was natural for him to seek an emotional substitute; in the absence of actual certainty in the midst of a precarious and hazardous world, men cultivated all sorts of things that would give them the *feeling* of certainty. And it is possible that when not carried to an illusory point, the cultivation of the feeling gave man courage and confidence and enabled him to carry the burdens of life more successfully.[31]

Not only did Dewey suggest a theory of the dependence of systems of thought on the type of community in which they were being propounded, but he further outlined a theory of the relation between occupational roles and styles of thought:

Occupations, determine the fundamental modes of activity, and hence control the formation and use of habits. These habits, in turn, are something more than practical and overt. . . . The occupations determine the chief mode of satisfaction, the standards of success and failure. Hence they furnish the working classifications and definitions of value; they control the desire processes. Moreover, they decide the sets of objects and relations that are important, and thereby provide the content or material of attention, and the qualities that are interestingly significant. The directions given to mental life thereby extend to emotional and intellectual characteristics. So fundamental and pervasive is the group of occupational activities that it affords the scheme or pattern of the structural organization of mental traits.[32]

Pragmatic philosophy is not the only intellectual trend native to America which influenced the development of the sociology of knowledge. American critical scholarship in history, especially the work of Charles A. Beard, may be said to have implicitly appropriated a number of the orientations of European sociology of knowledge, especially in its Marxian form. Beard's *An Economic Interpretation of the Constitution of the United States,* attempting to trace in detail the relationship of the thought of the Founding Fathers to their economic interests, provided a model for later sociological interpretations of systems of political ideas. Similarly, Vernon

L. Parrington's brilliant *Main Currents in American Thought* opened many a new perspective on the development of American letters by relating currents of thought in America to economic and social conditions.

At times American thinkers within a broad pragmatist tradition developed themes concerning the social roots of knowledge and ideas which antedate by a number of years specific contributions of their European counterparts. Consider only the amazing similarity between the approach developed by the economist A. B. Wolfe in his *Conservatism, Radicalism and Scientific Method,* published in 1923,[33] and the later formulations of Karl Mannheim. Wolfe writes:

A man's point of view, determines the perspective and the light in which he looks at things. The apparent shape of an object depends upon the direction from which it is viewed. Two individuals looking at a cylinder, the one broadside, the other endwise, would differ hopelessly as to its shape, if they could not shift their positions. One would hold it to be rectangular, the other circular. . . . It is much the same in human affairs. . . . Our social viewpoints determine both the direction, the perspective, and the light in which we see the social landscape, so far as it comes within our vision at all. . . . Whether an individual thinks or not, whether his thinking is connected and logical or fragmentary and full of fallacies, whether he has intellectually supported opinions or merely sentiments, whether he is credulous or critical, open-minded or narrowly prejudiced and intolerant, he has some viewpoint from which he looks out upon life. He cannot escape having attitudes toward the world of his experience and the issues which come to his attention, however transitorily. Judgments and prejudgments (prejudices), sentiments, opinions, valuations . . . are always the product of experience (taking the word in a broad sense), which has determined the individual's point of view and attitudes.[34]

Many of these strains of ideas had only an indirect influence on American sociology. It remains to draw attention to the contributions of two American thinkers who did, we believe, explicitly influence American sociology of knowledge to a significant extent: Thorstein Veblen and George Herbert Mead.

Among the most persistent themes that run through Thorstein Veblen's work is the attempt to show how thoughtways can be traced to the institutional framework in which they function. In *The Place of Science in Modern Civilization* he writes:

This question of a scientific point of view, of a particular attitude and animus in matters of knowledge, is a question of the formation of habits of thought; and habits of thought are an outcome of habits of life. A scientific point of view is a consensus of habits of thought current in the community, and the scientist is constrained to believe that this consensus is formed in response to a more or less consistent discipline of habituation to which the community is subjected, and that the consensus can extend only so far and maintain its force only so long as the discipline of habituation exercised by the circumstances of life enforces it and backs it up.[35]

But Veblen, not content simply to assert the dependence of thought styles on the community in which they are prevalent, went on to develop a theory linking such styles of thought to specific structural positions and roles within the community. He proposed a theory of the dependence of thought styles on the occupational position of their proponents.

. . . the scheme of life which men perforce adopt under the exigencies of an advanced industrial situation shapes their habits of thought on the side of their behavior, and shapes their habits of thought to some extent for all purposes. Each individual is but a single complex of habits of thought, and the same psychical mechanism that expresses itself in one direction as conduct expresses itself in another direction as knowledge. The habits of thought formed in the one connection . . . must therefore, have their effect when the same individual comes to respond to stimuli that call for a response in terms of knowledge. The scheme of thought or of knowledge is in good part a reverberation of the scheme of life. So that, after all has been said, it remains true that with the growth of industrial organization and efficiency there must, by selection and by adaptation, supervene a greater resort to the mechanical or dispassionate method of apprehending facts.[36]

Thorstein Veblen's savage onslaughts in *The Higher Learning in America,* should not be regarded simply as superb polemics (though they are that) but as significant contributions to the sociology of the academy and the roots of the ideas which it breeds. Thus, when Veblen wishes to account for the fact that the members of the leisure class are drawn to classical studies, law, and politics, rather than to natural science, he attempts to establish a functional relation between position in society and types of knowledge cultivated:

Further, as regards the direct participating of the members of the leisure class in the furtherance of knowledge, the canons of reputable living act to throw such intellectual interest as seeks expression among the class on the side of classical and formal erudition, rather than on the side of the sciences that bear some relation to the community's industrial life. The most frequent excursions into other than classical fields of knowledge on the part of members of the leisure class are made into the discipline of law and the political, and more especially the administrative, sciences. . . . The interest with which this discipline is approached is therefore not commonly the intellectual or cognitive interest simple. It is largely the practical interest of the exigencies of that relation of mastery in which the members of the class are placed.[37]

George Herbert Mead's social behaviorism, with its insistence that mind itself is a social product and is of social origin, provided a much needed social psychological basis for some of the assertions of previous researchers and theorists in the sociology of knowledge. For Mead communication was central to an understanding of the nature of mind: "Mind arises through communication by a conversation of gestures in a social process or context of experience—not communication through mind." [38] If mind is socially constituted and grounded in social communication, then a social determination of knowledge and thought cannot be questioned.

The self-conscious human individual . . . takes or assumes the organized social attitudes of the given social group or community (or of some one section thereof) to which he belongs, toward the social problems of various kinds which confront that group or community at any given time, and which arise in connection with the correspondingly different social projects or organized co-operative enterprises in which that group or community as such is engaged; and as an individual participant in these social projects or co-operative enterprises, he governs his own conduct accordingly.[39]

. . . the society in which we belong represents an organized set of responses to certain situations in which the individual is involved, . . . in so far as the individual can take those organized responses over into his own nature, and call them out by means of the symbol in the social response, he has a mind in which mental processes can go on, a mind whose inner structure he has taken from the community to which he belongs.[40]

It would seem that the key contribution of George Herbert Mead to the sociology of knowledge consists in the elaboration of a social psychology more adequate to an understanding of the functional relations between knowledge and society than some of its European counterparts. As a recent commentator has written: "His extraction of mind, self, thinking, and meaning from the context of the social act via the delineation of such mechanisms as role-taking, the generalized other, symbolization, and attitude systems, constitutes an expansion of the frame of reference of the sociology of knowledge." [41] Mead's work seems to have established that whatever determinants of thought do exist other than society, they can structure, mind only through the intermediary of the social realities by which it is circumscribed.[42]

CONTEMPORARY TRENDS IN THE SOCIOLOGY OF KNOWLEDGE IN AMERICA

It is difficult to assess the contribution of the sociology of knowledge to contemporary American social thought. As the sociology of knowledge has been incorporated into American theory, it has often merged with other areas of research, and in such cases it is no longer explicitly referred to as sociology of knowledge. Thus the research of Robert K. Merton [43] and Bernard Barber [44] in the sociology of science, the work of such men as E. C. Hughes,[45] Oswald Hall,[46] Talcott Parsons,[47] and others in the sociology of the professions, or, even more generally, much of the research concerned with social roles may be related to, and in part derived from, the orientations of the sociology of knowledge. On the other hand, the sociology of knowledge has been relatively neglected as a separate and distinct field of inquiry. Many practitioner of what is in fact sociology of knowledge may at times be rather surprised when it is pointed out that, like Monsieur Jourdain they have been talking prose all along.

This state of affairs may in itself provide an excellent field for research in the sociology of knowledge. One might inquire, for example, whether the relative stability of the American social structure and the relative homogeneity of the American systems of political and social thought have not contributed to a deflection of the original aims of the European sociology of knowledge. To the extent that the latter developed in response to the emergence, in a conflict-ridden social structure, of separate and contending universes of discourse and conflicting group perspectives and orientations, it is not too surprising that in contemporary America, where such differences have as yet been successfully minimized, the sociology of knowledge has assumed a somewhat different character. As Merton has pointed out, the sociology of public opinion and mass communication, a specifically American field, has to some extent taken the place of the sociology of knowledge in America and has tended to shift emphasis from concern with the structural determinants of thought to questions about the impact of mass media upon their audience.[48] Where the European tradition centered upon the production of ideas, the American is more concerned with their consumption. While European thought assumed as axiomatic that different strata in the society produced different types of ideas, the main trend in American research assumes that strata are chiefly differentiated by the ways in which they consume standardized thought products. Hence American research is noticeably more concerned with the reception than with the production of ideas, with audience research rather than with the perspectives and orientations of intellectual spokesmen.

Yet concern with the problems of the sociology of knowledge has led in America to significant attempts at stock taking in the field and at clarification of the key methodological questions involved. Merton's "paradigm for the sociology of knowledge," [49] which is intended to introduce a basis of comparability among the various types of studies and theories which have appeared in the field and to provide a classificatory scheme, is especially noteworthy. This paradigm draws attention to the variant and often quite contradictory approaches to the field and helps one to detect lacunae and weaknesses in current or past investigation. In particular he addresses himself to such questions as, "Where is the existential basis of mental production located?" and then discusses the various solutions to this question which have been proposed, such as social position, class generation, and occupational role. Also he asks, "How are mental productions related to the existential basis?" He points to variant responses in terms of causal or functional relations such as determination, cause, necessary condition, etc., and symbolic or organismic or meaningful relations such as harmony, coherance, symbolic expression and inner connection.

Among other notable contributions to the methodology and theoretical clarification of the sociology of knowledge, those of the philosopher Arthur Child [50] and the sociologists Hans Speier,[51] Gerard De Gré, Kurt H. Wolff [52] and C. Wright Mills [53] are especially valuable.

Within the area of substantive American contributions in the field, the work of Pitirim A. Sorokin is of special note.[54] Blending an earlier European tradition of large-scale speculation with American statistical research methods, Sorokin's encyclopedic historical sociology raises a number of significant questions for the sociology of knowledge. Sorokin's theories are basically at variance with such thinkers as Mannheim, who propose to consider classes, or other economic and social groups as the independent variable in the functional relations between knowledge and society. To Sorokin the independent variable is composed of variant "cultural mentalities." Thus we have here an idealist theory which rejects concern with the existential basis of thought and attempts instead to relate particular systems of knowledge and truth to the cultural premises on which they are alleged to be dependent. Sorokin attempts to show that there are three dominant cultural tendencies which appear alternatively in the course of human history: the ideational mentality, the idealistic mentality and the sensate mentality. Systems of truth and knowledge are then said to be dependent on or meaningfully integrated with one of these predominant "culture mentalities." This view presents a number of serious difficulties. For example, it obscures differences within a dominant culture, it totally neglects the existential basis of thought, and it may often involve a kind of gerrymandering of history in order to fit its fluctuations into the basic categories provided by Sorokin's all-embracing system. Nevertheless, the sociologist of knowledge, even if he rejects Sorokin's idealist system, will be able to profit from many of the stimulating investigations that Sorokin and some of his students have initiated. His researches in the idea of social time and the idea of causality are especially noteworthy.

Another fruitful contribution to the field in recent American work is Florian Znaniecki's The Social Role of the Man of Knowledge.[55] Znaniecki introduces the notion of the "social circle," that is, the audience or the public to which a thinker addresses himself. This notion allows us to deal more precisely with the relation between the thought of particular men and the culture of which they are part. Znaniecki shows that thinkers, at least in heterogeneous societies, are not likely to address the total society but rather tend to address selected segments or publics. He contends that their thinking is importantly related to the demands of their social circle. The thinker is expected to live up to certain demands of his circle, and his circle in turn grants him certain rights. "Every social role pre-supposes that between the individual performing the role . . . and a smaller or larger set of people who participate in his performance and may be termed his 'social circle' there is a common bond constituted by a complex of values which all of them appreciate positively." [56] Men of knowledge anticipate the demands of their public, and they tend to form self images, define data, and seize upon problems in terms of these actual or anticipated audiences. Men of knowledge may thus be classified, according to Znaniecki, in terms of their social position and their public, so that it becomes possible to establish such types of men of knowledge as the Sage, the Technologist, and the Scholar. Some of the clashes between doctrines, especially in differentiated societies, can then be accounted for in terms of the differentiated roles and the differentiated publics of their originators.

It cannot be the task of this paper to discuss or even exhaustively enumerate the recent American studies which either directly or indirectly contribute to the further development of the sociology of knowledge. We must therefore be content with only a few more references to recent work. Many researches in the field of social role, the sociology of professions, the sociology of communications and public opinion, as we have already mentioned, may be said to contain important contributions to the sociology of knowledge. The student would be well advised to consult specialized bibliographies in these fields. In other areas we may list here, more or less at random, the studies exploring the relation between minority status and originality or intellectual perspectives, of which the recent work by Melvin Seeman [57] seems an excellent example; or the studies in the history of sociological theories in which sociology of knowledge techniques have been utilized, for example the work of Bernard Rosenberg [58] on Veblen and of C. Wright Mills [59] and Lewis A. Coser [60] on modern American sociology; or studies which relate thought styles among American academic men to the structure and functioning of the academy, like Logan Wilson's work *The Academic Man*,[61] or attempts to account for divergent interpretations of the same culture by different social scientists in terms of the divergent backgrounds and social perspectives of these scientists, such as a perceptive paper by John W. Bennett.[62]

The sociology of knowledge was marked in its early history by a tendency to set up grandiose hypothetical schemes which contributed a number of suggestive leads of the highest importance. Recently it has on occasion been caught in a tendency that should have been outgrown, toward eschewing speculation in favor of ever more trivial investigation. While this may be an antidote to the earlier types of premature generalization, it carries with it a danger of overlooking the significant on behalf of the provable. But such oscillation (Saint Simon called it the law of alternativity between the generalizing and the particularizing approach to the sciences) is part of the development of any science. The future sociology of knowledge may well return to the more daring formulations of its founders, but such generalizations as might be attempted at a later date can then be based upon the mass of careful and detailed work that preceding generations of researchers will have amassed.[63]

NOTES

1. *The Advancement of Learning*, Everyman's Library Edition, pp. 169 ff. Quoted in Hans Speier, see note 51 below.
2. *The German Ideology*, New York, 1939, p. 6.
3. *The Communist Manifesto* (ed. by Ryazanov), New York, 1939, p. 47.
4. *A Contribution to the Critique of Political Economy*, Chicago, 1904, pp. 11–12.
5. *The Communist Manifesto*, p. 50.
6. Engels, letter to Heinz Starkenburg, in Marx, *Selected Works*, Moscow, 1935, vol. I, p. 392.
7. Robert K. Merton, *Social Theory and Social Structure*, Glencoe, Ill., 1949, pp. 238–239.
8. Esp. in his *Geschichte und Klassenbewusstsein*, Berlin, 1923.
9. *Ideology and Utopia*, New York, 1936, p. 67.
10. *Ibid.*, p. 69.
11. *Ibid.*, p. 3.
12. *Ibid.*, pp. 239–240.
13. *Essays on the Sociology of Knowledge*, New York, 1952, p. 176.
14. H. Otto Dahlke, "The Sociology of Knowledge" in *Contemporary Social Theory* (ed. by Barnes, Becker and Becker), New York, 1940, p. 87.
15. *Ideology and Utopia*, p. 4.
16. *Ibid.*, p. 256.
17. *Ibid.*, p. 4.
18. in Mannheim, *Essays on Sociology and Social Psychology*, New York, 1953.
19. in *Essays in the Sociology of Knowledge*.
20. *Die Wissensformen und die Gesellschaft*, Leipzig, 1926, contains Scheler's most elaborate treatment of his sociology of knowledge. For discussions of Scheler's work in English, see Merton, *op. cit.*, esp. Chapter 8, also Dahlke, *op. cit.*, and Howard Becker and H. O. Dahlke "Max Scheler's Sociology of Knowledge," *Philosophy and Phenomenological Research*, II, 1942, pp. 310–322.
21. *l'Année Sociologique*, 6, 1–72.
22. *The Elementary Forms of Religious Life*, Glencoe, Ill., 1947, p. 12.
23. *Ibid.*, pp. 10–11.
24. *Contemporary Sociological Theories*, New York, 1928, p. 477.
25. "French Sociology" in *Twentieth Century Sociology* (ed. by Gurvitch and Moore), New York, 1945, p. 518.
26. *La Pensée Chinoise*, Paris, 1934.
27. *Themis*, Cambridge, England, 1912.
28. *From Religion to Philosophy*, London, 1927.
29. *Les Cadres Sociaux de la Mémoire*, Paris, 1925.
30. Louis Wirth, Introduction to *Ideology and Utopia*.
31. *The Quest for Certainty*, New York, 1929, p. 33.
32. "The Interpretation of the Savage Mind," *Psychological Review*, IX (1902), pp. 219–220.
33. Macmillan, New York.
34. *Ibid.*, p. 1–2
35. New York, 1932, p. 39.
36. *The Place of Science in Modern Civilization*, p. 105.
37. *The Theory of the Leisure Class*, Mentor ed., p. 247.

38. *Mind, Self and Society,* Chicago, 1934, p. 50.
39. *Ibid.,* p. 156.
40. *Ibid.,* p. 270.
41. John C. McKinney, "The Contribution of George Herbert Mead to the Sociology of Knowledge," *Social Forces,* 34, 2, p. 149.
42. Cf. Arthur Child, "The Theoretical Possibility of the Sociology of Knowledge," *Ethics* 51, pp. 392–418.
43. *Science, Technology and Society in Seventeenth Century England,* Osiris History of Science Monographs, Bruges, 1938; and Part IV in *Social Theory and Social Structure.*
44. *Science and the Social Order,* Glencoe, Ill., 1952.
45. See f. expl. his "Institutional Office and the Person," *American Journal of Sociology* 43, pp. 404–13.
46. See his work on the medical profession in *American Journal of Sociology* 53,5 and 55,3.
47. See Chapter VIII of his *Essays in Sociological Theory,* Glencoe, Ill., 1949. For an excellent bibliography on the literature on occupations see *The Sociology of Work* by Theodore Caplow, Minneapolis, 1954. Caplow's chapters on "Occupational Institutions" and "Occupational Ideologies" are also valuable in this context.
48. pp. 200 ff.
49. Chapter VIII.
50. See his series of 5 articles on problems of the sociology of knowledge in *Ethics,* vols. 51, 52, 54, and 58.
51. "The Social Determination of Ideas" in *Social Order and the Risks of War,* New York, 1952.
52. *Society and Ideology,* New York, 1943; "The Sociology of Knowledge" *Philosophy of Science,* 10, pp. 104–123.
53. "Language, Logic and Culture," *American Sociological Review,* 4, pp. 70–680; "Methodological Consequences of the Sociology of Knowledge," *American Journal of Sociology,* XLVI, pp. 316–330; "Situated Actions and Vocabularies of Motives." *American Sociological Review,* 5, pp. 904–913.
54. *Social and Cultural Dynamics,* 4 vols., 1937–41. See also *Sociocultural Causality, Space and Time,* New York, 1943.
55. New York, 1940. (See Section 10).
56. *Ibid.,* pp. 14–15.
57. "Intellectual Perspective and Minority Status," *Social Problems* III, 3, pp. 141–153.
58. *The Values of Veblen: A Critical Appraisal,* Washington, D. C., 1956.
59. "The Professional Ideology of Social Pathologists," *American Journal of Sociology,* 49, pp. 165–190.
60. *The Functions of Social Conflict,* Glencoe, Ill., 1956, Chapter 1.
61. New York, 1942.
62. "The Interpretation of Pueblo Culture: a question of values," *Southwestern Journal of Anthropology,* II, 4, pp. 361–374.
63. For extensive bibliographies see Merton, *op. cit.;* Mannheim, *Ideology and Utopia, op. cit.,* and Jacques Maquet, *The Sociology of Knowledge,* Boston, 1951.

INDEX